UNVEILING THE RETIREMENT MYTH

Advanced Retirement Planning based on Market History

Jim C. Otar

First edition published in 2009 Printed in Canada

Cover picture: my loving parents and all their children, 1952
Visit www.retirementoptimizer.com for bulk orders or additional copies of this book.

Library and Archives Canada Cataloguing in Publication

Otar, Jim C.
Unveiling the retirement myth: advanced retirement planning based on market history / Jim C. Otar.

Includes index.
ISBN 978-0-9689634-2-5

1. Retirement income--Planning. 2. Stocks--Rate of return. 3. Investment analysis. 4. Portfolio management. I. Title.

HG179.O838 2009 332.024'01 C2009–904683–0

To my parents, with whom I wish I had spent more time

To Rita, who has always been beside me

To those advisors who try to do their best for their clients

Author's Preface

This book is based on my research of retirement planning involving one hundred and nine years of market history.

It provides comprehensive analysis of methods and strategies for retirement planning. Detailed, step–by–step examples that are based on actual market history are included. These methods and strategies will take the reader to the next step, the advanced retirement planning. It will also help fellow advisors to reduce their exposure to liability when more and more retirees realize the devastating shortfalls of existing models.

What you read will be depressing. The light at the end of the tunnel will not be visible until you start reading the zone strategy. There, you can find strategies for lifelong income, no matter how much you might have saved for your retirement.

Jim C. Otar
CFP, CMT, BASc, MEng
Toronto, October 1, 2009
www.retirementoptimizer.com
jim@retirementoptimizer.com

Acknowledgements

In life, there are two kinds of luck: The first kind simply drops into your lap without you even asking for it. Many either do not experience it more than once in their entire lifetime or miss it altogether when it happens. The second kind of luck does not fall into your lap; it happens because of your hard work, tenacity, persistence, curiosity, and sometimes by you just being there.

Fifty–eight years ago, I experienced the good luck of the first kind at birth: I was welcomed into this world by my wonderful parents. The values and the sense of humor they instilled in the early years of my childhood have been my greatest resource throughout my life. I thank them for their encouragement to complete this book.

Thirty–two years ago, good luck of the first kind struck me again. I met Rita, my better half. She asked me a simple question in 1999, “Do we have enough money to retire?”. That question triggered my first book on this topic in 2001. Six years ago, when I decided to re–write this expanded edition, she gave me unbounded encouragement. I thank her for that.

I thank my older brother Yavuz for teaching me everything from how to ride a bicycle, to building radios, to the basics of economics, and how to fill out my first tax return. He gave me some of his unique combination of skepticism and self–confidence wrapped in one package. This attribute became my biggest asset for what I have been doing in the last fifteen years.

I owe thanks to readers, advisors, friends, clients and editors of my articles, as well as sponsors of my live presentations. They asked numerous questions, gave me their feedback, suggested wonderful improvements to my retirement calculator, made my Wall–Street–bashing more compliant for my live presentations, and encouraged me to write more. I thank you all. In addition, a special thanks to Michael Baney for converting me from a “road worrier” to a “road warrior”. He is one of the finest people that I have met in this business.

Finally, Boris Krivy did an excellent job of leaving my accent intact in my writings. I thank him for his fine editing. I also thank Kevin Reperowitz, Brian Janssen, Jim Lorenz, James Gebert, Bruce Semple and Gail Bebee for their editing feedback.

I am a typical engineer: I am skeptical of everything that I hear or read about, especially in the investment world. If I come across a strategy that looks interesting, then I like to work through the numbers until I can clearly see if and how it works. That is how I discovered nine years ago while writing “High Expectations & False Dreams”, that most research and innovative strategies you hear or read about, are just plain garbage.

This book is mostly a collection of my articles. I wanted to gather them all under one cover for your convenience. There are numerous tables and charts in each chapter. Some of the material might appear to be repetitious. For some readers, this can be overwhelming.

There are two kinds of readers: Those who like details and those who don’t.

- If you like details, then read the entire book. Some topics are heavy. Do not be discouraged; you may need to read some chapters more than once.
- If you dislike details or hate math, then you do not need to read the entire chapter. I designed many of the chapters in such a way that you can skip the details and still make sense of the topic. Here is how it works:

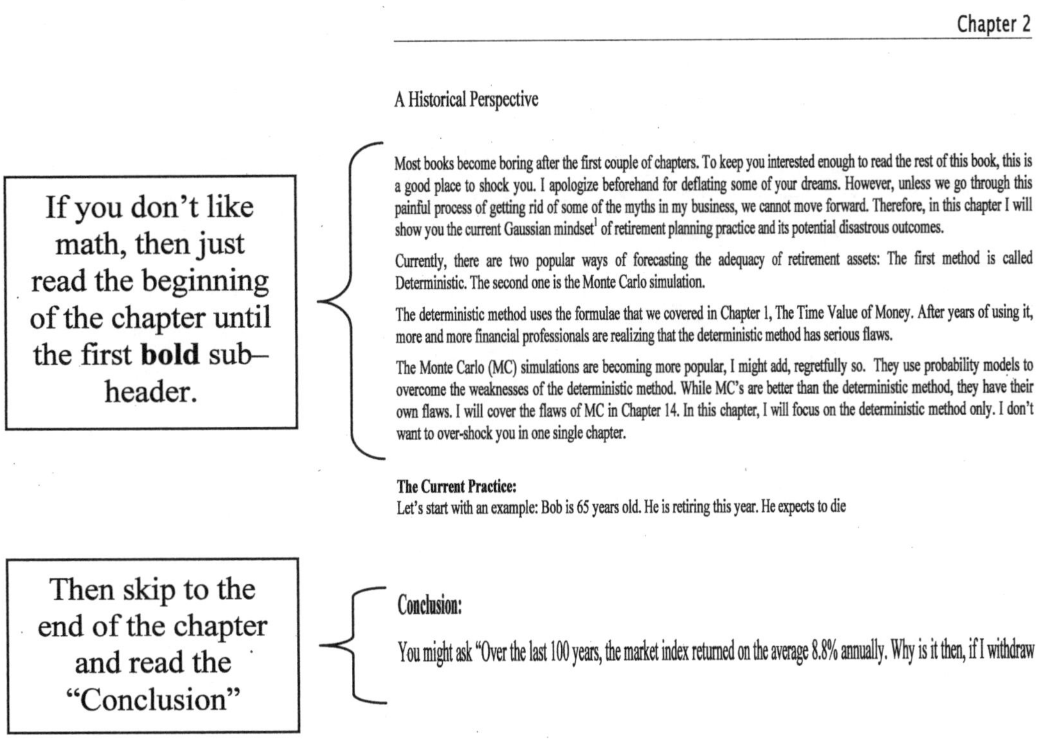

Chapter 2

A Historical Perspective

Most books become boring after the first couple of chapters. To keep you interested enough to read the rest of this book, this is a good place to shock you. I apologize beforehand for deflating some of your dreams. However, unless we go through this painful process of getting rid of some of the myths in my business, we cannot move forward. Therefore, in this chapter I will show you the current Gaussian mindset[1] of retirement planning practice and its potential disastrous outcomes.

Currently, there are two popular ways of forecasting the adequacy of retirement assets: The first method is called Deterministic. The second one is the Monte Carlo simulation.

The deterministic method uses the formulae that we covered in Chapter 1, The Time Value of Money. After years of using it, more and more financial professionals are realizing that the deterministic method has serious flaws.

The Monte Carlo (MC) simulations are becoming more popular, I might add, regretfully so. They use probability models to overcome the weaknesses of the deterministic method. While MC’s are better than the deterministic method, they have their own flaws. I will cover the flaws of MC in Chapter 14. In this chapter, I will focus on the deterministic method only. I don’t want to over-shock you in one single chapter.

The Current Practice:

Let’s start with an example: Bob is 65 years old. He is retiring this year. He expects to die

Conclusion:

You might ask “Over the last 100 years, the market index returned on the average 8.8% annually. Why is it then, if I withdraw

In the old country, when I was little, my parents owned a small hobby farm. We had a flock of sheep, a dog, a few stray turtles and the neighbor's donkey. My older brother raised chickens, ducks and geese for fun. Ali, the watchman, grew vegetables and looked after the sheep and the fruit trees.

I had occasional talks with Ali. One day, I don't know how it started, I found myself discussing the merits of cabbage with him. He mentioned that cabbage, unlike okra, is a hardy plant, easy to grow, easy to pick, easy to sell. I started thinking about it. I calculated the cost of planting an acre of cabbage. Then I calculated the yield. Only then did I realize how much money I could make in just a few months.

I could probably plant a cabbage field every year and overcome my biggest phobia: asking my father for an allowance. The poor guy was already burdened up to his neck helping out the Crimean Tatars escaping from Russia, and they kept coming and coming. He was an accountant. Sometimes, his little office looked more like a refugee camp.

Wow! I was only eleven years old and thanks to this cabbage enterprise, I was set for life.

I shared my thoughts with Ali. He responded –trying not to discourage my enthusiasm, "you'll never know how much money you'll make until it is in your pocket. We may lose some seedlings to birds and sheep, but perhaps we can put a new fence around the sheep flock. That may solve the sheep problem. Then there is the neighbor's donkey. They love cabbage; he may break his rope and eat our crop, but perhaps we can buy a stronger rope for the donkey and solve the donkey problem. Then there are the passers–by, especially the poor ones. They will certainly help themselves and you can never put them on a rope! As if this is not enough, on the harvest day the local deputy will undoubtedly show up and he would want to fill up his trunk with gifted cabbage!"

I did not like at all what Ali was saying. "These farmers are so stupid", I said to myself, "that is why they must be so poor". I always hated asking my father for allowance. This was my only way out, through the cabbage field. The next day, I cashed in all my life savings. I also broke my piggy–bank for additional funding, just in case. Ali and I went to the nursery and bought seedlings. You need lots of manure to grow cabbage. So, I bought a truck–load. Finally, I spent the last bit of my money on a new rope for the donkey and a new fence for the sheep. That was my risk management.

As tradition dictates, we planted several baskets of seedlings under the bright full moon. Then, I spread the entire mountain of manure carefully with my own bare hands around each seedling.

Weeks went by. It was a good season; the cabbage grew unbelievably well. We had less damage than we expected from birds, sheep, donkey and people. My dreams were coming true. No more asking my father for the weekly allowance!

But the winter was approaching fast. I asked Ali when we should harvest the cabbage. He gazed at the distant horizon for a long moment and then said, "We should wait two more weeks. The cabbage will weigh more then. You'll make more money."

Two weeks later, I went back to our hobby farm. On the way, I prepared myself mentally for the inevitable confrontation with the local deputy for his cut of my crop. Other than that, I was overflowing with joy, as I anticipated my new wealth.

When I arrived there, Ali did not look too happy. He said that there was a premature frost the night before. Now, the cabbage was useless. "Only the donkey can eat it now", he added, "that is, if he cannot find anything better to eat".

An unexpected unlucky event, just one day before the harvest, turned my dreams of financial freedom into financial ruin. As a result of that premature frost, I continued to feel a deep embarrassment weekly; each time I asked my father for my allowance. "Why did I listen to Ali? Why did I not harvest my cabbage one day earlier? Why? Why!"

Several years later, at age twenty, as hippies from the West were traveling to the East, I went in the opposite direction. I moved to Canada. I enrolled in the Faculty of Engineering at the University of Toronto. I made a living driving a taxi part–time during my student days. Finally, I no longer needed my father's allowance.

The chances are, if that frost forty–seven years ago had come one day later, I would not have moved to Canada, have would have never met Rita, and you would not be reading this book. Remember, I mentioned earlier that there are two kinds of luck? Moving to Canada was good luck of the second kind. Many years later, I still cannot believe that happened at age twenty.

During the next ten years, over 90 million Americans and Canadians are hoping to retire. We have successfully landed robots on Mars and observed their amazing findings. We have successfully discovered cures for many diseases. We have found solutions to numerous other problems.

Yet our financial planning community still does not have the tools to give realistic answers to some of the most basic questions:

- When can I retire?
- Do I have enough money to retire?
- How much do I need to save for my retirement?
- How long will my money last?
- Is there a shortfall?
- How much do I need to save between now and retirement?

You will find dozens of books in your local bookstore that attempt to answer these questions. Almost all of them use certain assumptions about future market growth and future inflation. You will find some of their arguments reasonable and logical. Others make outrageous claims. Most ignore one thing: averages do not apply to individuals.

When I changed my career from engineering to financial planning, I was appalled by the current design practice: we assume an "average" growth rate for the portfolio and then design a retirement plan accordingly.

If you design for the "average", when things get worse –as they always do–, your design will collapse:

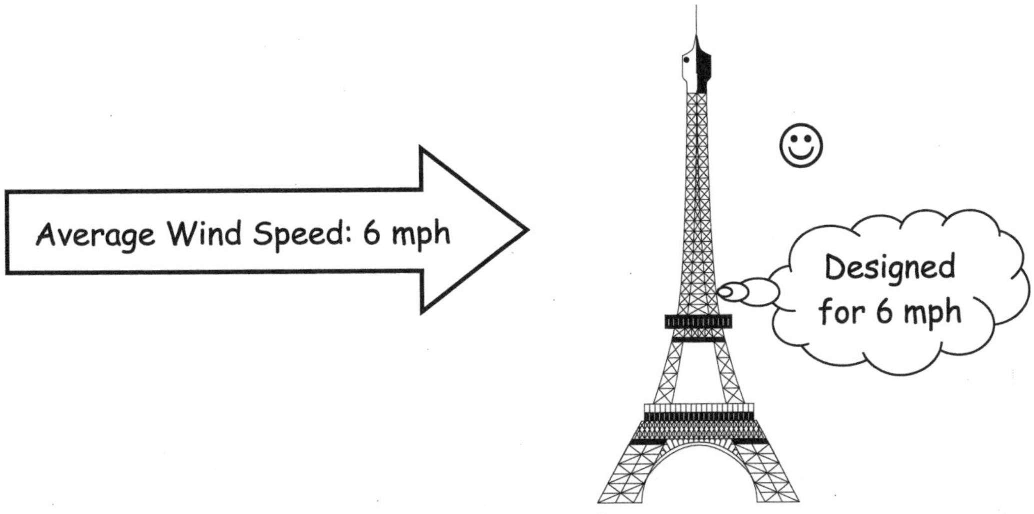

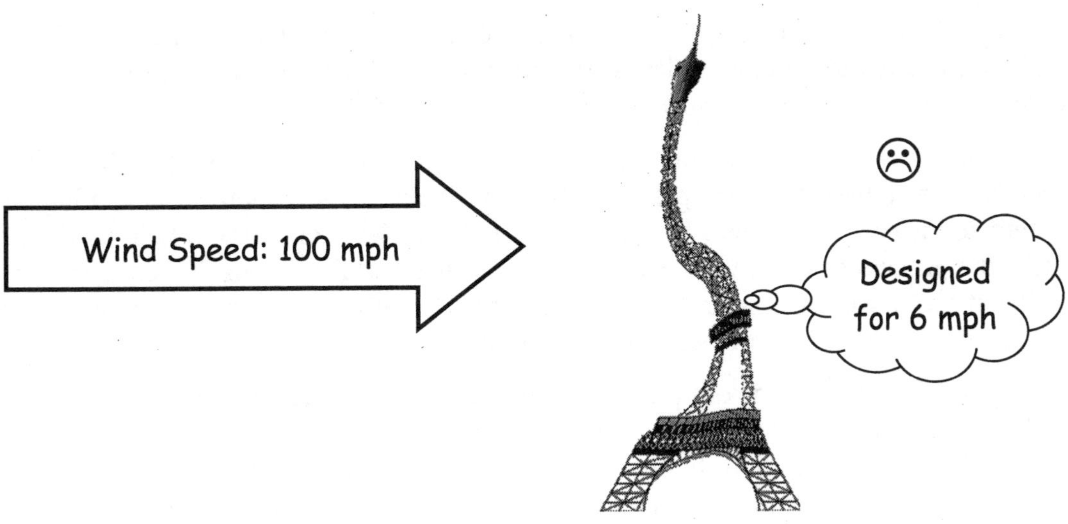

In engineering, you would never design anything for the "average"; you would design it for the "worst", and then some. Only then can your design overcome or withstand adverse conditions. Similarly, it is wise to design your retirement plan, not for "average", but for adverse conditions. Yes, I am a positive person, but that is because I prepare for the worst.

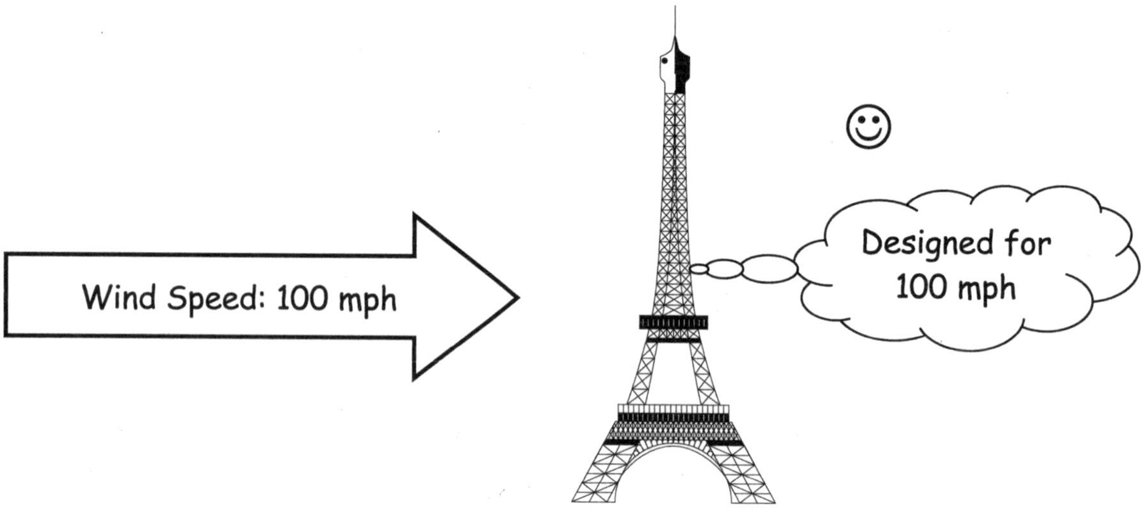

In this book, there are no assumptions of future portfolio growth rates or future inflation rates. When I present a retirement plan to my clients, I don't pretend to be a fortuneteller. I don't say "assuming a portfolio growth rate of 8% and inflation of 3%..."

I give my clients a range of outcomes based on market history since 1900. I show them what can happen to their financial picture if they are lucky. I show them what can happen if they are unlucky. I give them the whole picture and let them make their choices. I transform the process of retirement planning from a **forecast** that spans 30 years or more, to an **aftcast** that covers 109 years. I convert the process of making wrong assumptions – a liability– into increased client awareness –an asset–.

What you will find in this book is pure historical data applied to retirement planning. In my earlier book on this topic[1], I wrote about market history and how it applies to retirement planning. I brought to light some of the perils, such as sequence of returns and the luck factor. In this book, I expand on this and present my findings in a more practical and detailed way. Several examples and solutions are presented throughout the text.

This book can help you only if you are willing to learn from history. Since no crystal ball can tell us the future, for the time being, history is our only guide.

[1] author, "High Expectations & False Dreams", October 2001, ISBN 0–9689634–0–4

Chapter 1

Time Value of Money

The time value of money is the foundation of current retirement planning practice. Therefore, it is a good place to start.

Most retirement plans are based on steady growth of the markets over the life of the portfolio. The future value of the investment is based on an "average" growth rate. This is generally called the "time value of money".

There are two types of calculations for estimating future value. If we have currently a pool of investments and no money added or removed, then we are talking about the "future value of a single sum". Its equation has four variables. They are: the present value of investments, the assumed interest or growth rate, the compounding time period and the future value. If you know any three of these four variables you can then calculate the fourth. Here is the equation to calculate the future value of a single sum:

$$FV = PV \times (1 + i)^n \qquad \text{(Equation 1.1)}$$

where:

FV	is the future value
PV	is the present value
i	is the interest rate during the period
n	is the number of periods

Example 1.1

Bob invests \$100,000 in a 2-year CD compounded annually at 3%. Calculate its future value.

$$FV = \$100{,}000 \times (1 + 0.03)^2$$
$$FV = \$106{,}090$$

The future value of \$100,000 invested in a 2-year CD compounded annually at 3% is \$106,090.

If the future value is known, here is the formula to calculate the present value:

$$PV = FV \ / \ (1 + i)^n \qquad \text{(Equation 1.2)}$$

> Example 1.2
>
> Bob needs to save $100,000 in 5 years. How much does he need to invest today if he decides on a zero-coupon government bond[2] maturing in 5 years and yielding net 4% annually?
>
> $$FV = \$100{,}000 \ / \ (1 + 0.04)^5$$
> $$FV = \$82{,}192.71$$
>
> It will cost Bob $82,192.71 to buy this bond.

The second type equations are used to estimate a future value for a series of periodic cash flows of equal amount. This is called an annuity calculation. To find the future value of an annuity stream, we simply take the cash flow at each period, figure out its future value and then add them up. Here is the formula that does that for cash flows of equal amount:

$$FV = \{PMT \times [(1 + i)^n - 1]\} \ / \ i \qquad \text{(Equation 1.3)}$$

where:
PMT is the amount of the periodic cash flow

> Example 1.3
>
> Bob saves $10,000 each year for the next three years. Assuming that interest rate is 4% and never changes during that time, how much does Bob have at the end of 3 years?
>
> $$FV = \{\$10{,}000 \times [(1 + 0.04)^3 - 1]\} \ / \ 0.04$$
> $$FV = \$31{,}216$$
>
> Bob's total savings are $31,216 at the end of 3 years.

[2] also known as "strip bonds", zero coupon bonds pay no interest but are purchased at a discount, so the interest is built into the price difference between their cost and maturity value

If the amount of periodic cash flow is unknown, then the formula is:

$$PMT = \{FV / [(1 + i)^n - 1]\} / i \qquad \text{(Equation 1.4)}$$

Example 1.4

Bob wants to accumulate $200,000 during the next 10 years. How much does he need to set aside if he is getting 5% interest throughout the entire 10-year period?

$$PMT = \{\$200{,}000 / [(1 + 0.05)^{10} - 1]\} / 0.05$$
$$PMT = \$15{,}901$$

Bob needs to save $15,901 each year for the next 10 years to accumulate $200,000.

The present value of a periodic cash flow is calculated as:

$$PV = PMT \times \{1 - [1 / (1 + i)^n]\} / i \qquad \text{(Equation 1.5)}$$

Example 1.5

Bob wins a lottery, which will pay him $10,000 at the end of each year for the next 25 years. The lottery corporation also offers him a one-time lump sum payment instead. Assuming a discount rate of 6%, how much can Bob expect as a lump sum?

$$PV = \$10{,}000 \times \{1 - [1 / (1 + 0.06)^{25}]\} / 0.06$$
$$PV = \$127{,}834$$

Bob can expect $127,834 as a lump sum payment.

When we talk about retirement savings, we need to take into account the increases in cash flow. For example, before retirement, you may be increasing the periodic deposit amounts in line with your increased earnings as time goes on. On the other hand, after retirement, you will likely increase your withdrawals over time to keep up with inflation. Let's look at formulae at each life stage.

Accumulation Stage:

Equation 1.6 is used to calculate the future value of retirement savings[3]. It includes the future value of current savings as well as periodic deposits that occur at the end of each year and increase each year.

$$FV = [PV \times (1 + i)^n] + \sum_{t=0}^{n-1} PMT \times (1 + k)^t \times (1 + i)^{n-t-1} \qquad \text{(Equation 1.6)}$$

where:

k is the annual increase of the periodic deposits

If the deposits are made at the beginning of the year, then the growth of this deposit during the year has to be accounted for as well. If this is the case, the equation 1.6 is rewritten slightly differently:

$$FV = [PV \times (1 + i)^n] + \sum_{t=0}^{n-1} PMT \times (1 + k)^t \times (1 + i)^{n-t} \qquad \text{(Equation 1.7)}$$

These last two equations can be calculated using a standard financial hand calculator. However, it can be time–consuming. That is where the retirement calculation software comes in. A retirement calculator computes these formulae instantly and displays the results for each age, line–by–line. Let's look at two examples.

---

[3] For those who do not have a math background: the summation sign, $\sum_{t=0}^{n-1}$ indicates that the expression following it must be calculated for all values of t starting at 0, and ending at n–1, and then added together.

Example 1.6

Bob's current savings are $50,000. At the end of the first year, he deposits $5,000. In subsequent years, he increases this deposit amount by 2% each year. The investments grow by 6% each and every year.

Calculate the portfolio value at the end of 5 years.

Using equation 1.6:

$$FV = [PV \times (1+i)^n] + \sum_{t=0}^{n-1} PMT \times (1+k)^t \times (1+i)^{n-t-1}$$

First, calculate the components of the summation:

$$\sum_{t=0}^{n-1} PMT \times (1+k)^t \times (1+i)^{n-t-1} = 5{,}000 \times (1+0.02)^0 \times (1+0.06)^{5-0-1}$$

$$+ 5{,}000 \times (1+0.02)^1 \times (1+0.06)^{5-1-1}$$
$$+ 5{,}000 \times (1+0.02)^2 \times (1+0.06)^{5-2-1}$$
$$+ 5{,}000 \times (1+0.02)^3 \times (1+0.06)^{5-3-1}$$
$$+ 5{,}000 \times (1+0.02)^4 \times (1+0.06)^{5-4-1}$$
$$= 5{,}000 \times (1.262477+1.214836+1.68993+1.124880+1.082432)$$
$$= 29{,}268$$

Now, calculate FV:

$$FV = [50{,}000 \times (1+0.06)^5] + 29{,}268$$
$$= \$96{,}179$$

At the end of 5 years Bob accumulates $96,179. You can also calculate this using a spreadsheet:

Year	Beginning Value $	Growth $	Annual Deposit $	End Value $
1	50,000	3,000	5,000	58,000
2	58,000	3,480	5,100	66,580
3	66,580	3,995	5,202	75,777
4	75,777	4,547	5,306	85,630
5	85,630	5,138	5,412	96,180

In year 1, the beginning value of the savings is $50,000. At the end of the year, the deposit of $5,000 is added to the portfolio. The 6% growth of the $50,000 is $3,000. Therefore the total year-end value is the sum of the beginning value, the growth and the savings, which works out as $58,000. This amount now becomes the beginning value of the second year. Repeat each row until the table is completed.

Here is the same example when deposits are made at the beginning of each year instead of at the end:

Example 1.7

Same as Example 1.6 except Bob adds $5,000 to his account at the beginning of each year, instead of at the end.

Using equation 1.7:

$$FV = [PV \times (1+i)^n] + \sum_{t=0}^{n-1} PMT \times (1+k)^t \times (1+i)^{n-t}$$

First, calculate the components of the summation:

$$\sum_{t=0}^{n-1} PMT \times (1+k)^t \times (1+i)^{n-t-1} = 5{,}000 \times (1+0.02)^0 \times (1+0.06)^{5-0}$$
$$+\ 5{,}000 \times (1+0.02)^1 \times (1+0.06)^{5-1}$$
$$+\ 5{,}000 \times (1+0.02)^2 \times (1+0.06)^{5-2}$$
$$+\ 5{,}000 \times (1+0.02)^3 \times (1+0.06)^{5-3}$$
$$+\ 5{,}000 \times (1+0.02)^4 \times (1+0.06)^{5-4}$$
$$= 5{,}000 \times (1.338226+1.287726+1.239133+1.192373+1.147378)$$
$$= 31{,}024$$

Now, calculate FV:

$$FV = [50{,}000 \times (1+0.06)^5] + 31{,}024$$
$$= \$97{,}935$$

At the end of 5 years Bob accumulates $97,935. If you use a spreadsheet:

Year	Beginning Value $	Annual Deposit $	Growth $	End Value $
1	50,000	5,000	3,300	58,300
2	58,300	5,100	3,804	67,204
3	67,204	5,202	4,344	76,750
4	76,750	5,306	4,923	86,980
5	86,980	5,412	5,544	97,935

In year 1, the beginning value of the savings is $50,000 plus the deposit of $5,000. The 6% growth of the $55,000 is $3,300. Therefore the total year-end value is the sum of the beginning value, the growth and the savings, which works out as $58,300. This amount now becomes the beginning value of the second year. Repeat each row until the table is completed.

Distribution Stage:

After retirement, we begin withdrawing money from the portfolio. This is known as the "distribution" stage. This is because money is distributed out of the portfolio on a periodic basis.

Some people use the term "decumulation" to describe this stage. This implies that portfolios will decumulate, i.e. their value will decline over time during the retirement stage. However, just because you take money out of a portfolio does not necessarily mean its value will decline. You could be taking out money while the portfolio value increases. Decumulation refers to asset value, distribution refers to cash outflow.

I believe the term "distribution" describes this stage more accurately. We can't always tell in advance whether an investment portfolio will accumulate (i.e. increase in value) or "decumulate" (i.e. decrease in value). I use "distribution portfolio" or "distribution stage" to describe this stage throughout this book..

Figure 1.1: An accumulation portfolio, accumulating

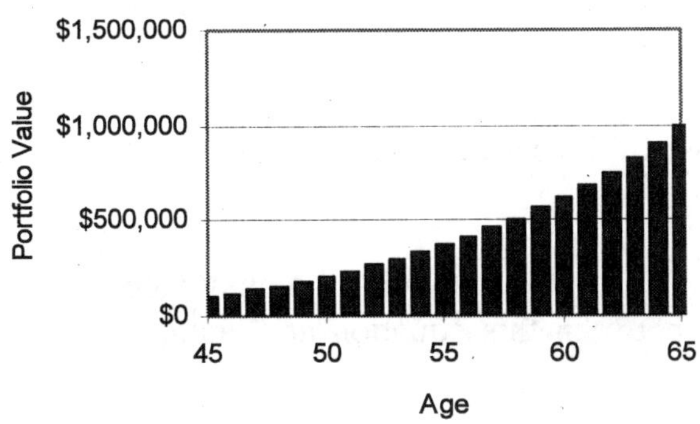

Figure 1.2: A distribution portfolio, decumulating

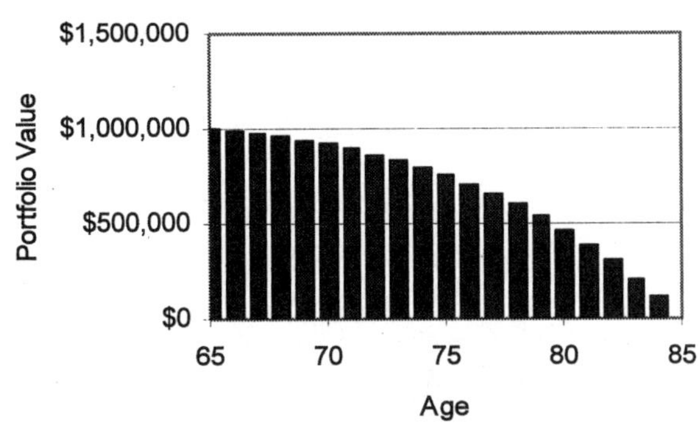

Figure 1.3: A distribution portfolio, accumulating

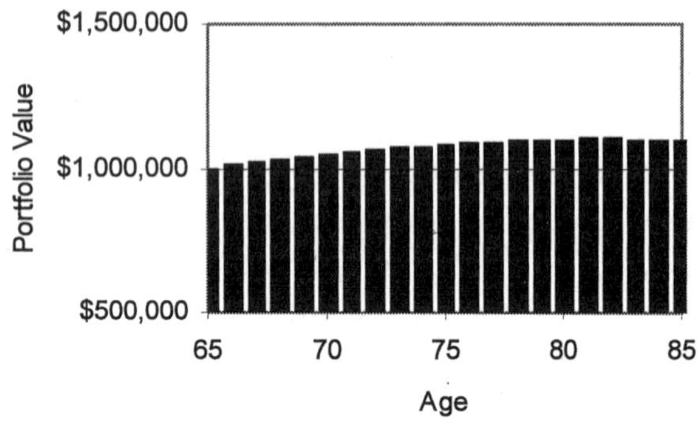

Here is the formula to calculate the future value of the portfolio if an increasing periodic income (PMT) is taken out of the portfolio, at the end of each year:

$$FV = [PV \times (1 + i)^n] - \sum_{t=0}^{n-1} PMT \times (1 + k)^t \times (1 + i)^{n-t-1} \qquad \text{(Equation 1.8)}$$

where:
k is the annual increase of the periodic withdrawals

Keep in mind; the periodic cash flow PMT is now the amount of money taken out of the portfolio. Therefore, the only difference between this equation and equation 1.6 is the "minus" sign before the summation.

If the withdrawal occurs at the beginning of the year then the equation 1.8 is:

$$FV = [PV \times (1 + i)^n] - \sum_{t=0}^{n-1} PMT \times (1 + k)^t \times (1 + i)^{n-t} \qquad \text{(Equation 1.9)}$$

Here is an example when withdrawals occur at the end of each year:

Example 1.8

Bob has $500,000 in his retirement savings growing at 6% each and every year. He needs $30,000 at the end of each year, indexed at 3% annually.

Calculate the portfolio value at the end of 5 years.

Using equation 1.8:

$$FV = [PV \times (1+i)^n] - \sum_{t=0}^{n-1} PMT \times (1+k)^t \times (1+i)^{n-t-1}$$

First, calculate the components of the summation:

$$\begin{aligned}\sum_{t=0}^{n-1} PMT \times (1+k)^t \times (1+i)^{n-t-1} &= 30{,}000 \times (1+0.03)^0 \times (1+0.06)^{5-0-1}\\ &+ 30{,}000 \times (1+0.03)^1 \times (1+0.06)^{5-1-1}\\ &+ 30{,}000 \times (1+0.03)^2 \times (1+0.06)^{5-2-1}\\ &+ 30{,}000 \times (1+0.03)^3 \times (1+0.06)^{5-3-1}\\ &+ 30{,}000 \times (1+0.03)^4 \times (1+0.06)^{5-4-1}\\ &= 30{,}000 \times (1.262477+1.226746+1.192027+1.158291+1.125509)\\ &= 178{,}952\end{aligned}$$

Now, calculate FV:

$$\begin{aligned}FV &= [500{,}000 \times (1+0.06)^5] - 178{,}952\\ &= \$490{,}161\end{aligned}$$

At the end of 5 years, the portfolio value is $490,161.

Here is the projection of the portfolio value using a spreadsheet:

Year	Begin Value $	Growth $	Withdrawal $	End Value $
1	500,000	30,000	30,000	500,000
2	500,000	30,000	30,900	499,100
3	499,100	29,946	31,837	497,219
4	497,219	29,833	32,782	494,270
5	494,270	29,656	33,765	490,161

In a retirement plan, the accumulation and distribution projections are typically shown on the same chart, covering the entire lifespan, as indicated in Figure 1.4.

The left hand portion of the chart, which is the part that is increasing parabolically, represents the portfolio value during the accumulation years. The right hand portion of the chart, which is the part that is decreasing parabolically, shows the portfolio value over time during the distribution or retirement years. While this chart depicts an idealized life cycle, it is possible to see a decreasing portfolio value during the accumulation stage in adverse markets, as well as increasing portfolio value during the distribution stage when withdrawals are below sustainable rates.

Figure 1.4: A typical chart in a retirement plan forecasting the value of portfolio value over time

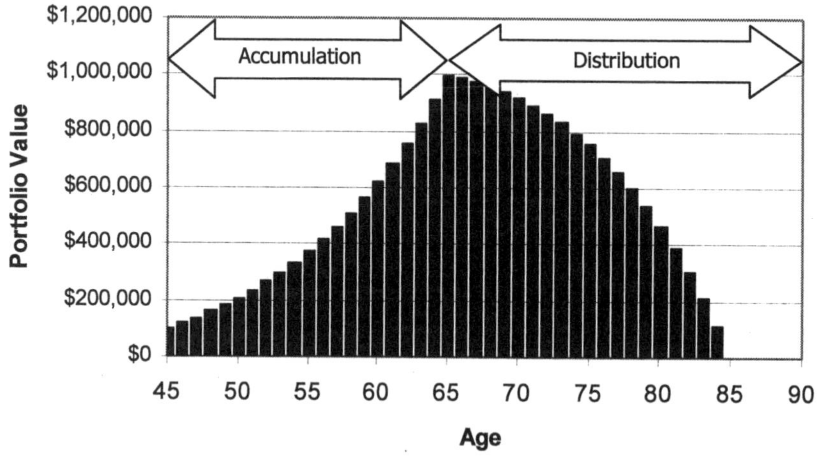

Annuitized Withdrawal Rate (AWR):

Equations 1.8 and 1.9 help us calculate the future value of a portfolio. If we want to calculate the annuitized withdrawal rate, all we need to do is to rearrange these two equations for the periodic income. Once we know the periodic income, PMT, then the annuitized withdrawal rate is PMT divided by the present value of current savings expressed as a percentage.

Here is the formula to calculate the starting amount of the increasing periodic income taken out of the portfolio. The income is taken out at the end of each year.

$$PMT = \frac{PV \times (1+i)^{n} - FV}{\sum_{t=0}^{n-1} (1+k)^{t} \times (1+i)^{n-t-1}} \qquad \text{(Equation 1.10)}$$

where:

FV	is the future value of savings
PV	is the present value of savings
PMT	id the first periodic withdrawal amount
i	is the constant interest rate
n	is the number of periods
k	is the annual increase of periodic withdrawals

If the periodic withdrawal occurs at the beginning of each year then the formula is:

$$PMT = \frac{PV \times (1+i)^{n} - FV}{\sum_{t=0}^{n-1} (1+k)^{t} \times (1+i)^{n-t}} \qquad \text{(Equation 1.11)}$$

The formula for the annuitized withdrawal rate is:

$$AWR = \frac{PMT}{PV} \times 100\% \qquad \text{(Equation 1.12)}$$

When you calculate the annuitized withdrawal rate using these formulae, you are making certain assumptions:

- The growth rate (or the interest rate – if you are from a bank or insurance background) is constant throughout the entire time period.
- The indexation is constant throughout the entire time period.

The only time that these assumptions are realistic is when you buy a single–premium immediate annuity. Regretfully, the financial planning community still uses this simplistic (also known as "deterministic") model for fluctuating investment portfolios. The results for doing so can be devastating, as we will see in future chapters.

Example 1.9

Bob has $500,000 in his retirement savings growing at 6% each and every year. He wants to withdraw money at the end of each year for the next 5 years, indexed at 3% annually. He wants $100,000 left in his account at the end of the five years. How much can he take out? What is his AWR?

Using equation 1.10:

$$PMT = \frac{PV \times (1+i)^n - FV}{\sum_{t=0}^{n-1}(1+k)^t \times (1+i)^{n-t-1}}$$

First, calculate the components of the summation:

$$\sum_{t=0}^{n-1} (1+k)^t \times (1+i)^{n-t-1} = (1+0.03)^0 \times (1+0.06)^{5-0-1}$$

$$+ (1+0.03)^1 \times (1+0.06)^{5-1-1}$$
$$+ (1+0.03)^2 \times (1+0.06)^{5-2-1}$$
$$+ (1+0.03)^3 \times (1+0.06)^{5-3-1}$$
$$+ (1+0.03)^4 \times (1+0.06)^{5-4-1}$$

$$= 1.262477+1.226746+1.192027+1.158291+1.125509$$

$$= 5.96505$$

Now, calculate PMT:

$$PMT = \{[500{,}000 \times (1+0.06)^5] - 100{,}000\} / 5.96505$$

$$= \$95{,}408$$

The first withdrawal is $95,408. The subsequent withdrawals are indexed by 3% each year.

Bob's annuitized withdrawal rate is:

AWR = ($95,408 / $500,000) x 100%

= 19.08%

You can also use a standard (deterministic) retirement calculator. The following table depicts the outcome:

Year	Begin Value $	Growth $	Withdrawal $	End Value $
1	500,000	30,000	95,408	434,592
2	434,592	26.076	98,270	362,398
3	362,398	21,744	101,218	282,923
4	282,923	16,975	104,255	195,644
5	195,644	11,739	107,382	100,000

Tables 1.1, 1.2 and 1.3 show the annuitized withdrawal rates for 4%, 6% and 8% annual growth (or interest rate), respectively, for various retirement ages. Each table shows three levels of indexation, 2%, 3% and 4%. The future value of savings is assumed to be zero, the age of death is assumed to be 95, and withdrawals are made at the end of each year.

Table 1.1: Annuitized withdrawal rates based on a steady portfolio growth of 4% annually

Retirement Age	Annuitized Withdrawal Rate (AWR) at 2% indexation	at 3% indexation	at 4% indexation
55	3.7%	3.1%	2.6%
60	4.1%	3.5%	3.0%
65	4.5%	4.0%	3.5%
70	5.2%	4.7%	4.2%
75	6.2%	5.7%	5.2%

Table 1.2: Annuitized withdrawal rates based on a steady portfolio growth of 6% annually

Retirement Age	Annuitized Withdrawal Rate (AWR)		
	at 2% indexation	at 3% indexation	at 4% indexation
55	5.1%	4.3%	3.8%
60	5.4%	4.7%	4.1%
65	5.8%	5.2%	4.6%
70	6.5%	5.9%	5.3%
75	7.5%	6.9%	6.3%

Table 1.3: Annuitized withdrawal rates based on a steady portfolio growth of 8% annually

Retirement Age	Annuitized Withdrawal Rate (AWR)		
	at 2% indexation	at 3% indexation	at 4% indexation
55	6.7%	5.9%	5.1%
60	6.9%	6.2%	5.5%
65	7.3%	6.6%	5.9%
70	7.9%	7.2%	6.5%
75	8.8%	8.2%	7.5%

Instead of using Equations 1.10 or 1.11, you can calculate the periodic withdrawal amount simply by looking up the AWR in Tables 1.1 through 1.3 and the present value of retirement savings:

$$PMT = AWR \times PV \qquad \text{(Equation 1.13)}$$

Example 1.10

Bob, 65, is retiring this year. His retirement savings amount to $500,000. Assuming Bob's portfolio grows 8% and inflation is 3% each and every year until he dies at age 95, what is the maximum annual income he can take out?

Table 1.3 shows the annuitized withdrawal rate for portfolio growth rate of 8%. For 3% indexation and retirement age of 65, we read the annuitized withdrawal rate as 6.6%.

PMT = 6.6% x $500,000 = $33,000

Therefore Bob can take out $33,000 annually starting at age 65, indexed at 3% each year until age 95. No money would be left at age 95.

Asset Multiplier:

The asset multiplier (AM) is the dollar amount of capital required at the beginning of retirement for each dollar of lifelong withdrawal. The withdrawal amount is indexed in subsequent years.

In the context of time value of money, the asset multiplier is calculated as 100 divided by the annuitized withdrawal rate. The annuitized withdrawal rate tables (Tables 1.1 through 1.3) already account for the indexation. Therefore, it is unnecessary to make further inflation adjustments.

During accumulation years, the typical question is "How much savings do I need to finance my/our retirement?" The asset multiplier answers this question.

To figure out the total savings required to finance the retirement, simply take the dollar amount of withdrawals required during the first year of retirement and multiply it with the asset multiplier.

$$AM = \frac{100}{AWR} \qquad \text{(Equation 1.14)}$$

The total savings required (SR) to finance retirement at the beginning of retirement is calculated as:

$$SR = PMT \times AM \qquad \text{(Equation 1.15)}$$

Tables 1.4, 1.5 and 1.6 show the asset multiplier for 4%, 6% and 8% annual growth (or interest) rates, respectively, for various retirement ages. Each table shows three levels of indexation, 2%, 3% and 4%. The future value of savings is assumed to be zero, i.e. no money left at death. The age of death is assumed to be 95. The periodic withdrawals are made at the end of each year.

Table 1.4: Asset multiplier based on a steady portfolio growth of 4% annually

Retirement Age	Asset Multiplier at 2% inflation	Asset Multiplier at 3% inflation	Asset Multiplier at 4% inflation
55	27.0	32.3	38.5
60	24.4	28.6	33.3
65	22.2	25.0	28.6
70	19.2	21.3	23.8
75	16.1	17.5	19.2

Table 1.5: Asset multiplier based on a steady portfolio growth of 6% annually

Retirement Age	Asset Multiplier at 2% inflation	at 3% inflation	at 4% inflation
55	19.6	23.3	26.3
60	18.5	21.3	24.4
65	17.2	19.2	21.7
70	15.4	16.9	18.9
75	13.3	14.5	15.9

Table 1.6: Asset multiplier based on a steady portfolio growth of 8% annually

Retirement Age	Asset Multiplier at 2% inflation	at 3% inflation	at 4% inflation
55	14.9	16.9	19.6
60	14.5	16.1	18.2
65	13.7	15.2	16.9
70	12.7	13.9	15.4
75	11.4	12.2	13.3

When calculating out the savings required for financing retirement, the first step is to establish a detailed retirement budget. A budget indicates the expected annual income from all sources on one hand, and all living expenses on the other hand. A shortfall of income exists if annual expenses are greater than expected annual income.

Next, calculate the future value of this shortfall of income at retirement age.

Finally, using the future value of the expected shortfall of income and the asset multiplier, calculate the total retirement savings required at the time of retirement.

Example 1.11

Bob, 60, is planning to retire at age 65. He needs $30,000 of income yearly in current dollars, indexed by 3% each year to keep up with inflation. Assuming Bob's portfolio grows 6% each year until he dies at age 95, how much total savings does he need to finance his entire retirement?

Table 1.5 shows the asset multiplier for 6% average portfolio growth. Look up for 3% inflation and retirement age of 65 and read the asset multiplier, 19.2.

Next, figure out the future value of $30,000 at age 65. Using Equation (1.1), 3% inflation and 5 year time period, calculate the future value of $30,000. It is $34,778 at age 65.

Savings Required, SR= $34,778 x 19.2 = $667,738

Bob needs to accumulate $667,738 by age 65 for his retirement.

Effect of Indexation Lag:

If indexation for inflation occurs once a year then there is a gap (loss) for the retiree throughout the year. This is because the purchasing power of the income stream decreases gradually over the year before the indexation kicks in. This can be significant during high inflation periods. In the eyes of the retiree, it seems that "he is never catching up with inflation", and rightfully so.

The effect of inflation lag is calculated by figuring out the difference between the purchasing power and payment streams for each period. You can use Equation 1.16 to calculate the *approximate* average loss of purchasing power by the end of the year.

$$LPP = \frac{k}{1.5 \times C} \qquad \text{(Equation 1.16)}$$

where:

k is the annual inflation

C is the number of indexations per year (1= annual, 2=semiannual, 4=quarterly)

LPP is the approximate loss of purchasing power in percentage by the end of year

In Equation 1.16, the following assumptions are made:

- inflation is steady throughout the year (prices increasing linearly over time)
- indexation frequency is annual, semiannual or quarterly
- the delay between the publication of the recent CPI and the actual indexation of the payments based on that data is insignificant (in reality, this may be a few months)

Table 1.7: Loss of purchasing power at the end of the year as a result of indexation lag

Annual Inflation	Indexation Frequency		
	Annual	Semiannual	Quarterly
	Loss of Purchasing Power		
0%	0.0%	0.0%	0.0%
2%	1.3%	0.7%	0.3%
4%	2.7%	1.3%	0.6%
6%	4.0%	2.0%	1.0%
8%	5.3%	2.7%	1.3%
10%	6.7%	3.3%	1.7%

Limitations of Time Value of Money:

The equations and tables cited in this chapter were developed to calculate annuities, loans, mortgages, interest amounts and other applications related to the time value of money. In these types of applications, the inputs are generally known for the duration of the contract.

Regretfully, we conveniently took these equations and applied them to retirement planning without blinking an eye. If you are using these equations and tables for retirement planning –as they are used in all standard retirement calculators– you are making two assumptions:

- the portfolio grows at the assumed rate *exactly, each and every year*
- the inflation rate is *exactly as assumed each and every year*

Don't fool yourself into thinking that, if you assume average historical returns, then everything will be fine. For these equations to reflect reality, averages are just not enough.

Conclusion:

There are many factors that influence the outcome of a retirement plan. Some of these factors are luck, variations in inflation, interest rate, portfolio performance, market cycles, investment strategies, asset allocation, asset selection, and management fees. As we will see in following chapters, many factors render the equations and tables cited in this chapter –as impressive looking as they might be– basically useless for realistic retirement planning.

Therefore, while it is important to know the tools that are currently used in financial planning, avoid using any of them. It is not enough to master the "Time Value of Money"; we must also be cognizant of the concept of "The Time Value of Fluctuations" which is what this book is all about.

A Historical Perspective

Most financial books become boring after the first couple of chapters. To keep you interested enough to continue reading this is a good place to shock you. I apologize beforehand for possibly deflating some of your dreams. However, unless we go through this painful process of exposing some of the common myths in financial planning, we cannot move forward. In this chapter, I will show you the current Gaussian mindset[4] of retirement planning practice and its disastrous outcomes.

Currently, there are two popular ways of forecasting the adequacy of retirement assets: the first method is called deterministic; the second is Monte Carlo simulations.

The deterministic method uses the formulae that we covered in Chapter 1, The Time Value of Money. After years of using it, more and more financial professionals are realizing that the deterministic method has serious flaws.

The Monte Carlo (MC) simulations are becoming more popular, I might add, regretfully so. They use probability models to overcome the weaknesses of the deterministic method. While MCs are better than the deterministic method, they also have serious flaws. I will cover those flaws in Chapter 15. In this chapter, I will focus on the deterministic method only. I don't want to over–shock you in one single dose.

The Current Practice:

Let's start with an example: Bob is 65 years old. He is retiring this year. He expects to live until age 95. His retirement savings are valued at one million dollars. He assumes an average annual index growth rate of 7.3%. By the way, this happens to be the average annual growth rate of DJIA between the years 1900 and 2004, inclusive.

The average dividend yield of DJIA was 4.4% between the years 1900 and 2004, inclusive. However, since the early 1980s, the dividend yields dropped precipitously. Going forward, Bob assumes that he will receive an average dividend of 2% annually. Bob calculates his portfolio's total average annual return as 8.8% – index return of 7.3% plus 2% dividend minus 0.5% for management fees.

He needs to withdraw $60,000 each year, indexed by 3% annually to maintain his purchasing power.

I plug in these numbers to a standard retirement calculator and obtain the portfolio value for each year during retirement, as shown in Table 2.1:

---

4 For a definition of Gaussian mindset, please read: Nassim Nicholas Taleb, "The Black Swan – The Impact of Highly Improbable" by Random House, 2007.

Table 2.1: Bob's asset projection based on the standard retirement plan

Age	Year	Begin Value $	Growth $	Withdrawal $	End Value $
65	1	$1,000,000	$88,000	$60,000	$1,028,000
66	2	$1,028,000	$90,464	$61,800	$1,056,664
67	3	$1,056,664	$92,986	$63,654	$1,085,996
68	4	$1,085,996	$95,567	$65,563	$1,116,000
69	5	$1,116,000	$98,208	$67,529	$1,146,679
70	6	$1,146,679	$100,907	$69,554	$1,178,032
71	7	$1,178,032	$103,666	$71,640	$1,210,058
72	8	$1,210,058	$106,485	$73,789	$1,242,754
73	9	$1,242,754	$109,362	$76,002	$1,276,114
74	10	$1,276,114	$112,298	$78,282	$1,310,130
75	11	$1,310,130	$115,291	$80,630	$1,344,791
76	12	$1,344,791	$118,341	$83,048	$1,380,084
77	13	$1,380,084	$121,447	$85,539	$1,415,992
78	14	$1,415,992	$124,607	$88,105	$1,452,494
79	15	$1,452,494	$127,819	$90,748	$1,489,565
80	16	$1,489,565	$131,081	$93,470	$1,527,176
81	17	$1,527,176	$134,391	$96,274	$1,565,293
82	18	$1,565,293	$137,745	$99,162	$1,603,876
83	19	$1,603,876	$141,141	$102,136	$1,642,881
84	20	$1,642,881	$144,573	$105,200	$1,682,254
85	21	$1,682,254	$148,038	$108,356	$1,721,936
86	22	$1,721,936	$151,530	$111,606	$1,761,860
87	23	$1,761,860	$155,043	$114,954	$1,801,949
88	24	$1,801,949	$158,571	$118,402	$1,842,118
89	25	$1,842,118	$162,106	$121,954	$1,882,270
90	26	$1,882,270	$165,639	$125,612	$1,922,297
91	27	$1,922,297	$169,162	$129,380	$1,962,079
92	28	$1,962,079	$172,662	$133,261	$2,001,480
93	29	$2,001,480	$176,130	$137,258	$2,040,352
94	30	$2,040,352	$179,550	$141,375	$2,078,527

Figure 2.1: Projected value of retirement assets over time

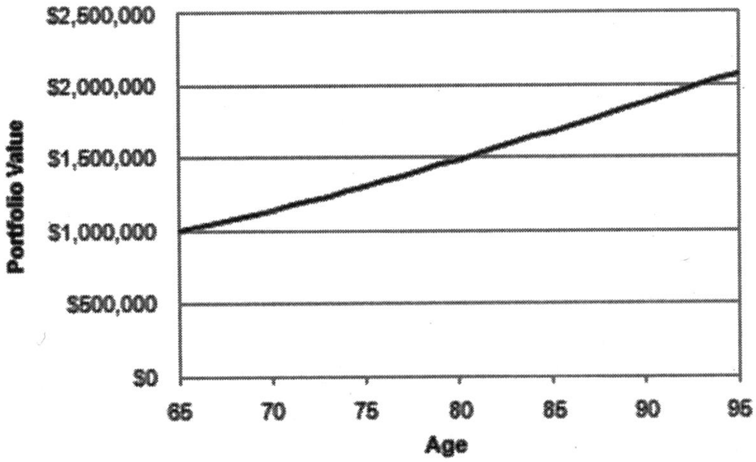

We depict Bob's retirement assets in Figure 2.1: Bob's retirement plan shows a smooth line that indicates an increasing value of his investments. Looking at this chart, with a sigh of relief, Bob is happy to see that his million–dollar portfolio should last him over his lifetime and leave an estate worth over $2,000,000 at age 95.

Bob thinks, just because I, the financial planner, can forecast 30 years into the future so neatly and precisely using very reasonable assumptions, that I must be a very smart advisor. He is elated. Needless to say, if he switches his account from the other advisor to me, I will be also happy.

The Reality:

We all know that investments do not grow on a straight line. Let us make two seemingly minor changes to our assumptions:

- Instead of using an average growth rate of 8.8%, let's use the actual market growth.
- Instead of using an average inflation of 3%, let's use the actual inflation.

It is no secret that since 1900, the worst market crash occurred between 1929 and 1932. On a monthly chart, the DJIA[5] lost about 90% peak–to–trough during that time. Therefore, it is logical that we should look at what would have happened to Bob's portfolio if he retired at the beginning of 1929.

[5] DJIA (Dow Jones Industrial Average) is developed, maintained and licensed by Dow Jones Indexes, part of Dow Jones & Company, Inc.

Bob's son, Bob II, retires in 1966. This happens to be the start of a long–term sideways trend that lasted until 1982. We go through the same steps and figure out what would have happened in real life during Bob II's retirement.

Bob's grandson, Bob III, retires at the beginning of 2000, when the last secular bullish trend ended. The ensuing three–year back–to–back market losses were the worst since the 1929 crash.

Retiring in 1929:

Continuing with our example, let us work out Bob's portfolio value, starting at the beginning of 1929. Table 2.2 shows the historical data that we used to recreate Bob's hypothetical portfolio value. We assume that he pays an average of 0.5% management fees, which is probably low by today's standards.

Table 2.2: Historical data used, retiring at the beginning of 1929

End of Year	% Change of DJIA	Dividend Yield %	Mgmt Cost %	Net Growth %	Inflation %
1929	–17.17%	4.10%	0.50%	–13.57%	0.6%
1930	–33.77%	4.70%	0.50%	–29.57%	–6.4%
1931	–52.67%	6.10%	0.50%	–47.07%	–9.3%
1932	–23.07%	7.20%	0.50%	–16.37%	–10.3%
1933	66.69%	4.10%	0.50%	70.29%	0.8%
1934	4.14%	3.70%	0.50%	7.34%	1.5%
1935	38.53%	3.80%	0.50%	41.83%	3.0%
1936	24.82%	4.30%	0.50%	28.62%	1.4%
1937	–32.82%	5.30%	0.50%	–28.02%	2.9%
1938	28.06%	3.80%	0.50%	31.36%	–2.8%
1939	–2.92%	4.30%	0.50%	0.88%	0.0%

Table 2.3: Bob's portfolio value if he had retired at the beginning of 1929

Bob's Age	Year	Begin Value $	Growth $ (Loss $)	Withdrawal $	End Value $
65	1	$1,000,000	($135,700)	$60,000	$804,300
66	2	$804,300	($237,832)	$60,360	$506,108
67	3	$506,108	($238,225)	$56,497	$211,386
68	4	$211,386	($34,604	$51,242	$125,540
69	5	$125,540	$88,242	$45,964	$167,818
70	6	$167,818	$12,318	$46,332	$133,804
71	7	$133,804	$55,970	$47,027	$142,747
72	8	$142,747	$40,854	$48,438	$135,163
73	9	$135,163	($37,873)	$49,116	$48,174
74	10	$48,174	$15,107	$50,540	$12,741
75	11	$12,741	$112	$49,125	$0

Figure 2.2: Value of retirement assets over time, projection of a standard retirement calculator versus retiring at the beginning of 1929

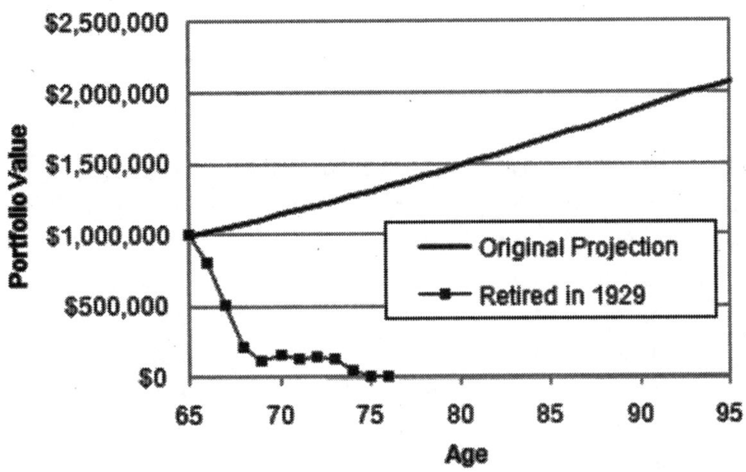

So much for the $2,000,000 projected estate value at age 95. Bob is broke ten years and three months into his retirement.

If this were one of my retirement planning workshops, usually at this point someone in the audience would shout: "You picked the worst year of the last century. Surely, the government won't let it happen again!"

Yes, it is a fact that I picked seemingly[6] the worst year of the last century. Whether future governments, the Federal Reserve or any other central bank will have any power to prevent a similar financial disaster is yet to be seen. The prevailing budget deficits in most of the industrialized nations, the ever–increasing enormous trade deficits of the greatest economic power in the world and the appalling human greed in the financial industry, make me believe that a financial crisis of 1929 proportions can easily happen again.

Nevertheless, setting aside my personal opinion, let us continue.

Retiring in 1966:

This is when Bob II retired. The year 1966 was the start of a secular sideways trend that finally ended in 1981. During that time, the index just went up and down in a cyclical fashion for sixteen years. In 1981, it was basically at the same place as where it had been in 1966. Table 2.4 shows the historical data used.

Table 2.4: Historical data used, retiring at the beginning of 1966

End of Year	% Change of DJIA	Dividend Yield %	Mgmt Cost %	Net Growth %	Inflation %
1966	–18.94%	3.70%	0.50%	–15.74%	3.5%
1967	15.20%	3.40%	0.50%	18.10%	3.0%
1968	4.27%	3.50%	0.50%	7.27%	4.7%
1969	–15.19%	3.90%	0.50%	–11.79%	6.2%
1970	4.82%	4.20%	0.50%	8.52%	5.6%
1971	6.11%	3.50%	0.50%	9.11%	3.3%
1972	14.58%	3.40%	0.50%	17.48%	3.4%
1973	–16.58%	3.80%	0.50%	–13.28%	8.7%
1974	–27.57%	5.00%	0.50%	–23.07%	12.3%
1975	38.32%	4.70%	0.50%	42.52%	6.9%
1976	17.86%	4.20%	0.50%	21.56%	4.9%
1977	–17.27%	5.10%	0.50%	–12.67%	6.7%
1978	–3.15%	5.90%	0.50%	2.25%	9.0%
1979	4.19%	6.00%	0.50%	9.69%	13.3%

[6] Seemingly: If one were to pick a more conservative asset allocation, say 40% equity and 60% fixed income, 1929 would not be the worst year to retire during the last century.

Table 2.5: Bob II's portfolio value if he had retired at the beginning of 1966

Bob II's Age	Year	Begin Value $	Growth $ (Loss $)	Withdrawal $	End Value $
65	1	$1,000,000	($157,400)	$60,000	$782,600
66	2	$782,600	$141,651	$62,100	$862,151
67	3	$862,151	$62,678	$63,963	$860,866
68	4	$860,866	($101,496)	$66,969	$692,401
69	5	$692,401	$58,993	$71,121	$680,273
70	6	$680,273	$61,973	$75,104	$667,142
71	7	$667,142	$116,616	$77,582	$706,176
72	8	$706,176	($93,780)	$80,220	$532,176
73	9	$532,176	($122,773)	$87,199	$322,204
74	10	$322,204	$137,001	$97,924	$361,281
75	11	$361,281	$77,892	$104,681	$334,492
76	12	$334,492	($42,380)	$109,810	$182,302
77	13	$182,302	$4,102	$117,167	$69,237
78	14	$69,237	$6,709	$127,712	$0

If Bob II were to retire at the beginning of 1966, his portfolio would have lasted only 13 years and 7 months.

Figure 2.3: Value of retirement assets over time, projection of a standard retirement calculator versus retiring at the beginning of 1966

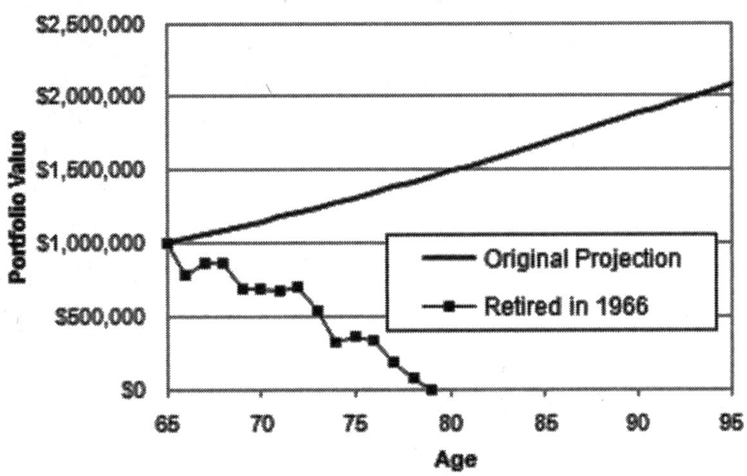

Retiring in 2000:

This is when the grandson, Bob III, retired. The years leading to 2000 were the longest bull–run of the 20th century. Let's see what happens to his portfolio. This time, we use the S&P500 index[7] as the proxy of equity returns. The historical data is depicted in Table 2.6.

Table 2.6: Historical data used, retiring at the beginning of 2000

End of Year	% Change of S&P500	Dividend Yield %	Mgmt Cost %	Net Growth %	Inflation %
2000	–10.14%	1.2%	0.50%	–9.44%	3.4%
2001	–13.03%	1.5%	0.50%	–12.03%	1.6%
2002	–23.36%	1.3%	0.50%	–22.56%	2.4%
2003	26.38%	1.8%	0.50%	27.68%	1.9%
2004	8.99%	1.4%	0.50%	9.89%	3.3%
2005	3.00%	1.9%	0.50%	4.40%	3.4%
2006	13.6%	2.0%	0.50%	15.12%	2.5%
2007	3.5%	1.5%	0.50%	4.5%	4.1%
2008	–38.5%	3.0%	0.50%	–36.0%	0.1%

Table 2.7: Bob III's portfolio value if he had retired at the beginning of 2000

Bob III's Age	Year	Begin Value $	Growth $ (Loss $)	Withdrawal $	End Value $
65	1	1,000,000	(94,400)	60,000	845,570
66	2	845,570	(101,722)	62,040	681,808
67	3	681,808	(153,816)	63,033	464,959
68	4	464,959	128,701	64,545	529,115
69	5	529,115	52,329	65,772	515,672
70	6	515,672	22,690	67,942	470,420
71	7	470,420	71,128	70,252	471,296
72	8	471,296	21,208	72,009	420,495
73	9	420,495	(151,378)	74,961	194,156
74	10	194,156		75,036	

The portfolio value at the end of 2008 would have been $194,156.

[7] S&P 500 is developed, maintained and licensed by Standard & Poor's Financial Services LLC, a subsidiary of The McGraw–Hill Companies, Inc.

Figure 2.4: Value of retirement assets over time, projection of a standard retirement calculator versus retiring at the beginning of 2000

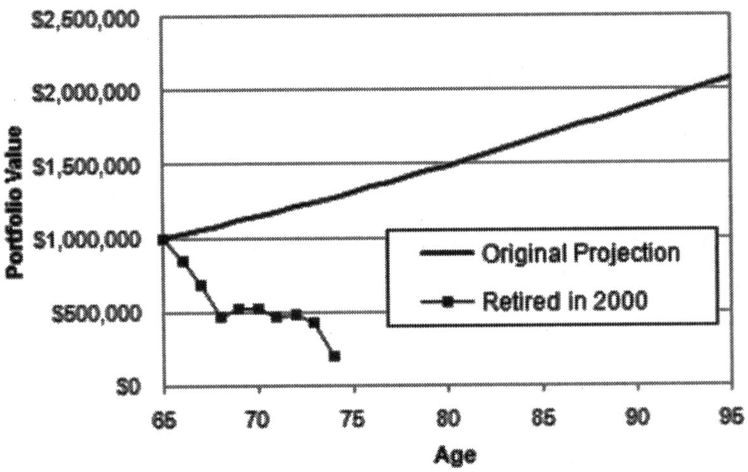

Going forward from 2008 (the last year of available data at the time of writing), we can make a new projection using the historical 8.8% average growth rate and 3% indexation. This projection indicates that Bob will run out of money in 3 years, at age 77. This new and improved projection is probably as unrealistic as our original one. He will likely run out of money sooner than that.

Figure 2.5: Value of retirement assets over time, projection of a standard retirement calculator versus retiring at the beginning of 2000

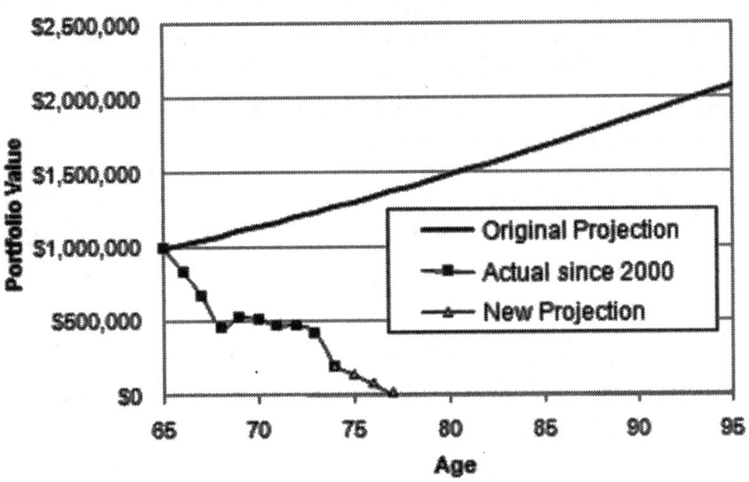

This was the tale for the three generations of retirees: The grandfather, Bob, ran out of money at age 75. His son, Bob II, ran out of money at age 79. His grandson, Bob III, is likely to run out of money by age 77, if not sooner.

What about the $2 million that we originally projected based on averages? Don't worry about that; it is just another pipedream, similar to what we have been selling to all our clients.

Averages do not apply to individuals!

Retiring in Any Year since 1900:

Still not convinced? What if I run the same calculation for each and every one of the years since 1900? This would be the real test. I can then draw the portfolio value for each starting point of retirement on the same chart. That way, I create a bird's eye view of the entire market history. It shows us the luckiest outcome, the unluckiest outcome, and everything in between. Remember, this chart does not have any assumed growth rates or assumed inflation. This is no forecast, but an **aftcast**.

The weather people (i.e. meteorologists) use aftcasting all the time. They analyze atmospheric patterns. When you watch the weather report on your TV, you can see it in a fast–forward motion. In a second or two, you can see how clouds have been moving all day long in your area. It is the ultimate reality show. By looking at it, the weatherman can then easily determine what kind of weather to expect the next day.

This is exactly what I am doing by aftcasting a retirement plan; showing you the financial patterns of the past. Some people say "Past is past, future results will be different". By saying that, they try to justify their misguided projections and assumptions. However, with our ingrained human emotions over thousands of years, we like to believe in forecasts. It is just that we now have different tools and communication methods of expressing it or dealing with them. Aftcasting will at least show you the *range* of what to expect during your retirement and help you prepare for it.

Figure 2.6 depicts the portfolio value of all portfolios as if one were to start his retirement in any one of the years since 1900. I used the actual historical market performance, actual historical dividends, 0.5% management fee and actual historical inflation for each year to construct each line on the chart.

Earlier, we made seemingly reasonable assumptions for the average growth rate, dividends, management costs and inflation. Then, we entered these figures into the standard retirement calculator. When we observe Figure 2.6, we realize that all this careful consideration was totally and absolutely meaningless. If you are lucky, your initial one million dollars would have grown to over $3 million in ten years, at age 75. If you are unlucky, you'd run out of money in ten years! There is nothing average about it.

Figure 2.6: Comparison of projection of a standard retirement calculator versus retiring in each of the years since 1900 using historical data, equity portfolio

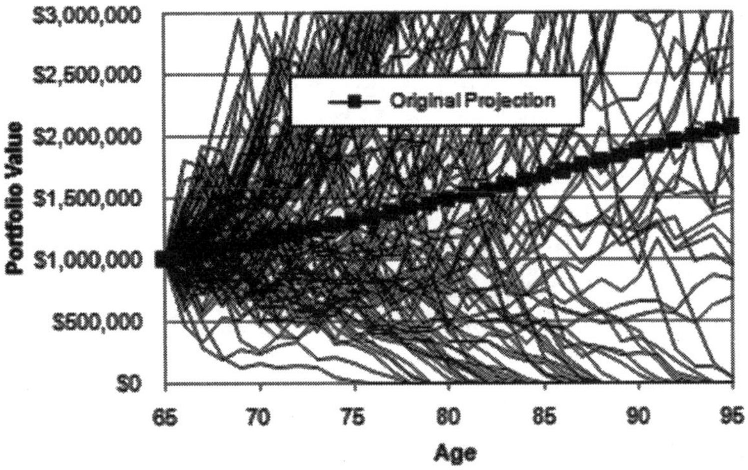

The asset projection line generated by the standard retirement calculator (the heavy line) appears far from forecasting any outcome. You could as easily have picked an average portfolio growth rate of 15% and come up with delightful results. Or, you could have picked a growth rate of 2% and you would be just as accurate, but less happy with the outcome. As a matter of fact, you can assume any growth rate in your standard retirement and be "right" occasionally!

In reality, using Bob's example, over 62% of portfolios had a lower asset value at age 95 than the projected amount of $2,087,527. By the time Bob reached age 95, 45% of portfolios would have run out of money completely. Not a pretty sight, is it?

What is Retirement Planning?

Before we can answer the question "What is retirement planning?" let's first try to answer "What is *not* retirement planning?" We, the financial advisors, produce all kinds of retirement plans for our clients. Also, investors can go to financial websites, enter their own numbers and produce retirement plans[8].

---

[8] Example: The retirement calculator on the web site of "Investor Education Fund" established by Ontario Securities Commission, (www.investored.ca/IefCalculators/Calculators/RrspSavings/) allows you to enter an average annual portfolio growth rate of 30%! This certainly has nothing to do with retirement planning. If you do not like what you read in this chapter, go to their website, use their calculator and all your retirement worries will likely disappear. Then come back and continue reading this book.

In reality, most of these plans are produced for only one reason: to sell dreams. Many financial planners do that, many stockbrokers do that, mutual funds do that, hedge funds do that, many pension managers do that. Just about anyone in the financial industry is here to sell you some form of dreams. Throughout history, emperors were guided by clairvoyants, fortune tellers and dream–interpreters. Now that we are a more advanced society, we are guided by the dream–makers of the financial industry.

We might tweak portfolio growth and inflation by 1% here and 1% there and *voila* you have a perfect plan. "Save this much each year, take more risk", we say, "and if your portfolio grows by an average of 8% each year, you'll have enough money to retire at 65 and live happily ever after. Now, that you know you will have this much money, let's do some estate planning. We need to set up this trust, that foundation, buy life insurance to pay taxes at death…" and so on and so forth. "You are set for life" That is **not** retirement planning.

To protect ourselves, we include a disclaimer with the written plan, something like "markets are subject to fluctuation". In my vocabulary, the word "fluctuation" implies a deviation from some "normal" number. In reality, what might happen is not just a fluctuation, but it can be a disaster or bliss. If you are lucky your portfolio can triple in value in ten years. And if you are not lucky, it can deplete totally in ten years. That certainly is a lot more than a fluctuation. So, our first step must be to design a retirement plan that is as foolproof as possible.

Now, let's answer what retirement planning is. From the financial aspect, retirement planning is the process of designing and following a strategy that will provide a lifelong income for the retiree. When we are designing a plan, we must focus on the lower part of the aftcast chart. This is where all bad things happen. This is where a good design can protect you. It is not about wishful thinking, it is not about making assumptions, and it is not about selling dreams. It is about confronting reality.

Figure 2.7: Planning zones on the asset chart

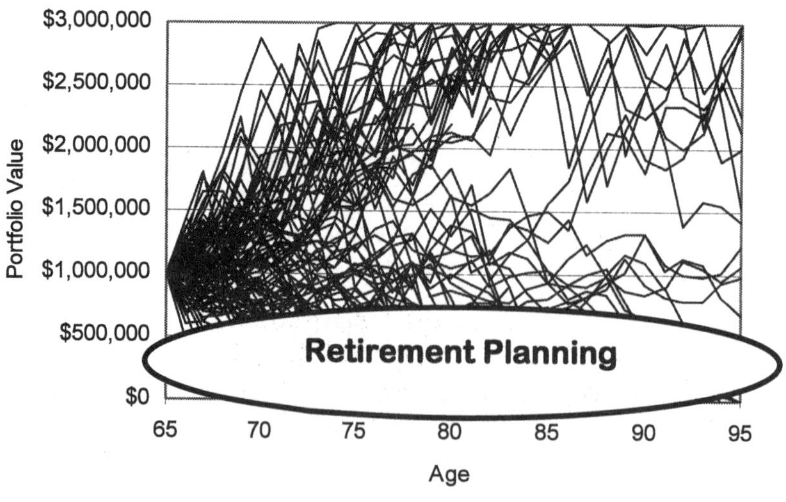

Figure 2.8: Planning zones on the asset chart

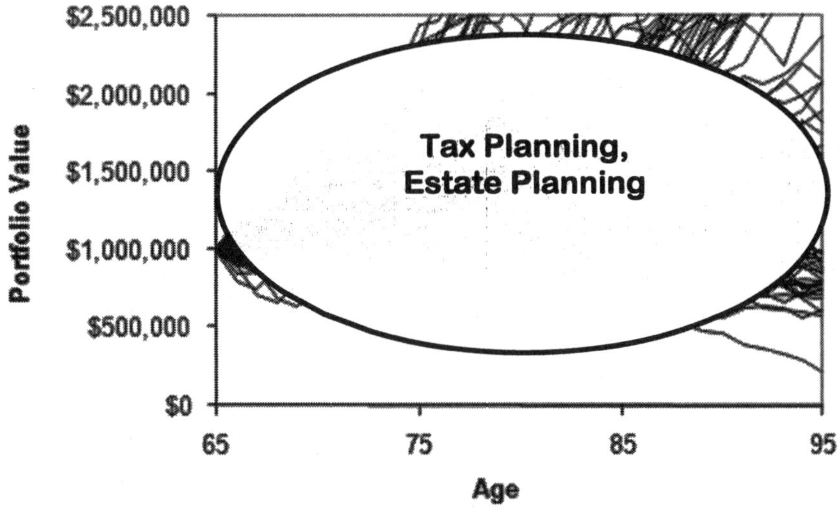

Focus on the lower part, as indicated on Figure 2.7. Make sure a lifelong income is provided under any circumstance. Fix the situation so that the chart looks like Figure 2.8. Only after that can you start talking about "...set up this trust, that foundation, buy life insurance to pay taxes at death..." Estate planning and tax planning cannot proceed until a solid retirement plan covering the *unlucky* outcomes is firmly in place.

Conclusion:

You might ask "Over the last 100 years, the market index returned on average 8.8% annually. Why is it then, if I withdraw 6% (initial withdrawal rate, indexed to inflation), the probability of running out of money is so high?" The reason is a little known concept called the "Time Value of Fluctuations". It is covered in Chapter 13.

At this point, you need to know that any assumptions, reasonable or not, have no bearing on the outcome of a retirement plan unless one considers the concept of the time value of fluctuations. However, before we get there, I need to expose some more of the myths and aberrations prevalent in our world.

Chapter 3

Dividends

I love dividends. I had a portfolio of five DRIP[9] stocks over twenty years ago. It kept growing and growing by about 15% annually despite the Latin American crisis, Russian debt crisis, market crash of 2000, another crisis by LTCM –a hedge fund created by some smart Nobel Prize winning academics[10].

I wrote a book[11] about Canadian dividend reinvestment plans (DRIPs) in 1996 to share my experience with others. The publisher of a magazine used to call me whenever he had some blank space to fill. In particular, he would ask me to write an update about my DRIP portfolio. Each time, I did so with pleasure because it was almost always good news.

Traditionally, companies shared their profits with investors in the form of dividends. Between 1900 and 1990, the average dividend yield was about 4.5% (see Figure 6). Since early 1990s this tradition was gradually abandoned. Nowadays[12] the average dividend is around 2%.

Figure 3.1: Historical dividend yields

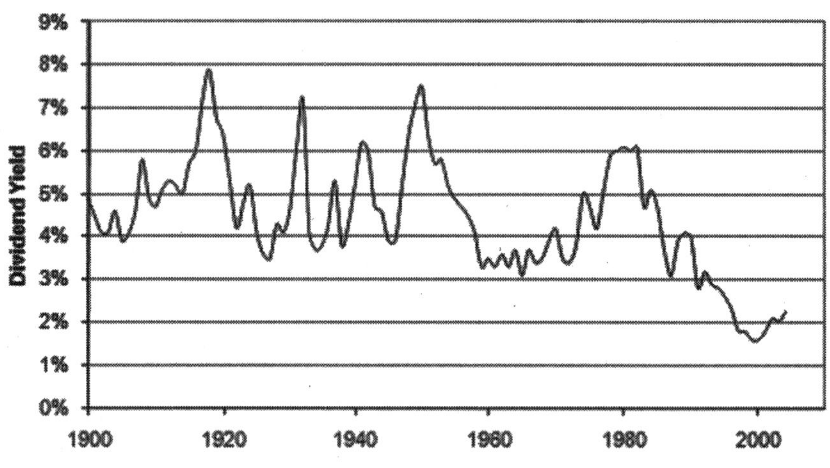

[9] DRIP is an acronym for Dividend ReInvestment Plan.
[10] After the 2008 crisis, many other hedge funds collapsed or shut down.
[11] author, “Commission Free Investing – Handbook of Canadian DRIPs and SPPs”, Uphill Publishing
[12] at the time of writing this chapter, early 2007.

While dividends are a significant part of the total return in accumulation portfolios, the scenario is different for distribution portfolios. Statements such as "over the long term half of the total return is from dividends" may apply to accumulation portfolios of the past, but they certainly do not apply to distribution portfolios. If you used historical dividends for your retirement planning, you would be generating unrealistically optimistic projections.

There are four reasons for not using historical dividends for retirement planning:

- Compounding of dividends takes time. If a distribution portfolio depletes in fifteen years, there is no significant compounding. That is because you would not only be drawing down the capital, but also cashing out some or all of the dividends. In other words, the compound return from dividends becomes significant only if you are lucky, catch a secular bull market and don't rely on dividends.
- Dividends compound only if they are present. From their current low levels, dividends can go back to their historical levels only (a) if markets lose more than half[13] of their value while earnings and dividends remain the same, (b) if companies decide to double their current dividends immediately, (c) some combination of both. Until that happens, apply prevailing dividend rates and not historical rates for your retirement planning.
- If you invest in mutual funds, the portfolio costs will eat away most, if not all, of the dividends.
- Last but not least, as long as generous stock options are the preferred method of rewarding the voracious appetite of company executives, their preference will be to increase the stock price. This can be achieved by buying back company shares instead of distributing the profits as dividends. Dividends don't increase the value of their options; the increased stock price (due to the share buy–backs) does. This is a serious conflict of interest between short–sighted corporate executives and long–term shareholders. This conflict of interest must eventually be resolved for the sake of preserving capitalism. However, as long as there is an abundance of capital in the markets, there is little incentive to change the status quo. Scarcity of capital might trigger such a positive change in the future.

Another common misconception is that it is feasible to withdraw the sustainable withdrawal rate (SWR) *plus* the dividend. That may be mathematically correct for average portfolios in average times, but when we talk about the SWR for individuals, we anticipate and design for the worst case situation. During these time periods, the benefit of dividends diminishes significantly.

---

[13] After the 2008 market crash, the average dividend yield became higher. At the end of 2008, the average dividend yield for DJIA reached 4%. However, reported earnings can drop significantly throughout 2009. Looking forward, many companies may not be able to maintain their dividends.

For example, if you had retired at the beginning of 1929, by 1932 stocks had lost 85% of their value and the dividend payout of surviving stocks changed from about 3.5% to about 7%. If you were counting on receiving $100 per month of income from dividends, now you'd be receiving only $30 per month for that year[14]. The shortfall of $70 per month must come from the capital, but most of that was lost too.

Some academics argue that the past stock market performance is an essential part of the higher historical dividends. I agree with that wholeheartedly. The flaw that many fall into subsequently is this: they go on to conclude that only the historical dividends should be used with historical index returns when forecasting retirement portfolio value. This is an incorrect conclusion. A lower dividend environment creates weaker stock price support. That means in a lower dividend environment, we can expect lower appreciation and higher volatility of stock prices. Both of these factors will cause faster depletion of a distribution portfolio for those who are planning to retire in the next ten years or so.

Remember Bob II in the previous chapter? He was 65 years old when he retired in 1966. His retirement savings were valued at one million dollars. He needed to withdraw $60,000 each year, indexed to actual inflation.

Figure 3.2 depicts the difference in portfolio life for retiring in 1966 when using the historical dividend, 2% dividend or no dividend (index return only). Higher historical dividends hardly made a difference in portfolio life for this distribution portfolio.

Figure 3.2: Retiring in 1966, effect of dividends, initial withdrawal rate of 6%

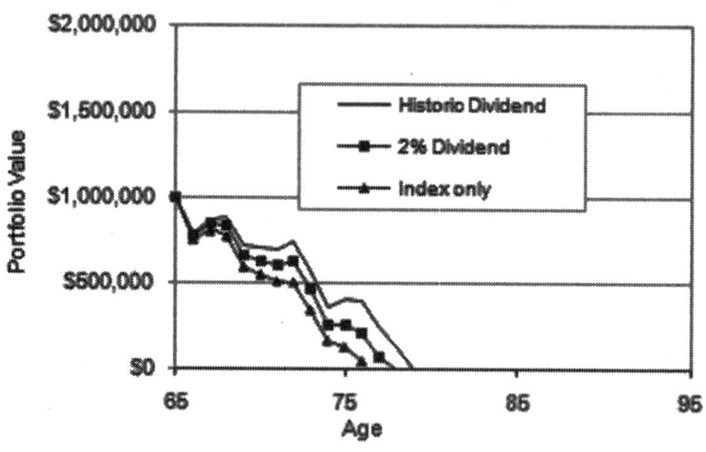

By the way, in an accumulation portfolio, this 1966 picture would be entirely different. Dividends would be the most important component of the portfolio growth.

---

[14] Calculated as (100% – 85%) X 7% / 3.5%

Looking at the market history since 1900, we compare the effect of using the current dividend yield versus using historical dividends. Figures 3.3 and 3.4 depict the difference. When a 2% dividend yield was used, the probability of depletion by age 95 was 71%. When historical dividend yield was used, then the probability of depletion was 45%. Don't trick yourself into thinking that your plan is OK by using the better looking historical dividend rates in your plans.

Figure 3.3: Using historical dividend yield less 0.5% management costs, equity portfolio, all years since 1900

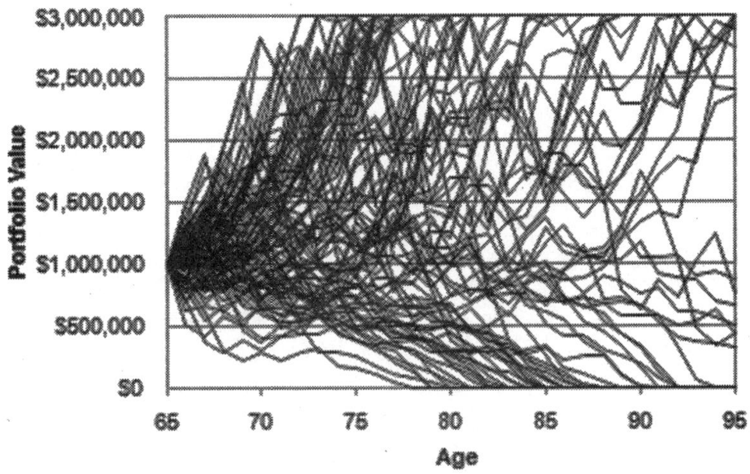

Figure 3.4: Using 2% dividend yield less 0.5% management fees, equity portfolio, all years since 1900

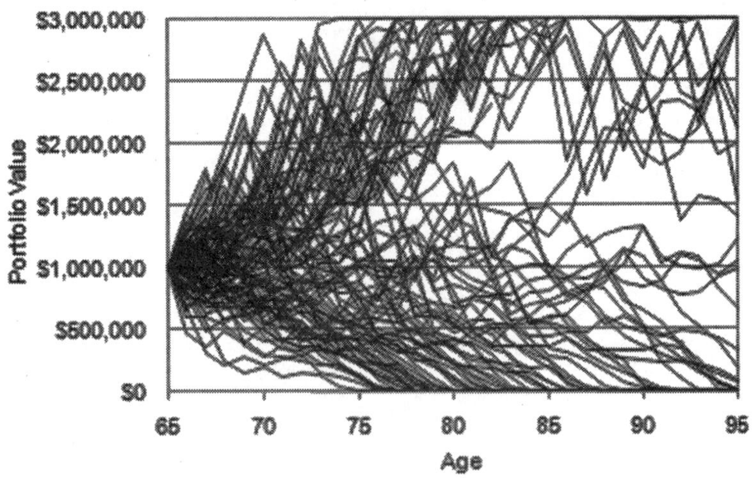

Conclusion:

It is important to understand that dividends do not convert an unlucky retirement portfolio into a lucky one. Dividends merely make the lucky portfolios luckier. At best, dividends add one or two years to an unlucky portfolio life.

And please stop saying “over the long term half of total return is from dividends”. It is just not true for the majority of retirement portfolios.

There are several academic studies that use the historical dividend yield to arrive at some conclusions on retirement planning strategies. Ignore them entirely. Their authors are confusing the past with the future. Use the prevailing dividend yield (2% at the time of writing) less portfolio management fees when preparing retirement plans.

Chapter 4

The "Importance" of Asset Allocation

> *"Research has shown that asset allocation is the single largest contributor to a portfolio's success. It is much more important than security selection. In fact, one study concluded that asset allocation accounted for over 90% of the difference in a portfolio's investment return."*

Different variations of this mantra appear in articles, sales brochures, and newsletters in the financial media. Each time I read it, I imagine myself at an auction: I can almost hear the auctioneer shouting: "I have 90% for asset allocation, do I hear 100%!"

What was this research? It is based on the study by Gary P. Brinson, Randolph L. Hood, and Gilbert L Beebower, "Determinants of Portfolio Performance II," Financial Analysts Journal, January/February 1995. This was a follow–up study to their original one in 1986.

What did this research encompass? It analyzed data from 91 large corporate pension plans with assets of at least $100 million over a 10–year period beginning in 1974.

What was its conclusion? The components of the *difference in success* of a portfolio are: Asset allocation: 93.6%; Security selection 2.5%; Other: 2.2%; Market timing 1.7%.

I have no doubt this study is very important for large pension funds. Keep in mind that pension fund managers usually come from the same school[15] and investments usually come from the same pool[16]. That being the case, it is no wonder that asset allocation may appear to be one of the most important contributors to the success of large pension funds.

Here is the problem: The findings of the Brinson study cannot be transferred, scaled or applied to individual retirement portfolios. Here are the reasons:

- The dynamics of cash flow in a pension fund are entirely different from the dynamics of cash flow in an individual retirement account. When there is a shortfall in a pension fund, then contributions are increased to meet this shortfall. A pension fund is an "open–perpetual" system; an individual retirement account is a "closed–finite" system.
- A pension fund has a continuous inflow of money over time. In an individual retirement account, inflow of money occurs up to a point. After that point there is no more inflow, but only outflow.
- The portfolio management costs are vastly different. This makes a big difference over time.

[15] meaning, "school of thought", "school of investment concepts and philosophies"
[16] meaning, "pool of standard investments available", like bonds and widely–held common stocks

- In an individual retirement account, once the withdrawals start, the effect of "reverse dollar–cost–averaging" becomes important. In a pension fund, since there is a continuous inflow of money, this effect is insignificant.
- In an individual account, inflation is important. Withdrawals must be increased over time to maintain the same purchasing power. In pension funds, there is no such concern; as inflation goes up, salaries also go up and pension contributions increase as well. This ensures that the effect of inflation is insignificant in the pension account as far as cash flow is concerned.
- The twenty–year time frame of the study is too short. It basically rides on a single secular bullish trend. Such a short time frame will miss significant events that might be present only in other types of secular market trends.

Figure 4.1: Time period covered in the Brinson study

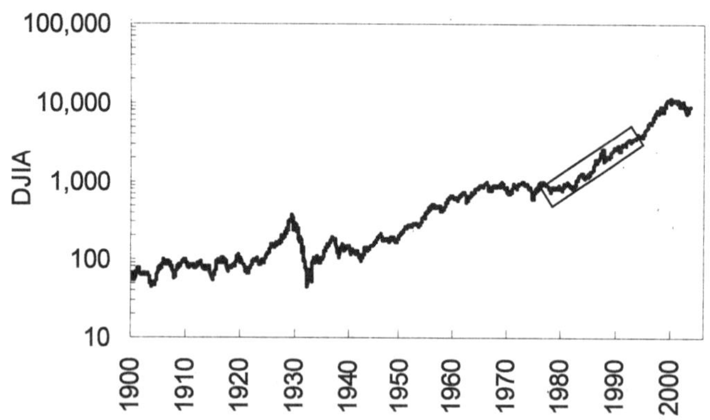

The Brinson study is a valuable research work. There is no doubt that asset allocation is important for a pension fund's success, subject to the limitations mentioned above. However, it is abused by many, sometimes to the point of outright lying. In one of my presentations, the speaker before me was from a well–known mutual fund company. These were his words: "Asset allocation contributes to over 90% of a portfolio's success. All you have to do is sit down with your client, decide on an asset allocation, and leave the rest to us". He conveniently dropped *difference in success* from his utterance, as well as the importance of asset selection (his funds were performing at a mediocre level at best).

Many in our profession try hard to make investors believe that asset allocation is the Holy Grail of investing. When a new account is opened, the first thing a client does is to fill out a risk–assessment questionnaire. Based on the client's answers, he or she is then pigeonholed into one of four or five investment portfolios. Is this the right thing to do?

The Reality:

Let's look at an example: Bill is 65 years old. He is retiring this year. He expects to live until age 95. His retirement savings are valued at one million dollars. He needs to withdraw $60,000 each year, indexed to actual inflation. On the equity side, his equity proxy is S&P500. He expects an average of 2% dividend yield, pays 0.5% management fees. On the fixed income side, he expects a return of 0.5% over and above the historical 6–month CD rates after all management fees.

Bill, like many others, has been bombarded with the asset allocation hype in the past. Therefore, he now questions whether the asset allocation between equities and fixed income is that important. He wants to know the probability of running out of money by age 95. He looks at the market history for answers.

Let's look at how his portfolios would have performed if he were to start his retirement in any of the years between 1900 and 1999. We calculate for six different asset mixes: 100/0, 80/20, 60/40, 40/60, 20/80, 0/100 of equity/fixed income. Figures 4.2 through 4.7 depict the asset value.

Figure 4.2: Asset allocation: 100% equity, 0% fixed income
Probability of depletion 71%, median portfolio expiry age: 87

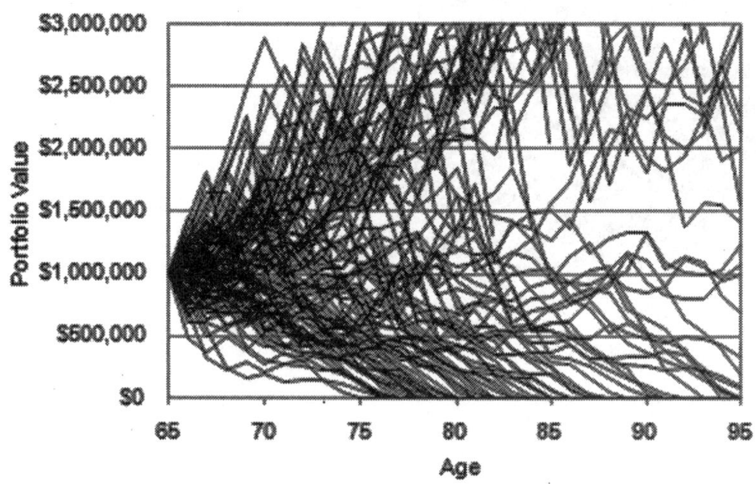

Figure 4.3: Asset allocation: 80% equity, 20% fixed income
Probability of depletion 69%, median portfolio expiry age: 87

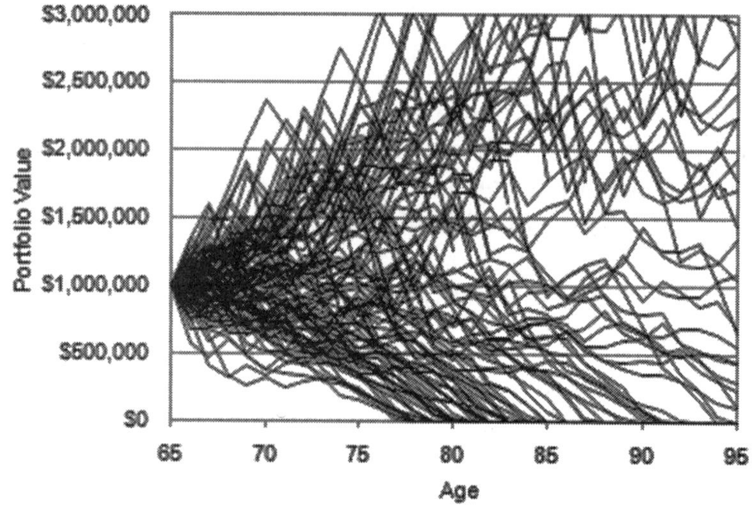

Figure 4.4: Asset allocation: 60% equity, 40% fixed income
Probability of depletion 76%, median portfolio expiry age: 87

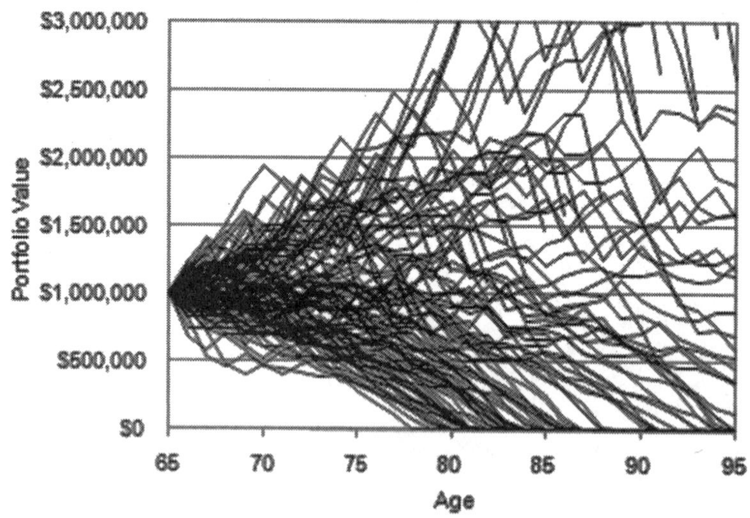

Figure 4.5: Asset allocation: 40% equity, 60% fixed income
Probability of depletion 81%, median portfolio expiry age: 87

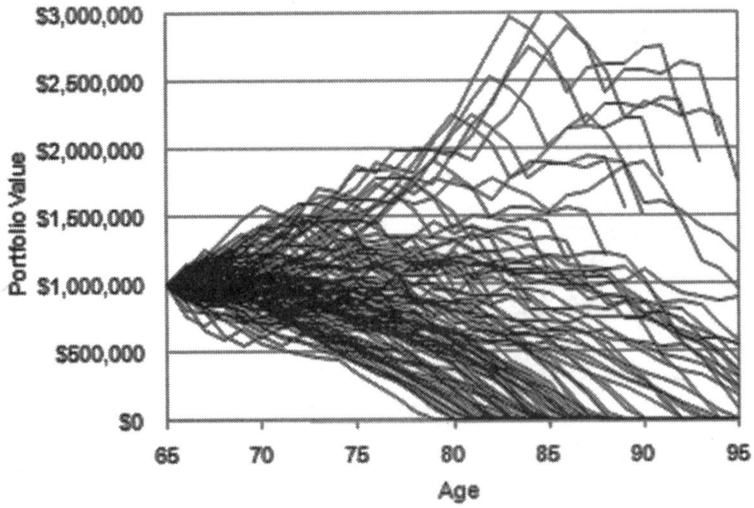

Figure 4.6: Asset allocation: 20% equity, 80% fixed income
Probability of depletion 95%, median portfolio expiry age: 87

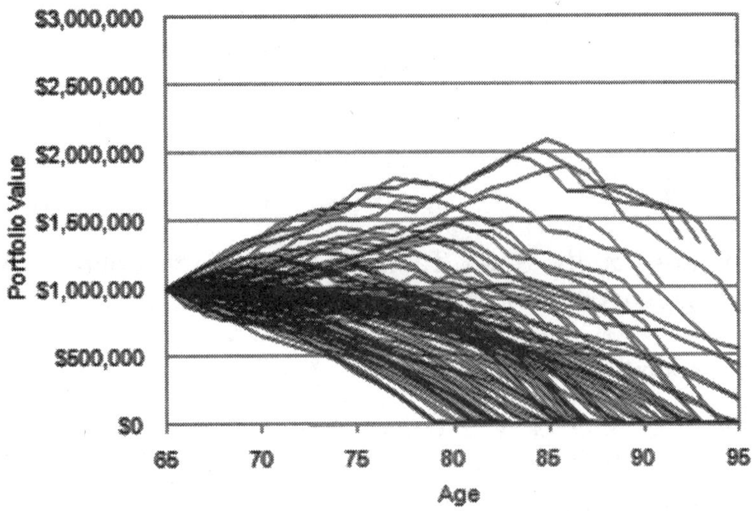

Figure 4.7: Asset allocation: 0% equity, 100% fixed income
Probability of depletion 96%, median portfolio expiry age: 87

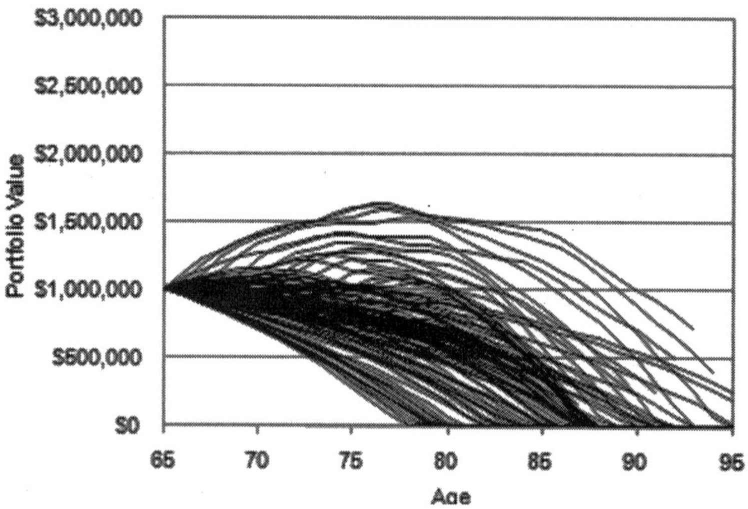

Table 4.1: Probability of depletion for all portfolios from very conservative to very aggressive

Asset Mix Equity / Fixed Income	Probability of Depletion by Age 95	Median Portfolio depleted at Age
100% Equity	71%	87
80 / 20	69%	87
60 / 40	76%	87
40 / 60	81%	87
20 / 80	95%	87
100% Fixed Income	96%	87

Observe Figures 4.2 through 4.6 carefully. Study Table 4.1. What do you notice? What happens as we go from most aggressive (100% equity) to most conservative (0% equity)?

This is what asset allocation accomplished:

- As the portfolio becomes more conservative, its volatility decreases. The advisor will receive panicky phone calls from clients less often. The risk of losing a client or litigation as a result of higher losses is also reduced.
- As the portfolio becomes more conservative, the potential for making "a lot" of money decreases. In the portfolio with 100% fixed income (Figure 4.7), Bill's portfolio value never exceeds $1.6 million. In the portfolio with 100% equity (Figure 4.2), there is a much higher chance of making "a lot" more money.

This is what asset allocation did *not* accomplish:

- If Bill is unlucky[17], the portfolio life does not improve significantly. When bad things happen, portfolios start to run out of money somewhere between ages 75 and 79.
- The probability of depletion does not improve significantly. The chance of Bill going broke varies between 69% and 96%. When the probability of depletion by the age of death is above 10% then it really does not make any difference whether it is 70% or 90%; it is just too high.
- The median portfolio life remained at age 87, regardless of the asset mix. Once you exceed the sustainable withdrawal rate, the median portfolio life does not change much by varying the asset mix.

Keep in mind that these observations apply to this example with 6% initial withdrawal rate. Higher withdrawals make these observations more pronounced, and lower withdrawals make them less so.

Measuring the Effect of Asset Allocation:

We can measure the effect of asset allocation by observing the difference of the compound annual returns (CAR) of the median portfolio for the asset mix with the best and the worst CAR.

> Example 4.1
>
> Bob, 65, is just retiring. He has $1,000,000 savings for retirement; he needs $30,000 each year, indexed to inflation. His equities grow the same as the S&P500 index, plus 2% for dividends, less 2% management fees. His fixed income yields 6-month CD plus 0.5%. He rebalances his asset mix annually if equities deviate by more than 3%.
>
> Based on market history, the compound annual return (CAR) of the median portfolio for various asset mixes are as follows:

[17] Throughout this book, the median portfolio is the line where half of all historically observed outcomes are better and half are worse. Unlucky is the bottom decile or bottom 10% of all observations. If you have an unlucky outcome and you have 100 observations, you have the 10th worst outcome. Lucky is the top decile or top 10% of all outcomes. If you have a lucky outcome and you have 100 observations, you have the 10th best outcome.

	Asset Mix (Equity / Fixed Income)					
	0/100	20/80	40/60	60/40	80/20	100/0
CAR, (median)	4.73%	4.78%	5.03%	5.27%	5.07%	4.07%

For this example, based on market history, the highest growth rate was at 5.27% and the lowest was 4.07%. If Bob makes the worst asset allocation decision, the maximum penalty is a 1.2% difference in CAR in absolute terms, or in relative terms, the difference is 29.5%, calculated as 1.2% divided by 4.07%.

Tables 4.2 and 4.3 indicate the impact of asset allocation on the portfolio for S&P500 and the Canadian market index, SP/TSX.

Table 4.2: The effect of asset allocation on portfolio growth, equity proxy S&P500

	Initial Withdrawal Rate						
	0%	2%	3%	4%	6%	8%	10%
CAR of worst asset mix	4.63%	4.50%	4.07%	3.65%	4.09%	4.56%	5.51%
CAR of best asset mix	6.10%	4.78%	5.27%	5.12%	5.36%	5.55%	5.98%
Impact of the worst possible asset allocation decision	31.7%	6.2%	29.5%	40.3%	31.1%	21.7%	8.5%

Table 4.3: The effect of asset allocation on portfolio growth, equity proxy SP/TSX

	Initial Withdrawal Rate						
	0%	2%	3%	4%	6%	8%	10%
CAR of worst asset mix	4.90%	4.66%	4.78%	5.12%	5.38%	5.54%	5.73%
CAR of best asset mix	6.43%	6.18%	5.97%	5.69%	5.69%	6.06%	6.42%
Impact of the worst possible asset allocation decision	31.2%	32.6%	24.9%	11.1%	5.8%	9.4%	12.0%

Conclusion:

In this chapter, I walked you through a process where we saw clearly the unimportance of asset allocation in distribution portfolios.

Asset allocation, as practiced today, protects the advisor and retains the client with the same advisor for as long as possible. As for the client, a "suitable" allocation makes the fluctuations in a distribution portfolio less painful. As for the portfolio longevity, its effect is of no consequence in most cases.

I am not saying asset allocation is not important. In some unlucky cases, maintaining the optimum asset mix might add up to four years to portfolio life at reasonable withdrawal rates compared to holding 100% equity. It also gives to the investor the essential "staying power". But its contribution is nowhere near 94%. On the average (if I may use that term), it is no more than 30%. Please, don't make a mountain out of a molehill.

At this point, you might be wondering "Why so?" The answer is simple. During the accumulation stage, the most important thing is the "**Volatility** of Returns". Asset allocation can manage the volatility of returns reasonably well.

On the other hand, during the distribution stage, the most important thing is the "**Sequence** of Returns". Asset allocation does not manage well the bad effects of sequence of returns. Therefore, it has little impact on portfolio longevity except in borderline cases. This is also why a new fad on the block, called Target Date funds, cannot provide much protection for you as you get closer to retirement. It is the wrong fix for the sequence of returns.

However, if you believed in the miracle of asset allocation up to this point, don't feel bad. You are not alone. The entire pension fund industry fell into that trap a long time ago. They too favor of the volatility of returns at the expense of the sequence of returns because that is what their Gaussian models can simulate. Unless they broaden their peripheral vision, many of them will not make it. They might then ask you, the taxpayer, to bail them out. If you want to lose your money again and again, keep giving it to a loser, again and again.

Chapter 5

The "Magic" of Diversification

" Divide your portion to seven, or even to eight, for you do not know what misfortune may occur on the earth" (Ecclesiastes 11:2).

One of the most frequently cited recommendations in investing is the concept of diversification. Dividing up the portfolio and investing each part in different asset classes can minimize the risk. It is a simple concept that can reduce the pain when extreme events happen that may ruin your wealth.

The basic asset classes are equities, bonds, cash, income producing real estate, land, gold, natural resources, inflation indexed bonds, cash, art, collectibles and so on. In our business, this is another area where I find incompetence is gaining ground; not satisfied with the number of asset classes that we can sell to our clients (stock and bonds), our industry continues to invent "new" asset classes. Several years ago, we created six asset classes from one; large cap, mid cap, small cap – each in either growth or value. We have asset classes based on geography: emerging, developed, Latin America, BRIC and so on. Some even call the different strategies in hedge funds as different asset classes: long–short, convertible arbitrage, merger arbitrage, and so on. I hope that this madness of giving artificial birth to new asset classes stops soon and common sense returns.

In the context of this book, my investment universe includes equities and variations of fixed income (cash, conventional and inflation indexed bonds). I will try to demonstrate you what diversification can and cannot do using these two particular asset classes.

Accumulation Portfolios:

Let's work through a few examples to demonstrate the effect of diversification:

Example 5.1

Steve lives in the U.S.A. He is 30 years old. He is just starting to save for his retirement. He saves $10,000 each year for the next 30 years. His asset allocation is 60% equity and 40% fixed income, rebalanced annually. On the equity side, he has four choices:

- Portfolio A: Least diversified - Invest all his equity allocation in DJIA.
- Portfolio B: A little more diversified - Invest all his equity allocation in S&P500, which includes 500 stocks.
- Portfolio C: More diversified - Invest in 40% S&P500 (USA), 20% NIKKEI (Japan)

- Portfolio D: Most diversified - Invest in 33% S&P500, 12% NIKKEI, 8% FTSE (United Kingdom), and 7% SP/TSX (Canada)

On the equity side, he expects an average of 2% dividend yield. He pays 0.5% management fees. On the fixed income side, he expects a return of 0.5% over and above the historical 6-month CD rates after all management fees. The fixed income side remains the same in all cases, based on historical data of US fixed income markets.

Ignore the exchange rate fluctuations between currencies (assume foreign currency is hedged). The question is "After 30 years, which portfolio has the highest market value?"

Portfolio A - Portfolio value over time

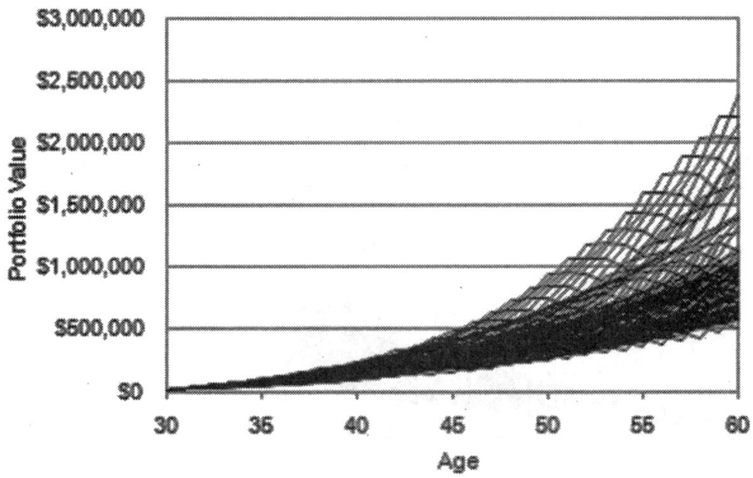

We calculate the portfolio value over time based on market history:

	Average Portfolio Value after 30 Years	Lucky (Top decile)	Unlucky (Bottom decile)
Portfolio A	USD$1,038,081	USD$1,749,011	USD$623,720
Portfolio B	USD$1,064,272	USD$1,688,347	USD$562,500
Portfolio C	USD$1,284,629	USD$1,796,420	USD$587,932
Portfolio D	USD$1,214,676	USD$1,821,193	USD$584,951

Example 5.2

Jane lives in Canada. She is 30 years old. She is just starting to save for her retirement. She saves $10,000 each year for the next 30 years. Her asset allocation is 60% equity and 40% fixed income, rebalanced annually. On the equity side, she has two choices:

- Portfolio A: Least diversified - Invest all her equity allocation in the Canadian index SP/TSX.
- Portfolio D: Most diversified - Invest in 33% SP/TSX, 12% S&P500, 7% FTSE and 8% NIKKEI

On the equity side, she expects an average of 2% dividend yield. She pays 1.5% management fees. On the fixed income side, use same data as Example 5.1.

Portfolio A - Portfolio value over time

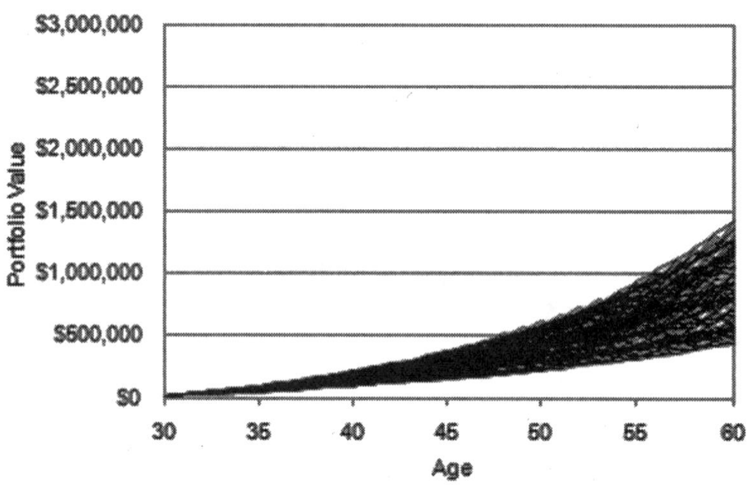

	Average Portfolio Value after 30 Years	Lucky (Top decile)	Unlucky (Bottom decile)
Portfolio A	CAD$902,075	CAD$1,265,530	CAD$547,354
Portfolio D	CAD$1,020,491	CAD$1,503,553	CAD$537,144

Example 5.3

Yoshie lives in Japan. She is 30 years old. She is just starting to save for her retirement. She saves ¥10,000 each year[18] for the next 30 years. Her asset allocation is 60% equity and 40% fixed income, rebalanced annually. On the equity side, she has two choices:

- Portfolio A: Least diversified - Invest all her equity allocation in the Japanese index NIKKEI.
- Portfolio D: Most diversified - Invest in 33% NIKKEI, 12% S&P500, 7% FTSE and 8% SP/TSX

On the equity side, she expects an average of 2% dividend yield. She pays 1.0% management fees. On the fixed income side, use same data as Example 5.1.

Portfolio A - Portfolio value over time

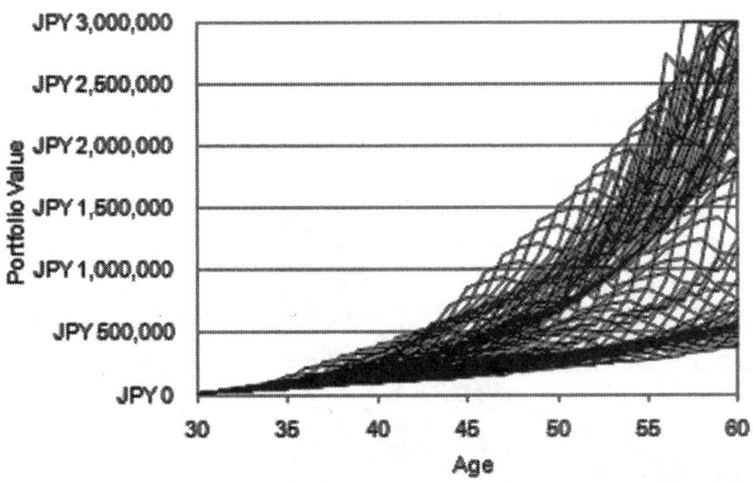

	Average Portfolio Value after 30 Years	Lucky (Top decile)	Unlucky (Bottom decile)
Portfolio A	¥1,776,289	¥3,198,983	¥530,732
Portfolio D	¥1,398,884	¥2,058,724	¥556,020

[18] I know this is not a lot of money in Japan, but I like to keep the same figures across all examples.

Example 5.4

Charles lives in the United Kingdom. He is 30 years old. He is just starting to save for his retirement. He saves £10,000 each year for the next 30 years. His asset allocation is 60% equity and 40% fixed income, rebalanced annually. On the equity side, he has two choices:

- Portfolio A: Least diversified – Invest all his equity allocation in the FTSE index.
- Portfolio D: Most diversified – Invest in 33% FTSE, 12% S&P500, 7% SP/TSX and 8% NIKKEI

On the equity side, he expects an average of 2% dividend yield. He pays 1.0% management fees. On the fixed income side, use same data as Example 5.1.

Ignore the exchange rate fluctuations between currencies (assume foreign currency is hedged). The question is "After 30 years, which portfolio has the highest market value?"

Portfolio A – Portfolio value over time

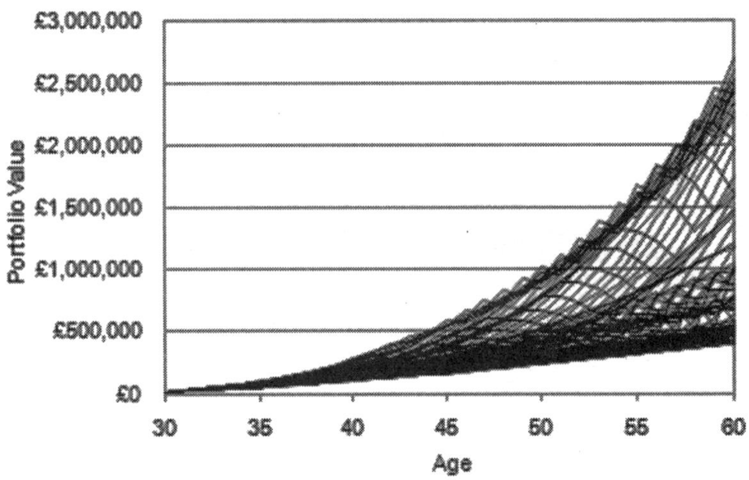

	Average Portfolio Value after 30 Years	Lucky (Top decile)	Unlucky (Bottom decile)
Portfolio A	£1,142,412	£2,413,275	£463,570
Portfolio D	£1,172,067	£2,078,400	£530,642

In these examples, portfolios include indices from four different geographies: U.S.A., Japan, Canada and the United Kingdom (UK). The United Kingdom was arguably *the* world power until the beginning of Second World War. U.S.A. is *the* world power since then. Some were victors of both world wars; one was the loser. Canada has been more resource based and the others were less so. There were diverse cultures and social structures. Remembering that during the last century, globalization was nothing like it is today; we would expect diversification to create improvements.

Table 5.1: Ranking of the effect of diversification for accumulation portfolios, portfolio A is least diversified, portfolio D is most diversified

Base Country		Average Portfolio Value	Lucky Portfolio Value	Unlucky Portfolio Value
		Rankings:		
U.S.A.	Best	Portfolio C	Portfolio D	Portfolio A
	⇩	Portfolio D	Portfolio C	Portfolio C
		Portfolio B	Portfolio A	Portfolio D
	Worst	Portfolio A	Portfolio B	Portfolio B
Japan	Best	Portfolio A	Portfolio A	Portfolio D
	Worst	Portfolio D	Portfolio D	Portfolio A
United Kingdom	Best	Portfolio D	Portfolio A	Portfolio D
	Worst	Portfolio A	Portfolio D	Portfolio A
Canada	Best	Portfolio D	Portfolio D	Portfolio A
	Worst	Portfolio A	Portfolio A	Portfolio D

Here are my observations for accumulation portfolios:

- Diversification improved Steve's (U.S.A.) outcome somewhat. Portfolio "C' did best for the average portfolio: It included only two countries: Japanese and US equities. Adding Canada and the UK worsened the outcome. When we look at the unlucky outcome, the portfolio "A", least diversified, had the best outcome. One would think that Portfolio D, which was the most diversified, should have the best outcome. So, my question is: "Is it really diversification at play here? Or was it sheer luck that the combination of these two indices (S&P500 and NIKKEI–225) gave the best results?"
- Diversification improved Jane's (Canada) outcome, except when she is unlucky.
- Diversification worsened Yoshie's (Japan) outcome significantly, except when she is unlucky.

- Diversification improved Charles' (UK) outcome slightly, except when he is lucky.
- In all cases, the effect of whether one is lucky or unlucky (top decile versus bottom decile portfolio values) was at least three times more significant than the effect one might possibly attribute to diversification.

Do you see a pattern as we go from the least diversified portfolio to the most diversified across different countries? I don't. As we diversify more, sometimes the portfolio does better, sometimes it does not.

Ask yourself this: Could it be that the performance of a particular portfolio has little to do with diversification, but it has more to do with asset selection?

Let's move on to distribution portfolios and see what we can uncover there.

Distribution Portfolios:

Let's go through similar calculations for distribution portfolios:

Example 5.5

Steve lives in the U.S.A. He is 65 years old, just retiring. He has $1 million in his portfolio and needs $60,000 each year, indexed to inflation. His asset allocation is 40% equity and 60% fixed income, rebalanced annually. On the equity side, he has four choices:

- Portfolio A: Least diversified - Invest all his equity allocation in DJIA.
- Portfolio B: A little more diversified - Invest all his equity allocation in S&P500, which includes 500 stocks.
- Portfolio C: More diversified - Invest in 30% S&P500, 10% NIKKEI
- Portfolio D: Most diversified - Invest in 25% S&P500, 8% NIKKEI, 4% FTSE and 3% SP/TSX

The dividend yield, currency exchange rate considerations, equity and fixed income performance are same as in Example 5.1.

Portfolio A - Portfolio value over time

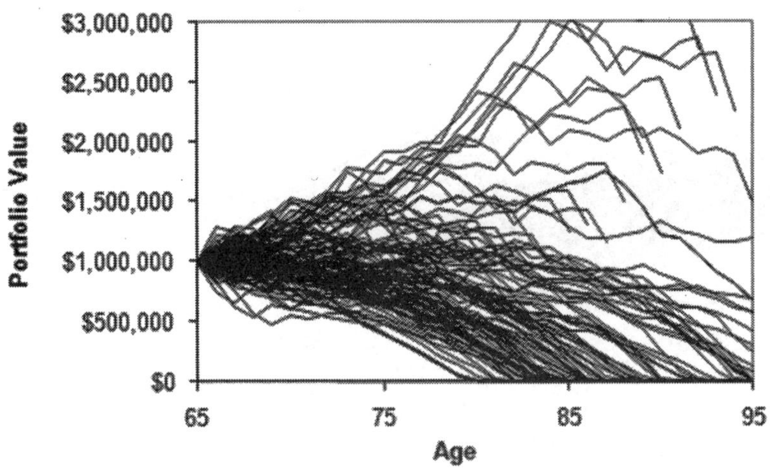

	Earliest Portfolio Depletion at Age	Probability of depletion by age 95
Portfolio A	80	87%
Portfolio B	79	81%
Portfolio C	80	66%
Portfolio D	80	64%

Example 5.6

Jane lives in Canada. She is 65 years old, just retiring. She has $1 million in her portfolio and needs $60,000 each year, indexed to inflation. Her asset allocation is 40% equity and 60% fixed income, rebalanced annually. On the equity side, she has two choices:

- Portfolio A: Least diversified - Invest all her equity allocation in the Canadian index SP/TSX.
- Portfolio D: Most diversified - Invest in 25% SP/TSX, 8% S&P500, 3% FTSE and 4% NIKKEI

The dividend yield, currency exchange rate considerations, equity and fixed income performance are same as in Example 5.2.

Portfolio A - Portfolio value over time

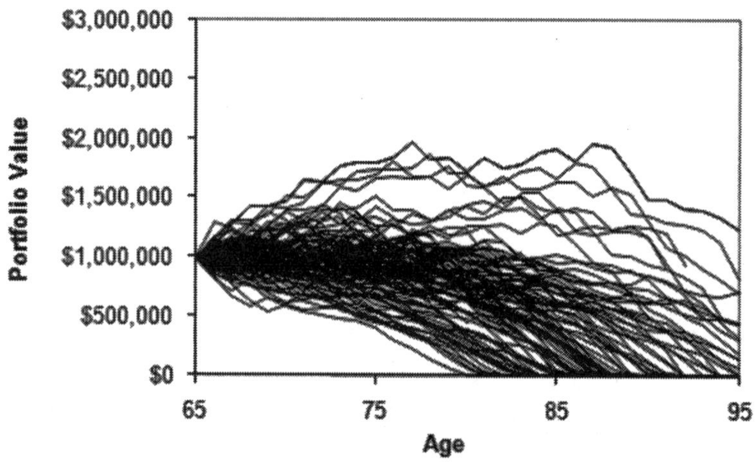

	Earliest Portfolio Depletion at Age	Probability of Depletion by Age 95
Portfolio A	79	92%
Portfolio D	80	85%

Example 5.7

Yoshie lives in Japan. She is 65 years old, just retiring. She has ¥1 million in her portfolio and needs ¥60,000 each year, indexed to inflation. Her asset allocation is 40% equity and 60% fixed income, rebalanced annually. On the equity side, she has two choices:

- Portfolio A: Least diversified - Invest all her equity allocation in the Japanese index NIKKEI.
- Portfolio D: Most diversified - Invest in 25% NIKKEI, 8% S&P500, 3% FTSE and 4% SP/TSX

The dividend yield, currency exchange rate considerations, equity and fixed income performance are same as in Example 5.3.

Portfolio A - Portfolio Value over Time based on Market History

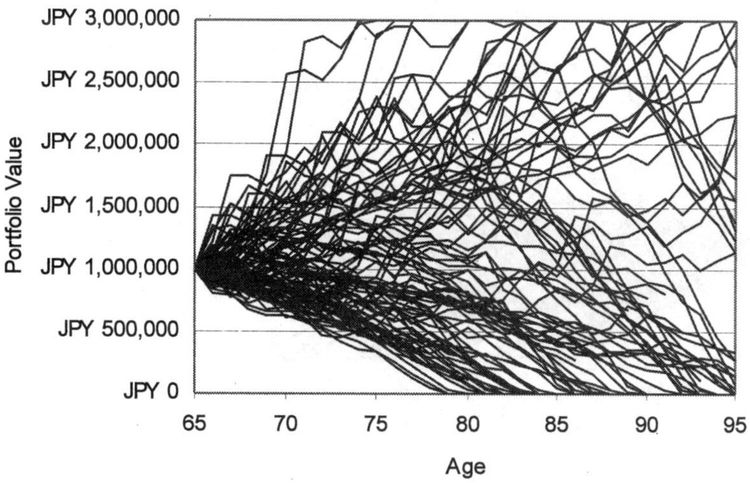

	Earliest Portfolio Depletion at Age	Probability of depletion by age 95
Portfolio A	79	42%
Portfolio D	81	47%

Example 5.8

Charles lives in the United Kingdom. He is 65 years old, just retiring. He has £1 million in his portfolio and needs £60,000 each year, indexed to inflation. His asset allocation is 40% equity and 60% fixed income, rebalanced annually. On the equity side, he has two choices:

- Portfolio A: Least diversified - Invest all his equity allocation in the FTSE index.
- Portfolio D: Most diversified - Invest in 25% FTSE, 8% S&P500, 3% SP/TSX and 4% NIKKEI

The dividend yield, currency exchange rate considerations, equity and fixed income performance are same as in Example 5.4.

Portfolio A - Portfolio value over time

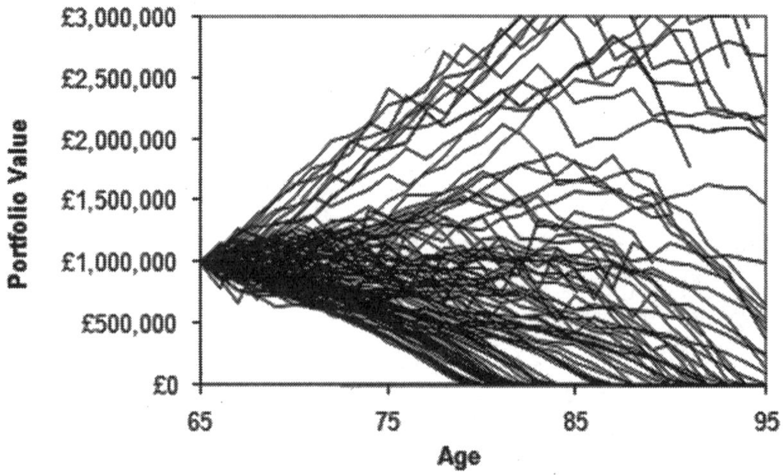

	Earliest Portfolio Depletion at Age	Probability of depletion by age 95
Portfolio A	79	82%
Portfolio D	80	73%

Here are my observations for the distribution portfolio examples:

- When bad things happen, no amount of diversification provided much help. In such cases, all portfolios ran out of many between ages 79 and 81, regardless of where the money was invested or how much it was diversified. At times of crisis, there is nothing you can do because all markets move down together.
- Diversification did not improve the probability of depletion in any meaningful way. The slight improvement is only academic and it has no practical meaning for a retiree.

Conclusion:

Deep down, I believe in the benefit of diversification, especially across different asset classes[19]. However, it appears that diversification in the same asset class and across different geographies does little good, other than perhaps in the short term during routine fluctuations. Considering the additional currency risk, I am more inclined to invest at home and not diversify too much across the globe. In my client portfolios, I usually don't recommend allocating more than 20% of the equities to foreign content, especially for buy–and–hold portfolios. The rest stays in domestic equities and fixed income. In my experience, finding a few good portfolio managers and hanging on to them as long as they continue to perform well, was a lot better than stuffing umpteen funds into the account under the guise of diversification.

Ignore tables and charts that show the correlation factors between different mutual funds and/or asset subclasses. They are not too meaningful. These correlation tables are based on "normal" distribution of volatility of the recent past. This has little use in "extreme" markets that make or break your retirement planning. Because of this asymmetry, any benefit of diversification in "normal" markets is wiped out in "extreme" markets.

Disregard any advice such as "Diversification prevents losses" or even "Diversification minimizes losses". It is simply not so, especially when you need it most. When markets are against you, they all move together – down.

As for *real* diversification –that is outside the immediate realm of the financial industry–, I am all for that. Venture investments of the third kind (i.e. children's and grandchildren's education) and charitable donations are a great form of diversification. I know it sounds crazy but that kind of diversification always paid me back handsomely, so far anyway.

[19] I don't consider value, growth, large/mid/small cap as different asset classes, just subgroups of equities.

Chapter 6

Rebalancing

Recently, I had a meeting with a mutual fund wholesaler. He introduced his company's new product, which was a fund of funds. Among many of its bells and whistles, one was especially intriguing: The advisor can specify how often to rebalance: annually, quarterly, monthly or weekly. All you have to do is check the appropriate box and you are in business: No more meeting the client to explain the rebalancing activities, no more wasted time. It seems so convenient to delegate this task to the fund manager.

In the first edition of this book, I analyzed this topic at length. Here, I will rework my earlier findings and present simpler guidelines.

When it comes to rebalancing, many investment professionals believe often is better. Rebalancing is done, supposedly, to reduce the portfolio volatility. Does frequent rebalancing really decrease volatility? How does it affect portfolio longevity? Let's try to answer these questions by observing historical data.

Volatility has two components. The first component is short–term random fluctuations. Every second, every minute, every day, some event happens somewhere in the world that influences investor psychology. As investors make trading decisions, markets move up or down. This is how random volatility is created.

The second component of volatility occurs over the longer term. Markets respond to the collective expectation of investors and a trend forms. If we agree with the notion that price movements within a one–year time horizon are mostly random, then we cannot expect a reduction in volatility by rebalancing more frequently than annually. So you can rebalance all you want, daily or hourly, and you won't be able to reduce the random volatility at all.

Rebalancing can reduce volatility only if it is done after an *observable trend.* An observable trend can occur in two ways:

- After a cyclical trend, or
- After high rate of withdrawals, which creates a downtrend because of the cash outflow.

When does a portfolio experience an observable trend? There are several known market cycles; the 54–year Kondratieff cycle, 10–year decennial cycle, and the 4–year U.S. Presidential election cycle, to name a few. We will focus on the U.S. Presidential Election cycle as the basis of our rebalancing study. It is the shortest market cycle that is meaningful to retirement planning that we can work with.

Let's look at an example: Steve, 65, is retiring this year. He has put aside $1 million for his retirement, 40% equity and 60% fixed income. He needs $50,000 income each year, indexed to inflation. He takes his withdrawal from the fixed income portion of his portfolio.

Retiring into a Bearish trend – 1929:

Figure 6.1 shows Steve's portfolio value if he had retired at the beginning of 1929, the beginning of a secular bear market. At the market bottom of 1932, Steve's portfolio experienced a smaller loss when rebalanced every four years than if he rebalanced every year. The portfolio that was rebalanced every four years provided Steve with 28 years of income. On the other hand, if rebalanced annually, the portfolio would run out of money after 21 years. Rebalancing every four years on the Presidential election year increased the portfolio life by a respectable 38%.

Figure 6.1: Retiring at the start of the 1929 secular bear market

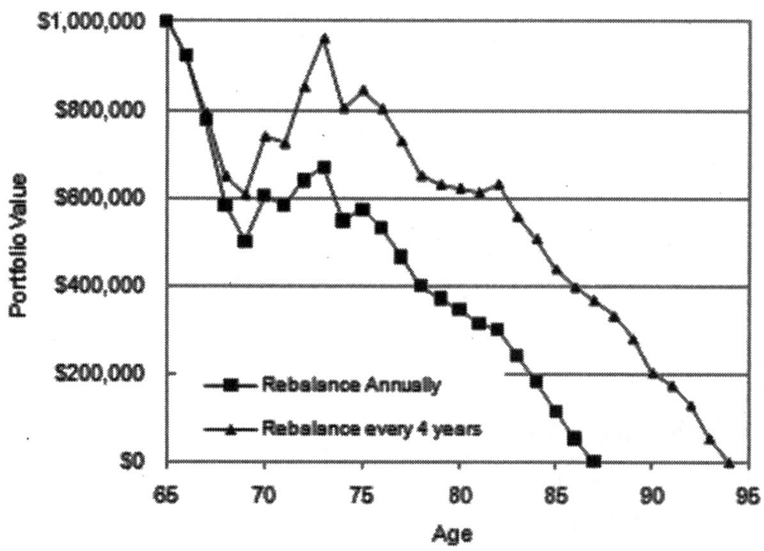

Retiring into a Bullish Trend – 1921:

Figure 6.2 shows the portfolio value if Steve had retired in 1921, the beginning of the first secular bull market of the last century. At the end of 30 years, Steve was one million dollars richer if he rebalanced every four years at the end of the U.S. Presidential election year than if he were to rebalance annually. The volatility was about the same for either. Imagine this: you make more money by doing less work! A novel concept, isn't it?

Figure 6.2: Retiring at the start of the 1921 secular bull market

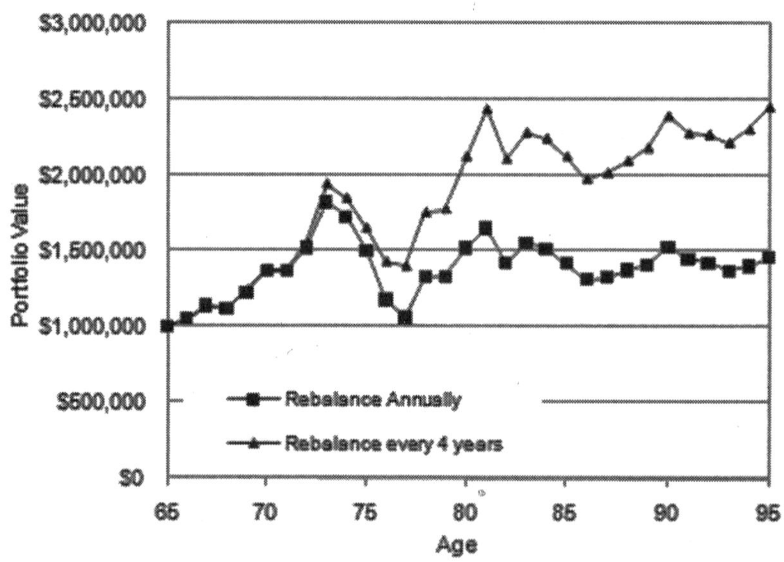

Retiring into a Bullish Trend – 1949:

Figure 6.3 shows Steve's portfolio value if he had retired at the beginning of the second secular bullish trend of the 20th century that prevailed between 1949 and 1965. It demonstrates that there was a slight increase – about 10%– in the portfolio value when rebalanced every four years on the Presidential election year as opposed to rebalancing annually. The portfolio volatility was essentially identical.

Figure 6.3: Retiring at the start of a bull market, in 1949

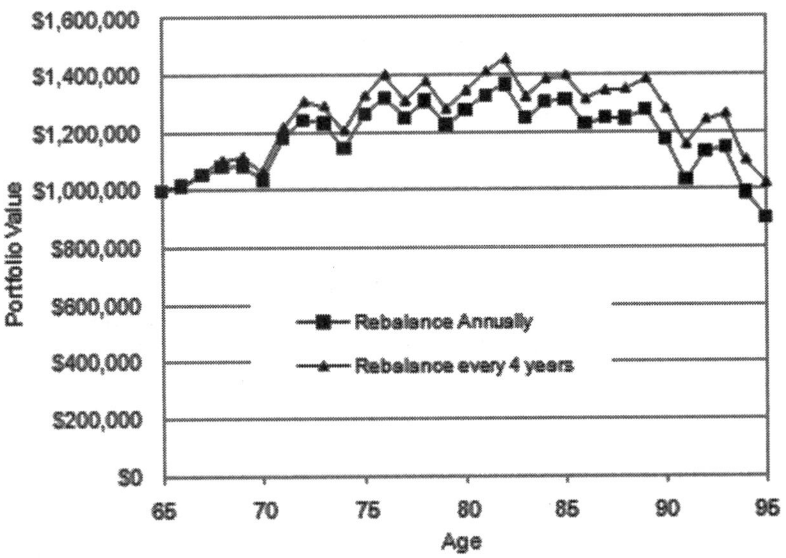

Retiring into a Sideways Trend – 1966:

Figure 6.4 shows Steve's portfolio value if he had retired at the beginning of a secular sideways trend that prevailed between 1966 and 1981. It demonstrates that there was no perceivable difference in the portfolio value when rebalanced every four years on the Presidential election year as opposed to rebalancing annually. The portfolio volatility was essentially identical.

Figure 6.4: Retiring at the start of a bull market, in 1966

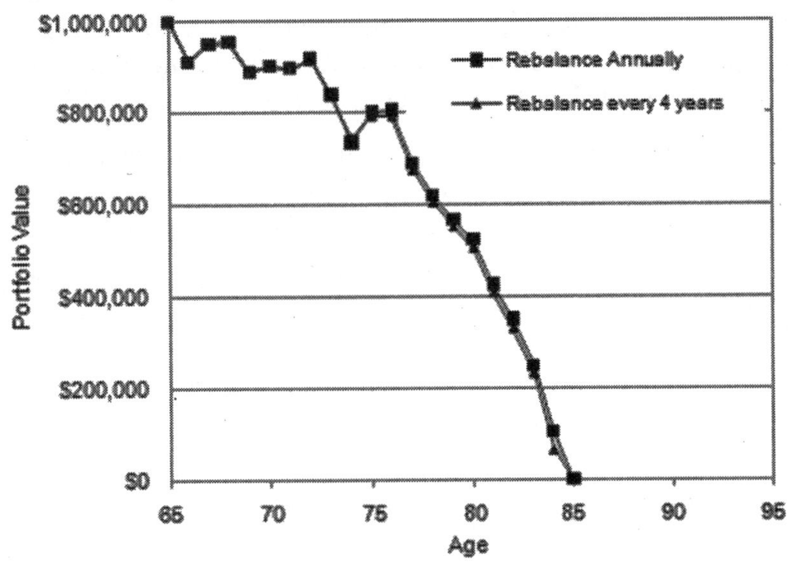

I studied charts for all years between 1900 and 1999 and came to the following conclusions:

- The long term volatility was about the same whether you rebalanced annually or once every four years on the Presidential election year.
- Rebalancing too often stunted the portfolio growth in secular bull markets. In many cases, the portfolio that was rebalanced based on the Presidential cycle had a slightly higher value at the market peak than rebalancing annually.
- Rebalancing too often compounded losses in secular bear markets. The real benefit of synchronizing the rebalancing activity with the U.S. Presidential election cycle was a significant improvement in preserving capital. This made a considerable difference in portfolio longevity.
- In sideways markets, it did not matter how often you rebalanced. The portfolio life varied slightly at random.

You might be wondering why I am so specific about when to rebalance. Why not rebalance every 4th anniversary of retirement? Why choose the US Presidential election year?

I rebalanced at different intervals, from annually to every ten years and everything in between. Then I looked at the 4–year cycle and all its permutations, including rebalancing every second, third, fourth year of the Presidential term. I even tried rebalancing every second (i.e. rebalance every eight years), as well as third (every twelve years), and fourth (every sixteen years) election.

The answer lies in how markets behave with respect to the presidential election cycle. Generally, in a broad interpretation of this cycle, the markets grow below average during the first and second years of the Presidential term. They are stronger in the third and fourth years of the term. The average DJIA growth between 1900 and 1999 was 6%, 3%, 12%, 10% for the first, second, third and fourth year of the Presidential term, respectively. Keep in mind; there are large deviations from these averages and one must never make trading decisions based on this cycle alone.

It turned out that rebalancing at the end of each Presidential election year gave the best results because this synchronized with the high point of this cycle. Rebalancing at any other frequency or at any other time in the cycle did not add as much value.

Figure 6.4 demonstrates the portfolio life based on a 5% initial withdrawal rate for annual as well as the Presidential cycle rebalancing frequency, using a rebalancing threshold of 3%.

Figure 6.4: Comparing the effect of rebalancing frequency on portfolio life

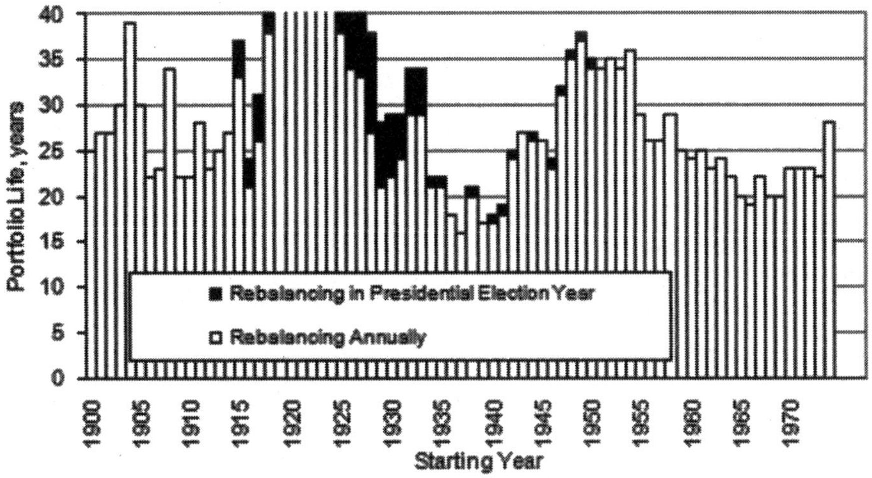

Measuring the Effect of the Frequency of Rebalancing:

A good way of measuring the effect of the frequency of rebalancing is to observe the difference of the compound annual returns (CAR) of the median portfolio for both scenarios. Table 6.1 indicates the impact of rebalancing frequency on the CAR for a portfolio consisting of 40% S&P500 and 60% fixed income. On the equity side, the investor expects an average of 2% dividend yield, pays 2% management fees. On the fixed income side, he expects a return of 0.5% over and above the historical 6–month CD rates after all management fees. Table 6.2 is the same information for the Canadian SP/TSX.

Table 6.1: The effect of rebalancing frequency on portfolio growth, equity proxy S&P500

	Initial Withdrawal Rate					
	0%	2%	4%	6%	8%	10%
Compound Annual Return, annual rebalancing	4.80%	4.85%	4.82%	4.69%	5.51%	5.89%
Compound Annual Return, rebalance 4th year of Presidential term	4.97%	5.43%	5.06%	4.75%	5.59%	6.01%
Impact of rebalancing frequency on compound annual return	3.5%	12.0%	5.0%	1.3%	1.5%	2.0%

Table 6.2: The effect of rebalancing frequency on portfolio growth, equity proxy SP/TSX

	Initial Withdrawal Rate					
	0%	2%	4%	6%	8%	10%
Compound Annual Return, annual rebalancing	6.65%	6.17%	5.28%	5.55%	5.96%	5.98%
Compound Annual Return, rebalance 4th year of Presidential term	6.65%	6.23%	5.51%	5.71%	6.11%	6.37%
Impact of rebalancing frequency on compound annual return	0.0%	1.0%	4.4%	2.9%	2.5%	6.5%

Rebalancing Threshold:

Threshold is the amount by which you allow the equity percentage to deviate before triggering a rebalancing event. For example, if the normal asset mix is 50/50 and your threshold is 3%, then you would only rebalance if the equity percentage at the end of the year were less than 47% or over 53%.

I experimented with various thresholds for all withdrawal rates up to 8%. I rebalanced annually and every four years. The largest difference in the compound annual growth rate was less than 0.07% for any threshold between 0% and 5%, randomly distributed. Therefore, do not waste your time trying to figure out what is the best threshold. I use a 3% threshold. If you want less work, use a 5% threshold.

Figure 6.5 demonstrate the median portfolio value based on a 5% initial withdrawal rate for 2% and 6% rebalancing thresholds. This is for a portfolio consisting of 40% S&P500 and 60% fixed income. On the equity side, the average dividend yield is 2% and the management fees are 2%. On the fixed income side, the return is 0.5% over and above the historical 6–month CD rates after all management fees.

Figure 6.5: Comparing rebalancing threshold, median portfolio value

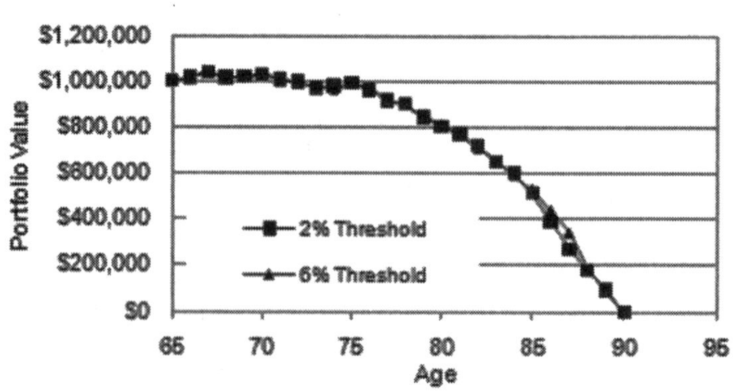

One–Way Rebalancing:

Here, rebalancing means the money can flow only one–way: from equities to fixed income. If equities do well, the excess is sold and the proceeds are added to fixed income. However, when equities lose, no fixed income holdings are sold to top off equities.

It sounds logical, except it does not work. I discovered that in all cases up to an 8% withdrawal rate, this strategy added no value. On the contrary, it reduced the compound annual growth rate by as much as 0.6% in some cases.

As the withdrawal rate approached 8%, the difference between the two strategies (i.e. one way rebalancing and two–way rebalancing) decreased to zero. That is because at higher withdrawal rates, the cash/fixed income portion of the portfolio needed replenishing by selling more and more equities each year, which created a "de facto" one–way rebalancing even if you allowed two–way rebalancing.

Figure 6.6 demonstrates the difference based on portfolio value based on a 5% initial withdrawal rate. This is for a portfolio consisting of 40% S&P500 and 60% fixed income. On the equity side, the average dividend yield is 2% and the management fees are 2%. On the fixed income side, the return is 0.5% over and above the historical 6–month CD rates after all management fees.

Figure 6.6: Comparing the rebalancing both ways versus one way, median portfolio value

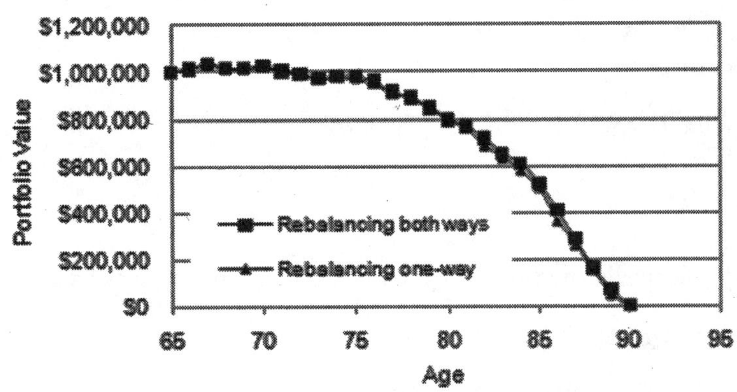

Never–Rebalancing:

There are some academic studies that suggest that you should not rebalance your asset mix, ever. It works like this: You start with an asset mix, say 40% equity and 60% fixed income. The withdrawals are always taken out of the fixed income portfolio until it is depleted. After that, income is taken out of the equities. The asset mix is never rebalanced. The intent is to allow equities to "grow" while you take your withdrawals from the fixed income portion of the portfolio.

I discussed the merits and pitfalls of this strategy in my earlier book, "High Expectations and False Dreams" in 2001. This strategy works better only if the equity side of the portfolio outperforms its underlying equity benchmark index by at least 3% annually. Beware of rebalancing research that uses historically high dividends in their model. This creates an artificially higher degree of outperformance compared to prevailing dividend yields. It is misleading, going forward. For most investors, consistently beating the index by over 3% after paying all portfolio expenses is not a realistic assumption.

Here is the danger: Say you think you can beat the index by 3% annually. So, you decide never to rebalance your asset mix. After a while you realize that you were wrong. Most likely, this realization comes after a large loss. When you make a change in your strategy, it is most damaging if this change is made after a loss. When adopting a strategy, always be mindful of the potential damage if things don't work out as planned.

Figure 6.7 demonstrates the difference based on portfolio value based on a 5% initial withdrawal rate. This is for a portfolio consisting of 40% S&P500 and 60% fixed income. On the equity side, the average dividend yield is 2% and management fees are 2%. On the fixed income side, the return is 0.5% over and above the historical 6–month CD rates after all management fees.

Keep away from the "never rebalancing" strategy.

Figure 6.7: Comparing the median portfolio value for rebalancing annually versus never

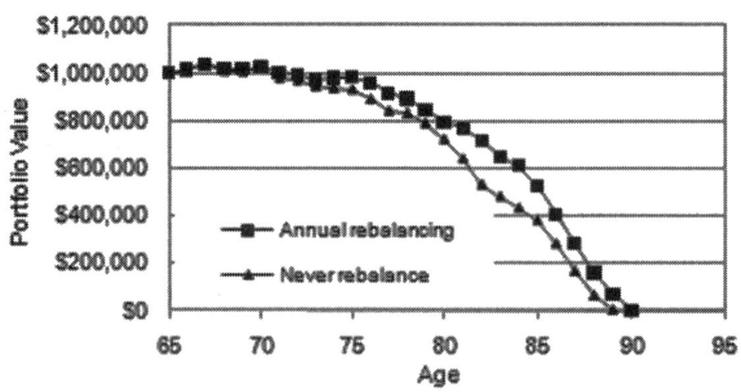

Other Rebalancing Techniques:

I also looked at several other rebalancing strategies over the years using the actual market history since 1900:

- Asymmetric Rebalancing: Generally equities have a higher volatility than the fixed income portion of the portfolio. Therefore, it is only logical to use a lower rebalancing threshold for equities, say 4%, and a higher threshold for bonds, say 8%. In other words, the proceeds of rebalancing flows from equity to fixed income a lot more often than from fixed income to equities.

  Example: Target asset mix is 50/50. Equity rebalancing threshold is 4% and for the fixed income, it is 8%.

  Equities move up and now they are over 54% of the portfolio. Sell the excess equity and buy more bonds.

  Conversely, if equities move down to under 42% of the portfolio, sell the excess bond and buy more equity.

- Growth Rebalancing: Here, the rebalancing activity depends on the growth of the equities and not on a preset time interval. Rebalance if equities grow more than a preset growth rate, for example 15%, from a previous value. The previous value may be a recent low value or a "high water mark" value.

- Over–rebalancing: Say your original asset mix is 50/50. Equities grow during the year and they are now 55% of the portfolio. Instead of bringing equities back to 50%, you sell additional equities and bring it down to 45%.

Many seemingly logical ideas popped into my head over the last nine years. I spent plenty of time rewiring my spreadsheets and then analyzing the results. At end of each episode, I felt that it was a waste of time. A few months would go by and another seemingly bright idea would appear out of nowhere; and another wasted week.

Finally, as a consolation, I convinced myself that writing about what does not work is probably as valuable as writing about what does work. Many strategies that sound logical end up failing the test of time because markets are seldom logical.

Conclusion:

What is the purpose of rebalancing? Before you can answer this question, you need to remember the most important thing for a buy–and–hold portfolio:

- In an accumulation portfolio: the important thing is the **volatility** of returns. Thus, the purpose of rebalancing in an accumulation portfolio is to contain the volatility of returns.
- In a distribution portfolio: the important thing is the **sequence** of returns. Thus, the purpose of rebalancing in a distribution portfolio is to minimize the effect of a bad sequence of returns.

Having defined these two purposes of rebalancing, here are my general guidelines:

Accumulation Portfolios:

- If retirement is at least five years away:
  Excess equity: rebalance whenever the equity percentage exceeds its target by more than 5%. There is no time limit for that; you may need to rebalance several times in a year if the market happens to be bullish.

  Excess fixed income: when the fixed–income portion of the portfolio exceeds its target percentage by more than 5%, then rebalance on the anniversary of the most recent rebalance, never more often.
- Within five years of retirement:
  Rebalance at the end of the presidential election years only.

Distribution Portfolios:

- If the withdrawal rate is 5% or less:
  Rebalance at the end of the presidential election years only.
- If the withdrawal rate is over 5%:
  Rebalance annually.

There is no holy grail for rebalancing. Following these guidelines can help you reduce large losses in extreme markets. In normal markets, rebalancing sells high and buys low. For a buy–and–hold portfolio, that is good enough for me.

If you want to do anything more sophisticated than that, you need to step up from the "rebalancing school" into the "market timing school". It is important to differentiate between these two schools. Many people don't or cannot see the difference. I have seen several studies on rebalancing that look like poor imitations of market timing strategies. Rebalancing is rebalancing. Market timing is market timing. If you confuse the two, then your returns will suffer. Whatever you do, not only in investments but in life in general, make sure that the purpose of each one of your actions is very clear to you.

And the next time you are asked to sign the form for automatic rebalancing, stop and think. You may be –unknowingly– signing away years of portfolio life or years of growth. The right way of investing is about being careful with strategies. It has absolutely nothing to do with convenience.

Chapter 7

Market Trends

When we talk about fluctuating asset values, we mainly consider equities because generally they have the highest volatility in a portfolio. Equity markets are made up of waves of four sizes:

- Secular trends
- Cyclical trends
- Seasonality
- Random fluctuations

Let's look at each of these categories.

Secular Trends:

These are the long–term market trends that can last as long as twenty years. They are also known as megatrends or generational trends. They exert the strongest effect on market behavior. There are three kinds of secular trends: bullish, bearish and sideways. Figure 7.1 depicts the secular equity market trends since 1900.

Figure 7.1: Secular trends in equity markets

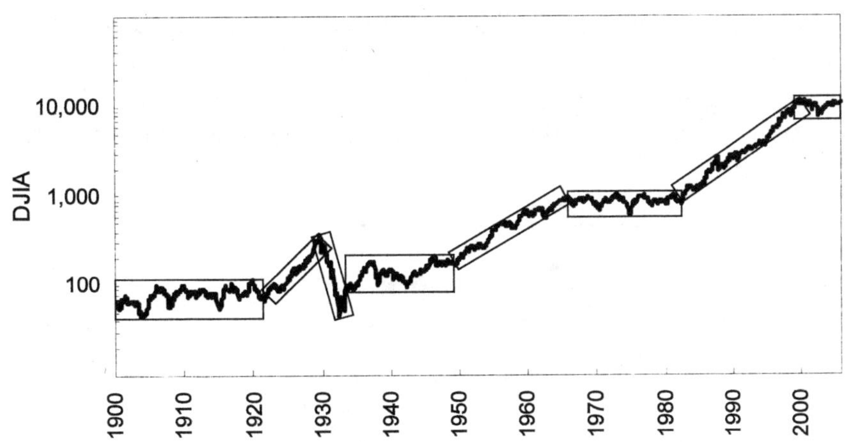

We can describe the shape of the secular trends as a "sloped staircase". In secular bullish trends, markets move up strongly for a number of years, dismissing any bearish factors along the way. As more and more people become aware of this seemingly endless uptrend, more money flows into equities. This fuels the bullish trend further. Towards the end of this trend, speculative money starts rolling in. Eventually, an unpredictable and otherwise an insignificant event triggers the end of it.

When the secular bullish market ends, the speculative money can be destroyed or "digested", in one of two ways:

1. Vertical compression: A secular bearish market wipes out the excess froth by compressing the value of the index in a short period of time, resulting in a large loss. This is like a river expending its energy by means of waterfalls or rapids. The 1929 market crash lasted 32 months:

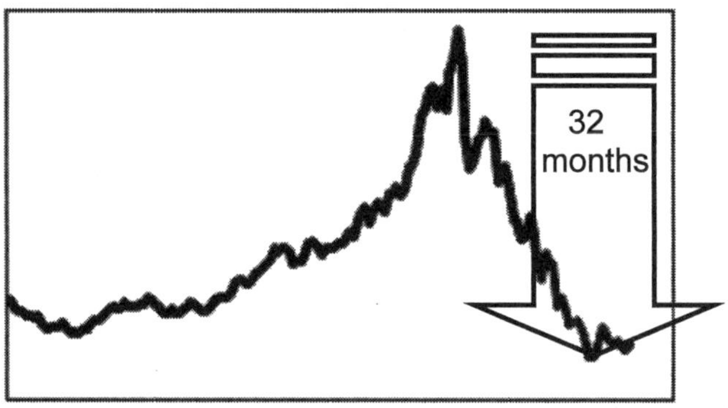

2. Horizontal expansion: A secular sideways market sets in. It wipes out the excess froth of the preceding secular bullish trend over a long period of time by moving up and down in a channel, typically within a range of ±30%. This is like a river expending its energy by meandering in the plains. The 1966 secular sideways trend lasted more than 170 months; five times longer than the 1929 crash:

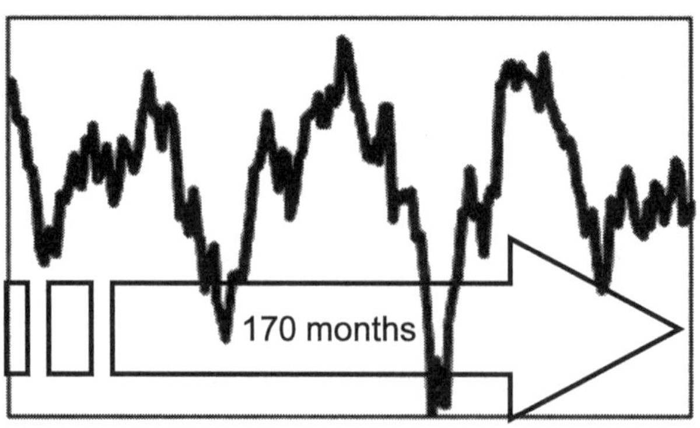

Don't try to guess which one of these two routes the markets will choose to follow after the secular bullish trend. For example, in 1929, the secular bullish trend ended catastrophically. Some blame the U.S. Federal Reserve for continuing to raise interest rates even after the precipitous losses in the markets during that time period. While there may be some truth to it, it is probably not that significant. In the late 60's and 70's, interest rate hikes were much more severe, but this did not create a secular bearish trend, only a secular sideways trend.

The vertical compression creates a large loss of *money*. The horizontal expansion creates a large loss of *time*. Since "time is money", you end up losing a combination of both time and money in either event.

Table 7.1 depicts the secular trends of the twentieth century. Looking at it as a whole, secular sideways trends lasted between twelve and twenty–one years. Secular bullish trends lasted between eight and eighteen years. The only secular bearish trend was the 1929 – 1932 market crash.

Markets spent about 49% of their time in secular sideways trends and about 43% in secular bullish trends. That means a "buy–and–hold" market–index fund made money in about 43% of the time during the accumulation stage. The rest of the time, it was plenty of sizzle, but no steak.

Table 7.1: Secular trends (1900 – 1999)

Trend		Average Annual DJIA Growth	Length, years
All Trends	1900 – 1999	**7.7%**	
Secular Sideways[20]:		**2.4%**	
	1900 – 1920	4.2%	21
	1937 – 1948	1.4%	12
	1966 – 1981	0.8%	16
Secular Bull:		**15.0%**	
	1921 – 1928	20.6%	8
	1949 – 1965	11.5%	17
	1982 – 1999	15.9%	18
Secular Bear:		**–31.7%**	
	1929 – 1932	–31.7%	4
Other:			
Cyclical Bull	1933 – 1936	33.5%	4

[20] the average indicated for each trend type is a weighted average (in bold) and it is weighted by the length of each secular trend

Cyclical Trends:

The next category is the cyclical trend. Cycles occur in all aspects of life. Sunspot activity, wars, insect population and many other events follow cycles[21]. Similarly, economic activities move in cycles[22]. The expectation of the onset of a new phase in an economic cycle triggers fluctuations in bond markets, equity markets, inflation, interest rates and commodity prices.

Figure 7.2 illustrates economic and market cycles. In general, bond and equity markets foresee economic expansion or contraction well in advance. That is then reflected in the price of securities.

Figure 7.2: Economic cycle and market cycle

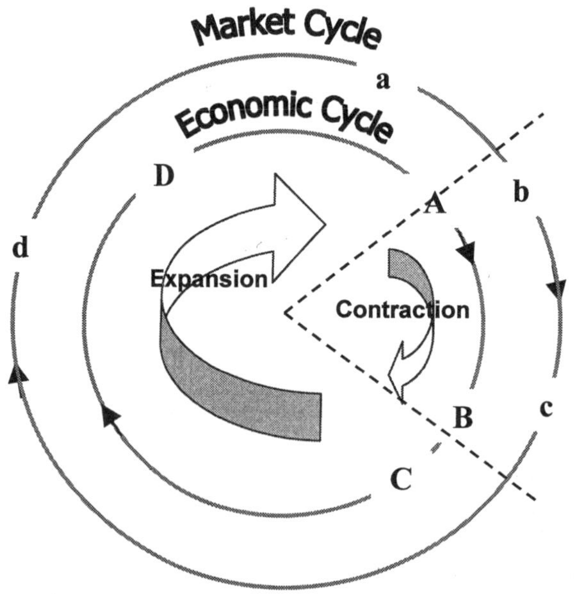

Here are the stages of the *economic* cycle (Figure 7.2, the inner circle):

	A	B	C	D
Economic Activity	recession starts	recession bottoms out	growth starts	growth peaks
Inflation	starts declining	steady	bottoms out	peaks

21 Edward R. Dewey & Og Mandino, "Foundation for the Study of Cycles", July 1998

22 for more information on cycles: National Bureau of Economic Research, "U.S. Business Cycle Expansions and Contractions", www.nber.org/cycles.html

Here are the stages of the *market* cycle (Figure 7.2, the outer circle):

	a	b	c	d
Bonds	continue declining	bottom out on the average 6–7 months before the economic bottom	continue rising	peaks on the average of 2 years before the economic top
Stocks	start declining months before economic peak	continue declining	start rising several months before the economic bottom	continue rising

The cyclical trends occur within larger secular trends as depicted in Figure 7.3. At least two complete cyclical trends are required to create a secular trend. If the peak of the current cycle is higher than the peak of the previous cycle, they form a secular bullish trend (1921–1928, 1949–1965, and 1982–1999). If they are about the same as the previous cycle, they form a secular sideways trend (1900–1920, 1937–1948, and 1966–1981). If the trough of the current cycle is lower than the trough of the previous cycle, they create a secular bearish trend (1929–1932).

Figure 7.3: Cyclical trends in equity markets

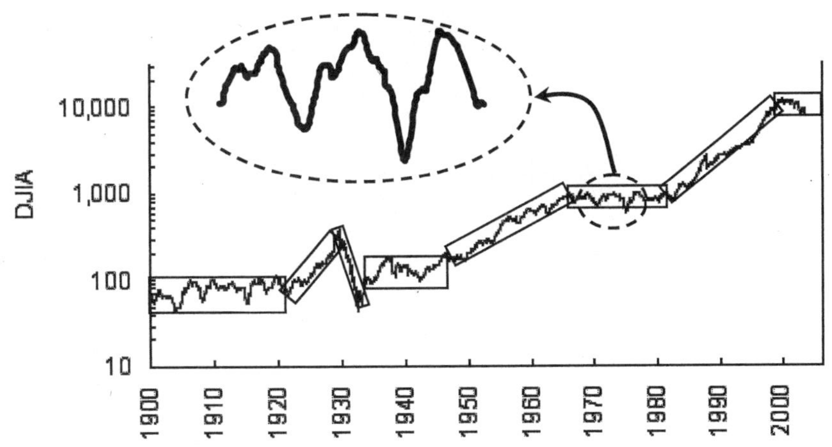

Generally, cyclical trends are more recognizable inside the secular sideways trends (Figure 7.4). They are less visible during secular bullish trends. During the late stages of a secular bullish trend, they seem to disappear altogether because of the strength of the speculative demand on equities. The length of a secular trend tends to be a multiple of the length of the underlying cyclical trends.

Figure 7.4 Cyclical trends during 1966 –1979

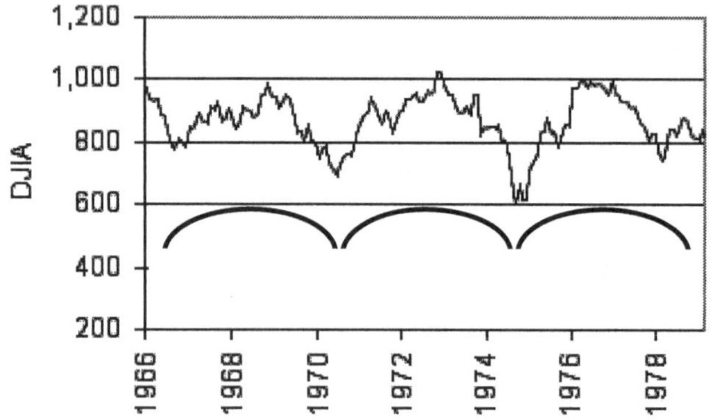

Since 1854, an average business cycle lasted 55 months. The average expansion was 38 months and the average contraction was 17 months in duration. Between 1945 and 2001, the average expansion was 57 months and the average contraction was 10 months[23]

For equity markets, the most commonly known cyclical trend is the US Presidential Election Cycle, which has a 4–year time cycle.

[23] National Bureau of Economic Research, "U.S. Business Cycle Expansions and Contractions", www.nber.org/cycles.html

Seasonality:

Seasonality is defined market movements that have a recurrence rate of one year. They have no long–term influence on portfolio longevity. However, the strongest three months of the year for stocks have historically been November, December and January[24]. Accordingly, if you are withdrawing income annually, the best time to do so might be at the end of January, after the seasonal rise. If you don't need the money, but are forced to withdraw (tax–deferred portfolios), then make your withdrawals at the end of December.

Also, if you are withdrawing income monthly, you might want to do so early in the month to take advantage of the Day–of–the–Month effect[25], when statistically markets are slightly higher.

Other than these two tips, any other portfolio activity related to seasonality should be of interest only to professional traders and not to average retirees.

Random Fluctuations:

Apart from secular, cyclical and seasonality trends, markets fluctuate randomly. Many investors and advisors pay excessive attention to the randomness of markets. Secular or cyclical trends, investment strategies, risk management strategies and management costs each have far more influence on the longevity of a retirement portfolio than random fluctuations.

My analysis based on market history indicates that portfolio longevity varies no more than 8% as a result of random fluctuations. Random fluctuations can help short–term traders, but they have no significant effect on buy–and–hold retirement portfolios.

Conclusion:

Markets move at random in the short term, cyclically in the mid–term and in secular trends in the long term. A sound understanding of market trends is essential for proper investment planning, meaningful academic research and good practice management.

Be wary of any research that shows any type of historical market statistics (index growth rate, dividend yields, earnings, PE ratios, investment strategies and so on) based on man–made, fixed time intervals; such as ten–year time periods. Any such time interval is incongruent with the duration of secular market trends. Conclusions from such statistics are generally useless for developing any investment or retirement planning strategies.

---

24 Yale Hirsch, "Stock Trader's Almanac"

25 Research indicates that the last trading day and first three trading days of the month have a higher return than any other days of the month. Bruce Jacobs and Kenneth Levy, "Calendar Anomalities, MTA Journal, Winter 1989–1990

Chapter 8

Mathematics of Loss

If you are a trader, the mathematics of loss is a simple calculation: If you had paid $10 per share last week and it is now $8, you lost $2. The loss is 20%, based on the original share price of $10. To go back to the break–even point, you have to make $2, which is 25% of the current share price of $8.

Equation 8.1 shows how to calculate the gain you need to break even from a loss:

$$GR = 100\% \times \left(\frac{100}{100 - \text{Loss}\%} - 1 \right) \qquad \text{(Equation 8.1)}$$

where:
GR is the percent growth required to breakeven

> Example 8.1: Brian has an investment portfolio worth one million dollars. He does not withdraw any income from his portfolio. Suddenly, a bear market appears out of nowhere. Brian's portfolio loses 20% of its value. How much does Brian's portfolio need to gain to break even?
>
> $$\text{\% Gain Required to break even} = 100\% \times \left(\frac{100}{100 - 20} - 1 \right) = 25\%$$

Table 8.1, shows how much you need to gain to break even after a loss:

Table 8.1: Percent gain required to breakeven

% Loss	% Gain required to break even
5%	5.26%
10%	11.11%
20%	25.00%
30%	42.86%
50%	100.00%
80%	400.00%

When we talk about distribution portfolios, we are talking about withdrawals from fluctuating investments. If there is a periodic withdrawal from the portfolio, does the same table apply? No, it does not. Each withdrawal at a loss creates a permanent loss. Not only you do need to recover from earlier market losses, but you also need to recover from these seemingly small chunks of permanent losses created along the way.

To keep things simple, let's ignore the indexation of periodic withdrawals. Assuming a steady recovery after the initial loss, you can use the following formulas to calculate the total gain required after a loss:

$$FA = PI \times (1 + GI)^{M+N} - \frac{WA \times \left[(1 + GI)^{M+N} - 1\right]}{GI} \qquad \text{(Equation 8.2)}$$

$$FB = PC \times (1 + GR)^{M} - \frac{WA \times \left[(1 + GR)^{M} - 1\right]}{GR} \qquad \text{(Equation 8.3)}$$

$$TG = (1 + GR)^{M} - 1 \qquad \text{(Equation 8.4)}$$

where:

PI	the original portfolio value
PC	the current portfolio value
FA	the future portfolio value calculated on the original retirement plan
FB	the revised future value
GI	the original assumed annual growth rate
GR	the annual growth rate required to match the portfolio value of the original plan
N	the number of years since the original plan
M	the number of years required to catch up
WA	the annual withdrawal amount on the original plan
TG	the total gain in percentage required to meet the original retirement plan portfolio value

Keep in mind; since we ignored the effect of inflation, these equations apply only to short periods of time, perhaps a few years.

To calculate these formulas manually, follow these steps:

Step 1: Calculate the future value, FA, of the portfolio based on your original assumptions at the beginning of retirement, using Equation 8.2.

Step 2: Assume a growth rate required, GR and calculate FB using equation 8.3

Step 3: Vary the value of assumed GR and repeat step 2 until FB is equal to FA.

Step 4: Calculate total gain required in the next "M" years using equation 8.4

To calculate these formulas using a standard financial calculator, follow these steps:

Step 1: Calculate FA:

Enter Value	Press
PI +/–	PV
WA	PYMT
GI	I/YR
M + N	N

Read the value of FA by pressing the FV key. Do not clear.

Step 2: Calculate GR:

Enter Value	Press
PC +/–	PV
M	N

Read the value of GR by pressing I/YR. This is the value of GR. Do not clear.

Step 3: Calculate TG

Enter Value	Press
	/
100	+
1	=
	y^x
M	–
	=

Example 8.2

Steve retired 4 years ago. He then believed that stocks are for the long run. He had 100% equities in his portfolio. Originally, he had $1,000,000 in his portfolio. When he prepared his retirement plan four years ago, he assumed a long-term annual portfolio growth rate of 10%. He withdraws $60,000 annually from his portfolio.

Because of adverse market conditions and his periodic withdrawals totaling $240,000 over the last four years, his portfolio is now worth $610,000. Steve wants his portfolio to catch up with his original retirement plan in 3 years. Ignore inflation.

How much does Steve's portfolio need to gain?

Step 1: Using a financial calculator, calculate FA

Enter Value	Press
1,000,000 +/-	PV
60,000	PYMT
10	I/YR
7	N

Read FA by pressing FV = 1,379,487. Do not clear.

Step 2: Calculate GR:

Enter Value	Press
610,000 +/-	PV
3	N

Read the value of GR by pressing I/YR = 39%. Do not clear.

Step 3: Calculate Total Gain using equation 8.4:

$$TG = [(1 + 39/100)^3 - 1] \times 100\% = 169\%$$

Steve's portfolio needs to grow by 169% within the next 3 years to match his original retirement plan. Do you think this is possible?

Now, Steve thinks "Perhaps it is more realistic to expect a full recovery in five years instead of three". Reworking numbers, Steve calculates that he needs a total gain of 238% over the next 5 years. Again, this is an unlikely return for a retirement portfolio.

Steve now understands the concept of mathematics of loss.

For a typical cyclical bearish trend, you might be interested in knowing the total gain required within a 3–year time period. The following table shows how much you need to gain for various losses and withdrawal rates, assuming a steady increase of the portfolio value after the initial loss and no indexation of withdrawals over time:

Table 8.2: Percent gain required in three years:

	Initial Withdrawal Rate			
	0%	4%	6%	8%
Percent Loss:	Percent Gain Required over 3 years:			
10%	11%	26%	33%	41%
20%	25%	42%	51%	60%
30%	43%	63%	74%	86%
50%	100%	132%	150%	169%
80%	400%	525%	597%	676%

Retiring in 2000:

Equations 8.2 to 8.4 and Table 8.2 do not consider inflation, dividends and management costs. In real life, they are important.

Let's go back to Chapter 2 and follow up the case of retiring in the year 2000. Remember that Bob III retired at the beginning of year 2000 with $1 million retirement savings. He was taking out $60,000 each year. He projected his portfolio growth at the historical average rate of 8.8%. The reality turned out to be much grimmer than his projection. The last row on Table 2.7 indicated that he would have $194,156 left in his portfolio and his withdrawal after indexation was $75,036 at the end of 2008.

Here is the question: Bob III originally projected that his portfolio would be worth $1,415,992 in year 14 (Table 2.1). By how much does S&P500 need to increase over the next five years, so that Bob's portfolio value can catch up with his original projection, assuming a 3% indexation of his withdrawals going forward?

Now, I like to incorporate the inflation indexation to our calculation. I use a spreadsheet for that. Table 8.3 shows the results: The S&P500 needs to grow about 70.2% annually for the next five years for Bob III to catch up with his original projection. This sounds like a pipedream, even though his original assumptions were totally logical.

Table 8.3: Bob III's portfolio needs a growth of 70.2% to catch up with his original projection:

End of Year	Begin Value $	Withdrawal $	Growth $ @ 72.07108%	End Value $
2009	$194,156	$75,036	$139,930	$259,050
2010	$259,050	$77,287	$186,700	$368,464
2011	$368,464	$79,606	$265,556	$554,414
2012	$554,414	$81,994	$399,572	$871,992
2013	$871,992	$84,454	$628,454	$1,415,992
2014	$1,415,992	$86,987		

Figure 8.1: Bob III's portfolio needs a growth of 72.1% in each and every year for the next five years to catch up with his original projection:

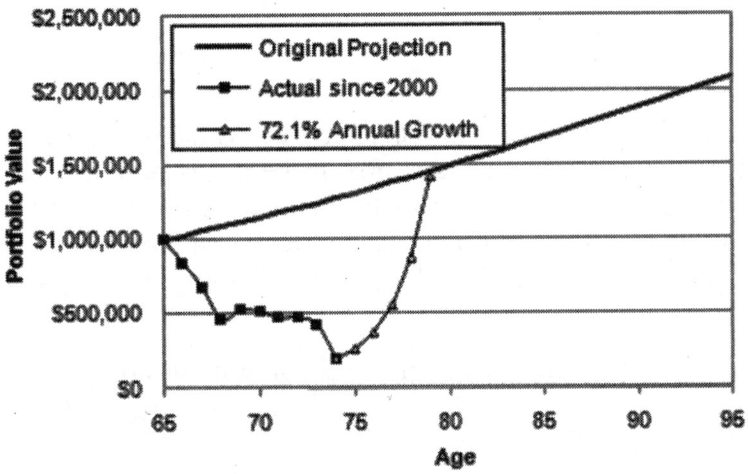

What if Bob III does not necessarily need a fast recovery? He can wait until age 95 to catch up. How much of a growth would you need then?

In this case, the S&P500 does not need to grow by 72.1% each year for the next five years. It needs to grow only by 41.9% each and every year for the next twenty–one years. Phew!

Figure 8.2: Bob III's portfolio needs a growth of 41.9% in each and every year for the next twenty–one years to catch up with his original projection:

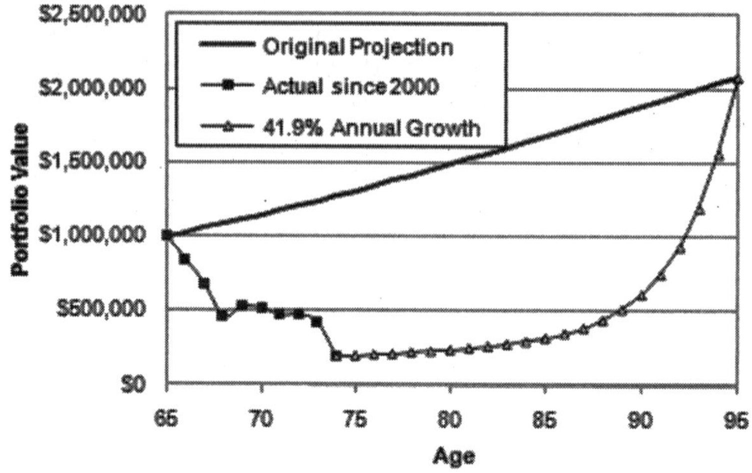

Finally, Bob III decides to forget about catching up with his original projection. He just wants to know how much of an average growth he needs until age 95 for income only. Here is the answer: He needs 41.6% growth each and every year until age 95 for lifelong income. Notice that it takes only a 0.3% difference (41.6% versus 41.9%) in annual growth rate to have about two million dollars or absolutely nothing in Bob III's portfolio in twenty–one years.

Now you might start wondering why so many pension funds are in trouble. Keep reading.

Figure 8.3: Bob III's portfolio needs a growth of 41.6% in each and every year for the next twenty–one years just to have a lifelong income:

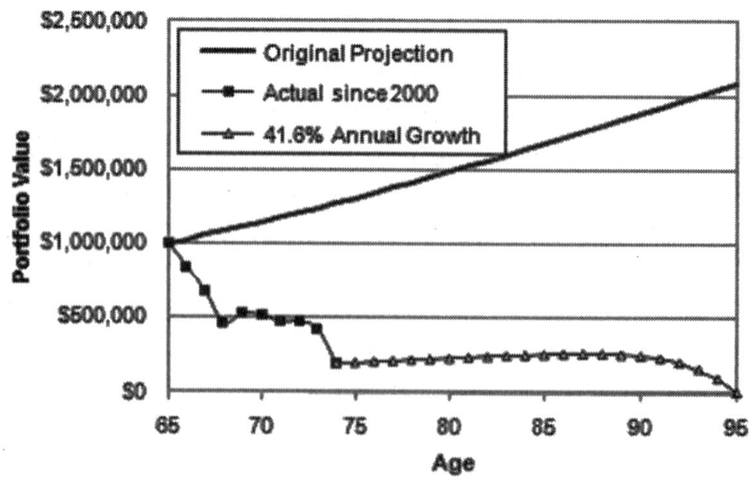

Probability of a Market Loss:

Sooner or later, every investor experiences a loss. Table 8.4 indicates the probability of loss in any one year for different markets based on historical index returns.

Table 8.4: Probability of occurrence of loss in any one calendar year

Index	The loss is less than 10%	The loss is 10% or more	Any amount of loss
	Probability of Occurrence of Loss:		
DJIA (since 1900)	14%	22%	36%
S&P500 (since 1900)	10%	22%	32%
Nikkei 225 (since 1914)	15%	25%	40%
FTSE All Shares (since 1900)	19%	21%	40%
SP/TSX (since 1919)	13%	21%	34%

Let's look at the probability of loss separately in secular bullish and sideways markets:

Table 8.5: Probability of Loss in a calendar year in secular bullish trends (1921–1928, 1949–1965, 1982–1999)

Index	Loss is less than 10%	Loss is 10% or more	Any Loss
	Probability of Occurrence of Loss in Secular Bullish Trends:		
DJIA (since 1900)	12%	5%	17%
S&P500 (since 1900)	12%	2%	14%

Table 8.6: Probability of loss in a calendar year in secular sideways trends (1900–1920, 1937–1948, 1966–1981)

Index	Loss is less than 10%	Loss is 10% or more	Any Loss
	Probability of Occurrence of Loss in Secular Sideways Trends:		
DJIA (since 1900)	18%	31%	49%
S&P500 (since 1900)	12%	31%	43%

Tables 8.5 and 8.6 indicate that in secular bullish trends, there is about a one in six chance of experiencing a losing year. In secular sideways trends, the chance of a losing year is one in two. What differentiates a secular bullish trend from a secular sideways trend is not only the depth, but also the frequency of losing years.

We will see later on that if you have *any* loss during the first four years of retirement, the chances of portfolio depletion during your life time increases dramatically. If you have a loss of 10% or more, it is nearly impossible to recover from it, *ever*. The market history shows that the probability of such a loss is between 21% and 25% for developed economies. That means your arm is tied behind your back before you are out of the gate for retirement, well before any other financial calamity knocks you down. If the start of your retirement coincides with a secular sideways trend, you have little chance of lifelong income.

Anatomy of Recovery:

Many people confuse the market direction with the portfolio direction. They think when markets go up, so does the portfolio. Nothing can be further from the truth. When markets go up, portfolios do not necessarily go up even though you may be holding the exact market index in your portfolio. Market action and portfolio action are two entirely different things.

A case in point: At the end of June 1932, the low point for the DJIA was 44.32. A few years later, at the end of February 1937, it was 187.68. This is a 324% increase. In an accumulation portfolio, this would have been fantastic.

How does this work out in a distribution portfolio? Remember in Chapter 2, Bob retires at the beginning of 1929 at age 65. Look at Figure 8.4. What happened to Bob's portfolio while the markets were rampantly bullish? Absolutely nothing! His portfolio was flat during this 4½–year bullish trend, between ages 69 and 73. At age 75, it just fizzled out.

Figure 8.4: Value of retirement assets over time, projection of a standard retirement calculator versus retiring at the beginning of 1929

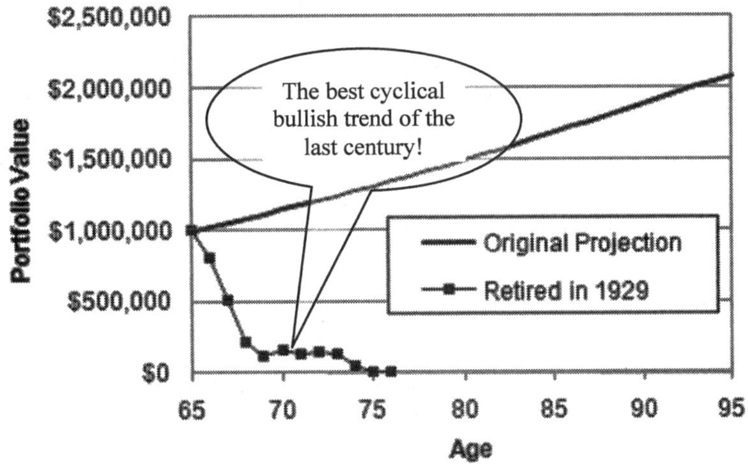

What about retiring in year 2000? See Figure 8.5. It shows a similar behavior to 1929, doesn't it? After three years of back–to–back losses, markets went up for four years between 2003 and 2007. How did this bullish trend manifest itself in the distribution portfolio? There is no bullish trend in the portfolio at all. It remained almost flat until the crash of 2008. One thing about financial history is this: it does repeat itself.

Figure 8.5: Value of retirement assets over time, projection of a standard retirement calculator versus retiring at the beginning of 2000

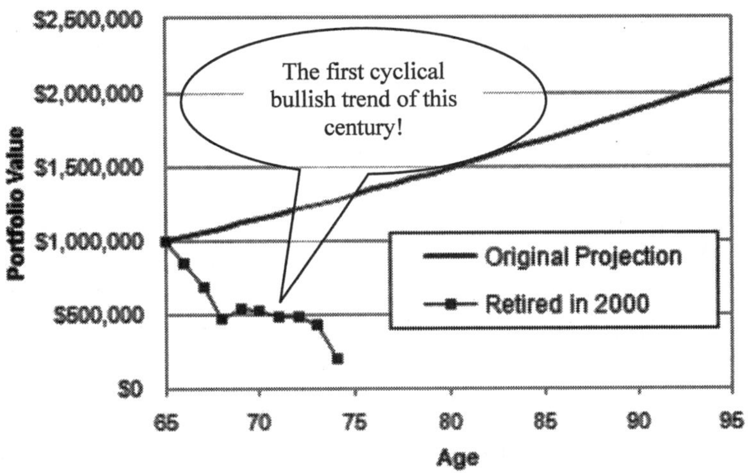

After the first loss, the die is already cast. Even the strongest bullish trend cannot save a distribution portfolio from its eventual demise. A withdrawal rate of 4% prior to a market downturn jumps to 5% after a 20% loss and to 8% after a 50% loss.

Once the withdrawal rate exceeds 4%, a distribution portfolio does not go up when markets go up. If you watch your portfolio on a daily basis, you may see higher portfolio values after strong days and feel good about it. But at the end of the year, the most you can hope for is a flat portfolio value, even when markets might be soaring.

Here is how portfolios behave in various market trends:

MARKET TREND:	**PORTFOLIO TREND:**	
	Accumulation Portfolio	**Distribution Portfolio,** (Withdrawal rate over 4%)
⇩ Bearish	⇩ Down	⇩ Down
⇔ Sideways	⇔ Sideways	⇩ Down
⇧ Bullish	⇧ Up	⇔ Sideways or ⇩ Down

Most of the educational curricula for advisors cover only accumulation portfolios. With that mindset, over the long term, one expects to recover from losses. The chart in Figure 8.6 depicts the probability of a lower portfolio value at each age after retirement, compared with the starting portfolio value at age 65. It is based on actual market history with an asset mix of 40% equity (DJIA) and 60% fixed income.

Figure 8.6: Probability of lower portfolio value, no withdrawals, 40% DJIA, 60% fixed income, since 1900

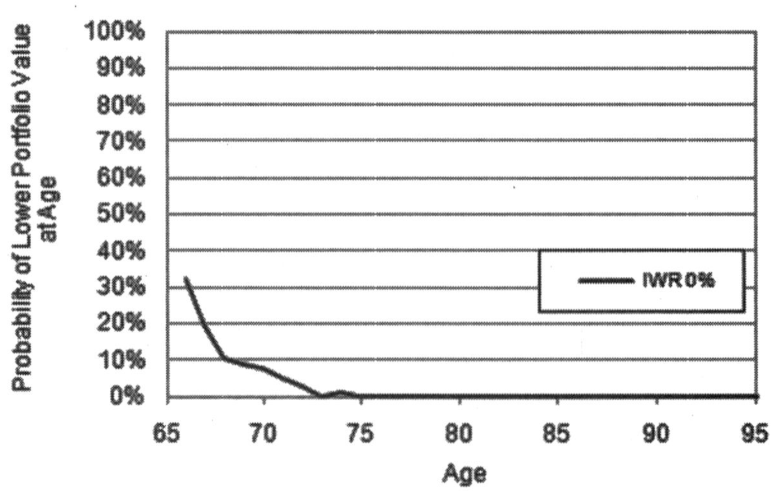

The solid black line on the chart indicates that, if you have no withdrawals (IWR=0%), there was about a 32% chance of a lower portfolio value in the following year, at age 66. However, the portfolio inevitably recovered from the loss and the probability of a lower portfolio value came down to 0% at age 73. In other words, when there were no withdrawals, after eight years, you always had a higher portfolio value than the starting amount in a balanced portfolio.

What happens if there are withdrawals from the portfolio? Keep in mind, you don't have to be retired for that. There are periodic withdrawals in accumulation portfolios too: fund fees, performance fees, management fees, trading costs and slippage, segregated fund guarantee costs, advisor fees, taxes and other leakages from your portfolio all create "withdrawals" continuously. These costs create de facto periodic withdrawals anywhere between 1% and 5%, depending on what you invest in, even in accumulation portfolios.

When there is even the smallest periodic withdrawal, a full recovery might never happen. I calculated and plotted in Figure 8.7 the probability of a lower portfolio value for a 3% initial withdrawal rate. This is well below the sustainable withdrawal rate. We observe that there is at least a 10% probability that a balanced portfolio *never* recovers from losses at a 3% initial withdrawal rate, no matter how long the time horizon is.

Figure 8.7: Probability of lower portfolio value after retirement, 3% IWR, 40% DJIA, 60% fixed income, since 1900

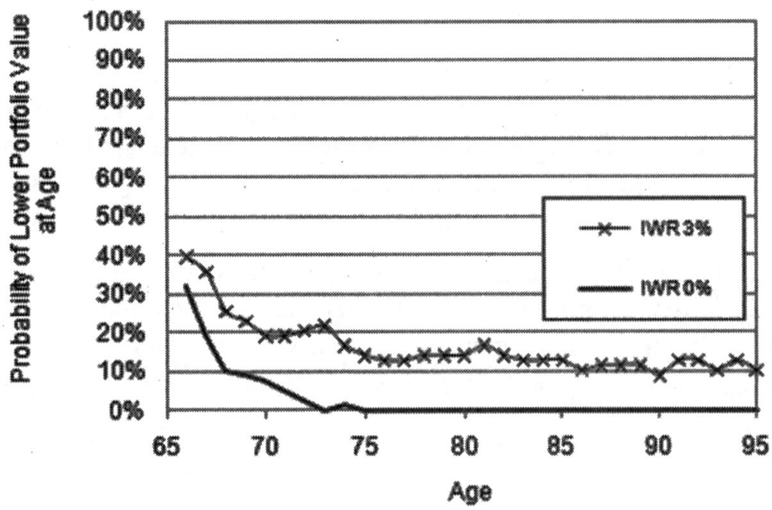

Going further, looking at Figure 8.8, when the initial withdrawal rate is 8%, the probability of a lower portfolio value by age 76 was 100%, regardless of what kind of a rip–roaring secular bullish market might be prevailing.

Figure 8.8: Probability of lower portfolio value after retirement, 40% DJIA, 60% fixed income, since 1900

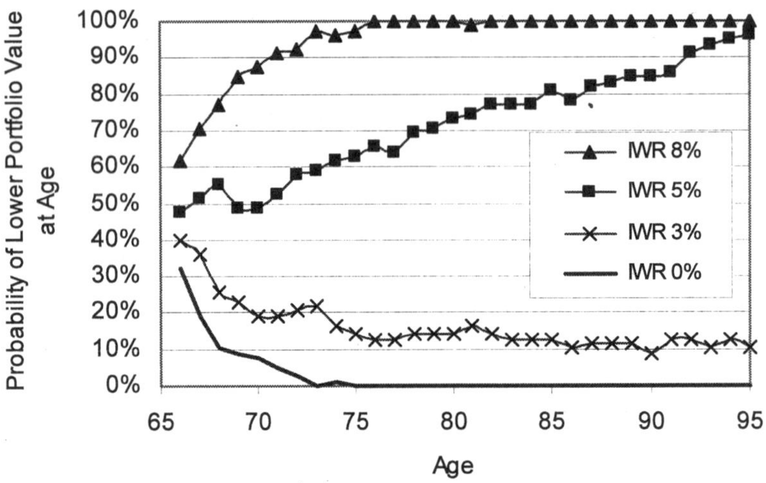

So, if you thought you were safe withdrawing 4% starting at the beginning of 2008, you are likely in for a rude awakening. If you were holding an aggressive portfolio, then after the crash, your withdrawals might have increased to about 8% of the portfolio value. Now, your initial withdrawal rate suddenly becomes 8%, starting in 2009. As such, you are 100% guaranteed *never* to recover fully from *any* future loss for the rest of your life.

Disregard any financial research, any words of wisdom, any gibberish from financial gurus in the media that "markets eventually recover in the long term." They are not telling you the full story: Yes, markets did always recover in the past, but your distribution portfolio retained a permanent loss for the rest of your life.

That is why most portfolios, including pension funds and other similar portfolios, fall more and more behind their benchmark over the long–term regardless of how well they might have been designed initially. Even if you are a Nobel prize winner in economics or in math, if you don't understand the concept of "Time Value of Fluctuations" then your portfolio's long–term underperformance will be an ever perplexing spectacle for you.

I also plotted similar charts for using other equity indices. Figures 8.9 through 8.12 depict the outcome when S&P500, SP/TSX, Nikkei225 and FTSE are the equity proxy. At 3% initial withdrawal rate, the probability of a permanent residual loss was over 20% with S&P500 and SP/TSX. With FTSE, it was more dismal, around 50%.

The concept of "long–term" exists only in accumulation portfolios.
There is no such thing as "long term" in a distribution portfolio.
As soon as your periodic withdrawals start, "long–term" ceases to exist, and the "luck factor" takes control of the outcome.

Figure 8.9: Probability of lower portfolio value after retirement, 40% S&P500, 60% fixed income, since 1900

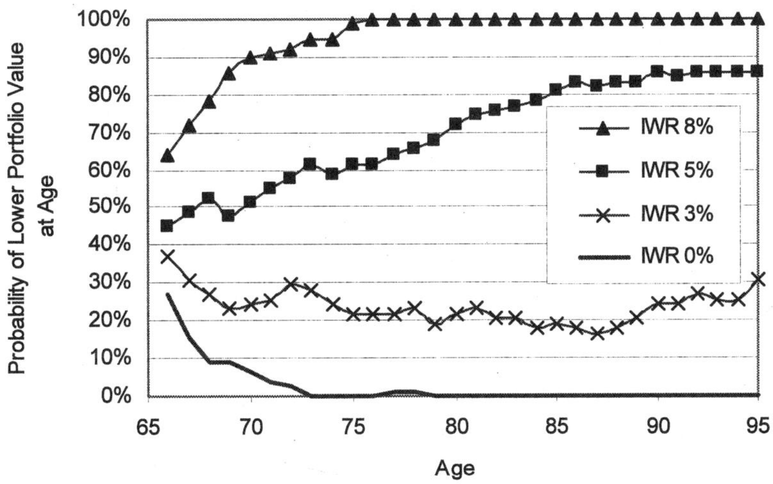

Figure 8.10: Probability of lower portfolio value after retirement, 40% SP/TSX, 60% fixed income, since 1919

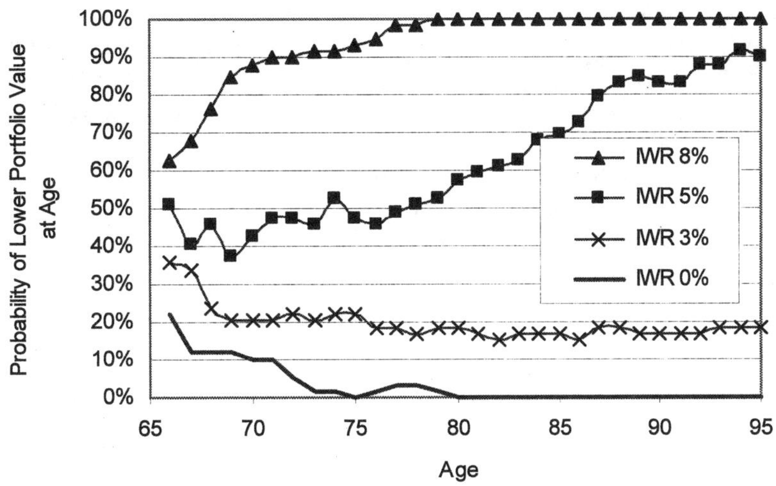

Figure 8.11: Probability of lower portfolio value after retirement, 40% Nikkei 225, 60% fixed income, since 1914

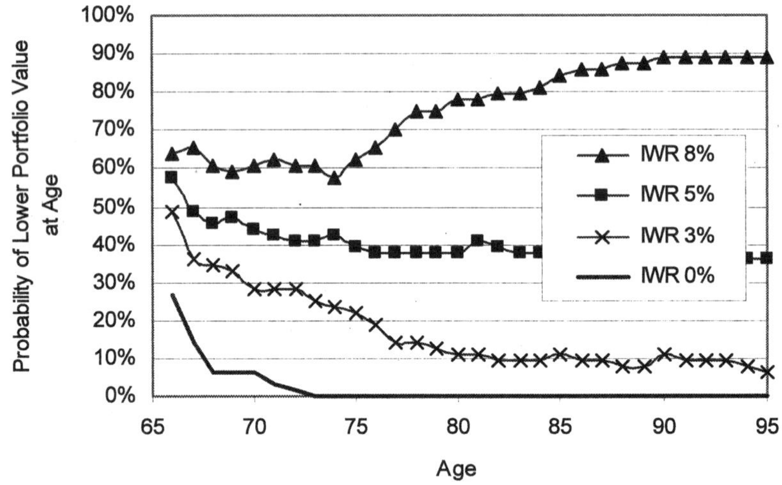

Figure 8.12: Probability of lower portfolio value after retirement, 40% FTSE All Shares, 60% fixed income, since 1900

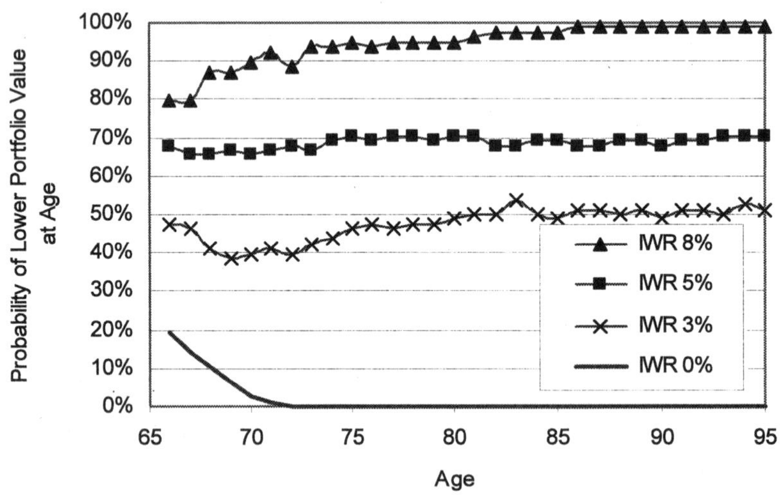

Conclusion:

So you thought that "markets always go up in the long term!" That is fine. You can continue thinking that way. The thing is, while markets go up, your distribution portfolio will not follow it up. This minor detail can deplete it in a very short time.

If you are following a "buy–and–hold" strategy and the initial withdrawal rate exceeds 3%, there is a good chance that your portfolio might never recover fully, even from routine fluctuations. The losses become permanent, even in the presence of strong bullish trends or a multi–country diversification.

Do not lose, give away, donate, part with, gift, help out or misplace any retirement savings, especially during the early years of retirement. I have homework for you: every morning, take a blank piece of paper. Write on it:

Don't lose today!

Read it to yourself throughout the day during your breaks. My best investment ever was a little sticky paper on my computer screen, where I do my occasional stock trades. It reads: "Greed kills". I pay attention to it.

Sometimes, investors tell me that they watch their investments very carefully and closely. That is great. However, the most effective way of containing the risk is the "bet" size. It should be small enough so that if you lose half of that particular investment, your retirement plan should not be derailed. If the "bet" size is the cake, watching it closely is only the icing on that cake.

In a distribution portfolio, there are three different luck factors that create permanent losses:

- Sequence of Returns
- Inflation, and
- Reverse Dollar Cost Averaging

In the next four chapters, we go into more detail about each of these topics.

Chapter 9

The Luck Factor

Luck is one of the most elusive concepts in retirement planning. We strive to portray our financial planning profession as a science. We talk about academic studies that conclude that “asset allocation accounts for over 90% of the variation in a portfolio's investment return.” We show our clients the efficient frontier charts produced by reputable research organizations. Some of us run one million (years of) simulations, well knowing that there is no recorded stock index history beyond the last 115 years.

Yet after this entire charade, when I open a new account for a couple, their parting words at the end of the meeting are invariably, “I hope we get lucky and our retirement savings lasts us until we die!”

Most clients know about luck. It is us, advisers, who shun the concept of luck because it is incongruent with our training and sales material. We have been brainwashed too much with the so–called “scientific” nonsense in our financial curriculum.

Deep down, most of us know the importance of luck in retirement planning. We avoid talking about it because we don’t know how to deal with it. After all, how can we gain the respect of our clients if we use terms like “luck” or “kismet” while giving them precise–looking forecasts thirty years into the unknown future? Otherwise, the sign at the entrance to my office might as well look something like this:

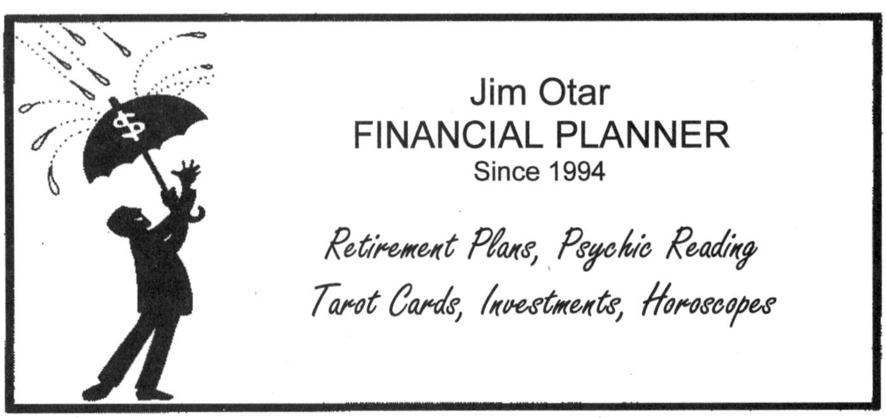

In this chapter, we'll look at how luck plays havoc with retirement plans. I'll expose some of the misconceptions in retirement planning. I will define and quantify the contribution of luck.

First of all, what creates the luck factor? *Any* deviation from *any* straight line growth and inflation creates the luck factor. All secular and cyclical trends create these deviations.

The most important thing in a distribution portfolio is the **sequence of returns.** In this context, luck refers to the timing of the start of your retirement relative to a *secular* trend. If you are lucky, the start of your retirement coincides with the start of a secular bull market and you experience a favorable sequence of returns during the initial years of retirement.

The second important luck factor is **inflation**. In this context, luck refers to the general inflation level that you will experience during your retirement. If you are lucky, you'll live in a low inflation environment during your retirement. This allows you to give yourself smaller pay increases to maintain your purchasing power.

The third important luck factor is **reverse dollar cost averaging (RDCA)**. This is caused by cyclical trends. RDCA speeds up the depletion of your portfolio.

Let's look at an example: Bob, 65, is retiring this year with $1 million for his retirement invested in a balanced portfolio. His asset mix is 60% fixed income and 40% equity. His fixed income yields a net income of historical 6–month CD plus 1%. His equities perform the same as the DJIA. He needs to withdraw $60,000 annually, indexed to inflation. Using historical data, I calculate the portfolio life, as if Bob were to retire in any of the years since 1900.

Figure 9.1 illustrates the outcome. The upper part of the graph shows the value of DJIA over time. The lower part of the chart shows the portfolio life depending on the year Bob retired. The happy faces on the top of the chart indicate the years of retirement that ended up as lucky; the unhappy faces are the unlucky years. Notice that the unlucky bands are a lot wider than lucky years.

Each of the starting portfolios had the same asset allocation, the same asset selection and the same management costs. The only variable was the timing of Bob's retirement; if Bob were lucky enough to retire during the early years of any secular bull market, early 1920's, early 1950's or late 1970's, then his portfolio would likely last him 30 years or more.

If Bob retired at any other time, 1900's, 1910's, 1930's, most of 1940's, late 1950's, 1960's or early 1970's, then the portfolio life is about 17 years. It would not matter what the asset allocation was or how much he diversified internationally.

The crosshatched area to the right of the portfolio life chart indicates the years for which we do not know the portfolio life yet. However, you may recall Bob III in Chapter 2. There, we calculated the portfolio performance from the beginning of year 2000 until the end of 2008, using actual historical data. We then estimated that the money would run out within about three years. This adds up to twelve years of total portfolio life and gives us an idea about the end–points of the crosshatched area.

Figure 9.1: The luck factor over the 20th century

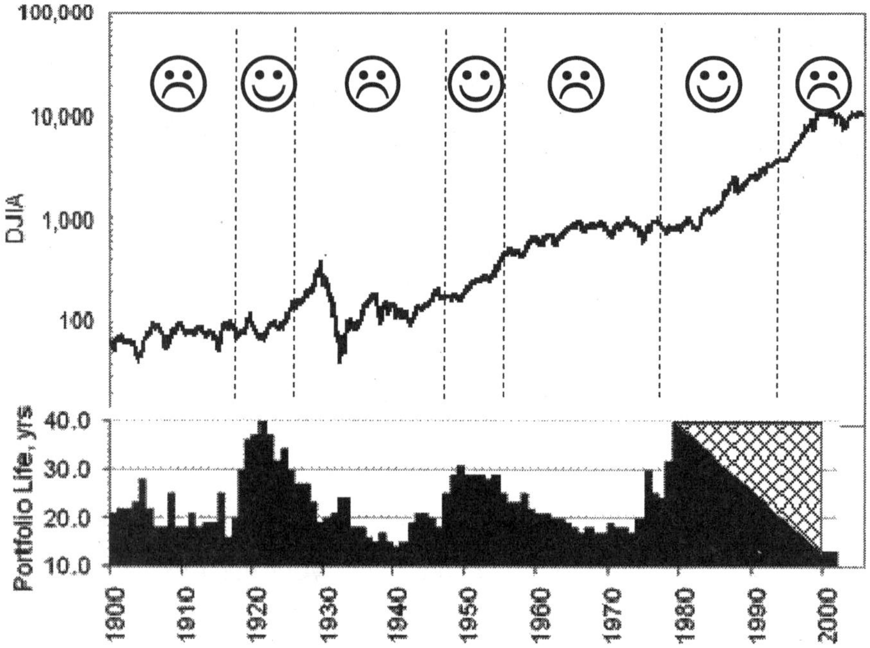

The transition from good luck to bad luck, or vice versa, is usually quick. For example: if Bob were to retire in 1973, his portfolio would have lasted only 17 years. If he were to retire in 1975, then his portfolio would last about 30 years.

The bottom line is, in 69% of time, Bob would have run out of money before age 90. While there is nothing we can do about luck, we can recognize and quantify its existence. This allows us to bypass the luck factor by looking at other income classes to create life–long income.

Conclusion:

Luck is by far one of the most important factors in retirement planning. It is second only to the withdrawal rate for influencing the portfolio life.

In the investment community, we generally ignore it. Many advisors feel uncomfortable conceding that the success of a retirement plan has more to do with luck than their talent and good counsel. If you ignore the luck factor, the chances are you will suffer financially during your retirement *and* this pain will continue for the rest of your life. On the other hand, if you accept it as large component of the outcome, then you will set yourself free to look for solutions.

In the next three chapters, we go into details of the three components of the luck factor: the sequence of returns, inflation, and reverse dollar cost averaging.

Chapter 10

The Sequence of Returns

The sequence of returns is the most important component of the luck factor. In my earlier book "High Expectations & False Dreams" in 2001, I wrote about this at length. At that time, I put together a spreadsheet to show the difference between retiring at the beginning of a bullish cycle versus retiring at the beginning of a bearish cycle. I made this spreadsheet available to readers free of charge to help them plan for their retirement. Eventually, I replaced it with my more sophisticated retirement calculator based on the actual market history.

Figure 10.1: The sequence of returns

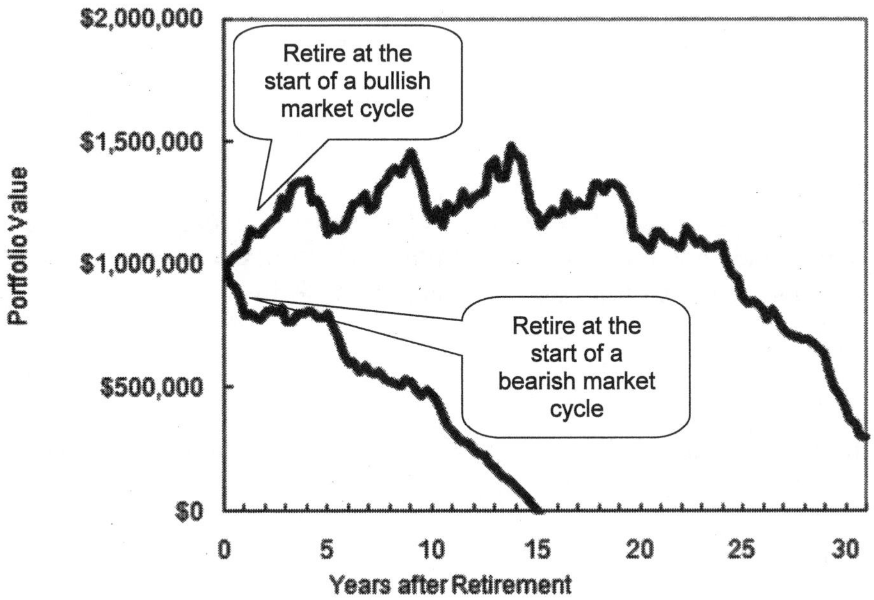

How can we calculate the effect of the sequence of returns in a retirement portfolio? Here are the steps:

1. Isolate and exclude the effect of the variability of inflation from secular trends. We do that by using a fixed "average" inflation rate during retirement. This leaves us with variations in the sequence of returns only[26].
2. Calculate the asset value of the portfolio over time for all years since 1900. I define the top 10% of all outcomes as the "lucky" outcome and the bottom 10% of all outcomes as the "unlucky" outcome.
3. Calculate the median outcome, where half of the outcomes are better and half are worse.
4. Calculate the compound annual return (CAR) of the lucky, unlucky and the median portfolios.
5. Finally, the luck factor is half of the difference between the CAR of the lucky and unlucky portfolios divided by the CAR of the median:

$$LF = \frac{(CAR_{90} - CAR_{10})}{2 \times CAR_{50}} \times 100\% \qquad \text{(Equation 10.1)}$$

where:

LF is the luck factor
CAR_{90} is the compound annual return of the lucky (top decile) portfolio
CAR_{10} is the compound annual return of the unlucky (bottom decile) portfolio
CAR_{50} is the compound annual return of the median portfolio

The luck factor measures the average difference of the compound annual returns between the extreme outcome and the median outcome, expressed in percentage.

[26] For the purposes of this book, the effect of reverse dollar cost averaging is not related to secular trends, but only to cyclical trends. In real life, there is a small interaction.

Example 10.1

Dan is 65 years old, just retiring. He has $1 million in his portfolio and needs $60,000 each year, indexed to inflation. His asset allocation is 40% DJIA and 60% fixed income, rebalanced annually. On the equity side, he expects the index return. On the fixed income side, he expects a return of 0.5% over and above the historical 6-month CD rates after all management fees. Using 3.3% annual increase of withdrawals, calculate his luck factor resulting from the sequence of returns.

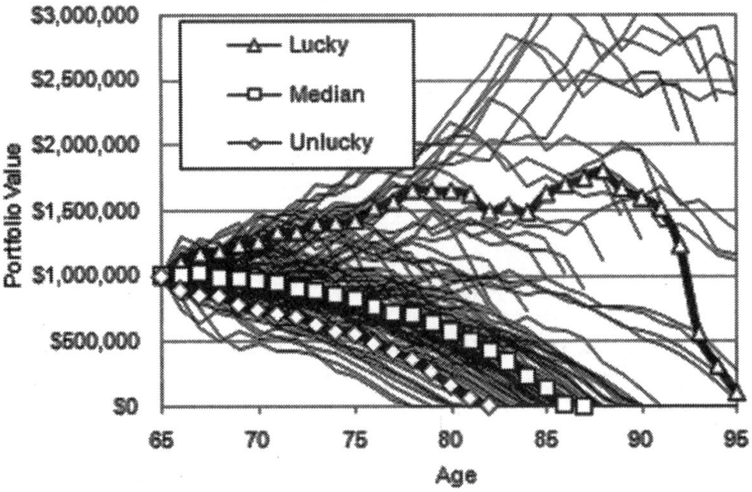

The lucky, unlucky and median portfolios are indicated on the chart. The compound annual returns[27] for the lucky, unlucky and median portfolios are 7.57%, 2.86% and 5.30%, respectively. Plug in these numbers into Equation 10.1 and calculate the luck factor resulting from the sequence of returns:

$$\text{Luck Factor} = \frac{7.57\%-2.86\%}{2 \times 5.30\%} = 44\%$$

Table 10.1 depicts the effect of sequence of returns for different indices and withdrawal rates based on an asset mix of 40% equity and 60% fixed income for a constant average annual inflation of 3.3%. In all cases, the fixed income returns are based on US historical data.

[27] using Otar Retirement Calculator

Table 10.1: The effect of the sequence of returns

	Initial Withdrawal Rate					
	0%	2%	4%	6%	8%	10%
Index:	**The Luck Factor created by Sequence of Returns:**					
DJIA (since 1900)	43%	42%	45%	44%	58%	65%
S&P500 (since 1900)	48%	49%	52%	46%	63%	66%
SP/TSX (since 1919)	35%	37%	44%	49%	54%	57%
FTSE All Shares (since 1900)	84%	87%	101%	98%	98%	105%
Nikkei 225 (since 1914)	39%	41%	45%	52%	62%	77%
ASX All Ordinaries (since 1900)	51%	52%	56%	52%	57%	61%

Conclusion:

Among the three components of the luck factor, the sequence of returns is by far the most important. Two negative years or four flat years at the beginning of retirement can cut the portfolio life by half. There is little one can do to mitigate a bad sequence of returns with buy–and–hold portfolios.

The financial planning community is now starting to understand this concept. However, many still think asset allocation and diversification will cure the problem. Asset allocation and diversification can only reduce the volatility of returns, but not the sequence of returns; therefore they are no cure. Unfortunately, many retirees are finding this out the hard way; by losing large chunks of their portfolio permanently when markets go against them.

Chapter 11

Inflation

Inflation is the second most important component of the luck factor. It forces a retiree to withdraw higher and higher amounts from his portfolio, just to keep his purchasing power the same. Many times, this depletes retirement portfolios prematurely.

Over time, inflation reduces a portfolio's lifespan in two ways:

- Initially, more and more money is withdrawn from investments to maintain purchasing power.
- Subsequently, to fight inflation, central banks increase short–term interest rates. This ultimately pushes down share prices, which in turn reduces the value of equity investments, at least temporarily. The net effect is that the retiree withdraws increasingly larger amounts from his investments, and must do so from a shrinking asset base.

Figure 11.1 depicts the US inflation rate over the 20th century. Before 1950, the average inflation was 2.6% but this came with a high volatility[28]. During the second half of the last century, the Federal Reserve was able to rein in the volatility of inflation, but this came with a higher average inflation rate of 4.0%.

Figure 11.1: Inflation since 1900

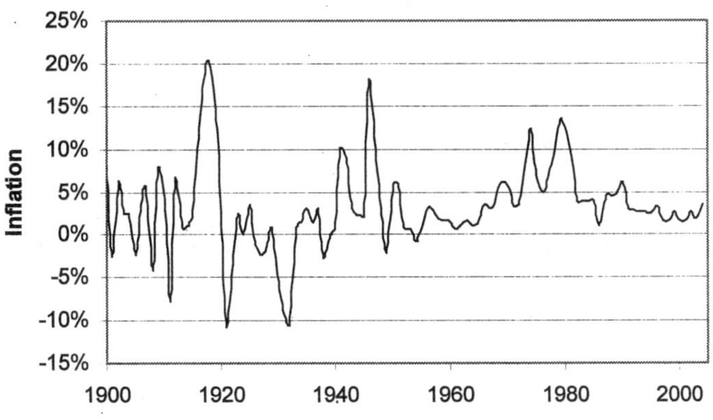

[28] The standard deviation of annual inflation was 6.7 between 1900 and 1950, and it was only 3.2 between 1951 and 1999

When we looked at cyclical trends in Chapter 7, we correlated inflation to economic activity. Inflation generally increases as economic activity peaks. However, this applies only to cyclical trends and not to secular trends. While we can expect higher inflation as the economy heats up within a cycle, this plays differently in the context of the larger secular trends.

Let's look at secular trends to see the interrelation between inflation and market growth. Table 11.1 indicates the average annual inflation and DJIA growth over each secular trend.

Table 11.1: Inflation in secular trends (1900 – 1999)

Trend		Average Annual DJIA Growth	Average Annual Inflation	Length, years
All Trends	1900 – 1999	**7.7%**	**3.3%**	
Secular Sideways[29]**:**		**2.4%**	**5.6%**	
	1900 – 1920	4.2%	4.8%	21
	1937 – 1948	1.4%	4.8%	12
	1966 – 1981	0.8%	7.1%	16
Secular Bull:		**15.0%**	**1.8%**	
	1921 – 1928	20.6%	–1.5%	8
	1949 – 1965	11.5%	1.7%	17
	1982 – 1999	15.9%	3.3%	18
Secular Bear:		**–31.7%**	**–6.4%**	
	1929 – 1932	–31.7%	–6.4%	4
Other:				
Cyclical Bull	1933 – 1936	33.5%	1.7%	4

We observe that:

- In secular bullish trends: the average inflation was 1.8%. The average growth of equities was 15%, which handily beats the inflation.
- In secular sideways trends: the average inflation was 5.6%, much higher than in secular bullish trends. The average growth in equities was only 2.4%, far short of inflation. Markets spend about half of their time in secular sideways trends and equities do not provide an inflation hedge during those time periods.
- In secular bearish trends: there was only one such trend, between 1929 and 1932. Here, the concern is not inflation (or deflation, as it was in this case) but devastating losses.

29 weighted average; weighted by the length of each secular trend

Consider a retiree with an asset mix of 40/60 equity/fixed income and a 6% initial withdrawal rate. Use historical dividend rates and assume no management fees.

If he were to retire at the beginning of the market crash of 1929, his portfolio would have lasted 24 years. On the other hand, if he were to retire in 1966, the beginning of a secular sideways market, his portfolio would have lasted only 18 years, as shown in Figure 11.2. Surprised?

The high average inflation rate of 7.1% between 1966 and 1981 would have forced the retiree to withdraw more and more income, eventually depleting his portfolio. This was worse than the secular bearish trend that started in 1929, when equities lost about 80% of their value.

Figure 11.2: High inflation can shorten portfolio life more than the worst market crash.

There is not much one can do but hope that in the future, the central banks continue to keep inflation in check. After the global market crash of 2008, governments around the world pumped stimulus and rescue packages amounting to trillions of dollars –money they don't have. This only shifts the crisis to the next generation. Unless the excessive greed of global capitalism is somehow curbed, we cannot continue rescuing ourselves from successions of greed and incompetence cycles, at least not without creating future inflation and other calamities.

Inflation is one of the most efficient ways of transferring wealth from those who derive their income from capital (most retirees) to those who derive their income from work. I have no doubt that the next generation, overburdened with the debt that our generation created, will be successful in bringing back inflation when the time is right for them. This, plus the ever–increasing costs of financing the final years of life (additional health care, home care and nursing home expenses), plus all the retirement plans floating around with bizarre growth projections, makes me think that the largest wealth transfer in history, anticipated eagerly by the financial industry, is likely a self–delusion.

Figure 11.3 shows the areas of the standard retirement plan where sequence of returns plays an important role and where inflation plays an important role on portfolio longevity. Generally, the sequence of returns impacts the portfolio in the early years and inflation impacts it in later years. If you see a retirement projection with a sharp decline of the portfolio value after about twenty years, it is almost always because of inflation. If that sharp drop occurs in the early years, it is generally because of the sequence of returns.

Figure 11.3: Influence of the Sequence of Returns and Inflation on distribution portfolio

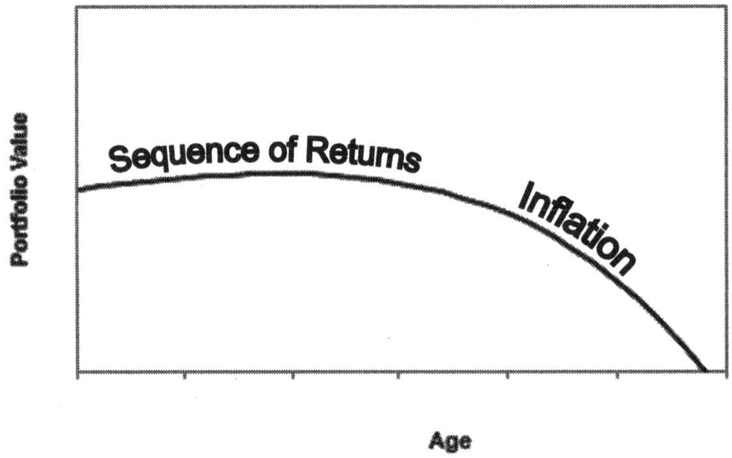

Observing the Effect of Inflation:

How can we demonstrate the impact of inflation? One way of doing this is to calculate portfolio life for all retirement years, first with fully indexed withdrawals[30] and then with no indexation. The difference is the impact of inflation on portfolio life.

Let's work through an example: Marco has $1,000,000 in his retirement portfolio. His portfolio consists of 40% S&P500 and 60% fixed income. He is planning to withdraw $60,000 annually. I calculate the portfolio life for all years of retirement, first with full indexation and then with no indexation.

Figure 11.4 shows the portfolio over time for both indexed and non–indexed withdrawals. Different withdrawal rates and market indices will result in different portfolio longevity.

30 Indexed to inflation

Figure 11.4: Portfolio life, with and without indexation

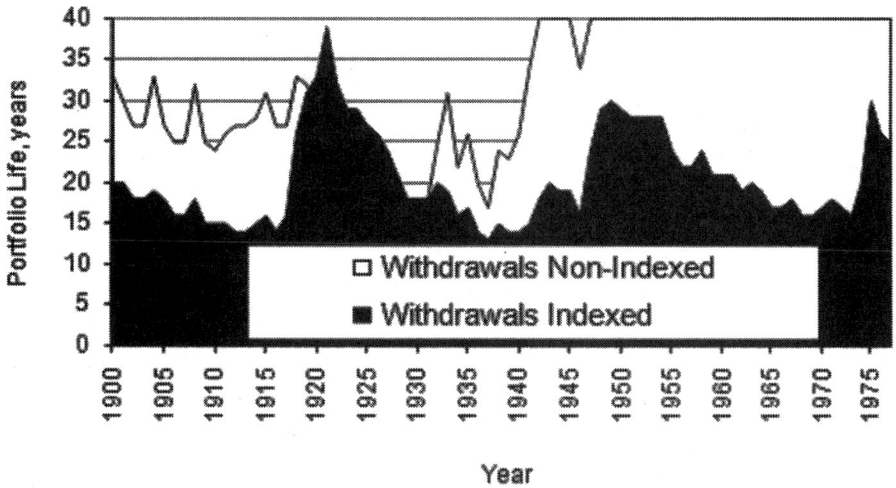

Indexation of withdrawals decreased the average portfolio life by about 65%. However, this varied wildly. Don't use this 65% for anything; it is just a number.

There are academic studies that recommend retirement income strategies which involve foregoing the CPI–indexation after negative years. They claim such strategies can provide lifelong income. Ignore such studies; they don't work (see Chapter 39).

How can we calculate the luck factor created by the effect of inflation in a retirement portfolio? It is very similar to calculating the effect of the sequence of returns. Here are the steps:

1. Isolate and exclude the effect of the sequence of returns. We do that by using a fixed "average" portfolio growth rate. This leaves us only with the historical inflation rates[31] that vary from year to year.
2. Calculate the compound annual return (CAR) of the lucky, unlucky and the median portfolios.
3. Calculate the luck factor due to inflation using equation 10.1.

---

[31] For the purposes of this book, the effect of reverse dollar cost averaging is related to cyclical trends only.

Example 11.1

Marco is 65 years old, just retiring. He has $1 million in his portfolio and needs $60,000 each year, indexed to inflation. His asset allocation is 40% equities and 60% fixed income, rebalanced annually.

Marco assumes that he will receive the index return, 7.3% (between the years 1900 and 2004) after all management fees. As for the fixed income side, the average increase was 5.1% for the same time period.

Therefore, the average return for a 40/60 asset mix portfolio would be about 6.0%, calculated as 40% of 7.3% (equity growth) and 60% of 5.1% (fixed income growth).

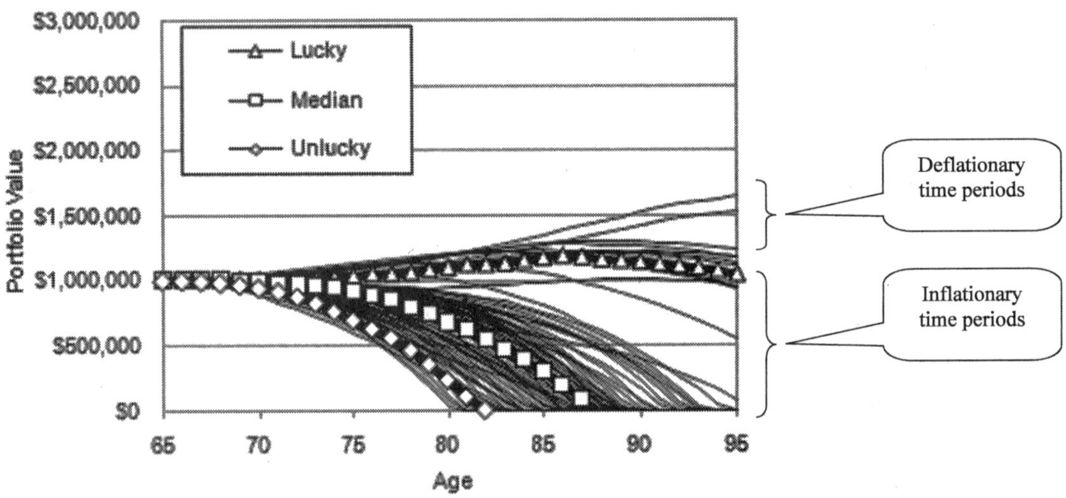

The lucky, unlucky and median portfolios are indicated on the aftcast chart above. The compound annual returns[32] for the lucky, unlucky and median portfolios are 8.33%, 3.17% and 5.87%, respectively. Plug these numbers into Equation 10.1 and calculate the luck factor that is attributable to inflation:

$$\text{Luck Factor} = \frac{8.33\% - 3.17\%}{2 \times 5.87\%} = 44\%$$

[32] using Otar Retirement Calculator

Table 11.2 indicates the impact of inflation on the CAR for a portfolio consisting of 40% equity and 60% fixed income.

Table 11.2: The luck factor created by inflation

	Initial Withdrawal Rate					
	0%	2%	4%	6%	8%	10%
The impact of inflation on compound annual return	0%	11%	31%	44%	55%	55%

Conclusion:

A retiree needs a strong inflation hedge, especially during secular sideways trends. And it just so happens that during these time periods, equities do not provide that inflation hedge.

You can consider holding some additional precious metal, resource and energy sectors in the portfolio, as these sectors can provide a better inflation hedge. But sector trading requires a disciplined approach. You cannot just buy and hold these sectors, hoping that in ten or twenty years they may protect your portfolio from inflation. Distribution portfolios don't have time on their side. In the meantime, their volatility will cause more damage to a distribution portfolio than their potential benefit.

A better strategy may be to use inflation–indexed bonds (a.k.a. TIPS, real return bonds).

Another strategy may be to purchase a guaranteed income stream which eliminates market and longevity risks. This will allow the retiree to use his remaining investment portfolio as an inflation "bucket" for inflation protection only. We will go over these strategies later on.

Chapter 12

Reverse Dollar Cost Averaging

Generally, cyclical trends run for periods of four or five years. During wealth accumulation, you are adding money to your investments on a periodic basis. This is called Dollar–Cost Averaging (DCA). Your average cost of shares will always be less than the average price of the shares, because you will be buying more shares during market troughs for the same dollar amount.

Here is an example of how dollar cost averaging (DCA) can benefit you in accumulation portfolios.

Example 12.1

Brian is planning to add $600 each year to his investment. The share price is $10 right now. The following year, a bear market arrives and the share price drops from $10 to $7. After hitting that low point, the share price recovers gradually. After a while, it recovers fully and the share price comes back to $10.

The following table shows the activity in the account:

Year	Share Price	Dollar Amount	Cumulative Cost	Shares traded	Share Balance	Market Value
Start	$10.00	$600	$600	60.00	60.00	$600
1	$7.00	$600	$1,200	85.71	145.71	$1,020
2	$8.00	$600	$1,800	75.00	220.71	$1,766
3	$9.00	$600	$2,400	66.67	287.38	$2,586
4	$10.00	$600	$3,000	60.00	347.38	$3,474

The average cost of shares over this time period is $8.80 per share, calculated as ($10 + $7 + $8 + $9 + $10) / 5

Brian's average cost was $8.63 per share, calculated as $3,000 / 347.38

For the same $600, Brian was able to buy more shares when the price was low. Therefore, when the share price went back up to $10, he had more shares to participate in the rise. At the end of the cycle, even though the share price was exactly the same as it was at the start of the bear cycle, his total cost was $3,000 and the total market value was $3,474.

Therefore, Brian's net profit attributable to DCA is 15.8%, calculated as [($3,474 / $3,000)-1] x 100%.

In a distribution portfolio, reverse dollar cost averaging (RDCA) works exactly the opposite of DCA. Investments are sold periodically to provide an income. During a bear market, you must sell more shares at a lower price to maintain the same income stream. Even though markets may recover subsequently, your loss is permanent. That is because the shares that you already sold are no longer in your portfolio and cannot participate in the recovery.

In Example 12.2, Ed has $5,000 in his portfolio and he withdraws $600 each year from his portfolio.

Example 12.2

Ed has $5,000 in his equity index investment. He is planning to withdraw $600 each year from this investment. The share price moves exactly same way as in the previous example.

Year	Share Price	Dollar Amount	Cumulative Cost	Shares traded	Share Balance	Market Value
Start	$10.00	$5,000	$5,000	500.00	500.00	$5,000
1	$7.00	($600)	$4,400	(85.71)	414.29	$2,900
2	$8.00	($600)	$3,800	(75.00)	339.29	$2,714
3	$9.00	($600)	$3,200	(66.67)	272.62	$2,454
4	$10.00	($600)	$2,600	(60.00)	212.60	$2,126

For the same $600 periodic income, Ed was forced to sell more shares when the price was low. Therefore, when the share price went back up to $10, he had fewer shares to participate in the rise. At the end of the cycle, his total cost was $2,600 and the total market value is $2,126.

Therefore, Ed's net loss due to RDCA is 18.1%, calculated as
[($2,126 / $2,600)-1] x 100%.

An average retiree can expect to endure between three and five bear markets during his retirement. If income is withdrawn from fluctuating assets such as equities, a significant portion of the portfolio life might be lost due to RDCA during a typical retirement. On average, RDCA can reduce the portfolio life by about 15%.

The way the math works, given the same bear market, the percentage loss from RDCA is always greater than the percentage profit from a DCA. This is because as you add money over time to an accumulation portfolio and as it gets larger, the effect of DCA diminishes. Table 12.1 shows the profit due to DCA and Table 12.2 shows the loss due to RDCA for different periodic amounts:

Table 12.1: Profit created by dollar cost averaging

Periodic Deposit as a Percentage of Starting Portfolio Value	Percent *Profit* due to the DCA
1%	0.8%
2%	1.5%
5%	3.3%
8%	4.8%
10%	5.6%
15%	7.4%

Table 12.2: Loss created by reverse dollar cost averaging

Periodic Withdrawal as a Percentage of Starting Portfolio Value	Percent *Loss* due to the RDCA
1%	0.8%
2%	1.7%
5%	4.9%
8%	9.3%
10%	13.8%
15%	29.6%

Keep in mind, figures in Tables 12.1 and 12.2 apply only to Example 12.2. A bear market with a different price pattern will produce different results. In any case, the percentage loss from RDCA is always higher than the percentage profit from a DCA for the same percentage money flow.

Example 12.3 demonstrates the effect of RDCA during a sideways market when withdrawals are monthly.

Example 12.3

Bob II has $1,000,000 in his retirement portfolio. His investment consists of the DJIA equity index. He is planning to withdraw $5,000 each month ($60,000 annual). We want to isolate the effect of inflation in this example, so we keep withdrawals constant over time.

Bob II retires on January 1st, 1966. The starting value of the DJIA then is 969.26. We calculate the portfolio value over time. Bob runs out of money after 177 months (14.75 years), in September 1980. At that time the index is 939.42. Plugging these numbers into a standard financial calculator and entering PV=-969.26, FV=939.42, n=14.75, we calculate the compound annual return as -0.212% during that time period.

Now, we calculate how much a portfolio would have lasted without any fluctuations using this calculated growth rate of -0.212%. We find out that it lasts 196 months. This is how long the portfolio would have lasted if there were no fluctuations to create reverse dollar cost averaging.

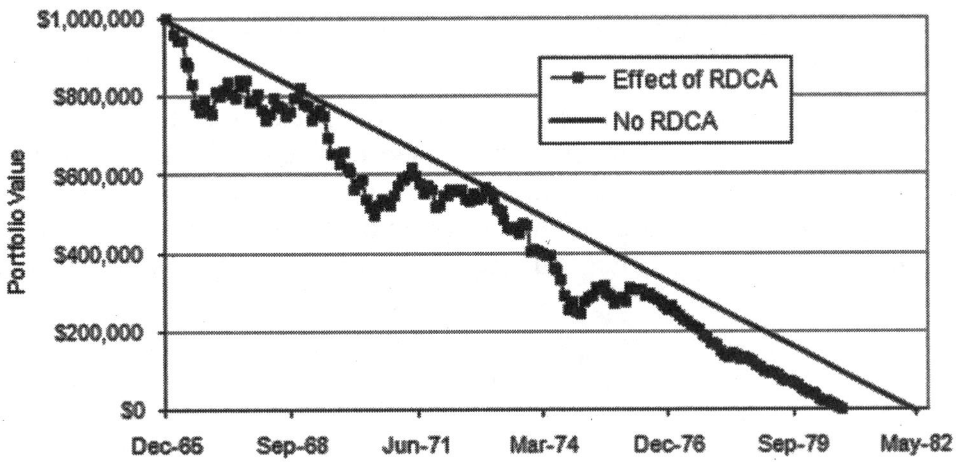

Bob II's portfolio would have lasted about 11% longer if there were no fluctuations to create the RDCA effect.

For depleting portfolios, the effect of RDCA becomes less pronounced as time goes on. In the example above (Example 12.3), during the final five years, the actual portfolio asset value declined steadily, parallel to the non–fluctuating line. This is because at this stage, withdrawals create a much larger decline than market fluctuations. This implies that for depleting portfolios, the RDCA is generally more damaging in the early years of retirement, just like the sequence of returns.

Conclusion:

Cyclical trends create reverse dollar cost averaging. This can shorten portfolio life. The following strategies will minimize the adverse effect of RDCA:

- Include cash or money market funds in your holdings. Periodic withdrawals should come only from the cash balance or money market funds. Do not withdraw from any fluctuating investment. (see also Optimum Asset Allocation – Chapter 16)
- Frequent rebalancing can cause significant damage to your distribution portfolio. Make sure to optimize rebalancing frequency (Chapter 6).

Be aware that these measures can help only to mitigate the effect of RDCA. They do nothing for the luck factor.

Many people think that by allocating a large portion of the portfolio to cash or cash–like "buckets" they can also remove the effect of the sequence of returns. This is not so. The other two components of the luck factor, i.e. the sequence of returns and inflation, are minimized only by exporting the risk. Holding large amounts of cash in a buy–and–hold portfolio will allow you to sleep better, but the portfolio will likely run out of money sooner.

Chapter 13

The Time Value of Fluctuations

Many retirees spend thirty years or more in retirement. In current retirement planning practice, we assume an "average" portfolio growth rate and an "average" inflation rate for the entire time horizon. The reality is that all asset values fluctuate. Many naively think that if they use historical averages, then everything will be fine in the long run.

Unfortunately, this is not the case. There is always a permanent loss owing to the fluctuations in a distribution portfolio due to the luck factor. After any fluctuation, large or small, not only do you need to recover from the market losses, but you also need to recover from the differential losses between the original plan and the actual portfolio value *while you are withdrawing income.* In many cases, these losses can cut the portfolio life by half of what a standard retirement calculator forecasts. That is why many pension funds appear to be in a downward spiral in recent years. The pension administrators and managers routinely blame markets, demographics and other factors for what is actually their failure to incorporate the concept of "Time Value of Fluctuations" in their forecast. Since this is one of the most misunderstood concepts in retirement planning, it is well worth looking into it at this point.

Root Causes of Time Value of Fluctuations:

The time value of fluctuations exists only if money goes into or out of the portfolio periodically. If there are no withdrawals from or deposits to a portfolio, then there is no time value of fluctuations, just fluctuations.

If there are periodic withdrawals from the portfolio then *any* fluctuations shorten the portfolio life. There are two types of contributors to the time value of fluctuations: The first one is fluctuations in the growth rate. An analogy can be made to gas mileage when driving: If you drive along a straight road with no hills, you will use less gas than if you were to drive an identical distance with many curves, hills and valleys. Similarly, the more a portfolio fluctuates, the more money is exhausted going up and down the fluctuations, for lack of a better term, "friction losses".

The second contributing factor to the time value of fluctuations is caused by fluctuations in cash outflow. The further inflation deviates from the assumed "average", the more money is exhausted.

Figure 13.1: Components of the time value of fluctuations in distribution portfolios

The Source:	The Event:	The Resulting Luck Factor	Contribution to TVF:
Fluctuating Assets:			
Market	Secular Trends	Sequence of Returns	40% to 100%
Market	Cyclical Trends	Reverse Dollar Cost Averaging	0% to 20%
Market	Seasonality	Insignificant	Up to 5%
Market	Random Fluctuations	Insignificant	Up to 8%
Fluctuating Outflow:			
Economy	Inflation	Increased Withdrawals	30% to 60%

Calculating the Time Value of Fluctuations in Distribution Portfolios:

How can we measure the time value of fluctuations (TVF) in a distribution portfolio? We know the present value of the assets and we know the time horizon. We plan for zero future value of assets. Starting with these, we go through the following steps:

Step 1: Calculate the benchmark withdrawal rate:

Assume there are no fluctuations in the growth rate of assets or in the indexation of withdrawals. Calculate the annuitized withdrawal rate that leaves zero assets at the end of the time horizon. This is the benchmark.

Step 2: Calculate the sustainable withdrawal rate:

We want to make sure that portfolio assets survive, even for the unlucky outcome, which is defined as the bottom decile (bottom 10%) of all observations. By trial and error, we calculate the withdrawal rate where the unlucky portfolio lasts exactly as long the benchmark portfolio calculated in the first step.

Step 3: Calculate the Time Value of Fluctuations:

TVF is the difference in withdrawal rates, with and without fluctuations. Since we use the entire market history, this calculation reflects all effects of all possible events, i.e. the entire luck factor.

The formula for the TVF for a distribution portfolio is:

$$TVF = AWR - SWR_{10} \qquad \text{(Equation 13.1)}$$

Additional capital required to overcome the effect of the TVF is calculated using the following formula:

$$ACR = \frac{(AWR - SWR_{10})}{SWR_{10}} \times 100\% \qquad \text{(Equation 13.2)}$$

where:

AWR is the annuitized withdrawal rate

SWR_{10} is the sustainable withdrawal rate based on 90% portfolio survival

ACR is the additional capital required, over and above the calculated value using the average and steady growth rate of the portfolio and steady indexation of withdrawals; i.e. annuitized withdrawal rate

---

Example 13.1

Ron is 65 years old. He is retiring this year. He expects to die at age 95. His retirement savings are valued at one million dollars. His asset allocation is 40% DJIA, 60% fixed income.

On the equity side, he assumes an average annual growth rate of 7.3%, which happens to be the average annual growth rate of DJIA between the years 1900 and 2006. He expects an average dividend of 2% annually, but it will all be spent for management fees and portfolio expenses. On the fixed income side, he assumes a net yield of 5.2% after expenses, which also happens to be the average interest rate on a 6-month CD plus one half of one percent premium. Therefore, his average portfolio growth rate is 6.04% after all expenses.

Step 1: What is Ron's annuitized withdrawal rate? Calculate the annuitized withdrawal rate, using a spreadsheet. By trial and error, a withdrawal rate of $52,221 in the first year, indexed to inflation by 3% annually thereafter, lasts exactly 30 years.

Age	Year	Begin Value $	Growth $	Withdrawal $	End Value $
65	1	$1,000,000	$60,400	$52,221	$1,008,179
66	2	$1,008,179	$60,894	$53,787	$1,015,286
67	3	$1,015,286	$61,323	$55,401	$1,021,209
68	4	$1,021,209	$61,681	$57,063	$1,025,827
69	5	$1,025,827	$61,960	$58,775	$1,029,012
70	6	$1,029,012	$62,152	$60,538	$1,030,626
71	7	$1,030,626	$62,250	$62,354	$1,030,522
72	8	$1,030,522	$62,244	$64,225	$1,028,541
73	9	$1,028,541	$62,124	$66,152	$1,024,513
74	10	$1,024,513	$61,881	$68,136	$1,018,257
75	11	$1,018,257	$61,503	$70,180	$1,009,580
76	12	$1,009,580	$60,979	$72,286	$998,273
77	13	$998,273	$60,296	$74,454	$984,115
78	14	$984,115	$59,441	$76,688	$966,867
79	15	$966,867	$58,399	$78,988	$946,278
80	16	$946,278	$57,155	$81,358	$922,075
81	17	$922,075	$55,693	$83,799	$893,969
82	18	$893,969	$53,996	$86,313	$861,652
83	19	$861,652	$52,044	$88,902	$824,794
84	20	$824,794	$49,818	$91,569	$783,042
85	21	$783,042	$47,296	$94,316	$736,022
86	22	$736,022	$44,456	$97,146	$683,332
87	23	$683,332	$41,273	$100,060	$624,545
88	24	$624,545	$37,723	$103,062	$559,206
89	25	$559,206	$33,776	$106,154	$486,828
90	26	$486,828	$29,404	$109,338	$406,894
91	27	$406,894	$24,576	$112,619	$318,852
92	28	$318,852	$19,259	$115,997	$222,113
93	29	$222,113	$13,416	$119,477	$116,052
94	30	$116,052	$7,010	$123,061	$0

Assuming there are no fluctuations of the portfolio growth rate and indexation of the withdrawals, the annuitized withdrawal rate is 5.22% in the first year of retirement, calculated as $52,221 divided by $1 million expressed as a percentage. This is the benchmark.

Step 2: How much can Ron take out based on actual market history? I use my retirement calculator based on market history. The chart below depicts the portfolio value for all retirement years between 1900 and 2006. It also shows the annuitized withdrawal rate and at the sustainable withdrawal rate.

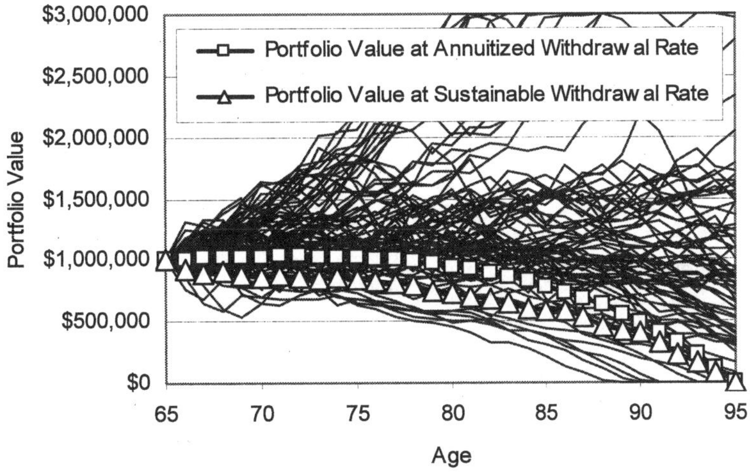

The sustainable withdrawal rate for the unlucky portfolio (90% probability of survival) using actual market history is calculated as $37,600 in dollars, or 3.76%.

Step 3: What is the time value of fluctuations? The time value of fluctuations is the difference between the withdrawal rates with and without fluctuations, i.e. the annuitized and sustainable withdrawal rates.

TVF = 5.22% - 3.76% = 1.46%

- In real life, with savings of $1 million at age 65, Ron's withdrawals must be 28% lower than the annuitized withdrawal rate (52,221), calculated as $\frac{1.46\%}{5.22\%} \times 100\%$, for his money to last 30 years.

- In real life, if Ron wants the same income as the annuitized withdrawal rate ($52,221) for life, the additional capital he needs is:

$$ACR = \frac{(5.22\% - 3.76\%)}{3.76\%} \times 100\% = 38.8\%$$

Ron needs 38.8% more than the $1 million he has, or $1,388,000 savings to start with, if he wants $52,221 at age 65 indexed to actual inflation until age 95.

Table 13.1 depicts the ACR, the additional capital required, using S&P500 as the equity proxy for various asset mixes and time horizons.

Table 13.1: Additional capital required to overcome TVF in distribution portfolios for different asset mixes and time horizons

Asset Mix:	Time Horizon 20 years	Time Horizon 30 years
	Additional Capital Required to account for TVF:	
100% Equity – S&P500	100%	117%
80 / 20	74%	78%
60 / 40	54%	53%
40 / 60	41%	41%
20 / 80	39%	51%
100% Fixed Income	60%	87%

If the asset mix is not at its optimum, i.e. if the portfolio volatility is too high or too low, then this creates a higher time value of fluctuations. This debunks another myth in our business: "If you want higher returns, you need to take a higher risk!" This is the wrong advice for *all* distribution portfolios.

Table 13.2 displays the ACR for different markets and time horizons for an asset allocation of 40% equity and 60% fixed income.

Table 13.2: Additional capital required to overcome TVF in distribution portfolios for different markets

Market:	Time Horizon 20 years	Time Horizon 30 years
	Additional Capital Required to account for TVF:	
40% DJIA, 60% Fixed Income	37%	39%
40% S&P500, 60% Fixed Income	41%	41%
40 % Nikkei 225, 60% Fixed Income	45%	46%
40% FTSE All Shares, 60% Fixed Income	49%	54%
40% SP/TSX, 60% Fixed Income	36%	41%

Table 13.3 depicts the historical average growth rates used in calculating the annuitized withdrawal rates for Table 13.2.

Table 13.3: Average growth rates, net after portfolio expenses

	Average Growth Rate
DJIA (1900 – 2006)	7.3%
S&P500 (1900 – 2006)	7.0%
Nikkei 225 (1914 – 2006)	10.9%
FTSE All Shares (1900 – 2006)	6.0%
SP/TSX (1919 – 2006)	7.3%
Fixed income (1900 – 2006) (historical 6–month CD interest plus 0.5%)	5.2%

If you like formulas, I have developed a formula based on empirical data to calculate the TVF *approximately* as a function of the time horizon. This formula applies only to distribution portfolios with optimum asset mix and only to DJIA, S&P500 and the SP/TSX indices.

$$\text{TVF} = \frac{20}{N^{0.735}} \qquad \text{(Equation 13.3)}$$

where:

N is the number of years, any number between 10 and 40

Time Value of Fluctuations in Accumulation Portfolios:

In accumulation portfolios, there are several forces at work:

- In secular bullish trends, asset values surge up; the luck factor works for you.
- In secular sideways trends, the dollar–cost–averaging (DCA) works for you. However, the benefit of DCA does not compensate for the adverse luck factor in such trends.
- In secular bearish trends, if you have the patience and fortitude to continue investing, dollar–cost–averaging and rebalancing create a positive outcome eventually. Keep in mind that most of us do not have the discipline and the patience for that.

The logic for calculating the TVF in accumulation portfolios is the mirror image of that of distribution portfolios. We know the present value of the assets, the time horizon and the desired future value of assets.

<u>Step 1:</u> Calculate the benchmark deposit rate:
Calculate the benchmark deposit rate, which is the first year's savings as a percentage of the future target amount of the median portfolio. Assume a constant growth rate of the portfolio with no fluctuations of deposits over the entire time horizon.

<u>Step 2:</u> Calculate the deposit rate based on market history:
Using the actual market history by trial and error, calculate the deposit rate that you need. This is the dollar amount you need to save periodically to reach the desired median portfolio value over the same time horizon as the benchmark.

<u>Step 3:</u> Calculate the Time Value of Fluctuations:
The difference between the two deposit rates is the time value of fluctuations, which reflects the gains, or the losses as the case might be, due to the fluctuations in asset value and inflation over the entire time period.

The formula for the TVF in an accumulation portfolio is:

$$TVF = RDR - ADR \qquad \text{(Equation 13.4)}$$

The following formula is for calculating the additional periodic savings required to overcome the effect of the TVF:

$$ASR = \frac{(RDR - ADR)}{ADR} \times 100\% \qquad \text{(Equation 13.5)}$$

where:

ADR is the deposit rate, first year's deposits as a percentage of the future target amount, where growth rate and indexation rate are constant

RDR is the deposit rate required, first year's savings as a percentage of the future target amount of the median portfolio, growth rate and inflation varies using actual market history

ASR is the additional periodic savings required, over and above the ADR

Example 13.3

Steve wants to accumulate $2 million in his portfolio in 30 years. He wants to start saving right now, and increase his annual saving amount by 3% each year. Currently, he has nothing in his account. His asset allocation is 60% DJIA and 40% fixed income.

On the equity side, he assumes an average annual growth rate of 7.3%, which happens to be the average annual growth rate of DJIA between the years 1900 and 2006. He assumes an average dividend of 2% annually which will be spent entirely for management fees. On the fixed income side, he assumes a net yield of 5.2% after expenses, which is the historical average interest rate on a 6-month CD plus 0.5% premium. Therefore, he calculates his average portfolio growth rate is 6.46% after all expenses.

Step 1: What is his deposit rate?

Use a spreadsheet. By trial and error, we calculate an accumulation rate as $15,506 in the first year, indexed by 3% annually thereafter.

Year	Begin Value $	Growth $	End of Year Deposit $	End Value $
1	$15,506	$1,002	$15,972	$32,480
2	$32,480	$2,098	$16,451	$51,029
3	$51,029	$3,296	$16,944	$71,270
4	$71,270	$4,604	$17,453	$93,326
5	$93,326	$6,029	$17,976	$117,331
6	$117,331	$7,580	$18,516	$143,426
7	$143,426	$9,265	$19,071	$171,763
8	$171,763	$11,096	$19,643	$202,502
9	$202,502	$13,082	$20,232	$235,816
10	$235,816	$15,234	$20,839	$271,889
11	$271,889	$17,564	$21,465	$310,917
12	$310,917	$20,085	$22,108	$353,111
13	$353,111	$22,811	$22,772	$398,694
14	$398,694	$25,756	$23,455	$447,904
15	$447,904	$28,935	$24,159	$500,997
16	$500,997	$32,364	$24,883	$558,245
17	$558,245	$36,063	$25,630	$619,937
18	$619,937	$40,048	$26,399	$686,384
19	$686,384	$44,340	$27,191	$757,915
20	$757,915	$48,961	$28,006	$834,883
21	$834,883	$53,933	$28,847	$917,663
22	$917,663	$59,281	$29,712	$1,006,656
23	$1,006,656	$65,030	$30,603	$1,102,289
24	$1,102,289	$71,208	$31,521	$1,205,018
25	$1,205,018	$77,844	$32,467	$1,315,329
26	$1,315,329	$84,970	$33,441	$1,433,741
27	$1,433,741	$92,620	$34,444	$1,560,805
28	$1,560,805	$100,828	$35,478	$1,697,110
29	$1,697,110	$109,633	$36,542	$1,843,286
30	$1,843,286	$119,076	$37,638	$2,000,000

Therefore, assuming there are no fluctuations of growth rate, the deposit rate is 0.775%, calculated as $15,506 divided by $2 million (the final-year target amount). This is the benchmark, ADR.

Step 2: How much should Steve deposit based on market history? He increases his deposits each year by the same amount as inflation. He is targeting a total portfolio value of $2 million in 30 years.

Using my retirement calculator based on market history. I calculate that Steve needs to deposit $18,470 in the first year, indexed to actual inflation for the next 30 years, to accumulate $2 million in his median portfolio. The required deposit rate (RDR) is 0.924%, calculated as $18,470 / $2,000,000 X 100%.

Here is the aftcast:

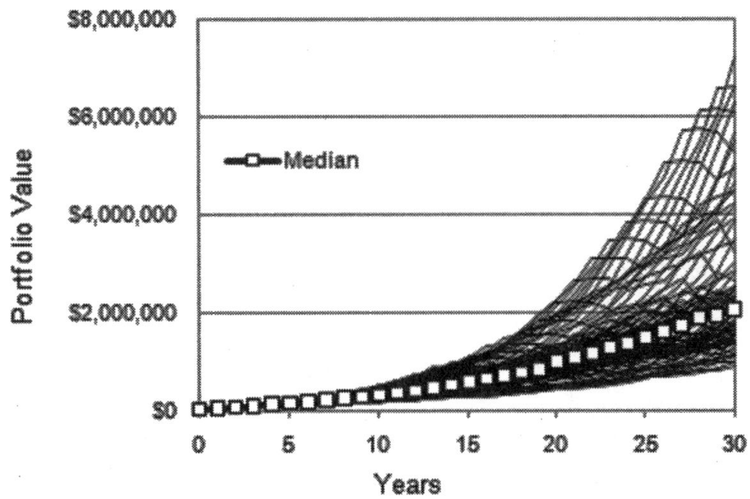

What is the time value of fluctuations? The time value of fluctuations is the difference between the deposit rates with and without fluctuations.

TVF = 0.924% - 0.775% = 0.149%

If the portfolio growth rate were steady, Steve would need to deposit $15,506, indexed by 3% annually. In real life, both the growth rate and inflation fluctuate. How much more does he need to deposit periodically?

The additional periodic savings required is calculated using equation 13.5:

$$ASR = \frac{(0.924\% - 0.775\%)}{0.775\%} \times 100\% = 19.2\%$$

Steve needs to save periodically 19.2% more than he calculated using the steady growth and inflation rates for the next 30 years to accumulate $2 million in the median portfolio.

Table 13.4 depicts the ASR, the additional periodic savings required, using S&P500 as the equity proxy for various asset mix and time horizons. Generally, if your asset mix is near the optimum, the dollar amount of your deposits is the lowest to achieve the same target.

Table 13.4: Additional periodic savings required in an accumulation portfolio

Asset Mix:	**Time Horizon** 20 years	30 years
	Additional Periodic Savings Required to account for TVF:	
100% Equity – S&P500	1%	10%
80 / 20	2%	9%
60 / 40	–1%	5%
40 / 60	5%	10%
20 / 80	5%	18%
100% Fixed Income	7%	19%

Conclusion:

The Time Value of Fluctuations is defined as losses created by long and short–term market fluctuations and inflation. It is the missing link between the annuitized (steady) withdrawal rate and the sustainable withdrawal rate in distribution portfolios. The TVF describes and quantifies the chronic losses which are outside the control of the investor.

It is essential to understand that it exists. It is especially important if you are preparing retirement plans or administering pension funds. You don't need to remember the formulas or memorize the tables in this chapter; the TVF has a more qualitative use than a quantitative one. In Chapter 16, we will use this knowledge as our starting point for optimizing the asset allocation process. But first, we need to discover the flaws of the tool that is most commonly used for optimization, the efficient frontier.

Chapter 14

The Efficient Frontier

The Efficient Frontier (EF) is one of the pillars of current investment practice. First defined in 1952 by Harry Markowitz, it shifted the investment focus from individual securities to the entire portfolio. Nowadays, it is used for everything from selling mutual funds to determining the "right" asset mix.

To refresh your memory on the concept of EF: The portfolio return and the risk –defined as the standard deviation of returns– of two securities are plotted on a chart (Figure 14.1). The vertical axis indicates the return –growth–; the horizontal axis represents the risk. The return and the risk of the portfolio consisting of these two securities (let's call them "A" and "B"), at different proportions are plotted on the same chart, as shown in the example below. These points are then connected. The top part of the line –the heavy line– is called the efficient frontier.

Figure 14.1: A typical efficient frontier diagram

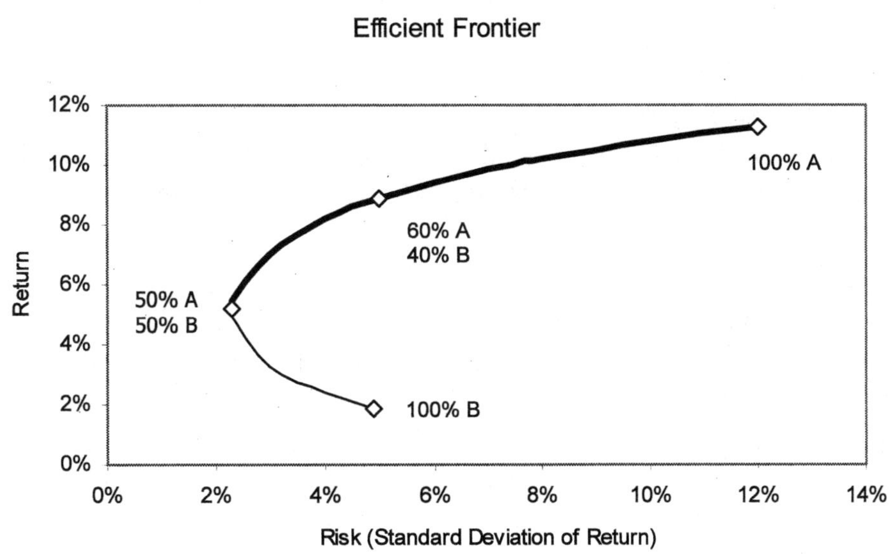

Looking at this chart, we can reach the following conclusions:

- Investing all of the money in "B" produces the lowest return. Instead, if you invest 60% in "A" and 40% in "B", you end up with a significantly higher return for the same level of risk.
- Investing 50% in each of "A" and "B" produces the highest return at the lowest risk.
- Investing all of the money in "A produces a higher return than investing 60% in "A" and 40% in "B", but at a significantly higher risk.

After observing this chart, an unsuspecting investor might conclude, "Gee, this is wonderful, let's invest 60% of the money in A and 40% in B." Actually, this is the generally accepted method[33] of optimizing the asset allocation.

What is the flaw of in the EF? There are a few:

1. The look–back time:
   The first one is the time frame. EF charts are based on historical performance of a limited time. Many use a 3–year or a 5–year history. Such a short time period mismatches the length of the two most prominent market cycles.

   Secular trends can last up to 20 years. Even if you use a 20–year history for your EF, it may reflect one specific secular trend which may never repeat again in your lifetime.

   Cyclical trends last 4 to 6 years. If you use a 5–year history, you may be applying the events of one cyclical trend to your EF analysis, which is usually irrelevant during the subsequent cycle.

2. Recent past will repeat itself:
   The second flaw of the EF is that it inherently assumes that the risk and return profile of investments will remain essentially the same in the future as it was in the recent past. This is usually not the case.

3. Gaussian Mindset:
   The third and the most important flaw of the EF is that it defines risk as the standard deviation of returns (volatility). This may be reasonable in a "normal" Gaussian model, but it is incongruent with what happens in real life.

   In distribution portfolios, the primary risk is the sequence of returns and not the volatility of returns. What makes or breaks the outcome of a portfolio is not what happens 95% of the time in "normal" markets, but what happens in 5% of the time in "extreme" markets, up or down (see Chapter 27). Therefore, 95% of the data included in the statistical analysis corrupts its conclusions to the point of uselessness.

---

[33] To be more exact, the point where a one-unit increase in risk results in a one-unit increase in return (45 degree tangent line, if the vertical and horizontal scales are the same), is considered as the optimum point by many.

Conventional EF analysis totally ignores the cash flows in and out of the portfolio. They start with a fixed portfolio value and vary only as a result of the growth of its underlying assets. To overcome this shortfall, here is what I did: I considered one accumulation and one distribution portfolio. In the accumulation portfolio, the investor saves $10,000 each year. In the distribution portfolio, the investor starts with $1 million and takes out $50,000 each year, indexed to inflation. My objective is to find the "right" asset mix using the efficient frontier to establish an optimum mix of stocks and bonds for each portfolio.

Assume it is 1910. I draw the efficient frontier line using the preceding ten year history, i.e. 1900–1909 similar to Figure 14.1. From this EF curve, I optimize the asset mix using the annual returns and volatility of each asset class.

Next, I move on to 1911. I repeat the same process using the preceding 10 years of data. Calculate the EF for 1911. I repeat the same process for all the years until the end of 2005. Now, I have an efficient frontier curve for each year since 1900. Based on each year's EF curve, I figured out the optimum asset mix.

So, I was very happy to have created a model that can automatically draw the EF curve based on the client's assets *and* included his cash flow.

However, my joy was short lived once I plotted these findings. A very interesting picture appeared. Observe Figure 14.2 for accumulation and Figure 14.3 for distribution portfolios. Notice that it took the efficient frontier four years to recognize the devastating 1929 crash and to go from 100% to 0% equity. Ironically, this happened just prior to the greatest cyclical bull market of the last century (1933–1936). In effect, what disappointed me was, this looked very much like a market–timing model. The equity percentage swings from 0% to 100% in short periods of time. This cannot be described in anything other than a complicated market–timing model, a very bad one, I might add.

Figure 14.2: Optimum asset mix for an accumulation portfolio

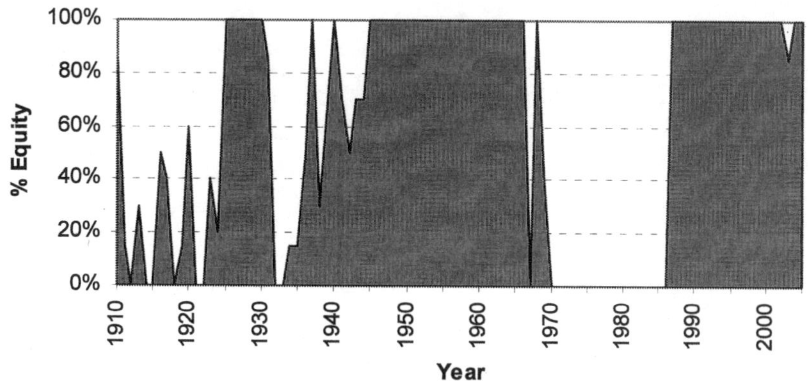

Figure 14.3: Optimum asset mix for a distribution portfolio

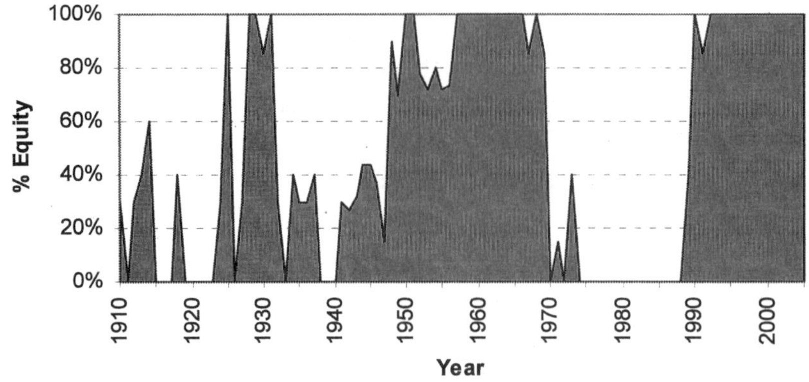

I tried the same procedure with a 20–year history instead of a 10–year history. This smoothened some of the jagged edges, but the general picture remained the same. The efficient frontier still worked like a bad market–timing model. It was then I realized that EF might be a great idea for randomly moving events 100% of the time, but it does not work well if that randomness prevails only 95% of the time.

Regretfully, that is what we have been selling to unsuspecting investors. No wonder only 15% of fund managers can *randomly* beat the index over the long term. No wonder less than 1% of fund managers can *consistently* beat the index over the long term. We all have been using the wrong tool.

Conclusion:

Here are my rules for the efficient frontier analysis:

Do not use EF:

- For optimizing the optimum asset allocation unless the historical data covers at least two secular trends, i.e. a minimum of forty years of look–back.
- For the purpose of market/sector/country timing by applying a shorter history. Analysis based on three or five years is useless for this purpose. Much better timing tools are available in the realm of technical and intermarket analysis.
- For distribution portfolios.

You can use EF:

- For comparing different mutual funds of the same asset class using a minimum of ten years of history, as long as each mutual fund maintains the same fund manager over that time period.
- For individual stocks within a portfolio with a shorter history.

Chapter 15

Monte Carlo Simulators

The term "Monte Carlo method" was coined in the 1940s by physicists working on nuclear weapon projects in the Los Alamos National Laboratory[34]. They are computational algorithms that rely on repeated random sampling to compute their results.

Since the start of the last secular sideways in year 2000, more and more advisors have been switching from using standard retirement calculators to Monte Carlo (MC) simulators to forecast portfolio asset values. What makes the MC different from a standard retirement calculator is that it adds random fluctuations to an average, steady growth rate. The user selects a base line (the average base growth rate) and a standard deviation from that base line. The model then runs thousands (or millions, if you choose so) of projections by randomly varying this base line. Finally, it reports the range and probability of these projections.

While the MC model is a step forward from the standard, single line retirement calculator, it has significant shortcomings. Here are some of its flaws.

Flaw #1:

The first flaw of the MC is how it generates randomness. It is generated using a distribution curve. There are many types of distribution curves, such as: Normal, Lognormal, Triangular, Uniform, Binomial, Exponential, and Geometric, to name a few. The uniform and normal distribution curves are used most commonly in MC simulators.

Figure 15.1: Typical distribution curves:

Uniform | Normal (Gaussian curve)

[34] Nicholas Metropolis (1987), "The beginning of the Monte Carlo method", Los Alamos Science (1987 Special Issue dedicated to Stanislaw Ulam)

The uniform distribution curve generates random numbers with equal frequency. For example, if the average growth rate is 8% and the specified range is between –16% and +16%, then the probability of running a 15% growth rate in one of the simulations is the same as running a 5% growth rate.

The normal distribution curve (also known as the Gaussian or the bell curve) is based on generating more of the random numbers that are closer to the average growth rate and fewer that are further from it. For example, if the average growth rate is 8% and the stated range is between –16% and +16%, then a 10% growth rate is forecast more often than a 3% growth rate.

In real life, the distribution curve is significantly different than these idealized distribution curves. Not only that, market history shows that the distribution curve changes its shape over time. Many factors affect the shape of the distribution curve, such as different withdrawal rates, time passed since the beginning of retirement, asset allocation and rebalancing models. Figure 15.2 shows the actual distribution curve of a portfolio after five years and then, after twenty years. As time passed, the distribution curve flattened significantly in this particular case.

The distribution curve in MC models does not cover the entire retirement time period accurately. Therefore, the resulting simulations are significantly different from the actual market history.

Figure 15.2: Actual probability curve for a distribution portfolio

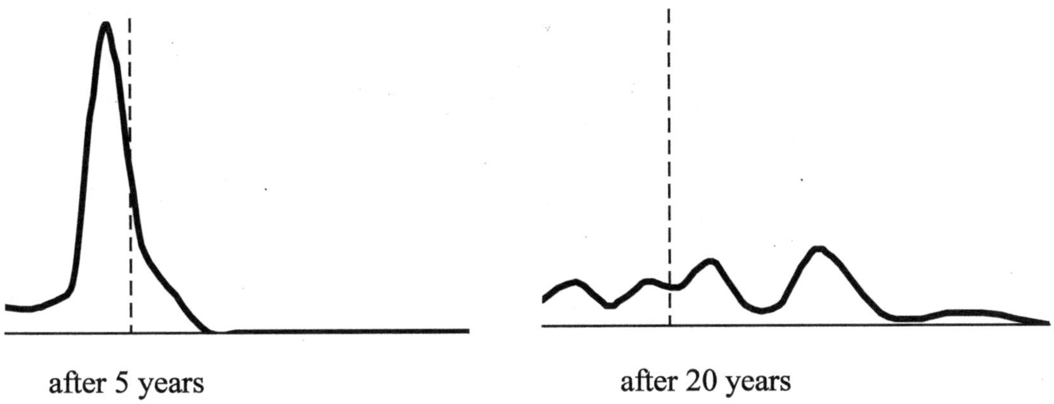

Flaw #2:

The second flaw of MC is that its outcomes are generated randomly in a single, long trend as depicted in Figure 15.3. It ignores the effects of cyclical and secular trends. It ignores the existence of the secular **trend discontinuities**, which are transitions from one type of the secular trend to another (see Figure 15.4).

Figure 15.3: MC simulated trend, the index value on a logarithmic scale

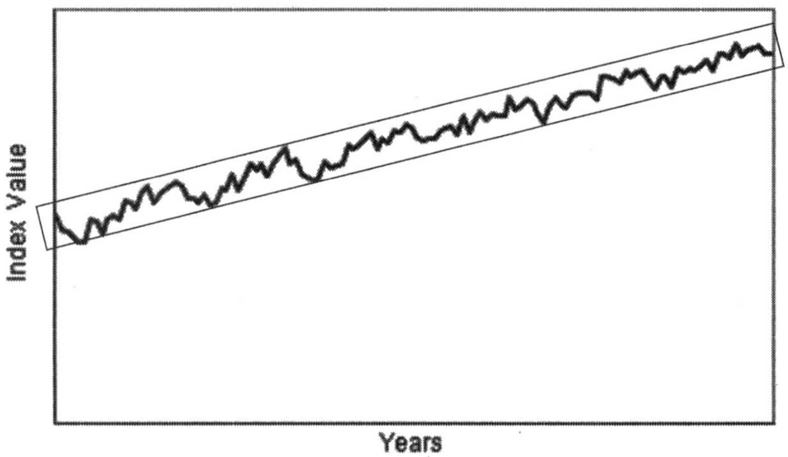

Figure 15.4: Actual market history with trend discontinuities, the index value on a logarithmic scale

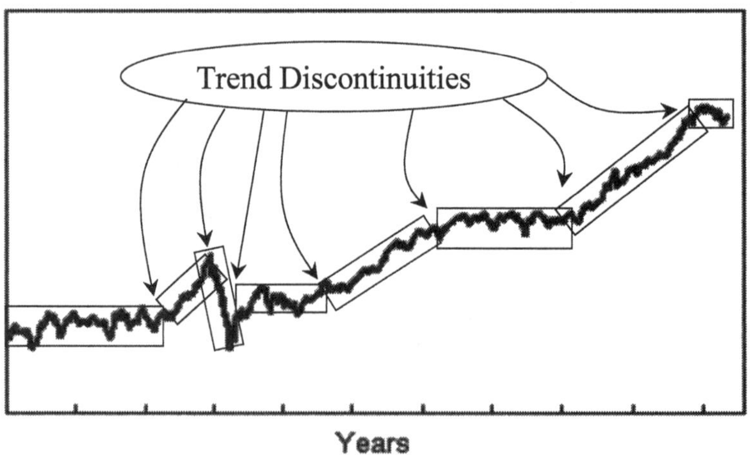

When we look at history, we observe that markets are random in the short term, cyclical in the mid–term, and trending (up, down or sideways) in the long term. Furthermore, the sequence of market events is not random, they are correlated: higher inflation eventually causes the short term interest rates to rise, which can have bearish effects on the stocks and bonds, and vice versa. Picking growth rates at random for different asset classes and attaching these to a randomly selected inflation rate is not congruent with what happens in real life.

Consequently, the user ends up increasing the range of outcomes, say from ±15% to ±30% to cover this deficiency. Doing so only masks this problem, but it does not solve it.

MC simulation is based on statistical randomness around a predefined straight line. Increasing the envelope of these outcomes does not make it more accurate. If the model does not fit well, then running one million simulations instead of one hundred does not make it any more accurate.

Flaw #3:

The third flaw of MC is the unrealistic sequence of returns.

In real life, usually during the last one third of a secular bullish trend, good news begets more good news. The index moves up sharply higher just because many more investors bet that it will continue moving higher. On the other hand, when a bear market starts, bad news begets more bad news. These events create the market "extremes."

Most MC simulators ignore these as "extreme" or "won't–happen–again" types of events[35]. They will rarely produce multi–year, back–to–back "streaks" of multiple bear or bull outcomes, as happens in real life.

Some simulators add two additional, smaller distribution curves to each side of the main distribution curve. This is (supposedly) to account for the higher than "normal" occurrence of such market extremes. These are also known as the "fat tails." Yes, this can definitely simulate the higher occurrence of the volatility of returns at these extremes, but their random occurrence in the simulator (Flaw #1) prevents it from simulating the sequence of returns of such extremes in any realistic way.

[35] That is why "once–a–century events" such as floods, fires, markets crashes, other types of crises can and do occur more often than simulators forecast.

Figure 15.5: Fat Tails

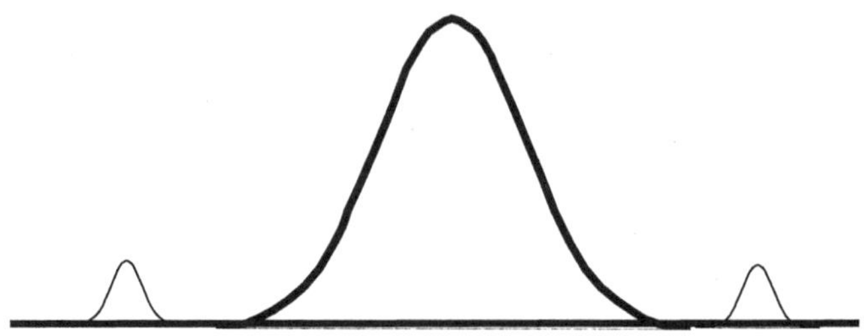

When we look at market history (DJIA or S&P500), we see that there is not one main distribution curve with two tails, but we have (at least) two main curves with two tails, as shown in Figure 15.6:

Figure 15.6: Major US indices, the distribution curve for the 20th century

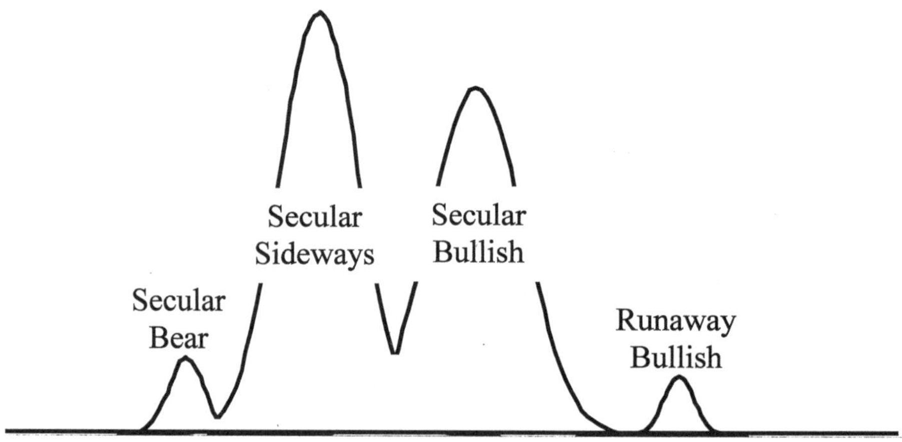

The leftmost curve (the left tail) represents the "unlikely" sharp, multi–year market crashes like the 1929 crash. During the last century, markets spent about 4% of their time there. This is the secular bear zone.

The taller distribution curve to the right of the secular bear trend is the secular sideways trend. In this region, the growth rates are insignificant and the inflation is about 5% per year. Markets spend about 50% of their time here.

To the right of that is the secular bullish distribution curve. Here, the average growth rate is 15% and the average inflation is 2%. Markets spend about 38% of their time in secular bullish trends.

The right–most curve represents the runaway bullish trends where markets spent about 8% of their time during last century. Keep in mind; I am only reporting what happened during the last century. I make no claims that this century will be the same.

Even if an MC simulator could be designed to incorporate the distribution curves depicted in Figure 15.6, it would still not be good enough. Such a model would simulate the frequency of these events correctly; however, it would still miss the sequence of them.

Here is how the sequence of returns works in real life: once markets decide to be in the bullish area, they stay in that bullish distribution curve for as long as 20 years (sometimes less). Then some invisible hand (a seemingly unimportant event) pushes the trend either under the leftmost fat tail where it can stay a number of years or under the secular sideways distribution curve, where it may stay for up to 20 years (sometimes less). It stays there until this infamous hand (another seemingly unimportant event) pushes it back under the secular bullish distribution curve.

The easiest way of demonstrating this flaw is to look at retirement portfolios using actual market history (Figure 15.7). The median line is a lot closer to the unlucky than the lucky line, even though both lucky and unlucky portfolios have the same probability of occurrence (10%). In other words, after retirement, it is much easier to become unlucky than to become lucky. All it takes is one or two mishap and your portfolio travels to the unlucky region quickly. It would take a whole series of good moves and strategies to nudge towards the lucky region, a much longer distance to travel.

No advisor should ignore that the path to an unlucky outcome is a lot shorter than the path to a lucky outcome.

A well–designed MC simulator should be able to simulate the frequency of growth rates and inflation, as well as the sequence of returns. Whether or not such a model can have any predictive power is, of course, another question.

Figure 15.7: The actual market history: median, lucky and unlucky outcomes during retirement:

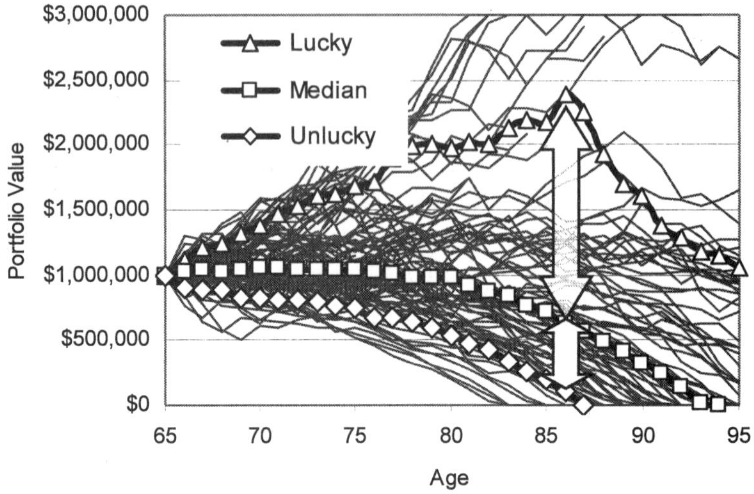

I compared the outcomes of one MC simulator with actual market history using the same case. Table 15.1 depicts the outcome:

Table 15.1: Comparing MC simulator with actual history

Years after Retirement	Monte Carlo	Actual
10	0%	0%
15	1%	3%
20	14%	36%
25	37%	68%
30	55%	86%

In the final analysis, most Monte Carlo simulations create outcomes that are too optimistic. Using the actual market history eliminates these shortfalls. However, if you insist on using an MC simulator instead of actual historical data, then I suggest that you should at least use a better MC model, as described below.

A Better Simulator:

For a better model, you need to start with the big picture. You need to include the effect of secular trends as well as random fluctuations. The following model is such a two–layer simulator. Let's call this an MC2 simulator.

The first layer selects a particular secular trend at random. The only rule at this first level is that the same secular trend cannot be repeated: a secular bullish trend can only be followed by a secular sideways trend or a secular bearish trend. A secular bearish trend can only be followed by a secular sideways trend or a secular bullish trend. A secular sideways trend can only be followed by a secular bullish trend.

The second layer of the simulator is identical to models in use today. However, it uses different base rates for each type of secular trend. I the use following base rates:

- If the first layer of simulation is in a secular bullish trend, then the second layer is set to the following limits: Growth: 15% annually, range ±15%. Inflation: 2% annually, range ±1%. Length of time: 20 years
- If the first layer of simulation is a secular sideways trend, then the second layer is set to: Growth: 2%, ±20%. Inflation: 5%, ±2%. Length: 20 years
- If the first layer of simulation is a secular bearish trend, then the second layer is set to: Growth: –20%, ±15%. Inflation: –5%, ±2%, Length: 4 years
- Both the trend type and the stage of the trend are randomly selected at the starting point of simulations. For example, the simulation may start in the 6th year of a bullish trend or it may start in the 9th year of a secular sideways trend.

The two–layer simulation minimizes, even eliminates all three flaws that I described earlier. These particular parameters apply only to DJIA and S&P500 indices since 1900. Other markets have different rules based on their own historical experience. You can download this MC2 simulator[36] and change any of these parameters to fit your needs.

Keep in mind; a man–made simulator is still a man–made simulator. It is still not the real thing. Do yourself a favor; use the actual history.

[36] It is available free at www.retirementoptimizer.com.

The Evolution of Retirement Calculator Models:

The following four charts compare retirement projections using different models based on a starting capital of $1 million and withdrawals of $60,000, indexed to inflation, starting at age 65. All charts are based on holding a balanced portfolio:

- The first chart (Figure 15.8) is based on a standard retirement calculator with a steady growth rate and inflation. This is the most popular model used by financial planners and it is also available at many financial websites. In this example, it shows the projection using an assumed average growth rate of 8% and an assumed inflation of 3%. It is generally useless for retirement planning.
- The second chart (Figure 15.9) is a typical Monte Carlo simulation, which is becoming more and more popular and available at some financial websites. The probability of depletion in this particular run of simulations[37] was 53% by age 95.
- The third chart (Figure 15.10) is a two–layer Monte Carlo simulation as described above. The probability of depletion in this particular run of simulations was 77% by age 95.
- The fourth chart (Figure 15.11) indicates outcomes based on actual market history. The probability of depletion in this run by age 95 was 74%.

The two–layer simulation reflected the historical experience significantly more realistically than the standard Monte Carlo simulator. Occasionally, I get questions like "Why do I get different probabilities of portfolio survival each time I run the simulator?" The results will fluctuate each time you run the simulation with any MC simulator. That is the way they work.

Figure 15.8: Standard retirement calculator

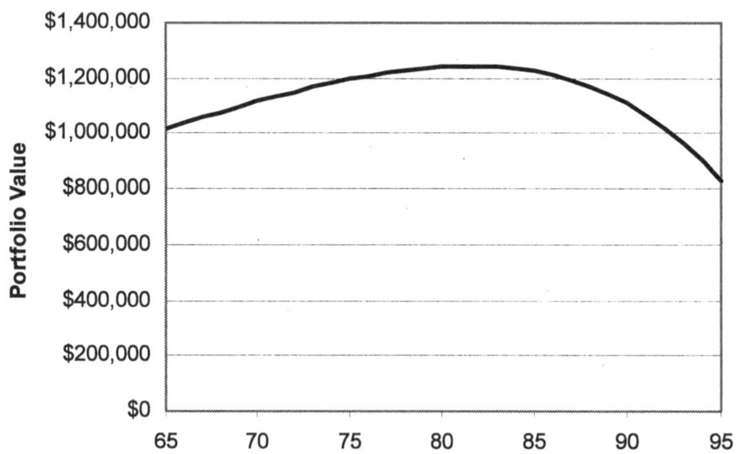

[37] Keep in mind, when you run a simulator, each run will give you a different probability of depletion

Figure 15.9: Typical Monte Carlo simulator

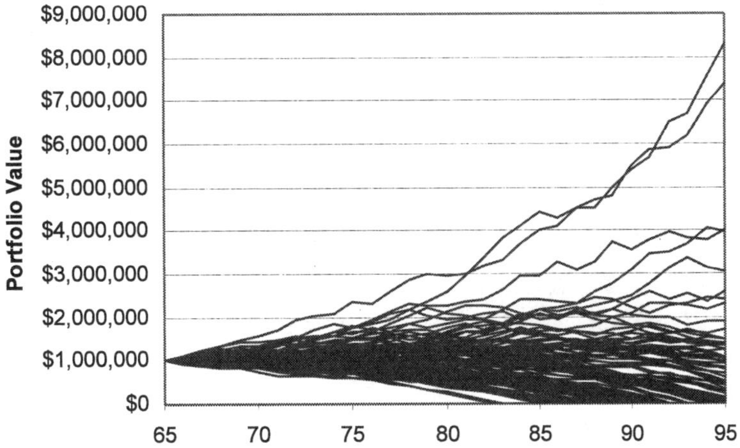

Figure 15.10: Two–Layer Monte Carlo simulator (MC2)

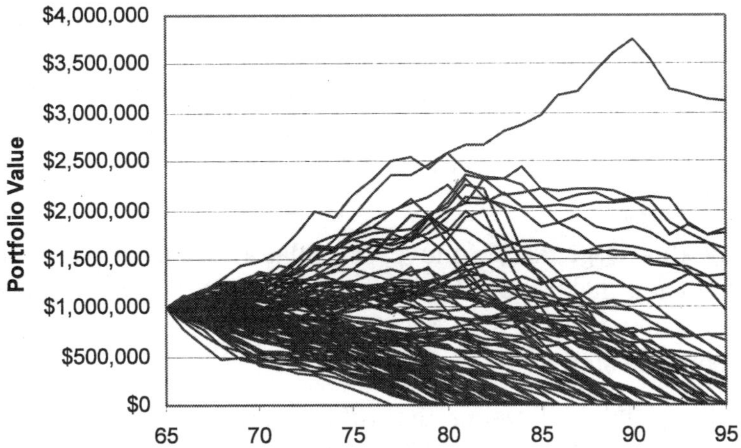

Figure 15.11: The actual market history

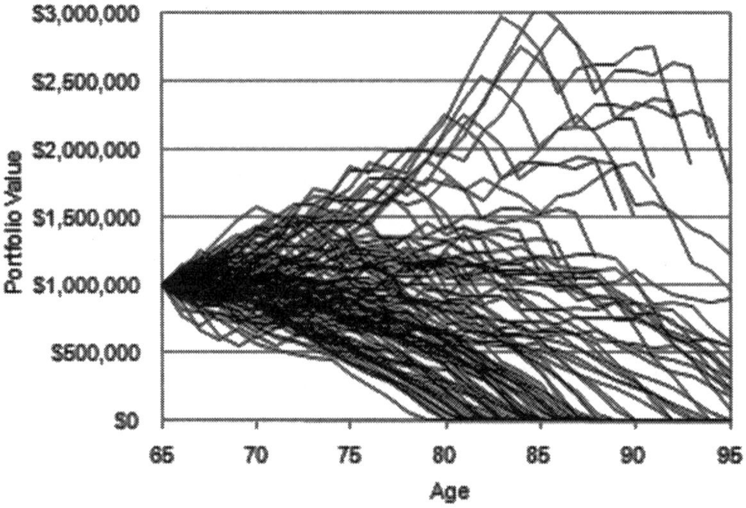

Conclusion:

The flaws of MC simulators are probably rooted in our own flaws as human beings. Human nature likes observations to fit into a neat, easily explainable, Gaussian mindset. We must go beyond that. Many in the financial industry already know that market events do not fit into neat models, but in more complex non–linear observations. We must move beyond "projecting 30 years into the future" based on our limited assumptions and simulations.

Every so often, usually after large market moves, simulator designers tweak their models to reflect these events. They make the fat tails larger, smaller, narrower, wider, further apart or closer together. None of these can help, because the structure of the model does not reflect market behavior to start with.

When I talk about the pitfalls of using the MC versus the actual market history, sometimes I hear this objection: "Aftcasting gives you only one of the possible outcomes. If you use the MC simulator, you can get millions of outcomes!" Just ask yourself this question: how was the MC developed initially? It was developed using the only set of market data that we have, historical data. The Gaussian randomness was piggybacked onto this data. If the model is wrong, it does not matter how many millions of simulations you run. The outcome will still be wrong.

If you still don't believe me, just answer this question:"You claim you can simulate 10,000 years of market history. Fantastic! Can you please tell me how long my portfolio would have lasted if I were to retire in 1450 B.C., around the time the Red Sea was rumored to have parted?"

Figure 15.12 shows the portfolio life[38] for a 6% initial withdrawal rate (IWR) over the last century. You can observe the cyclical nature of the portfolio life. Figures 15.13 and 15.14 show the portfolio life according to the MC simulator as a random outcome.

Figure 15.12: The portfolio life over the last century

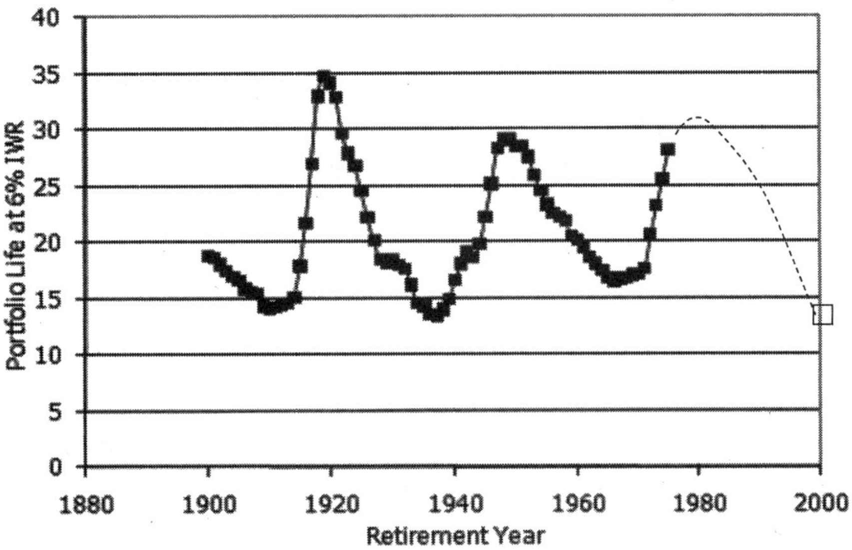

Figure 15.13: The portfolio life according to a MC simulator, one simulation

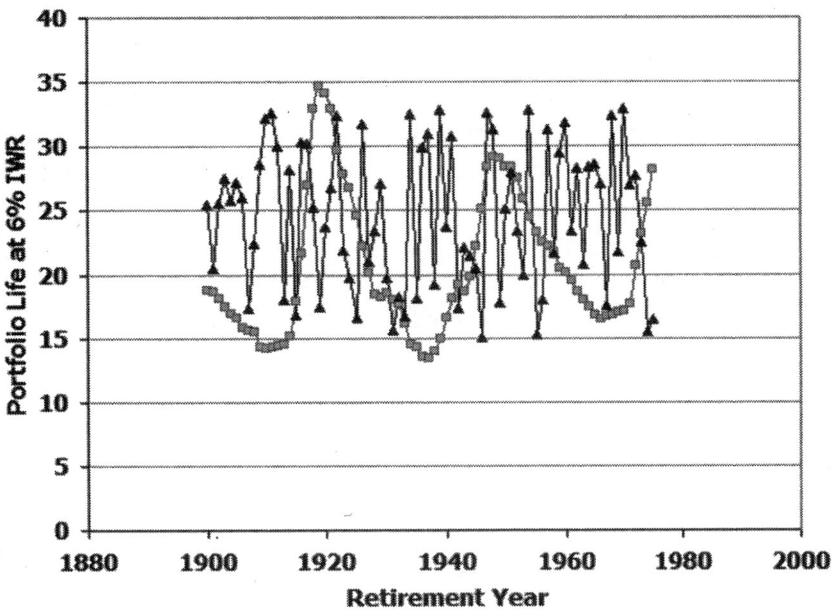

[38] To smoothen this chart for cyclical trends, I used a 4–year moving average of the actual portfolio life for a balanced portfolio 40/60 asset mix.

Figure 15.14: The portfolio life according to a MC simulator, 34 simulations

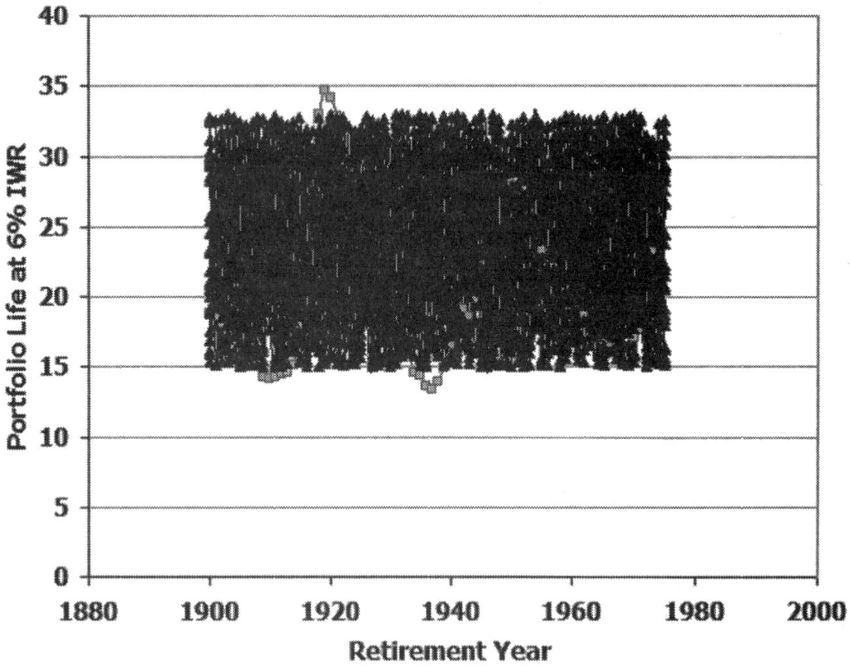

Picture this: You are watching different animals grazing on the African plains from the safety and comfort of your safari vehicle. Hundreds of zebras, giraffes, gazelles, wildebeests and antelopes are grazing. They move about in a random fashion, feeding, enjoying their day and playing around. Suddenly, you hear the roar of a lion at a distance. All animals stop grazing, first they lift their heads fearfully, assess the direction of the lion's roar, then they start running away from where the lion's roar originated. Some of the animals that somehow missed the lion's roar at first, now notice that all others are running and they also join this stampede. Once they start running in one direction, theirs is no longer a random movement. As a matter of fact, if any prey animal ignores this non–randomness and still maintains its random grazing mode, it will be dinner for the lion. This entire episode takes only five minutes. Once the lion's stomach is full, he goes back to sleep. All of the zebras, giraffes, gazelles, wildebeests and antelopes resume their grazing. For them, the non–randomness ends and the randomness resumes. As for the animal that just became dinner for the lion, it is no longer able to care for randomness or non–randomness; it will turn into dung in a few days and start a whole new exciting life cycle!

The same thing happened in the markets during the last century. In about 95% of the time, nothing happened and it remained random. In 2.5% of the time, you had non–random, extreme down markets. In the other 2.5% of the remaining time, they recovered all that was lost and then some. In Chapter 27, I will discuss what happens if you miss the best and the worst of the markets.

We fooled our clients far too long with models using steady growth rates. Many educated clients don't fall for that anymore. Now, we are again trying to fool them, this time with randomness, using sophisticated simulators.

> The greatest danger and impediment to the advancement of the mathematics of distribution is the fabrication of useless studies by researchers using Monte Carlo simulators. Their findings from these flawed research studies are applied to asset allocation, portfolio optimization, diversification, risk management and all other aspects of retirement planning, investment management, pension management and actuarial calculations.
>
> I cringe every time I look at a publication that includes the words, "using a Monte Carlo simulator", "scientific study", "our conclusion is..." in the same article. Our money, trillions of dollars, is managed based on such flawed models and assumptions.

I feel sorry for insurance companies and pension funds. They hire top math wizards to design risk management strategies for them. What happens? They work in 95% of the time and don't work in 5% of the time. Their Gaussian minds create models that sit right on the financial fault lines. A few years later, it blows up in their faces. This happens over and over. When you think about it, it is no different than barbers performing surgeries in medieval ages. The players are different, but the sting is the same.

Unless you are a short–term trader, purge your simulator from all your computers! Using the actual market history goes a long way in protecting the naked retiree from calamities.

Chapter 16

Optimum Asset Allocation – Distribution Stage

When it comes to investment planning, asset allocation is one of the important decisions. A proper asset allocation can maximize portfolio value, decrease the probability of depletion, increase portfolio life. It limits portfolio volatility to within the investor's tolerance level. It can make a difference to the portfolio's success.

The asset allocation decision involves two main areas:

- The **optimum** asset mix is the asset allocation that fulfills a particular objective. This objective can be maximizing the portfolio value, minimizing the probability of running out of money or seeking the longest portfolio life. It is based on market history.
- The **tolerable** asset mix is the asset allocation that limits the portfolio volatility to a level that you can tolerate. Your risk tolerance is determined during the initial discovery process when you open your account. Subsequently, it is fine–tuned as you gain a better understanding of risk over time.

You need to go through three steps to accomplish the proper asset mix.

<u>Step 1:</u> Figure out the optimum asset mix. This is where the portfolio life is longest, the probability of depletion is lowest and the portfolio value is highest.

<u>Step 2:</u> Figure out how much loss is tolerable for you. Is a 5% loss in a month too much? How about losing 40% in a year? Of course, nobody likes to lose money. What is important is not that you like losses or not, but how you react to such losses. If your asset mix is too aggressive to start with, you might end up liquidating your holdings at a market low and create a permanent loss. Stay within your risk tolerance

<u>Step 3:</u> The proper asset mix is the least aggressive of the tolerable and the optimum.

Figure 16.1: Suitable asset mix

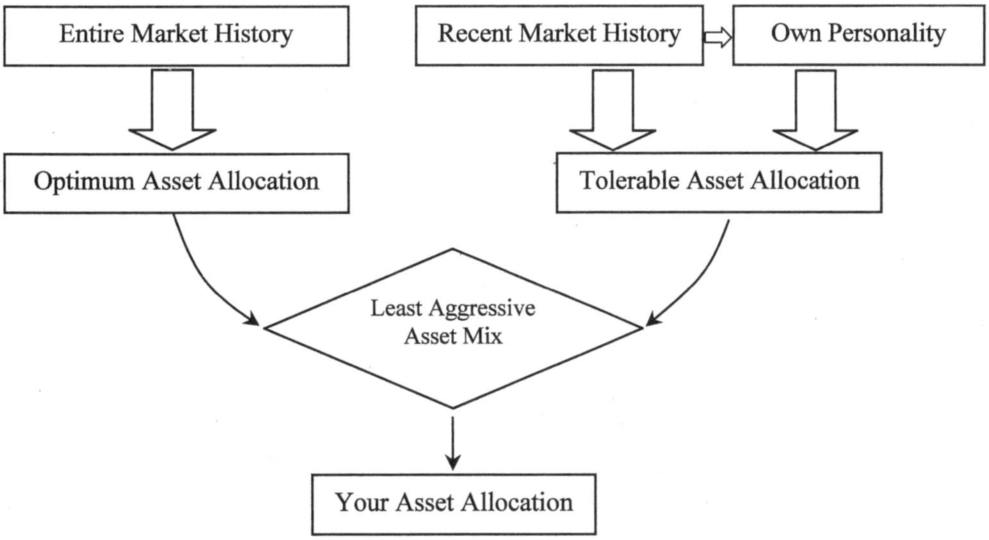

Optimizing the Asset Allocation:

We discussed in Chapter 14 the shortcomings of the efficient frontier (EF) for asset allocation. Therefore, we are not going to use EF or any similar method that is based on the Gaussian mindset. We will approach the optimization process from a different angle.

One of the most important factors in the optimization process is the time horizon. A longer time horizon means that equities might have more chance of spending time in a secular bullish trend. When the time horizon is long, the luck factor plays a smaller role.

Many confuse the time horizon of the portfolio with the time horizon of the investor. In a distribution portfolio, the time horizon is the life of the portfolio. It is not the time horizon of the portfolio's owner. A portfolio does not care how long its owner lives, but how much is taken out each month. A 65–year old person may have a 30–year time horizon but this has nothing to do with the time horizon of the portfolio or its optimum asset mix. The retiree may live 30 years, but at a 6% initial withdrawal rate, the portfolio will likely expire in 16 to 20 years. For optimization, you must use the time horizon of the *portfolio* and not of the *investor*.

The only exception is when the withdrawal rate is very low, 2% or lower. In this case, the portfolio life is practically infinite and the retiree's time horizon becomes the governing factor.

Three factors determine the time horizon: the withdrawal rate, the luck factor and alpha[39]. The most important factor in optimizing the asset mix is the withdrawal rate. If it is low, then the portfolio lasts longer.

The second important factor is the luck factor. For that, I use the time value of fluctuations (TVF) as the basis for portfolio optimization.

- Secular Trends: While asset allocation does not convert an unlucky outcome to a lucky one, it can improve it somewhat. Here our objective is to find the optimum mix of the two main asset classes, equity and fixed income.
- Cyclical Trends: We need to maintain sufficient liquidity in the portfolio to minimize the effects of the reverse dollar cost averaging (RDCA). The optimization tells us how much we need to allocate to money market and short–term bonds in the fixed income portion of the portfolio.
- Inflation: Optimization tells us how much we need to allocate to inflation indexed bonds in the fixed income portion of the portfolio. This is to minimize the inflation risk.

Let us look at each of these steps.

Equity / Fixed Income Allocation:

A distribution portfolio may be in one of the two distinct regimes: the withdrawal rate is either lower or it is higher than the SWR.

A different objective applies for each regime. When the withdrawal rate is lower than the SWR, we seek to maximize the portfolio growth. When the withdrawal rate is higher than the SWR, we seek to minimize the probability of depletion of the portfolio.

<u>Maximize Growth:</u> When the withdrawal rate is below the sustainable withdrawal rate, then the portfolio value increases over time. If you are lucky, you end up with plenty of money. If you are unlucky, there won't be as much left for the estate. In either case, the portfolio continues accumulating and no portfolio runs out of money.

In such cases, our purpose is to maintain an asset mix that creates the maximum dollar value of the median portfolio.

[39] Alpha is the excess return of the equity portfolio over and above its benchmark index, see Chapter 18.

Example 16.1

Steve retires at age 65 with $1 million in his portfolio. He needs to withdraw $20,000 annually from his portfolio, indexed fully to inflation. What is his optimum asset allocation?

Note: Equity history is based on S&P500 index, plus 2% dividends, less 2% management fees. Fixed income return: historical 6-month term deposit interest rate plus 0.5%, net of all management fees, annual rebalancing.

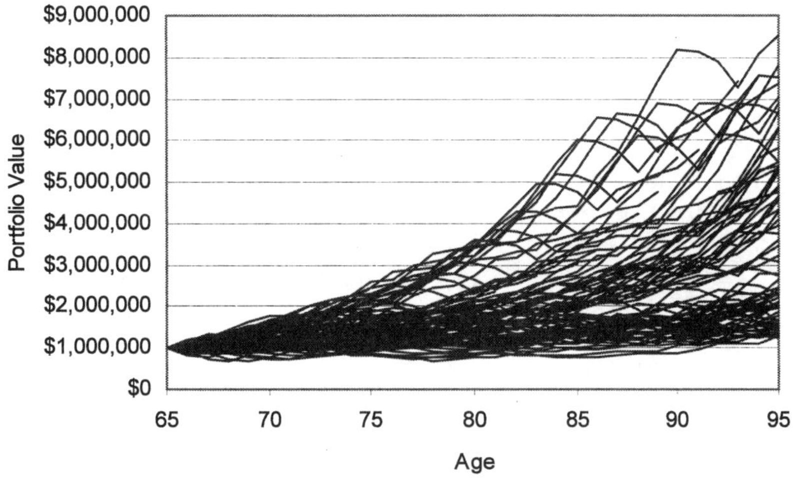

Equity / Fixed Income	Portfolio Value at age 90 Unlucky (Bottom Decile)	Median	Lucky (Top Decile)	Probability of Depletion by age 90	Worst-Case Portfolio Life
0 / 100	$703,145	$2,051,716	$4,940,407	0%	Over 25 years
15 / 85	$1,003,572	$2,041,855	$4,905,574	0%	Over 25 years
30 / 70	$1,304,024	$2,033,930	$4,982,303	0%	Over 25 years
40 / 60	$1,272,932	$2,133,259	$5,268,260	0%	Over 25 years
50 / 50	$1,206,841	$2,414,093	$5,486,145	0%	Over 25 years
60 / 40	$1,083,190	**$2,461,104**	$5,627,046	0%	Over 25 years
70 / 30	$925,694	$2,389,216	$5,865,163	0%	Over 25 years
85 / 15	$670,001	$2,060,350	$6,471,478	0%	Over 25 years
100 / 0	$398,340	$1,856,537	$6,724,709	0%	Over 25 years

The median portfolio value is highest when the asset mix is 60% equity and 40% fixed income, as indicated in bold. Therefore, the optimum asset mix is 60/40.

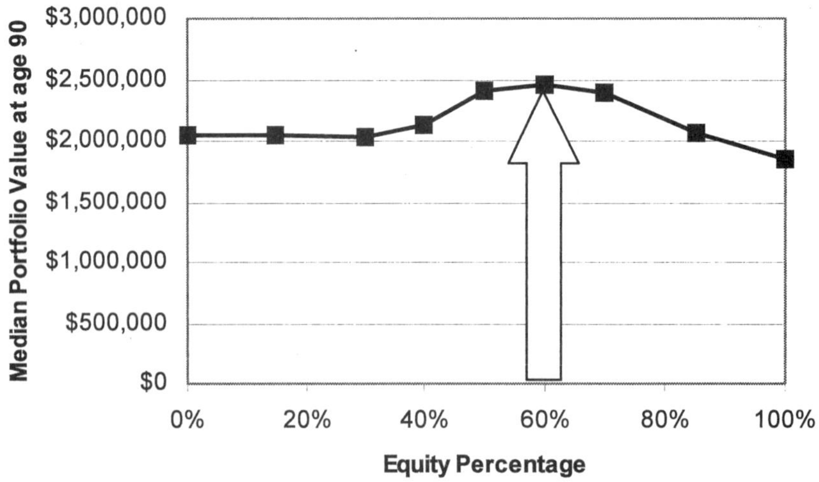

Minimize Probability of Depletion: When the withdrawal rate is near or above the sustainable withdrawal rate (over 3.5%), then some portfolios will survive and some will deplete, depending on the luck factor. In this regime, our purpose is to seek an asset mix that minimizes the probability of depletion.

Example 16.2

Same as Example 16.1 except Steve withdraws $40,000 annually. What is his optimum asset allocation?

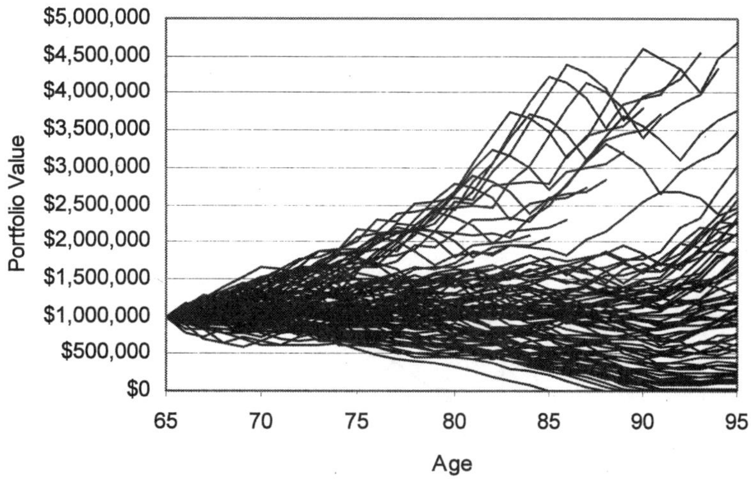

Equity / Fixed Income	Portfolio Value at age 90: Unlucky (Bottom Decile)	Median	Lucky (Top Decile)	Probability of Depletion by age 90	Worst-Case Portfolio Life
0 / 100	$0	$854,492	$2,345,497	18%	18 years
15 / 85	$0	$847,619	$2,372,879	12%	20 years
30 / 70	$197,445	$913,745	$2,373,697	8%	20 years
40 / 60	$100,294	$826,164	$2,392,678	**5%**	20 years
50 / 50	$5,362	$774,303	$2,413,962	11%	19 years
60 / 40	$0	$711,873	$2,679,973	20%	19 years
70 / 30	$0	$632,006	$3,103,795	25%	18 years
85 / 15	$0	$494,076	$3,656,894	40%	16 years
100 / 0	$0	$307,426	$4,417,842	43%	13 years

In this case, the 40/60-asset mix (indicated in bold) resulted in the lowest probability of depletion. At this asset mix, the probability of depletion was 5% and in the worst case, his portfolio would have lasted for 20 years.

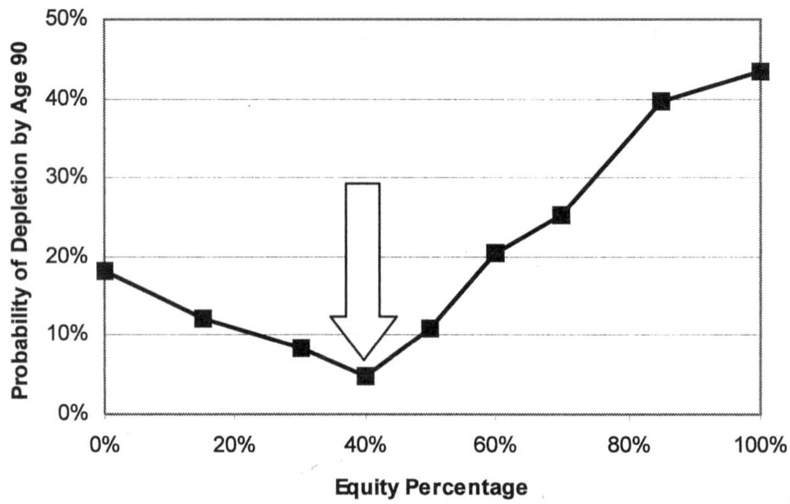

At high withdrawal rates, the probability of depletion is meaningless because it will be high for all asset mixes. In such cases, use a lower age, such as 80, instead of age of death, and then redraw this chart.

At this point, we optimized the asset mix of equities and fixed income. Next, we need to look at how much to allocate to the money market within the fixed income portion of the portfolio, to minimize the effect of the RDCA.

Money Market and Short–Term Bonds:

Now, we want to minimize the effect of RDCA by maintaining sufficient liquidity in the portfolio. The following rules will help you minimize, even eliminate, most of the adverse effects of RDCA in the distribution portfolio:

Rule #1: Allocate two years' of withdrawals to a money market fund as part of the fixed income portion of the portfolio. The money market fund is for immediate–term liquidity.

All periodic withdrawals must come from the money market fund only. Do not set up automatic withdrawals from any fluctuating investments such as equity funds, income trust funds, balanced funds or even bond funds.

Don't confuse the effects of RDCA and the luck factor. Holding more cash does not reduce the effect of other components of the luck factor. If you hold more than two years of income in the money market fund, then the performance will be impeded.

Rule #2: Allocate three years' of withdrawals to short–term bonds as part of the fixed income portion of the portfolio. This is used to top off the money market fund as it depletes over time.

Rule #3: If rebalancing from equities to fixed income, the money should first top off the money market fund, then the short–term bond, and finally other bonds in the fixed income portion of the portfolio.

Figure 16.4: Flow of money, rule #3

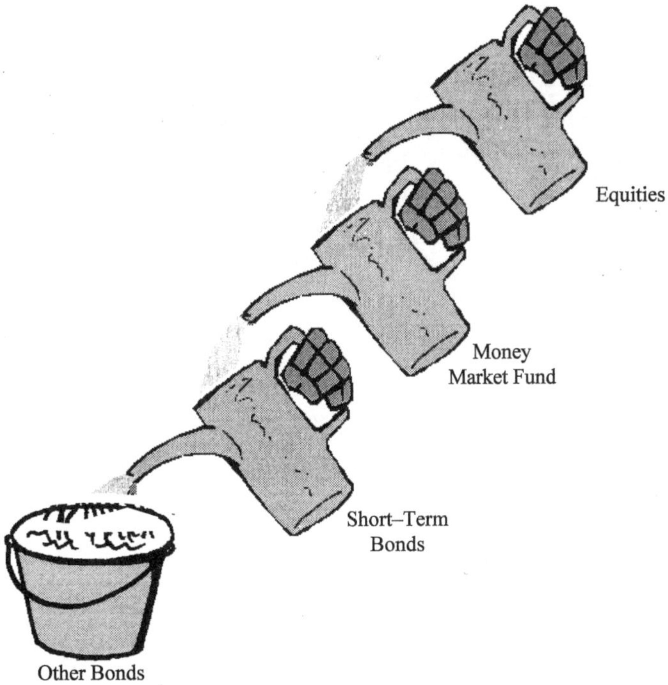

Rule #4: If rebalancing from fixed income to equities: the money should go from longer–term bonds to money market first, then to short–term bonds, and finally to equities.

Generally, if you are planning to hold a bond ladder, you may be able to stagger bond maturities. As each bond matures, you can use this money to top off the money market funds.

Figure 16.5: Flow of money, rule #4

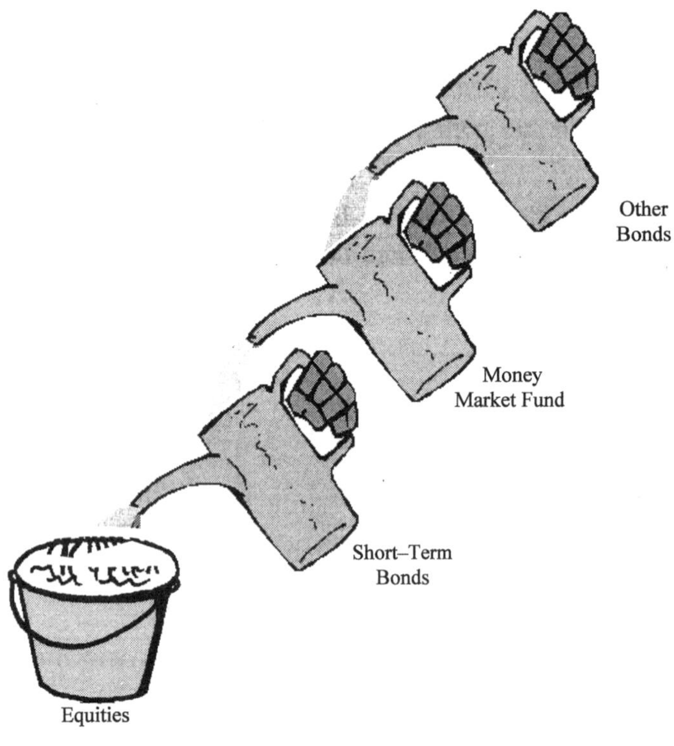

Rule #5: If there is cash inflow into the portfolio, such as dividends, interest or other cash distributions, add these to the money market fund first. Do not reinvest them until the money market and short–term bond portfolio is fully topped up.

Figure 16.6: Flow of money, rule #5

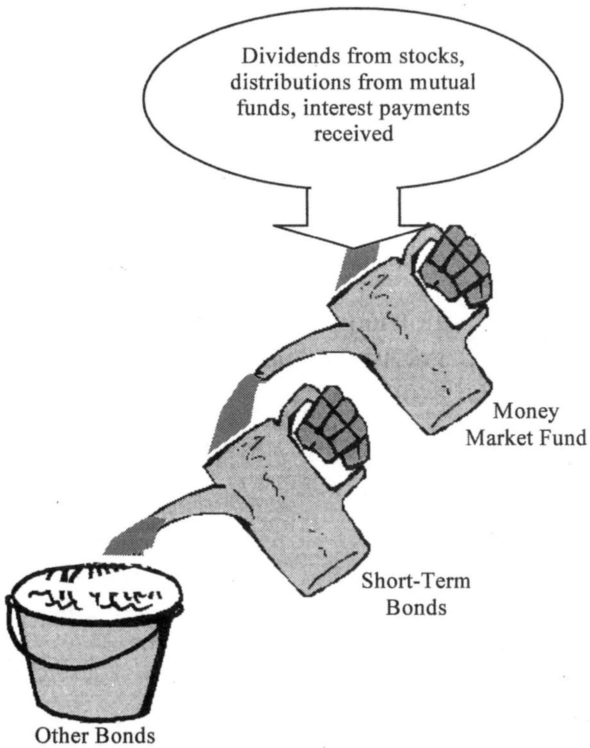

The money market fund is always the first one to be topped off, then the short–term bond and then remaining asset classes.

Rule #6: Do not rebalance the equity/fixed income holdings too often. If you rebalance too often, this has the same effect as withdrawing periodically from equities with a short time delay. Frequent rebalancing can cause significant damage to a distribution portfolio. If the withdrawal rate is 5% or less, it is better to rebalance once every four years at the end of the US Presidential election year (see Chapter 6).

Inflation Protection:

Optimizing for inflation protection is the final step. There are two ways of reducing the effect of inflation: 1. Equities, or 2. Inflation indexed bonds.

On the equity side, you can hold hard assets or shares of companies holding/producing hard assets. These are commodities, resources, energy, precious metals and real estate. Among the equity markets with a long history, the Canadian and Australian markets provide better inflation protection than other markets because their market indices contain a higher portion of commodity–based companies.

On the fixed income side, you can use inflation–indexed bonds for inflation protection. The face value of the inflation–indexed bonds is reset to inflation periodically and the coupon payments track inflation.

In distribution portfolios, it is more efficient to hold inflation–indexed bonds instead of resource–based equities. Lower volatility and steady price appreciation of these bonds can create a lower time value of fluctuations.

Generally, adding any fixed income to a portfolio "squeezes" the envelope of probable outcomes, as depicted in Figure 16.7. This can increase the predictability of the outcome because of this narrower range. The inflation–indexed bonds do that more effectively than the conventional bonds because they also minimize the inflation risk.

However, there is a price to pay: while adding fixed income to a portfolio narrows the envelope of outcomes, it also reduces the occurrence of "lucky" outcomes. You make less money when markets do well. This is significantly more so with inflation–indexed bonds than with conventional bonds. The inflation–indexed bonds have a lower return in secular bullish trends where inflation is generally lower. Because of that, inflation indexed bonds should not be held in the portfolio when the withdrawal rate is lower than the sustainable withdrawal rate. This would be no different than filling up the gas tank with "nitro" just to go for a Sunday ride.

Figure 16.7: Envelope of outcomes

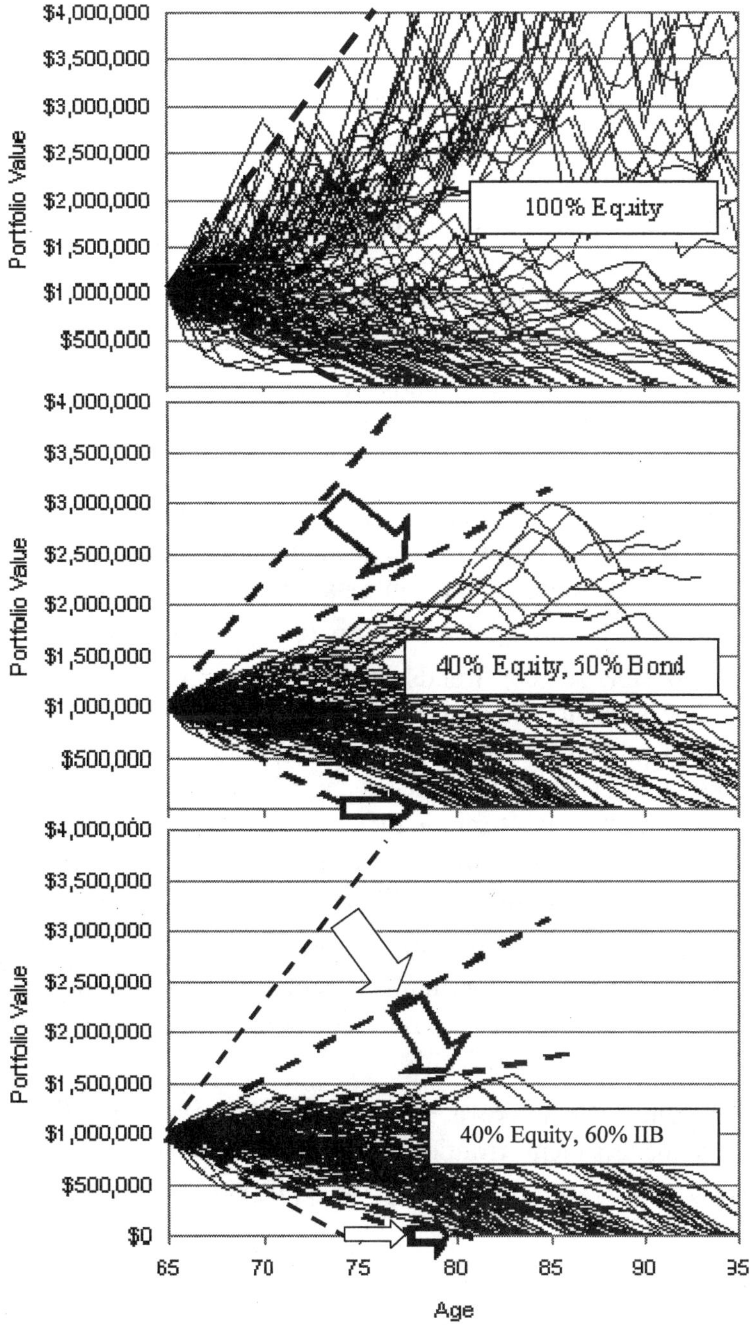

Optimum Asset Mix:

If the withdrawal rate is *below* the sustainable withdrawal rate then you need to hold money market funds, short–term bonds, and medium-term bonds in the fixed income part of your portfolio. The maturity of the medium-term bonds should remain below eight years or so. Holding bonds with longer maturities can create a higher time value of fluctuations than the potential benefit of extra yield that they might generate. Also, keep only high quality bonds to keep the risk low.

If the withdrawal rate is *higher* than the sustainable withdrawal rate, then you need to hold money market funds, short-term bonds, medium-term bonds and inflation–indexed bonds in the fixed income part of your portfolio.

Ideally, you would get the best of both worlds if you hold conventional bonds during a secular bullish trend and inflation–indexed bonds during a secular sideways trend. But that means stepping into some sort of technical analysis which is beyond most fixed income investors.

The optimum asset allocation depends also on alpha. It is the excess equity return relative to its benchmark. If your equity holdings outperform the index then the time horizon stretches longer. Therefore, the optimum mix contains a higher percentage of equities if the alpha is higher.

Another observation is this: the secular trends in the US markets exhibit a "sloped–staircase" formation. With this formation, markets may be flat in a secular sideways trend for 20 years. After that, in a secular bullish trend, markets may rise for 20 years. At low withdrawal rates, it makes a difference whether the portfolio owner has a 20–year or a 30–year time horizon. The optimum asset mix is different for each time horizon. Once the initial withdrawal rate exceeds 2%, this difference becomes insignificant because the *portfolio*'s time horizon becomes more important than the *portfolio owner*'s time horizon.

In Canadian markets, secular trend discontinuities are less pronounced than for US markets. Therefore, the optimum asset mix remains essentially the same for different time horizons. In addition, because there is a higher resource component in Canadian markets, there is a lesser need for inflation–indexed bonds.

These seemingly minor points can make a large difference over long time horizons. However, when you run the efficient frontier analysis with only ten or twenty–year historical data or use Monte Carlo simulators for optimizing the asset mix, these important details are missed entirely.

Tables 16.1 through 16.4 depict the optimum asset mix for distribution portfolios for the US and Canadian markets. The tables indicate the optimum asset mix based on two different alpha values: equities performing the same as the index and also outperforming it by 1%.

Table 16.1: Optimum asset mix in US distribution portfolios optimized for time value of fluctuations
Equity: S&P500, the net alpha (after management fees) is 0% (index return only), the net fixed income yield is 6–month CD plus 1%, inflation–indexed bond yield is inflation plus 1%

		Initial Withdrawal Rate					
		0%	2%	3%	4%	5%	6% and over
		Asset Mix:					
Equity	20–yr time horizon	40%	39%	42%	30%	30%	20%
	30–yr time horizon	67%	60%				
Money Market		0%	4%	6%	8%	10%	2 year's withdrawals
Short Term Bonds		6%	6%	9%	12%	15%	3 year's withdrawals
Mid–term Bonds	20–yr time horizon	54%	51%	43%	35%	0%	0%
	30–yr time horizon	27%	30%				
Inflation Indexed Bonds		0%	0%	0%	15%	45%	Remaining assets

Table 16.2: Optimum asset mix in US distribution portfolios optimized for time value of fluctuations
Equity: S&P500, the net alpha (after management fees) is 1%, the net fixed income yield is 6–month CD plus 1%, inflation–indexed bond yield is inflation plus 1%

		Initial Withdrawal Rate					
		0%	2%	3%	4%	5%	6% and over
		Asset Mix:					
Equity	20–yr time horizon	70%	49%	61%	45%	35%	28%
	30–yr time horizon	85%	77%				
Money Market		0%	4%	6%	8%	10%	2 year's withdrawals
Short Term Bonds		6%	6%	9%	12%	15%	3 year's withdrawals
Mid–term Bonds	20–yr time horizon	24%	41%	24%	35%	0%	0%
	30–yr time horizon	9%	13%				
Inflation Indexed Bonds		0%	0%	0%	0%	40%	Remaining assets

Table 16.3: Optimum asset mix in Canadian distribution portfolios optimized for time value of fluctuations, equity: SP/TSX, net alpha (after management fees) is 0%, net fixed income yield is 6–month CD plus 1%, inflation–indexed bond yield is inflation plus 1%

	Initial Withdrawal Rate					
	0%	2%	3%	4%	5%	6% and over
Asset Mix:						
Equity	83%	54%	57%	43%	40%	32%
Money Market	0%	4%	6%	8%	10%	2 year's withdrawals
Short Term Bonds	6%	6%	9%	12%	15%	3 year's withdrawals
Mid–term Bonds	11%	36%	28%	37%	20%	½ of remaining assets
Inflation Indexed Bonds	0%	0%	0%	0%	15%	½ of remaining assets

Table 16.4: Optimum asset mix in Canadian distribution portfolios optimized for time value of fluctuations, equity: SP/TSX, net alpha (after management fees) is 1%, net fixed income yield is 6–month CD plus 1%, inflation–indexed bond yield is inflation plus 1%

	Initial Withdrawal Rate					
	0%	2%	3%	4%	5%	6% and over
Asset Mix:						
Equity	83%	75%	62%	48%	45%	40%
Money Market	0%	4%	6%	8%	10%	2 year's withdrawals
Short Term Bonds	6%	6%	9%	12%	15%	3 year's withdrawals
Mid–term Bonds	11%	15%	23%	32%	20%	2/3 of remaining assets
Inflation Indexed Bonds	0%	0%	0%	0%	10%	1/3 of remaining assets

Example 16.3

Joe needs annually $20,000 of income, indexed to inflation, from his portfolio of $300,000. His equities are invested in the S&P500 index. What asset mix would you recommend?

His initial withdrawal rate is 6.7%, calculated as $20,000 divided by $300,000. Look up Table 16.1:

Equity: allocate $60,000, calculated as 20% of $300,000
Money Market: $40,000, calculated as 2 years of withdrawals
Short term bonds: $60,000, calculated as 3 years of withdrawals
Inflation-indexed Bonds (TIPS): $140,000, calculated as remaining assets from the $300,000

By the way, at this high rate of withdrawal, there is a 69% chance that his portfolio will deplete within 20 years.

Example 16.4

Steve needs annually $20,000 of income, indexed to inflation, from his portfolio of $300,000. His equities are invested in the Canadian SP/TSX index. His net return is index plus 1% after accounting for dividends less management fees. What asset mix would you recommend?

His initial withdrawal rate is 6.7%, calculated as $20,000 divided by $300,000. Look up Table 16.4:

Equity: allocate $120,000, calculated as 40% of $300,000
Money Market: $40,000, calculated as 2 years of withdrawals
Short term bonds: $60,000, calculated as 3 years of withdrawals
Conventional, mid-term bonds: $53,000, calculated as 2/3 of the remaining $80,000
Inflation-indexed bonds (Real Return Bonds): $27,000, calculated as 1/3 of the remaining $80,000

At this high rate of withdrawal, there is a 46% chance that his portfolio will deplete within 20 years.

Tolerable Asset Allocation:

Historically, equities have been outperforming fixed income investments over the long term. In this context, long term means 20 years or more. However, when it comes to short–term fluctuations, many of the asset allocation surveys that look like glorified restaurant menus, will not help you much.

Higher levels of volatility can be intolerable for many. You want to make sure that you can ride out the short–term fluctuations in order to achieve your long–term objectives. The purpose of tolerable asset allocation is to limit losses to within *your* risk tolerance.

Table 16.5 depicts the worst monthly and annual losses based on market history. Tables 16.6 and 16.7 depict maximum short–term losses for various asset mixes. You can select an asset mix that will minimize the "statement shock" after a bad month or after a bad year. For example, you might want to limit the loss to 10% in any given month.

Keep in mind; if you limit your loss to 10% in a month, you may still have another 10% loss in the following month in bad markets. Using the tolerable asset allocation, you are not limiting your total loss, but only the loss within that time period.

If the *optimum* asset mix (from Tables 16.1 through 16.4) indicates a higher equity content than your *tolerable* asset mix, then choose the lower equity content of the tolerable asset mix.

Table 16.5: Monthly and annual historical equity losses

	Worst Loss	99 out of 100 times, the loss is less than	19 out of 20 times, the loss is less than
Monthly	32%	15%	8%
Annual	48%	35%	24%

Table 16.6: Asset allocation to limit risk, monthly loss

Asset Mix (Equity / Fixed Income)	**Monthly** Maximum Historical Loss		
	Worst	99 times out of 100 less than:	19 times out of 20 less than
0 / 100	0%	0%	0%
15 / 85	5%	2%	1%
30 / 70	10%	5%	2%
40 / 60	13%	6%	**3%**
50 / 50	16%	8%	4%
60 / 40	19%	9%	5%
70 / 30	22%	11%	6%
85 / 15	27%	13%	7%
100 / 0	32%	15%	8%

Table 16.7: Asset allocation to limit risk, annual loss

Asset Mix (Equity / Fixed Income)	**Annual** Maximum Historical Loss		
	Worst	99 times out of 100 less than:	19 times out of 20 less than:
0 / 100	0%	0%	0%
15 / 85	7%	5%	4%
30 / 70	14%	11%	7%
40 / 60	19%	14%	10%
50 / 50	24%	18%	12%
60 / 40	29%	21%	14%
70 / 30	34%	25%	17%
85 / 15	41%	30%	20%
100 / 0	48%	35%	24%

Example 16.5

Michael is a US investor. He needs annually $20,000 of income, indexed to inflation. He has savings of $1 million. He has a 30-year time horizon. He does not want to see a loss of more than 3% in any month in his portfolio, 19 times out 20. What asset mix would you recommend?

Optimum Asset Mix: Look up Table 16.1. Accordingly, for a 2% withdrawal rate ($20,000 from $1 million), his optimum asset mix is: 60% equity, 4% money market, 6% short-term bonds and 30% conventional bonds.

Tolerable Asset Mix: Michael does not want to see a loss over 3% in any month, 19 times out 20. Look up Table 16.6. A 40/60-asset mix limits the risk to 3% (indicated in bold). This is Michael's risk tolerance.

Therefore, the recommended asset mix is: 40% equity, 4% money market, 6% short term bonds and 50% mid-term conventional bonds.

Conclusion:

I developed this asset allocation philosophy because I was not satisfied with the existing methods. Many asset allocation questionnaires that I have seen have little to do with optimization and a lot to do with protecting the financial industry. I wanted to be a little more scientific than that.

This process also brings secularism to asset allocation. It places a clear separation between market behavior and the client's psychology. The optimum asset allocation looks at the actual market history. The tolerable asset allocation focuses on the client. The division of each domain is crystal clear. Yet, all you need to do is look up one table for the optimum asset mix and another for the tolerable asset mix[40].

Another benefit of this process is that it is easy to explain. You only need to say, "This asset mix gives you the lowest probability of running out of money based on market history". This is a lot easier than explaining standard deviations and other statistical jargon. Many in our business have difficulty understanding the efficient frontier. So, they resort to name–dropping, "This is based on the research of Nobel prize winning…" This certainly does not create much trust, does it?

If you find this chapter too complicated, don't fret. Here is an optimization you can do in your sleep:

- If you do not need money from your portfolio allocate 50% in equities and 50% in fixed income.
- If you need a small periodic income, 4% or less, then allocate 40% in equities and 60% in fixed income.
- If you need a larger periodic income, over 4%, then allocate 35% in equities and 65% in fixed income.

If you follow these guidelines, you will not be far from the optimum. Keep it in perspective: if your withdrawal rate is over 5%, then asset allocation counts for less than 15% of the whole picture. So, even if you are a little wrong, it just does not matter.

[40] Or, click on the "optimize" button on my retirement calculator for an instant answer.

Chapter 17

Sustainable Withdrawal Rate

Before I go into the details of the sustainable withdrawal rate (SWR), let's first talk about the financial risks during retirement.

Proper retirement planning requires planning for the worst. There are three significant financial risk factors for a retiree:

- Longevity risk: longevity risk means living "too long".

  When designing a retirement plan, make sure to use an *age of death* where the probability of survival does not exceed 15%. In most cases, that age is 95.

- Market risk: market risk quantifies the *probability of portfolio depletion.*

  Make sure the probability of depletion does not exceed 10% at the age of death. Otherwise, irreversible calamities can happen. If the market risk is over 10%, even slightly, you would need an exponentially higher level of genius or luck to recover from a routine market correction.

- Inflation risk: inflation risk refers to the *ability to maintain the purchasing power.*

  My limit is 10%, i.e. purchasing power must stay above 90% of the requested amount. This becomes important when we talk about guaranteed income classes such as variable annuities, variable pay annuities or index linked annuities. Many of these income classes do not provide inflation protection.

A retirement plan must meet each of these three criteria to be considered a well–designed plan. We have already covered market and inflation risks in earlier chapters, but this is a good place to discuss longevity risk.

Longevity Risk:

Some people go to great lengths to calculate their life expectancy. The average life expectancy is important for insurance companies, health care professionals, and morticians for their planning. However, I find little use for it in the financial planning practice for individuals. I can best explain the reason by sharing a personal experience with you.

On my 50th birthday, I received a phone call. As the phone was ringing, I saw my family doctor's name on the call display. While I was reaching for the handset, I cheerfully mumbled to myself "Such a thoughtful doctor. He remembers my birthday!"

His phone call was not about what I naively expected. He went on to explain that my PSA (prostate specific antigen) level was abnormally high and I needed to have a prostate biopsy right away. He further added that, based on my PSA level, I had about a 15% probability of having prostate cancer.

It was not a happy day for me. Later on, I started thinking about this 15% probability. You see, this information may be useful for prostate clinics or cancer treatment centers. Probabilities are valuable for them in planning their business, facilities and resources. However, it has no use for me whatsoever. You see, I cannot have 15% cancer. I either have it (100%) or I don't have it (0%).

The same analogy applies for retirement planning: I don't attempt to figure out my client's life expectancy by asking numerous questions. One such question is "Did you have any traffic violations in the last three years!" The answer to this question may be significant for estimating one's life expectancy. However, I just don't think financial planners should turn into actuaries. The term "life expectancy" measures the age at which half of the people will die and the other half will survive for that group. What if a seemingly incurable ailment becomes treatable in five years with a routine procedure? Would that create a sufficient excuse for running out of money? Can a financial planner defend himself in court with this following argument? "The doctor estimated that my client will die in three years. I planned for five. But doctors were wrong. The client kept living and living. Now, the client is broke, he is suing me. He should go and sue his doctor!"

One of my clients was told by a cancer specialist that he should prepare himself and his family for the inevitable. Supposedly, he had only a few months left to live. That was twelve years ago. He died just over a year ago.

No, we are neither statisticians nor actuaries. Of course, there are some situations where one should use some judgment. However, if you do that, you must be cognizant of where the ultimate judgment comes from. Unless someone looks as if they are at death's door, I am not going to waste my time trying to figure out whether his life expectancy is 83 or 86 years.

I use age 95 as the age of death in my plans. This gives me between a 5% and a 15% survival rate, which I am comfortable with. In some specific situations, I may use age 100 and in some other cases, age 90; but I don't venture outside this range.

Withdrawal Rate:

In a distribution portfolio, the withdrawal rate is the most important contributor of portfolio longevity. It is far more important than asset allocation, asset selection, management fees, dividends, and reverse dollar cost averaging.

A seemingly small increase in withdrawals can change the outcome drastically. A case in point: If you have savings of $1 million at age 65 and your annual withdrawals are $38,000 indexed to inflation, market history shows that the probability of running out of money is only 9% by age 95. If you increase annual withdrawals by $4,000 to $42,000, then the probability of going broke by age 95 increases from 9% to 29%. Suddenly, an acceptable risk becomes a totally unacceptable one. You can play with any of the other variables such as asset allocation and management fees, and this will not likely change the picture.

Withdrawal rate is the annual periodic withdrawal amount expressed as a percentage of the total retirement savings in the current year.

$$WR = (PMT / PV) \times 100\% \qquad \text{(Equation 17.1)}$$

where:
WR is the withdrawal rate in percentage
PMT is the dollar amount of the annual withdrawal
PV is the present value of savings

For example, I make the following statement: "At 3.6% WR, your portfolio should last you for at least 30 years". What that means is, "if you start with $1 million capital at age 65, and take out $36,000 annually, indexed to inflation each year, this capital should last at least until age 95". During these 30 years the portfolio will fluctuate and the withdrawals will increase with inflation. But that does not matter; you would have income until age 95. In this case, this 3.6 % withdrawal rate is also referred to as the Initial Withdrawal Rate (IWR).

The withdrawal rate is only a measure of the "drain" of retirement savings. Always keep in mind that you cannot spend, give away or donate percentages, only dollars. Don't get stuck on percentages.

Yet many people confuse the two. Here is the give–away question I am asked occasionally during my talks: "If the sustainable withdrawal rate at age 65 is 3.6%, does it mean that each year I can only take out 3.6% of my portfolio?"

At the risk of being repetitive, here is my answer: "No! Don't confuse percentage with dollars. All it means is this: if you have one million dollars in your portfolio at age 65, you can take out $36,000 annually from your portfolio. You can continue taking out $36,000 –indexed– each and every year until age 95, regardless of what the portfolio value is at any future age and regardless of what the indexation amount is."

If you still get stuck in percentages, just remember the following: You can take out 99% of your portfolio each and every year for the rest of your life. In theory, your portfolio will never run out of money. But after a short time, your periodic withdrawals will drop very sharply – to pennies. This is definitely not a realistic retirement plan!

Example 17.1

Carl is retiring this year. He has $500,000 for his retirement. He needs $25,000 each year from these savings, indexed to inflation.

Carl's withdrawal rate is 5%, calculated as

($25,000 / $500,000) x 100% = 5%

Four years later, Carl develops some health problems. He needs to increase his withdrawals substantially to meet his additional expenses. His withdrawals jump to $42,000. His portfolio is valued at $350,000.

Carl's withdrawal rate is now 12%, calculated as

($42,000 / $350,000) x 100% = 12%

Example 17.2

Steve's retirement portfolio has $250,000. He withdraws $12,500 each year, indexed to inflation.

Jane's retirement portfolio has $750,000. She withdraws $37,500 each year, indexed to inflation.

Assuming both Steve and Jane have identical investments with identical management costs, whose portfolio will run out of money first?

Steve's withdrawal rate is 5%, calculated as

($12,500 / $250,000) x 100% = 5%

Jane's withdrawal rate is 5%, calculated as

($37,500 / $750,000) x 100% = 5%

The withdrawal rate measures the "drain" on the portfolio. Jane and Steve have the same withdrawal rate, 5%. Therefore, both portfolios will run out of money at the same time.

Sustainable Withdrawal Rate:

Retirement planning is an exercise in balancing assets and cash flow over the entire retirement period. One of the key questions is this: "How much can I safely withdraw from my portfolio for the rest of my life?"

In real life, the time value of money (TVM) model does not work well. The time value of fluctuations (TVF) causes the sustainable withdrawals to be significantly lower than the projections using TVM.

In theory, the sustainable withdrawal rate (SWR) is the maximum amount of money one can withdraw from a retirement portfolio on a periodic basis with no probability of depleting these savings during one's lifetime. It is based on market history and expressed as a percentage of portfolio value.

In practice, I use 90% probability of portfolio survival, i.e. 10% probability of depletion. This allows a slightly higher withdrawal without being too punitive. If things don't work out as planned, this provides just enough leeway to adjust the income allocation strategy without causing much damage to lifelong income.

Another definition for the SWR is this: the SWR is the borderline between an accumulation portfolio and a decumulation portfolio. If the withdrawal rate is below the SWR –even just slightly– then the median asset value of the portfolio continues to increase, i.e. accumulate, in spite of withdrawals during the distribution stage (Figure 17.1). On the other hand, if the withdrawal rate is higher than the SWR, then the median line declines in value, i.e. decumulates, during the retirement stage (Figure 17.2).

Figure 17.1: WR less than SWR, asset value continues to accumulate during the distribution stage

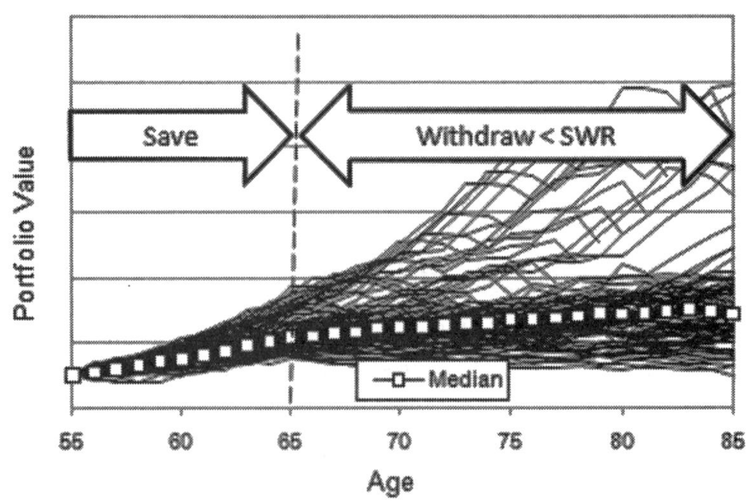

Figure 17.2: WR larger than SWR, asset value decumulates during the distribution stage

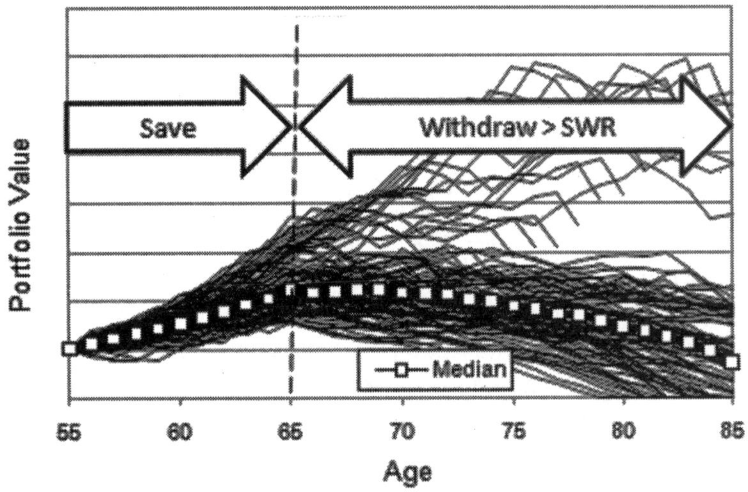

Some of the factors that affect the SWR are:

- Retirement time horizon
- Asset mix
- Asset allocation and rebalancing strategy
- Asset selection strategy
- Portfolio management expenses
- Mandatory minimum cash withdrawal requirements from tax–advantaged portfolios
- Long–term performance of investments relative to the benchmark

Beware that many of the academic studies that talk about sustainable withdrawal rates are flawed because of one of the following reasons:

- Start–date bias: Many studies use 1926 as a starting year. This start–date treats the 1929 crash as a "one–time" event. Start in 1900 and you will see how the 1929 crash appears like a black hole.
- The wrong market history may be used. You cannot take the US market, run a research, and then use it for Canadian or Japanese retirees.
- Some studies include the high historical dividends. For realistic retirement planning, only the index plus prevailing dividend yields minus the portfolio costs should be used.
- Management fees may not be included. Count on spending annually 2% to 3% of the account value as management and trading costs.
- Most research is based on data generated by Monte Carlo simulators. Their results are presented as "proven science" in decisions involving asset allocation, diversification, portfolio success rate, sustainable withdrawal rate, and so on. I described the serious flaws of Monte Carlo simulators in Chapter 15.

The SWR tables below (Tables 17.1 to 17.4) are based on actual market history. For each equity index, there are two different tables: one with alpha equals 0% and another with 1%. All portfolios are rebalanced at the end of the Presidential election year. On the fixed income side, the net fixed income yield is the historical 6–month CD yield plus 0.5%. For the inflation–indexed bonds, a net yield of historical inflation plus 0.5% was used.

It is important to recognize that SWR does not guarantee that you will die broke. On the contrary, in over 90% of cases, if you limit your withdrawals to SWR, there will be assets left for the estate.

The SWR in these tables is based on 90% survival of all portfolios. This should give sufficient time to revise the retirement plan if things don't go well with the luck factor. Generally, if the luck factor turns against you, you need to change the income class from the investment portfolio to guaranteed products, such as annuities.

Table 17.1: Sustainable withdrawal rate, equity: S&P500, net alpha (after management fees) is 0%, net fixed income yield is 6–month CD plus 0.5%, inflation–indexed bond yield is inflation plus 0.5%

Time Horizon	SWR	for the Asset Mix			
		Equity	Money Market	Bond	TIPS
20 years	5.2%	25%	10%	20%	45%
25 years	4.3%	30%	9%	35%	26%
30 years	3.8%	35%	8%	57%	0%
35 years	3.4%	40%	7%	53%	0%
40 years	3.1%	42%	6%	52%	0%

Table 17.2: Sustainable withdrawal rate, equity: S&P500, net alpha (after management fees) is 1%, net fixed income yield is 6–month CD plus 0.5%, inflation–indexed bond yield is inflation plus 0.5%

Time Horizon	SWR	for the Asset Mix			
		Equity	Money Market	Bond	TIPS
20 years	5.4%	25%	10%	20%	45%
25 years	4.5%	30%	9%	45%	16%
30 years	4.0%	39%	8%	53%	0%
35 years	3.7%	40%	8%	52%	0%
40 years	3.4%	45%	7%	48%	0%

Table 17.3: Sustainable withdrawal rate, equity: SP/TSX, net alpha (after management fees) is 0%, net fixed income yield is 6–month CD plus 0.5%, inflation–indexed bond yield is inflation plus 0.5%

Time Horizon	SWR	for the Asset Mix: Equity	Money Market	Bond	RRB[41]
20 years	5.4%	35%	10%	25%	30%
25 years	4.5%	43%	9%	34%	14%
30 years	4.0%	50%	8%	42%	0%
35 years	3.6%	50%	7%	43%	0%
40 years	3.3%	54%	6%	40%	0%

Table 17.4: Sustainable withdrawal rate, equity: SP/TSX, net alpha (after management fees) is 1%, net fixed income yield is 6–month CD plus 1%, inflation–indexed bond yield is inflation plus 1%

Time Horizon	SWR	for the Asset Mix: Equity	Money Market	Bond	RRB
20 years	5.6%	43%	11%	28%	18%
25 years	4.7%	45%	10%	30%	15%
30 years	4.3%	48%	9%	39%	4%
35 years	4.0%	50%	8%	42%	0%
40 years	3.7%	59%	7%	34%	0%

Example 17.3

Caleb, 65, is retiring right now. He has $980,000 in his retirement portfolio. Assume that his equities in the portfolio outperform the S&P500 index by 1% annually. Plan for a 30-year time horizon; until age 95.

How much can he take out this year, how much next year?

Table 17.2 shows the SWR for a 30-year time horizon, 4.0%.

He can take out a total of $40,000 from his portfolio this year. Next year, he can increase this amount by the amount of inflation. He can take this dollar amount, indexed to inflation until age 95. The plan should be reviewed periodically.

[41] Inflation–indexed bonds in Canada are called real return bond (RRB)

Sustainable Asset Multiplier:

During accumulation years, the typical question is "How much savings do I need to finance my retirement?" The sustainable asset multiplier (SAM) makes this a simple question to answer.

The SAM is the dollar amount of savings (portfolio assets) required at the beginning of retirement, sufficient to a last a specified number of years, for each dollar of withdrawal required during the first year of retirement. It is calculated as 100 divided by the sustainable withdrawal rate. Tables 17.1 through 17.4 already account for the inflation. Therefore, it is unnecessary to make any further inflation adjustments.

$$SAM = \frac{100}{SWR} \qquad \text{(Equation 17.2)}$$

To figure out the total savings required (SR) at the start of retirement to finance the retirement, simply take the dollar amount of withdrawals required during the first year of retirement and multiply it by the asset multiplier.

$$SR = PMT \times SAM \qquad \text{(Equation 17.3)}$$

When figuring out the savings required for financing your retirement, you first need to prepare a detailed retirement budget. A budget indicates the expected annual income from all sources on one side, and all living expenses on the other side. If your annual expenses are greater than your expected annual income then, you have a shortfall of income.

Next, calculate the future value of this shortfall of income at retirement age. Finally, calculate the total retirement savings required at the time of retirement.

Example 17.4

Charles, 60, is planning to retire at age 65. He needs $30,000 of income yearly in current dollars. Assume 3% inflation for the next 5 years. Assume that equities in his portfolio outperform the S&P500 index by 1% annually. Assume he will live until 95. How much total savings does he need to finance his entire retirement?

Table 17.2 shows the SWR of 4% for a 30-year time horizon. The sustainable asset multiplier is 25, calculated as 100 / 4%.

Next, figure out the future value of $30,000 at age 65. Using Equation (1.1), 3% inflation and a 5-year time period, calculate the future value of $30,000. It is $34,778 at age 65.

Savings Required at age 65, SR = $34,778 x 25 = $869,450

Charles needs to accumulate a total of $869,450 by age 65.

Portfolio Survival Rate:

Tables 17.5 through 17.8 indicate portfolio survival rates based on actual market history. On the fixed income side, the net fixed income yield is the historical 6–month CD yield plus 0.5%. On the equity side, there are two different alphas, 0% and 1%.

Table 17.5: Portfolio survival rates, equity: S&P500, net alpha (after management fees) is 0%, net fixed income yield is 6–month CD plus 0.5%

Initial Withdrawal Rate	Time Horizon	Asset Mix: Equity/Fixed Income					
		0 / 100	20 / 80	40 / 60	60 / 40	80 / 20	100 / 0
		PROBABILITY OF SURVIVAL					
2%	40 years	100%	100%	100%	100%	100%	84%
3%	20 years	100%	100%	100%	100%	100%	97%
	30 years	87%	99%	100%	100%	85%	65%
	40 years	76%	85%	91%	76%	65%	56%
4%	20 years	97%	100%	100%	99%	86%	70%
	30 years	78%	78%	73%	59%	50%	46%
	40 years	31%	37%	29%	38%	40%	34%
6%	10 years	100%	100%	100%	100%	100%	97%
	20 years	69%	59%	51%	51%	49%	47%
	30 years	4%	5%	8%	15%	18%	18%
	40 years	0%	0%	0%	1%	3%	4%
8%	10 years	99%	100%	99%	94%	88%	82%
	20 years	8%	17%	24%	25%	26%	26%
	30 years	0%	0%	0%	0%	0%	4%
10%	10 years	80%	83%	81%	72%	66%	62%
	20 years	0%	0%	0%	0%	0%	0%

Table 17.6: Portfolio survival rates, equity: S&P500, net alpha (after management fees) is 1%, net fixed income yield is 6–month CD plus 0.5%

Initial Withdrawal Rate	Time Horizon	Asset Mix: Equity/Fixed Income 0 / 100	20 / 80	40 / 60	60 / 40	80 / 20	100 / 0
		PROBABILITY OF SURVIVAL					
2%	40 years	100%	100%	100%	100%	100%	99%
3%	20 years	100%	100%	100%	100%	100%	99%
	30 years	100%	100%	100%	100%	97%	79%
	40 years	76%	87%	97%	93%	78%	66%
4%	20 years	97%	100%	100%	99%	86%	70%
	30 years	78%	81%	83%	74%	62%	54%
	40 years	31%	46%	41%	49%	49%	47%
6%	10 years	100%	100%	100%	100%	100%	99%
	20 years	69%	66%	58%	56%	55%	53%
	30 years	4%	5%	18%	22%	27%	26%
	40 years	0%	0%	1%	4%	12%	21%
8%	10 years	99%	100%	99%	96%	91%	85%
	20 years	8%	17%	27%	30%	34%	34%
	30 years	0%	0%	0%	1%	5%	15%
10%	10 years	80%	83%	82%	76%	71%	67%
	20 years	0%	1%	1%	7%	16%	17%

Table 17.7: Portfolio survival rates, equity: SP/TSX, net alpha (after management fees) is 0%, net fixed income yield is 6–month CD plus 0.5%

Initial Withdrawal Rate	Time Horizon	Asset Mix: Equity/Fixed Income 0 / 100	20 / 80	40 / 60	60 / 40	80 / 20	100 / 0
		PROBABILITY OF SURVIVAL					
2%	40 years	100%	100%	100%	100%	100%	98%
3%	20 years	100%	100%	100%	100%	100%	99%
	30 years	100%	100%	100%	100%	97%	93%
	40 years	76%	82%	90%	94%	88%	82%
4%	20 years	97%	100%	100%	100%	97%	96%
	30 years	78%	71%	83%	81%	75%	66%
	40 years	31%	47%	47%	49%	51%	53%
6%	10 years	100%	100%	100%	100%	100%	99%
	20 years	69%	72%	71%	65%	62%	58%
	30 years	4%	7%	7%	12%	19%	19%
	40 years	0%	0%	0%	0%	0%	10%
8%	10 years	99%	100%	100%	100%	96%	92%
	20 years	8%	14%	12%	19%	12%	20%
	30 years	0%	0%	0%	0%	0%	3%
10%	10 years	80%	86%	89%	85%	78%	76%
	20 years	0%	0%	0%	0%	1%	6%

Table 17.8: Portfolio survival rates, equity: SP/TSX, net alpha (after management fees) is 1%, net fixed income yield is 6–month CD plus 1%

Initial Withdrawal Rate	Time Horizon	Asset Mix: Equity/Fixed Income 0 / 100	20 / 80	40 / 60	60 / 40	80 / 20	100 / 0
		PROBABILITY OF SURVIVAL					
2%	40 years	100%	100%	100%	100%	100%	100%
3%	20 years	100%	100%	100%	100%	100%	99%
	30 years	100%	100%	100%	100%	98%	97%
	40 years	76%	82%	98%	98%	96%	94%
4%	20 years	97%	100%	100%	100%	99%	96%
	30 years	78%	80%	86%	95%	86%	81%
	40 years	31%	59%	63%	67%	73%	71%
6%	10 years	100%	100%	100%	100%	100%	99%
	20 years	69%	77%	77%	74%	70%	72%
	30 years	4%	7%	17%	31%	37%	34%
	40 years	0%	0%	0%	2%	14%	18%
8%	10 years	99%	100%	100%	100%	96%	92%
	20 years	8%	19%	20%	26%	39%	38%
	30 years	0%	0%	0%	0%	2%	12%
10%	10 years	80%	87%	90%	86%	84%	78%
	20 years	0%	0%	0%	0%	4%	10%

Conclusion:

Don't confuse the average portfolio growth rate with the sustainable withdrawal rate, they are two different things. The answer to the question, "How much can I take out of my portfolio?" is not a pleasant one: "A lot less than you think".

I admit; there are too many tables and numbers in this chapter. In my live presentations, I have to keep things simple. So, I show the following table in my presentations:

Table 17.9: Simplified sustainable withdrawal rates[42]

Time Horizon	Sustainable Withdrawal Rate for USA	Sustainable Withdrawal Rate for Canada
20 years	5.2%	5.6%
30 years	3.8%	4.3%
40 years	3.1%	3.7%

Table 17.10: Simplified sustainable asset multipliers, the portfolio size required for a $10,000 annual income fully indexed to CPI

Time Horizon	Sustainable Asset Multiplier for USA	Sustainable Asset Multiplier for Canada
	Minimum Portfolio Size Required for $10,000 annual income indexed fully to CPI, maximum 10% probability of depletion	
20 years	$192,300	$178,600
30 years	$263,200	$232,600
40 years	$322,600	$270,300

Do not round up the sustainable withdrawal rate to an even 4%. We have seen earlier in "Mathematics of Loss" (page 96) that for Bob III's portfolio, a difference of 0.3% can make a difference between $2 million or nothing over 21 years.

42 You will find slight differences in the SWR in my earlier publications and articles. That is because the SWR will vary depending on portfolio costs and fees, dividend yield, asset mix, etc.

Chapter 18

How Much Alpha Do You Need?

Many of the ideas in this book came from questions asked by some very smart advisors at my workshops. As the boomer wave rolls from accumulation stage into the retirement stage, advisors are more and more eager to learn about distribution planning. In one of my meetings, one advisor asked me: "Are you are telling me that I can only take out 3.8%? What if I hold the best managed funds, the funds with the highest alpha?" Good question.

Let's first define alpha: It is a measure of how a portfolio performs relative to the market, the so–called "excess return". It is a common measure of assessing a manager's performance compared to a benchmark index.

For the purpose of keeping it simple, I will lump together all factors that affect this excess return. What are the factors that increase alpha? The dividends received, proper diversification and the manager's talent, all increase alpha. On the other hand, management fees, portfolio fees and charges, mismanagement and bad luck, all decrease the alpha.

For example, say your benchmark is the S&P500 index. In a particular year, it returns 8%. During the same year, your equity portfolio has a net return of 10%. In this case, your alpha is 2%, calculated as 10% less 8%. This includes all dividends, expenses, fees, talent, luck, and –yes– stupidities for that entire year.

You have a certain amount of savings to finance your retirement. You need to withdraw periodically from these savings. If your withdrawals are less than or equal to the sustainable withdrawal rate mentioned in the previous chapter (Table 17.9), then index funds may be just fine for you. Otherwise, your portfolio needs to beat the index. The question is: what is the minimum alpha to create a lifelong income?

Here is the problem: In the long term, over 80% of actively managed funds do not beat the index. If you want to have an alpha greater than zero, then fund selection becomes a critical issue for generating lifelong income.

Here is an example: Jamie, 65, is just retiring. He has $1 million in his portfolio. He needs $30,000 from his portfolio each year, indexed to CPI until the end of his life. For planning purposes, we use age 95 as the age of death. His asset mix is 40% S&P500 and 60% fixed income. Figure 18.1 depicts the aftcast.

Figure 18.1: The aftcast of 3% initial withdrawal rate since 1900

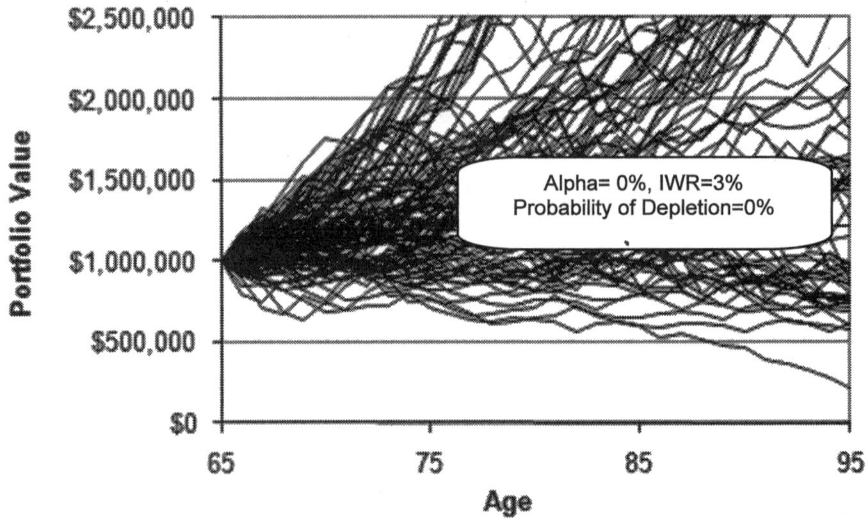

If Jamie had just the index return on his equity investments, he would have lifelong income. After 30 years in retirement, he would leave a sizable estate somewhere between $200,000 and $6.8 million, depending on his luck. So, in addition to retirement planning, you also need to do estate planning and tax planning. This is the good news.

We can go a little further than that. We decrease alpha until the probability of depletion at the age of death reaches 10%. This alpha would then indicate by how much the equity portion of Jamie's portfolio can safely underperform the S&P500 index. I know, I know, nobody plans to underperform the index, but let's calculate it anyways.

Market history shows us that if Jamie were to attain an alpha of negative 4.5% for 30 years, he would still have lifelong income, as depicted in Figure 18.2. So, this is the "Minimum Required Alpha" for lifelong income.

Figure 18.2: The aftcast of 3% initial withdrawal rate using the minimum required alpha (minus 4.5%)

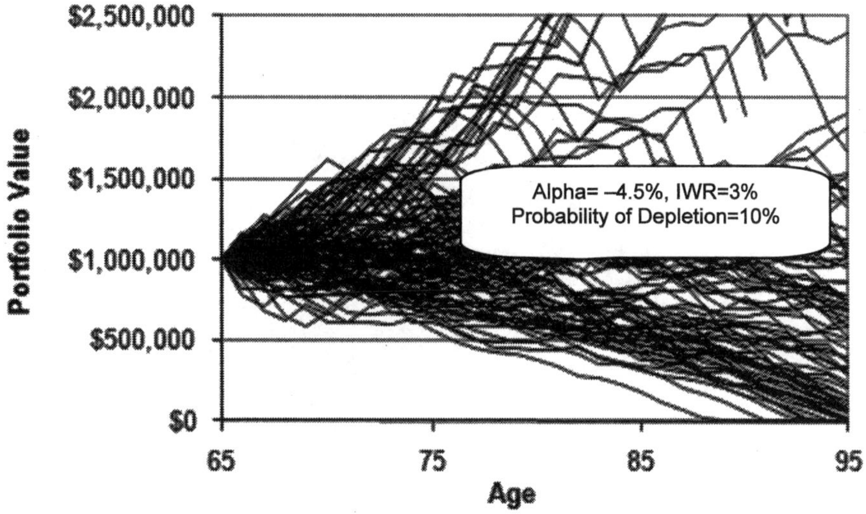

In this example, Jamie was lucky; he only needed $30,000 from his portfolio. Most of us need larger withdrawals.

What if Jamie were to need $50,000 at age 65, indexed to CPI annually for 30 years? This is an initial withdrawal rate of 5%. Now the plot thickens. Figure 18.3 depicts the outcome. The probability of depletion is 68% at age 95. Not a pretty figure is it.

So, Jamie`s equity portfolio needs to perform better than the index. How much higher alpha does he need so that the probability of depletion remains below 10% at age 95? The aftcast shoes a whopping 5.3%! Figure 18.4 depicts this aftcast.

Figure 18.3: The aftcast of 5% initial withdrawal rate, alpha = 0

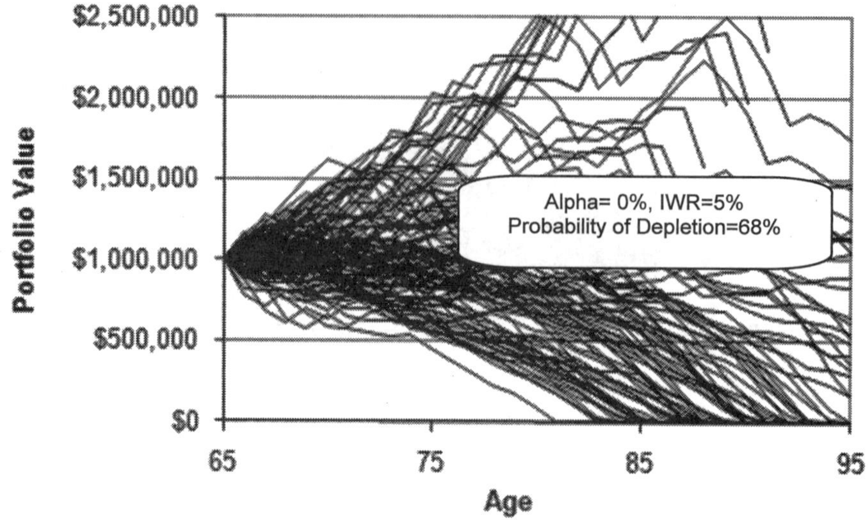

Figure 18.4: The aftcast of 5% initial withdrawal rate, alpha = +5.3%

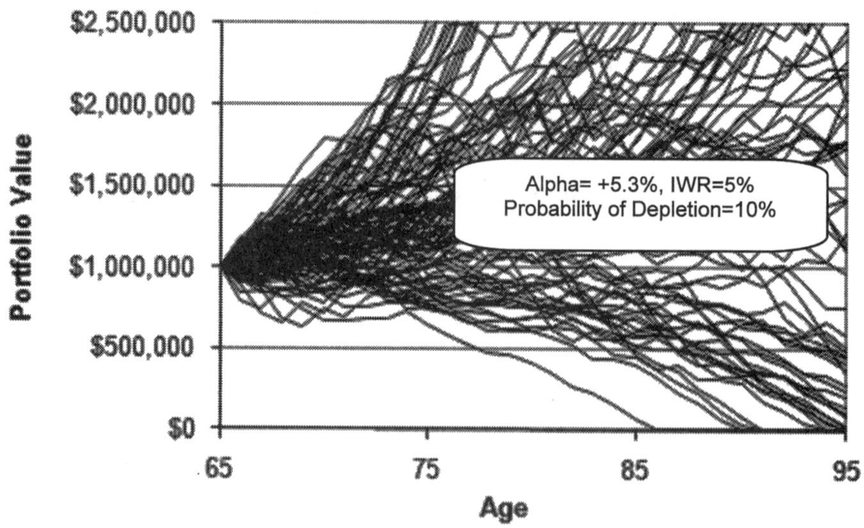

Similarly, I calculated the minimum required alpha for various initial withdrawal rates and various time horizons. Table 18.1 shows the results:

Table 18.1: Minimum required alpha

Initial Withdrawal Rate	Minimum Required Alpha for Retirement Time Horizon		
	20 years	30 years	40 years
3%	–11.8%	–4.5%	–0.8%
4%	–5.5%	+0.8%	+3.6%
5%	+0.1%	+5.3%	+7.5%
6%	+5.0%	+9.3%	+11.1%

This table quantifies what most of us already know:

- The higher the withdrawal rate, the higher is the required alpha for the same time horizon.
- The longer the time horizon, the higher is the required alpha for the same initial withdrawal rate.

Figure 18.5 depicts this table in a visual format. Now, you can make a clear and precise decision about choosing between the index funds versus actively managed funds in your retirement portfolio:

- If the minimum required alpha is 0% or less, then you can successfully use the index fund in your portfolio for lifelong income. For example, for a 30–year time horizon, if the initial withdrawal rate is less than about 3.8%, you can use the index fund for a lifelong income.
- If the minimum required alpha is above 0% (the gray–shaded area on the chart), then index funds will likely not give you a lifelong income. You need actively managed equity portfolios and/or strategies that can deliver this minimum alpha, and nothing less.

Figure 18.5: The minimum required alpha for various initial withdrawal rates and time horizons

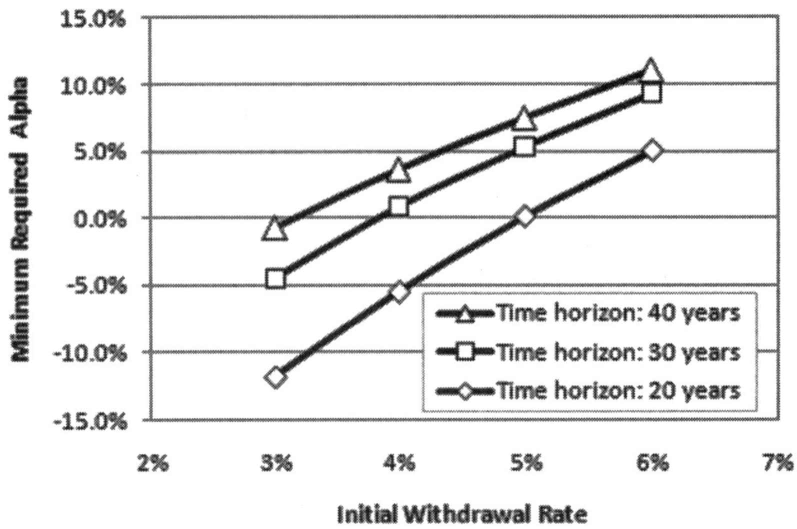

Going back to Jamie's example, he wants a 5% initial withdrawal rate for 30 years. For that, he needs to find a portfolio manager who can deliver an alpha of +5.3% for the next 30 years. This is not easy. The law of averages tells me that I'd be better off exporting the risk to an insurance company by buying a life annuity at such high withdrawal rates than trying to chase the star fund managers.

The Effect of Beta:

Let's complete this chapter by introducing another Greek letter, beta. It measures the volatility of a portfolio in relation to a benchmark. If beta is 1 then the portfolio moves exactly the same as the benchmark, if it is 0.5 it has half of the volatility of the market. Using the same methodology, I calculated the effect of beta on the minimum required alpha. Table 18.2 shows the minimum required alpha for various initial withdrawal rates, time horizon and beta.

Essentially, a lower beta requires a higher alpha. That is mostly because of how the index moves. Generally, it takes a longer time for the index to go up than to go down for the same percentage change. The downward moves are usually sharper than the upward moves, like the edge of a carpenter's saw, held upside down. That means if you reduce the volatility (beta) then you need to increase the average upward slope (alpha) because withdrawals are exposed to a lesser benefit of the upside move, where more time is spent.

Therefore, if you want to suppress the volatility of your investments to reduce your anxiety, you would need to work harder to increase the alpha. You have to decide for your own situation which objective is easier to attain: a high alpha/low beta combination or a low alpha/high beta combination. It is not an easy choice; each has its own limitations and constraints. Depending on what combination works for you, you then need to optimize[43] the asset mix accordingly. One thing is for sure: if you follow a "buy–and–hold" strategy, index funds will not make the cut for most retirees. And, if you hunt for alpha through mutual funds, the vast majority of them underperform the index. This is the "alpha–hunter's paradox".

Table 18.2: Minimum required alpha for various beta values

Initial Withdrawal Rate	Beta	Minimum Required Alpha for Retirement Time Horizon		
		20 years	30 years	40 years
3%	0.7	–11.1%	–3.0%	+0.5%
	1.0	–11.8%	–4.5%	–0.8%
	1.3	–12.2%	–5.1%	–1.4%
4%	0.7	–4.8%	+2.0%	+4.7%
	1.0	–5.5%	+0.8%	+3.6%
	1.3	–5.8%	+0.3%	+3.2%
5%	0.7	+0.7%	+6.2%	+8.7%
	1.0	+0.1%	+5.3%	+7.5%
	1.3	–0.1%	+5.1%	+7.2%
6%	0.7	+5.4%	+10.4%	+12.5%
	1.0	+5.0%	+9.3%	+11.1%
	1.3	+4.8%	+9.1%	+10.9%

Conclusion:

If you are attempting to create lifelong income from your portfolio, now you know what you are up against: most retirees need a much higher alpha than what an index provides. Furthermore, reducing the beta of your equities does not improve the situation. The recent stampede from mutual funds to ETF's will not make a typical retirement plan workable either. It is just another "solution bubble" that will burst in time.

Instead of hoping and wishing to attain these performance levels throughout retirement, you should consider exporting your risk to insurance companies. Life can be too agonizing if you have to depend on your children for help, or worse, move in with them.

[43] Click on the "optimize" button on the Otar Retirement Calculator after entering your own alpha and beta.

Chapter 19

Optimum Asset Allocation – Accumulation Stage

After the market crash of 2000, many investors moved from pure equity to balanced funds. One of the benefits of holding balanced funds is that you can fall asleep at the switch for a few years and portfolios will not get hurt beyond the normal fluctuations.

The financial industry moved a step beyond the balanced funds. Target date funds were invented. These funds are designed to start with an aggressive asset mix and become more conservative over time. For example, if you are 35 years away from your retirement, they would typically start with 85% in equities and that would come down to 25% by age 65. Different fund companies follow different levels of asset mix, so you need to read the prospectus very carefully. The idea is, if I buy these funds, I can then fall asleep at the switch not only for a few years, but a few decades. Is this a good strategy? In this chapter, we look at that.

There are three stages during accumulation: seed money formation stage, mid–life growth stage and pre–retirement consolidation stage.

Figure 19.1: Life stages during accumulation:

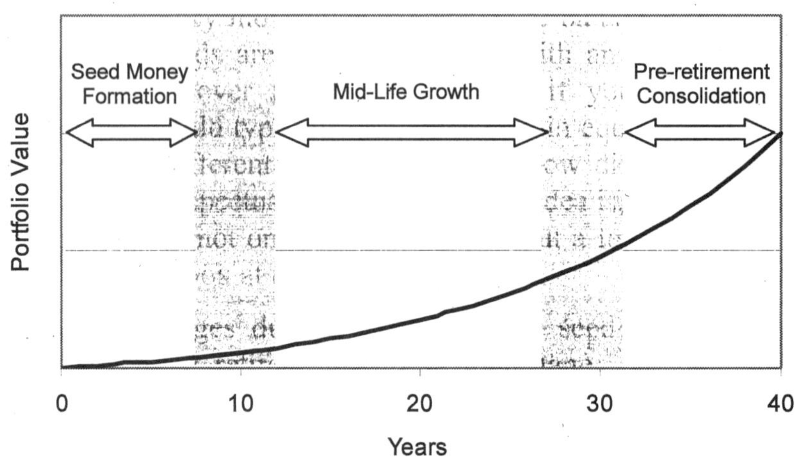

Seed Money Formation:

At this stage, the objective is to accumulate sufficient seed money to create a base for future growth. Some people start saving for retirement in their 20's, some start later. Generally, the range is between the ages of 20 and 40. I don't want to be the bearer of bad news, but if you do not accumulate the seed money by age 40, then it will likely be too late to grow sufficient assets by age 65. Of course, you may get lucky and receive an inheritance, marry a rich spouse or write a book on retirement that sells a million copies. But these are exceptions.

This stage should be considered complete when you have saved twice your estimated post–retirement withdrawals. For example, you might estimate that you need $60,000 per year at retirement in current dollars. If the projected government benefits provide $15,000 annually, then you need $45,000 from your portfolio upon retirement. Since the target at the seed money formation stage is to save twice as much as the post–retirement withdrawals, then this stage is completed once your savings exceed $90,000.

In theory, income earners with a pension plan need a smaller amount of savings to finance their retirement. However, companies and pension plans are not infallible; many are already in trouble. So, having a pension plan should not stop you from setting a larger target, if you can. If it turns out that you don't need these savings in the future, you can use them to finance other dreams.

The seed formation stage is your most important and most vulnerable stage. Because there is little money in the account, you may easily be swayed from your long–term objectives. You may think that you'll never be able to save enough money at this rate. Or, you may be discouraged by the market's ups and downs. Family expenses and unfavorable career changes can make this process even more difficult.

Many researchers and academics consider the time horizon as the most important asset allocation factor. Conventional asset allocation guidelines point to an aggressive portfolio consisting of 70% to 90% equities for younger investors, just because this group has a longer time horizon. Ignore any such counsel.

While the time horizon is an important factor, in real life, behavioral risk is probably a more important factor at this stage. An investor with little investment experience is more likely to make wrong decisions based on emotions. The largest risk here is short–term losses that might scare the inexperienced investor out of the market. Once out, it may take years to gather enough confidence to return to investing, perhaps not until the late stages of the next bull market. After some experience with investing, about two market cycles later (about eight to ten years), this behavioral risk might decrease to a more manageable level.

Your investments might be a small amount at this point; this is *all* the money that you have saved *all* your life. You would perceive any loss to your seed money as a big loss. It does not matter how diligently you might have educated yourself about the benefits of long–term investing, when your dream is bruised, it is hard to recover.

Figure 19.2: Typical risk levels:

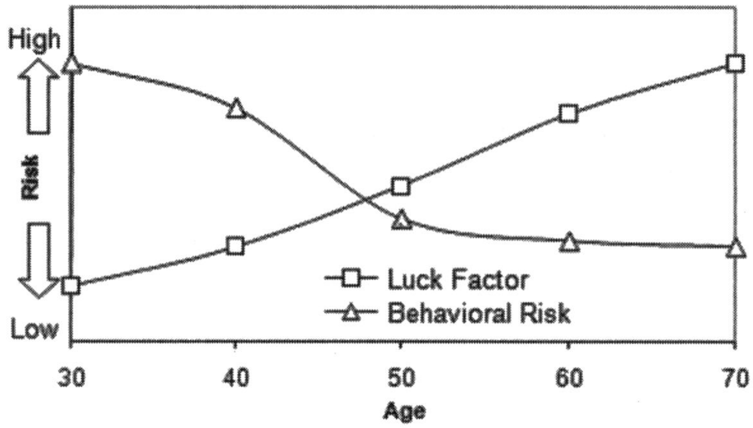

Picture this: you just have your first baby boy. His average life expectancy is 84 years. Being overjoyed, you grab the baby and start tossing him up towards the ceiling, over and over again. Everyone witnessing this dangerous spectacle in the delivery room is screaming at you, in shock. Finally, you stop and explain: "Why should I worry? His life expectancy is 84 years. He has a long time horizon!" Well, not so, if *you* put the poor baby at undue risk.

As absurd as this scenario may appear to you, this is exactly what the financial industry counsels you to do when your portfolio is only a "baby", i.e. during the seed money formation years. Remember, when you don't have much money, an advisor might not be able to spend much time with you; it just does not pay. Your entire education process might consist of one single sentence: "You have a long time horizon young man, be aggressive!" Not knowing any better, you sign all the papers that he pushes in front of you on his way out to the next meeting.

I suggest that you do the opposite of the conventional wisdom; be conservative with your seed money. Do not waste it. Do not take big chances. You may have a long time horizon, but you can take advantage of it only if you have the staying power. Using the rule of 72, if your portfolio grows annually at 8%, then that means it doubles every 9 years. If you lose half of your seed money, you need an additional 9 years to catch up with that loss at the other end, at least in theory. The financial establishment will love you more if you have to linger in the accumulation stage, even for a few additional years.

Assume you have a balanced portfolio growing at 6% annually. If you start with nothing in your account and save 15% of your income regularly, it takes five years and ten months until the account value exceeds your annual earnings. On the other hand, a more aggressive portfolio that grows at 10% per year will reach the same dollar amount in five years and four months.

The difference between the two portfolios is six months. In other words, 91% of the portfolio growth can be attributed to your discipline of investing and only 9% is attributable to the difference in the growth rate (the difference of six months divided by 5 years and 10 months). Skipping a few months of deposits at this seed formation stage will hurt the portfolio ten times more than the modesty of its growth rate. During this stage it almost does not matter how much your portfolio grows, so stay conservative.

According to the US–based TIAA–CREF Institute[44], a surprisingly high number of young people invest in low–interest bearing fixed accounts. They are instinctively doing the wise thing, which is preserving their seed money as best as they can. Unfortunately, the wise men of the financial establishment find this "inefficient".

Let's look at market history to compare two different asset allocation strategies at the seed formation stage: Target Date Asset Allocation and Graduated Asset Allocation.

<u>Target Date Asset Allocation (TDAA):</u> In this portfolio, the asset mix is 85/15 (85% of the portfolio is invested in equities and 15% in fixed income) during the first eight years. After that, it is 70/30.

Figure 19.3 Target date asset allocation

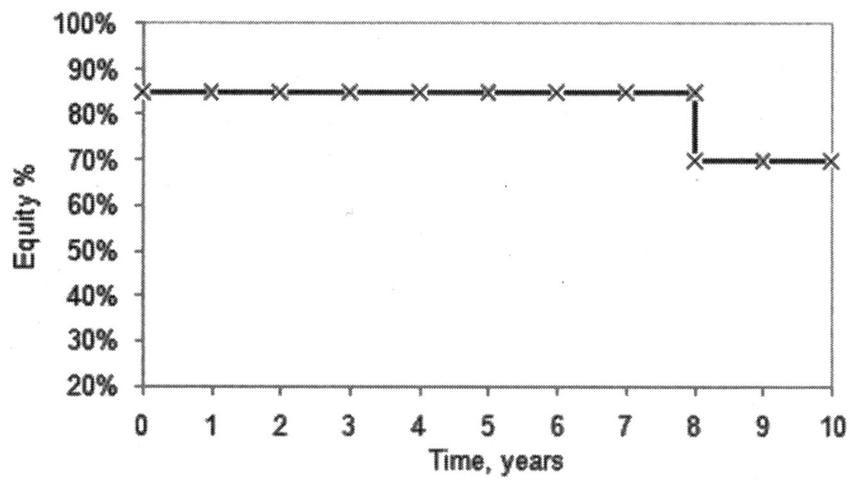

---

[44] Jacob S. Rugh, "Premium and Asset Allocations of Premium–Paying TIAA–CREF Participants as of March 31, 2004" TIAA–CREF Institute, www.tiaa–crefinstitute.org

Graduated Asset Allocation (GAA): Here is my suggestion for the seed formation stage. It reduces the behavioral risk during the early years and enables the investor to stick to his plan. This is how it works:

- Figure out your long–term asset allocation. Say, it is 70/30 equity/fixed income. This will be your asset mix in 8 years, but not yet, not now.
- Start with a 30/70–asset mix. Keep this conservative asset mix for four years.
- After 4 years, increase the equity allocation to halfway between the current (30%) and the long term (70%). In this case, the half way of the 30% and 70% is 50%. Keep this 50/50 mix for the following 4 years.
- After 8 years, set the asset allocation to 70/30, your long–term mix.

Figure 19.4 Graduated asset allocation

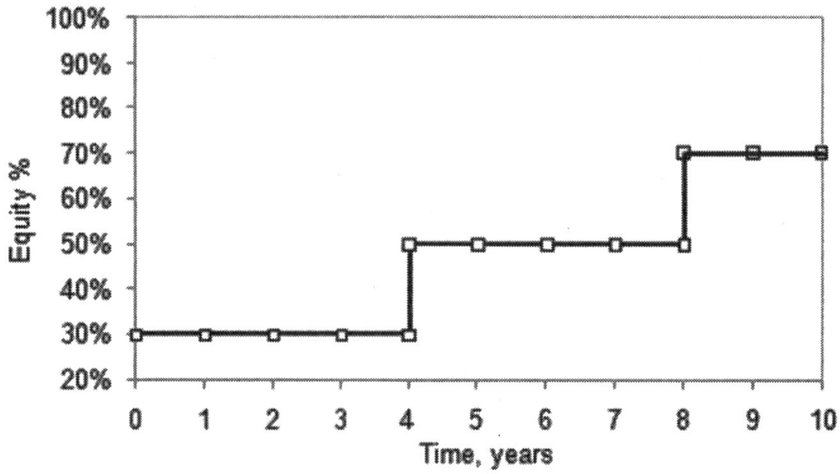

The most important element during the seed money formation years is to invest with discipline, month after month, year after year. The reduced volatility of a conservative portfolio will give you much–needed staying power. Once this critical survival period is over, then you have more experience to handle volatility with a larger portfolio and you will be more understanding of how markets work.

Yes, you might give up some potential for higher growth. By the same token, you will also avoid higher potential losses, which might tempt you to abandon your long–term plans. Abandoning the long term plan is much more damaging than the small benefit derived from a potentially higher growth rate at this stage. Wall Street would not care less about your losses. Ignore their drummers.

Let's look at an example using historical market data.

Example 19.1

Steve is just starting to save for his retirement. He is planning to save $10,000 each year for the next 8 years.

In the first case, according to his target date asset allocation guidelines, the asset mix is 85% equities (S&P500) and 15% fixed income.

In the second case, he follows the graduated asset allocation strategy. During the first four years his asset mix is 30/70 (S&P500/Fixed Income). During the subsequent 4 years, it is 50/50.

In both cases, his asset mix is rebalanced annually.

Here are the portfolio values after eight years for each strategy, based on market history for his total deposits of $80,000 over 8 years:

	Portfolio Value at the end of 8 years	
	Target Date AA 85/15 - First 8 years	Graduated AA 30/70 - first 4 years 50/50 - the next 4 years
Median Portfolio	$97,083	$96,863
Worst Case Portfolio	$50,421	$67,875

The median portfolio value of the aggressive TDAA portfolio was only $220 more than the more conservative GAA portfolio. This is only a 0.2% difference. To put this in perspective, this amounts to 8 days of deposits!

What if things go bad? The TDAA portfolio lost $29,579 ($80,000 less $50,421), or 3.7 years of deposits. On the other hand, the GAA portfolio showed a loss of $12,125, a 59% lower loss than with TDAA. This may be just enough for Steve not to abandon his long-term goals, while sacrificing almost nothing under "normal" conditions, i.e. the median outcome.

Median Portfolio Value:

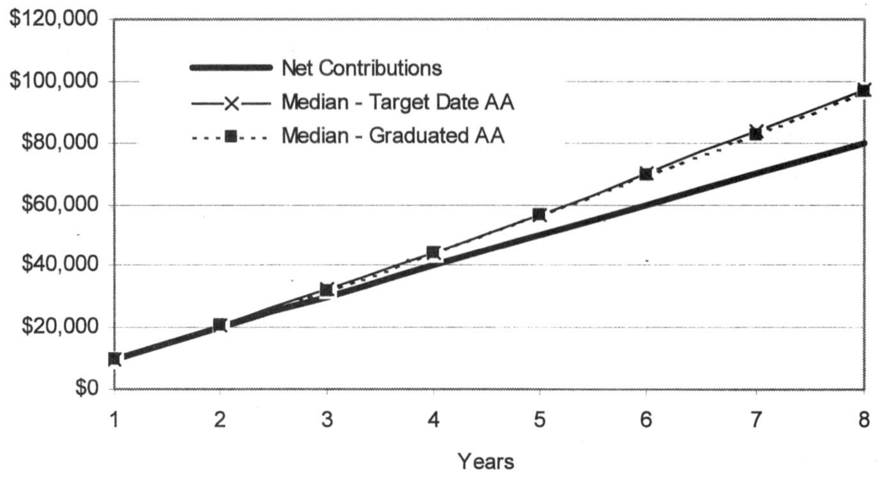

Worst Case Portfolio Value:

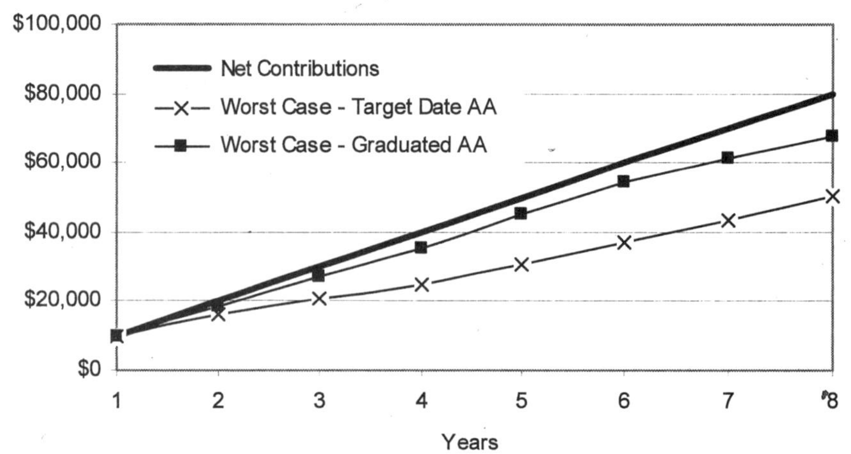

You might wonder why I suggest an 8–year time period. It covers approximately two market cycles. This should provide enough time to accumulate the seed money that you require. If you cannot save 15% of your annual income each year during this stage, you will need to spend more time to cross this finish line.

Having survived this most vulnerable stage without permanent scars, you are now ready to proceed to the next stage, the mid–life growth.

Mid–Life Growth:

The mid–life growth years are generally between ages 35 and 60. The emphasis during this stage is to focus on the long term goals and to continue saving. At this point, you have a good idea of where you are going with your life goals. Your portfolio moved from its most vulnerable "baby" stage to its "youth" stage. Now, it can grow faster.

The mid–life growth stage is complete when the asset to withdrawal ratio reaches twenty. For example; if you need $50,000/year from the portfolio after retirement and have $1,000,000 in your portfolio, this ratio is twenty; our mid–life growth stage is completed.

Over the last 75 years, great advances were made in investment research. While many strategies, methods and tools help the investor to make better investment choices, the importance of the luck factor should not be ignored. Historically, the market spent about 43% its time in secular bullish trends. The rest of the time, it just meandered sideways or went down. You should always keep in mind, in spite of great strides in investment research; the element of luck is still the most important factor.

The objective during the mid–life growth stage is to maximize median portfolio growth. Based on that, the optimum asset mix for the mid–life growth stage (including some effect of dollar–cost averaging) is depicted in Tables 19.1 and 19.2 for US and Canadian investors.

Table 19.1: Optimum asset mix during the mid–life growth stage, equity: S&P500, fixed income: historical 6–month CD yield plus 1%

Time Horizon	Equity	Fixed Income
10 years	50%	50%
20 years	60%	40%
30 years	70%	30%

Table 19.2: Optimum asset mix during the mid–life growth stage, equity: SP/TSX, fixed income: historical 6–month CD yield plus 1%

Time Horizon	Equity	Fixed Income
10 years	65%	35%
20 years	80%	20%
30 years	85%	15%

Example 19.2:

Steve is 35. He has $100,000 in his portfolio. He is adding $10,000 each year to his portfolio. What is his optimum asset allocation for the next 20 years? Assume he uses S&P500 as his equity proxy.

Using Table 19.1, his optimum asset mix is 60% equity and 40% fixed income.

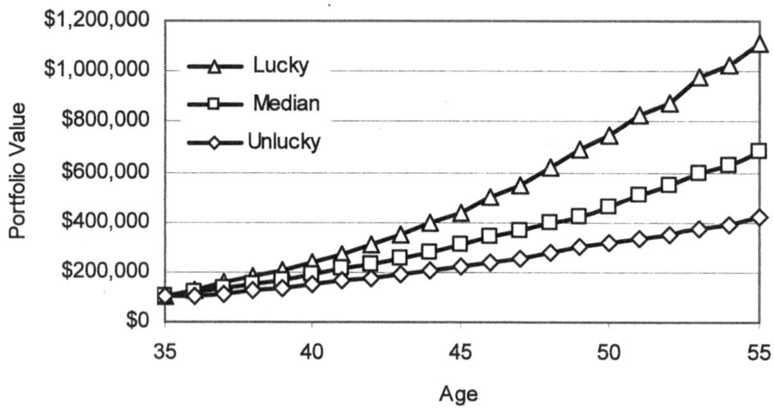

Even though the asset mix is optimum, the larger factor is luck. Based on market history, at age 55, Steve could end up with $421,000 if he is unlucky. On the other hand, if he catches a secular bullish trend, he might end up with over $1.1 million.

Pre–Retirement Consolidation:

Pre–retirement consolidation usually occurs between ages 55 and 70. Most of the capital formation, whether it is the investment portfolio, real estate or business, is completed during this stage. Your portfolio value goes from twenty times to thirty times of your estimated post–retirement withdrawals.

If you have been saving diligently over the years, when you enter this stage, you should have sufficient savings for a life annuity to provide you lifelong income. If you are still working or you are retired from work but do not need periodic income from your savings, this will allow your portfolio to grow further. Taking the portfolio from twenty times to thirty times of your estimated post–retirement withdrawals, will allow you to finance your retirement totally from your portfolio without the need of life annuities. This will also give you the opportunity to accumulate for your legacy.

Here, the first task is to preserve the funds. Secondly, where possible, create some growth. The equity portion of the portfolio should be somewhere between what is indicated on tables 16.1 through 16.4 (the optimum asset mix during retirement) and what is indicated on tables 19.1 and 19.2, the asset mix for the mid–growth stage. For the U.S. portfolios, this optimum asset mix is 40/60 equity/fixed income. For the Canadian portfolios, it is 50/50.

If you have not been saving for retirement sufficiently or you were unlucky with your investments, then this stage can disappear entirely. In this case, you would go from the mid–life growth stage right into retirement with inadequate savings. If this applies to you, then you should consider nothing but life annuities for lifelong income. Unfortunately for the vast majority of retirees, this is the predicament.

Conclusion:

The following table summarizes the approximate optimum asset mix for different life stages as well as the milestones. Both tables are based on an initial withdrawal rate of 5% after retirement. If your numbers are somewhat different, don't worry; you can still use this table. You will be approximately right. As I mentioned a few times already, asset allocation is not the most important factor, but luck is.

Table 19.3: Optimum asset mix over the entire life cycle, US markets

Stage	Asset to Withdrawals Ratio	Equity S&P500	Fixed Income
Seed Money Formation	Under 1	30%	70%
	1 – 2	50%	50%
Mid–Life Growth	2 – 10	70%	30%
	11 – 16	60%	40%
	17 – 20	50%	50%
Pre–Retirement Consolidation	20–30	40%	60%
Retirement (See Table 16.1 for further breakdown of asset classes)		30%	70%

Figure 19.5: Suggested equity percentage over the life of the perfect saver, US markets

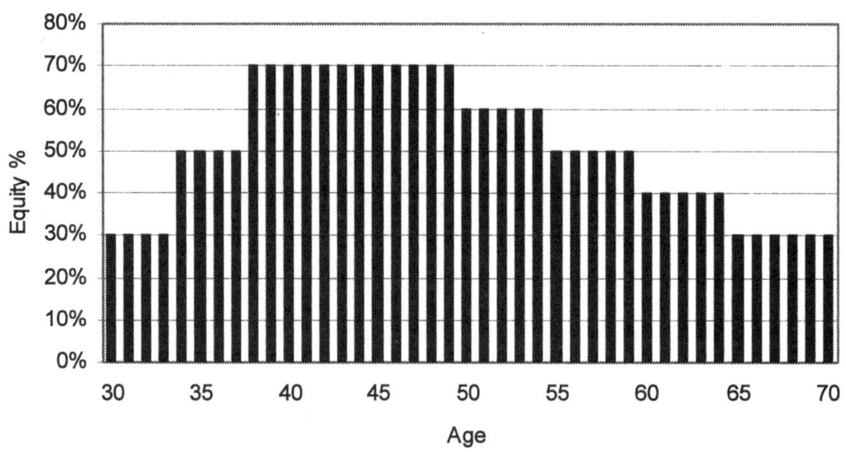

The following table summarizes the approximate optimum asset mix for Canadian readers.

Table 19.4: Optimum asset mix over the entire life cycle, Canadian markets

Stage	Asset to Withdrawals Ratio	Equity SP/TSX	Fixed Income
Seed Money Formation	Under 1	30%	70%
	1 – 2	55%	45%
Mid–Life Growth	2 – 15	85%	15%
	16 – 20	65%	35%
Pre–Retirement Consolidation	20 – 30	50%	50%
Retirement (See Table 16.3 for further breakdown of asset classes)		40%	60%

Figure 19.6: Suggested equity percentage over the life of the perfect saver, Canadian markets

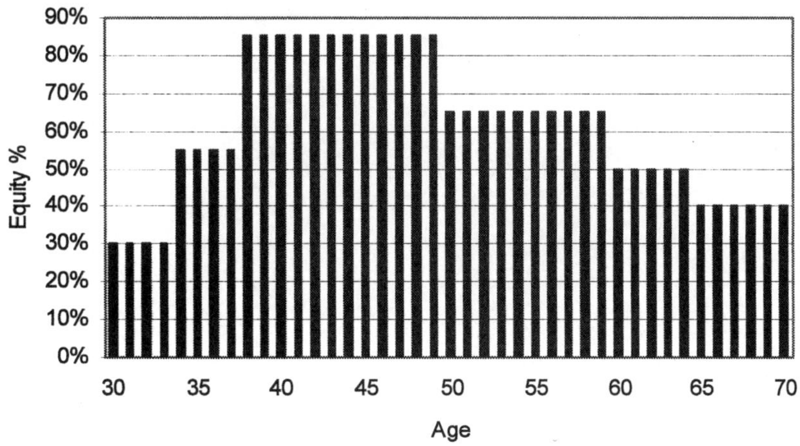

In conclusion, the keys to success during the accumulation stage are:

- Save religiously; put aside 15% of your income for your retirement each year, no matter what.
- Stay well within your own risk tolerance
- Keep yourself clear of risky investments and anything you don't totally understand, no matter how attractive they look
- Review your plan regularly

Chapter 20

Effective Growth Rate

So far, we have learned quite a bit about the market history and the time value of fluctuations. Now our question is: "Is there an effective growth rate that we can plug into a standard retirement calculator and make projections that are in line with the market's historical performance?"

The answer is a qualified "yes".

Distribution Portfolios:

There is not one single effective growth rate, but there are many to choose from, depending on several factors. Some of the important factors are: initial withdrawal rate, asset mix, and alpha.

The effective growth rate (EGR) is calculated by trial and error. First, we do an aftcast. Then we calculate out the lucky (top decile), median and the unlucky (bottom decile) asset values. Next, we calculate the effective growth rates using a standard retirement calculator until we match the lucky, median and unlucky asset values of the aftcast.

When we look at an aftcast, we observe that there are two possible outcomes: either the portfolio depletes within the retirement time horizon or it goes up in value (non–depleting).

- In depleting portfolios, the EGR is the growth rate that forecasts the same *portfolio longevity* as the historical outcome. This is shown in Figure 20.1, the upper chart.
- In non–depleting portfolios, the EGR is the growth rate that projects the same *portfolio dollar value* as the historical outcome at the end of 30 years. See the lower chart in Figure 20.1.

Keep in mind; the EGR is accurate in forecasting either the portfolio's longevity or its value in its 30th year, but it is not always accurate for the years in between. However, using the effective growth rate is a giant leap forward compared to using an "average" growth rate. That is because it includes all of the effects of the time value of fluctuations for the entire investment time horizon.

Figure 20.1: Effective growth rate versus historical outcomes

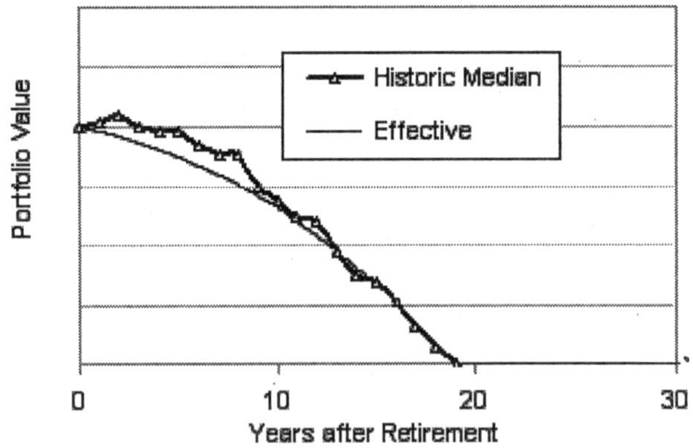

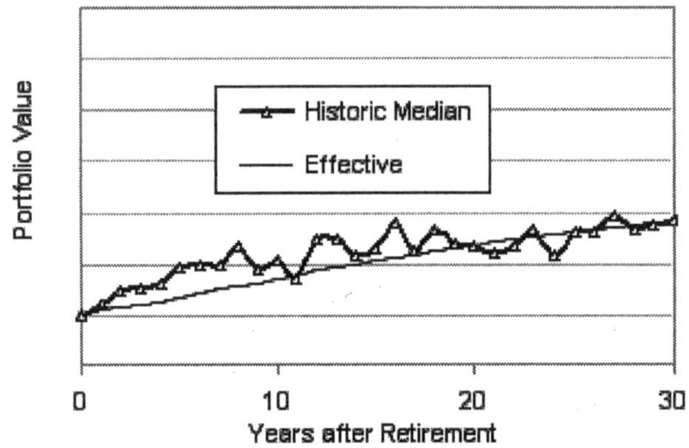

Table 20.1 shows the effective growth rate for various indices and distribution portfolios for all years of retirement between 1900 and 2008, inclusive[45]. Equity returns are the pure index return, conventional bond returns are the historical 6–month CD yield plus 0.5%, inflation index bond returns are historical inflation rate plus 1%.

If you are using a standard retirement calculator, take the EGR figure from Table 20.1, and enter 3% "average" inflation rate. This is the closest you can come to actual market history on your standard retirement calculator, probably better than any simulator.

The unlucky and lucky outcomes draw the envelope where 80% of outcomes can be expected. For retirement planning, the unlucky outcome should be used. For tax and estate planning, the median outcome should be used.

[45] For the SP/TSX, the market history starts in 1919. For the Nikkei225, the market history starts in 1914.

Table 20.1: Effective growth rate, distribution portfolios

Initial Withdrawal Rate	Portfolio	Outcome		
		Unlucky	Median	Lucky
		Effective Growth Rate:		
2%	S&P500	0.8%	4.9%	7.5%
	DJIA	1.4%	4.0%	7.3%
	SP/TSX	4.1%	5.8%	8.0%
	FTSE	–0.9%	4.5%	9.3%
	NIKKEI	2.0%	9.8%	16.0%
	50% S&P500, 50% Fixed Income	3.4%	5.2%	7.7%
	60% SP/TSX, 40% Fixed Income	4.5%	6.3%	7.2%
	100% Fixed Income	2.1%	5.0%	7.7%
	100% Inflation Indexed Bonds	3.0%	4.6%	5.6%
4%	S&P500	–2.0%	3.8%	7.7%
	DJIA	–1.7%	3.6%	6.8%
	SP/TSX	1.7%	5.2%	7.8%
	FTSE	–1.9%	4.1%	8.5%
	NIKKEI	–4.4%	9.4%	16.0%
	35% S&P500, 65% Fixed Income	3.4%	5.1%	6.5%
	45% SP/TSX, 55% Fixed Income	3.4%	5.6%	6.8%
	100% Fixed Income	1.0%	5.5%	6.7%
	100% Inflation Indexed Bonds	3.9%	4.1%	4.2%
6%	S&P500	–3.3%	4.2%	8.2%
	DJIA	–2.9%	4.4%	7.7%
	SP/TSX	0.4%	5.6%	8.1%
	FTSE	–2.7%	3.6%	7.3%
	NIKKEI	–5.8%	8.3%	16.0%
	25% S&P500, 75% Fixed Income	2.2%	4.9%	6.9%
	35% SP/TSX, 65% Fixed Income	3.0%	5.6%	7.1%
	100% Fixed Income	0.6%	5.5%	7.0%
	100% Inflation Indexed Bonds	3.6%	4.0%	4.5%
8%	S&P500	–3.6%	4.7%	9.4%
	DJIA	–3.7%	4.7%	9.3%
	SP/TSX	–0.2%	5.8%	9.2%
	FTSE	–2.7%	3.5%	9.5%
	NIKKEI	–6.7%	7.4%	15.7%
	20% S&P500, 80% Fixed Income	1.3%	5.6%	8.1%
	30% SP/TSX, 70% Fixed Income	2.7%	5.8%	7.9%
	100% Fixed Income	1.0%	5.6%	7.6%
	100% Inflation Indexed Bonds	3.3%	4.0%	4.6%
10%	S&P500	–4.5%	5.5%	11.0%
	DJIA	–4.2%	5.6%	10.9%
	SP/TSX	–1.4%	6.3%	9.5%
	FTSE	–3.6%	3.4%	10.4%
	NIKKEI	–6.2%	6.1%	16.0%
	20% S&P500, 80% Fixed Income	0.7%	5.8%	8.6%
	30% SP/TSX, 70% Fixed Income	2.6%	6.2%	8.3%
	100% Fixed Income	1.6%	5.5%	8.3%
	100% Inflation Indexed Bonds	2.9%	4.0%	4.7%

Example 20.1

Josh retires at age 60 with $1,000,000 in his investment portfolio. He invested 35% of his money in S&P500 and 65% in fixed income.

He withdraws $40,000 from his portfolio each year, indexed to inflation.

1. Calculate the portfolio life if Josh is unlucky.
2. Calculate the estate value at age 90 if Josh is lucky.

Josh's initial withdrawal rate is 4%, calculated as $40,000 divided by $1,000,000 expressed in percentage.

1. Look up the effective growth rate on Table 20.1 under the "unlucky" column, 4% initial withdrawal rate: it is 3.4%. Using an average growth rate of 3.4%, starting with one million dollars, withdrawing $40,000 per year indexed to 3% inflation, the standard retirement calculator predicts that Josh will have no money left in his portfolio at age 87, if he is unlucky.
2. Look up the effective growth rate under the "lucky" column: it is 6.5%. Using an average growth rate of 6.5%, starting with $1,000,000, withdrawing $40,000 per year indexed to 3% inflation, the standard retirement calculator predicts that Josh will have about $1.8 million at age 90, if he is lucky.

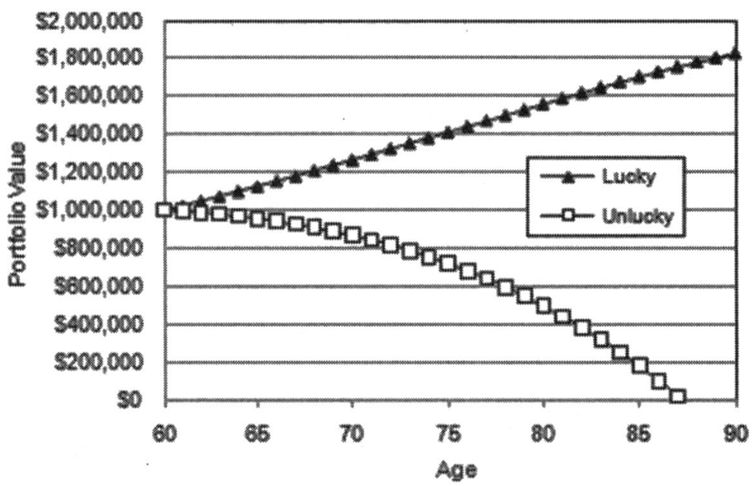

Based on market history, there is about an 80% chance that the outcome is somewhere in between these two lines.

Accumulation Portfolios:

In accumulation portfolios, dollar cost averaging (DCA) increases the effective growth rates. Tables 20.3 and 20.4 depict the values of EGR. The asset mix is taken from Tables 19.1 and 19.2, which is the optimum asset mix for the mid–life growth stage.

The EGR values in these tables are based on index return only. Because this an accumulation portfolio and dividends compound, if you are reinvesting dividends, then you have to add part of that to the indicated EGR. For example, if you reinvest an average of 2% dividend yield (net of all portfolio costs and management fees) of the equity portion of your portfolio and you have 60% of your portfolio in equities, then you need to add 1.2% to each figure, calculated as 60% of 2%.

Table 20.3: Effective growth rate, US accumulation portfolios, equity: S&P500

Time Horizon	Asset Mix (Equity/Fixed Income)	Outcome		
		Unlucky	Median	Lucky
		Effective Growth Rate:		
10 years	50/50	1.8%	5.6%	10.3%
20 years	60/40	2.2%	6.0%	9.3%
30 years	70/30	2.7%	6.0%	8.7%

Table 20.4: Effective growth rate, Canadian accumulation portfolios, equity: SP/TSX

Time Horizon	Asset Mix (Equity/Fixed Income)	Outcome		
		Unlucky	Median	Lucky
		Effective Growth Rate:		
10 years	65/35	1.3%	6.1%	9.9%
20 years	80/20	2.4%	7.0%	8.1%
30 years	85/15	5.0%	6.7%	7.7%

Example 20.2

Marilyn is 45. She currently has $100,000 in her retirement account. Her money is invested 60% S&P500 and 40% fixed income. How much money does she need to save each year to end up with $500,000 at age 65? Assume her equity dividend yield is 1.5% and that is reinvested.

1. For proper retirement planning, Marilyn needs to save enough money to cover the unlucky outcome. Look up Table 20.3, for the 20-year time horizon; the unlucky EGR is 2.2%. Add to this the benefit of dividends 0.90%, calculated as 60% of 1.5%. Now the EGR is 3.1%, including the reinvested dividends. Using a standard financial calculator, key in PV=-$100,000, I/YR=3.1, FV=$500,000, N=20. Press PMT, which calculates that Marilyn needs to save $11,635 each year. Do not clear the calculator.
2. The median growth rate from the table is 6%. With dividends, it is 6.9%. Enter 6.9% for I/YR, and pressing PYMT, Marilyn reads that she needs to save $2,964/year. Do not clear the calculator.
3. What if Marilyn gets lucky? The growth rate for the lucky portfolio is 9.3%. With dividends, it is 10.2%. Enter 10.2% for I/YR, 0 for PYMT, press FV; it is $697,641. If Marilyn knew in advance that she would be lucky, she would not need to add any more money to her investments and she would still end up with substantially more assets than her target.

Ideally, Marilyn should save $11,635 each year to cover the unlucky outcome, if she can. She should review her plan each year to see if she can reduce this amount and still meet her target.

In practice, she may not be able to save that much. If so, then she should at least save $2,964 annually, which is the amount necessary to meet the median outcome.

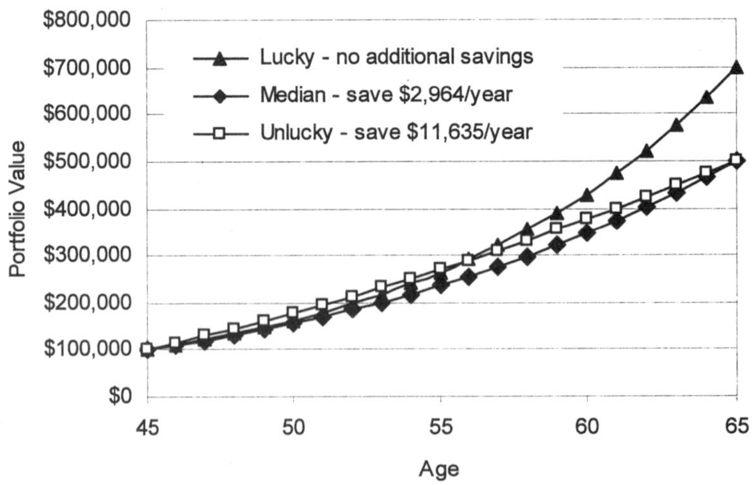

This example shows that, depending on what happens in the markets, Marilyn may need to deposit a lot of money, some money or no money at all to reach her target. Planning should start as early as possible. It should be followed up with an annual review to ensure adequate savings in changing market conditions.

Optimum Asset Allocation:

In Chapter 16, we discussed the optimum asset allocation for distribution portfolios. The effective growth rate can also help us to develop a better understanding of our asset allocation philosophy.

First, we want to know how a combination of two asset classes, equity and fixed income, can work together. We plot the effective growth rates of both asset classes for various initial withdrawal rates in Figure 20.2. The solid black area indicates the range of lucky and unlucky effective growth rates for fixed income. The white area indicates the range of lucky and unlucky effective growth rates for equities.

Figure 20.2: The range of effective growth rates for pure equity and pure fixed income portfolios. The top of each range indicates the effective growth rate for the lucky outcome. The bottom of each range indicates the effective growth rate for the unlucky outcome. Equity growth: historical S&P500 index. Fixed income yield: historical 6–month CD yield plus 0.5%.

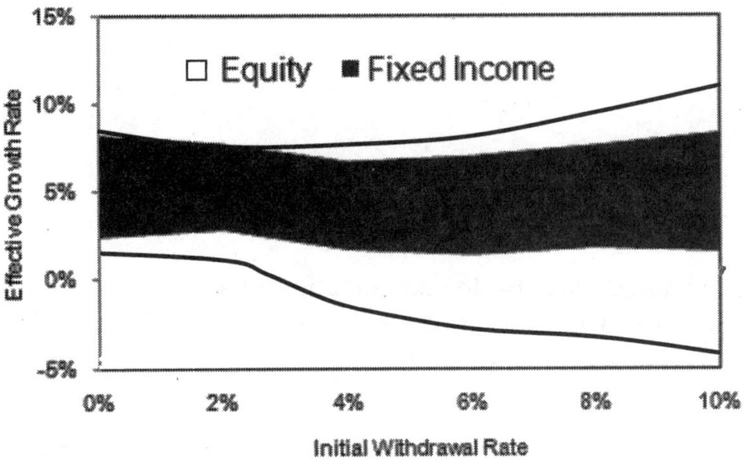

We do the same exercise by combining an equity portfolio and an inflation indexed bond portfolio (ILB). Figure 20.3 depicts the range of effective growth rates.

We observe that when the withdrawal rate is greater than 4%, the overlap is very narrow. The inflation indexed bonds provide a sharp “floor” against unlucky equity outcomes. This suggests that these two asset classes can be combined very effectively at higher withdrawal rates.

Figure 20.3: The range of effective growth rates for pure equity and pure inflation indexed bond portfolios. The top of each range indicates the effective growth rate for the lucky outcome. The bottom of each range indicates the effective growth rate for the unlucky outcome. Equity growth: historical S&P500 index. ILB yield: historical inflation rate plus 1%.

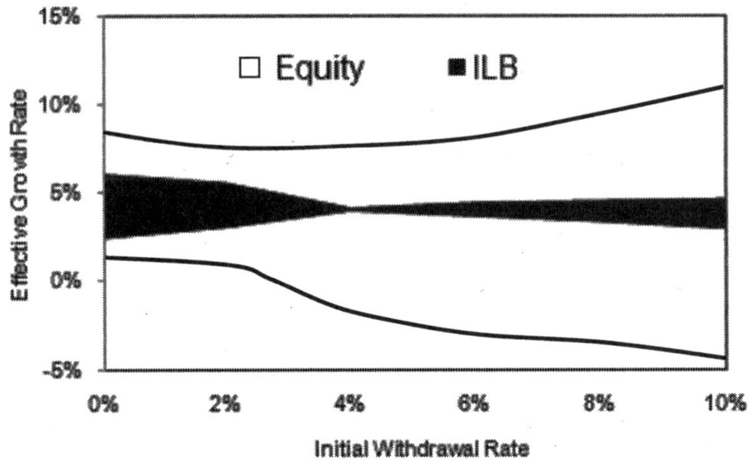

Finally, we plot a similar chart for the combination of an inflation indexed bond portfolio and a conventional fixed income portfolio, as depicted in Figure 20.4. For withdrawal rates under 4%, the conventional fixed income portfolio has a larger EGR. This indicates that at lower withdrawal rates, conventional fixed income can be a better choice.

However, once the withdrawal rate exceeds 4%, the range of effective growth rates of the inflation indexed bonds becomes narrower. Here, the inflation indexed bonds provide a “floor” against unlucky fixed income outcomes. The ILBs seem to provide a higher return when unlucky. This suggests that at higher withdrawal rates, the inflation indexed bonds should be preferred over conventional bonds in the fixed income portion of the portfolio.

Figure 20.4: The range of effective growth rates for pure equity and pure inflation indexed bond portfolios. The top of each range indicates the effective growth rate for the lucky outcome. The bottom of each range indicates the effective growth rate for the unlucky outcome. Fixed income yield: historical 6–month CD yield plus 0.5%. ILB yield: historical inflation rate plus 1%.

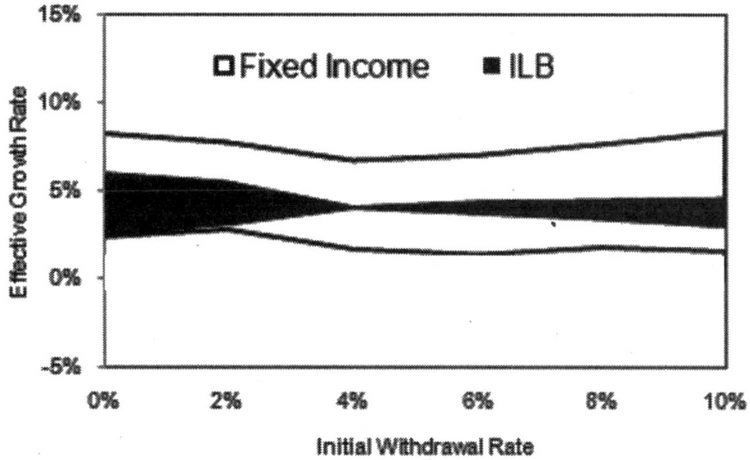

Minimum Mandatory Withdrawals:

When you invest money in a tax–sheltered retirement account, eventually the government likes to recapture the deferred taxes. Minimum mandatory withdrawals apply once you reach a certain age. How do these mandatory withdrawals affect assets and cash flow?

That depends on your assets and your withdrawals. On the asset side, you have three categories of outcome: lucky, median and unlucky. On the cash flow side, there are two categories of withdrawals: larger than the sustainable withdrawal rate (SWR) and smaller than SWR.

Let's first look at the scenario where a retiree needs less income than the SWR from a tax–sheltered account. In this case, he is forced to withdraw the minimum mandatory amount, which is usually higher than the SWR. He will likely have an excess income. If he does not spend it all, he can invest it in his open investment account.

Figure 20.5 depicts the difference in portfolio assets with and without the mandatory minimum withdrawal rates when the retiree only needs 2% IWR. We observe that the minimum mandatory withdrawal creates a lower portfolio value. This is true in all outcome categories, lucky, median or unlucky.

Next, we look at the situation where the required initial withdrawal rate is greater than the sustainable withdrawal rate. The retiree requires 6% IWR. Figure 20.6 depicts the difference of portfolio value over time for lucky, median and unlucky outcomes. The mandatory minimum withdrawals reduce the portfolio value only if the retiree is lucky. Otherwise, there is no perceivable difference in portfolio values. That is because the retiree is forced to withdraw more than he needs only in a lucky scenario.

Figure 20.5: The effect of mandatory minimum withdrawal rates (Uniform Distribution Table) on the all–equity portfolio value, the 65–year old retiree requires only 2% WR

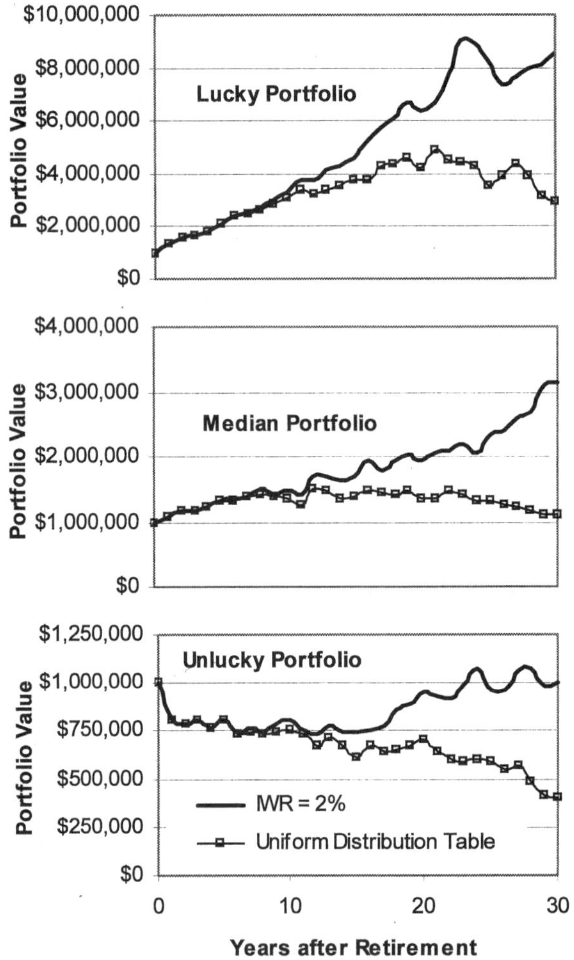

Figure 20.6: The effect of mandatory minimum withdrawal rates (Uniform Distribution Table) on the all–equity portfolio value, the 65–year old retiree requires only 6% WR

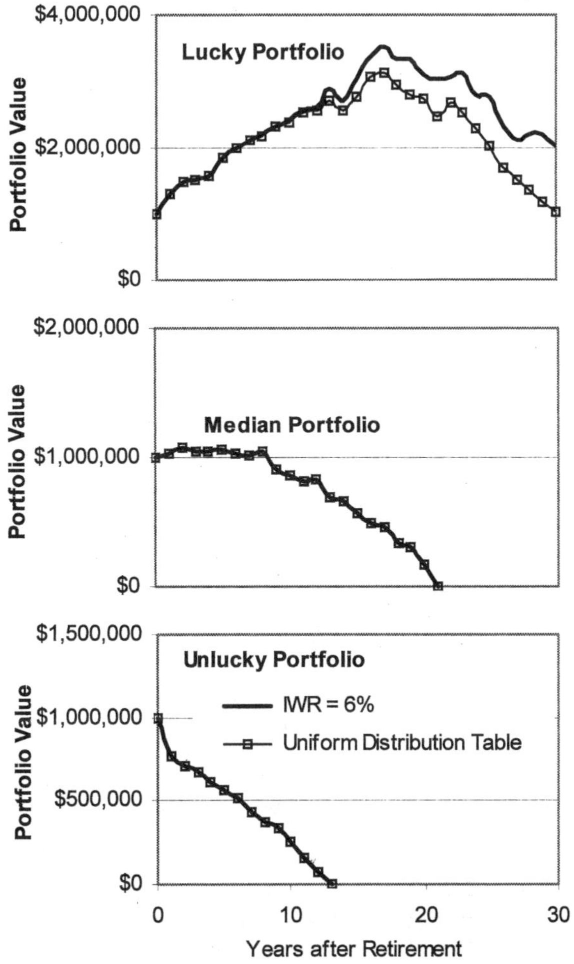

Here is the effect of minimum mandatory withdrawal:

- If the retiree is lucky *or* he needs less than the sustainable withdrawal rate, then the growth of his portfolio is reduced significantly in a tax–sheltered account.
- If the retiree needs more money than the sustainable withdrawal rate *and* is not lucky, then the mandatory minimum withdrawal rates have little or no effect on portfolio longevity.

Table 20.5: Effect of the minimum mandatory withdrawals

	Required withdrawals are less than SWR	Required withdrawals are larger than SWR
	Effect of Minimum Mandatory Withdrawals:	
Lucky	Significant	Significant
Median	Significant	Insignificant
Unlucky	Significant	Insignificant

In Canada, the minimum mandatory withdrawals from the tax–advantaged retirement accounts (RRIFs) are significantly higher than in the U.S.A. Therefore, they are significantly more vulnerable to running out of money -even if lucky- than U.S. retirees, as depicted in Figure 20.7.

Figure 20.7: The effect of applying mandatory minimum withdrawals (Canadian–RRIF) on the portfolio value when a retiree requires 6% WR rate

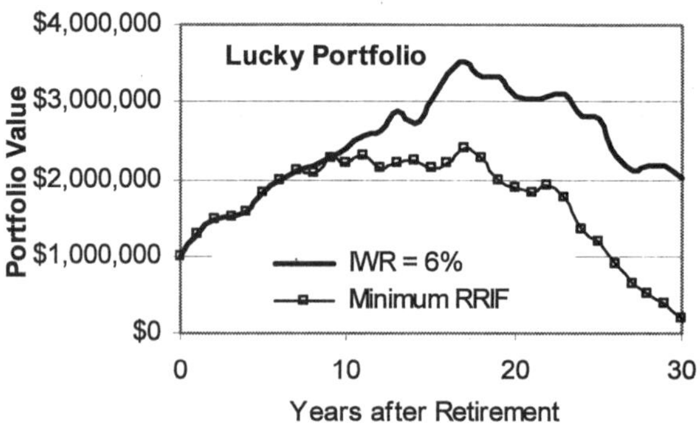

Tables 20.6 and 20.7 show the effective growth rate for tax–sheltered distribution portfolios. Keep in mind, the required initial withdrawal rate that is indicated on this table is what the retiree actually wants. He may be forced to withdraw more than that because of the minimum mandatory withdrawal requirements. Table 20.6 is for the US (Uniform Distribution Table). Table 20.7 is for Canadian (RRIF, post 1992) accounts. In all cases, retirement starts at age 65.

Take the most suitable EGR figure from this table. Using a 3% "average" inflation rate, enter these numbers into a standard retirement calculator. The results will be the closest you can come to actual market history on a standard retirement calculator for a tax–sheltered portfolio.

Table 20.6: Effective growth rate, distribution portfolios, US (Uniform Distribution Table applies)

Required Initial Withdrawal Rate	Portfolio	Outcome		
		Unlucky	Median	Lucky
		Effective Growth Rate:		
2%	S&P500	0.8%	5.6%	8.2%
	DJIA	1.2%	4.0%	8.1%
	50% S&P500, 50% Fixed Income	3.2%	5.4%	8.4%
	100% Fixed Income	2.4%	4.7%	8.2%
4%	S&P500	–2.0%	3.8%	7.2%
	DJIA	–1.7%	3.4%	6.8%
	35% S&P500, 65% Fixed Income	3.4%	4.9%	7.3%
	100% Fixed Income	1.3%	4.8%	7.9%
6%	S&P500	–3.3%	4.2%	7.9%
	DJIA	–2.9%	4.4%	7.6%
	25% S&P500, 75% Fixed Income	2.2%	4.9%	6.9%
	100% Fixed Income	1.0%	5.4%	6.8%
8%	S&P500	–3.6%	4.7%	9.4%
	DJIA	–3.7%	4.7%	9.3%
	20% S&P500, 80% Fixed Income	1.3%	5.6%	8.1%
	100% Fixed Income	1.3%	5.4%	7.6%
10%	S&P500	–4.5%	5.5%	11.0%
	DJIA	–4.2%	5.6%	10.9%
	20% S&P500, 80% Fixed Income	0.7%	5.8%	8.6%
	100% Fixed Income	1.3%	5.6%	7.9%

Table 20.7: Effective growth rate, distribution portfolios, Canada (RRIF tables apply)

Required Initial Withdrawal Rate	Portfolio	Outcome		
		Unlucky	Median	Lucky
		Effective Growth Rate:		
2%	SP/TSX	4.1%	6.1%	7.7%
	60% SP/TSX, 40% Fixed Income	4.0%	6.5%	7.9%
4%	SP/TSX	1.6%	4.8%	7.7%
	45% SP/TSX, 55% Fixed Income	3.5%	5.4%	7.1%
6%	SP/TSX	0.4%	5.2%	7.3%
	35% SP/TSX, 65% Fixed Income	3.0%	5.6%	7.0%
8%	SP/TSX	–0.2%	5.8%	9.2%
	30% SP/TSX, 70% Fixed Income	2.7%	5.8%	7.9%
10%	SP/TSX	–1.4%	6.3%	9.5%
	30% SP/TSX, 70% Fixed Income	2.6%	6.2%	8.3%

Conclusion:

The point of the two examples in this chapter is not necessarily to give you precise numbers, but to inspire you to be flexible and adaptable when planning for retirement.

The effective growth rate, when used in a standard retirement calculator, can help to project outcomes that are congruent with market history. Since we define the unlucky as the bottom 10% of all outcomes, there is still a 10% chance that the outcome may be worse than predicted. Nevertheless, this is a better method than using the traditional average growth rates. This way, your retirement plan will be much more robust.

In addition, the effective growth rate can help develop a more effective asset allocation philosophy by indicating what works when and at what withdrawal rates.

Chapter 21

Price–Earnings Ratio as a Predictor of Portfolio Life

The PE ratio is calculated by dividing the stock price by its earnings. When you take the average Price–Earnings Ratio (PE) of all stocks in an index, then you have the average market PE for that index. It is a way of measuring the fair value of the stock market. If the average PE of the equity index is high, then markets are considered overvalued. If the average PE is low, then markets are considered undervalued.

There is another good use of the PE ratio for retirement planning. It can be a good predictor of portfolio longevity[46].

The reciprocal of the PE ratio is called the Earnings Yield (EY). The EY is calculated by dividing earnings by the stock price expressed as a percentage. I use the EY in this analysis because its correlation with the portfolio life is much easier to observe.

Let's look at an example: A retirement portfolio starts with $1 million in total assets, invested 40% in S&P500 and 60% in fixed income. The withdrawal in the first year is $60,000, indexed to inflation in subsequent years. Thus, the initial withdrawal rate (IWR) is 6%, calculated as $60,000 as a percentage of $1 million. On the equity side, going forward, I used the prevailing dividend rate of 2%. As for the management costs, I assumed 1.5% for the equity holdings and 1.0% for the fixed income holdings.

First, I calculate the portfolio life for each year of starting the retirement for all years since 1900. Then, I take the 4–year moving average of the portfolio life. This is to smooth the fluctuations of the portfolio life within a market cycle. Figure 21.1 depicts the portfolio life.

Figure 21.1: Portfolio life

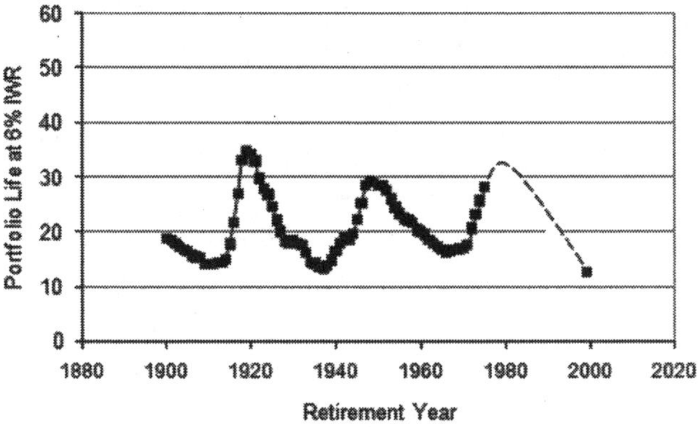

46 Otar, Jim "Can the Prevailing PE be a Good Predictor of the Portfolio Longevity", IMCA Monitor, December 2007

The portfolio life between the years 1978 and 2000 is indicated with a dotted line. That is because we don't know the actual portfolio life for these years yet. However, we know from Chapter 2, that Bob III retired in the year 2000 and his portfolio life is about 12 years.

Let's turn to EY. As for the data source, between the years 1900–1935, I used the historical earnings data available in Shiller's book[47]. For the years after 1935, the historical PE's were available at the Standard & Poor's database[48]. Then, I took the 4–year moving average of the EY to smoothen the fluctuations within a market cycle.

Subsequently, I observed that the EY needed two modifications. The first one accounts for the survivor bias after the market crash of 1929. Many companies went under during the Great Depression. The EY during this time period includes only the surviving companies. Therefore, I reduced the EY by one third between 1935 and 1945 to compensate for the survivor bias.

The second adjustment was for the years between 1900 and 1934. Before 1934, companies were not required to disclose detailed financial information. I observed a three–year shift between the observed portfolio life and the EY. Therefore, I allowed for a three–year time lapse in the dissemination of real company information for all years before 1935. Other than these two modifications, I made no other adjustments for any year after 1945. Figure 21.2 depicts the earnings yields over the last century.

Figure 21.2: Earnings yield

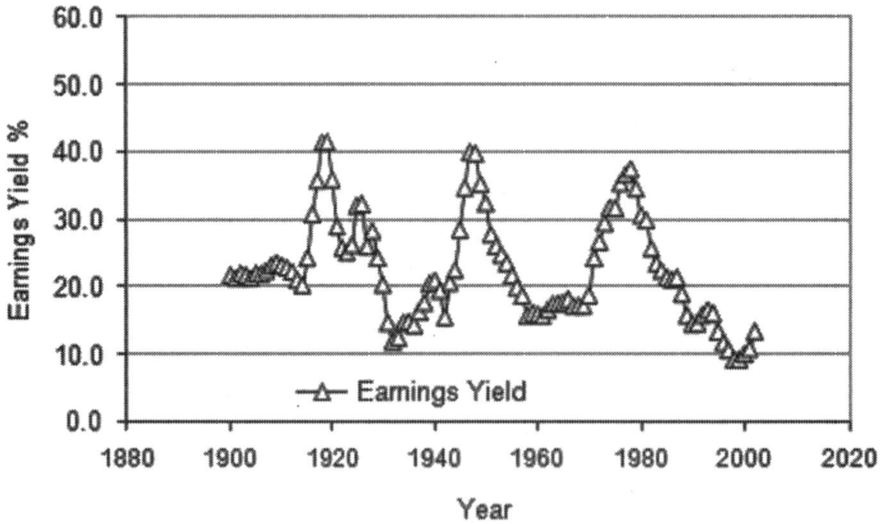

[47] Robert J. Shiller, "Market Volatility", MIT Press
[48] www.standardsandpoors.com

Next, I plotted both the earnings yield and the portfolio life onto the same graph (see Figure 21.3). Can you spot the parallel between these two curves?

Figure 21.3: Earnings yield and portfolio life

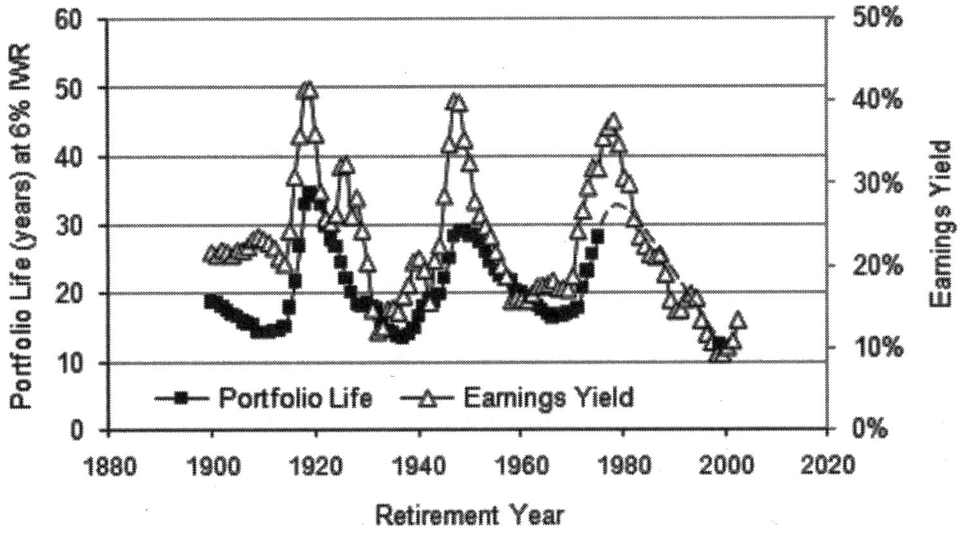

A simple curve–fitting reveals the magic formula which can help you estimate the average expected life for a well–diversified portfolio:

$$\text{Estimated Portfolio Life} = 4 + \frac{A}{PE_4} \qquad \text{(Equation 21.1)}$$

where:

PE_4 is the average PE ratio of the S&P500, recent four years

A 250 if the initial withdrawal rate is 6%,
360 if the initial withdrawal rate is 5%

Example 21.1

The PE ratio for the S&P500 was 28, 20, 19, and 17 at the end of June 2003, 2004, 2005, and 2006 respectively. The average of these four years is 21.

Calculate the expected approximate life of a diversified portfolio at 5% initial withdrawal rate, fully indexed to inflation, retiring at the end of June 2006.

Portfolio Life for 5% IWR = 4 + (360 / 21) = 21 years

What if the initial withdrawal rate was 6%?

Portfolio Life for 6% IWR = 4 + (250 / 21) = 16 years

I am sometimes asked for formulas for other withdrawal rates, such as 4% or 7%? The answer is simple:

- If your withdrawal rate is over 6%, you don't need any formulas; you will likely run out of money well before 30 years.
- On the other hand, if your withdrawal rate is 4% or less, you don't need any formulas either, you'll likely have lifelong income.
- The P/E ratio warning signal works well between 4% and 6% initial withdrawal rates. Inside this range, use Equation 21.1. Outside this range, use common sense.

Going further, I wanted to create a simple "rule of thumb". I thought it would be nice to know a threshold PE level, above which the risk is too high. After some trial and error, I noticed that a PE ratio of 12.5 was a good indicator.

So, I divided the historical data into two groups. The first group includes the observation points where the PE ratio is less than 12.5. The second group includes the points where the PE ratio is larger than 12.5. Figure 21.4 depicts the portfolio life for the two sets of numbers.

Figure 21.4: PE ratio and portfolio life

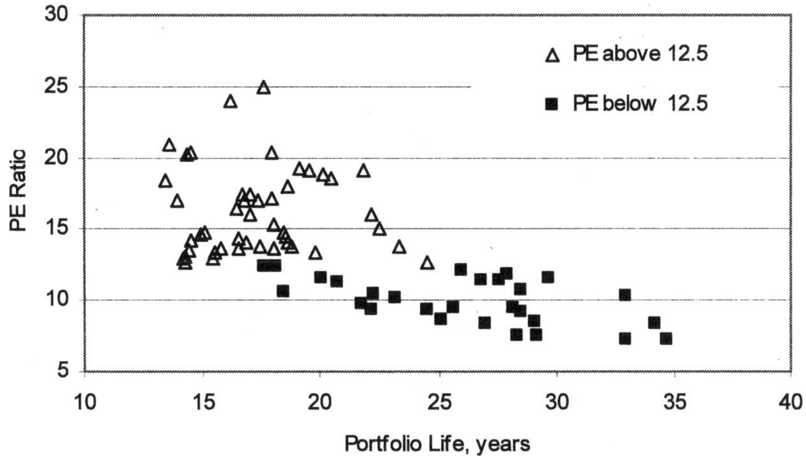

We observe in Figure 21.4 two clusters of data. When the PE ratio was larger than 12.5 (indicated by small triangles on the chart), then the subsequent portfolio life was generally shorter than the other group, where the PE ratio was lower than 12.5 (indicated by small squares on the chart).

I calculated that when the PE was less than 12.5, then the average portfolio life for the group was 25.8 years. When the PE was greater than 12.5, then the average portfolio life was 17.4 years. The difference in the average portfolio life was 49%, which is significant.

So, here is the rule of thumb: If you retire when the PE ratio is higher than 12.5, you can count on a shorter portfolio life, usually less than 20 years. However, the opposite is not always true, just because the PE ratio is low does not necessarily mean your portfolio will have a long life. It just means the wind will be at your back, helping you sail through your retirement a lot easier.

Retiring in Year 2000:

In Chapter 2, we observed the shrinkage of the portfolio value that belonged to the grandson, Bob III, who retired at the beginning of the year 2000. This is how it looked (see Figure 21.5):

Figure 21.5: Value of retirement assets over time, projection of a standard retirement calculator versus retiring at the beginning of 2000

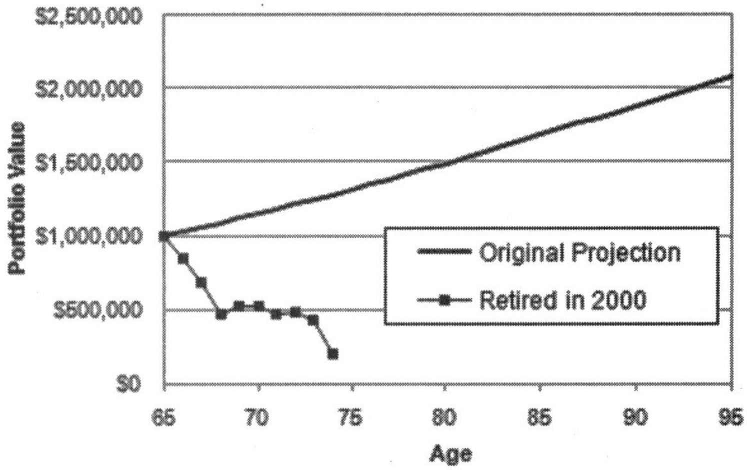

Going forward from 2008, the final year of available market data at the time of writing, we made a new projection using the historical 8.8% average growth rate and 3% indexation. This projection indicated that the portfolio is expected to deplete at age 77 as seen in Figure 21.6.

Figure 21.6: Value of retirement assets over time, projection of a standard retirement calculator versus retiring at the beginning of 2000

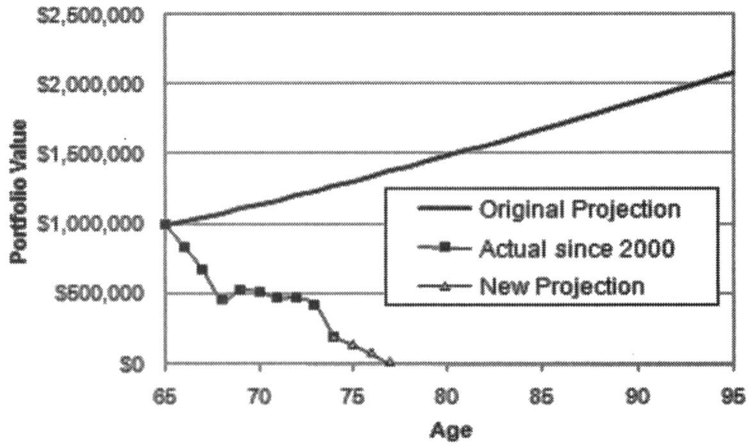

Imagine that it is now the beginning of the year 2000. Let's calculate the approximate portfolio life. The PE ratios for the years 1996, 1997, 1998 and 1999 were 19, 24, 33, and 31 respectively. The average PE for these four years is 27. This is our PE_4. Applying equation 21.1:

Estimated Portfolio Life = 4 + (250/27) = 13 years

In the year 2000, just prior to retirement, we were able to estimate the portfolio life as 13 years by simply knowing the PE ratio of the market. Nine years later, at the end of 2008, we observe that this portfolio will deplete within the next two or three years.

The PE ratio predicted a 13–year portfolio life. The reality is that the portfolio will deplete somewhere between 11 and 13 years. This is close enough for me. If the retiree was aware of this predicament in 2000, he might have decided to delay his retirement or buy life annuities. Now, it is too late for any strategic rescue.

Figure 21.7: Projection of a standard retirement calculator versus estimation using the PE ratio at the beginning of year 2000

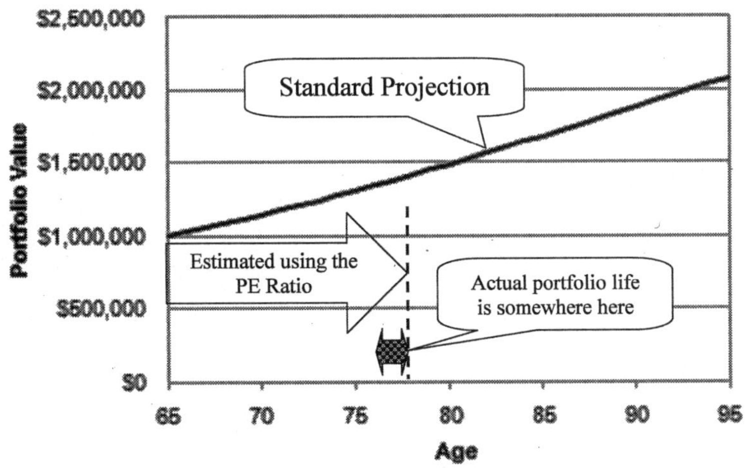

Keep in mind that this is just an estimate. But it is far more realistic than the standard projection at the beginning of the year 2000, which indicated portfolio assets of over $2 million at age 95, using an "assumed" average 8.8% growth rate.

Conclusion:

A high PE ratio is an indicator of overvalued equity prices. Eventually, such trends go through a correction. If you are just retiring, this correction will create a bad sequence of returns in your portfolio.

Prior to retirement, check the average market PE ratio. If it is over 12.5, then it should serve as a warning signal. Ignore any projections based on average returns and focus on unlucky outcomes *only*. Proceed to estimate your portfolio life using the formula above. If it is shorter than what is acceptable to you, then this is the best time to export the risk to insurance companies by way of a life annuity.

Chapter 22

Other Warning Signals of Diminishing Luck

After the withdrawal rate, the luck factor is the second largest determinant of a portfolio's longevity. Therefore, it is important to keep an eye out for warning signals that indicate diminishing luck. I describe four different warning signals in this chapter. Each one works a little differently than the other.

Warning Signal #1: Current Price Earnings Ratio

We covered this warning signal in Chapter 21 in detail. The current market PE ratio indicates whether markets are overvalued or undervalued. If markets are overvalued, they eventually go through a correction and that creates a bad sequence of returns. Therefore, a high PE ratio is an indicator of a pending, unfavorable sequence of returns for the retiree.

You need only to look for this signal once, and that is at the beginning of retirement. It gives you 12 to 30 years of advance notice.

Warning Signal #2: The Fourth–Year Check–Up

The fourth–year checkup indicates the presence or absence of a bad sequence of returns in the early years of retirement. As its name suggests, it is tested only once during the retirement, at the fourth anniversary of the start of withdrawals.

While warning signal #1 (the prevailing PE Ratio) is predictive of a bad sequence of returns, the fourth–year check–up is "after–the–fact" evidence of a bad sequence of returns.

I calculated the asset value of all portfolios over the entire retirement time period for each starting year since 1900. These are the aftcast charts that we have seen many times before. Then, I examined the portfolio value of each retirement year four years after the start of periodic withdrawals. Some were higher and some were lower when compared to their initial value. I separated these into two buckets: the winners and the losers. The winners are those portfolios which had a higher value after four years. The losers are those portfolios which had a lower value after four years. Next, I looked at each bucket after 20 years. The winners had a much higher survival rate than the losers. Here are the numbers:

Table 22.1: Fourth–year check–up, US markets[49]

Initial Withdrawal Rate	Is the portfolio value higher or lower on the 4th anniversary of retirement? HIGHER	LOWER
	Probability of Depletion by 20th Year:	
5%	0%	7%
6%	2%	38%
8%	6%	72%

Table 22.1: Fourth–year check–up, Canadian markets[50]

Initial Withdrawal Rate	Is the portfolio value higher or lower on the 4th anniversary of retirement? HIGHER	LOWER
	Probability of Depletion by 20th Year:	
5%	0%	5%
6%	0%	30%
8%	10%	75%

Here is how this warning signal works: On the fourth anniversary of the start of withdrawals, ask this: "Do I have more money or less money compared to four years ago?" If you have more money, don't worry; be happy. This is an indication that the sequence of returns is going your way. The chances of having a lifelong income are high.

On the other hand, if you have less money, the sequence of returns is working against you. Thus, the risk of running out of money during your lifetime is too high.

This warning signal gives you up to 20 years of advance notice.

Warning Signal #3: Withdrawals Exceed the Sustainable Withdrawal Rate

If the current withdrawal rate exceeds the sustainable withdrawal rate, then retirement assets will likely expire before its owner. Use figures in Table 17.9 for your sustainable withdrawal rates.

[49] for an asset mix of 40% DJIA and 60% fixed income

[50] for an asset mix of 40% SP/TSX and 60% fixed income

Example 22.1

Sarah is 65 years of age, just retired. She has $1 million in her portfolio. She needs $48,000 each year, indexed to actual inflation. She wants her money to last until age 95. What are the chances?

Answer: Sarah's time horizon is 30 years. Her sustainable withdrawal rate for 90% survival is 3.8% (Table 17.9), which is less than her actual withdrawal rate of 4.8% ($48,000 is 4.8% of $1 million). Therefore it is likely that her portfolio will deplete before age 95.

This warning signal gives you 15 to 25 years of advance notice. You need to check for this signal after each significant market event.

Warning Signal #4: The Final Warning Signal

This is your last call. If you ignore this signal, no amount of luck (historically speaking) will help you recover financially.

I observed all aftcasts starting in each year since 1900. I plotted the current withdrawal rate against the remaining portfolio life. Figure 22.1 depicts the results.

Figure 22.1: The remaining portfolio life

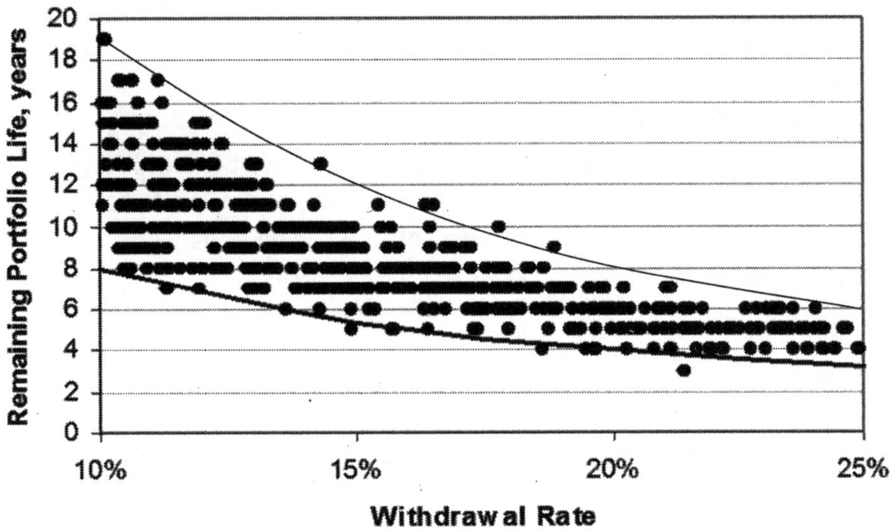

Once the withdrawal rate touches or exceeds 10% of the portfolio value, history shows that no retirement portfolio will last more than 19 years. Consider this warning signal as served even if the withdrawal rate subsequently retreats to below 10%.

The following formulas will give you a rough estimate of the maximum and minimum remaining portfolio life for a withdrawal rate exceeding 10%:

- Maximum Remaining Portfolio Life = 160 / Current Withdrawal Rate
- Minimum Remaining Portfolio Life = 80 / Current Withdrawal Rate

This warning signal gives you 8 to 18 years of advance notice. Check for this signal annually.

Retiring in Year 2000:

Going back to Chapter 2, we observed the portfolio of the grandson, Bob III. He was retiring at the beginning of year 2000. Let's look at all of the warning signals that Bob III should have heeded:

- At the start of retirement

  Warning Signal #1: The current PE ratio
  We already estimated this portfolio life in Chapter 21: It is only 13 years. Bad news!

  Warning Signal #3: Withdrawals exceed the sustainable withdrawal rate
  Bob III plans to withdraw $60,000 annually from an initial asset base of $1,000,000. This is a 6% withdrawal rate, which is a lot higher than the sustainable withdrawal rate. Bad news!

- Three years after retirement

  Warning Signal #4: The Final Warning Signal
  At age 68, Bob III withdraws $63,670 from an asset base of $466,806 (see Table 2.7). The current withdrawal rate is close to 14%, calculated as $63,670 / $466,806 x 100%. Once the current withdrawal rate touches or exceeds 10% then you have a problem. Bad news!

- Four years after retirement

  Warning Signal #2: The fourth–year check–up
  On the fourth anniversary of retirement, the portfolio value is definitely lower than its starting value. Bad news!

Figure 22.2: Warning signals, retiring at the beginning of year 2000

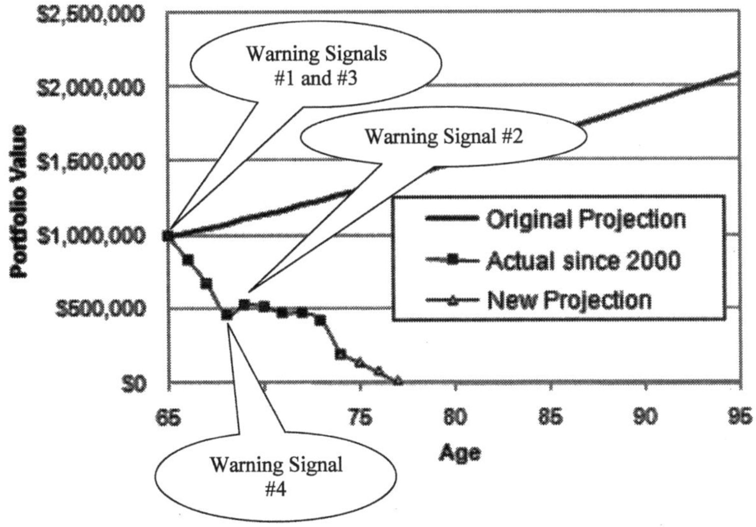

Bob III saw four warning signals during the first four years of his retirement. His portfolio will deplete at age 77. What did he do wrong? He ignored all warning signals.

He should have considered purchasing a life annuity after seeing the first warning signal, right at the beginning of retirement. That would have given him lifelong income. Now, it is too late.

Figure 22.3 displays the annual review flowchart for the warning signals after retirement starts. The PE ratio warning signal is not indicated on this diagram because it applies only at the beginning of retirement.

Figure 22.3: Annual review of warning signals after retirement

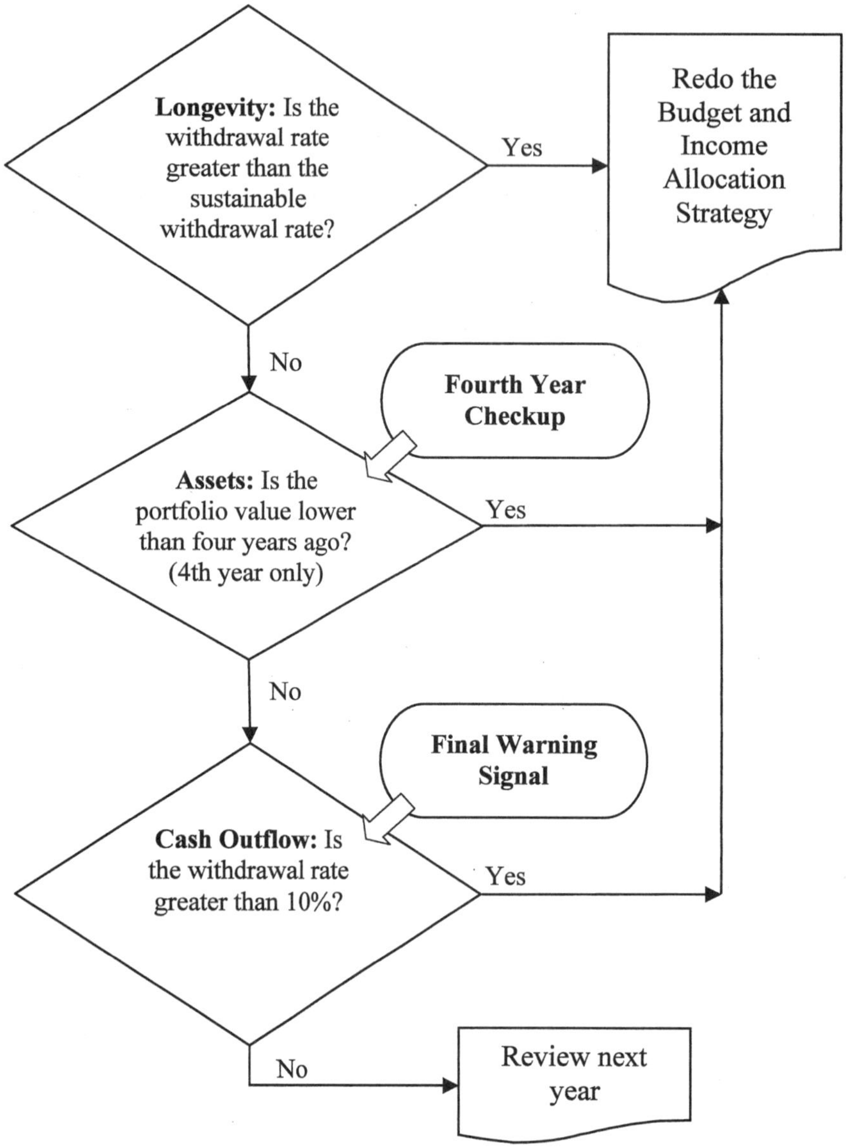

Conclusion:

Here, we have four different warning signals that will give you 8 to 30 years of advance notice of declining luck. If you detect any of these warning signals, you will have to consider guaranteed income classes such as life annuities.

Keep in mind that these findings are based on market extremes of the last century. The current century may create market extremes beyond those extremes. Future outcomes will likely be less favorable for the retiree.

Chapter 23

Age Based Asset Allocation

This is one of the asset allocation strategies followed by some investors. With this strategy, the amount allocated to an asset class is based on one's age. The basic premise of this strategy is "as the retiree gets older, his portfolio should be more conservative". I call this strategy Age Based Asset Allocation (ABAA).

For example, you might say: "I will allocate to equities 100 minus my age". Here, the number 100 is called the base number. Subtract the age from this base number to determine the percentage of assets allocated to equities.

$$\text{Equity \%} = \text{Base number} - \text{Current Age} \qquad \text{(Equation 23.1)}$$

Using this formula, examples of the asset allocation for various ages are indicated in Table 23.1.

Table 23.1: Age based asset allocation for the base number 100:

Age	% Fixed Income	% Equity
65	65%	35%
66	66%	34%
94	94%	6%
101	100%	0%

You can use a different base number. For example if you use a base number of 105 then the asset allocation would be as depicted in Table 23.2

Table 23.2: Age based asset allocation for the base number 105:

Age	% Fixed Income	% Equity
65	60%	40%
66	61%	39%
94	89%	11%
101	96%	4%

Example 23.1

Jack is 65 years old. He is retiring this year. He expects to die at age 95. His retirement savings are valued at one million dollars. He needs to withdraw $60,000 each year, indexed to actual inflation. On the equity side, his equity proxy is S&P500. On the fixed income side, he expects a return of 0.5% over and above the historical 6-month CD rates after all management fees.

Jack follows the age based asset allocation strategy. He selects "100" as the base number. His target asset allocation until age 95 is:

Age	Fixed Income %	Equity %	Age	Fixed Income %	Equity %
65	65%	35%	81	81%	19%
66	66%	34%	82	82%	18%
67	67%	33%	83	83%	17%
68	68%	32%	84	84%	16%
69	69%	31%	85	85%	15%
70	70%	30%	86	86%	14%
71	71%	29%	87	87%	13%
72	72%	28%	88	88%	12%
73	73%	27%	89	89%	11%
74	74%	26%	90	90%	10%
75	75%	25%	91	91%	9%
76	76%	24%	92	92%	8%
77	77%	23%	93	93%	7%
78	78%	22%	94	94%	6%
79	79%	21%	95	95%	5%
80	80%	20%			

Here is the aftcast:

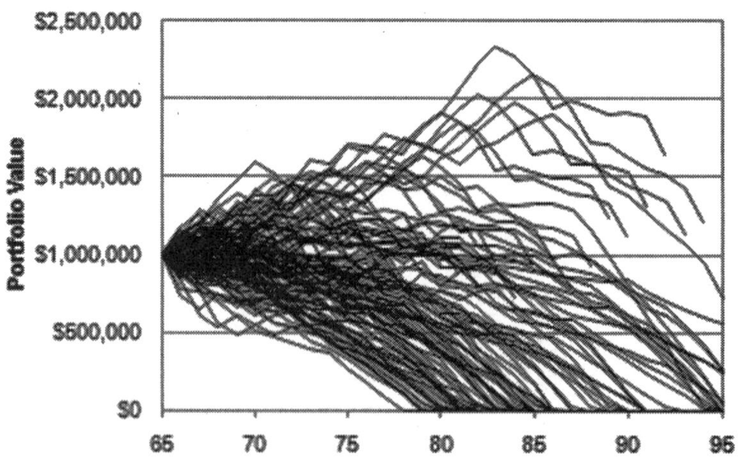

Here is a comparison of age based asset allocation and strategic asset allocation. The vertical axis indicates the probability of receiving the full $60,000 indexed income at various ages:

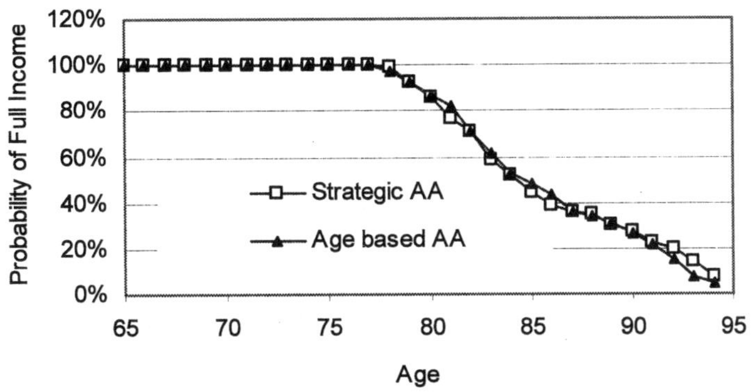

Accelerated Age Based Asset Allocation:

As the name implies, the accelerated age based asset allocation (AABAA) is a more aggressive version of the ABAA. The equity allocation is:

$$\text{Equity \%} = \text{Base number} - \frac{\text{Age}^2}{100} \qquad \text{(Equation 23.2)}$$

Example 23.2

Mark is 65 years old. He is retiring this year. He expects to die at age 95. His retirement savings are valued at one million dollars. He needs to withdraw $60,000 each year, indexed to actual inflation. On the equity side, his equity proxy is S&P500. On the fixed income side, he expects a return of 0.5% over and above the historical 6-month CD rates after all management fees.

Mark follows the accelerated age based asset allocation. He selects "100" as the base number. His target asset allocation until age 95 is:

Age	Fixed Income %	Equity %
65	42%	58%
66	44%	56%
67	45%	55%
68	46%	54%
69	48%	52%
70	49%	51%
71	50%	50%
72	52%	48%
73	53%	47%
74	55%	45%
75	56%	44%
76	58%	42%
77	59%	41%
78	61%	39%
79	62%	38%
80	64%	36%

Age	Fixed Income %	Equity %
81	66%	34%
82	67%	33%
83	69%	31%
84	71%	29%
85	72%	28%
86	74%	26%
87	76%	24%
88	77%	23%
89	79%	21%
90	81%	19%
91	83%	17%
92	85%	15%
93	86%	14%
94	88%	12%
95	90%	10%

Here is the aftcast:

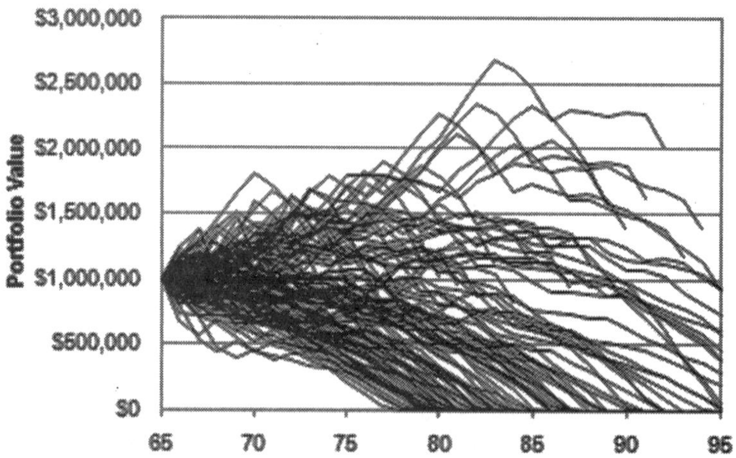

Here is a comparison of accelerated age based asset allocation and strategic asset allocation. The vertical axis indicated the probability of receiving the full $60,000 indexed income across different ages:

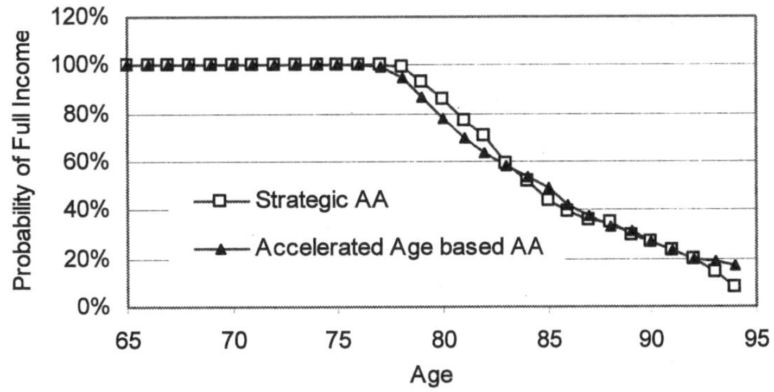

Sustainable Withdrawal Rates:

The sustainable withdrawal rates for age based asset allocation are calculated for the 90% probability of portfolio survival, i.e. for 10% probability of depletion.

In all cases the base number is 100 and retirement starts at age 65. These results are case specific. The results will be different for different retirement ages and the base numbers.

Table 23.3: Sustainable withdrawal rates for age based asset allocation, US markets, S&P500

Time Horizon	Age Based AA		Accelerated Age Based AA	
	Equity Alpha=0	Equity Alpha=1	Equity Alpha=0	Equity Alpha=1
	SUSTAINABLE WITHDRAWAL RATE:			
20 years	4.9%	5.1%	4.5%	4.8%
30 years	3.4%	3.7%	3.4%	3.7%
40 years	2.8%	2.9%	2.8%	3.0%

Table 23.4: Sustainable withdrawal rates for age based asset allocation, Canadian markets, SP/TSX

Time Horizon	Age Based AA		Accelerated Age Based AA	
	Equity Alpha=0	Equity Alpha=1	Equity Alpha=0	Equity Alpha=1
	SUSTAINABLE WITHDRAWAL RATE:			
20 years	5.1%	5.4%	4.9%	5.0%
30 years	3.4%	3.6%	3.6%	3.8%
40 years	2.7%	2.8%	2.9%	3.1%

Effective Growth Rates:

Table 23.5 and 23.6 show the effective growth rate (EGR) for the US and Canadian markets and distribution portfolios for age based asset allocation. Use a 3% "average" inflation rate for the indexation of withdrawals in a standard retirement calculator. Enter the EGR figure from this table as the "average growth rate". This will help you to forecast the portfolio value or longevity. All numbers are based on equity alpha equals zero and the base number equals 100.

Table 23.5: Effective growth rate, age based asset allocation, US markets, equity is S&P500

Initial Withdrawal Rate	Strategy	Outcome		
		Unlucky	Median	Lucky
		Effective Growth Rate:		
2%	Age based	3.4%	4.7%	7.4%
	Accelerated	3.2%	4.7%	7.2%
4%	Age based	3.2%	5.0%	6.6%
	Accelerated	2.5%	4.7%	7.2%
6%	Age based	2.1%	4.9%	7.0%
	Accelerated	0.77%	5.0%	7.5%
8%	Age based	0.50%	5.6%	8.4%
	Accelerated	0.15%	5.5%	8.7%
10%	Age based	1.1%	5.8%	8.7%
	Accelerated	–0.12%	5.9%	9.4%

Table 23.6: Effective growth rate, age based asset allocation, Canadian markets, equity is SP/TSX

Initial Withdrawal Rate	Strategy	Outcome		
		Unlucky	Median	Lucky
		Effective Growth Rate:		
2%	Age based	3.0%	6.0%	7.5%
	Accelerated	3.6%	6.5%	7.4%
4%	Age based	2.8%	5.6%	6.7%
	Accelerated	3.1%	5.5%	7.1%
6%	Age based	2.9%	5.5%	7.0%
	Accelerated	2.6%	5.7%	7.3%
8%	Age based	2.7%	5.9%	7.9%
	Accelerated	2.1%	6.0%	8.2%
10%	Age based	2.7%	5.9%	8.4%
	Accelerated	1.7%	6.3%	8.6%

Sustainable Asset Multiplier:

Table 23.7 shows the sustainable asset multiplier for the age based and accelerated age based asset allocation strategies.

Table 23.7: Sustainable asset multiplier, portfolio size required for $10,000 annual income fully indexed to CPI

Time Horizon	Minimum Portfolio Size Required for $10,000 annual income indexed fully to CPI, maximum 10% probability of depletion	
	Alpha = 0%	Alpha = 1%
	Age based asset allocation:	
20 years	$196,100	$185,200
30 years	$294,100	$277,800
40 years	$370,400	$357,100
	Accelerated age based asset allocation:	
20 years	$204,100	$200,000
30 years	$277,800	$263,200
40 years	$344,800	$322,600

Conclusion:

The problem with age based asset allocation is this: As you get older, more of the assets are placed into fixed income. Thus, the portfolio's ability to participate in a secular bullish trend diminishes when it is most needed during the later years. In the long term, it is not a better technique than strategic asset allocation. In all cases, accelerated or not, it generated a sustainable withdrawal rate that was lower than for the strategic asset allocation that was covered in Chapter 16.

You can optimize the base number for better outcomes. The problem is that any such optimization amounts to data mining for a specific age. I consider this to be a meaningless exercise.

In the final analysis, age based asset allocation is too much work for nothing. It gives a false impression of a reduced risk. It does not reduce the effect of the sequence of returns effectively during the early years of retirement. And it does not reduce the effect of inflation during the later years of retirement. The market history shows that strategic asset allocation has been a better solution than the age based asset allocation during retirement.

Chapter 24

Tactical Asset Allocation

In the conclusion of Chapter 6 on rebalancing, I wrote, "If you want anything more sophisticated, you will need to step up from the rebalancing school into the market timing school. It is important to be able to differentiate between these two schools."

There is only one problem: The expression "market timing" is a near blasphemy in the financial planning profession. So, instead of calling the next four chapters "market timing", I gave them different names. This chapter is about "tactical asset allocation". The next one is "flexible asset allocation". The one after that is the "combo". The last one is "If you Miss the Best..." Now, that sounds less scary. But, please keep this as a secret; I don't want other people thinking that I do market timing. I don't want to be "disbarred" from my profession.

Tactical asset allocation (TAA) is based on the premise that the growth rate of equities eventually reverts to its historical mean. It assumes that markets move at random, piggy–backed onto their average historical growth rate. The portfolio is reviewed annually: if equity markets did well in the preceding year, then the probability of reverting to the mean –doing poorly in the following year– is higher. The asset mix is then positioned in a more defensive stance.

On the other hand, if equity markets did poorly in the preceding year, then the probability of a good market in the following year is higher. The portfolio asset mix is then positioned in a more aggressive stance.

This brings up several questions:

- What is the historical growth rate? Do you consider the entire market history?
- What is the defensive stance? Is a 20% allocation to equities better than 45%?
- What is the aggressive stance? Is a 70% allocation to equities better than 100%?

Let's look at the length of time. If you use the entire market history to calculate an average growth rate, then you would be ignoring the existence of secular trends. The average index growth rate since 1900 is about 7.7% for the DJIA. In a secular bullish trend, where the average is about 15%, you may be sitting in a defensive position for several years and miss all that growth. This is definitely not good.

So, we need to use a shorter market history. It should be just long enough to cover at least one market cycle. That gives us a 4–year time frame. However, this would then still ignore secular trends outside a cyclical trend. By trial and error, I observed that a 6–year history (one and one–half market cycle) gives me a long enough history to recognize the change in a secular trend. And, it is short enough to recognize overvalued/undervalued decisions for my asset mix in a timely manner.

Once a year, during the first week of January, you have to decide whether or not the portfolio should be made more defensive or more aggressive for the coming year. Here is the procedure to follow:

- Make a list of the annual percent growth of the equity index for the previous six years.
- Take the average of the last six years of the change in the equity index. If you do that every year, then this is called a moving average.
- Look at the percent growth of the equity index of last year: If it is higher than the average, sell some equity and become defensive in your portfolio. If it is lower than the average, this may be an opportunity to turn aggressive. Of course, there is no guarantee that markets will move higher next year, but the odds are more in your favor.

The intent of the tactical asset allocation is "buy low, sell high". In my model, the trade decision is made only once a year. It takes about 10 minutes of your time. It is not a lot of work, but it can reward you handsomely.

Example 24.1:

The annual index growth rate for DJIA between 1897 and 1910 is depicted in the following table. Decide for each year whether the asset mix should be defensive or aggressive.

End of Year	Annual Growth of the Index
1897	22.2%
1898	22.5%
1899	9.2%
1900	7.0%
1901	-8.7%
1902	-0.4%
1903	-23.6%
1904	41.7%
1905	38.2%
1906	-1.9%
1907	-37.7%
1908	46.6%
1909	15.0%
1910	-17.9%

Calculate the moving average of the growth of the index for the preceding 6 years. The 6-year moving average for the year 1902 is calculated by adding all annual growth rates between 1897 and 1902 (inclusive) and dividing by 6, (22.2%+22.5%+9.2%+7.0%-8.7%-0.4%)/6 = 8.6%.

Year	Annual growth of the index at the end of year	6-year moving average of the annual growth
1897	22.2%	
1898	22.5%	
1899	9.2%	
1900	7.0%	
1901	-8.7%	
1902	-0.4%	8.6%
1903	-23.6%	1.0%
1904	41.7%	4.2%
1905	38.2%	9.0%
1906	-1.9%	7.5%
1907	-37.7%	2.7%
1908	46.6%	10.6%
1909	15.0%	17.0%
1910	-17.9%	7.0%

Decide whether the most recent growth of the index is higher or lower than the moving average:

Year	Annual growth of the index at the end of year	6-year moving average of the annual growth	Is the recent annual growth of the index higher or lower than its moving average?
1897	22.2%		
1898	22.5%		
1899	9.2%		
1900	7.0%		
1901	-8.7%		
1902	-0.4%	8.6%	Lower
1903	-23.6%	1.0%	Lower
1904	41.7%	4.2%	Higher
1905	38.2%	9.0%	Higher
1906	-1.9%	7.5%	Lower
1907	-37.7%	2.7%	Lower
1908	46.6%	10.6%	Higher
1909	15.0%	17.0%	Lower
1910	-17.9%	7.0%	Lower

Decide whether the asset mix should be aggressive or defensive in the coming year:

Year	Annual growth of the index at the end of year	6-year moving average of the annual growth	Is the recent annual growth of the index higher or lower than its moving average?	Asset mix in the current year
1897	22.2%			
1898	22.5%			
1899	9.2%			
1900	7.0%			
1901	-8.7%			
1902	-0.4%	8.6%	Lower	
1903	-23.6%	1.0%	Lower	Aggressive
1904	41.7%	4.2%	Higher	Aggressive
1905	38.2%	9.0%	Higher	Defensive
1906	-1.9%	7.5%	Lower	Defensive
1907	-37.7%	2.7%	Lower	Aggressive
1908	46.6%	10.6%	Higher	Aggressive
1909	15.0%	17.0%	Lower	Defensive
1910	-17.9%	7.0%	Lower	Aggressive
1911				Aggressive

Now, we know for each year (historically) whether the portfolio should be aggressive of defensive. Every year, we add another line and decide the asset mix for that year. For example; adding one line at the end of 2009 will guide you to be defensive or aggressive for the year 2010.

If you were doing this exercise at the beginning of 1911, because the growth rate (negative 17.9%) in 1910 was lower than the 6-year moving average (7.0%), the portfolio is set to aggressive during the first few days of 1911 and it remains as such until the next review, at the beginning of 1912.

Figure 24.1 depicts the annual change in the growth rate of the index as well as the asset mix signals. The down–arrow indicates the defensive asset mix and the up–arrow indicates an aggressive asset mix. In the majority of cases, especially during secular sideways trends, the signals were very timely. However, since this is based on probabilities, these signals are not foolproof. There are occasional false signals.

Figure 24.1: The S&P500 index growth and the tactical asset allocation signals:

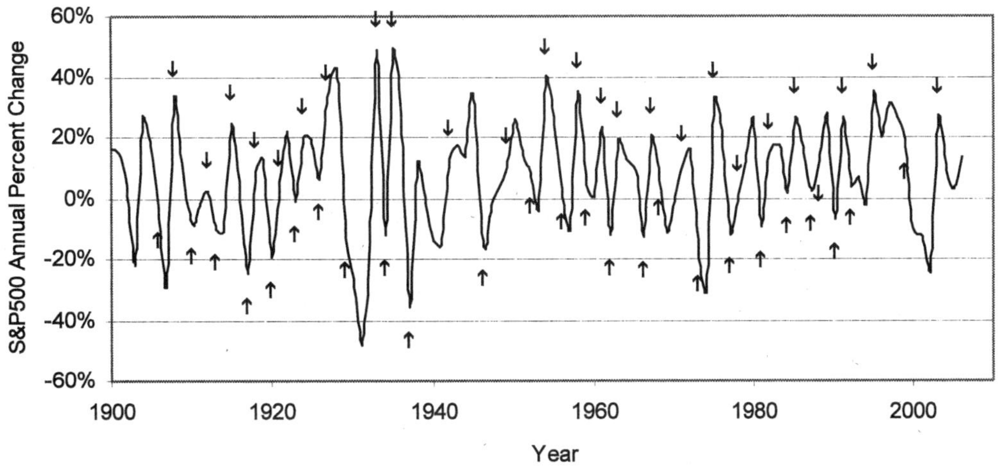

Table 24.1 indicates whether the portfolios were aggressive or defensive for different market histories. A check mark means that the asset mix was aggressive during that year. If there is no check mark, the asset mix was defensive. Each column is for a different equity index:

A – DJIA (US),
B – S&500 (US),
C – SP/TSX (Canada),
D – FTSE AllShares (UK),
E – Nikkei 225 (Japan),
F – ASX All Ord. (Australia)

Table 24.1: Aggressive/Defensive asset mix for tactical asset allocation for various markets.

Year	A	B	C	D	E	F
1900						
1901						
1902						
1903	✓					
1904	✓					
1905						
1906						
1907	✓	✓				
1908	✓	✓		✓		✓
1909						
1910	✓					
1911	✓	✓		✓		✓
1912	✓	✓				✓
1913				✓		✓
1914	✓	✓		✓		✓
1915	✓	✓		✓		
1916				✓		✓
1917	✓					✓
1918	✓	✓		✓		
1919						
1920						
1921	✓	✓		✓	✓	
1922				✓		✓
1923					✓	
1924	✓	✓		✓		
1925						✓
1926						✓
1927	✓	✓		✓	✓	
1928					✓	✓
1929					✓	✓
1930	✓	✓	✓	✓	✓	✓
1931	✓	✓	✓	✓	✓	✓
1932	✓	✓	✓	✓		✓
1933	✓	✓	✓			
1934						
1935		✓			✓	
1936					✓	
1937					✓	
1938	✓	✓	✓	✓	✓	✓
1939		✓	✓	✓	✓	✓
1940	✓	✓	✓			✓
1941	✓	✓	✓	✓	✓	✓
1942	✓	✓	✓			✓
1943					✓	✓
1944					✓	
1945					✓	
1946				✓	✓	
1947	✓	✓	✓		✓	
1948	✓	✓	✓	✓		
1949	✓	✓	✓	✓		✓
1950				✓		✓
1951					✓	
1952						
1953	✓	✓	✓	✓		✓
1954	✓	✓	✓		✓	✓
1955					✓	
1956				✓	✓	
1957	✓	✓	✓	✓	✓	✓
1958	✓	✓	✓	✓	✓	
1959						
1960	✓	✓	✓			
1961	✓	✓	✓	✓		
1962				✓	✓	✓
1963	✓	✓	✓	✓	✓	✓
1964				✓	✓	✓
1965				✓	✓	
1966			✓			✓
1967	✓	✓	✓	✓		✓
1968					✓	
1969	✓	✓				
1970	✓	✓	✓	✓		✓
1971		✓	✓	✓	✓	✓
1972						✓
1973				✓		
1974	✓	✓	✓	✓	✓	✓
1975	✓	✓	✓	✓	✓	✓
1976					✓	
1977				✓	✓	
1978	✓	✓			✓	✓
1979	✓			✓		
1980				✓		
1981				✓	✓	
1982	✓	✓	✓	✓	✓	✓
1983			✓		✓	✓
1984						
1985	✓	✓	✓			
1986				✓		
1987			✓			
1988	✓	✓	✓	✓	✓	✓
1989	✓		✓	✓		
1990						✓
1991	✓	✓	✓	✓	✓	✓
1992					✓	
1993	✓	✓	✓		✓	✓
1994		✓				
1995	✓	✓	✓	✓		✓
1996						
1997				✓		✓
1998					✓	✓
1999	✓		✓	✓	✓	✓
2000		✓				
2001	✓	✓	✓	✓	✓	✓
2002	✓	✓	✓	✓	✓	✓
2003	✓	✓	✓	✓	✓	✓
2004						
2005	✓					
2006	✓					
2007						
2008		✓	✓	✓	✓	
2009	✓	✓	✓	✓	✓	✓

Now, we know when to switch between the aggressive and the defensive asset mix. The next question is defining what is aggressive and what is defensive. Is allocating 90% to equities aggressive? Is 10% equity too conservative?

If your withdrawal rate is higher than the SWR, then you have a depleting portfolio. In this case, calculate the worst–case portfolio life for each one of the aggressive/defensive asset mix combinations in 10% increments. Fill these numbers into a matrix as shown in Example 24.2. The combination with the longest portfolio life is the optimum aggressive/defensive equity allocation. If there is more than one optimum, choose the one that is most conservative.

Example 24.2

Bob, 65, is just retiring. He has $1,000,000 savings for retirement; he needs annually $44,000 in current dollars.

His equities grow the same as the S&P500 index, plus 2% for dividends, less 0.8% for management fees. The net yield of the fixed income portion of his portfolio is the same as the historical 6-month CD yield plus 1%.

Bob wants to follow the tactical asset allocation strategy. What is his optimum aggressive and defensive asset mix?

The aggressive/defensive asset mix matrix is given below. The maximum age at which the portfolio expires in the worst case is age 86, as highlighted in bold.

Worst Case Portfolio Life, years

Aggressive Equity % \ Defensive Equity %	0	10	20	30	40	50	60	70	80	90	100
100	84	84	84	83	83	83	82	80	79	78	78
90	**86**	**86**	85	85	85	84	83	82	81	80	
80	**86**	**86**	**86**	85	85	84	84	83	82		
70	**86**	**86**	**86**	85	85	84	84	83			
60	**86**	**86**	85	85	85	84	84				
50	85	**86**	85	85	85	84					
40	85	85	85	85	84						
30	85	85	85	84							
20	84	85	84								
10	83	84									
0	82										

In his aggressive posture, Bob can allocate between 70% and 80% to equities. In his defensive posture, he can allocate between 0% and 20% to equities for the best results.

How does this compare to strategic asset allocation?

Look at the bottom diagonal line. Here, the equity mix is the same for the aggressive and defensive portfolios. In other words, this is the outcome for the strategic asset allocation. Along this line, the worst-case portfolio lasted until age 84 for any equity percentage between 10% and 60%. By using the tactical asset allocation and spending 10 minutes a year to decide whether he should have an aggressive or defensive stance in his portfolio, Bob was able to add two years to his worst-case portfolio life.

The following charts compare the strategic asset allocation (50/50 asset mix) and the tactical asset allocation. In the tactical asset allocation, 20% is allocated to equities when defensive and 70% when aggressive.

The median portfolio values:

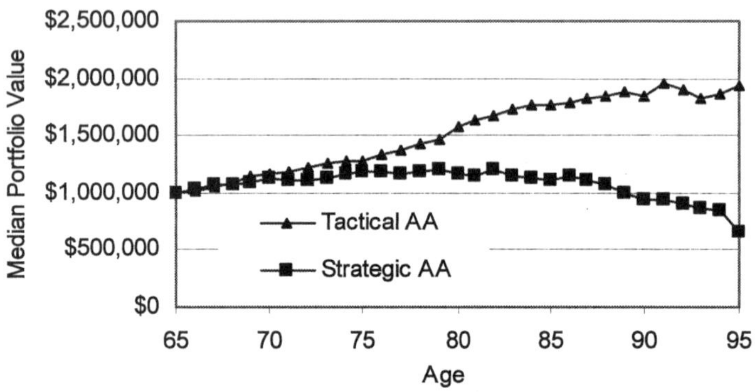

The unlucky portfolio values:

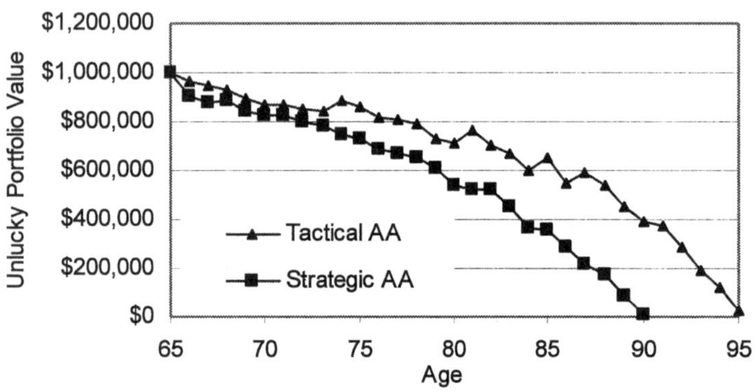

The lucky portfolio values:

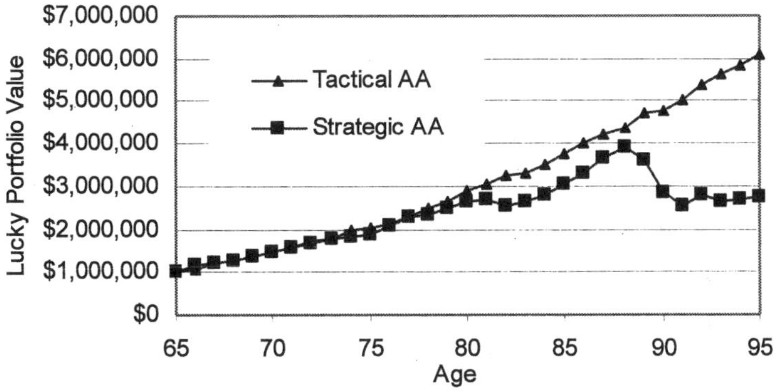

The probability of receiving the full income:

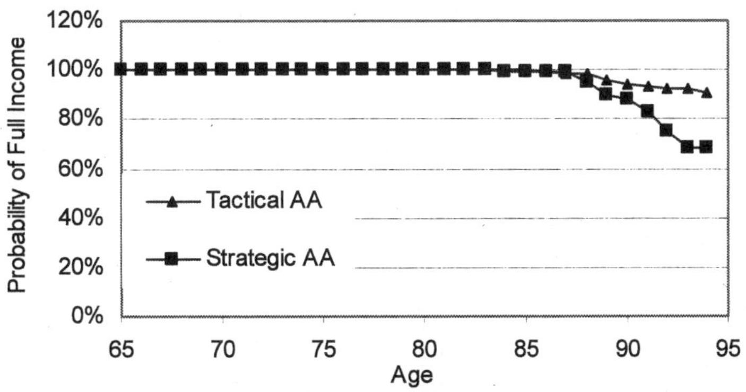

In all of the outcomes, the tactical asset allocation provided a higher portfolio value and a higher probability of full income. In lucky outcomes, it was able to preserve the capital better than the "buy-and-hold" philosophy of the strategic asset allocation. At age 95, Bob had more than twice the estate value than he would have had following the "buy-and-hold" strategy. All for 15 minutes of work per year!

If Bob is holding a fund of funds, all he has to do is write one trade ticket. Switch from aggressive growth to conservative income portfolio or vice versa once a year during the first week of January. That is, of course, if there is a switch signal. If there is no switch signal, nothing needs to be done.

If you have an accumulation portfolio or you have a distribution portfolio with a withdrawal rate lower than the SWR, then you have a non–depleting portfolio. In this case, calculate the median portfolio value for each one of the aggressive/defensive asset mix combinations in 10% increments. Insert these numbers into a matrix as shown in Example 24.3. The combination with the highest median portfolio value is the optimum aggressive/defensive equity allocation.

Example 24.3

Steve, 35, has $100,000 in his savings for retirement. He saves annually $15,000.

His equities grow the same as the S&P500 index, plus 2% for dividends, less 0.8% for management fees. The net yield of the fixed income portion of his portfolio is the same as the historical 6-month CD yield plus 1%.

Steve wants to follow the tactical asset allocation strategy for the next 20 years. He does not want to allocate more than 70% (when aggressive) or less than 30% (when defensive) to equities in his portfolio. What is his optimum aggressive and defensive asset mix?

The aggressive/defensive asset mix matrix is given below. The number in each box is the median portfolio value after 20 years for all combinations of asset mixes. The highest amount of money is made when Steve allocates 100% to equities when aggressive and 0% when defensive. This generated $1.43 million.

Median Portfolio Value x$1million

Aggressive Equity % \ Defensive Equity %	0	10	20	30	40	50	60	70	80	90	100
100	1.43	1.37	1.33	1.28	1.23	1.24	1.23	1.13	1.06	1.04	1.00
90	1.36	1.31	1.28	1.23	1.21	1.16	1.16	1.08	1.02	0.99	
80	1.28	1.24	1.22	1.17	1.17	1.10	1.10	1.03	0.98		
70	1.19	1.17	1.18	**1.13**	1.11	1.04	1.02	0.99			
60	1.13	1.10	1.11	1.08	1.05	1.00	0.96				
50	1.06	1.05	1.03	1.01	0.99	0.95					
40	1.00	0.99	0.97	0.95	0.93						
30	0.96	0.93	0.90	0.88							
20	0.92	0.88	0.84								
10	0.88	0.84									
0	0.84										

However, Steve does not like such broad swings in his asset mix. He knows that any market timing system is not perfect and can give wrong signals. He wants to keep his equity percentage between 30% (when defensive) and 70% (when aggressive). That box reads $1.13 million, indicated in bold.

How does this compare to the strategic asset allocation?

Look at the bottom diagonal line on the matrix, the outcome for SAA. The median portfolio made the most money when 70% was allocated to equities, $990,000. This is the outcome for the strategic asset allocation. On the other hand, with tactical asset allocation, Steve was able to accumulate $140,000 more in his portfolio.

The following charts compare the strategic asset allocation with 70/30-asset mix with the tactical asset allocation. In the tactical asset allocation, 30% is allocated to equities when defensive and 70% when aggressive.

The median portfolio values:

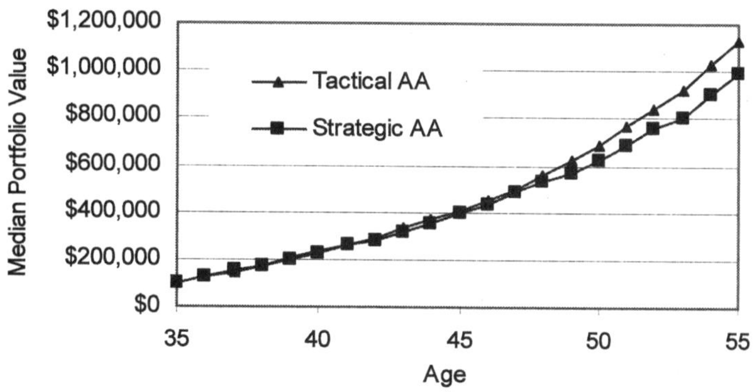

The unlucky portfolio values:

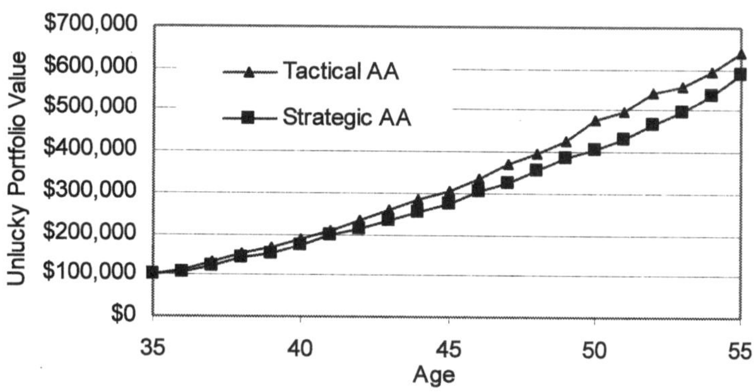

The lucky portfolio values:

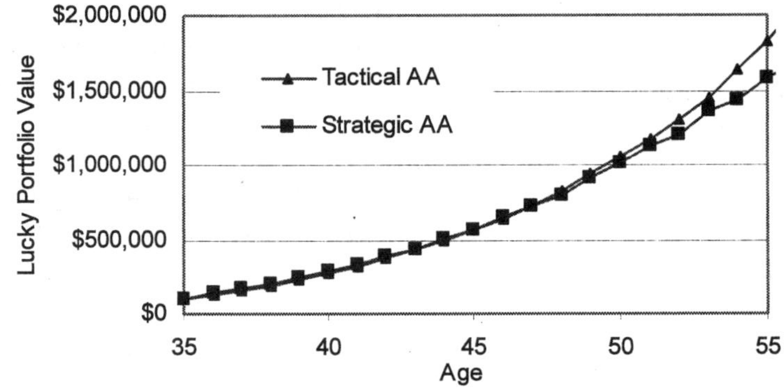

Sustainable Withdrawal Rate:

Sustainable withdrawal rates for tactical asset allocation strategy are depicted in Table 24.2. The equity proxy is the S&P500 index. The equity allocation is 70% when the portfolio is aggressive and 30% when the portfolio is defensive. The net yield on the fixed income portion of the portfolio is the historical 6–month CD yield plus 0.5%.

Table 24.2: Sustainable withdrawal rates for tactical asset allocation, US markets, S&P500

Time Horizon	Tactical Asset Allocation	
	Equity Alpha=0	Equity Alpha=1
20 years	5.1%	5.4%
30 years	4.0%	4.3%
40 years	3.3%	3.6%

Effective Growth Rate:

Table 24.3 shows the effective growth rate (EGR) for the tactical asset allocation strategy as described in this chapter. Enter 3% as the "average" inflation rate for indexation of withdrawals in a standard retirement calculator. Enter the EGR figure from this table as the "average growth rate". This will help you to forecast the portfolio value or its longevity with reasonable accuracy using a standard retirement calculator.

The numbers in Table 24.3 are based on the equity allocation of 70% when the portfolio is aggressive and 30% when the portfolio is defensive. The equity alpha is zero. The net yield on the fixed income portion of the portfolio is the historical 6–month CD yield plus 0.5%.

Table 24.3: Effective growth rate, tactical asset allocation, equity is S&P500

Initial Withdrawal Rate	Outcome		
	Unlucky	Median	Lucky
	Effective Growth Rate:		
0%	3.7%	6.6%	8.8%
2%	4.0%	6.5%	8.5%
4%	4.1%	6.3%	8.1%
6%	2.3%	6.0%	8.0%
8%	1.9%	6.3%	9.0%
10%	1.3%	6.5%	9.6%

Sustainable Asset Multiplier:

Table 24.4 shows the sustainable asset multiplier for the tactical asset allocation strategy. The equity allocation is 70% when the portfolio is aggressive and 30% when the portfolio is defensive. The net yield on the fixed income portion of the portfolio is the historical 6–month CD yield plus 0.5%.

Table 24.4: Simplified sustainable asset multiplier, tactical asset allocation, portfolio size required for $10,000 annual income fully indexed to CPI

Time Horizon	Minimum Portfolio Size Required for $10,000 annual income indexed fully to CPI, maximum 10% probability of depletion	
	Alpha=0%	Alpha=1%
20 years	$193,000	$184,600
30 years	$246,200	$232,200
40 years	$299,700	$275,800

The Effect of Tactical Asset Allocation Strategy:

In distribution portfolios, tactical asset allocation strategy can produce better results than strategic asset allocation.

We can measure the effect of timing based on tactical asset allocation by measuring the difference in the compound annual return of the median portfolio. Table 24.5 indicates the impact of this timing strategy.

Table 24.5: The effect of timing – tactical asset allocation

	Initial Withdrawal Rate					
	0%	2%	4%	6%	8%	10%
Strategic Asset Allocation – compound annual return of the median portfolio (from Tables 20.1, 20.3)	6.0%	5.2%	5.1%	4.9%	5.6%	5.8%
Tactical Asset Allocation – compound annual return of the median portfolio (from Table 24.3)	6.6%	6.5%	6.3%	6.0%	6.3%	6.5%
Impact of TAA timing strategy on compound annual return	10%	25%	24%	22%	13%	12%

Conclusion:

Tactical asset allocation works well in the US markets where the formation of secular trends resembles a sloped staircase. Spending ten minutes a year can add a significant value to portfolio longevity and estate value.

In markets where cyclical trends are more pronounced than secular trends, such as in Canada and Australia, tactical asset allocation does not work as well. In those markets, the "buy–and–hold" philosophy of strategic asset allocation seems to work better than the "buy low, sell high" approach of tactical asset allocation.

Tactical asset allocation is an automated market timing system. As it is with such systems, not all trade decisions will be successful. In some years, you will get false signals.

Chapter 25

Flexible Asset Allocation

Flexible asset allocation (FAA) attempts to increase portfolio returns by tracking secular trends. It works exactly the opposite way of tactical asset allocation. When it detects a secular bullish trend, the equity allocation is increased. This aggressive stance is maintained until a second signal indicates the end of the secular bullish trend.

Here is how we can compare these three strategies qualitatively:

Asset Allocation Strategy	Philosophy	When markets have done well	When markets have done poorly
Strategic	"Buy and hold"	Stay the course	
Tactical	" Buy low, sell high"	Reduce equity holdings	Add money to equities
Flexible	"Buy high, sell higher"	Add money to equities	Reduce equity holdings

History[51] tells us that markets are in a secular bullish trend in about 43% of the time. Here is how flexible asset allocation works: once a year, during the first week of January, you need to figure out whether markets are in a secular bullish trend. Observe the following:

- If your portfolio is in a defensive stance, decide whether the markets are entering a secular bullish mode. If so, make the portfolio more aggressive. Otherwise, stay defensive.
- If your portfolio is in an aggressive stance, decide if the bullish trend still exists. If so, stay aggressive. If markets are no longer bullish, switch to a more defensive posture.

This sounds logical, but it is easier said than done. How can we tell when the markets start a secular bullish trend? How can we differentiate between a cyclical and a secular bullish trend?

We saw in Chapter 7 that you need at least two cyclical trends to create a secular trend. If the peak of the current cycle is higher than the peak of the prior cycle, they form a secular bullish trend. If they are about the same as the previous cycle, they form a secular

[51] Broad–based indices with long–term history such as S&P500 and DJIA.

sideways trend. If the trough of the current cycle is lower than the trough of the previous cycle, they create a secular bearish trend.

So, we need to compare the current cycle with its recent history. How long a history do you need? If you take too short a history, cyclical bullish trends as opposed to secular bullish trends will trigger false signals. If you take too long a history, you might miss a large part of the secular bullish trend. By trial and error, I found that six years gives the best results, the same as the time frame for the tactical asset allocation.

Here are the actual steps for this analysis:

1. List the equity index value (Column A).
2. Take the average of the index value of the last 6 years (Column B).
3. Calculate the annual change in the index value (Column C).
4. Take the average of the annual change of the index value for the preceding 6 years (Column D).
5. Divide the most recent index value by the 6–year moving average of the index value, minus one. Enter this number into the next column. This is the cyclical growth (Column E).

Example 25.1

The annual index values are given below. Decide for each year whether the asset mix should be defensive or aggressive.

Year	Column A STEP 1: Index Value at the End of the Year	Column B STEP 2: 6-Year Moving Average of the Index Value	Column C STEP 3: Annual Change in Index Value	Column D STEP 4: 6-Year Moving Average of the Annual Change of The Index Value	Column E STEP 5: Cyclical Growth
1	1020.02				
2	850.86		-16.6%		
3	616.24		-27.6%		
4	852.41		38.3%		
5	1004.65		17.9%		
6	831.17	862.56	-17.3%		-3.6%
7	805.01	826.72	-3.1%	-1.4%	-2.6%
8	838.74	824.70	4.2%	2.1%	1.7%
9	963.99	882.66	14.9%	9.1%	9.2%
10	875.00	886.43	-9.2%	1.2%	-1.3%
11	1046.54	893.41	19.6%	1.5%	17.1%
12	1258.64	964.65	20.3%	7.8%	30.5%
13	1211.57	1032.41	-3.7%	7.7%	17.4%
14	1546.67	1150.40	27.7%	11.6%	34.4%
15	1895.95	1305.73	22.6%	12.9%	45.2%
16	1938.83	1483.03	2.3%	14.8%	30.7%
17	2168.57	1670.04	11.8%	13.5%	29.9%
18	2753.20	1919.13	27.0%	14.6%	43.5%

In the next set of columns, we calculate if the markets are in a bullish trend. I call this the "Secular Bullish Indicator" or SBI for short.

How is the SBI calculated? Here are the rules to determine the start of a secular bullish trend:

- Current trend: If the most recent cyclical growth (Column E) is less than zero, then there is no indication of a secular bullish trend. The SBI is zero.
- Large Loss: If the index value (Column C) drops 15% or more, there is no secular bullish trend. The SBI is zero.
- Persistent Loss: If the last two years' annual change in index value (Column C) is negative (two years of negative markets, regardless of how benign) then the SBI is zero.
- Otherwise, if the cyclical growth (Column E) is larger than 10%, we have the start of a possible secular bullish trend. The SBI is set equal to the value in this column.

Once the secular bullish trend starts, here is how the SBI is calculated in subsequent years:

- Change of current trend: If the most recent cyclical growth (Column E) is less than zero, then the secular trend is over. SBI is set to zero.
- Large Loss: If the index value (Column C) drops 15% or more, then the secular trend is over. SBI is set to zero.
- Persistent Loss: If the last two years' annual change in index value (Column C) is negative (two years of negative markets, regardless of how benign), then the secular trend is over. SBI is set to zero.
- Otherwise: If the cyclical growth (Column E) plus the previous year's SBI is greater than 10%, then the secular bullish trend continues. The SBI is set equal to the cyclical growth plus the previous year's SBI.

If you are writing these on a spreadsheet, here are the formulas:

Cell A1: Enter index values in this column.

Cell B6: AVERAGE (A1:A6), drag down to fill formulas

Cell C2: (A2–A1) / A1, drag down to fill formulas

Cell D7: AVERAGE (C2:C7), drag down to fill formulas

Cell E6: (A6/B6) –1, drag down to fill formulas

Cell F6 calculates the value of SBI. The formula is:

```
MAX(0,IF(OR(E6<0,C6<–0.15,AND(C6<0,C5<0)),0,IF(E6+F5>0.1,E6+F5,0)))
```

Don't forget to drag down to fill formulas

Example 25.2

Calculate SBI, the secular bullish indicator

Year	Column C STEP 3: Annual Change in Index Value	Column D STEP 4: 6-Year Moving Average of the Annual Change of The Index Value	Column E STEP 5: Cyclical Growth	Column F: SBI Secular Bullish Indicator
1				
2	-16.6%			
3	-27.6%			
4	38.3%			
5	17.9%			
6	-17.3%		-3.6%	0.00
7	-3.1%	-1.4%	-2.6%	0.00
8	4.2%	2.1%	1.7%	0.00
9	14.9%	9.1%	9.2%	0.00
10	-9.2%	1.2%	-1.3%	0.00
11	19.6%	1.5%	17.1%	0.17
12	20.3%	7.8%	30.5%	0.48
13	-3.7%	7.7%	17.4%	0.65
14	27.7%	11.6%	34.4%	0.99
15	22.6%	12.9%	45.2%	1.45
16	2.3%	14.8%	30.7%	1.75
17	11.8%	13.5%	29.9%	2.05
18	27.0%	14.6%	43.5%	2.49

Now, we know when the market is in a bullish trend. However, that does not mean we can trade yet, for that we need to create some rules.

Trading Rules:

Going Aggressive: A non–zero SBI indicates the start of a bullish trend. At this point, we don't know yet if it is the beginning of a secular or a cyclical bullish trend. If you switch to an aggressive asset mix too soon and later it turns out to be only an extended cyclical bullish trend, you may be in for an unpleasant loss.

You need to wait until you see a confirmation. Yes, the market might move higher in the meantime, but patience is a virtue in trend trading. A secular trend is confirmed when you see three consecutive, non–zero SBIs. Also, the most recent SBI must not be the smallest of the three. Once you see this formation, you are officially in a multi–year, secular bullish trend. Now, you can take an aggressive stance in your portfolio

Going Defensive: Sooner or later, a bullish trend comes to an end. There are two events that signal the end of a secular bullish trend.

The first signal is when the SBI turns zero. That means the secular trend has ended. Go defensive.

The second signal is more of a predictive signal. In a continuing secular bullish trend that has lasted at least four years, if the number in column D (the 6–year moving average of the annual change of the index value) exceeds 20%, that means markets are overheated and everyone is entering the market. For the Gaussian mind, this is the right–fat tail of the distribution curve. Don't wait until SBI turns zero; the risk is too high. Move to a defensive asset mix now.

Staying out of trouble: Once you go defensive, stay defensive for the next three years. Give yourself permission to preserve your investments. Allow others to lose their money during such volatile time periods.

Example 25.3

Here is a complete secular bullish event:

Year	Column C STEP 3: Annual Change in Index Value	Column D STEP 4: 6-Year Moving Average of the Annual Change of The Index Value	Column E STEP 5: Cyclical Growth	Column F: SBI Secular Bullish Indicator	Portfolio Asset Mix
1					
2	-16.6%				
3	-27.6%				
4	38.3%				
5	17.9%				
6	-17.3%		-3.6%	0.00	
7	-3.1%	-1.4%	-2.6%	0.00	
8	4.2%	2.1%	1.7%	0.00	Defensive
9	14.9%	9.1%	9.2%	0.00	Defensive
10	-9.2%	1.2%	-1.3%	0.00	Defensive
11	19.6%	1.5%	17.1%	0.17	Defensive
12	20.3%	7.8%	30.5%	0.48	Defensive
13	-3.7%	7.7%	17.4%	0.65	Defensive
14	27.7%	11.6%	34.4%	0.99	Aggressive
15	22.6%	12.9%	45.2%	1.45	Aggressive
16	2.3%	14.8%	30.7%	1.75	Aggressive
17	11.8%	13.5%	29.9%	2.05	Aggressive
18	27.0%	14.6%	43.5%	2.49	Aggressive
19	-4.3%	14.5%	22.1%	2.71	Aggressive
20	20.3%	13.3%	30.6%	3.01	Aggressive
21	4.2%	10.2%	24.1%	3.25	Aggressive
22	13.7%	12.1%	26.7%	3.52	Aggressive
23	2.1%	10.5%	18.3%	3.70	Aggressive
24	33.5%	11.6%	40.8%	4.11	Aggressive
25	26.0%	16.6%	51.0%	4.62	Aggressive
26	22.6%	17.0%	56.3%	5.19	Aggressive
27	16.1%	19.0%	52.0%	5.71	Aggressive
28	25.2%	**20.9%**	56.8%	6.27	Defensive
29	-6.2%	19.5%	27.1%	6.54	Defensive
30	-7.1%	12.8%	7.7%	0.00	Defensive
31	-16.8%	5.7%	-13.3%	0.00	Defensive
32	25.3%	6.1%	4.0%	0.00	Defensive
33	3.2%	3.9%	4.5%	0.00	Defensive
34	-0.6%	-0.4%	5.2%	0.00	Defensive
35	16.3%	3.4%	19.1%	0.19	Defensive
36					Defensive

First week of Year 14: At the end of each one of the three preceding years, the SBI was greater than zero. The SBI at the end of year 13 is 0.65. Furthermore, it is not the smallest of the last three SBI's. That means we have a confirmed secular bullish trend at the beginning of year 14. Go aggressive.

Stay aggressive until the SBI turns zero or the figure in column D exceeds 20% after at least four years of aggressive asset mix. Column D exceeds 20% at the end of year 28, so turn defensive at the beginning of year 29.

Figure 25.1 depicts the SBI for the DJIA for all years since 1900. The columns show the value of the SBI. The vertical bars in the unconfirmed years are white. The solid black columns indicate the confirmed secular trends.

Figure 25.1: Historical SBI and secular bullish trends, DJIA

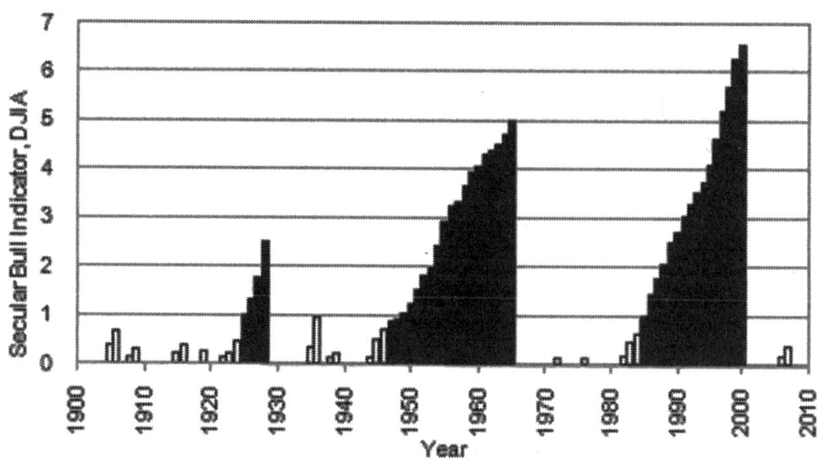

Table 25.1 indicates whether the portfolios were aggressive or defensive for different market histories. A check mark means that the asset mix was aggressive during that year. If there is no check mark, then the asset mix was defensive. Each column is for a different equity index:

A – DJIA (US),
B – S&500 (US),
C – SP/TSX (Canada),
D – FTSE AllShares (UK),
E – Nikkei 225 (Japan),
F – ASX All Ord. (Australia)

Table 25.1: Aggressive/Defensive asset mix for flexible asset allocation for different markets.

Year	A	B	C	D	E	F
1900						
1901						
1902						
1903						
1904						
1905						
1906						
1907						✓
1908						✓
1909						✓
1910						✓
1911						✓
1912						✓
1913						✓
1914						✓
1915						✓
1916						✓
1917						
1918						
1919						
1920						
1921						
1922						
1923						✓
1924						✓
1925	✓	✓				✓
1926	✓	✓				✓
1927	✓	✓	✓	✓		✓
1928	✓	✓	✓	✓		✓
1929		✓	✓	✓		✓
1930		✓	✓	✓		✓
1931						
1932						
1933						
1934						
1935					✓	
1936					✓	
1937				✓	✓	✓
1938					✓	✓
1939						✓
1940						

Year	A	B	C	D	E	F
1941						
1942						
1943						
1944						
1945				✓		
1946				✓		
1947	✓		✓	✓		
1948	✓		✓	✓		✓
1949	✓		✓			✓
1950	✓		✓			✓
1951	✓		✓		✓	✓
1952	✓		✓		✓	✓
1953	✓	✓	✓		✓	
1954	✓	✓			✓	
1955	✓	✓				
1956	✓	✓				
1957	✓	✓	✓	✓		
1958	✓	✓			✓	
1959	✓	✓			✓	
1960	✓	✓			✓	✓
1961	✓	✓	✓	✓	✓	✓
1962	✓	✓	✓			✓
1963	✓	✓	✓			✓
1964	✓	✓	✓			✓
1965	✓	✓	✓			✓
1966	✓	✓	✓			✓
1967		✓	✓			
1968		✓	✓			
1969		✓	✓			
1970		✓	✓			✓
1971						✓
1972						
1973						
1974						
1975						
1976						
1977						
1978					✓	
1979					✓	
1980				✓	✓	
1981			✓	✓	✓	✓

Year	A	B	C	D	E	F
1982		✓	✓	✓	✓	✓
1983		✓	✓	✓	✓	
1984		✓	✓	✓	✓	
1985	✓	✓	✓		✓	
1986	✓	✓	✓		✓	✓
1987	✓	✓	✓		✓	✓
1988	✓	✓	✓	✓	✓	
1989	✓	✓	✓	✓		
1990	✓	✓	✓	✓		
1991	✓	✓		✓		
1992	✓	✓		✓		
1993	✓	✓		✓		
1994	✓	✓		✓		
1995	✓	✓		✓		
1996	✓	✓	✓	✓		
1997	✓	✓	✓	✓		
1998	✓	✓	✓	✓		✓
1999	✓	✓	✓	✓		✓
2000		✓	✓	✓		✓
2001		✓	✓	✓		✓
2002			✓			✓
2003						
2004						
2005						
2006						
2007			✓			✓
2008			✓	✓	✓	✓
2009						

Now, we know when to switch between the aggressive and the defensive asset mix. The next question is "how aggressive, how defensive?"

If your withdrawal rate is higher than the SWR, calculate the worst case portfolio life for each one of the aggressive/defensive asset mix combinations in 10% increments. Fill these numbers into a matrix as shown in Example 25.4. The combination with the longest portfolio life is the optimum aggressive/defensive equity allocation. If there is more than one optimum, chose the one that is most conservative.

Example 25.4

Judy, 65, is just retiring. She has $1,000,000 savings for retirement; she needs annually $44,000 in current dollars.

Her equities grow the same as the S&P500 index, plus 2% for dividends, less 0.8% for management fees. The net yield of the fixed income portion of her portfolio is the same as the historical 6-month CD yield plus 1%.

Judy wants to follow the flexible asset allocation strategy. What is her optimum aggressive and defensive asset mix?

The aggressive/defensive asset mix matrix is given below. The maximum age at which the portfolio expires in the worst case is age 85, as highlighted in bold.

Worst Case Portfolio Life, years

Aggressive Equity % \ Defensive Equity %	0	10	20	30	40	50	60	70	80	90	100
100	77	78	79	79	79	79	79	79	78	78	78
90	79	80	81	81	81	81	81	80	80	80	
80	81	82	82	83	83	83	83	83	82		
70	83	84	84	84	**85**	84	84	83			
60	84	**85**	**85**	**85**	84	84	84				
50	84	**85**	**85**	**85**	84	84					
40	83	**85**	**85**	**85**	84						
30	83	84	**85**	84							
20	83	84	84								
10	82	84									
0	82										

In her aggressive posture, Judy can allocate between 30% and 60% to equities. In her defensive posture, she can allocate between 10% and 30% to equities.

How does this compare to the strategic asset allocation?

Look at the bottom diagonal line, the outcome for the strategic asset allocation. Along this line, the worst case portfolio lasted until age 84 for any equity percentage between 10% and 60%. By using the flexible asset allocation and spending 30 minutes a year to decide whether she should have an aggressive or defensive stance in her portfolio, Judy was able to add one year to her worst case portfolio life.

The following charts compare the "buy-and-hold" of the strategic asset allocation (50/50 asset mix) with the flexible asset allocation. In the flexible asset allocation, 30% is allocated to equities when defensive and 60% when aggressive.

The median portfolio values:

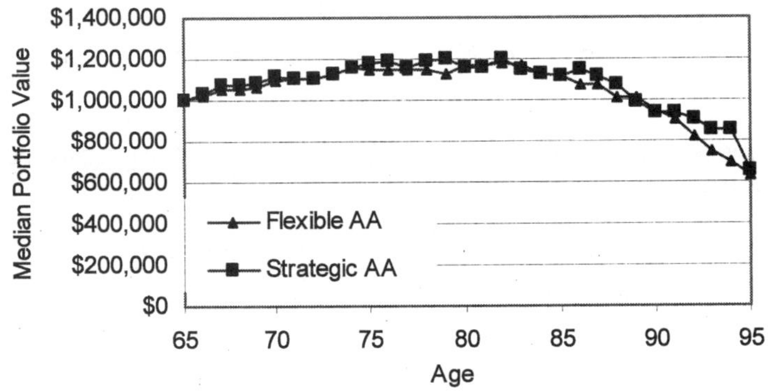

The unlucky portfolio values:

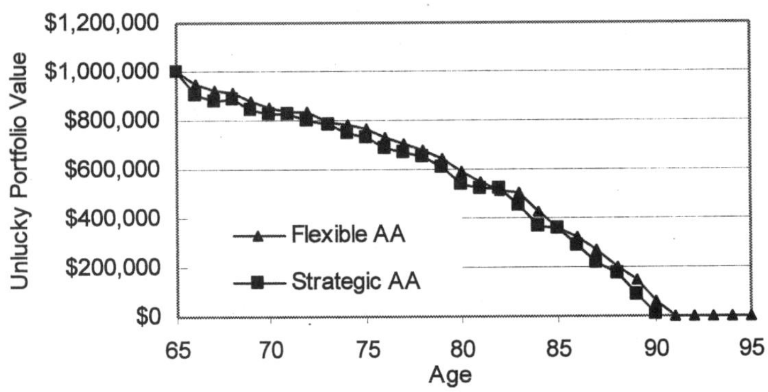

The lucky portfolio values:

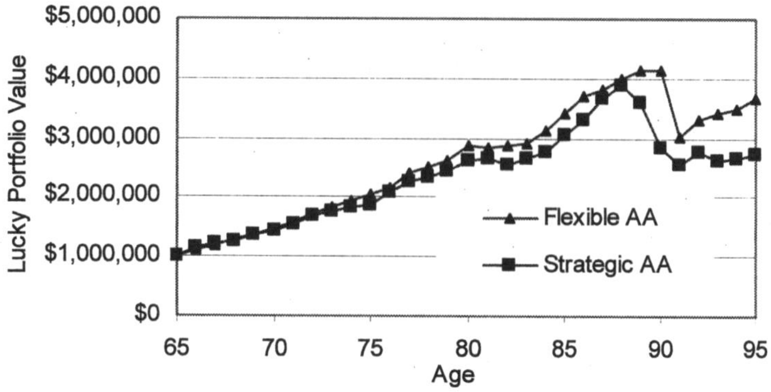

The probability of receiving the full income:

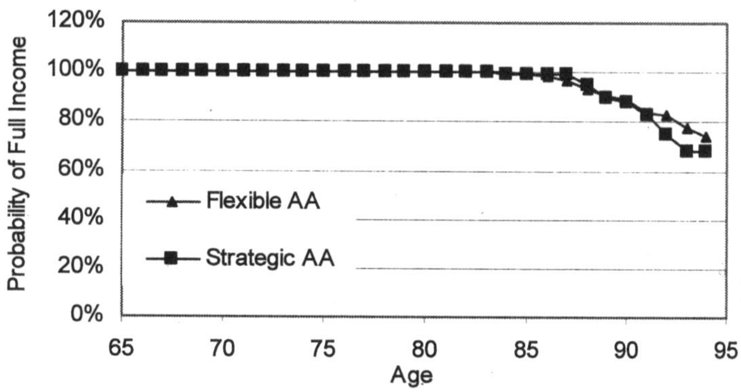

Compared with the strategic asset allocation, the flexible asset allocation improved the outcome only slightly in this example.

If you have an accumulation portfolio or you have a distribution portfolio with a withdrawal rate lower than the SWR, then you have a non–depleting portfolio. In this case, calculate out the median portfolio value for each one of the aggressive/defensive asset mix combinations in 10% increments. Insert these numbers into a matrix as shown in Example 25.5. The combination with the highest median portfolio value is the optimum aggressive/defensive equity allocation.

Example 25.5

Steve, 35, has $100,000 in his savings for retirement. He saves annually $15,000. His equities grow the same as the S&P500 index, plus 2% for dividends, less 0.8% for management fees. The net yield of the fixed income portion of his portfolio is the same as historical 6-month CD yield plus 1%.

Steve wants to follow the flexible asset allocation strategy for the next 20 years. What is his optimum aggressive and defensive asset mix?

The aggressive/defensive asset mix matrix is given below. The number in each box is the median portfolio value after 20 years for all combinations of asset mixes. The greatest amount of money is made when Steve holds an aggressive portfolio with 100% equities and a defensive one with 40% equities. This generated $1.06 million.

Median Portfolio Value x$1 million

Aggressive Equity % \ Defensive Equity %	0	10	20	30	40	50	60	70	80	90	100
100	1.03	1.06	1.05	1.04	1.06	1.04	1.04	1.01	1.00	1.00	1.00
90	1.00	1.03	1.04	1.02	1.03	1.03	1.83	1.00	0.99	0.99	
80	0.99	1.00	1.03	1.01	1.00	1.01	1.02	0.99	0.98		
70	0.99	0.98	0.99	**1.01**	0.99	0.98	0.99	0.99			
60	0.96	0.97	0.96	0.98	0.99	0.96	0.96				
50	0.95	0.95	0.95	0.95	0.95	0.95					
40	0.90	0.92	0.92	0.93	0.93						
30	0.88	0.87	0.87	0.88							
20	0.88	0.85	0.84								
10	0.87	0.84									
0	0.84										

However, Steve does not like such high swings in his asset mix. He wants to keep his equity percentage between 30% (defensive) and 70% (aggressive). That box reads $1.01 million as indicated in bold.

How does this compare to the strategic asset allocation? Look at the bottom diagonal line. The median portfolio grew most when 70% was allocated to equities, $0.99 million. This is the outcome for the strategic asset allocation. In this case, the difference between these two asset allocation strategies was insignificant.

The following charts compare the strategic asset allocation (70/30-asset mix) with the flexible asset allocation. In the flexible asset allocation, 30% is allocated to equities when defensive and 70% when aggressive.

The median portfolio values:

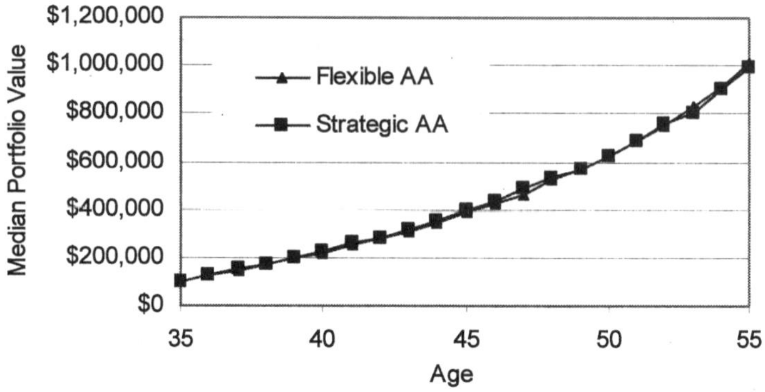

The unlucky portfolio values:

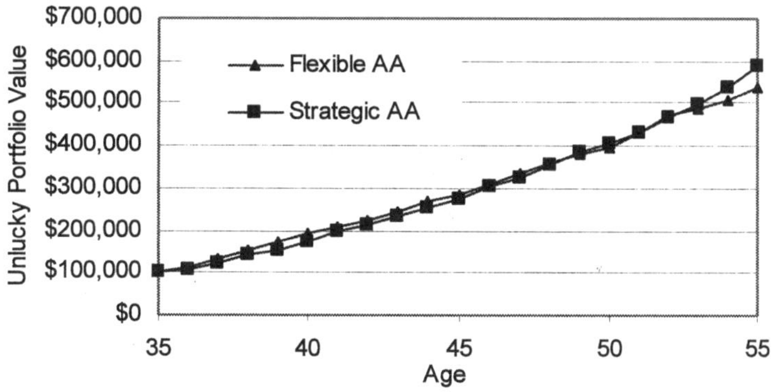

The lucky portfolio values:

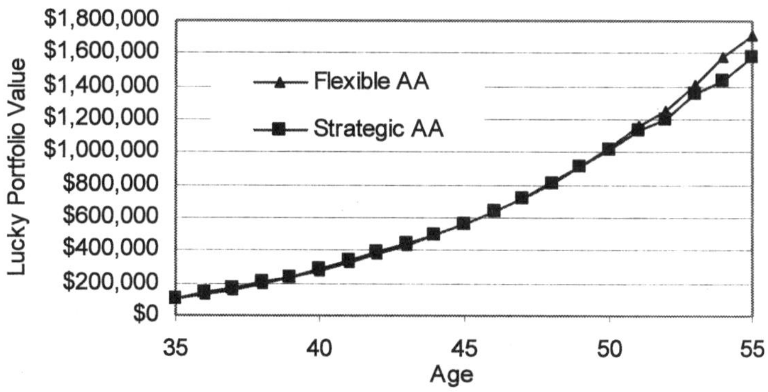

Sustainable Withdrawal Rates:

Sustainable withdrawal rates for the flexible asset allocation strategy are depicted in Table 25.2. The equity proxy is the S&P500 index. The equity allocation is 70% when the portfolio is aggressive and 30% when the portfolio is defensive. The net yield on the fixed income portion of the portfolio is the historical 6–month CD yield plus 0.5%.

Table 25.2: Sustainable withdrawal rates for flexible asset allocation, US markets, S&P500

Time Horizon	Flexible Asset Allocation	
	Equity Alpha=0	Equity Alpha=1
20 years	4.8%	5.0%
30 years	3.6%	3.8%
40 years	2.8%	3.0%

Effective Growth Rates:

Table 25.3 shows the effective growth rate (EGR) for the flexible asset allocation strategy as described in this chapter. Enter 3% as the "average" inflation rate for indexation of withdrawals in a standard retirement calculator. Enter the EGR figure from this table as the "average growth rate". This will help you to forecast the portfolio value or its longevity with reasonable accuracy using a standard retirement calculator.

The numbers in Table 25.3 are based on the equity allocation of 70% when the portfolio is aggressive and 30% when the portfolio is defensive. The equity alpha is zero. The net yield on the fixed income portion of the portfolio is the historical 6–month CD yield plus 0.5%.

Table 25.3: Effective growth rate, flexible asset allocation, equity is S&P500

Initial Withdrawal Rate	Outcome		
	Unlucky	Median	Lucky
	Effective Growth Rate:		
0%	2.6%	5.6%	8.9%
2%	3.1%	5.0%	8.5%
4%	3.1%	4.9%	7.7%
6%	1.7%	4.7%	7.6%
8%	0.7%	5.3%	8.9%
10%	–0.1%	5.6%	9.7%

Sustainable Asset Multiplier:

Table 25.4 shows the sustainable asset multiplier for the flexible asset allocation strategy. The equity allocation is 70% when the portfolio is aggressive and 30% when the portfolio is defensive. The net yield on the fixed income portion of the portfolio is the historical 6–month CD yield plus 0.5%.

Table 25.4: Simplified sustainable asset multiplier, flexible asset allocation, portfolio size required for $10,000 annual income fully indexed to CPI

Time Horizon	Minimum Portfolio Size Required for $10,000 annual income indexed fully to CPI, maximum 10% probability of depletion	
	Alpha=0%	Alpha=1%
20 years	$206,000	$199,500
30 years	$275,200	$264,300
40 years	$348,700	$325,700

The Effect of Timing Strategy:

We can measure the effect of timing based on flexible asset allocation by measuring the difference in the compound annual return of the median portfolio. Table 25.5 indicates the impact of this timing strategy.

Table 25.5: The effect of timing – flexible asset allocation

	Initial Withdrawal Rate					
	0%	2%	4%	6%	8%	10%
Strategic Asset Allocation – compound annual return of the median portfolio (from tables 20.1, 20.3)	6.0%	5.2%	5.1%	4.9%	5.6%	5.8%
Flexible Asset Allocation – compound annual return of the median portfolio (from Table 25.3)	5.6%	4.9%	4.8%	4.7%	5.2%	5.6%
Impact of FAA timing strategy on compound annual return	–7%	–6%	–6%	–4%	–7%	–3%

Conclusion:

Flexible asset allocation is a trend following system. Unlike tactical asset allocation, it is more prone to market risks because it may be too slow to recognize and react to trend changes. Tactical asset allocation *anticipates* market events, while the trend following system *reacts* to market events.

The secular bullish trends come few and far in between. If you are not lucky, you may spend your entire retirement in a secular sideways market and the flexible asset allocation will do nothing for you. If you are lucky, then you may be able to take advantage of it. That is, if you catch it in time. If you want better results, you need to follow the market trends more frequently than once a year.

Always keep in mind that future performance will not be the same. As it is with any automated market timing system, not all trade decisions will be successful. You will get occasional false signals.

The bottom line is that the strategic asset allocation produced better results than the flexible asset allocation.

Chapter 26

Combo Asset Allocation

Can we combine the flexible asset allocation with the tactical and try to make use of the best of both worlds? Sure, we can. This way, you can "buy low, sell high" in sideways trends and "buy high, sell higher" in bullish trends.

For the lack of creativity on my part, let's call this the "Combo Asset Allocation" or CAA for short. Here is how CAA it works:

- When the secular trend is bullish, then use the signals from the flexible asset allocation strategy and go aggressive. Ignore the tactical asset allocation signals during the secular bullish trend.
- After a secular bullish trend ends (as per the rules of the flexible asset allocation), go defensive. Ignore the signals from the tactical asset allocation for the three years that follow the secular bullish trend and stay defensive during that time.
- Otherwise follow the signals from the tactical asset allocation strategy until a new secular bullish trend is confirmed.

Table 26.1 indicates whether the portfolios were aggressive or defensive for different market histories. A check mark means that the asset mix was aggressive during the year. Otherwise, the asset mix was defensive. Each column is for a different equity index:

A – DJIA (US),
B – S&500 (US),
C – SP/TSX (Canada),
D – FTSE AllShares (UK),
E – Nikkei 225 (Japan),
F – ASX All Ord. (Australia)

Table 26.1: Aggressive/Defensive asset mix for combo asset allocation for different markets.

Year	A	B	C	D	E	F
1900						
1901						
1902						
1903	✓					
1904	✓					
1905						
1906						
1907	✓	✓				✓
1908	✓	✓		✓		✓
1909						✓
1910	✓					✓
1911	✓	✓		✓		✓
1912	✓	✓				✓
1913				✓		✓
1914	✓	✓		✓		✓
1915	✓	✓		✓		✓
1916				✓		✓
1917	✓					
1918	✓	✓		✓		
1919						
1920						
1921	✓	✓		✓	✓	
1922				✓		✓
1923					✓	✓
1924	✓	✓		✓		✓
1925	✓	✓				✓
1926	✓	✓				✓
1927	✓	✓	✓	✓	✓	✓
1928	✓	✓	✓	✓	✓	✓
1929		✓	✓	✓	✓	✓
1930		✓	✓	✓	✓	✓
1931					✓	
1932	✓					
1933	✓	✓	✓			
1934						
1935		✓			✓	
1936					✓	
1937					✓	✓
1938	✓	✓	✓	✓	✓	✓
1939		✓	✓	✓		✓
1940	✓	✓	✓			
1941	✓	✓	✓	✓	✓	
1942	✓	✓	✓			✓
1943					✓	✓
1944					✓	
1945				✓	✓	
1946				✓	✓	
1947	✓	✓	✓	✓	✓	
1948	✓	✓	✓	✓		✓
1949	✓	✓	✓			✓
1950	✓		✓			✓
1951	✓		✓		✓	✓
1952	✓		✓		✓	✓
1953	✓	✓	✓	✓	✓	
1954	✓	✓			✓	
1955	✓	✓				
1956	✓	✓		✓		
1957	✓	✓	✓	✓		✓
1958	✓	✓	✓	✓	✓	
1959	✓	✓			✓	
1960	✓	✓	✓		✓	✓
1961	✓	✓	✓	✓	✓	✓
1962	✓	✓	✓	✓		✓
1963	✓	✓	✓	✓		✓
1964	✓	✓	✓	✓	✓	✓
1965	✓	✓	✓	✓	✓	✓
1966	✓	✓	✓			✓
1967		✓	✓	✓		
1968		✓	✓		✓	
1969	✓	✓	✓			
1970	✓	✓	✓	✓		✓
1971				✓	✓	✓
1972						✓
1973				✓		
1974	✓	✓	✓	✓	✓	✓
1975	✓	✓	✓	✓	✓	✓
1976					✓	
1977				✓	✓	
1978	✓	✓			✓	✓
1979	✓			✓	✓	
1980				✓	✓	
1981			✓	✓	✓	
1982	✓	✓	✓	✓	✓	✓
1983		✓	✓	✓	✓	✓
1984		✓	✓	✓	✓	
1985	✓	✓	✓		✓	
1986	✓	✓	✓		✓	
1987	✓	✓	✓		✓	
1988	✓	✓	✓	✓	✓	✓
1989	✓	✓	✓	✓		
1990	✓	✓	✓	✓		✓
1991	✓	✓		✓		✓
1992	✓	✓		✓	✓	
1993	✓	✓	✓	✓	✓	✓
1994	✓	✓		✓		
1995	✓	✓	✓	✓		✓
1996	✓	✓	✓	✓		
1997	✓	✓	✓	✓		✓
1998	✓	✓	✓	✓	✓	✓
1999	✓	✓	✓	✓	✓	✓
2000			✓	✓		✓
2001			✓	✓	✓	✓
2002			✓		✓	✓
2003	✓	✓			✓	
2004						
2005	✓					
2006	✓					
2007			✓			✓
2008			✓	✓	✓	✓
2009	✓	✓				

Now that we know when to switch between the aggressive and the defensive asset mixes, the next question is defining what is aggressive and what is defensive.

If your withdrawal rate is higher than the SWR, then you have a depleting portfolio. In this case, calculate the worst case portfolio life for each of the aggressive/defensive asset mix combinations in 10% increments. Enter these numbers into a matrix as shown in Example 26.1. The combination with the longest portfolio life is the optimum aggressive/defensive equity allocation. If there is more than one optimum, choose the one that is most conservative.

Example 26.1

Carol, 65, is just retiring. She has $1,000,000 in savings for retirement; she needs annually $44,000 in current dollars.

Her equities grow the same as the S&P500 index, plus 2% for dividends, less 0.8% for management fees. The net yield of the fixed income portion of her portfolio is the same as the historical 6-month CD yield plus 1%.

Carol wants to follow the combo asset allocation strategy. What is her optimum aggressive and defensive asset mix?

The aggressive/defensive asset mix matrix is shown below. The maximum age at which the portfolio expires in the worst case is age 86, as highlighted in bold.

For that, Carol can allocate 50% to equities when aggressive and 10% to equities when defensive.

Worst Case Portfolio Life, years

Aggressive Equity % \ Defensive Equity %	0	10	20	30	40	50	60	70	80	90	100
100	77	78	78	79	79	79	79	78	78	78	78
90	79	80	80	80	81	81	81	80	80	80	
80	81	82	82	83	83	83	83	83	82		
70	83	84	84	84	85	84	84	83			
60	85	85	85	85	85	84	84				
50	85	**86**	85	85	85	84					
40	85	85	85	85	84						
30	84	85	85	84							
20	84	85	84								
10	83	84									
0	82										

How does this compare to the strategic asset allocation?

Look at the bottom diagonal line, the outcome for the strategic asset allocation. Along this line, the worst case portfolio lasted until age 84 for any equity percentage between 10% and 60%. By using the combo asset allocation, Carol was able to add 2 years to her worst case portfolio life.

The following charts compare the outcomes of the strategic asset allocation (50/50 asset mix) with the combo asset allocation strategy. In the combo asset allocation, 10% is allocated to equities when defensive and 50% when aggressive.

The median portfolio values:

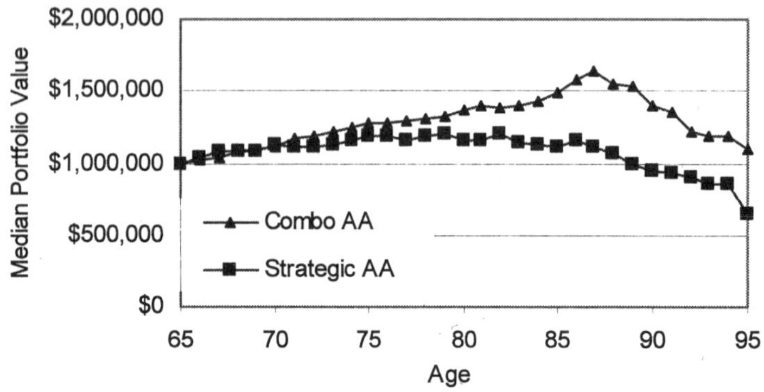

The unlucky portfolio values:

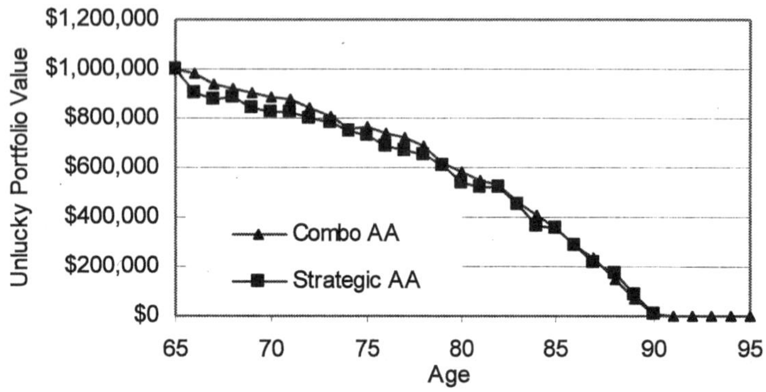

The lucky portfolio values:

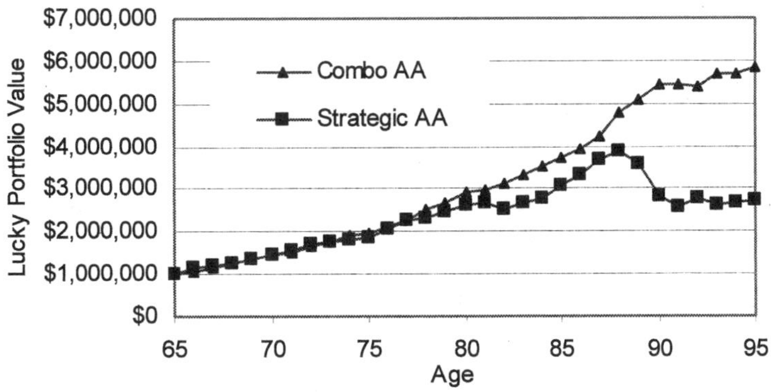

The probability of receiving the full income:

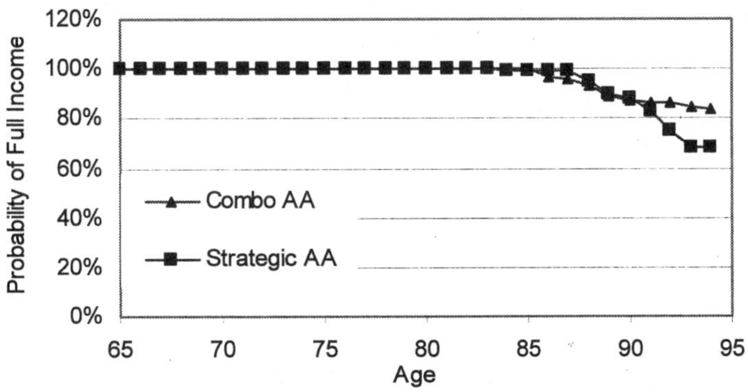

In this example, the combo strategy outperformed the strategic asset allocation.

If you have an accumulation portfolio or you have a distribution portfolio with a withdrawal rate lower than the SWR, then you have a non–depleting portfolio. In this case, figure out the median portfolio value for each of the aggressive/defensive asset mix combinations in 10% increments. Enter these numbers into a matrix as shown in Example 26.2. The combination with the highest median portfolio value is the optimum aggressive/defensive equity allocation.

Here is an accumulation example.

Example 26.2

Steve, 35, has $100,000 in his savings for retirement. He saves annually $15,000.

His equities grow the same as the S&P500 index, plus 2% for dividends, less 0.8% for management fees. The net yield of the fixed income portion of his portfolio is the same as the historical 6-month CD yield plus 1%.

Steve wants to follow the combo asset allocation strategy for the next 20 years. What is his optimum aggressive and defensive asset mix?

The aggressive/defensive asset mix matrix is given below. The number in each box is the median portfolio value after 20 years for all combinations of asset mixes. The highest amount of money is made when Steve holds an aggressive portfolio with 100% equities and a defensive one with 0% equities. This generated $1.34 million.

Median Portfolio Value x$1 million

Aggressive Equity % \ Defensive Equity %	0	10	20	30	40	50	60	70	80	90	100
100	1.34	1.33	1.24	1.21	1.17	1.17	1.15	1.10	1.07	1.03	1.00
90	1.29	1.27	1.19	1.14	1.14	1.12	1.12	1.06	1.02	0.99	
80	1.23	1.18	1.14	1.11	1.10	1.08	1.07	1.02	0.98		
70	1.17	1.14	1.09	**1.08**	1.06	1.04	1.02	0.99			
60	1.13	1.06	1.04	1.05	1.03	0.99	0.96				
50	1.05	1.01	1.00	0.99	0.98	0.95					
40	0.98	0.96	0.94	0.94	0.93						
30	0.94	0.92	0.89	0.88							
20	0.91	0.88	0.84								
10	0.89	0.84									
0	0.84										

However, Steve does not like such high swings in his asset mix. He wants to keep his equity percentage between 30% (when defensive) and 70% (when aggressive). That box reads $1.08 million, indicated in bold.

How does this compare to the strategic asset allocation?

Look at the bottom diagonal line. The median portfolio made the most money when 70% was allocated to equities, $990,000. This is the outcome for the strategic asset allocation. By using the combo asset allocation and spending an hour a year to decide whether he should have an aggressive or defensive stance in his portfolio, Steve was able to accumulate $90,000 more in his portfolio.

The following charts compare the strategic asset allocation (70/30-asset mix) with the flexible asset allocation. In the flexible asset allocation, 30% is allocated to equities when defensive and 70% when aggressive. In this example, the combo strategy slightly outperformed the strategic asset allocation.

The median portfolio value:

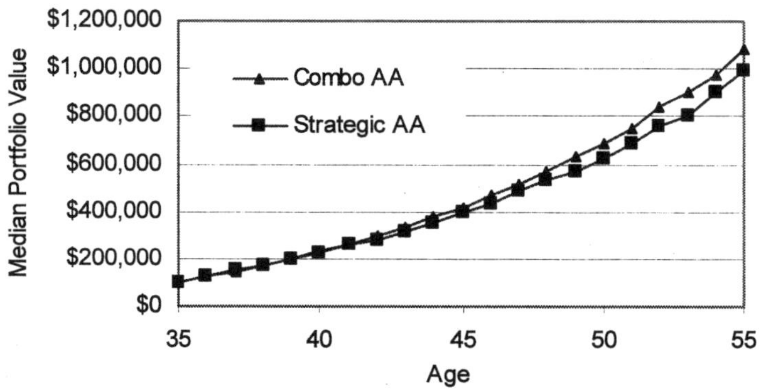

The unlucky portfolio value:

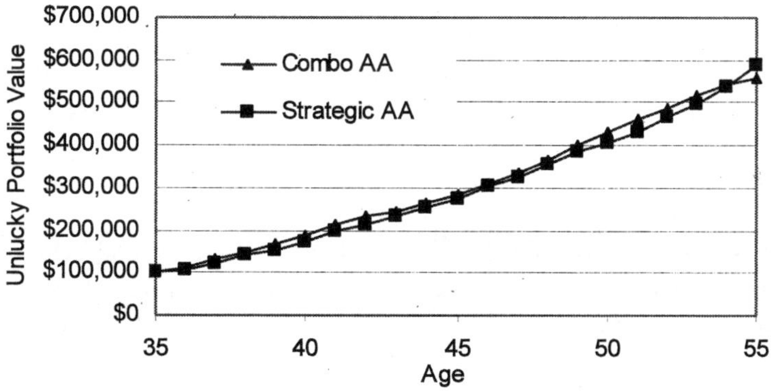

The lucky portfolio value:

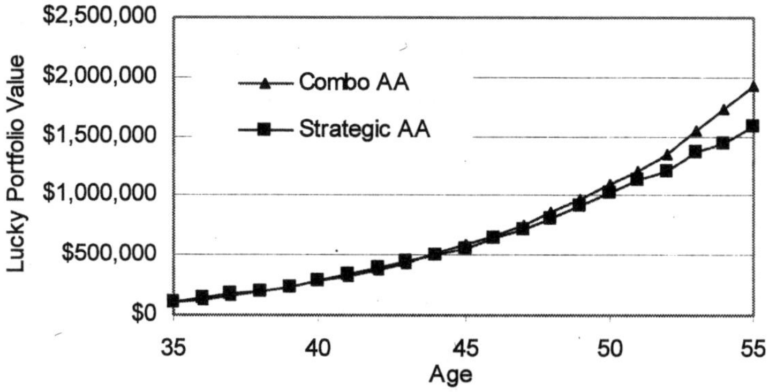

Sustainable Withdrawal Rates:

Sustainable withdrawal rates for the combo asset allocation strategy are depicted on Table 26.2. The equity proxy is the S&P500 index. The equity allocation is 70% when the portfolio is aggressive and 30% when the portfolio is defensive. The net yield on the fixed income portion of the portfolio is the historical 6–month CD yield plus 0.5%

Table 26.2: Sustainable withdrawal rates for combo asset allocation, US markets, S&P500

Time Horizon	Flexible Asset Allocation	
	Equity Alpha=0	Equity Alpha=1
20 years	5.1%	5.4%
30 years	3.8%	4.1%
40 years	3.1%	3.3%

Effective Growth Rates:

Table 26.3 shows the effective growth rate (EGR) for the combo asset allocation strategy as described in this chapter. Enter 3% as the "average" inflation rate for the indexation of withdrawals in a standard retirement calculator. Enter the EGR figure from this table as the "average growth rate". This will help you to forecast the portfolio value or its longevity with reasonable accuracy using a standard retirement calculator.

The numbers in Table 26.3 are based on the equity allocation of 70% when the portfolio is aggressive and 30% when the portfolio is defensive. The equity alpha is zero. The net yield on the fixed income portion of the portfolio is the historical 6–month CD yield plus 0.5%.

Table 26.3: Effective Growth Rate, combo asset allocation, equity is S&P500

Initial Withdrawal Rate	Outcome		
	Unlucky	Median	Lucky
	Effective Growth Rate:		
0%	3.1%	6.1%	9.7%
2%	3.5%	5.9%	9.3%
4%	3.8%	5.6%	8.6%
6%	2.3%	5.5%	7.9%
8%	1.5%	5.8%	9.1%
10%	0.6%	5.9%	10.0%

Sustainable Asset Multiplier:

Table 26.4 shows the sustainable asset multiplier for the combo asset allocation strategy. The equity allocation is 70% when the portfolio is aggressive and 30% when the portfolio is defensive. The net yield on the fixed income portion of the portfolio is the historical 6–month CD yield plus 0.5%.

Table 26.4: Simplified sustainable asset multiplier, combo asset allocation portfolio size required for $10,000 annual income fully indexed to CPI

Time Horizon	Minimum Portfolio Size Required for $10,000 annual income indexed fully to CPI, maximum 10% probability of depletion	
	Alpha=0%	Alpha=1%
20 years	$193,000	$184,800
30 years	$260,300	$240,500
40 years	$321,000	$294,300

The Effect of Timing Strategy:

We can measure the effect of timing based on the combo asset allocation by measuring the difference in the compound annual return of the median portfolio. Table 26.5 indicates the impact of this timing strategy.

Table 26.5: The effect of timing – combo asset allocation

	Initial Withdrawal Rate					
	0%	2%	4%	6%	8%	10%
Strategic Asset Allocation – compound annual return of the median portfolio (from tables 19.1, 19.3)	6.0%	5.2%	5.1%	4.9%	5.6%	5.8%
Combo Asset Allocation – compound annual return of the median portfolio (from Table 26.3)	6.1%	5.9%	5.6%	5.5%	5.8%	5.9%
Impact of timing strategy on compound annual return	2%	13%	10%	12%	4%	2%

Conclusion:

The combo asset allocation attempts to combine the anticipatory characteristics of the tactical asset allocation with the reactive characteristics of the trend following system.

History shows that it performs better than the flexible asset allocation strategy, but worse than the tactical asset allocation. In all cases the timing decision is done once a year, which may be not frequent enough. Keep in mind that this conclusion applies only to a typical retirement time horizon. If you use a different time horizon, the results will be very different, as we will see later on.

Always keep in mind that the future performance will be different. As it is with any automated market timing system, not all trade decisions will be successful. You will get occasional false signals.

Chapter 27

If You Miss the Best …

Every so often, markets go down. Since 1900, about one in three years experienced a negative equity index return[52]. It is to the advantage of the financial industry that you stay in the markets through thick and thin. How else would we –the investment industry– make money? We don't make money if you don't invest.

After every market crash, I get piles of communications from mutual funds and other financial circles. Many of them explain how we as advisors should deal with nervous and difficult clients. I don't know if they realize it, but this in itself is an insult to the client. Think about it: the poor client just lost half of his life savings and the industry has the audacity to call him "nervous" and "difficult".

One of the typical "education" pieces I receive after each market crash reads something like this: "If you missed the best 50 days of the market, your return over the last 10 years would be –1%". You will find a different number of days, years and growth rates in different sales materials. But in essence, what they try to tell you is "stay in the market, because nobody can time the markets"

It is amazing that all these publications appear *after* a market crash, telling you stay invested. If they are so good in telling you what to do after the crash, why don't they tell you *before* the crash something like "If you missed the worst 50 days in the last 25 years, your annual return would be 25%?"

First of all, it is impossible to miss only the 50 best days in 25 years. The chances of missing only the best 50 days are one in 1.681 followed by 125 zeros[53]. Don't worry; it is not going happen to you or anyone you know. But this is how Wall Street tries to scare you into staying invested and paying them management fees all your life.

However, this raises an interesting point. Go back to Table 7.1 in Chapter 7. During a secular bullish trend, the average index grows about 15% per year. Sounds great, but maybe just like any other "average" number, this is meaningless too. All you need to do is invest during the best ten or fifteen days, make your 15% and then get out. Of course, in reality, this would also be impossible; market timing is not so easy.

Here is my research based on DJIA between January 1st, 1900 and December 31, 2008. I used a pure index return, no dividends, no transaction fees and no interest income while the money sits in cash. We invest $1,000 at the beginning of 1900.

[52] DJIA

[53] 25 years, average 250 trading days per year, 6250 of available trading days, assuming you are allowed one trade on any trading day. Using Excel's COMBIN(6250,50) function

I also changed my time interval from days to months. If I am going to miss anything, it is more logical to miss months rather than days. There are 1305 months during this time period[54]. Table 27.1 shows the results.

Table 27.1: The effect of missing the best or the worst months

Number of Months Missed	Percent of Time out of the Market	Missed Best Months		Missed Worst Months	
		$1,000 invested becomes	Compound Annual Return	$1,000 invested becomes	Compound Annual Return
0 (Buy and hold)	0.00%	$132,815	4.54%	$132,815	4.54%
1	0.08%	$95,031	4.22%	$194,557	4.90%
3	0.23%	$56,994	3.74%	$337,041	5.43%
5	0.38%	$37,307	3.34%	$551,493	5.90%
10	0.77%	$18,680	2.70%	$1,612,958	6.94%
20	1.53%	$5,559	1.57%	$7,563,091	8.45%
30	**2.30%**	$1,933	**0.60%**	$26,351,084	9.69%
50	3.83%	$310	–1.06%	$224,575,874	11.84%
100	7.66%	$8.46	–4.24%	$10,392,962,546	15.81%
150	11.49%	$0.44	–6.77%	$201,317,127,876	18.97%

A buy–and–hold investor might look at this table and say "I had better stay invested for the entire term to maximize my return" A market–timer might look at this same table and say "Gee, if I miss the worst 150 months, I may end up three times richer than Bill Gates and Warren Buffett combined". Wishful thinking.

However, one thing is true: look at Table 27.1, the row with "30" months missed. Read the compound annual return: if you miss the best 30 months, which is 2.3% of the time, then your return is only 0.60%. I calculated that if you miss the best 2.5% of the months, your return is 0%. Furthermore, these 2.5% best months not only make up for the huge losses that happen in the worst 2.5% months, but also gives you an average return that the "stocks for the long run" people rave about.

The bottom line is that what happens in 5% of the time (good or bad) determines the success or failure of your portfolio. In the other 95% of the time, basically no significant returns happen. During that time, your pursuit of your dreams helps us create wealth, not necessarily for you but for ourselves, i.e. the players in the financial industry.

[54] Markets were closed for a some months in 1914.

Another argument might be this: You can't really miss just the best 10 months or the worst 10 months. How about missing the best and the worst 10 months? Now, that is more likely isn't it? Not really. Missing the best *and* the worst 10 months is much more improbable[55] than missing the best *or* the worst 10 months. However, let's continue our journey in this fantasyland. Table 27.2 shows the results.

Table 27.2: The effect of missing the best and the worst months

		Missed Best and Worst Months	
Number of Months Missed	Percent of Time out of Market	$1,000 invested becomes	Compound Annual Return
0 (Buy and Hold)	0.00	$132,815	4.54%
2	0.15	$139,209	4.59%
6	0.46	$144,633	4.62%
10	0.77	$154,913	4.69%
20	1.53	$226,861	5.05%
40	3.07	$316,565	5.37%
60	4.60	$383,551	5.55%
100	7.66	$524,888	5.85%
200	15.33	$661,776	6.08%
300	22.99	$672,313	6.09%

Why is it that if you miss the same number of best *and* worst months, your portfolio grows *always* more than a buy–and–hold portfolio? This has to do with how markets move:

- Generally, it takes a longer time for the index to go up than to go down for the same percentage change. The downward moves are usually sharper than the upward moves, like the teeth of a carpenter's saw, held upside down.

> If you are hoping "to miss" or "not to miss" anything, it is better to miss the worst month(s) than not–to–miss the best month(s).

[55] If you make one trading decision each month (buy, hold, sell), then missing ten specific months in 1305 months is a one in 2.5E31 chance, missing twenty is a one in 3.3E57 chance.

> After a loss, you need a much higher percentage growth than the percentage loss. If you lose 50% of your portfolio, you need a 100% gain to break even in an accumulation portfolio. In a distribution portfolio, you need significantly more than a 100% gain to break even, depending on your withdrawal rate.

Now that the theory is behind us, the question remains: can we find a way of avoiding at least some of the worst months and participating in some of the best months with our portfolio?

In Chapter 25, with flexible asset allocation strategy, we tried to accomplish that. But the results indicated that looking at the markets once a year did not work well. If you research markets correctly, you will find that regardless of how logical a theory might sound initially, many ideas fail in the real world.

So, let's move one step forward. Instead of looking at the markets annually, let's look at the market index once a month. This should increase our ability to follow the developing trends more closely.

When you invest your money there are only five possible outcomes:

1. Large loss
2. Small loss
3. Break even
4. Small gain
5. Large gain

If you can eliminate large losses as much as possible, then markets will take care of the rest. All we need is a method that gives us some indication of peaking or bottoming out. You are still not going to catch the exact top or bottom, but you might be able to avoid some of the worst market crashes. It is important to know, that you do not need to catch the top and the bottom perfectly for a profitable market timing strategy. You could be right only 50% of the time and still be ahead of buy–and–hold.

I use a technical analysis tool called the "simple moving average". Here is how the procedure works:

- Make a list of the equity index value for each month.
- Take the average of the last five months for each row. This is the 5–month moving average.
- Take the average of the last twelve months for each row. This is the 12–month moving average.
- If the 5–month moving average is lower than the 12–month moving average and the 12–month moving average is declining, then markets may be going into a bearish trend. Go defensive.
- Otherwise, stay aggressive.

Example 27.1 on the next page shows how it works step–by–step.

Example 27.1

Calculate the aggressive or defensive position of the portfolio for the dates shown below.

Month	Index Value	5-month Moving Average	12-month Moving Average	Is the 5-month MA below the 12-month MA?	Is the 12-month MA declining?	Aggressive or Defensive?
Oct-05	10440.1					
Nov-05	10805.9					
Dec-05	10717.5					
Jan-06	10864.9					
Feb-06	10993.4					
Mar-06	11109.3	10764.3				
Apr-06	11367.1	10898.2				
May-06	11168.3	11010.4				
Jun-06	11150.2	11100.6				
Jul-06	11185.7	11157.7				
Aug-06	11381.2	11196.1				
Sep-06	11679.1	11250.5				
Oct-06	12080.7	11312.9	11071.9	No	No	Aggressive
Nov-06	12221.9	11495.4	11208.6	No	No	Aggressive
Dec-06	12463.2	11709.7	11326.6	No	No	Aggressive
Jan-07	12621.7	11965.2	11472.1	No	No	Aggressive
Feb-07	12268.6	12213.3	11618.5	No	No	Aggressive
Mar-07	12354.4	12331.2	11724.8	No	No	Aggressive
Apr-07	13062.9	12386.0	11828.5	No	No	Aggressive
May-07	13627.6	12554.1	11969.8	No	No	Aggressive
Jun-07	13408.6	12787.0	12174.8	No	No	Aggressive
Jul-07	13212.0	12944.4	12363.0	No	No	Aggressive
Aug-07	13357.7	13133.1	12531.8	No	No	Aggressive
Sep-07	13895.6	13333.8	12696.5	No	No	Aggressive
Oct-07	13930.0	13500.3	12881.2	No	No	Aggressive
Nov-07	13371.7	13560.8	13035.4	No	No	Aggressive
Dec-07	13264.8	13553.4	13131.2	No	No	Aggressive
Jan-08	12650.4	13564.0	13198.0	No	No	Aggressive
Feb-08	12266.4	13422.5	13200.4	No	No	Aggressive
Mar-08	12262.9	13096.7	13200.2	Yes	Yes	Defensive
Apr-08	12820.1	12763.2	13192.6	Yes	Yes	Defensive
May-08	12638.3	12652.9	13172.3	Yes	Yes	Defensive
Jun-08	11350.0	12527.6	13089.9	Yes	Yes	Defensive
Jul-08	11378.0	12267.5	12918.3	Yes	Yes	Defensive
Aug-08	11543.5	12089.9	12765.5	Yes	Yes	Defensive
Sep-08	10850.7	11946.0	12614.3	Yes	Yes	Defensive
Oct-08	9325.0	11552.1	12360.6	Yes	Yes	Defensive
Nov-08	8829.0	10889.5	11976.8	Yes	Yes	Defensive
Dec-08	8776.4	10385.3	11598.3	Yes	Yes	Defensive

Figure 27.3 shows the S&P500 index for the 20–year period ending March 4, 2009. The arrows pointing up are the "buy" signals. The down arrows indicate the "sell" signals. During the past 20 years, there were two buy and two sell signals. If you had followed this technique, you would have avoided large losses, twice.

The problem with the technical analysis is this: most people do not have the discipline to check and follow the charts regularly. Once we make money, we confuse luck with talent. After a while, we become complacent and start trusting our own instincts instead of our methodology. Unfortunately, so does every other loser.

If you want to use any technical analysis to guide you, then you must trust *your methodology* and not *your instincts* at all times. No exceptions.

Figure 27.3: The buy and sell signals using 5–month / 20–month moving averages, courtesy of StockCharts.com

Comparing Strategies:

In the conclusion of the previous chapter, I noted that the results of tactical asset allocation were superior to the other asset allocation strategies for a typical retirement time horizon.

In this chapter, we are looking at DJIA between January 1, 1900 and December 31, 2008. Let's compare buy–and–hold, tactical, flexible and combo strategies with the moving average strategy we discussed above. Imagine that you can invest for the entire 109 years. With each timing strategy, we will hold 100% equity when aggressive and 100% cash when defensive. For the fun of it, let's add a 3% annual dividend yield to the equity return. When the money is parked in cash, assume it collects 3% interest annually.

We analyze each of these timing strategies with and without the overriding of the moving averages. For example, in the first case, we use only the tactical asset allocation decision–making process described in Chapter 24. In the second case, we will make portfolios aggressive (100% equity) only if *both* the tactical asset allocation *and* the 5–month / 12–month moving average crossover indicate an aggressive portfolio.

Table 27.3 indicates the portfolio values on December 31, 2008 if you were to invest $1,000 on January 1, 1900.

Table 27.3: Comparing Strategies

Strategy	Number of Months in Cash	Percent of Time out of the Market	$1,000 invested becomes	Compound Annual Return
Buy and Hold	0	0%	$3,432,919	7.66%
5–month / 12–month MA cross over	400	31%	$5,961,418	8.22%
Tactical Asset Allocation	685	52%	$210,235	4.98%
Tactical Asset allocation with 5–month 12–month MA cross over	957	73%	$292,620	5.29%
Flexible Asset Allocation	837	64%	$1,402,513	6.80%
Flexible Asset allocation with 5–month 12–month MA cross over	904	69%	$817,074	6.28%
Combo Asset Allocation	493	38%	$6,595,706	8.32%
Combo Asset allocation with 5–month 12–month MA cross over	739	57%	$3,292,753	7.64%

How do these strategies compare?

The highest growth happened with the combo asset allocation without using the moving average override. The portfolio was in cash in 38% of the time. Its compound annual growth rate was 8.32% versus the 7.66% of the buy–and–hold strategy. This translates into a 0.66% alpha with a greatly reduced market risk. Don't take that 0.66% alpha too lightly; it created a 92% larger portfolio during that same time period.

The next highest growth occurred with the 5–month / 12–month moving average crossover strategy alone. Its compound annual growth rate was 8.22% versus the 7.66% of the buy–and–hold strategy. That portfolio was in cash 31% of the time.

All other strategies performed worse than the buy–and–hold portfolio. The tactical asset allocation that I raved about in the previous chapter, had the worst outcome. What is the catch? Well, there is no catch. However, here is an important point that you must always keep in the back of your mind when evaluating strategies.

Every timing strategy has at least three legs that support it:

1. The characteristics of the equity index that it is based on,
2. The time horizon that you have,
3. The cash outflow that you require.

There are also other factors such as the alpha, management costs, and availability of different asset classes, trading costs, etc. However, these three legs are the most important ones.

No matter how smart a strategy might sound, if one these three legs do not match closely to your profile, then that strategy will likely not work for *you*. What works for an accumulation portfolio will fail for a distribution portfolio. What works for a 109–year market history will fail miserably for a 30–year time horizon. What works for the DJIA probably won't work as well for the NASDAQ. What works for a day–trader, will likely not work for a swing–trader who has an investment time horizon of a few weeks.

Throw away any research that includes strategies (including technical, asset allocation or timing strategies) that do not match *all* three legs. I have seen far too many publications that look at an accumulation portfolio using a 100–year history and then go on to conclude –without blinking an eye– that it should also work for a distribution portfolio with a 25–year retirement time horizon. That just does not work.

> If a research study involves a market index, a time horizon and a cash inflow/outflow that is not very similar to your own situation, then stay away from it.
>
> Don't waste your time, don't waste your money.

I have had to educate far too many of my retired clients who insisted on putting all of their money into stocks, after reading books that promote stocks for the long run. Some clients left me and went for "higher" returns with little understanding of risk, only to lose large chunks of their wealth. They became victims to research that does not apply to their specific situation. I hate to imagine how many billions of dollars must have been destroyed as a result of applying unsuitable research.

The opposite is also as bad. There are publications by prominent academics that promote retirement portfolios that include TIPS and bonds only –and nothing else. Their underlying research has one or more of the three legs missing.

Why do you think there is such great disappointment with the state of most pension funds? Most of them use the research based on models that ignore trend discontinuities. As a result, they miss the second and third legs of the list above. But they need to keep their jobs, so they will craft ridiculous excuses year after year to explain their shortfall.

Conclusion:

Before you go to work every day, do you listen to the weather report? If not, do you at least look up to see if there are any dark clouds in the sky? Doing so might prompt you to take an umbrella with you. Is it timing? No, it is common sense. How many times did you see the dark clouds before going to work and then said, "Maybe it will not rain today" or "I'll make it back home before the rain starts". What happened then? Did you get soaked in the downpour?

Market timing strategies are here to protect you from that downpour. Sometimes, you carry the umbrella with you but it does not rain. So what, a little prevention goes a long way in protecting you. Remember in the introduction I said, "Only if the frost had come one day later…" If you have to say, "I would have…" or "I should have..." too often, then what you have been doing is probably not working for you. Change your tack.

There are hundreds of timing methods in technical analysis. Moving average is just one of them. Make sure though, that any strategy that you decide to use is back–tested for the conditions that match your portfolio, your time horizon and your withdrawal strategy.

Don't fall into a trap that I fell into a few times in the past: I spent too much time in my early years for developing sophisticated trading methods. You can spend days, even weeks, developing advanced technical analysis indicators and procedures. What is worse, after spending so much time and effort, it is a lot easier to convince yourself that your system is "the best ever". The truth is that a well–designed set of moving averages or the century old point–and–figure method probably works better than anything that I invented. Don't waste too much time on reinventing the wheel. Those before us did all the work; benefit from them.

If the marketing material of an investment says something like "our sophisticated propriety computer model…", then avoid that fund. Either they are lying (they may just be using the same old technical and/or fundamental techniques) or if their model is indeed "sophisticated", it may eventually backfire with your money in it. It is better to avoid a sophisticated investment unless it has successfully gone through several different secular trends in real life, not just in computer simulations.

Always keep in mind that any timing system is based on past experience. Future performance will not be the same. And yes, you will get false signals occasionally and you will never catch the exact market tops and bottoms.

Market timing strategies tell you *when* to invest. In the next chapter, the fingerprinting technique will show you *what* to invest in.

Chapter 28

Asset Selection & Monitoring: Fingerprinting

As investors, we want our investments do better than the markets when they rise. And when markets fall, of course, we want them to retain their value. In this chapter, I will share with you a technique that I have used for many years for asset selection and monitoring.

Active versus Passive:

In 1952, Harry Markowitz published[56] the modern portfolio theory (MPT). This technique strives to create the perfect portfolio by analyzing the risk and return of each individual investment. His portfolios include securities that are "hand–picked" on the efficient frontier of the risk–return curve. This is called active investing.

Towards the end of the secular bull market of 1949–1962, Mr. Sharpe developed the Capital Asset Pricing Model (CAPM), which seemingly made life easier for investors. With the CAPM, you did not need to analyze individual stocks. CAPM claims that buying the index gives as good returns as active portfolio management over the long term. This is called passive investing. However, during the secular sideways markets of 1966–1981, index funds did not make much headway.

Index funds found favor again towards the end of the 1982–1999 secular bullish markets. Lazy money found its way into passive funds as the bullish trend peaked. Subsequently, once the bull markets ended in 2000, many investors found out the hard way that buying the index was not such a good idea during bear or sideways markets. Since then, other types of passive investing, such as enhanced indexing and fundamental indexing, evolved.

Many actively managed funds, as well as some of the passively managed funds, follow various styles, such as value, growth, momentum, contrarian or sector rotation. Others have no style at all. Regardless, each fund manager convincingly claims that he/she can beat the market over the long term. In fact, less than 20% have been able to beat the index at any given time.

The proponents of index funds try to convince you that since only a small portion of active managers beat the index, why not buy the whole market, i.e. the index? To me this sounds like, "since only a small number of scientists find a cure for a disease, why bother looking for a cure at all?" Just remember this: if you invested $100,000 in the Dow Jones Industrial Average[57] in 1965 and kept it until 1982, your investment would have grown to $100,072. During the same time period, $100,000 invested in the Templeton Growth fund would have become $1,400,235. Which one would you pick?

[56] Harry M. Markowitz, "Portfolio Selection", Journal of Finance, Vol. 7, No. 1 (March 1952)
[57] index return only

I don't believe that an active fund manager can beat the index consistently over the long term. Neither do I like to settle for the returns of an index fund. I search for talented and/or lucky managers. I search for sectors that are on the rise. I keep them as long as they add value to my portfolio. Once they stop adding value, I replace them with others that do. It is no different than managing "who–plays–when" in a hockey game.

It does not really matter which philosophy you follow as long as you don't do worse than the index. If your portfolio outperforms the index, you'll have a better chance of a lifetime income.

If you hold mutual funds, how are you going to build your winning team of mutual funds? How are you going to decide when a player is tired and needs replacing?

If you hold ETFs, how are you going to decide which sector is in the lead?

Fingerprinting:

Here is an asset selection method that I call "Fingerprinting". It is a visual technique for analyzing performance. You can use it for mutual funds, stocks or bonds. All you need is a benchmark against which you can measure performance. You can even use it to compare two funds. It gives clear "buy", "hold" and "sell" signals

An investment portfolio is a moving target, a work–in–progress. The fund manager must adjust its course as events occur. After each market crash, new patterns of strength and weakness develop. Fingerprinting allows you to detect these changes and guide you towards being more proactive in selecting the right funds for your portfolio.

This technique helps visualize fund behavior separately in both rising and falling markets. It will assist you to evaluate fund excellence, regardless of whether you are a buy–and–hold investor or a market–timer.

Fingerprinting has two main objectives:

- Detect the best performing funds
- Outperform the index

A portfolio manager may excel in rising markets and outperform the index when it is going up. Another portfolio manager may excel in falling markets by playing defensively and losing less than the market. In the final analysis, both of these managers may outperform the market, because one plays well offensively, and the other plays well defensively.

The fingerprint chart depicts their performance in two dimensions. In essence, the vertical scale of the chart shows how a fund behaves relative to the rising market (see Figure 28.1). The higher the point on the chart, the better the fund is at outperforming a rising market. You can define this as "alpha in rising markets".

The horizontal scale shows how the same fund behaves in a falling market (see Figure 28.2). The further the point is to the left on the chart, the better the fund is at protecting itself in a falling market. You can define this as "alpha in falling markets".

Figure 28.1: Fingerprint in rising markets

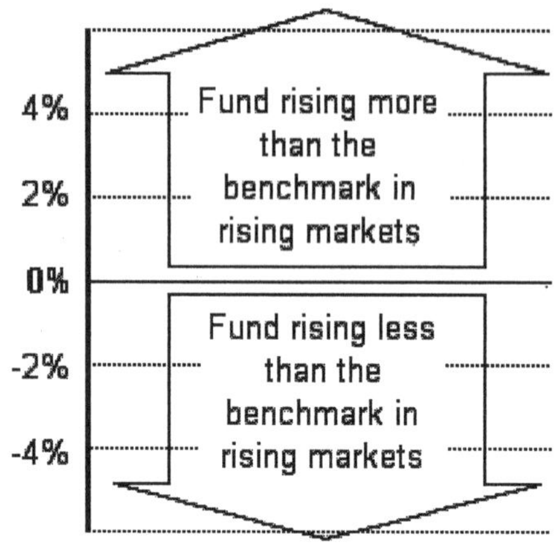

Figure 28.2: Fingerprint in falling markets

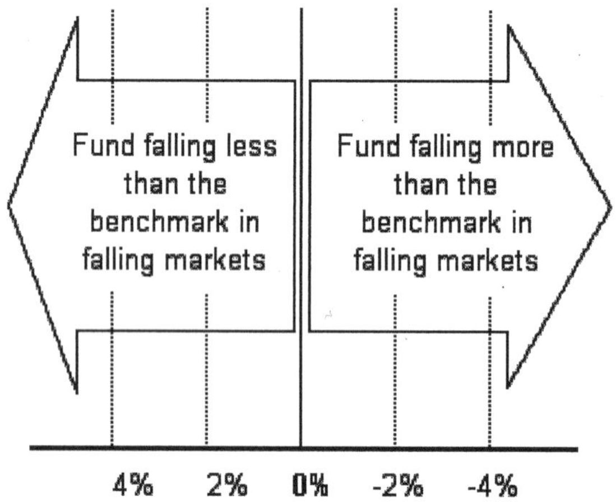

When these two charts are combined into one, it is called a "worm chart" in technical analysis. The chart is made up of four quadrants or zones. The significance of each zone is described in Figure 28.3.

Figure 28.3: Fingerprint of fund performance relative to the benchmark

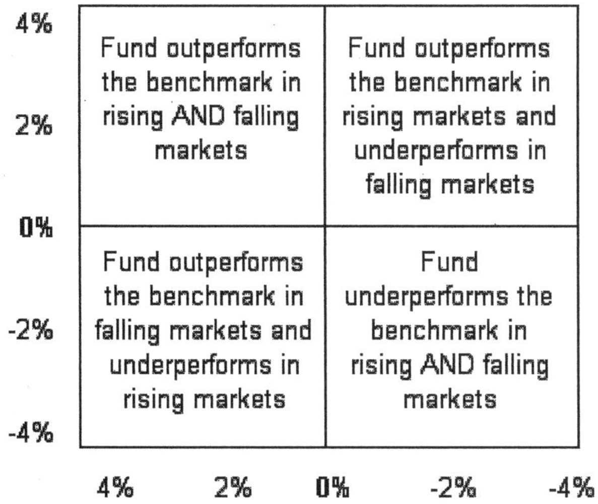

Constructing the Fingerprint Chart:

The following example shows how to create a fingerprint of your fund, step by step.

Step 1: Choose a fund that you want to fingerprint. Then, choose a benchmark. The benchmark can be any market index, like S&P500 or any fund that you want to compare your fund to.

Step 2: Fill out the month and year in Column A, the growth of the benchmark index in Column B, and the growth of the fund in Column C.

Step 3: Take the difference of the fund growth and index growth (Column C minus Column B). If Column B is a positive number (i.e. market is up), enter this difference in Column D. If Column B is a negative number (i.e. market is down), enter the difference in Column E.

You need at least six months of data to start your fingerprint chart. Repeat Step 2 until the first six lines are completed.

Month Year	Benchmark Growth	Fund Growth	Difference in Rising Benchmark	Difference in Falling Benchmark	6-month Moving Average Rising Benchmark	6-month Moving Average Falling Benchmark
Column A	**Column B**	**Column C**	**Column D**	**Column E**	**Column F**	**Column G**
Nov-95	4.7%	4.5%	-0.2%			
Dec-95	1.4%	4.2%	2.8%			
Jan-96	5.6%	6.0%	0.4%			
Feb-96	-0.5%	4.8%		5.3%		
Mar-96	1.0%	2.7%	1.7%			
Apr-96	3.6%	3.6%	0.0%		0.9%	5.3%
May-96	2.1%	2.4%	0.3%		1.0%	5.3%
Jun-96	-3.6%	-0.5%		3.2%	0.6%	4.2%
Jul-96	-2.2%	-1.2%		1.0%	0.7%	3.1%
Aug-96	4.5%	7.9%	3.3%		1.3%	2.1%
Sep-96	3.1%	8.8%	5.7%		2.3%	2.1%
Oct-96	5.9%	6.3%	0.4%		2.4%	2.1%

Step 4: Calculate the average of the last six numbers in Column D and enter it in Column F. When calculating the average, if there is no number in the box do not include it in the calculation. For instance, the average in April, 1996 in Column F is calculated as (–0.2 + 2.8 + 0.4 + 1.7 + 0.0) /5 = 0.94, rounded to 0.9. We did not include February, 1996 because that month was blank in Column D. Since we had only five numbers to average, we divided the total by 5 and not by 6.

Step 5: Calculate the average of the last six numbers in Column E and enter them in Column G. Use only non–blank numbers. For example, the average in April, 1996 in Column F is calculated as (–5.3) / 1 = 5.3. We included only February, 1996 because that was the only[58] non–blank number in Column E.

Step 6: Plot the values of Columns F and G on the graph[59]. The value in Column F measures the relative performance of the fund in a rising market. It is plotted on the vertical scale. The value in Column G measures the relative performance of the fund in a falling market, and it is plotted on the horizontal scale. Join each new point with the previous month's point to track its path.

[58] If this column is blank for all past six months then there is no average number to calculate, then just carry forward the previous average to the current month.

[59] Hint: for diversified funds, use a range between plus and minus 6%. For sector, country and other volatile funds, use a range between minus/plus 25%.

Figure 28.4 Fingerprint of the fund

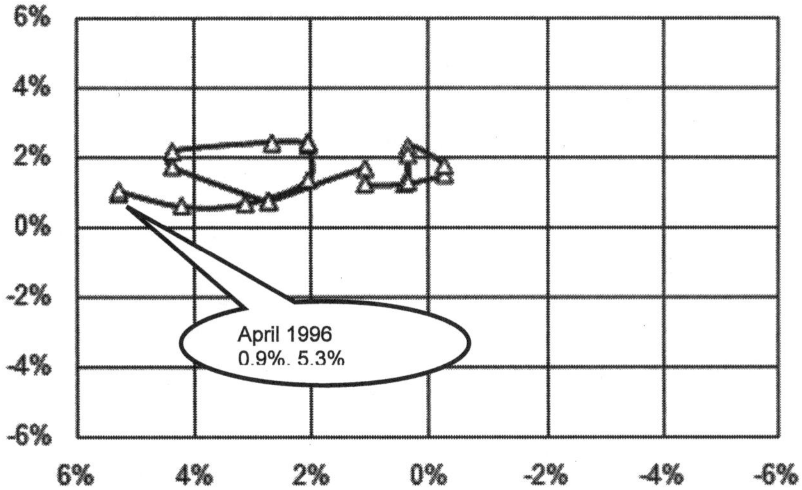

The location of the fingerprint reveals whether the fund is outperforming the markets. In this case in Figure 28.4 the fingerprint is in the upper left quadrant, meaning it has been outperforming its benchmark both in up and down markets.

During the time period studied, this fund outperformed its benchmark between 0.6% and 3% per month in rising markets (vertical scale). In falling markets, it outperformed its benchmark by 0% to 5% per month (horizontal scale). This is a remarkable performance. I would hold this fund in my portfolio as long as its fingerprint remains in the top left quadrant.

One of the amazing powers of fingerprinting is that it can pack all this price information into a single point. In the next few pages, Figures 28.5 through 28.9 show examples of how a price line is reflected in the fingerprint chart.

If the data point is in the top left quadrant (Figure 28.5), then this is an indication of a fund outperforming the benchmark when it is either rising or falling. If you can find it, this is a great fund to hold.

Figure 28.5: Fingerprint of a fund with alpha larger than zero

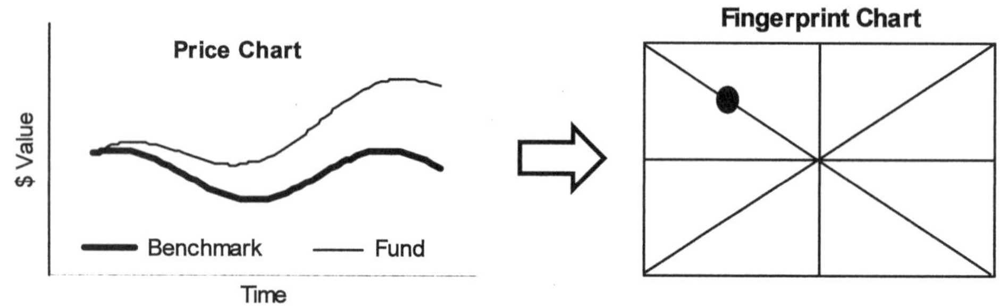

If the data point is in the bottom right quadrant (Figure 28.6), then this is an indication of a portfolio underperforming the benchmark when it is either rising or falling. This is typical of many equity funds, most bond funds, or funds with high management fees. Not a great fund to hold.

Figure 28.6: Fingerprint of a fund with alpha less than zero

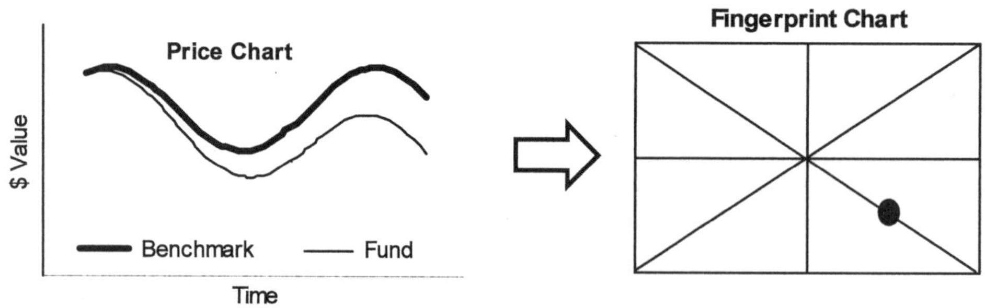

If the data point is exactly at the center (Figure 28.7), it means that the portfolio is performing exactly the same as the benchmark. This is typical of index funds or, to some extent, closet–index funds.

Figure 28.7: Fingerprint of a fund with alpha equals zero and beta equals one

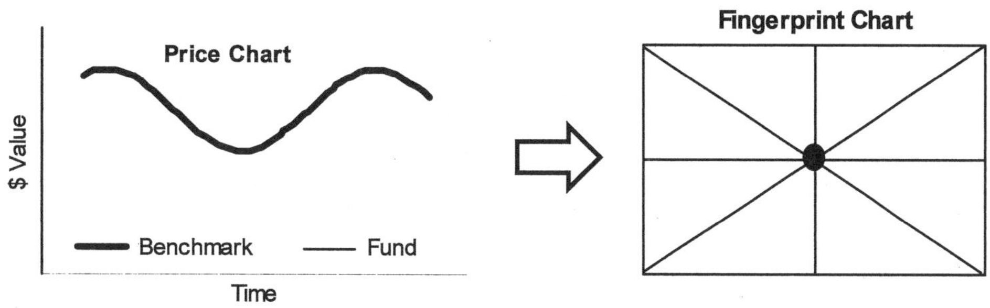

If the data point is in the bottom left quadrant (Figure 28.8), this is an indication of a portfolio underperforming the benchmark when it is rising and outperforming when it is falling. This is typical of well–run balanced funds.

Figure 28.8: Fingerprint of a fund with beta less than one

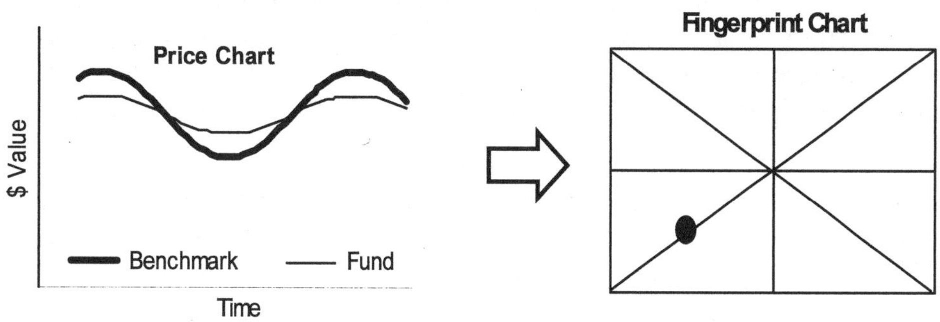

If the data point is in the top right quadrant (Figure 28.9), this is an indication of a portfolio underperforming the benchmark when it is falling and outperforming it when it is rising.

Figure 28.9: Fingerprint of a fund with beta larger than one

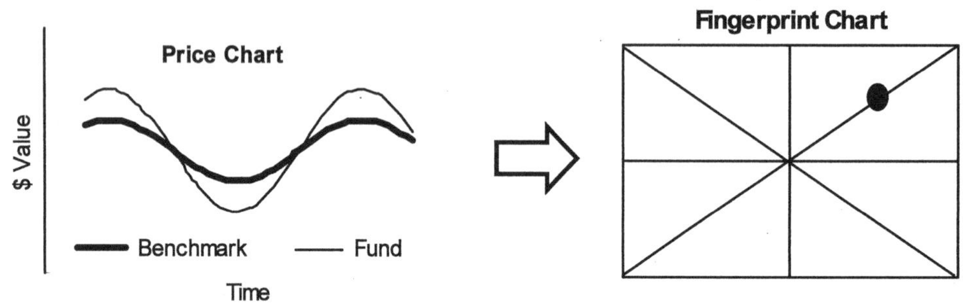

Equivalence Lines:

You may have noticed that I have two diagonal lines on fingerprint chart. The diagonal line running from the top right corner to the bottom left corner is the equal–beta line. As you move along this line, beta will vary and alpha is zero. At any point along this line, beta is the same for rising and falling markets.

In the top right quadrant, along this line, the fund outperforms the benchmark in rising markets exactly as much as underperforming it in falling markets. A fund in this area has a higher volatility for no higher reward (beta higher than one). Not a good place to be.

In the bottom left quadrant along this line, the fund underperforms the benchmark in rising markets exactly as much as outperforming it in falling markets (beta is less than one). Over the long term –assuming it remains at the same spot– it produces the same growth rate as the benchmark, regardless of its beta. It may be a desirable area for some investors.

The other diagonal line, the one going from the top left corner to the bottom right corner is the equal alpha line. Alpha is defined as the excess return over the benchmark. If you move along this line, alpha will vary and beta is one. At any given point along this line, alpha is the same both in rising and falling markets. This is great if the point is in the top left quadrant (positive alpha), and bad when it is in the bottom right quadrant along this line (negative alpha).

Selecting a Fund or Portfolio Manager:

Now that we have covered everything there is to know about the fingerprinting technique, the next question is, how do we make our decisions?

There are three zones on the fingerprint chart based on where the most recent data point is located.

- "Buy" zone; the top left quadrant. When one of the funds in your watch list migrates into this area, buy it.
- "Sell" zone; below the diagonal line. When one (or more) of the funds you are holding moves to this area, then sell it.
- "Hold" zones; between the diagonal line and the "buy" zone, as indicated in Figure 28.10. If the fund you are holding moves to this area, you may want to replace it with a better performing one. If you cannot find a better fund, keep a close watch.

In essence, you want to own a fund if its fingerprint is in the top left quadrant. Some of the best managers leave fingerprints in this area for several years. Choose funds with a good track record so you don't have to trade frequently. Eventually, most funds either become big and inefficient, or their managers leave for greener pastures. Then the fingerprint moves out of the "buy" zone. When this happens, replace it with a fund with its fingerprint in the "buy" zone.

Figure 28.10: Buy, hold and sell zones on the fingerprint chart

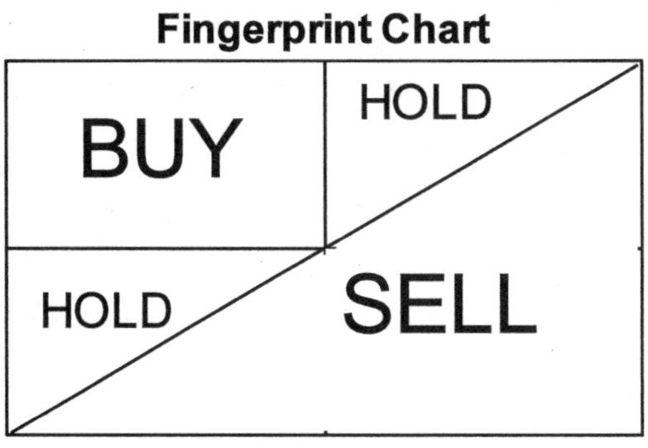

Comparing Two Funds:

You can use fingerprinting to compare two funds and decide which one should be in your portfolio. Example 28.1 illustrates the procedure.

Example 28.1

Richard has a choice of including fund "A" or fund "B" in his portfolio. Both funds are invested in the same asset class. Here is the monthly history of each fund.

Month End	Fund B	Fund A
November-06	0.0%	2.0%
December-06	3.3%	3.9%
January-07	1.0%	3.0%
February-07	3.6%	4.0%
March-07	-1.2%	2.0%
April-07	1.7%	3.0%
May-07	1.8%	2.0%
June-07	1.8%	2.0%
July-07	-1.0%	0.5%
August-07	-0.9%	3.0%
September-07	3.6%	3.0%
October-07	2.9%	4.0%

Should Richard choose fund "A" or fund "B"?

Enter the monthly growth rates of fund "B" as benchmark. Calculate and draw the fingerprint.

Month Year	Benchmark Growth	Fund Growth	Difference in		6-month Moving Average	
			Rising Benchmark	Falling Benchmark	Rising Benchmark	Falling Benchmark
	Fund B	**Fund A**				
November-06	0.0%	2.0%		2.0%		
December-06	3.3%	3.9%	0.6%			
January-07	1.0%	3.0%	2.0%			
February-07	3.6%	4.0%	0.4%			
March-07	-1.2%	2.0%		3.2%		
April-07	1.7%	3.0%	1.3%		1.1%	2.6%
May-07	1.8%	2.0%	0.2%		0.9%	3.2%
June-07	1.8%	2.0%	0.2%		0.8%	3.2%
July-07	-1.0%	0.5%		1.5%	0.5%	2.3%
August-07	-0.9%	3.0%		3.9%	0.6%	2.9%
September-07	3.6%	3.0%	-0.6%		0.3%	2.7%
October-07	2.9%	4.0%	1.1%		0.2%	2.7%

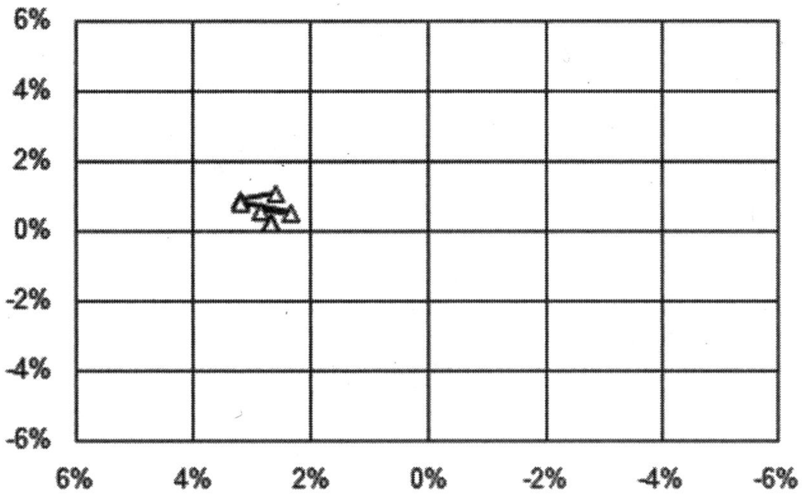

Fund "A" is in the top left quadrant compared to the benchmark, fund "B". Therefore Richard should choose fund "A" in his portfolio instead of fund "B".

If these points were in any other quadrant, Richard would choose fund "B".

Conclusion:

Fingerprinting is a great method to select, monitor and evaluate mutual funds, pension managers, portfolio managers. If applied in a disciplined manner and monitored monthly, it can add 2% to 3% of alpha to your portfolio.

You can use it to track how your own portfolio performs against your own benchmark. Whether you manage your own portfolio or an advisor manages it for you, you can evaluate its progress against your own blended benchmark.

I know it may look complicated at first reading. With time, it becomes easier to apply. Especially if you use a spreadsheet, it becomes a lot simpler to maintain. The single–page fingerprint graph describes several years of performance visually in both rising and falling markets on a single chart.

Even if you don't like technical analysis, you might like the simplicity of fingerprinting. The market timing systems that we discussed in the previous chapters tells me *when* to be defensive or aggressive with my equity holdings. The asset selection method described in this chapter tells me *what* to buy.

If you are still convinced that fingerprinting is not for you, then buy broadly diversified index funds for the equity portion of your portfolio. That way, you will know that your portfolio will be in the center point of the fingerprint chart in the worst case. I prefer index funds that are based on fundamentals (such as the RAFI index), rather than the conventional, market cap based index funds.

Chapter 29

Portfolio Management Expenses

Portfolio management expenses can significantly reduce portfolio longevity. Like inflation, its effect is not readily apparent in a short period of time.

Let's look at three examples to visualize the effect of management costs.

Example 29.1

Consider three retirees, 65 years old, each with an identical portfolio: $1 million savings, asset mix of 40% S&P500 and 60% fixed income, rebalanced each year, $53,000 annual withdrawal, adjusted for inflation.

Retiree "A": On the equity side of his portfolio, he holds an exchange tradable index fund (ETF). The index has an average of 2% dividends yield. He pays portfolio and management expenses of 0.2%. His total equity return is "index plus 1.8%", calculated as 2% minus 0.2%.

His net yield for the fixed income side is the historical 6-month CD yield plus 1.5%.

Retiree "B": On the equity side of his portfolio, he holds an average mutual fund. He collects 2% annually in dividends. He pays portfolio and management fee of 2%. His total equity return is exactly same as the index, calculated as 2% minus 2%. His fixed income portfolio is the same as Retiree "A".

Retiree "C": Holds a balanced mutual fund with 40% equity and 60% fixed income. Management costs are 2%. The equity side of this fund returns the same as the S&P500 index.

The figure below shows the median portfolio value based on market history since 1900.

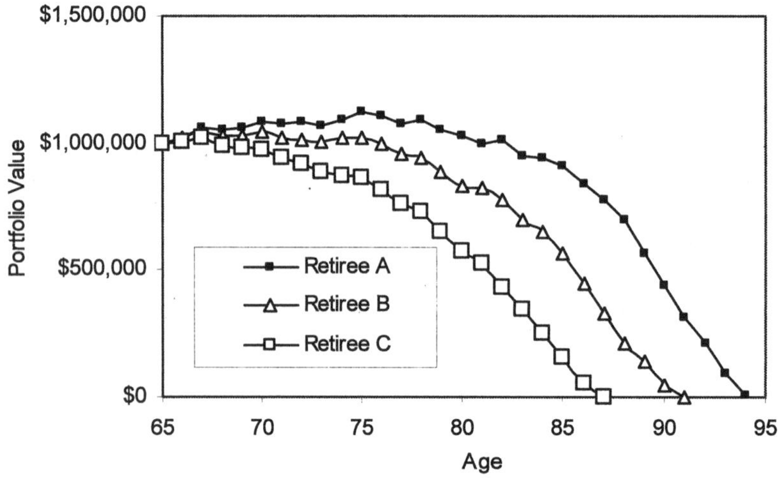

The median portfolio of Retiree A expired at age 94, of Retiree B at age 91, and of Retiree C, at age 87. The portfolio of Retiree A lasted about 32% longer than the median portfolio of Retiree C (22 years versus 29 years).

The Cumulative Cost:

Be aware of the portfolio costs at all times. Average management expenses look small in percentage terms, but they add up to big dollar amounts number over the years. The next example quantifies how your lifelong savings are "shared" between you and the financial industry.

Example 29.2

Using the figures from the previous example how much additional management fees did Retiree C pay over his life?

Age	Median Portfolio Value $	Average Income Taken	Portfolio Expenses, 2%
65	$1,000,000	$53,000	$20,000
66	$1,005,343	$54,741	$20,107
67	$1,018,502	$56,581	$20,370
68	$988,473	$58,544	$19,769
69	$978,544	$60,566	$19,571
70	$975,114	$62,659	$19,502
71	$940,970	$64,844	$18,819
72	$917,689	$67,160	$18,354
73	$887,488	$69,610	$17,750
74	$875,357	$72,138	$17,507
75	$864,110	$74,827	$17,282
76	$815,456	$77,609	$16,309
77	$763,838	$80,484	$15,277
78	$729,927	$83,526	$14,599
79	$651,343	$85,749	$13,027
80	$574,542	$86,370	$11,491
81	$524,297	$84,141	$10,486
82	$433,095	$80,764	$8,662
83	$344,791	$75,064	$6,896
84	$250,082	$66,474	$5,002
85	$154,552	$57,176	$3,091
86	$52,772	$50,225	$1,055
87	$0	$0	$0
	TOTAL $	$1,522,253	$314,926
	TOTAL %	83%	17%

Based on historical performance, this median portfolio paid out a total of $1,837,179 over the 22 years before it depleted totally. This includes withdrawals of $1,522,253 by the retiree and management expenses of $314,926.

In terms of percentages, Retiree C received about 83% of the total payout, pretax. The financial industry received the remaining 17%. If the advisor receives half of this 17%, then his total compensation will be about 10% of the total income received by Retiree C, or about 15% of his starting capital.

The Effect of Portfolio Costs:

I calculated the compound annual return of two different distribution portfolios. For both portfolios, the equity proxy is S&P500 and the asset mix is 40% equity and 60% fixed income, rebalanced annually.

In the base case, I used net alpha of 1.8% for equities, after all expenses. For the fixed income portion of the portfolio, I used the historical 6–month CD yield plus 1% as the net yield.

In the comparative case, I used 2% management fees for the entire portfolio.

I measured the effect of portfolio costs by measuring the difference in the compound annual return of the median portfolio in both cases. Table 29.1 indicates the impact of portfolio costs.

Keep in mind that these are just my assumptions. Some funds will cost more, some less. So, the impact of portfolio costs will vary from case to case.

Table 29.1: The effect of portfolio costs, equity proxy S&P500

	Initial Withdrawal Rate					
	0%	2%	4%	6%	8%	10%
Compound Annual Return, Equity: net alpha after portfolio costs: 1.8%, Fixed income: net yield: 6–month CD plus %1	5.99%	5.74%	6.22%	5.57%	6.48%	6.86%
Compound Annual Return, Portfolio management cost for the entire portfolio 2%	4.39%	4.16%	4.11%	4.16%	4.91%	5.36%
Impact of portfolio costs on compound annual return	36%	38%	51%	34%	32%	28%

Conclusion:

In the long–term, portfolio costs make a significant difference. If your holdings do not outperform the index, either find better ones or hold low cost index funds.

Chapter 30

Borrowing to Invest

I was not planning to write about borrowing money to invest. However, I recently came across another "academic" study[60] that concludes leveraging your retirement savings is good and that for all risk preferences, the results are better. As I read further, it said that historically equities have returned about 9%, the cost of margin was 5% and this equity premium of 4% served as the source of additional returns. Then, it reveals that they use Monte Carlo simulations to arrive at its claim.

By now, you should know that I cringe every time I read "historical averages" uttered by "academics" using "simulators", all on the same page. So, here is my take on leveraging.

By leveraging, I am only talking about borrowing money to invest. This can be a bank loan, a line of credit or a loan from an investment company. This money is then invested in stocks or mutual funds. I am not talking about leveraging in the context of commodities, futures, currencies or leveraging within hedge funds. I am also not talking about borrowing money to invest in the business in which you might have a controlling ownership. What I am talking about is borrowing to invest in a portfolio of stocks or mutual funds, nothing more and nothing less.

When you borrow money to invest, there may be as many as six participants in this transaction:

- You: the investor
- The lender: bank, brokerage or another financial institute
- The seller: mutual fund salesman, advisor or broker
- The dealer: the financial company that the seller works for
- The manufacturer: the fund company
- The overhead: the government tax department

When investments do well, then everyone in this list makes money one way or another. On the other hand, when things turn sour, then there is only one participant who definitely loses money, *you*. Other participants either still make money or they do not lose anything. The seller, dealer, manufacturer all make money in the form on commissions and trailer fees from investments, win or lose. The lender makes money on the interest of the money borrowed, win or lose. And finally, the overhead makes money if you win, otherwise, it does not.

[60] Ayres and Nalebuff, NBER , June 2008

The bottom line is this: the investor is always on the hook. Other participants would like you to make money, so they make more money. But if you lose, they usually don't. So, here is the first question: are you comfortable with this?

The second question is this: you need to be comfortable with the probabilities of outcome. What does history tell you? It is one thing to look at how your retirement savings would have fared from the perspective of market history. On top of that, do you really think you have any chance, especially if the underlying premise of leveraging is: "Win, we share. Lose, we don't care!"

The only reason you would borrow money to invest is that either you believe that the odds are on your side or someone convinced you that they are. You might be persuaded that a particular investment will do well. Or you believe that "markets go up in the long term". Or someone talked to you about the tax advantages. What convinced you does not matter, what matters is the outcome.

However, there is more to this than simply thinking that the odds are –or should be– on your side. When you borrow money to invest, you are in effect declaring that you are smarter than others. If that were not so, why would the bank lend you the money instead of investing it directly in that mutual fund? So, when you borrow money to invest, you are declaring silently that you are smarter and/or luckier than those who lend you the money.

Before going into more detail, let me clarify some of the terms and definitions that I used in my analysis:

Own–to–loan ratio: You might start with nothing of your own. You can simply go to a financial institution, borrow some money and invest it. In this case, the own–to–loan ratio is zero; basically, you have no investments other than those you bought using the borrowed money.

On the other hand, you might already have $100,000 in your investment account. Then, you borrow another $100,000 to invest. Now, you have $200,000 in investments, half of which is your own money, the other half is other people's money. Here the own–to–loan ratio is 1.

If you had $300,000 of your own money invested, and borrowed another $100,000 to invest, then your own–to–loan ratio would be 3.

Loan Repayments: You can repay interest only or you can pay a fixed amount. If you pay interest only, then the dollar amount of loan payments will fluctuate. If you pay a fixed amount, usually part of this money goes to paying down the loan principal, the rest is interest payments. If your payments are less than the interest amount, then the principal amount of the loan increases over time.

In all calculations, all loan repayments were paid from the portfolio, unless there was nothing left in the portfolio. If there are insufficient funds in the portfolio to cover all repayments (principle and interest), then the additional out–of–pocket loss is calculated and added to the loss created by leveraging.

To keep things simple, the money is borrowed at the beginning of the year. All repayments are made at the end of the year.

<u>Interest Rate:</u> The interest rate may be a fixed rate, for example, 8% of the remaining loan balance. It may also be a floating rate related to the prevailing interest rate, for example, prime rate plus 3%. This is the gross interest paid. If you get a tax write–off, then your net interest cost will be less. I use gross interest to keep things simple in my analysis.

<u>The Term of the Loan:</u> The term is the maximum length of time in years by which the loan is repaid to the lender. Generally, if the markets do well, repayments continue until end of the term. At the end of the term, the remaining loan balance is paid off. More than likely, you will get stopped out before the end of the term of the loan, in which case, the entire loan amount, plus accrued interest, is paid back.

<u>Stops:</u> There are many reasons why you may want to liquidate part or all of your portfolio, pay off the loan and call it quits. I have looked at three different "stop–loss" options.

1. Depleted Portfolio: If the portfolio depletes, you can either continue making your annual loan repayments as if nothing has happened. Or, you can liquidate the portfolio and pay off the loan when the portfolio value at any yearend is less than your annual loan repayments.
2. Margin Stop: You can have an option to pay off the loan if the portfolio asset value is below a certain percentage of the loan balance. For example, for risk management purposes, you may decide to liquidate the loan when the portfolio value drops to below 70% of the loan balance.
3. Trailing Stop: After investing, you may get lucky and the portfolio value may go up. Many times, an unlucky streak follows a lucky streak. If you invested using other people's money and get lucky with your investments, you may want to sell some of your holdings and pay off the loan before your luck turns around. This is called a "trailing stop". For example, when the portfolio value goes up and then starts going down to, say, 70% of its peak value, then sufficient investments are liquidated to pay off the loan.

The first two stops are to contain losses. The trailing stop is for preserving profits.

Let's work through examples to demonstrate the effects of leveraging.

Example 30.1

Allan is 30 years old. He has $100,000 in his portfolio. His portfolio is aggressive, 100% S&P500. For his portfolio growth, use the index return plus dividends, less his portfolio costs of 0.5%.

It is the beginning of 1990. If Allan had invested only his own money (no leveraging), here is how his portfolio would have fared:

Year	Assets
1990	$100,000
1991	$96,681
1992	$124,638
1993	$133,193
1994	$145,560
1995	$146,828
1996	$199,555
1997	$243,005
1998	$321,030
1999	$409,276
2000	$491,811

Allan's assets grew from $100,000 in the beginning of 1990, to $491,811 in the beginning of the year 2000, an increase of $391,811.

He decides to borrow $100,000 to enhance the return of his investments. He pays only the interest, which is paid out of his portfolio. The interest rate is equal to the 6-month CD yield plus 3%. At the end of 10 years, he is planning to pay back the loan principal from the portfolio as well. Here is how his portfolio would have grown:

Year	Assets	Loan Balance	Interest %	Interest Amount	Payments
1990	$200,000	$100,000	11.17%	$11,170	$11,170
1991	$182,192	$100,000	8.91%	$8,910	$8,910
1992	$225,966	$100,000	6.76%	$6,760	$6,760
1993	$234,716	$100,000	6.28%	$6,280	$6,280
1994	$250,230	$100,000	7.96%	$7,960	$7,960
1995	$244,449	$100,000	8.98%	$8,980	$8,980
1996	$323,252	$100,000	8.47%	$8,470	$8,470
1997	$385,166	$100,000	8.73%	$8,730	$8,730
1998	$500,106	$100,000	8.44%	$8,440	$8,440
1999	$629,138	$100,000	8.46%	$8,460	$108,460
2000	$647,550	$0		$0	$0

In this case, Allan's net assets grew from $100,000 to $647,550 in ten years, an increase of $547,550. Because he used other people's money to invest, he had a net benefit of $155,739 after paying all interest expenses, calculated as $547,550 less $391,811.

Example 30.2

Same as Example 30.1, but instead of starting in the year 1990, start in 1973.

If Allan invested only his own money, here is how his portfolio would have fared:

Year	Assets
1973	$100,000
1974	$85,834
1975	$64,558
1976	$87,275
1977	$106,980
1978	$99,607
1979	$105,536
1980	$123,835
1981	$161,002
1982	$153,499
1983	$182,957

Allan's assets grew from $100,000 in the beginning of 1973, to $182,957 in the beginning of the year 1983, an increase of $82,957.

Allan borrowed $100,000 to invest. Here is how his portfolio would have grown:

Year	Assets	Loan Balance	Interest %	Interest Amount	Payments
1973	$200,000	$100,000	10.93%	$10,930	$10,930
1974	$160,739	$100,000	14.03%	$14,030	$14,030
1975	$106,865	$100,000	10.24%	$10,240	$10,240
1976	$134,230	$100,000	8.70%	$8,700	$8,700
1977	$155,836	$100,000	8.28%	$8,280	$8,280
1978	$136,816	$100,000	10.78%	$10,780	$10,780
1979	$134,180	$100,000	13.88%	$13,880	$13,880
1980	$143,565	$100,000	14.37%	$14,370	$14,370
1981	$172,284	$100,000	20.63%	$20,630	$20,630
1982	$143,625	$100,000	17.60%	$17,600	$117,600
1983	$53,588	$0	0.00%	$0	$0

In this case, Allan's net assets shrank from $100,000 in the beginning of 1973, to $53,588 in the beginning of 1983, a decrease of $46,312.

The total cost attributable to leveraging is $129,369, calculated as the lost profit of $82,957 if he had not borrowed to invest, plus the loss of $46,312 due to leveraging.

I carried out the cost–benefit calculations for all years since 1900. Table 30.1 depicts the outcome. Figure 30.1 shows the same in graphic format.

Table 30.1: The Pre–tax cost–benefit analysis or loss of leveraging versus no leveraging:

Year	Profit / Loss	Year	Profit / Loss	Year	Profit / Loss	Year	Profit / Loss
1900	$27,250	1925	–$16,300	1950	$288,084	1975	$44,317
1901	–$10,295	1926	–$6,546	1951	$185,496	1976	–$10,886
1902	–$33,475	1927	$11,342	1952	$193,895	1977	–$51,850
1903	–$36,593	1928	–$57,342	1953	$135,363	1978	–$1,732
1904	$132	1929	–$90,174	1954	$190,345	1979	$22,507
1905	–$44,162	1930	–$72,652	1955	$105,959	1980	$31,511
1906	–$54,335	1931	–$46,184	1956	$60,429	1981	–$37,009
1907	–$44,413	1932	$29,729	1957	$35,645	1982	$88,122
1908	–$4,407	1933	$85,010	1958	$95,820	1983	$87,741
1909	–$40,982	1934	$34,523	1959	$28,224	1984	$66,574
1910	–$52,151	1935	$82,524	1960	$5,547	1985	$90,263
1911	–$52,987	1936	$42,234	1961	$5,367	1986	$81,486
1912	–$53,573	1937	–$16,627	1962	–$25,551	1987	$84,888
1913	–$47,212	1938	$58,671	1963	$16,884	1988	$156,335
1914	–$25,621	1939	$48,004	1964	–$36,107	1989	$193,493
1915	$18,428	1940	$70,718	1965	–$75,294	1990	$155,739
1916	–$16,201	1941	$159,834	1966	–$82,413	1991	$189,247
1917	–$20,587	1942	$261,986	1967	–$53,514	1992	$84,726
1918	$98,135	1943	$241,148	1968	–$84,556	1993	$38,981
1919	$149,052	1944	$178,399	1969	–$95,642	1994	$64,988
1920	$81,653	1945	$232,734	1970	–$75,702	1995	$97,366
1921	$119,291	1946	$184,511	1971	–$63,307	1996	$38,838
1922	$22,956	1947	$265,381	1972	–$94,197	1997	$23,385
1923	–$20,713	1948	$240,842	1973	–$129,369		
1924	$22,241	1949	$331,248	1974	–$83,160		

Let's observe Table 30.1 closely: starting in 1900, the cumulative profit/loss picture did not turn positive until 1938. In my circle of friends, I don't know of anyone who is rich enough, or for that matter dumb enough, to keep borrowing for 37 years, paying all that interest, only to break even at the end.

Figure 30.1: The pre–tax benefit and loss of leveraging:

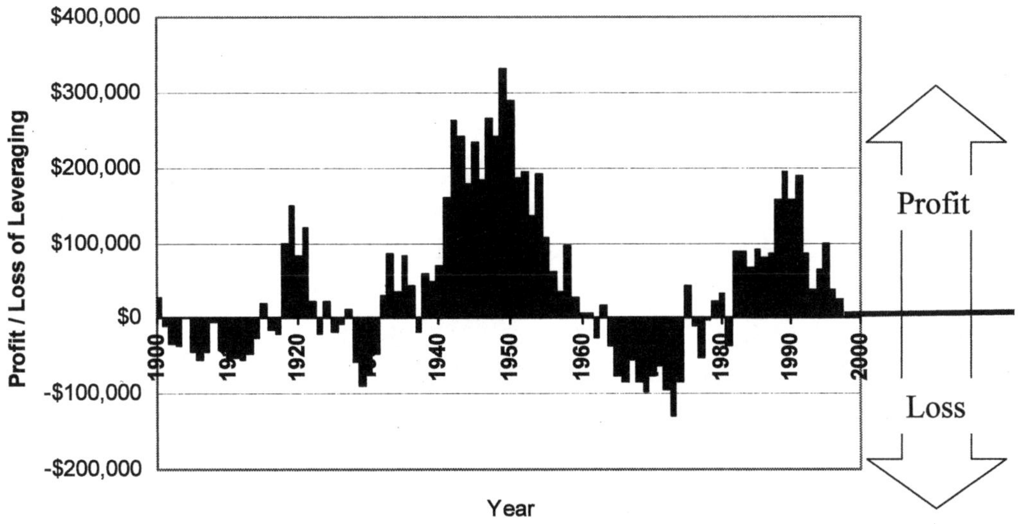

Allowing myself to wear a Gaussian hat for a moment, here are some statistics:

- Number of winning years: 59
- Number of losing years: 39
- Average win amount: $103,145
- Average loss amount: $47,790
- Median Profit due to leveraging: $25,318
- Lucky (top 10%): $189,572
- Median: $25,318
- Unlucky (bottom 10%): –$66,111
- Worst Case: –$129,369

How do we measure an acceptable risk? The profit factor measures the ratio of total dollars won to total dollars lost over the entire time period. It is calculated as:

$$\text{Profit Factor} = \text{PF} = \frac{\text{WY} \times \text{WA}}{\text{LY} \times \text{LA}} \qquad \text{(Equation 30.1)}$$

where:

WY	is the number of winning years
WA	is the average win amount
LY	is the number of losing years
LA	is the average loss amount

In this case, the profit factor is:

$$\text{Profit Factor} = \text{PF} = \frac{59 \times \$103{,}145}{39 \times \$47{,}790} = 3.27$$

Statistically speaking, if the profit factor is over two, then the outcome is good. However, considering that the average investing time horizon is between twenty and thirty years, a profit factor that is based on the entire one hundred years does not necessarily mean that an individual with a limited time horizon will see any of this high profit factor.

The general consensus in the investment world is that the emotional level of happiness from a three–dollar gain is same the emotional sadness from a one–dollar loss. Based on that, I will use a profit factor of three as my threshold for an acceptable risk. This is my first filter.

My second filter is the median portfolio value. Regardless of how high the profit factor might be, it is meaningless unless the historical median portfolio has a positive dollar value. If the median is negative, then I designated the profit factor as "nm" (not meaningful) in the following tables.

Let's look at each of these factors.

The Importance of Own/Loan Ratio:

If your entire investment portfolio consists of borrowed money, then the own/loan ratio is zero. If you have $100,000 in your portfolio and then you borrow $100,000 to invest, your own/loan ratio is 1.

I calculated the profit factor for different own/loan ratios and for different loan repayment methods for all years since 1900. They are indicated in Table 30.2

Table 30.2: The profit factor for different own/loan ratio and repayment methods

Own/Loan Ratio	**Repayment Method**			
	Pay Interest Only	Pay annually 10% of the initial loan amount	Pay annually 15% of the initial loan amount	Pay annually 20% of the initial loan amount
	Profit Factor			
0	2.85	2.53	3.04	3.28
1	3.27	2.97	2.57	2.34
3	2.68	2.56	2.48	2.32

This table indicates that:

- If your own/loan ratio is one or more, then you are better off paying only the interest over the term of the loan. Repay the loan principal at the end of the term.
- If the own/loan ratio is zero, i.e. the entire investment portfolio consist of other people's money, then you are better off paying at least 15% of the original loan amount each year until the end of the loan term, or until the loan is paid off, whichever comes first.

The Importance of Depletion Stop:

If the portfolio depletes during the term of the loan, you can continue making your loan repayments as if nothing has happened. Your other option is to liquidate the remaining assets in the portfolio and pay off the loan when the portfolio value falls below your annual loan payment amount.

If you continue paying interest after depletion, worst–case losses will increase significantly. From this point on in this chapter, it is assumed that the entire loan is repaid when the portfolio assets are below one year's loan repayment amount.

The Importance of Asset Allocation:

We have all been indoctrinated about the benefits of asset allocation and how it can decrease the risk. So, you may be tempted to hold some fixed income, supposedly to reduce risk.

Earlier, on the topic of optimum asset allocation, I talked about the virtues of keeping a conservative asset mix. The picture is different when you borrow to invest. For an individual investor, because the cost of borrowing is usually higher than the yield of a fixed income portfolio, it does not pay to borrow and then invest –even a small amount of that money– in a fixed income. The house always keeps the difference. If you are already taking a high risk by borrowing money to invest, then you might as well be prepared to invest 100% in equities.

One exception is the tax deductibility of interest payments. In some specific cases, your net cost of borrowing after taxes may be below the yield of fixed income investments. You need to evaluate each case on its own merits. To keep things simple in my analysis, I ignored the tax effects entirely. Generally, it is not a good idea to let tax benefits affect your investment decisions.

I calculated the profit factor for different asset mixes for all years since 1900, as indicated in Table 30.3 and Table 30.4. In Table 30.3, the own/loan ratio is zero. In Table 30.4, the own/loan ratio is one.

Table 30.3: The profit factor for different asset mixes, own/loan ratio is zero

Asset Mix	Repayment Method			
	Pay Interest Only	Pay annually 10% of the initial loan amount	Pay annually 15% of the initial loan amount	Pay annually 20% of the initial loan amount
	Profit Factor			
100% S&P500	2.85	2.53	3.04	3.28
80% S&P500 20% Fixed Income	2.24	1.97	2.39	2.58
60% S&P500 40% Fixed Income	1.50	nm	1.53	1.78

Table 30.4: The profit factor for different asset mixes, own/loan ratio is one

Asset Mix	Repayment Method			
	Pay Interest Only	Pay annually 10% of the initial loan amount	Pay annually 15% of the initial loan amount	Pay annually 20% of the initial loan amount
	Profit Factor			
100% S&P500	3.27	2.97	2.57	2.34
80% S&P500 20% Fixed Income	2.81	2.59	2.24	2.00
60% S&P500 40% Fixed Income	1.96	1.89	1.72	1.52

These two tables indicate that the highest profit factor occurs when the portfolio is most aggressive. For the balance of this chapter, the borrowed money is invested in S&P500 only and none is invested in fixed income.

The Importance of Margin Stop:

For risk management purposes, you may decide to liquidate the loan when the portfolio value goes below a certain percentage of the loan balance. In practice this is called a "margin call". Your broker will call you and notify you of a "margin call". That means you need either to add cash to your account to improve this ratio or liquidate some/all of your investments, reducing/eliminating your loan amount.

I calculated the profit factor for different margin stop levels for all years since 1900 for an own/loan ratio of zero as indicated in Table 30.5

Table 30.5: The profit factor for margin stop levels

Margin Stop Level	**Repayment Method** Pay Interest Only	Pay annually 10% of the initial loan amount	Pay annually 15% of the initial loan amount
		Profit Factor	
No Stop	2.85	2.53	3.04
60%	3.08	2.94	3.17
70%	3.23	3.13	3.20
80%	3.51	3.42	3.26
90%	2.93	2.89	2.89
100%	2.44	2.26	2.27

This table tells us at least two things:

- Never meet a margin call. Liquidate and pay off the loan.
- The optimum stop for leveraged portfolios is around 80%. Once the portfolio value is below 80% of the remaining loan balance, liquidate and pay off the loan. Don't wait in despair hoping that the markets will turn around and wipe out your losses; it will not happen.

A margin stop of 80% is used in all the remaining tables in this chapter.

The Importance of Trailing Stop:

The trailing stop forces you to liquidate your investments and pay off the loan on a high note if you are in a profitable position. On the other hand, if you are in a losing situation, it prevents further losses, similar to a margin stop.

I calculated the profit factor for different levels of trailing stop for all years since 1900. They are indicated in Table 30.6.

Table 30.6: The profit factor for different trailing stop levels

Trailing Stop Level	Repayment Method: Pay Interest Only, Own/Loan Ratio=1	Repayment Method: Pay annually 15% of the initial loan amount, Own/Loan Ratio=0
	Profit Factor	
No trailing Stop	3.24	3.26
5% from the peak value	nm	nm
10% from the peak value	nm	nm
15% from the peak value	3.42	nm
20% from the peak value	3.06	nm

Observing this table, we come to two conclusions:

- If the own/loan ratio is zero and you are paying down 15% of the initial loan amount each year (the optimum), then it is better not to implement any trailing stops.
- If the own/loan ratio is one or larger, and you are paying the loan interest only, then the optimum trailing stop is when the portfolio value goes below 15% of its peak level.

This test is only done once a year, at the end of the calendar year. During the year, ignore the signals for trailing stops.

You might ask, "Should I implement the trailing stop starting with the first year or after a few years of investing?" I analyzed the effects of starting the trailing stop after 2, 4 and 6 years. In all cases, the outcome was best by starting it immediately at the first year.

A trailing stop of 15% is used in all of the remaining tables for a own/loan ratio of one.

The Importance of Alpha:

Alpha is the excess return over and above the benchmark and it has a great influence on the profitability factor. It is one of the most important factors in the profit/loss picture of leveraging. I calculated the profit factor for different levels of alpha for all years since 1900. They are indicated in Table 30.7.

Table 30.7: The profit factor for different alphas

Alpha	Repayment Method: Pay Interest Only, Own/Loan Ratio=1	Repayment Method: Pay annually 15% of the initial loan amount, Own/Loan Ratio=0
	Profit Factor	
–4%	nm	nm
–2%	nm	nm
0%	nm	nm
2%	nm	nm
4%	3.93	3.07
6%	5.16	5.99
Historical S&P500 less 0.5% portfolio costs	3.42	3.26

Observing this table, we can conclude that if alpha is less than 4%, it is unlikely that there is any benefit in leveraging.

The Importance of the Interest Rate:

The interest rate has a great influence on the outcome. I overlaid the historical interest rate to the profit/loss chart in Figure 30.2. The vertical scale on the left of the chart indicates the profit/loss of leveraging. The vertical scale on the right indicates the interest rate.

We observe that there are two long–term waves of profitable leveraging. The first one started after 1932. The second one started 49 years later, after 1981. There is a common thread between these two waves: they both occurred immediately after sharp drops in the interest rates. They are indicated with arrows on the chart.

If you are lucky, you may be able to catch a similar wave once in your lifetime. That is, if you notice it in time. But, I think it is now well behind us boomers. The next such opportunity may not come until 2030, according to the 54–year Kondratieff cycle[61].

Figure 30.2: The correlation between the prevailing interest rate and profit/loss of leveraging

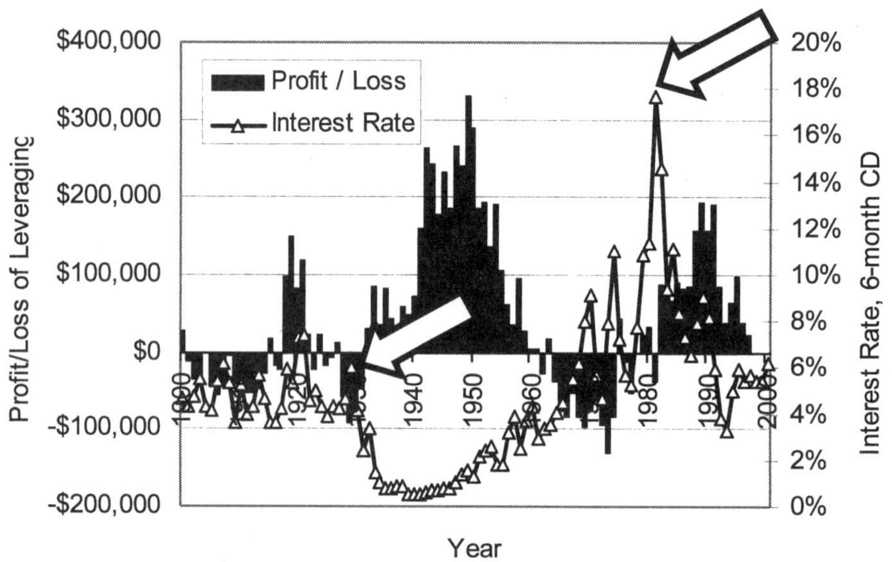

Table 30.8 indicates the profit factor for different interest rates.

61 For more information on cycles, refer to Technical Analysis of the Futures Markets, by John J. Murphy

Table 30.8: The profit factor for different net interest rate levels

Net Interest Rate	Repayment Method: Pay Interest Only, Own/Loan Ratio=1	Repayment Method: Pay annually 15% of the initial loan amount, Own/Loan Ratio=0
	Profit Factor	
6–month CD yield minus 1%	10.17	9.27
6–month CD yield plus 0%	7.70	7.18
6–month CD yield plus 1%	6.03	5.45
6–month CD yield plus 2%	4.39	4.29
6–month CD yield plus 3%	3.42	3.26
6–month CD yield plus 4%	2.57	nm

If the net interest rate you are paying is higher than the 6–month CD yield plus 3%, then leveraging is unlikely to be profitable.

The Importance of the Length of the Term of the Loan:

Time heals wounds. This is also true for leveraged investments. A longer loan term can create a higher profit factor, provided that you don't get stopped out. I calculated the profit factor for different loan terms as indicated in Table 30.9.

Table 30.9: The profit factor for different loan terms, own/loan ratio is zero

Loan Term	Repayment Method: Pay Interest Only, Own/Loan Ratio=1	Repayment Method: Pay annually 15% of the initial loan amount, Own/Loan Ratio=0
	Profit Factor	
5 years	1.80	nm
10 years	3.42	3.26
20 years	8.15	7.16

If your time horizon is less than ten years, then leveraging is unlikely to be profitable.

Canadians Borrowing Annually for Retirement Savings:

Many Canadians wait until the last day of the deadline to deposit money to their retirement plans (RRSP). Many don't have the cash at hand. So, they borrow to get the tax break. Example 30.3 shows the consequences.

> Example 30.3
>
> Chuck, 30, borrows $10,000 each year. The interest rate is 6-month CD plus 3% (approximately prime plus 1%). He pays it off at the end of each year. The funds are invested in a portfolio with 65% SP/TSX and 35% fixed income. The overall portfolio expenses are 2.5% year. He currently has $100,000 in his portfolio.
>
> What is the cost-benefit of this strategy for the next 20 years?
>
> Answer: The analysis based on market history indicates a profit factor of 0.48, a significant net loss over the long term, excluding the tax benefit.
>
> Suggestion: Chuck should stop borrowing each year. He should start monthly deposits that equals the loan payments he is making right now. He will definitely end up with a higher portfolio value.

Conclusion:

The three most important factors that determine the success of a leverage strategy are: luck, interest rate and alpha. You have no control over luck or the interest rate. As for alpha, most of us have insignificant control over it unless one follows a disciplined asset selection and monitoring strategy.

After all this discouragement, if you still want to borrow money to invest, here are some guidelines:

- Don't borrow more than the amount you already own in your investment portfolio
- Don't borrow if you are retired or plan to retire within the next ten years
- The loan term should be not less than ten years.
- Pay abundant attention to asset selection; you'll need to outperform the index by 4% or better.
- Make sure your net (after tax) interest cost is less than a 6–month CD plus 3%.
- Never meet a margin call. Liquidate if asset value is below 80% of the loan balance
- Use a 15% trailing stop

If you can fulfill *all* of these guidelines, then you have a good chance of making a profit.

Chapter 31

Determinants of a Portfolio's Success

Many people waste their lives by paying too much attention to unimportant things, investments or otherwise. They go around in circles trying to find the holy grail of financial success. As I wrote about asset allocation, rebalancing, the luck factor, reverse dollar cost averaging, inflation, portfolio expenses, market timing (tactical, flexible and combo) and asset selection (fingerprinting), I spelled out how each of these factors affect the outcome. Now, we can figure out what is important and what is not when it comes to retirement planning. After reading this chapter, you can decide how to allocate your time and resources more effectively to enhance your retirement finances.

Two sets of factors that determine a portfolio's success: the first one is the external factors, i.e. things you can do nothing about. This is the luck factor. I am not saying that there is nothing you can do about the luck factor or inflation; sure there is. You can buy life annuities and remove the luck factor entirely from the scene. But what I am talking about here is things there is nothing you can do about while holding an investment portfolio.

The second set includes factors that you can do something about to improve the outcome. They are asset selection and monitoring, optimum asset allocation and rebalancing, timing, and finally, portfolio costs. Let us recap these tables from earlier chapters.

Asset Allocation:

We calculated the impact of asset allocation in Chapter 4:

Table 31.1: The effect of rebalancing frequency on portfolio growth, equity proxy S&P500, from Table 4.2

	Initial Withdrawal Rate						
	0%	2%	3%	4%	6%	8%	10%
Impact of the worst possible asset allocation decision:	31.7%	6.2%	29.5%	40.3%	31.1%	21.7%	8.5%

Rebalancing:

We calculated the impact of rebalancing in Chapter 6:

Table 31.2: The effect of rebalancing frequency on portfolio growth, equity proxy S&P500, from Table 6.2

	Initial Withdrawal Rate					
	0%	2%	4%	6%	8%	10%
Impact of rebalancing frequency on compound annual return:	3.5%	12.0%	5.0%	1.3%	1.5%	2.0%

The Sequence of Returns:

We calculated the impact of the sequence of returns in Chapter 10:

Table 31.3: The effect of sequence of returns for various indices, from Table 10.1

	Initial Withdrawal Rate					
	0%	2%	4%	6%	8%	10%
DJIA (since 1900)	43%	42%	45%	44%	58%	65%
S&P500 (since 1900)	48%	49%	52%	46%	63%	66%
SP/TSX (since 1919)	35%	37%	44%	49%	54%	57%
FTSE All Shares (since 1900)	84%	87%	101%	98%	98%	105%
Nikkei 225 (since 1914)	39%	41%	45%	52%	62%	77%
ASX All Ordinaries (since 1900)	51%	52%	56%	52%	57%	61%

Reverse Dollar Cost Averaging:

We discussed reverse dollar cost averaging in Chapter 12. It is somewhat dependant on the withdrawal rate. It is also dependant on the volatility of markets in specific time periods. We calculated one example (Example 12.3), retiring in 1966 with 6% initial withdrawal rate. Reverse dollar cost averaging had an 11% impact on the portfolio longevity.

However, the effect of reverse dollar cost averaging can be minimized or even eliminated entirely by allocating some of the assets to money market and short–term bonds, by withdrawing income only from the non–fluctuating money market funds, and by optimizing the rebalancing frequency.

Since the impact of reverse dollar cost averaging is an avoidable one, we will exclude it from our list of the determinants of a portfolio's success.

Inflation:

We calculated the impact of inflation in Chapter 11:

Table 31.4: The effect of inflation, from Table 11.2

	Initial Withdrawal Rate					
	0%	2%	4%	6%	8%	10%
Impact of inflation on compound annual return:	0%	11%	31%	44%	55%	55%

Market Timing:

I use the tactical asset allocation strategy (see Chapter 24) to calculate the effects of market timing:

Table 31.5: The effect of timing – tactical asset allocation, from Table 24.5

	Initial Withdrawal Rate					
	0%	2%	4%	6%	8%	10%
Impact of TAA timing strategy on compound annual return:	10%	25%	24%	22%	13%	12%

Asset Selection:

We discussed asset selection in Chapter 28 on Fingerprinting. I believe that by carefully following the fingerprinting method you can add 2% to 3% to a portfolio's annual return. Using the low–end figure of 2%, Table 31.6 depicts the impact of asset selection.

I am not suggesting that one can necessarily outperform the index by 2% merely by paying more attention through skilful asset selection. I used 2% only as a possible upper limit for calculation purposes. Keep in mind; the impact of asset selection is dependent on how disciplined the investor is in following this strategy. Any degree of lack of discipline can do more harm than good.

I know this is not exact, but that is the best I can do unless you can provide me with your personal track record covering at least ten years.

Table 31.6: The effect of asset selection and monitoring, equity proxy S&P500

	Initial Withdrawal Rate					
	0%	2%	4%	6%	8%	10%
Strategic Asset Allocation – compound annual return of the median portfolio (from Table 20.3 and Table 20.1)	6.0%	5.2%	5.1%	4.9%	5.6%	5.8%
If asset selection and monitoring can add	2.0%	2.0%	2.0%	2.0%	2.0%	2.0%
Impact of properly applied asset selection and monitoring:	33%	38%	39%	41%	36%	34%

Portfolio Costs:

We discussed portfolio and management costs in Chapter 29. Keep in mind that portfolio costs can vary widely. Use this table with some latitude.

Table 31.7: The effect of portfolio costs, equity proxy S&P500, from Table 29.1

	Initial Withdrawal Rate					
	0%	2%	4%	6%	8%	10%
Impact of portfolio costs on compound annual return:	36%	38%	51%	34%	32%	31%

Determinants of Portfolio's Success:

Now we can combine all the figures from Tables 31.1 to 31.7 into one single table, as indicated in Table 31.8.

Table 31.8: The non–cumulative effect of different factors to a portfolio's success, equity proxy S&P500

	Initial Withdrawal Rate					
Factors:	0%	2%	4%	6%	8%	10%
Luck Factor:						
Sequence of Returns	48%	49%	52%	46%	63%	66%
Inflation	0%	11%	31%	44%	55%	55%
Manageable Factors:						
Asset Selection & Monitoring	33%	38%	39%	41%	36%	34%
Optimum Asset Allocation	32%	6.2%	40%	31%	22%	8.5%
Market Timing (Tactical AA)	10%	25%	24%	22%	13%	12%
Optimum Rebalancing	3.5%	12%	5.0%	1.3%	1.5%	2.0%
Portfolio Costs	36%	38%	51%	34%	32%	28%

Figures on this table indicate the percentage of impact on the growth rate caused by each factor alone. In other words, if you total each column, they do not add up to 100%.

To calculate the relative importance of each factor, we prorate these figures so that each column adds up to 100%. Table 31.9 shows the relative contribution of each factor for different initial withdrawal rates.

Table 31.9: The determinants of a portfolio's success, equity proxy S&P500

Factors:	**Initial Withdrawal Rate**					
	0%	2%	4%	6%	8%	10%
	Determinant's of a Distribution Portfolio's Success					
Luck Factor:						
Sequence of Returns	30%	27%	21%	21%	28%	32%
Inflation	0%	6%	13%	20%	25%	27%
Total – Luck Factor	**30%**	**33%**	**34%**	**41%**	**53%**	**59%**
Manageable Factors:						
Asset Selection & Monitoring[62]	20%	22%	16%	18%	16%	16%
Optimum Asset Allocation	20%	3%	17%	14%	10%	4%
Market Timing (Tactical AA)	6%	14%	10%	10%	6%	6%
Optimum Rebalancing	2%	7%	2%	1%	1%	1%
Portfolio Costs	22%	21%	21%	16%	14%	14%
Total – Manageable Factors	**70%**	**67%**	**66%**	**59%**	**47%**	**41%**

62 Because of rounding, the sum did not always add to 100%. In such situations, the asset selection and monitoring factor were adjusted up or down to ensure that the numbers in each column add to 100%

Conclusion:

At all withdrawal rates, the luck factor is the most important contributor to the success of a portfolio. If luck is not on your side, your investment portfolio can do little for you. The remedy is not in what you can do with your portfolio, but what you can do with your assets. Insurance products, specifically annuities, become a natural choice.

The next important factor is asset selection & monitoring, followed by portfolio costs. However, these two are at the opposite ends of the performance spectrum. If you minimize your portfolio costs, then you are likely buying index funds. In this case, you sacrifice the benefit of alpha through asset selection. You can try to compensate for this by timing the index funds.

In other words, these three factors, –asset selection, timing and portfolio costs– form a triangle. It takes an exceptional talent to combine the added value of the best managers, lowest portfolio costs and market timing, all in the same portfolio. For most, juggling only two of these three factors is a challenge. If you can only combine a strategy using index funds and timing successfully and consistently, consider yourself gifted. You can then enjoy the best of both worlds: a lower cost, a higher alpha and a lower beta. Otherwise, stick to buy–and–hold.

Optimizing asset allocation has a limited impact. The good thing about asset allocation is that you can easily implement it. In fact, this is the easiest part of the whole game. Otherwise, why would the financial industry push it so hard? Did you ever believe deep in your guts that asset allocation contributes to over 90% of the differences in a portfolio's success? If you did not believe it, now you know that you were right all along. If you did believe it, now you know why it has not been working for you.

Optimum rebalancing has a great impact on specific selected cases in history. It adds several years to portfolio life during secular bear markets by not permitting you to throw good money after bad, repeatedly. However, when we look at the entire market history, its "average" impact is rather small. It is included in this table only because you can put it into practice easily and it does work when you really need it – in bear markets.

Chapter 32

Retirement Income Classes

During the accumulation stage, we focus on *asset classes*. Allocating your assets to different and distinct asset classes reduces the overall risk in normal markets.

During the distribution stage, we focus on *income classes*. Each income class has a different way of providing income over life. You need to diversify income classes during the distribution stage. This can increase the probability of uninterrupted lifelong income.

The common income classes during retirement are:

- Government benefits and pensions
- Company pensions
- Annuities
- Rental income
- Investment portfolio
- Part–time work income
- Business income

When it comes to retirement finances, we have already covered the three main risk factors in Chapter 17: longevity risk, market risk and inflation risk. A retirement plan must minimize each of these three risk factors to be considered a well–designed plan.

Table 32.1 illustrates the risks in each of these income classes.

Table 32.1: Different income classes

Income Class	Longevity	Market	Inflation	Other Risks
	Risk Factors Covered			
Government Pensions and Benefits	✔	✔	✔	Sustainability of government programs, default of governments
Company and Other Pension				
Read the contract	Varies	Varies	Varies	Default, mismanagement, fraud
Rental Income				
Net positive cash flow	✔	✔	✔	Non–insurable property damage, mismanagement, bad tenants
Net negative cash flow	✘	✘	✘	
Investment Portfolio				
Withdrawals below sustainable	✔	✔	✔	Behavioral, mismanagement, bad investments, fraud, bad luck
Withdrawals above sustainable	✘	✘	✘	
Immediate Term Certain Annuity				
Straight – non–indexed	✘	✘	✘	Financial stability of the insurance company
Straight – indexed	✘	✘	Depends	
Immediate Life Annuity				
Straight – payments non–indexed	✔	✔	✘	
Straight – payments indexed at a fixed rate	✔	✔	Depends	
Straight – payments indexed partially for CPI	✔	✔	✘	Financial stability of the insurance company
Straight – payments indexed fully for CPI	✔	✔	✔	
Variable Pay – payments based on underlying index	✔	✘	✘	
Variable Annuity with GMWB or GMIB rider				
Straight & for Life – payments may increase based on performance of underlying investments	✔	✔	✘	Financial stability of the insurance company
Straight & for Term – payments may increase based on performance of underlying investments, term usually 20 years	✘	✘	✘	

Government Pension and Benefits:

Government pensions generally do not involve market risk, longevity risk or inflation risk. However, there is still the question of sustainability.

Here, I will only comment on the Canadian government pension system. I am not smart enough to learn fully and comment on the US social security system.

According to Canada's Chief Actuary's 2007 report, the Canada Pension Plan (CPP) is sustainable throughout the 75–year period covered by their report. I always get worried when actuaries make such claims. In principle, we are talking about the same body of knowledge that affects all other pension funds at work here as well. These methodologies gave birth to plenty of underfunded or insolvent company pension plans in the past. They all started with wonderful projections, not much different than your own personal retirement plans of the past. Eventually, most realize that there is something wrong with it. Surely, they will blame something or other, but mostly the adverse economy for their miscalculations. The only thing you need to know is this: the Gaussian mindset does not work for distribution portfolios. That is the deciding factor. For example, the CPP Investment Policy Statement states that they expect a 4.2% real return on the equity portion of their investments. This implies no consideration for the time value of fluctuations. When withdrawals start exceeding contributions in about ten years (their projection), using a 3% IWR[63] , including the time value of fluctuations, the Canadian equity index grew historically by about 2.4% in real dollars. I expect to see the dirt hitting the fan, perhaps in 2025, about three to five years after the cash outflow starts exceeding the cash inflow. At that time, managers will realize that it is a lot more difficult to achieve a positive alpha when cash is flowing out (reverse–dollar–cost averaging) than when it is flowing in (dollar–cost–averaging). In the meantime, they will continue dishing out generous bonuses and extras to themselves, all at our expense. What makes matters worse is that 40% of funds are invested in foreign equities. Recalling Chapter 5, The Magic of Diversification, this money should be invested in Canada to strengthen the Canadian economy, Canadian workers and Canadian retirees. Being one of the most stable and low–corruption economies in the world, why would anyone take that additional risk?

For my clients, I will assume that indexed government benefits will continue. Personally, I am old enough to let the next generation worry about these problems. Sorry, that is my easy way out!

[63] This is –very approximately– the reciprocal of asset/expenditure ratio in actuarial jargon

Rental Income:

If rental income creates a positive cash flow, then it is a great income class. It eliminates longevity and market risks. It minimizes inflation risk. Unlike a life annuity, your estate keeps your assets (rental property) at the end. You just have to make sure that there is sufficient insurance on the property to reduce the risk of unexpected calamities.

Keep in mind that a positive cash flow can turn negative quickly. You need to be good in dealing with tenants. Otherwise, you need to retain a property management company with an excellent track record.

If the cash flow is negative, then you need to turn that around before you begin your retirement. .

Investment Portfolio:

An investment portfolio can generate a reliable lifelong income only if withdrawals remain below the sustainable level.

Pay attention to the basic investment principles discussed throughout this book, such as strategies about asset allocation, rebalancing, asset selection, etc. However, even the best–laid plans involving investments have risks.

If things don't go as planned, switching to a safer **asset class** will not solve the problem; you must switch to a safer **income class**, such as annuities. That is your only stop–loss for lifelong income.

Immediate Term–Certain Annuity:

A term–certain annuity provides periodic payments for a fixed time period. Insurance companies are usually the main providers of this product. However, other financial institutions, such as trusts and banks, may also offer it in many jurisdictions. The periodic payments continue for the entire term, whether you are alive or dead. However, once the term expires, that is it, no more payments. Term annuities may be useful to create an income stream to bridge a gap. For example, if you want your investments to grow for five years untouched, you can buy a five–year term annuity for income to bridge those five years.

Immediate Life Annuity:

A life annuity is a contract between an individual and an insurance company. The person receiving the payments is called an annuitant. The annuitant makes a one–time payment, called the premium, to the insurance company. The insurance company makes periodic payments to the annuitant until annuitant's death. Immediate means that the payments start within one year of paying the premium.

With life annuity, both the market risk and longevity risks are eliminated. You have lifelong income, period. Depending on what type of annuity you choose, inflation risk may or may not be covered.

Variable Pay Annuity:

Variable pay annuity is a variation of the single premium immediate annuity. It pays a lifelong income, but the payments fluctuate in line with market performance. The retiree selects a benchmark index and an anticipated investment return (AIR). The starting amount of annuity payments, as well as how fluctuations of payments are calculated, depends on these two factors.

Variable pay annuity can be used as part of the retirement income solution if you are comfortable with fluctuating income.

Variable Annuity with GMWB:

Variable Annuities (VA) with Guaranteed Minimum Withdrawal Benefits (GMWB) were first introduced by Hartford Life in 2002. In 2004, sales of all variable annuities (with or without GMWB) in the US reached $128 billion, of which 69% of all sales had the GMWB rider. The total assets in VAs were about $1.1 trillion at the end of 2004. Most come with withdrawal benefits guaranteed for life, some have only a 20–year guarantee period. In this book, I will only consider those that come with a life guarantee. I use the acronym VA–GMWBL to refer to a variable annuity with guaranteed withdrawal benefits for life.

A VA–GMWBL has a market value which fluctuates just like a mutual fund. This is called the "Contract Value". In addition, there is another balance to track, which is called the "Guaranteed Withdrawal Base" (GWB). Its value does not fluctuate with day–to–day market fluctuations. It is used to calculate the income payments. The day you buy the VA–GMWBL, both the contract value and the GWB are the same, i.e. your initial premium.

When you buy a VA–GMWBL, you know exactly what your minimum income stream will be for the rest of your life. Even if the contract value might go down to zero in adverse markets, periodic payments continue for the life of the contract based on the GWB.

VA–GMWBL removes the market and longevity risks, but not the inflation risk. The dollar amount of payments never decreases, but its purchasing power will likely do so. I will cover the features of VA–GMWBL in detail in Chapter 35.

Variable Annuity with GMIB:

In many ways, a Guaranteed Minimum Income Benefits (GMIB) rider is similar to a GMWB. It has a market value that fluctuates like a mutual fund. This is the "Contract Value". In addition, there is the "Guaranteed Income Base" (GIB) which is used to calculate income payments. The day you buy the VA–GMIB, both the contract value and the GWB are the same, i.e. your initial premium.

Here is the difference: a GMIB is deemed to be annuitized when and if the contract value falls to zero. The deemed premium of this annuity is the value of the GIB at the time of annuitization. The annuity is based on the age of the retiree at the time of annuitization.

If the portfolio does not run out of money, then most GMIB plans will require you to annuitize at age 85 or 90.

Also, the account owner can annuitize his GMIB at a time of his own choosing. This is usually subject to some constrains, such as "no sooner than ten years after the last step–up reset". Annuitization usually creates a pay increase.

When you buy a VA–GMIB, you know exactly what your minimum income stream will be for the rest of your life. You also know the exact amount (in percentage) of the annuity payment rates for each annuitization age.

VA–GMIB removes market and longevity risks, but not inflation risk. The chances are, your purchasing power will decrease over time. I will cover the features of VA–GMIB in detail in Chapter 36.

Conclusion:

The income classes cited in this chapter are the most common ones in retirement planning. Which ones eliminate longevity, market and inflation risks? 1. Government benefits, 2. an investment portfolio where withdrawals are lower than the sustainable withdrawal rate, 3. rental income with a net positive cash flow, and 4. a life annuity with fully indexed payments.

We will first look at the details of annuities and then analyze how to create lifelong income by combining some of these and other income classes.

Chapter 33

Immediate Life Annuity

A life annuity is a contract between an individual and an insurance company. The person receiving the payments is called an annuitant. The annuitant makes a one–time payment, called the premium, to the insurance company. The insurance company pays periodic payments to the annuitant until death. Immediate means that the payments start within one year of paying the premium.

With a life annuity, both market risks and longevity risks are eliminated. You have lifelong income, period. Depending on what type of options you choose, inflation risk may also be eliminated.

There are many options, riders and types of life annuity. Here are a few:

- Joint and survivor: Also known as Joint–last to Die. The annuity pays out for as long as one of the spouses is alive.
- Reduction of payments: This applies only to joint and survivor life annuities. You can choose to have the payments reduced after one of the two spouses dies. There are many variations to this. You can specify a reduction after the first spouse dies, or after one of the primary or secondary annuitants dies. You can also request that this reduction occur immediately after death or after the minimum guarantee period.
- Minimum guarantee period: Also known as Life and Period Certain. When buying a life annuity, one of the concerns is a premature death. If the annuitant dies prematurely, the insurance company keeps the premium. To alleviate this concern, you can (and should) ask for a minimum guarantee period. This can be any number, but it is usually 10 or 15 years. It ensures that in the case of a premature death, the beneficiary continues to receive periodic payments until the end of the minimum guaranteed period. Usually, the beneficiary can also choose to receive the present value of the remaining annuity in a single, lump–sum payment.
- Refund certain: In the case of premature death, payments continue until the entire premium amount is paid back. Usually, the beneficiary can also choose to receive the present value of the remaining annuity in a single, lump sum payment.
- Indexation: Some insurance companies offer indexation of the payments. You can select fixed, partial or full indexation of payments for CPI.

  Fixed indexation means that your payments increase each year by a fixed percentage. On average, a 3% fixed indexation would keep the purchasing power steady over the long term. However, if you get caught in a high inflation time period, you may fall behind.

Full indexation means that payments are indexed to the CPI. Only a few insurance companies offer this option, so you may need to do some searching.

Partial indexation means that payments are indexed to part of the CPI and/or up to a limit. This may be suitable if full indexation is not necessary in your situation.

With many annuities, you can choose to trigger the indexation at the end of each calendar year or at the anniversary of the annuity contract.

This is only a short list of popular options. Many insurance companies offer other choices. Make sure to study each plan carefully before signing up. Weigh the consequences of each choice. Once you sign the contract, generally, you cannot change anything afterwards.

Table 33.1 shows the single premium required to pay $10,000 annually[64]. These figures are presented here only to give you a comparison purpose. The premiums will vary depending on many factors. Always get quotes from different insurance carriers before making a decision. Keep in mind that the highest quote may not be the wisest choice. You may want to sacrifice a little of the income stream for an insurer with better ratings and track record.

[64] in equal monthly installments of $833.33 per month during the first year

Table 33.1: Cost of life annuities for $10,000 annual income[65]

Life Annuity Type	Primary Annuitant Male, 65	Female, 65	Male, 70	Female, 70
No minimum guarantee period, no CPI indexation:				
Single Life Annuity	$127,886	$139,121	$112,113	$123,009
Joint & Survivor, spouse 60, 75% to survivor	$151,200	$150,255	$145,681	$143,482
Joint & Survivor, spouse 65, 75% to survivor	$143,224	$143,224	$136,768	$135,316
Joint & Survivor, spouse 70, 75% to survivor	$135,316	$136,768	$127,674	$127,674
15–yr minimum guarantee period, no CPI indexation:				
Single Life Annuity	$137,043	$144,033	$126,643	$131,824
Joint & Survivor, spouse 60, 75% to survivor	$151,550	$150,623	$146,228	$144,135
Joint & Survivor, spouse 65, 75% to survivor	$143,823	$143,823	$137,703	$136,379
Joint & Survivor, spouse 70, 75% to survivor	$136,379	$137,703	$129,337	$129,337
15–yr minimum guarantee period, annual 3% indexation:				
Single Life Annuity	$181,605	$195,298	$161,307	$170,835
J & S, spouse 60, 75% to survivor	$214,547	$211,620	$204,673	$198,822
J & S, spouse 65, 75% to survivor	$197,251	$197,251	$185,727	$182,483
J & S, spouse 70, 75% to survivor	$182,483	$185,727	$169,133	$169,133
15–yr minimum guarantee period, full annual CPI indexation:				
Single Life Annuity	$187,812	$201,716	$167,163	$177,029
J & S, spouse 60, 75% to survivor	$220,248	$217,608	$210,251	$204,774
J & S, spouse 65, 75% to survivor	$203,544	$203,544	$191,888	$194,527
J & S, spouse 70, 75% to survivor	$188,728	$191,888	$175,205	$175,205
Refund certain, annual 3% indexation:				
Single Life Annuity	$181,122	$196,141	$155,731	$168,653
J & S, spouse 60, 75% to survivor	$220,293	$216,600	$212,225	$204,764
J & S, spouse 65, 75% to survivor	$202,808	$202,808	$192,372	$188,257
J & S, spouse 70, 75% to survivor	$188,257	$192,372	$175,082	$175,082

[65] Where periodic payments are indexed, then this is the cost of buying a life annuity that pays $833.33/ month during the first year. Rates are as of March 2009. No taxes included

Laddering Life Annuities:

A life annuity provides a steady stream of income until death. It removes the possibility of outliving one's money. However, in most cases, there is no estate value upon death.

Some retirees want to keep control of their money as long as possible. Instead of buying a life annuity in one transaction, they buy several smaller life annuity contracts over time. This process is called "laddering" annuities. It is similar to laddering a bond portfolio or CD's with different maturities to reduce the interest rate risk.

Why would you ladder an annuity instead of buying it all at once? There are several reasons:

- The older you are, the higher the payout. As you add new "rungs" to your annuity ladder, you would receive higher payouts for the same amount of premium.
- Laddering will reduce the interest rate risk; the interest rate is blended over time.
- Portfolio value may go up over time, providing more funds to buy annuity.
- You have control of your money for a longer period of time.

To build an annuity ladder, we weigh the benefits of buying an annuity now against buying it in the future. The logic for laddering stems from two extreme constraints:

- If I know for sure that I will need more money to buy the same income stream next year, then I should buy the entire annuity now.
- If I know for sure that I will need less money to buy the same income stream next year, then I can delay buying the annuity until next year.

Obviously, we don't know what will happen next year; these two are just the extremes.

Let's calculate the probability of having a lower income stream next year, adjusted for inflation. Let's call this number AL. This probability, AL, depends on several factors:

- Luck factor – good markets mean more available money in the portfolio next year
- Interest rate – the higher the interest rate, the lower is the premium required for the same payout
- Inflation – inflation has a two–pronged effect: 1. the higher the inflation, the greater is the premium to buy a CPI indexed annuity paying the same income stream, and 2. the higher the inflation, the greater is the income you will need next year, and this will cost more in premium
- Age – the older you are, the lower is the premium for the same payout
- The time interval between the rungs of the annuity ladder is important when the withdrawal rate is greater than the sustainable withdrawal rate. The longer you

wait, the greater are the chances of having less money in the portfolio if the withdrawal rate exceeds the sustainable rate.

Many of these factors work in tandem. For example, a higher than expected inflation rate can create adverse market trends, which push your portfolio value down and require a higher withdrawal rate, which in turn increases the probability of having less money next year to purchase the next rung of the ladder.

I turn now to market history[66] to calculate AL for different levels of withdrawal rates, as shown in Table 33.2.

Table 33.2: Historical values of AL, the probability of a lower, inflation–adjusted income stream

Withdrawal Rate	Probability of lower income stream after one year	Probability of lower income stream after four years
2%	37%	27%
4%	49%	44%
6%	56%	55%
8%	62%	72%
10%	66%	85%

What is the significance of the AL? It tells you exactly how much of a life annuity to purchase for each rung of your ladder.

If you find this complicated, here is a simple rule of thumb: the dollar amount of the annuity premium for the current purchase should be half of the previous year's premium. This will give you approximately the optimum laddering based on market history. Keep in mind; each time you are buying the subsequent rung, you will likely need to recalculate this dollar amount to reflect the then current rates.

Example: You are buying a $300,000 annuity. How much money do you allocate to each rung? Table 33.3 shows the numbers:

[66] Assumptions: 1. Age factor: 1.8% lower premium required to buy the same annuity income on each birthday, 2. Inflation: 3% per annum, 3. Asset Mix: 40% DJIA and 60% fixed income portfolio

Table 33.3: Laddering a life annuity

Annuity Ladder:	Rungs:
No annuity ladder	No rungs, buy $300,000 life annuity now
Two–rung annuity ladder	First Rung: $200,000, buy now Second Rung: $100,000, buy one year from now
Three–rung annuity ladder	First Rung: $172,000, buy now Second Rung: $86,000, buy one year from now Third Rung: $42,000, buy two years from now
Four–rung annuity ladder	First Rung: $160,000, buy now Second Rung: $80,000, buy one year from now Third Rung: $40,000, buy two years from now Fourth Rung: $20,000, buy three years from now

The next question that you might ask is this: When is it unsafe to build an annuity ladder? At what point might laddering an annuity put the retiree at a risk of having a lower income than originally planned for?

This can happen when, after buying the first rung of the ladder:

- markets go down, taking your investment portfolio down. You may not have sufficient funds left to buy the subsequent rungs for your annuity ladder.
- inflation takes a sudden jump. If you are buying a CPI indexed annuity, the premium for the subsequent ladders might go up significantly.
- interest rates go down significantly. The premium for the subsequent ladders might go up significantly.

My rule of thumb is this: If the income requirement for a couple (joint and survivor annuity, indexed fully to CPI) is greater than the sustainable withdrawal rate, then it might be unsafe to ladder. If so, you would then just buy one life annuity, a single rung to pay the entire required income. This is as simple as it gets. If you want a more sophisticated answer to this, you need to download the retirement calculator available at my website, which will optimize the annuity ladder and indicate whether or not it is safe to ladder it for each specific scenario, at the push of a button.

Minimizing the Inflation Risk:

Most insurers do not offer a CPI–indexed life annuity. For inflation protection, you need to hold a separate investment portfolio, a separate "bucket". This bucket has only one purpose: it provides the funds to cover any loss of purchasing power from the life annuity that is not indexed to the CPI. In other words, it is the bucket where the pay increases come from[67] when and if needed.

Table 33.4 depicts the approximate size of this separate investment account to provide inflation protection for a $10,000 annual income for a 20–year and a 30–year time horizon. The core annual income of $10,000 is provided by the annuity. Any inflation shortfall is provided by this separate bucket. Table 33.4 shows the dollar amount that must be set aside to maintain purchasing power over the time horizon.

You can also use this table to calculate the additional investment bucket required to cover the shortfall from pension payments or any other income sources that are not indexed to the CPI.

Table 33.4: Additional assets required in an investment portfolio utilized as an inflation bucket for the life annuity

	Time Horizon: 20 years	Time Horizon: 30 years
	Additional Assets Required to make up for the inflation shortfall for a $10,000 annual base income :	
Base annuity is not indexed	$74,000	$109,000
Base annuity is indexed 1% each year	$65,000	$97,000
Base annuity is indexed 2% each year	$53,000	$84,000
Base annuity is indexed 3% each year	$38,000	$69,000
Base annuity is indexed 4% each year	$28,000	$50,000
Base annuity is indexed 5% each year	$18,000	$9,000
Base annuity is indexed 6% each year	$0	$0

Notes for the table: The asset mix of the investment portfolio used as the inflation bucket is 50% S&P500 index and 50% fixed income. Equity: dividend yield is 2%, management costs 2% for a net alpha of 0%. Fixed Income has a net yield of 6–month CD interest rate plus 0.5%.

[67] In a deflationary environment, excess income goes into this bucket.

After observing Table 33.4, those with eagle eyes might look at the second last row and ask two questions:

1. If the average historical inflation is 3.3%, why would I ever need any inflation bucket in combination with an annuity that is indexed by 5% each year?
2. Why would I need an inflation bucket of $18,000 for a 20–year time horizon, but only $9,000 for a 30–year time horizon?

The answer to the first question is: when it comes to making a plan, we do not design for the averages; we design for the unlucky outcomes. The average historical inflation may be 3.3%, but the average inflation in a secular sideways trend is 5.6%. So, you have to plan for adverse levels of inflation. If that does not happen in your lifetime, then good for you, the money goes to your estate.

The answer to the second question is: the longer time horizon allows more exposure to a lower inflation environment, on average. Therefore, you need less in your bucket for a 30–year time horizon than a 20–year time horizon for such extreme inflation waves.

Example 33.1

Howard, 65, is buying a life annuity. He needs $10,000 annual income at age 65. Which combination of an annuity and an inflation bucket will cost him the least amount of initial savings? Which one might provide the largest estate value?

Assume Howard wants inflation protection for 30 years.

We observe on Table 33.1 that an annuity that pays $10,000 annually with no indexation at all, costs $137,043. An annuity that pays $10,000 annually with 3% indexation, costs $181,605. An annuity that pays $10,000 annually with full CPI indexation costs $187,812.

We observe in Table 33.4 that you need an inflation bucket of $109,000 with an annuity that pays $10,000 annually with no indexation. The inflation bucket for an annuity with 3% indexation is $69,000. As for the annuity that is fully CPI indexed, you need no inflation bucket.

	Base annuity is not indexed	Base annuity is indexed 3% each year	Base annuity is indexed fully to CPI
Annuity Cost	$137,043	$181,605	$187,812
Inflation Bucket	$109,000	$69,000	$0
Total Savings Required	$246,043	$250,605	$187,812

Which strategy initially requires the least amount of savings? The initial cost of the annuity with full CPI is the lowest.

Which strategy leaves the highest estate value? The probability of depletion of the inflation bucket is no more than 10% based on market history. It is highly likely that a large part of the inflation bucket will remain unused and it is passed on to the estate.

Therefore, the combination of a straight, non-indexed annuity plus an inflation bucket costs initially more than the CPI-indexed annuity, but it leaves the largest estate value. By the way, the median portfolio value of the $109,000 inflation bucket grows to $167,800 after thirty years, based on actual market history.

What can we learn from Example 33.1? Here are the choices:

Choose the combination of non–indexed annuity plus inflation bucket:

- If you have large enough savings
- If you want to leave behind the maximum estate value

Choose the fully CPI–indexed life annuity:

- If you don't have sufficient savings for the non–indexed annuity plus the inflation bucket combination
- If it is not important for you to leave behind any money
- If you don't want to worry about investment performance in the inflation bucket.

Of course these are just general guidelines. You will need to review each case based on its own merits.

Conclusion:

Life annuities are one of the most foolproof income classes that money can buy. It creates a lifelong income and eliminates longevity and market risks. If required, it can also minimize the inflation risk to a level of your choice.

If you are retiring at age 65 and your asset to withdrawals ratio (asset multiplier, see Chapter 17) is less than thirty, you must consider life annuities as part of your income allocation strategy.

Chapter 34

Variable Pay Annuity

Variable pay annuity (VPA) is a variation of the single premium immediate annuity. It pays a lifelong income but the payments fluctuate. Payments are linked to market performance. The starting amount of annuity payments, as well as how subsequent payments are calculated, depends on two factors: The benchmark index selected and the anticipated investment return.

Before the arrival of VA–GMWB or VA–GMIB, variable pay annuities (VPA) were the annuity of choice for linking payments to market performance. The main difference between the VPA and the VA–GMWB is this: VPA is a true annuity. When you buy the VPA, you pay the premium to the insurance company, just like any other single premium immediate annuity. That premium goes to the general assets of the insurance company and it is no longer your money.

The VPA eliminates the longevity risk. There is a market risk because your income amount depends on market performance. For the same reason, there is also a significant inflation risk.

At the time of purchase, you need to decide on your "virtual portfolio". You don't own this portfolio and it has no monetary value. However, you can notionally allocate money to market index, bond index and various equity indexes. Next, you need to decide on the Anticipated Investment Return (AIR). Most plans allow you to choose one of 0%, 3%, 5%, and 6%. AIR is used to determine the initial payment of the VPA. The higher the AIR, the higher the starting income.

The AIR you select controls the future annual increases and decreases of your income. If you start with an AIR of 0%, you will receive the highest increases in good markets. In bad markets, an AIR of 0% will give you the least amount of pay cuts.

On the other hand, if you start with an AIR of 6%, you will have the lowest amount of increases in good markets. In bad markets, an AIR of 6% will give you the highest pay reduction. If inflation protection is important to you, always start with the lowest AIR.

The annual changes to your income are calculated using this formula:

$$\text{Change in Income} = \text{IC} = \left(\frac{(1+\text{VPR})}{(1+\text{AIR})} - 1 \right) \times 100\% \qquad \text{(Equation 34.1)}$$

where:
VPR is the investment return of the virtual portfolio
AIR is the anticipated investment return

Example 34.1

Chuck has a variable pay annuity. It pays him $2,000 per month. During the year, his virtual portfolio grows by 8%.

Calculate the increase in his monthly payment for the coming year:

- If his AIR is 0%

  Using equation 34.1:

  $$\left(\frac{(1+0.08)}{(1.00+0.00)}-1\right)\times 100\% \ = 8.0\% \text{ increase}$$

- If his AIR is 6%

  $$\left(\frac{(1+0.08)}{(1+0.06)}-1\right)\times 100\% \ = 1.9\% \text{ increase}$$

Example 34.2

Susan has a variable pay annuity. It pays her $2,000 per month. During the year, her virtual portfolio loses 8%.

Calculate the decrease in her monthly payment:

- If her AIR is 0%

  $$\left(\frac{(1+(-0.08))}{(1+0.00)}-1\right)\times 100\% \ = 8.0\% \text{ decrease}$$

- If her AIR is 6%

  $$\left(\frac{(1+(-0.08))}{(1+0.06)}-1\right)\times 100\% \ = 13.2\% \text{ decrease}$$

The Optimum AIR:

Insurance companies sometimes include striking examples in their sales materials. I came across something like this: A single 65–year old male buys a VPA in 1982 for a single premium of $100,000. The illustration showed monthly income increased from about $300 in June, 1982 to about $2,625 in June, 2002 (AIR is 0%). It showed another example using AIR of 6%: the monthly income went from $593 to $1,619 during the same 20–year time period. This is very impressive; the retiree beats the inflation during that time frame handily, regardless of the AIR he chooses.

There is only one problem: the years between 1982 and 2000 cover the best mega–bull market of the last century. We need to look at the entire market history to see what happens in a bear market and what happens in a high inflation time period.

Here is how I calculate the inflation risk:

1. Calculate the VPA payments for a 65–year old retiree for all starting years since 1900, using the actual market history. Note the VPA payment at age 85, 20 years after the initial payment.
2. Calculate the income that would have been required to keep up with inflation at age 85 –20 years after the start of payments– for each starting year since 1900. This is the real income required.
3. Divide the figure calculated in #1 by #2 and multiply by 100. This is the real purchasing power 20 years after the start of payments as a percentage of the starting amount.

Table 34.1 depicts the real purchasing power for a VPA indexed to the S&P500. The median real purchasing power after 20 years was 130% for 0% AIR, 105% for 3% AIR and 81% for 6% AIR.

Table 34.1: The Real Purchasing Power of VPA payments after 20 years:

Starting Year	Real Purchasing Power after 20 years			Starting Year	Real Purchasing Power after 20 years			Starting Year	Real Purchasing Power after 20 years		
	AIR 0%	AIR 3%	AIR 6%		AIR 0%	AIR 3%	AIR 6%		AIR 0%	AIR 3%	AIR 6%
1900	57%	46%	35%	1929	52%	42%	32%	1958	83%	67%	52%
1901	38%	30%	23%	1930	75%	61%	47%	1959	77%	62%	48%
1902	35%	28%	22%	1931	175%	140%	108%	1960	81%	65%	50%
1903	65%	52%	40%	1932	200%	161%	124%	1961	74%	59%	46%
1904	53%	43%	33%	1933	123%	99%	76%	1962	68%	54%	42%
1905	55%	44%	34%	1934	136%	110%	84%	1963	61%	49%	38%
1906	66%	53%	41%	1935	129%	104%	80%	1964	62%	50%	38%
1907	97%	78%	60%	1936	130%	105%	81%	1965	56%	45%	35%
1908	103%	83%	64%	1937	210%	169%	130%	1966	80%	64%	49%
1909	128%	103%	79%	1938	172%	138%	106%	1967	76%	61%	47%
1910	133%	107%	82%	1939	223%	179%	138%	1968	73%	59%	45%
1911	103%	83%	64%	1940	267%	214%	165%	1969	93%	75%	58%
1912	52%	41%	32%	1941	312%	251%	193%	1970	120%	97%	74%
1913	58%	46%	36%	1942	369%	297%	229%	1971	102%	82%	63%
1914	108%	87%	67%	1943	300%	241%	186%	1972	109%	88%	67%
1915	76%	61%	47%	1944	318%	256%	197%	1973	138%	111%	85%
1916	111%	89%	69%	1945	271%	218%	168%	1974	222%	179%	138%
1917	205%	165%	127%	1946	354%	285%	220%	1975	182%	146%	113%
1918	141%	114%	87%	1947	366%	295%	227%	1976	213%	171%	132%
1919	162%	130%	101%	1948	446%	359%	277%	1977	296%	238%	183%
1920	234%	188%	145%	1949	437%	352%	271%	1978	396%	319%	246%
1921	200%	161%	124%	1950	288%	232%	179%	1979	479%	385%	297%
1922	123%	99%	76%	1951	252%	203%	156%	1980	508%	408%	315%
1923	125%	100%	77%	1952	259%	209%	161%	1981	554%	445%	343%
1924	115%	92%	71%	1953	301%	242%	186%	1982	449%	361%	278%
1925	106%	85%	66%	1954	173%	139%	107%	1983	300%	241%	186%
1926	135%	109%	84%	1955	90%	72%	56%	1984	378%	304%	234%
1927	85%	68%	52%	1956	102%	82%	63%	1985	332%	267%	206%
1928	48%	39%	30%	1957	130%	105%	81%	1986	300%	241%	186%

Figure 34.1 shows the probability of the real purchasing power after 20 years for all years since 1900 in four different categories:

- less than 50%,
- between 50% and 70%,
- between 70% and 100%, and
- over 100%.

Figure 34.1: The real purchasing power of VPA for various AIR values after 20 years, equity index S&P500, all years

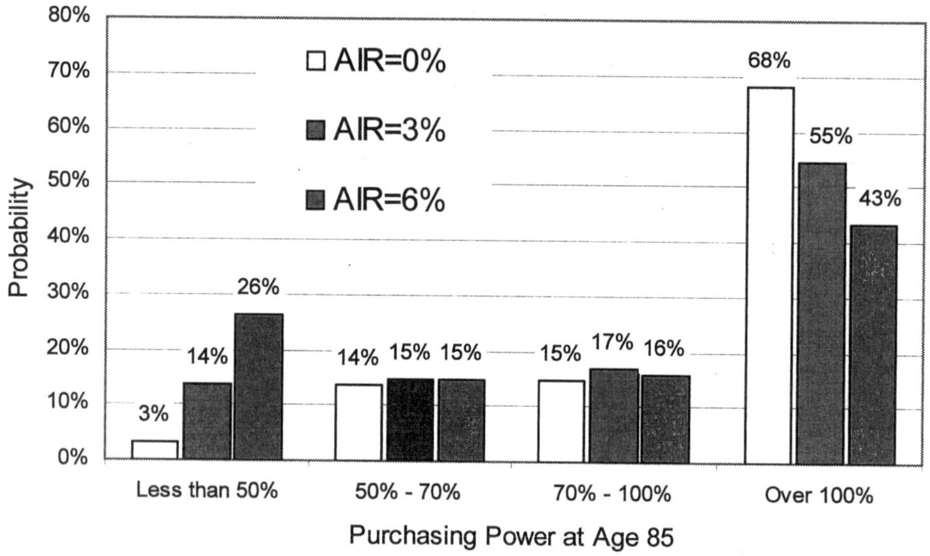

For example, with 0% AIR, the probability of the purchasing power decreasing to less than 50%, is only 3%. For 6% AIR, the probability is 26%.

In all cases, selecting 0% AIR gave the highest protection against inflation especially at the lucky or unlucky extremes. However, it comes at the greatest cost. For example, a 65–year old male needs a monthly income of $1,000 during the first year with a 15–year period–certain guarantee. He can pay a premium[68] of $313,945 for a 0% AIR or he can pay $168,588 for a 6% AIR. Which one should he buy?

This decision depends on several factors:

- The luck factor is most important. The increase or decrease of your pay largely depends on luck. This is beyond your control.
- Do you live until 85 or until 100? The inflation factor may affect your finances more adversely if you live longer. At the same time, the VPA gives you lifelong income, whereas an investment portfolio would be depleted.
- How much money do you have for the VPA? If you have insufficient savings and need the higher income, you may have no choice but to go for the highest AIR for the highest starting payments. This is probably the only factor that is in your control.

[68] These figures are only approximate. They will vary each day, for each insurance company.

For a $313,945 premium, the VPA with 0% AIR initially pays $1,000/month and protects you against inflation reasonably well. Alternatively, for the same premium, you can buy a VPA with 6% AIR that initially pays $1,862/month, but does not protect you for inflation as effectively. In theory, you could save this excess income in the early years for inflation protection during the later years.

When we plot the VPA payments starting in year 1982 (Figure 34.2), we have the following picture:

Figure 34.2: The crossover year for annuity payments, starting year 1982:

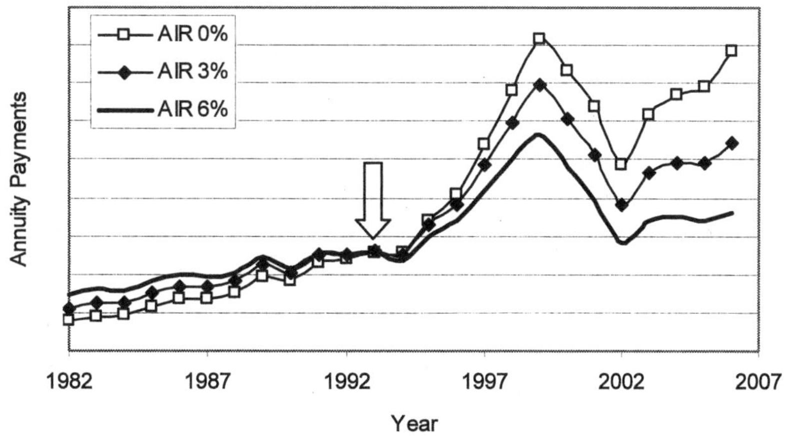

The crossover year is 1993, eleven years after the start of the payments. Historically, this crossover point does not change much for different starting years since 1900. However, this does not give us the whole picture. We need to use the internal rate of return (IRR) for a better evaluation. I calculated IRR based on the median VPA payout for all years since 1900. These are shown in Table 34.2 and Figure 34.3. Keep in mind that individual cases will differ based on various factors such as interest rate, market trend, age, costs of VPA, and others.

Table 34.2: The internal rate of return of VPA payments for various AIR values:

Time Period	AIR 0%	AIR 3%	AIR 6%
	Internal Rate of Return of the Median VPA Payments		
20 years	2.25%	2.80%	3.21%
30 years	5.95%	5.65%	5.36%
40 years	7.63%	6.86%	6.20%

Figure 34.3: The internal rate of return of VPA payments for various AIR values:

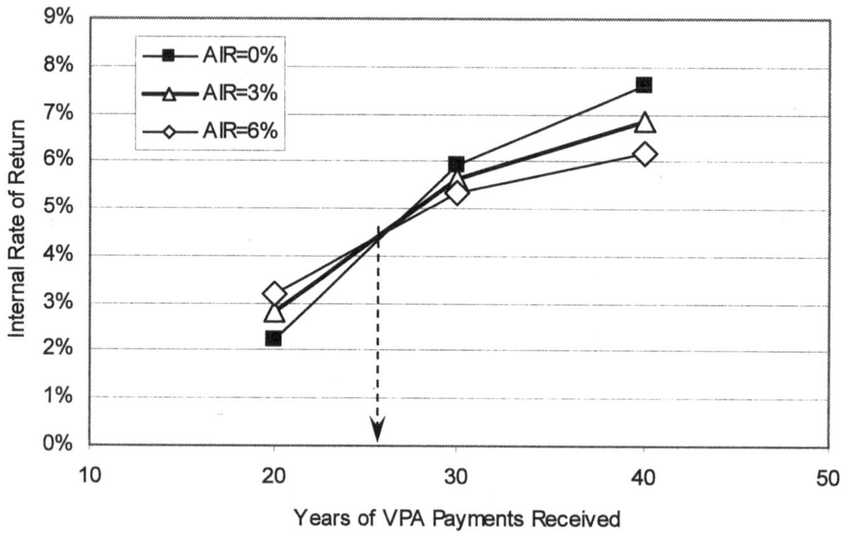

The IRR for various AIR levels cross over in year 26. Before 26 years, highest AIR gave the highest IRR. After 26 years, the lowest AIR gave the highest IRR. Keep in mind; these figures are all for the median portfolio. In real life, this crossover can occur anywhere between 15 years and 30 years, depending on your luck factor.

In the final analysis, I would choose the highest AIR only if all of these conditions are met:

- If reduction and fluctuation of income is not important
- If inflation protection is not important, and
- If you expect to live less than 25 years (either singly or jointly with your spouse) after the VPA payments start

If you don't want to agonize too long over this decision, then simply choose 3% AIR. It is a good compromise. Its premium for the same first–year income is closest to a life annuity that is fully indexed to CPI. Of course, while the life annuity with full CPI indexation will fully protect you against inflation, the VPA payments might go down or up substantially year–over–year.

Table 34.3 shows the typical cost[69] for various variable pay annuities for a starting income stream of $10,000 annually[70]. All figures are based on a 15–year period–certain guarantee. For all the joint and survivor annuities, after the death of the first spouse, the surviving spouse receives 75% of the full amount for life.

Table 34.3: Cost of different VPAs

Life Annuity Type	Male, 65	Female, 65	Male, 70	Female, 70
Conventional Life Annuity:				
Single life, CPI indexed	$187,812	$201,716	$167,163	$177,029
Variable Pay Annuity: AIR: 0%				
Single Life	$261,621	$288,467	$222,131	$240,030
Joint & Survivor, spouse 60	$331,733	$324,607	$312,988	$299,346
Joint & Survivor, spouse 65	$295,117	$295,117	$273,043	$265,898
Joint & Survivor, spouse 70	$265,898	$273,043	$240,241	$240,241
Variable Pay Annuity: AIR=3%				
Single Life	$186,073	$199,458	$166,291	$175,829
Joint & Survivor, spouse 60	$217,379	$214,921	$207,735	$202,583
Joint & Survivor, spouse 65	$201,512	$201,512	$190,269	$187,262
Joint & Survivor, spouse 70	$187,262	$190,269	$174,216	$174,216
Variable Pay Annuity: AIR=6%				
Single Life	$140,490	$147,518	$130,083	$135,374
Joint & Survivor, spouse 60	$155,209	$154,398	$149,888	$147,958
Joint & Survivor, spouse 65	$147,789	$147,789	$141,663	$140,380
Joint & Survivor, spouse 70	$140,380	$141,663	$133,308	$133,308

69 Rates are as of March 2009. No taxes included. The cost of buying an annuity changes daily.
70 Paid monthly, $833.33 per month during the first year.

Optimum Asset Allocation:

Our next step is to calculate the optimum asset mix. Keep in mind that this is a "virtual" asset allocation for calculating the payment streams; you actually own no assets.

Most variable pay annuities offer a range of indexes to choose from: money market, bond, and various equity indices. At one extreme, you can allocate everything into the equity market index. That will give you the highest chance of getting a pay increase. But, that will also give you the highest chance of a pay cut too. At the other extreme, you can allocate everything to the money market, set the AIR to 0% and you'll get a pay raise year–after–year. Where is the optimum allocation?

I calculated the median VPA payout for different values of asset mix at different AIRs for different time horizons. Figure 34.4 depicts the outcome for 0% AIR. The vertical scale shows the annual VPA payout. This is the median value for all years since 1900. On the horizontal scale, we have the time horizon. This is the number of years since the start of the VPA payments.

Figure 34.4: Optimum asset allocation for 0% AIR, equity index S&P500

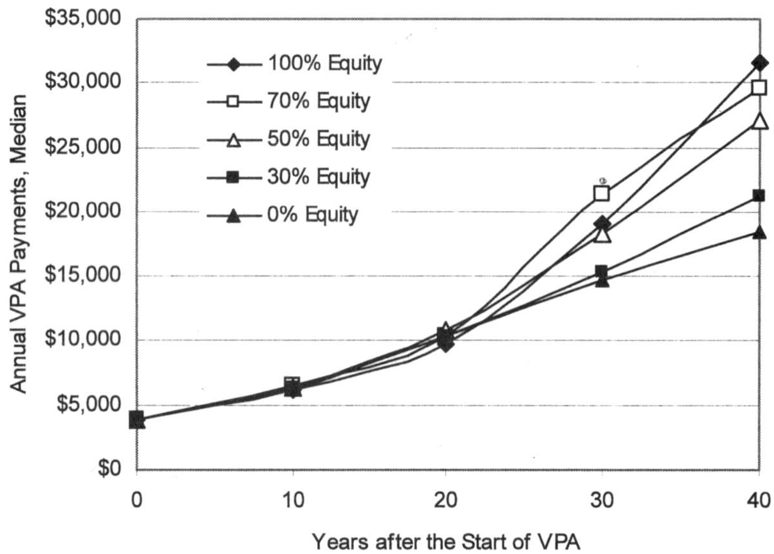

Assuming that most retirees may spend between 20 and 30 years in retirement, the optimum asset mix appears to be 70% equity index and 30% money market. This asset mix gives the highest payout between years 20 and 35, based on the entire market history. Of course, there is a wide fluctuation from the median.

The asset allocation decision is not cast in stone. Most insurance companies allow you to switch between different asset classes or equity indices. Some may limit the number of switches in a year. You can also try to improve the outcome by employing tactical asset allocation or moving average strategies for your VPA portfolio.

I analyzed similar charts for various levels of AIR. The 70% equity seemed to be the optimum. For Canadian readers, the Canadian market index also gave similar results.

The Conversion Privilege:

Most VPA policies allow you to convert to a regular annuity at anytime. You need to carefully analyze the benefits and consequences of this conversion.

Minimizing the Inflation and Income Volatility Risks:

VPA payments can vary wildly each year. If you have additional resources, then you need to hold a separate investment portfolio, a separate "bucket". This bucket provides the additional funds to cover any payment reductions and the inflation effect.

Table 34.4 depicts the approximate size of this separate investment account to provide income protection for a $10,000 annual VPA income. The core annual income of $10,000 is provided by the VPA. Any shortfall is provided by this separate bucket. Table 34.4 shows the dollar amount that must be set aside to maintain the purchasing power over the time horizon.

Table 34.4: Additional assets required as an investment portfolio for income protection

	Time Horizon	
	20 years	30 years
	Additional Assets Required to make up for the shortfall for a $10,000 starting base income :	
Base annuity is a VPA, AIR 0%	$26,000	$26,000
Base annuity is a VPA, AIR 3%	$69,800	$98,800
Base annuity is a VPA, AIR 6%	$97,900	$145,900

Notes for the table: The asset mix of the investment portfolio used as the inflation bucket is 50% S&P500 index and 50% fixed income. Equity: dividend yield is 2%, management costs 2% for a net alpha of 0%. Fixed Income has a net yield of 6–month CD interest rate plus 0.5%.

Example 34.3

Howard, 65, is buying a variable pay life annuity. He needs $10,000 annual income at age 65. Which combination of VPA and investment bucket will cost him the least amount of initial savings? Which one might provide the largest estate value?

Assume Howard wants inflation protection for 30 years.

We observe in Table 34.3 that an annuity that pays $10,000 in the first year with a 0% AIR costs $261,621; with a 3% AIR costs $186,073; with a 6%AIR costs $140,490.

We observe in Table 34.4 that you need an investment bucket of $26,000 with 0% AIR; $98,800 with 3% AIR; $145,900 with 6%AIR when the starting annual payment of the VPA is $10,000.

	VPA with 0% AIR	VPA with 3% AIR	VPA with 6% AIR
Annuity Cost	$261,621	$186,073	$140,490
Inflation Bucket	$26,000	$98,800	$145,900
Total Savings Required	$287,621	$284,873	$286,390

Which strategy initially requires the least amount of savings? They are all within 1% of each other, so it does not matter much which one you choose.

Which strategy leaves the highest estate value? The probability of depletion of the inflation bucket is no more than 10% based on market history. It is highly likely that a large part of the inflation bucket is unused and passed on to the estate. Therefore, the combination of a VPA with 6% AIR with an inflation bucket leaves the largest estate value. By the way, the median portfolio value of the inflation bucket is about $291,000 after 30 years, about twice as much as its starting value.

Conclusion:

Variable Pay Annuities can be part of your retirement income solution. However, the payments will fluctuate wildly. Over a 20–year time period, the payments may be as low as 20% or they may be as high as 600% of the initial pay in real dollars.

The charts in Figure 34.5 depict the percentage of initial income in real dollars over time for various AIR numbers. The heavy line is the median. Beware of what you are buying.

Figure 34.5: Variability of income with VPA

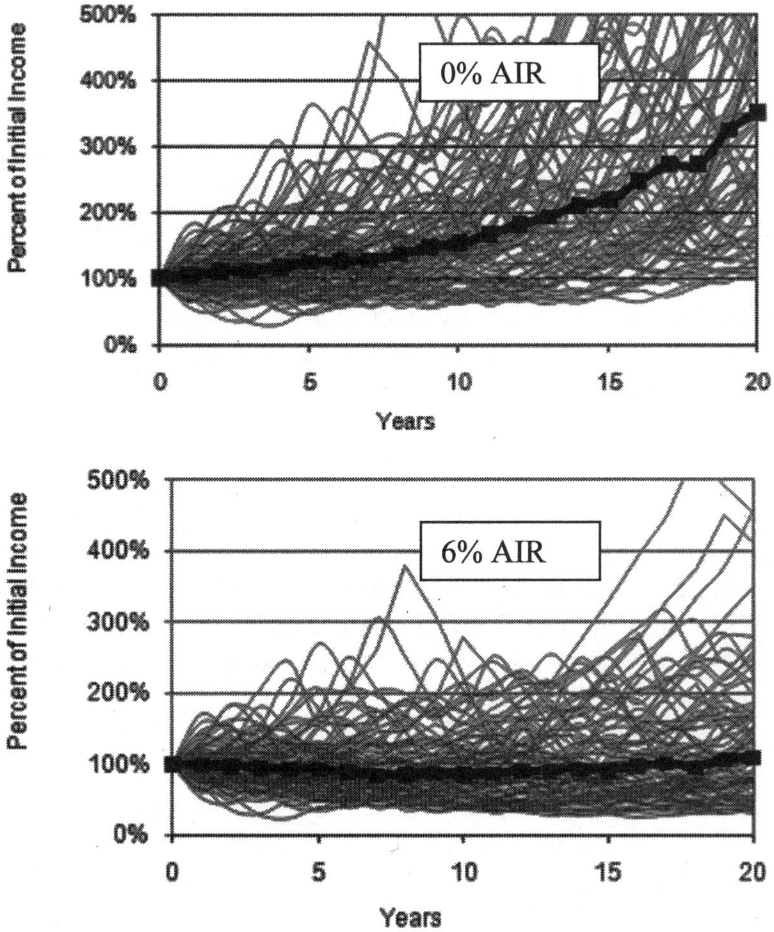

Chapter 35

Variable Annuity with GMWB

Variable annuities have been around for a long time. However, the guaranteed minimum withdrawal benefit as a living benefit has only been available since 2002. It was born as a timely response to the needs of retiring boomers. Unlike a life annuity, the retiree owns the investment assets as segregated funds. If and when the investment assets deplete, the insurer continues payments for life. It removes a large part of the fear because both market and longevity risks are eliminated for the retiree. In recent years, this income class became the first choice for many advisors and retirees.

When you purchase a VA, you are actually buying a segregated fund. They are similar to mutual funds; money is pooled to purchase investments and you can allocate it to various asset classes. But unlike mutual funds, they are considered insurance products. They are segregated from the assets of the insurance company. Their value is guaranteed (usually, 75% to 100% of the premium or reset value) after a certain holding time period (until its maturity) or upon death.

Originally, the earlier GMWB riders covered only a certain term, usually 20 years. Nowadays, most guaranteed withdrawal benefits are for life. In this book, I cover only those with a life guarantee. I use the acronym VA–GMWBL to refer to a variable annuity with guaranteed withdrawal benefits for life.

A VA–GMWBL has a market value, which fluctuates just like a mutual fund. This is called the "Contract Value". In addition, there is another balance to track, which is called the "Guaranteed Withdrawal Base" (GWB). Its value does not fluctuate with market conditions, but it is used to calculate the income payments. The day you buy the VA–GMWBL, both the contract value and the GWB are the same, i.e. your initial premium. Even if the contract value goes down to zero in adverse markets, annual payments continue for the life of the contract, based on the GWB.

There are several important features and benefits of VA–GMWBL:

- Guaranteed pay: Most plans pay, for life, 5% of the GWB each year. Some pay higher; however in this article we will use 5%. For example, if a client buys a VA–GMWBL with $100,000 at age 65, he is guaranteed to receive at least $5,000 each year for the rest of his life, regardless of how his investments perform.
- Step–up reset: If the portfolio does well and the contract value exceeds the GWB, then the GWB is reset higher, equal to the contract value. Most contracts allow for an annual reset. Many insurance companies put a time limit on step–up resets, such as 30 years from the initial contract date, or until age 80.

- Income credit: If you buy a VA–GMWBL prior to needing income, then an income credit is added to the GWB annually, usually 5%. A higher GWB pays a higher guaranteed income when it starts. For example, you are 55 years old and purchase a $100,000 VA–GMWBL. You start your periodic withdrawals at age 65. The GWB is increased by $5,000 each year until age 65. At age 65, the GWB is $150,000, even if the investments stay flat or go down.

  If there is a step–up reset that increases the GWB by more than the income credit amount in that year, then no income credit is added. There is usually a time or an age limit on income credit.

- Other benefits: The same benefits that are available for a regular variable annuity also apply to a VA–GMWBL; such as death benefits, principal protection, and conversion to a life annuity. Keep in mind that these benefits, or riders, differ from plan to plan, and usually come with additional costs. In this book I ignore these other riders and only focus on the guaranteed withdrawal benefit.

What happens if you need less money than the guaranteed 5%? Most contracts do not permit the carrying forward of withdrawals. Some allow up to a certain limit (10% or 15% – read the fine print) in a subsequent year. My suggestion is to take the entire guaranteed amount each year even if you don't need it and invest any surplus in a separate account. If you leave it in, you would be paying fees for guarantees for no additional benefit.

Can you take out all of your money at any time? Yes, you can cash out all of it (contract balance) at any time, subject to redemption fees, taxes and other charges.

The Accumulation Stage:

If you don't need the withdrawals immediately, then a VA may be a good way of creating a "guaranteed pension" during retirement. An income credit is added when:

- There are no withdrawals during the year and,
- If there is no step–up reset exceeding 5%

Thus, the insurance company guarantees a minimum increase of 5% annually as long as you are not withdrawing from the account. Many are confused about this; they think they can cash it out at will. You can't do that. The income credit is added to the GWB and **not** to the contract balance. In other words, the income credit cannot be cashed out, but it increases the guaranteed annual income for the remainder of the guarantee term.

The income credit feature allows one to be more aggressive. An aggressive portfolio will provide two benefits for the retiree: if markets do well, you'll end up with more step–up resets and higher future income. On the other hand, if markets don't do well, you still have the 5% income credit. However, a more aggressive portfolio generally runs out of money sooner, and it increases the liability of the insurance company. Therefore, many insurance companies limit how aggressively you can invest.

Here is an important question: you have 10 years before retirement and you have two choices: (a) Invest in a portfolio of mutual funds, or (b) Buy a VA–GMWBL contract and benefit from the income credit. Which would pay you more money at the end of 10 years? Let's try to answer this by using the following example:

Example 35.1

(A) Steve is 55. His investment portfolio is worth $100,000. His asset mix is 60% equities (S&P500) and 40% fixed income. His equities pay a dividend, but this dividend goes entirely to pay the portfolio costs, which is 2%. His fixed income portfolio return is the same as the historical 6-month CD rate plus 0.5%.

(B) Jane is also 55. She has $100,000. Unlike Steve, she buys a VA-GMWBL contract. Her asset mix is 80% equities and 20% fixed income. Her income credit increases her guaranteed withdrawal base by 5% each year, more if markets do well. At age 65, she takes out 5% of her guaranteed withdrawal base. She pays 2% for portfolio costs (same as Steve), but she pays an additional 1% of the GWB for the cost of the guarantees (GMWBL rider).

To keep it simple, we assume that neither Steve nor Jane add or withdraw any money from their portfolios until age 65. At age 65, both take out 5% of their portfolio value as income.

Question: Who has a greater income, starting at age 65?

Answer: For each retirement year since 1900, I calculated the value of the investment portfolio and the value of the guaranteed withdrawal base of the VA-GMWBL after 10 years.

Here are some statistics:

- At age 65, in 56% of the time, Jane's income was higher than Steve's. When Jane's income was higher than Steve's, it was on average 34% higher.
- At age 65, in 44% of the time, Jane's income was lower than Steve's. When Jane's income was lower than Steve's, it was on average 12% lower.

The following chart depicts the benefit of income credit: The bars indicate the increase or decrease of annual income when compared with the investment portfolio. On average, Jane would have done better than Steve. The income credit feature, combined with the annual step-up reset benefit, created a higher lifelong income. However, the outcome varied wildly in individual years.

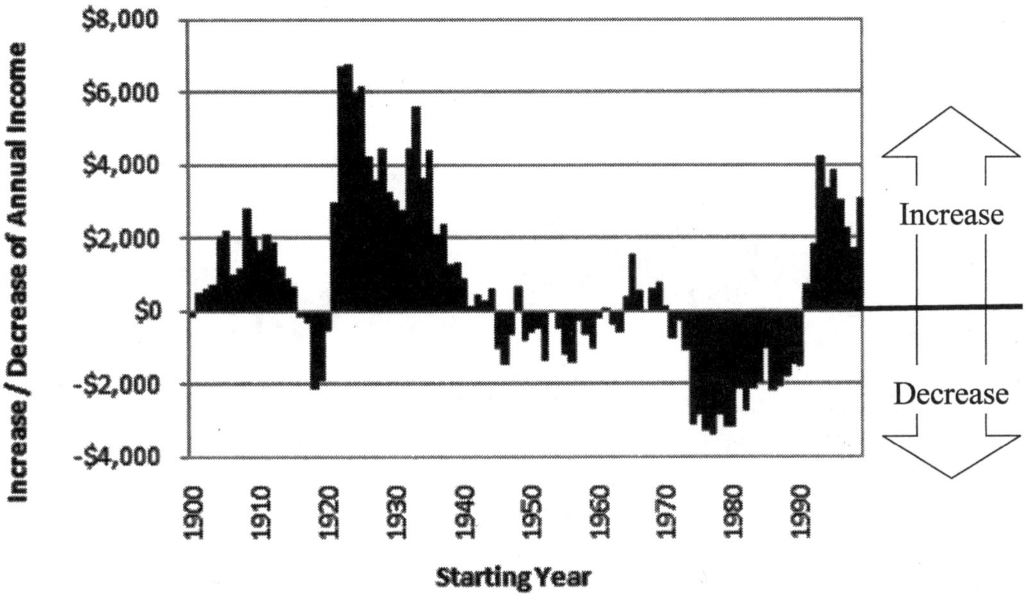

What if you have only a 5–year accumulation period? Do you: (a) Invest in a portfolio of mutual funds, or (b) Buy a VA–GMWBL contract and benefit from the income credit? Which would pay you more money at the end of 5 years? Let's look at Example 35.2:

Example 35.2

Same as Example 35.1, but both Jane and Steve are 60 years old and they have only 5 years before they start withdrawals.

The following chart depicts the benefit of income credit for the starting annual income:

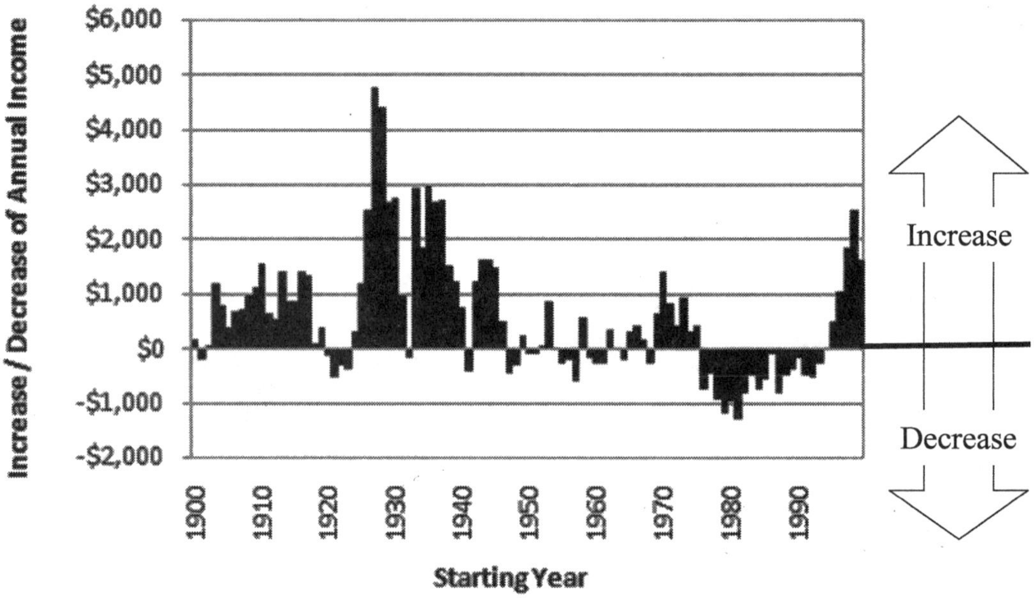

Here are some statistics:

- At age 65, in 61% of the time, Jane's income was higher than Steve's. When Jane's income was higher than Steve's, it was on average 23% higher.
- At age 65, in 39% of the time, Jane's income was lower than Steve's. When Jane's income was lower than Steve's, it was on average 6% lower.

On average, Jane would have done better than Steve. Most of the time, the income credit feature, combined with the annual step-up reset benefit, created a higher lifelong income.

Considering the peace of mind Jane will have when markets fluctuate, her decision to buy a VA-GMWBL was a better one than Steve's.

Doubling of the Guaranteed Withdrawal Base after 10 Years:

Some insurance companies provide an additional income credit: if the accumulation time period reaches ten years, the guaranteed withdrawal base is increased to twice the initial investment. This can be a significant benefit in many cases.

Example 35.3

Use example 35.1, but Jane's guaranteed withdrawal base doubles after ten years of no withdrawals. The following chart depicts the benefit of income credit:

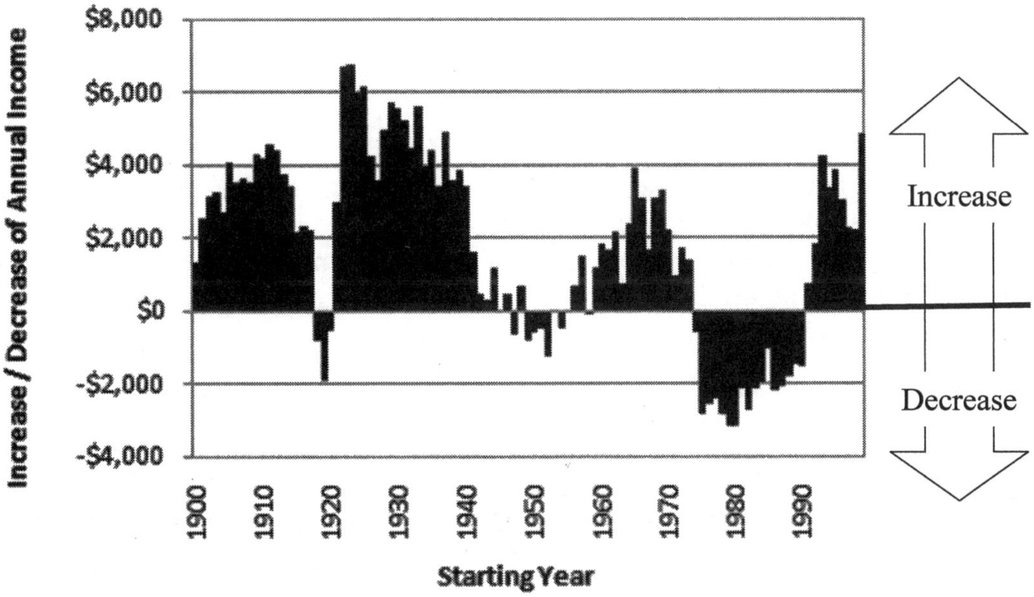

Here are some statistics:

- At age 65, in 70% of the time, Jane's income was higher than Steve's. When Jane's income was higher than Steve's, it was on average 47% higher.
- At age 65, in 30% of the time, Jane's income was lower than Steve's. When Jane's income was lower than Steve's, it was on average 11% lower.

This feature creates a significant improvement to Jane's income stream in most cases.

The Distribution Stage:

In the distribution stage, the retiree is paid a fixed percentage of the GWB. The value of the portfolio is reduced by the amount of withdrawals. Eventually, when and if the portfolio is depleted, the withdrawal guarantees kick in and payments continue for life. This is a seamless event; the retiree continues receiving his payments without missing a beat.

If the markets do well and the portfolio value goes up, then this may trigger step–up reset of the GWB. From that point on, the withdrawals are based on the percentage of the higher GWB.

There are two types of step–up resets:

- Lifetime High
- Annual High

Lifetime High Step–up Reset:

All VA–GMWBL plans except one[71], offer the lifetime high method. If markets do well and the contract value –net of all withdrawals– exceeds the value of the guaranteed withdrawal base, then the GWB is set equal to the higher market value. From that point on, the guaranteed withdrawals are proportionately higher for life. Generally, resets are activated at each contract anniversary.

Let's work through an example to see the difference between these two step–up reset methods.

Example 35.4

Scott, 65, is just retiring. He buys a VA-GMWBL for $100,000 that guarantees 5% withdrawal, or $5,000, for life. His contract allows him annual resets until age 95. The asset mix is 80% S&P500 index and 20% fixed income. Assume total costs of this contract - including management costs, portfolio costs, guarantee riders, other fees- is 3% of the contract value.

Let's assume Scott retired at the beginning of 1942. The step-up resets of his VA-GMWBL are based on the lifetime-high method.

The following chart shows the GWB if Scott were to retire at the beginning of 1942.

[71] At the time of writing this chapter (March 2009), only Allianz Life offered an annual high–water mark type of step–up reset.

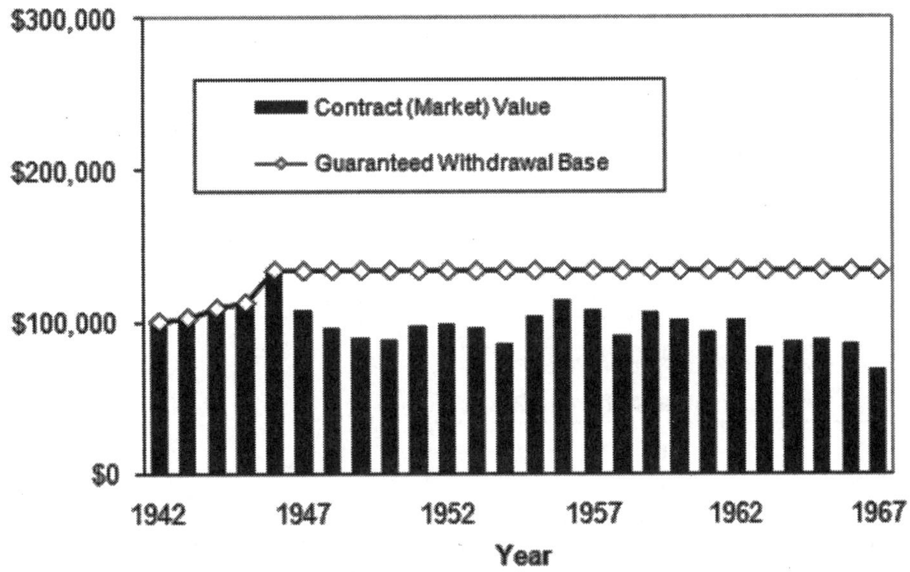

The portfolio made new highs from 1943 through 1946, reaching $134,606. After age 69, Scott's income was stepped-up to $6,730, which is 5% of $134,606. This sounds great, except that after 1946, no step-up resets happened.

At age 90, Scott received the same $6,730 as he did at age 70. Based on market history, he would have needed $10,611 at age 90 just to maintain his original purchasing power.

Let's move Scott's retirement year four years ahead and see what happens. Assume he is retiring in 1946 instead of 1942. How do step–up resets work then?

Example 35.5

Same as Example 35.4, but Scott is retiring at the beginning of 1946, not in 1942.

Here is the GWB chart.

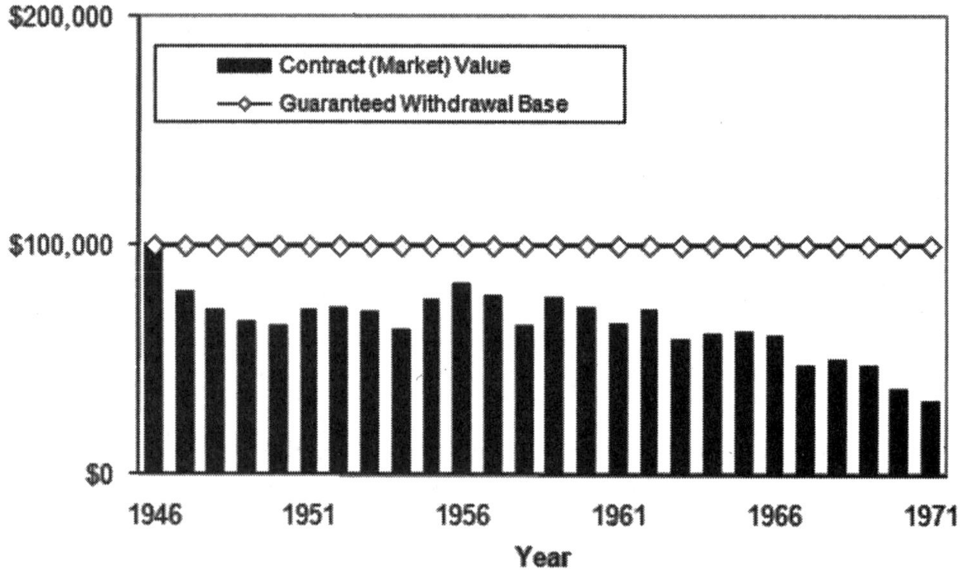

There were no resets at all. The payout remained at a constant $5,000 throughout Scott's life.

Based on market history, he would have needed $10,933 at age 90 just to maintain his original purchasing power. There was no inflation protection at all.

Finally, let's look at a more recent history and see what happens if Scott were to retire in 1982, the beginning of a long secular bullish trend in Example 35.6.

Example 35.6

Same as Example 35.4, but Scott is retiring at the beginning of 1982, not in 1942.

Here is the GWB chart.

There were 11 step-up resets. The last one occurred at age 83 and the GWB reached $257,793. From that point on, the annual payout was $12,890.

Based on market history, Scott would have needed $10,596 at age 90 just to maintain his original purchasing power. The VA-GMWBL more than covered his purchasing power.

Annual High Step–up Reset:

With the annual high method, the market value of the portfolio does not need to exceed the guaranteed withdrawal base to trigger a step–up reset. A reset is triggered if the market value is higher than its value at the last anniversary. The guaranteed withdrawals increase by the same percentage as the increase of the portfolio value (after all withdrawals, portfolio management costs and rider fees).

With this method, even if the portfolio is in the dumps, as long as its value is higher than the preceding year's value, you get a pay raise. The portfolio volatility becomes your true friend; the higher the volatility, the more chances for a higher lifelong income.

Let's look at the last three examples using the annual high–water mark method.

Example 35.7

Same as Example 35.4, but instead of lifetime high, the step-up resets are based on the annual high method.

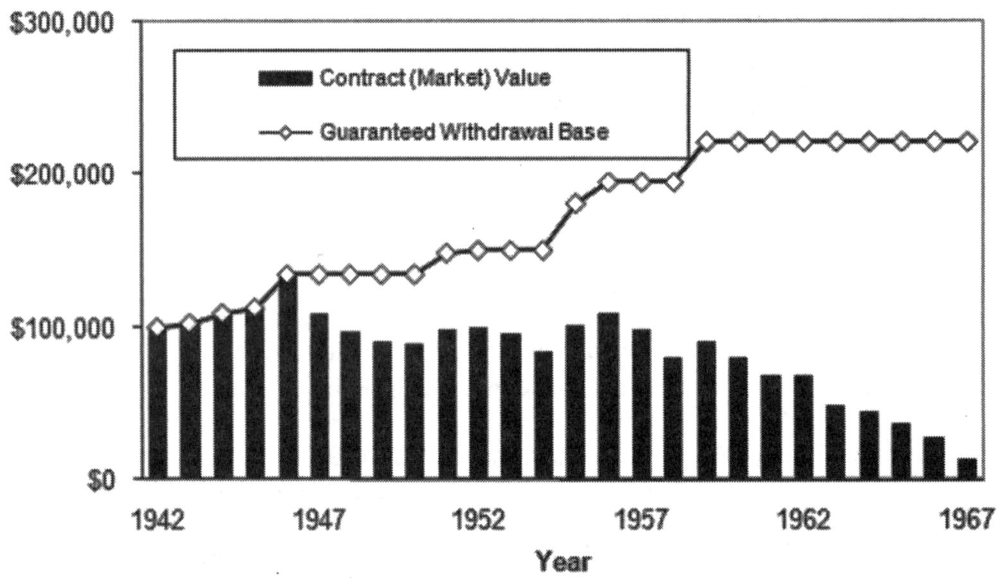

Each time the market value is higher over the previous year; there is a step-up reset for the same percentage growth. The final reset occurred at age 82, in the year 1959, and the guaranteed withdrawal base was set to $220,933. Therefore, his income after age 82 would be $11,047, which in this case handily beats the inflation. At age 90, it provided about 4% higher real purchasing power than the starting amount at age 65.

Example 35.8
Same as Example 35.5, but instead of lifetime high, the step-up resets are based on the annual high method.

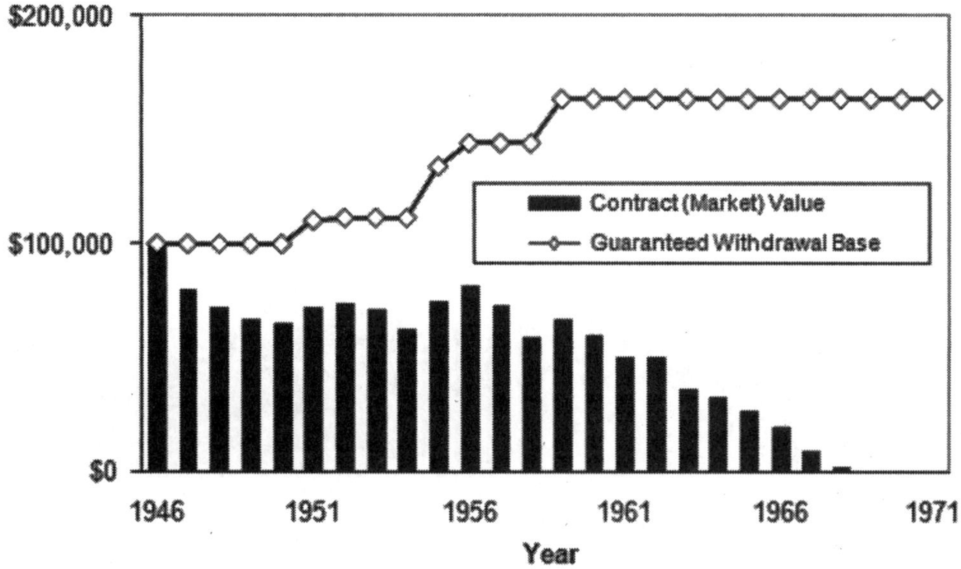

The annual-high reset method triggered five step-ups. These resets happened while the market value of the contract *never* exceeded the original $100,000 invested.

The final reset occurred at age 78, when his guaranteed payout climbed to $8,207 and remained constant after that. Seventeen years after his retirement, at age 82, Scott's payments still maintained the original purchasing power that he had at age 65.

Example 35.9
Same as Example 35.6, but instead of lifetime high, the step-up resets are based on the annual high method.

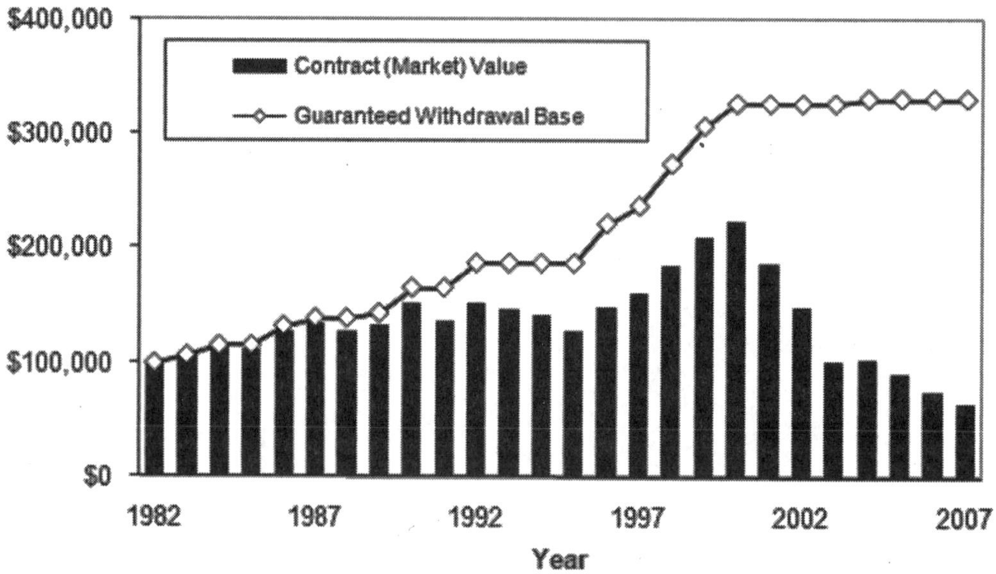

The annual-high step-up method created a substantially higher payment stream throughout the life of the retiree. If Scott were to save part of the payments that are over and above the inflation in a side account paying 3% interest, then these savings would grow to $106,683. Add this to the contract value and Scott would end up with a pretax estate value of $169,641. In the final analysis, Scott ends up with more than he originally planned for, both in higher income and higher estate value.

I calculated the same for all years of retirement starting in 1900 with a starting GWB of $100,000. Table 35.1 summarizes some statistics. Keep in mind that these figures will be different for each individual case.

Table 35.1: Comparison of lifetime and annual high step–up reset methods

	Lifetime–High Reset Method	Annual–High Reset Method
Probability of having one or more step–up resets	70%	100%
Probability of maintaining at least 85% of the original purchasing power at age 90	17%	41%
Average pay at age 90	$6,372	$8,217
Bottom quartile pay at age 90	$5,000	$6,410
Top quartile pay at age 90	$6,686	$9,473

Age Brackets:

Most plans pay a fixed percentage of the GWB for life, commonly 5% of the GWB. Some newer plans have age brackets where the age might determine the pay scale.

There are three types of age brackets:

- Static age brackets: The payments depend on the starting age of withdrawals and they remain the same for life. Example:

Age	Withdrawal %
59 – 64	4.5%
65 – 69	5.0%
70 – 74	5.5%
75 – 79	6.0%
80 – 84	6.5%
85 – 89	7.0%
90 – 94	7.5%
95+	8.0%

For example, based on the table above, if the retire starts his withdrawals at age 76, then he receives 6% of the GWB for the rest of his life.

- Dynamic age brackets: The payments depend on the actual age of the retiree. As he gets older, the payments *may* increase, depending on the market value of the portfolio. Example:

Age	Withdrawal %
50 – 59	4%
60 – 69	5%
70 – 79	6%
80 – 90	7%

  With dynamic age brackets, once the withdrawals start, the subsequent withdrawal percentage increases are based on the market value of the investments.

  For example, a retiree starts his withdrawals at age 68. His GWB is $100,000, so he receives $5,000 a year income. When he turns 70, his age bracket becomes 6%. His guaranteed withdrawals are now the higher of $5,000 and 6% of the market value of his portfolio during this new age bracket. If the market value of his portfolio is $112,000 at that time, then he will receive at least $6,720 each year for the rest of his life (6% of $112,000). If the market value of his portfolio is less than $100,000 at age 70, then he continues to receive $5,000 each year. Should the contract value go above the previous high ($112,000) at a later age, say at age 74, this will trigger a new pay increase.

- Absolute age brackets: The payments depend on the actual age of the retiree. As he gets older, the guaranteed withdrawals *will* increase. Example:

Age	Withdrawal %
69 and lower	5%
70 – 84	6%
85+	7%

  With absolute age brackets, the withdrawals are a percentage of the guaranteed withdrawal base. Since GWB can never go down as long as the guaranteed withdrawal rates are not exceeded, the pay increases are also guaranteed.

I calculated the effect of age brackets for retirement starting in all years since 1900 using the lifetime high step–up reset method. Table 35.2 summarizes some statistics. Keep in mind that these figures will be different for each individual case.

Table 35.2: Comparison of various age brackets

	Age Bracket based on		
	Static	Dynamic	Absolute
Probability of maintaining at least 85% of the original purchasing power at age 90	17%	22%	46%
Average pay at age 90	$6,344	$6,735	$8,484
Bottom quartile pay at age 90	$5,000	$5,000	$7,000
Top quartile pay at age 90	$6,696	$7,464	$9,374

Notes for Table 35.2:

1. Portfolio costs: 2.5% of the portfolio value at the end of the calendar year, rider costs: 1% of GWB, asset mix: 80% S&P500, 20% fixed income, all withdrawals start at age 65, initial purchase $100,000, lifetime high step–up reset
2. Guaranteed withdrawal rates:
   Static age bracket, starting at age 65: 5% of GWB
   Dynamic age brackets: 60–69: 5%, 70–79: 6%, and 80+ : 7% of portfolio value, if higher than present pay
   Absolute age brackets: 60–69: 5%, 70–84: 6%, and 85+ : 7% of GWB

The GMWBL Rider Costs:

The benefit of the VA–GMWBL does not come for free. You have to pay for it. In the insurance business, a benefit that you can attach to a plan is called a "rider". In this case, the GMWBL rider is attached to a VA.

Most insurance companies calculate these costs as a percentage of the GWB. Some base it on the market value. Over the long term, the portfolio value always declines more than the GWB. As a result, the rider costs that are based on the portfolio value cost about 30% to 35% less than those based on the GWB in the long term.

Table 35.3 summarizes some statistics for various rider costs for retirement starting at age 65 for all years since 1900.

Table 35.3: Costs for the GMWBL rider

	Rider cost percentage		
	0.8%	1.0%	1.5%
	Average total rider cost, first 10 years:		
If the rider cost based on the GWB	$8,862	$11,041	$16,391
If the rider cost based on the portfolio value	$7,055	$8,733	$12,732
	Average total rider cost, first 20 years:		
If the rider cost based on the GWB	$16,009	$19,597	$27,690
If the rider cost based on the portfolio value	$10,940	$13,369	$18,944
	Average total rider cost, first 30 years:		
If the rider cost based on the GWB	$19,385	$23,328	$31,823
If the rider cost based on the portfolio value	$12,846	$15,512	$21,386

Notes for Table 35.3:

1. Portfolio costs: 2.5% of the portfolio value at the end of the calendar year, asset mix: 80% S&P500, 20% fixed income, all withdrawals start at age 65, initial purchase $100,000, lifetime high step–up reset
2. Guaranteed withdrawal rate: 5% of GWB

The Portfolio Costs:

Over the long term, portfolio costs make a big difference on the occurrence and the size of step up resets. This directly affects the dollar amount of the guaranteed withdrawals. On average, a 1% higher portfolio management cost can create a 5% lower annual income at age 90.

Table 35.4 summarizes some statistics for various portfolio management costs for retirement starting at age 65 for all years since 1900.

Table 35.4: The effect of portfolio management costs

	Portfolio management cost, percentage of the portfolio value		
	1%	2%	3%
Probability of maintaining at least 85% of the original purchasing power at age 90	23%	20%	16%
Average pay at age 90	$6,959	$6,521	$6,185
Bottom quartile pay at age 90	$5,007	$5,000	$5,000
Top quartile pay at age 90	$7,419	$6,965	$6,572

Notes for Table 35.4:

1. GMWBL rider cost: 1.0% of the GWB, asset mix: 80% S&P500, 20% fixed income, all withdrawals start at age 65, initial purchase $100,000, lifetime high step–up reset
2. Guaranteed withdrawal rate: 5% of GWB
3. Average lifetime total rider cost is between ages 65 and 95.

The Benefit and Cost Analysis:

What makes a VA–GMWBL different from a fixed life annuity is this: While a fixed life annuity gives you only lifelong income protection, a VA gives you lifelong income protection *and* it gives back to you any residual assets that remain in the portfolio.

In cases where money is left in the portfolio at the time of death, it may appear that the income guarantees of a GMWBL did not provide any financial benefit. The portfolio provided all the income and the guarantees were never triggered[72]. You might think, "Why did I pay for these guarantees when I never had to use them?"

When you buy a life annuity, you pray that you live until 120 years old so that you get your money's worth. When you buy a VA–GMWBL, the money is yours anyway. Whether you die the next day or live until 120, you'll get either your own assets back, or you'll get income from the insurance companies. The only time you don't benefit from a VA–GMWBL is if you die in the same month as your portfolio runs out of money.

The life annuity removes the fear (of income disruption) during retirement. At the same time, it removes any hope (of portfolio growth), because the premium you paid no longer belongs to you. On the other hand, the VA–GMWBL removes the fear, but it does not remove the hope.

When evaluating the benefits of the VA–GMWBL, the guaranteed income as well as the remaining portfolio assets must both be considered in the analysis. We define the total benefit as the income that is collected from the guarantee benefits *or* any residual assets remaining in the portfolio.

The following charts depict the benefits and the costs of the VA–GMWBL for each year of retirement since 1900. The chart in Figure 35.1 shows a typical benefit and cost analysis chart with the following input: initial purchase amount is $100,000, GMWBL rider cost is 1.0% of the GWB, portfolio costs are 2.5% of the market value, asset mix is 80% S&P500 and 20% fixed income, lifetime high step–up reset, guaranteed withdrawal rate is 5% of GWB, withdrawals start at age 65 and they end at age 95. The cost is the total rider fees paid over the life of the plan. The income benefit is the total payments received after the portfolio depletes. The remaining assets (darker bars) indicate the years when withdrawals were made from the portfolio only until death, guarantees never were used, and the portfolio had money left for the estate.

[72] If you want to trigger guarantees while there is still money in the portfolio, then you need to look at another type of guarantee, GMIB.

Figure 35.1: Benefit and cost of GMWBL, age of death 95

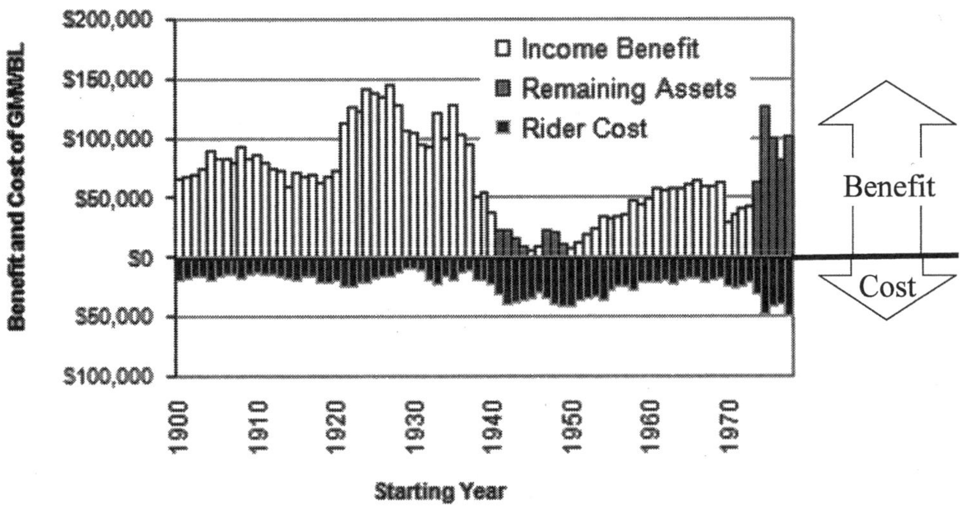

The total average periodic lifetime withdrawals from the portfolio (including the principal and growth, excluding the guaranteed income benefits) were $114,314. The average cost of the guarantees was $23,328. On the other hand, the average income benefit when there was no money left in the portfolio was $70,939. The average residual portfolio value –when no income benefit was received– was $49,298.

The following diagram (Figure 35.2) summarizes the *average* money flow for all years since 1900:

Figure 35.2: Average benefit and cost of a typical VA–GMWBL by age 95

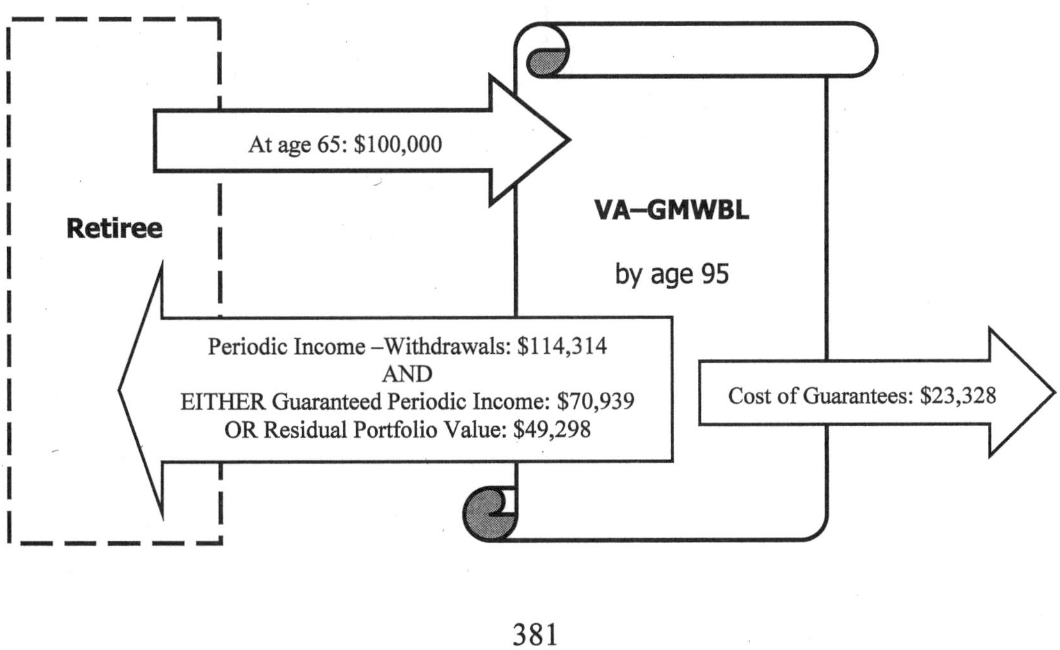

Since the average benefit was much greater than the average cost of the rider, does this mean the insurance company is losing money?

The insurance company hopes to benefit from the law of averages. The average age of death of a 65–year old male is about age 85. Those who are paying the GMWBL rider fees, finance the guaranteed income stream for those who exceed the average life expectancy *and* have no money left in their portfolio. Figures 35.3 and 35.4 depict the charts for age of death 85.

Figure 35.3: Benefit and cost of GMWBL, age of death 85

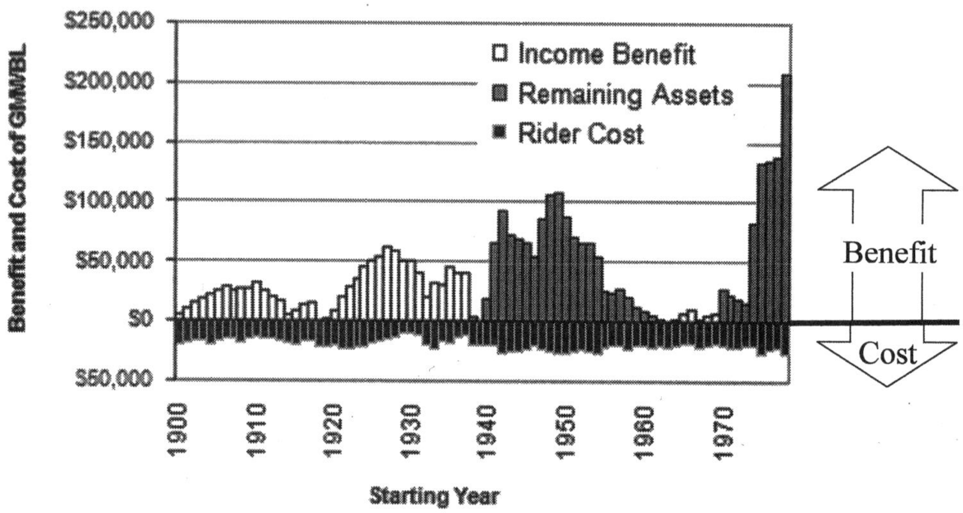

Figure 35.4: Average benefit and cost of a typical VA–GMWBL by age 85

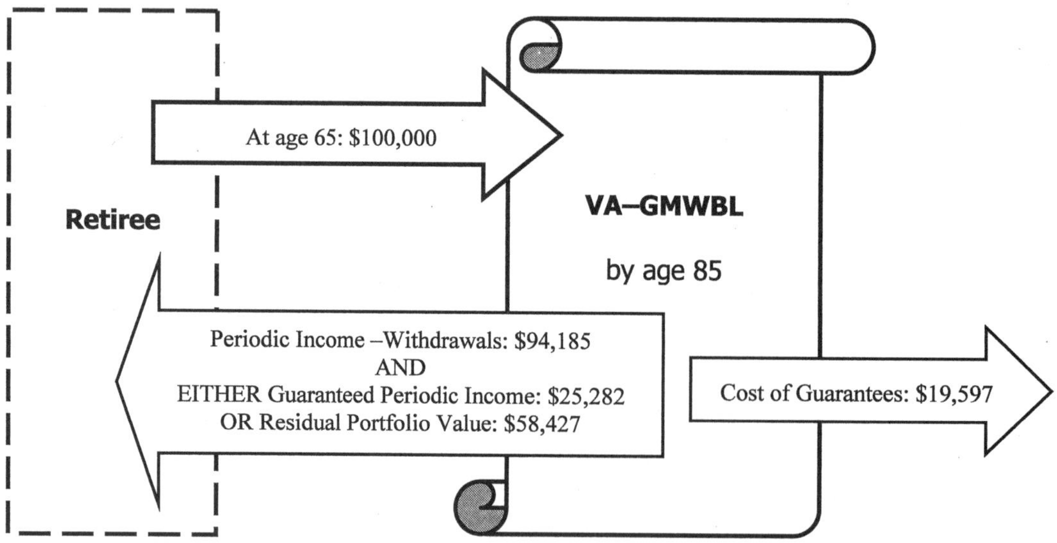

We observe in Figure 35.4, that the average guaranteed withdrawals that the insurance company has to pay –when assets deplete– are $25,282. The average GMWB rider paid is $19,597. There is still some shortfall for the average age of death of 85.

Insurance companies count on covering this shortfall by collecting rider fees from the surviving portfolios. This is one area of risk that might have been underestimated by actuaries. Since their Monte Carlo models fail to simulate the sequence of returns, they might not be estimating their costs accurately. When markets go into a secular bear or a secular sideways[73] trend, *all* VA portfolios that they manage suffer. You don't have the benefit of randomness here; this is unlike calculating the risks for life or disability insurance. Market events are not random, they are all correlated and they can create a simultaneous, larger–than–expected, "once–a–century" event occurring in *every* secular sideways trend.

You don't need to be a math wizard to expect that all cohorts[74] will have less money or no money in their VA portfolio in a bad market. The insurer then has to start paying larger and larger amounts from its pocket to that entire cohort group. To add to injury, because many VA portfolios eventually run out of money, there is a reduced supply of income from rider fees. More VA–GMWBs must be sold to create an additional source of income, which in turn can create an even larger future liability!

We saw in earlier chapters that there is no such a thing as an "average" portfolio life. If you are lucky then your "average" portfolio life can be 30 years or more. If you are not lucky, then the "average" portfolio life is around 16 years or so. There is not much in between. Add to this the effect of higher costs, and you can then expect a shorter "average" portfolio life of your VA–GMWBL.

For the most part, portfolio life is more important to the insurance company than the retiree. The retiree has a lifelong income regardless of his portfolio's value. However, once the portfolio runs out of money, the insurance company is on the hook from that point on..

In Figure 35.3, we saw that in *all* years between 1900 and 1938, portfolios ran out of money and the GMWBL guarantees kicked in within the first 20 years of withdrawals. That is a very long time for any insurer to withstand losses, year after year. Once actuaries understand the effects of the time value of fluctuations for VA–GMWBL portfolios, they will realize that the current rider fees are unsustainable. A more sustainable rider fee is somewhere between 2% to 3.5% of the GWB (depending on lapse rates, step–up reset methods and other factors) for sustainable guarantees by the insurer.

---

[73] Remember that, in a distribution portfolio, a secular sideways market behaves as a bear market.

[74] Cohorts: those who bought the VA–GMWBL plan during the same market cycle

With current levels of rider fees[75], a VA–GMWBL is beneficial to the retiree in *all* market trends. However, its benefit for the retiree is greater when purchased prior to certain market trends. The following list shows the ranking of the benefit of purchasing a VA–GMWBL prior to specific secular market trends:

The VA–GMWBL purchased just prior to a:	**For the retiree:**	**For the insurer:**
1. secular bullish market followed by a secular bear market	Most advantageous	Most risky
2. secular bear market		
3. secular bullish market followed by a secular sideways market		
4. secular sideways market	Least advantageous	Least risky
5. secular bullish market		

Inflation Risk:

Firstly, ignore all the sales mantra such as "step–up resets might provide inflation protection". This is just a myth. Variable annuities with guarantees (GMWBL or GMIB) convert the longevity and markets risks into the inflation risk. They do not remove the inflation risk.

Let's look at an example: the initial purchase amount is \$100,000, GMWBL rider cost is 1% of the GWB, portfolio costs are 3% of the market value, asset mix is 80% S&P500 and 20% fixed income, lifetime high step–up reset, guaranteed withdrawal rate is 5% of GWB, withdrawals start at age 65 and they end at age 95.

Chart 35.5 depicts the real purchasing power of GMWBL payments for all retirement years since 1900. It is interesting to note that once the deflationary period that followed the market crash of 1929 ended, the step–up resets were unable to increase the income sufficiently to keep up with inflation.

[75] As of December 2008

Figure 35.5: Real purchasing power at age 95 as percentage of starting amount at age 65

Table 35.5 depicts the probability of maintaining purchasing power. I considered three different types of VA–GMWBLs. In all cases, the initial purchase amount is $100,000, withdrawals start at age 65 and end at age 95, portfolio management costs are 3% of the market value, asset mix is 80% S&P500 and 20% fixed income:

A. The same as the VA–GMWBL used for Figure 35.5 above. GMWBL rider cost is 1% of the GWB, lifetime high step–up reset and the guaranteed withdrawal rate is 5% of GWB.

B. VA–GMWBL[76] with annual high step–up reset, guaranteed withdrawal rate is of the dynamic type and it is 5% of GWB between ages 65 and 69, 6% between ages 70 and 79, 7% for ages 80 and over. The GMWBL rider cost is 1.0% of the portfolio's market value.

C. VA–GMWBL[77] with lifetime high step–up reset, guaranteed withdrawal rate is 5% of GWB between ages 60 and 69, 6% between 70 and 84, 7% for ages 85 and over. The GMWBL rider cost is 1.0% of the GWB.

[76] B: This is similar to "Lifetime Plus II" by Allianz Life.
[77] C: This is similar to "Automatic Income Builder" by Pacific Life.

Table 35.5: Probability of maintaining purchasing power

	Type of VA–GMWBL		
	A	B	C
	Probability of Occurrence:		
Purchasing power at age 95 is 100% or higher than what it was at age 65	10%	16%	22%
Purchasing power at age 95 is between 85% and 100% of what it was at age 65	1%	10%	15%
Purchasing power at age 95 is between 50% and 85% of what it was at age 65	46%	52%	39%
Purchasing power at age 95 is less than 50% of what it was at age 65	43%	22%	24%

Table 35.5 demonstrates that the inflation risk is not handled well with VA–GMWBL, but "B" and "C" types provided better inflation protection than the "A" type.

Minimizing the Inflation Risk:

We now know that VA–GMWBL has a shortcoming when it comes to eliminating the inflation risk. Is there a practical way of getting around it? The answer is "yes".

Some think that you can just buy more of the same VA–GMWBL, more than you need, take the excess guaranteed income and save it for a future inflation shortfall. While this might work if you have abundant assets, it is not an efficient use of your money. If a particular income class does not give you full protection from the inflation risk, buying more of the same thing might just amplify the problem. For the most efficient use of your available assets, you need to hold a different income class; a separate investment portfolio, a separate "bucket". This bucket has only one purpose; it provides the funds to cover any loss of purchasing power from the VA–GMWBL payments.

Table 35.6 depicts the approximate size of this separate investment account required to provide inflation protection for $10,000 annual income starting at age 65 for 20–year and 30–year time horizons. The core income of $10,000 is provided by the VA–GMWBL, subject to increase if there are any resets. Any inflation shortfall is provided by this separate inflation bucket.

The three different portfolios (A, B, and C) are the same as described earlier. All figures are based on actual market history since 1900:

Table 35.6: Combined assets required for lifelong, CPI–indexed income

	Type of VA–GMWBL A	B	C
Assets Required for $10,000 annual, CPI–indexed income for a Retirement Time Horizon: 20 years			
VA–GMWBL required	$200,000	$200,000	$200,000
Inflation "bucket" required	$71,000	$55,000	$55,000
Total assets required	$271,000	$255,000	$255,000
Assets Required for $10,000 annual, CPI–indexed income for a Retirement Time Horizon: 30 years			
VA–GMWBL required	$200,000	$200,000	$200,000
Inflation "bucket" required	$106,000	$86,000	$81,000
Total assets required	$306,000	$286,000	$281,000

Notes for the table: The asset mix of the investment portfolio used as the inflation bucket is 50% S&P500 index and 50% fixed income. Equity: dividend yield is 2%, management costs 2% for a net alpha of 0%. Fixed Income has a net yield of 6–month CD interest rate plus 0.5%.

Asset Allocation in VA–GMWBL:

Before making a proper asset allocation decision in a VA–GMWBL, you need to ask yourself, "What is my objective?"

You need to choose one of these two objectives: (a) Maximize the guaranteed income benefit, or (b) Maximize portfolio assets.

Let's examine how we can achieve each objective.

Asset Allocation for Maximizing the Guaranteed Income Benefits:

In my live presentations, asset allocation in variable annuities is a popular question. The answer is not as straight forward as for your plain vanilla investment portfolios.

By purchasing a VA–GMWBL, you bypass the effects of market and longevity risks. The remaining risk factors are inflation and the financial strength of the insurance company.

Table 35.7 shows the probability of maintaining at least 85% of the purchasing power at age 85 for various asset mixes. The three different portfolios (A, B, and C) are the same as described earlier. All figures are based on actual market history since 1900.

Table 35.7: The effect of asset mix on purchasing power

	Type of VA–GMWBL		
	A	B	C
Equity Percentage in the VA–GMWBL portfolio	Probability of maintaining at least 85% of the purchasing power after 20 years of withdrawals:		
95%	43%	64%	58%
80%	38%	57%	57%
60%	35%	46%	54%
40%	21%	27%	41%
20%	15%	15%	34%

Generally, a higher equity component means larger and more frequent step–up resets. This increases your guaranteed lifelong income. With a VA–GMWBL, the volatility of returns works for the retiree[78]. Therefore, if you want the greatest inflation protection, you need to maximize the equity component of your asset mix.

One impediment in maximizing the equity component might be the current methods of risk assessment. Most compliance departments are still trapped in the mindset of accumulation portfolios. With that approach, they think that the volatility of returns is the most important thing. This may limit the advisor recommending a higher equity component in a VA portfolio for better inflation protection. The standard client risk analysis methods designed for non–guaranteed investment portfolios will not work for the VA–GMWBL portfolio because it is a different income class.

[78] Both the volatility of returns and the sequence of returns do matter greatly to the insurer.

Asset Allocation for Maximizing Portfolio Value:

If inflation protection is not important to you, then you need to consider a conservative asset mix. This might happen if you start receiving excess income from other sources unexpectedly, after having bought the VA–GMWBL.

A low equity component minimizes the occurrence of step–up resets, which in turn reduces withdrawal amounts. This allows the contract value to grow, or at least not to decrease as much.

In these cases, allocate between 30% and 50% to equities, which is generally the optimum asset mix for a non–guaranteed open investment.

However, before committing yourself to a specific asset mix, you must also examine the guaranteed death benefits for the plan. The final asset allocation decision has to be based on how all of the parts work.

Conclusion:

Variable annuities with guaranteed minimum withdrawal guarantees for life are one of the most versatile income classes in our toolbox. They convert the longevity and market risks to inflation risk. They go a long way in minimizing the "fear" for the retiree. It is very hard to put a price on the peace of mind that these guarantees provide: When and if assets deplete, you still have a lifelong income. That is priceless.

Also, keep in mind that unlike a fixed life annuity, VA–GMWBL does not remove the "hope." Assets may still grow and allow you to create an estate. With this income class, elimination of "fear" does not mean elimination of "hope."

However, there is one last factor. With VA–GMWBL, insurers might be exposed to large liabilities *occurring concurrently.* In adverse markets, portfolio values of nearly all VA–GMWBL accounts move down synchronously and eventually trigger the guarantees. If you want the highest protection, then you need to deal with insurance companies with the highest ratings. You need to weigh very carefully the immediate temptation of bigger promises offered by some VA–GMWBL providers against future "unknown unknowns."

Given the proliferation of different types, benefits and options available in the marketplace, it is critical to understand the details of each plan. The prospectus is "must–read" literature now more than ever.

Endnote: After the 2008 market crash, during the spring of 2009, many insurers suspended or redesigned their GMWBL plans. In many cases, the guaranteed withdrawal amounts were reduced, rider fees increased, step–up resets restrained, or some combination thereof. The information in this chapter might be outdated for future purposes, but it might be useful if you already hold such plans.

Chapter 36

Variable Annuity with GMIB

Guaranteed Minimum Income Benefit (GMIB) is a living benefit that is similar to a GMWBL in many ways. The following table shows the similarities and differences between the GMWBL and the GMIB:

Table 36.1: Comparing GMIB with GMWB:

	GMIB	GMWBL
Guarantee based on	Guaranteed Income Base (GIB)	Guaranteed Withdrawal Base (GWB)
Accumulation	The guaranteed income base increases each year, usually 6%, up to a certain age. You can take any amount up to 6% without disturbing the guarantees. Any amount not taken increases the future income.	Until withdrawals start, the guaranteed withdrawal base increases by a certain percentage (income credit) each year. Usually, there is an age limit (up to a certain age) or a term limit (up to a certain number of years).
Step–up Resets	Lifetime High: If portfolio value exceeds the GIB value, then this triggers an increase of the guaranteed income base. The age limit is usually more strict (up to age 75 or 80) Some plans have no step–up resets.	Lifetime High: If portfolio value exceeds the highest GWB value, then this triggers an increase of the guaranteed withdrawal base. Annual High: If portfolio value exceeds last anniversary portfolio value, then this triggers an increase of the guaranteed withdrawal base. There may be an age limit (up to a certain age) or a term limit (up to a certain number of years).
Variable annuity portfolio	Portfolio of segregated funds, nothing left after depletion or after annuitization	Portfolio of segregated funds, nothing left after depletion

	GMIB	GMWBL
When portfolio runs out of money	The plan is deemed to have annuitized based on a predetermined annuity rate table. The annuity rate table is clearly defined before you purchase the VA–GMIB. The "deemed annuity premium" is the value of the GIB. The age of the annuitization is the current age (the age at when the portfolio depletes) of the account owner.	Same withdrawals continue for life
Pay increase after income starts	• Age brackets, if any • Step–up resets • Annuitization	• Age brackets, if any • Step–up resets
Annuitization	• Portfolio depletion When portfolio depletes, annuitization is triggered immediately. • Age limit When the GMIB owner reaches a certain age (usually 85 or 90), annuitization is triggered. • Account owner's request After the waiting period (usually 10 years) since the last step–up reset, annuitization can be triggered at the request of the account owner.	N/A

Income Credit Accumulation:

One of the important features of the GMIB is how the income credit accumulates. With the GMIB, the income credit accumulation can continue whether or not you make withdrawals. This is different than most GMWBL plans, where the credit accumulation stops once you commence withdrawals.

For example, if the accumulation rate of the GMIB is 6%, then you can take any amount up to 6%. Whatever you don't take out continues to accumulate in the GIB. Say you purchased a $100,000 VA–GMIB. If you don't need any income, next year the guaranteed income base (GIB) becomes $106,000. If you take out $2,000, then the GIB becomes $104,000. If you need the full amount i.e. $6,000, then your guaranteed income base (GIB) remains at $100,000.

Credit accumulation ends when the age limit is reached or when annuitization occurs.

Annuitization:

Another important feature of GMIB is annuitization. When you purchase a VA–GMIB, your future annuity rates are stated in the prospectus. These rates are generally lower than the life annuity rates in the open market. Typical annuitization rates are shown in Table 36.2.

Table 36.2: Typical GMIB annuitization rates:

Age	Annuity Rate		
	Male	Female	Joint
65	5.3%	4.9%	4.4%
70	5.9%	5.5%	4.9%
75	6.8%	6.3%	5.5%
80	7.9%	7.3%	6.4%
85 +	10.1%	9.2%	7.5%

Annuitization can take place in the following situations:

1. Request by the account owner: The owner can choose to annuitize at any time after the waiting period, usually 10 years, from the last step–up reset. Using ble 36.2, since the annuity rates are over 6% after age 71, the retiree may want to annuitize if he needs an increase of income.

> Example 36.1
>
> Boris is 85. His GIB is $100,000. There were no step-up resets during the last 10 years. He has $25,000 left in his portfolio (the contract balance).
>
> He receives $6,000 each year (6% of the GIB) and he needs a pay increase.
>
> If Boris annuitizes his VA-GMIB, he can start collecting $10,100 (10.1% of the GIB) per year for the rest of his life, a 68% pay increase.
>
> Boris decides to annuitize. He hands over the $25,000 in his portfolio to the insurance company in exchange for this life annuity, and starts receiving $10,100 per year for the rest of his life.

2. Portfolio depletion: if and when the portfolio depletes, then the account owner is deemed to have purchased a life annuity.

> Example 36.2
>
> Jane is 75. Her GIB is $100,000. Because of bad markets, her portfolio just depleted this year.
>
> Her GMIB is annuitized automatically at the annuitization rate of 6.3%. From that point on, Jane receives $6,300 each year (6.3% of the GIB) for the rest of her life.

3. Age limit: When the account owner reaches a certain age (usually 85 or 90) and there is still some money left in the portfolio, then there is a forced annuitization.

> Example 36.3
>
> Steve just turned 85. His GMIB policy says that he has to annuitize at age 85. His GIB is $100,000. He has $12,000 left in his portfolio (contract balance).
>
> His GMIB is converted to a life annuity at age 85. His contract value is spent for annuitization. Now, he will collect $10,100 (10.1% of the GIB) per year for the rest of his life.
>
> If Steve does not want to annuitize at age 85, he can choose to withdraw his portfolio assets from the plan and cancel his GMIB before he reaches the forced annuitization age. Of course, by doing so, all the guarantees disappear and he is on his own.

When annuitization occurs, then the deemed premium for this annuity is the guaranteed income base. The annuity rate is based on the then current age at the time of annuitization. After annuitization, you will have life–long income from the annuity, but the income base and the account value ceases to exist. Depending on the age at annuitization, there is usually a minimum guaranteed payment period, in case of premature death.

The GMIB annuity rates are conservative. It is possible that the life annuity payments from the GMIB contract are less than the annuity payments that would be provided by applying your account value to the then–currently prevailing annuity rates. Most insurance companies will pay you the higher amount. However, this is an unlikely situation because most account values diminish as years go by.

The Accumulation Stage:

An income credit is added to the GIB when withdrawals are less than the stated income credit. Keep in mind that the income credit cannot be cashed out, but it only increases the guaranteed income base for future payments.

Let's look at an accumulation question: You have 10 years before retirement. You have two choices: (a) Invest in a portfolio of mutual funds, or (b) Buy a VA–GMIB contract and benefit from the income credit. Which would pay you more money at the end of 10 years? Let's try to answer by this using the following example:

Example 36.4

(C) Steve is 55. His investment portfolio is worth $100,000. His asset mix is 60% equities (S&P500) and 40% fixed income. His equities pay a dividend, but this dividend goes entirely to pay the portfolio costs. His fixed income portfolio return is the same as the historical 6-month CD rate plus 0.5%.

(D) Jane is also 55. She has $100,000. Unlike Steve, she buys a VA-GMIB contract. Her asset mix is 60% equities and 40% fixed income. Her income credit increases her guaranteed income base by 6% each year (compounding), more if the markets do well. At age 65, she takes out 6% of her guaranteed withdrawal base. She pays 3% for portfolio costs and 1% of the GIB for cost of the guarantees (GMIB rider).

To keep it simple, we assume that neither Steve nor Jane add or withdraw any money from their portfolios until age 65. At age 65, both take out 6% of their portfolio value as income.

Question: Who has a greater income starting at age 65?

Answer: For each retirement year since 1900, I calculate the value of the investment portfolio and the value of the guaranteed withdrawal base of the VA-GMWBL after 10 years.

Here are some statistics:

- At age 65, in 62% of the time, Jane's income was higher than Steve's. When Jane's income was higher than Steve's, it was on average 39% higher.
- At age 65, in 38% of the time, Jane's income was lower than Steve's. When Jane's income was lower than Steve's, it was on average 17% lower.

The Distribution Stage:

In the distribution stage, the retiree is paid a fixed percentage of the GIB. The value of the portfolio is reduced by the amount of withdrawals. When and if the portfolio is depleted, the GIB is annuitized and annuity payments continue for life. This is a seamless event; the retiree continues receiving his payments without missing a beat.

If the markets do well and the portfolio value goes up, then this may trigger a step–up reset of the GIB. From that point on, the income is based on the percentage of the higher GIB. Generally, resets are activated at each contract anniversary. However, step–up resets force the portfolio to deplete sooner and that triggers an earlier annuitization.

Example 36.5

Jeff, 65, is just retiring. He buys a VA-GMIB for $100,000 that guarantees 6% income, or $6,000, until annuitization. His contract allows him annual step-up resets until age 75. The age limit for annuitization is 85; i.e. if there is money left in the portfolio then an annuitization must occur at age 85. The asset mix is 60% S&P500 index and 40% fixed income. Assume management costs are 3% and GMIB rider is 1%.

Let's assume Jeff retired at the beginning of 1942. The step-up resets of his VA-GMWBL are based on the lifetime-high method.

The following chart shows the GIB if Jeff were to retire at the beginning of 1942.

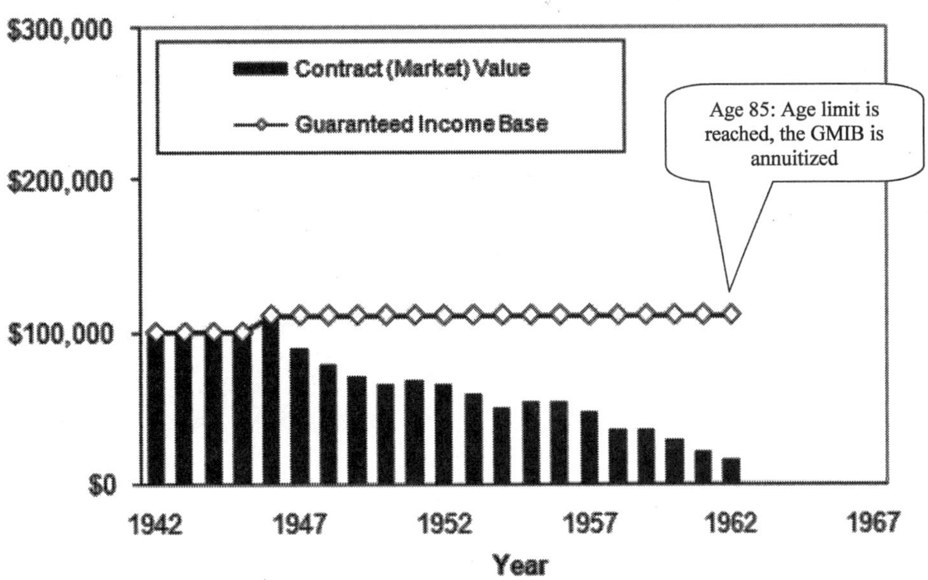

The portfolio created a step-up reset in 1946 (at age 69) and Jeff's GIB went from $100,000 to $111,092. After age 69, Jeff's annual income increased from $6,000 to $6,666, which is 6% of $111,092.

At age 85, when he reached his age limit for annuitization, his GMIB was annuitized with a deemed annuity premium of $111,092. His annuity payments increased to $11,220, which is 10.1% of $111,092. His contract value was $16,128 at age 85 and that was handed over to the insurance company for the annuitization.

The following chart shows Jeff's income over his life:

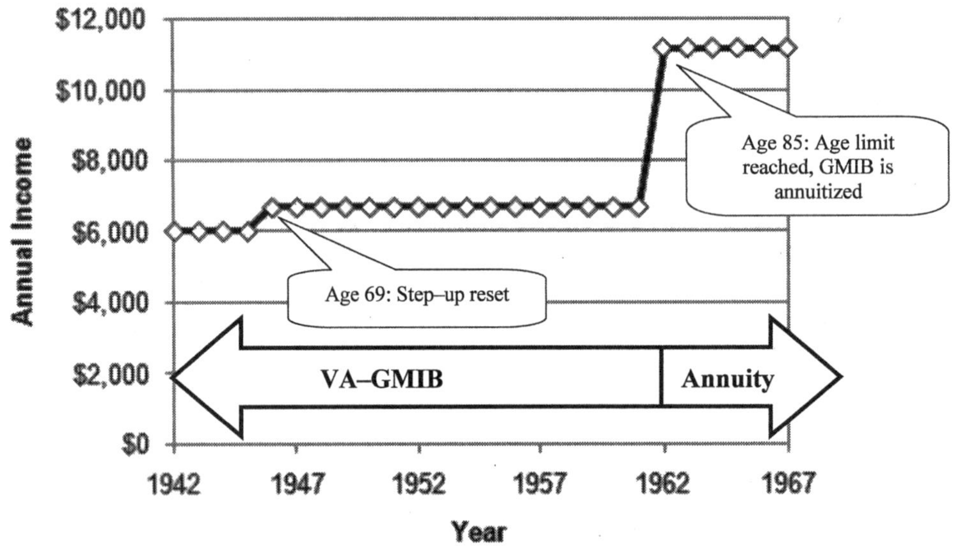

Let's move Jeff's retirement four years ahead to 1946 and see what happens.

Example 36.6

Same as Example 36.5, but Jeff is retiring at the beginning of 1946, not in 1942.

Here is the GIB chart.

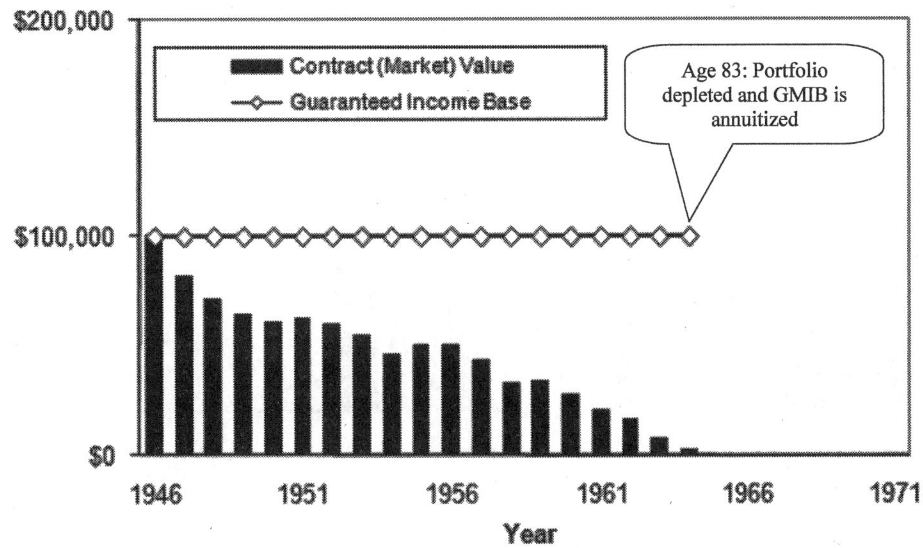

There were no step-up resets at all. The GIB remained constant at $100,000 until 1964, age 83. In that year, the annuitization took place, because then the portfolio depleted entirely. As a result of annuitization, at age 83, Jeff's annual income increased from $6,000 to $9,127. The following chart shows Jeff's income over his life:

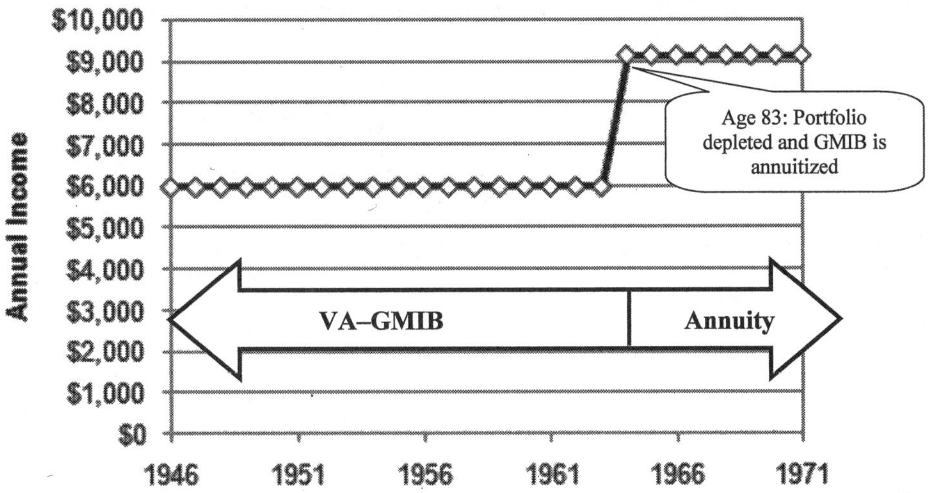

Let's move Jeff's retirement to 1982 and see what happens.

Example 36.6

Same as Example 36.5, but Jeff is retiring at the beginning of 1982.

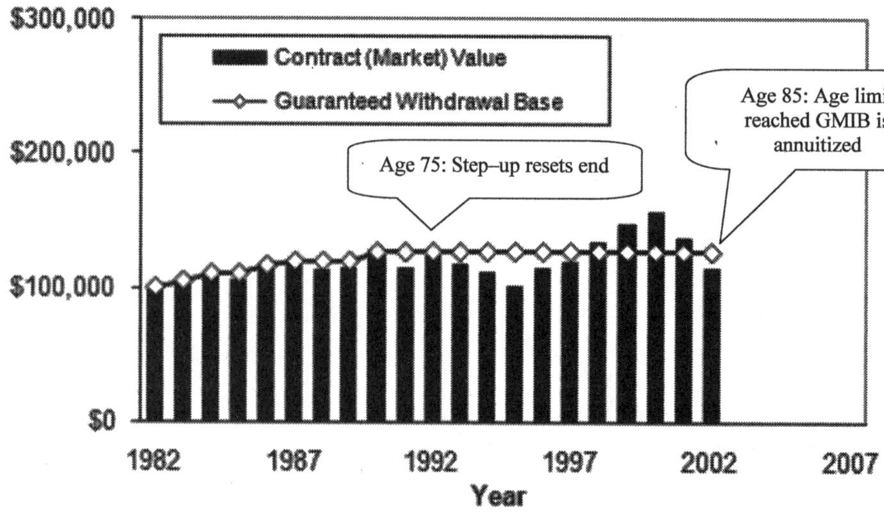

There were five step-up resets. The last one occurred at age 73 and the GIB increased to $126,994. From that point on, the annual payout was $7,620, 6% of $126,994. The GIB value remained constant after that age. At age 75, Jeff reached the age limit for the step-up resets and the GIB remained the same thereafter.

At age 85, the age limit for the GMIB is reached. At that point, the contract value is handed over to the insurance company and the GMIB is converted to an annuity. The annuity pays Jeff annually $12,826 for life. The income graph is depicted below:

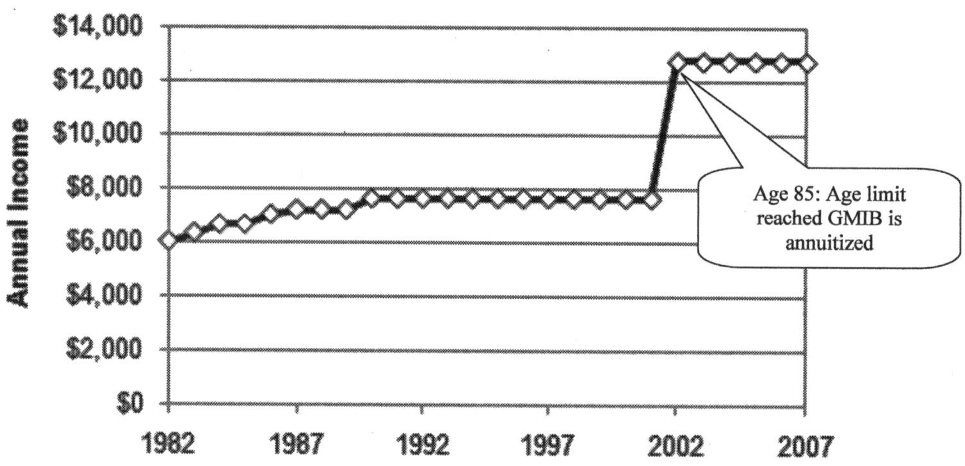

Jeff had another choice: His last reset occurred at age 73. He could have elected to annuitize at age 83, after the 10-year waiting period.

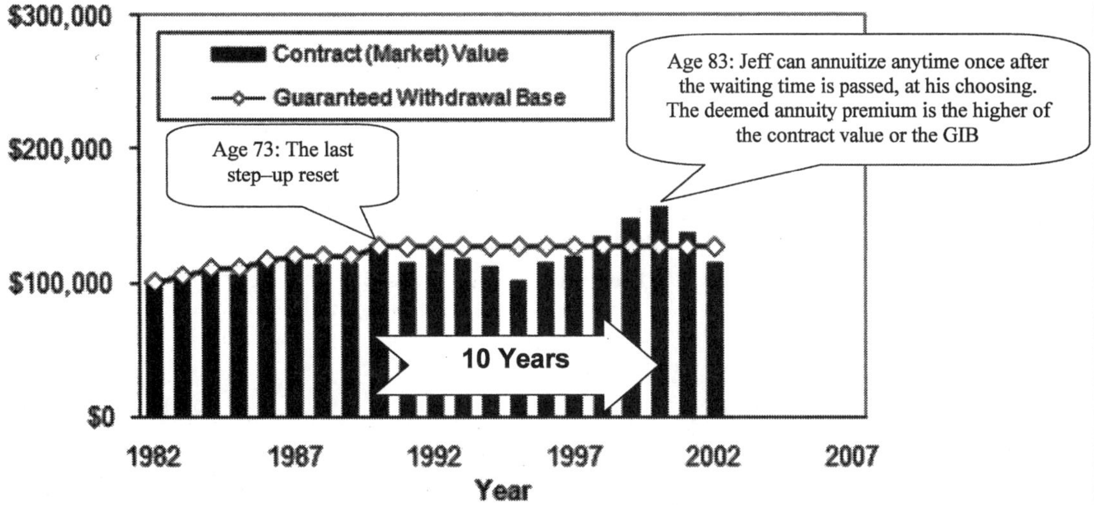

At age 83, his contract value is $155,511. Assuming the annuity rate in the open market for age 83 is 11.8%, he would then collect annually $18,350 from such an annuity. This is far better than waiting until age 85 and collecting only $12,826 of annual income. Here is the comparative income chart:

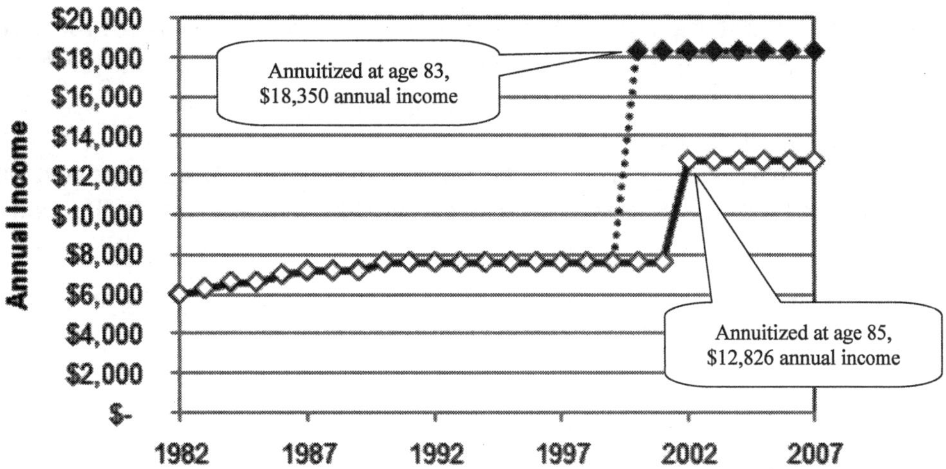

Example 36.6 shows the added benefit of the GMIB compared with the GMWBL. Once you buy the GMWBL, everything is on autopilot. Your pay increases depend on how your portfolio performs and on your age bracket, where applicable. With GMIB, you might still have an opportunity for one additional pay raise, the annuitization. So, the retiree has a little more leeway with the GMIB.

The insurance company is also a little ahead: not only do they make some money from rider fees, just like the GMWBL, but when you annuitize, the remaining contract value goes to the general revenues of the insurance company. This creates one last chunk of income for them, which covers a little more of the risk for the insurance company.

Once the waiting period from the last step–up reset is passed, watch your VA–GMIB statements more carefully. If the contract value is higher than the GIB or annuity rates are high enough, you might be better off annuitizing as soon as possible.

The Benefit and Cost Analysis:

When evaluating the benefit of the VA–GMIB, only the guaranteed income is considered. That is because eventually, any remaining portfolio assets are annuitized and no assets will be left.

Here is the input: initial purchase amount at age 65 is $100,000, GMIB rider cost is 1.0% of the GIB, portfolio costs are 3% of the market value, asset mix is 60% S&P500 and 40% fixed income, lifetime high step–up reset until age 75, guaranteed income is 6% of GIB until annuitization, age limit for annuitization is 90, annuity rates based on a male (see Table 36.2), income starts at age 65 and retiree dies at age 95. The retiree does not exercise his option to annuitize. He waits until the annuitization is forced upon him either due to portfolio depletion or the age limit.

Figure 36.1 depicts the benefit and the costs of the VA–GMIB for each year of retirement since 1900. The total cost is the total rider fees paid over the life of the plan (dark bars) plus the annuitization cost, which is the remaining portfolio value at the time of annuitization (gray bars). The income benefit is the total annuity payments received (white bars). By just observing the length of the income benefit bars and rider cost bars, you can see that GMIB benefits are generally richer than the average GMWBL plan we looked at in the previous chapter.

The diagram in Figure 36.2 summarizes the *average* money flow for all years since 1900.

Figure 36.1: Benefit and cost of GMIB, age of death 95

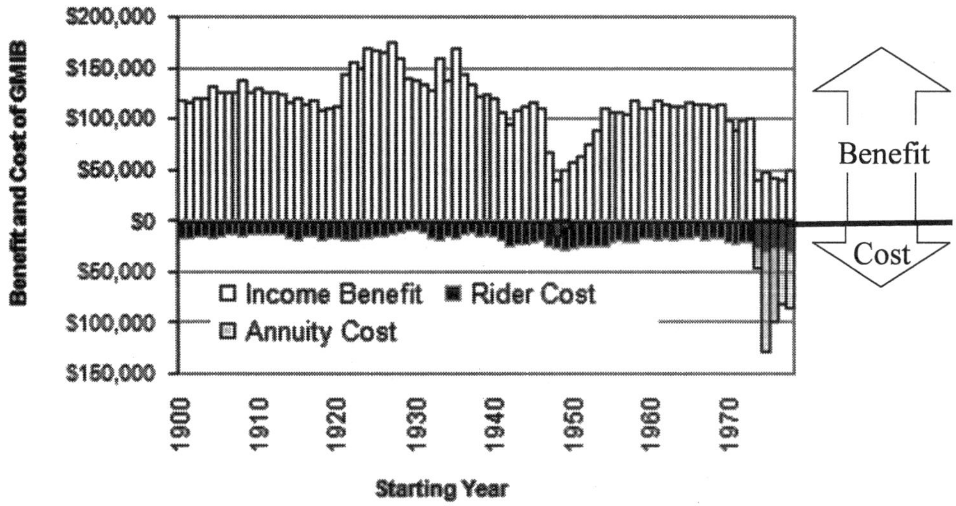

Figure 36.2: Average benefit and cost of a typical VA–GMIB by age 95

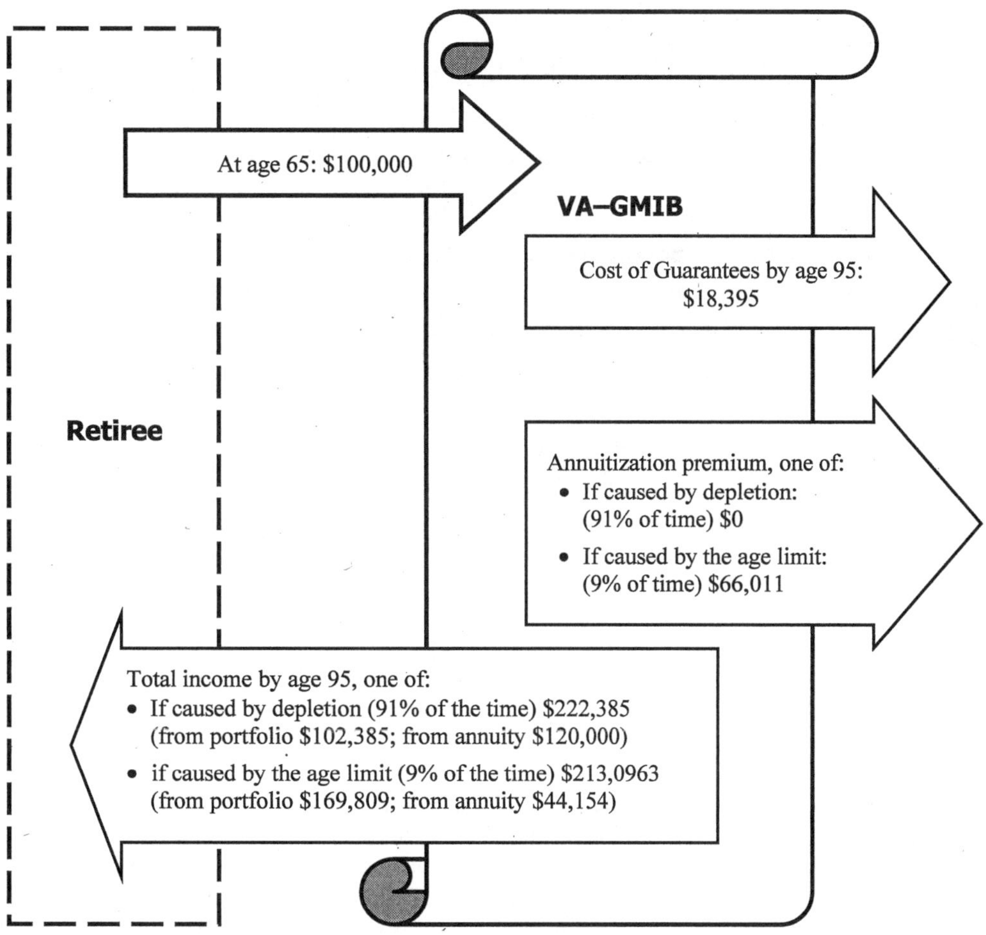

We observe in Figure 36.2 that in 91% of the time the portfolio depletes before age 90 and the retiree collects –on average– about $120,000 in annuity payments until age 95, after having paid –on average– only about $18,395 in rider fees. Not a bad deal at all!

What happens if the retiree decides to annuitize as soon as the waiting period is over?

I ran this case as well. Figure 36.3 depicts the year–by–year benefit and cost chart. Figure 36.4 summarizes the *average* money flow for all years since 1900. History shows that if you annuitize as soon as the waiting period is over, but not before age 75, you would have a higher benefit. That is true even if you were to die prematurely, because of the guarantee period[79] that comes with the annuity.

If you annuitize as soon as the waiting period is over, the rider fees paid to the insurer are reduced by about 30%.

Figure 36.3: Benefit and cost of GMIB, age of death 95, annuitized immediately after the waiting period

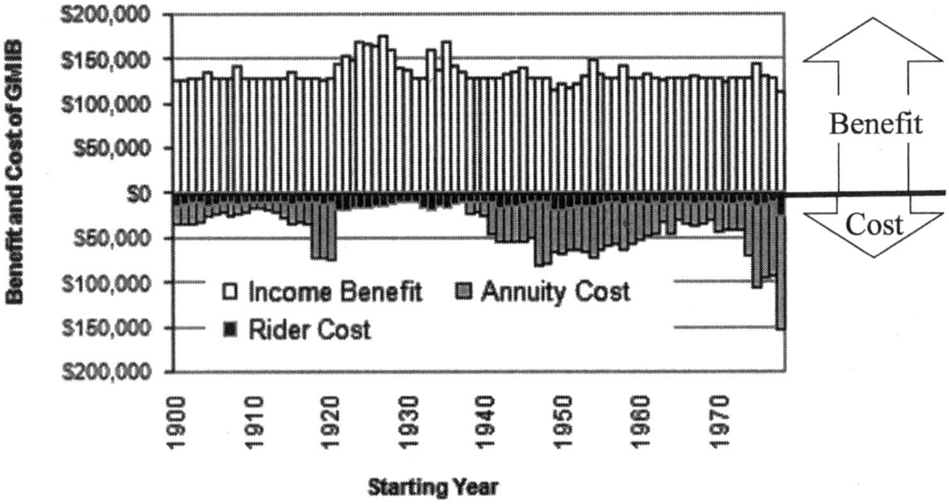

---

[79] Generally, annuities from GMIB plans have a minimum 10–year guarantee period if annuitized prior to age 80. If annuitized after 83, the minimum guarantee is 5 years. For joint and last survivor annuities and as long as the age difference between the joint annuitants is ten years or less in a qualified plan, the guarantee period is ten years. The payments continue to flow to the beneficiary even if the annuitant(s) die within the guarantee period. Read the prospectus carefully to verify this, as not all insurers offer the same terms and conditions.

Figure 36.4: Average benefit and cost of a typical VA–GMIB by age 95, annuitized immediately after the waiting period.

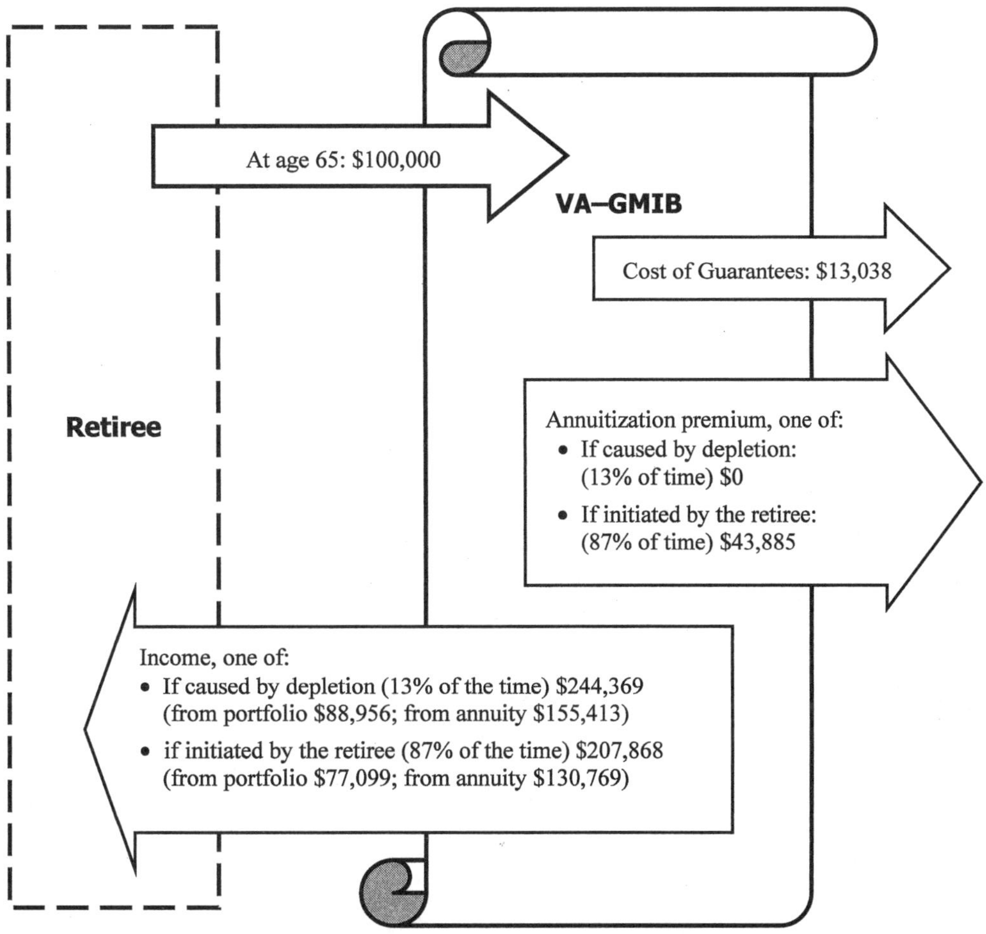

We observe here that in 13% of the cases the portfolios deplete and the annuity starts before the retiree has an opportunity to annuitize. When that happens, the retiree's average lifelong income is about $244,369. About 1/3 of this comes from his portfolio and 2/3 comes from annuity payments. The guarantee costs are –on average– only $13,038. Does this sound to good to be true?

In situations where the portfolio runs out of money, the insurance company is on the hook. A GMIB insurer loses more money than a GMWB insurer when the portfolio depletes. That is because when the annuitization occurs due to the portfolio depletion, there is usually a pay increase which has to be fully covered by the insurer. With GMWB, there is no pay increase when the portfolio depletes, so there is no added liability for that additional pay for the insurer. It is to the GMIB insurer's advantage when annuitization occurs due to the age limit. The next best scenario for the insurer is when an account owner requests annuitization immediately after the waiting period.

As for the GMIB rider costs, we observe a similar pattern to GMWBL. Generally, the prevailing GMIB costs might be too low for the long term.

With current levels of rider fees[80], a VA–GMIB is beneficial to the retiree in *all* market trends. However, its benefit is greater when purchased prior to certain market trends. In addition, if the retiree happens to be in an inflationary time period, he may want to annuitize sooner. This brings additional money to the insurer sooner. This is good for the insurer.

The following list shows the benefit of purchasing a VA–GMIB just prior to a specific secular market trend:

The VA–GMIB purchased just prior to a:	**For the retiree:**	**For the insurer:**
1. secular bullish market followed by a secular bear market	Most advantageous	Most risky
2. secular bear market		
3. secular bullish market followed by a secular sideways market	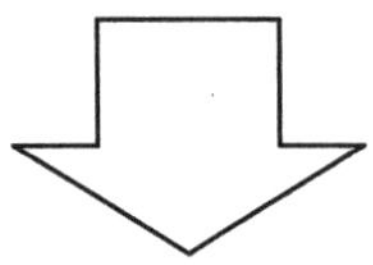	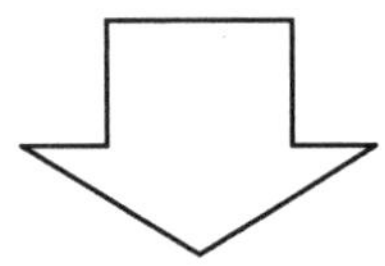
4. secular sideways market		
5. secular bullish market	Least advantageous	Least risky
6. high inflation time period		

---

[80] As of December 2008

Inflation Risk:

VA–GMIB converts the longevity and markets risks into the inflation risk. They do not remove the inflation risk.

Let's look at an example: the initial purchase amount is $100,000, GMIB rider cost is 1% of the GIB, portfolio costs are 3% of the market value, asset mix is 60% S&P500 and 40% fixed income, lifetime high step–up reset, guaranteed withdrawal rate is 6% of GIB until annuitization, income required starting at age 65 and ending at age 95.

Table 36.5 depicts the probability of maintaining the purchasing power of GMIB.

Table 36.5: Probability of maintaining purchasing power

	Probability of Occurrence:
Purchasing power at age 95 is 100% or higher than what it was at age 65	19%
Purchasing power at age 95 is between 85% and 100% of what it was at age 65	4%
Purchasing power at age 95 is between 50% and 85% of what it was at age 65	51%
Purchasing power at age 95 is less than 50% of what it was at age 65	26%

Table 36.5 demonstrates that the inflation risk is not handled well with VA–GMIB.

Minimizing the Inflation Risk:

While the GMIB removes the market risk and the longevity risk, it does not eliminate the inflation risk. If you have the resources, you need to hold a separate investment portfolio, a separate "inflation bucket", to maintain your purchasing power. This bucket has only one purpose: it provides the funds to cover any loss of purchasing power from the VA–GMIB payments.

Table 36.6 depicts the approximate size of this separate investment account to provide inflation protection for $10,000 annual income starting at age 65, for 20–year and 30–year time horizons. The core income of $10,000 is provided by the VA–GMIB, subject to increase if there are any resets or after annuitization. Any inflation shortfall is provided by this separate inflation bucket.

Table 36.6: Assets required for investment portfolio utilized as an inflation bucket

	Assets Required for $10,000 annual, CPI–indexed income
Retirement Time Horizon: 20 years	
VA–GMIB required	$166,666
Inflation "bucket" required	$66,334
Total assets required	$233,000
Retirement Time Horizon: 30 years	
VA–GMIB required	$166,666
Inflation "bucket" required	$100,334
Total assets required	$267,000

Notes for the table: The asset mix of the investment portfolio used as the inflation bucket is 50% S&P500 index and 50% fixed income. Equity: dividend yield is 2%, management costs 2% for a net alpha of 0%. Fixed Income has a net yield of 6–month CD interest rate plus 0.5%.

Asset Allocation in VA–GMIB:

The insurance company needs to collect the GMIB rider fees for as long as possible. Therefore, they would prefer that the retiree has a not–too–risky portfolio. As for the retiree, he wants to annuitize –eventually– to give himself a pay raise. Therefore, he would also prefer a not–too–risky portfolio.

This is different than the GMWBL. With the GMWBL, the retiree wants to be aggressive in order to maximize the potential for step–up resets. The insurance company prefers a lower risk portfolio to maximize the portfolio life and minimize the GMWBL payments from their own pocket. In a GMWBL, the insurance company and the retiree have differing objectives. In a GMIB, they have similar objectives.

Table 36.7 shows the probability of maintaining at least 85% of the purchasing power at age 86 for various asset mixes and genders for a GMIB based on actual market history since 1900.

Table 36.7: The effect of asset mix to purchasing power

Equity Percentage in the VA–GMIB portfolio	Gender	Probability of maintaining at least 85% of the purchasing power at age 86:
95%	Male	51%
	Female	41%
	Joint	36%
80%	Male	51%
	Female	47%
	Joint	33%
70%	Male	52%
	Female	45%
	Joint	28%
60%	Male	50%
	Female	45%
	Joint	22%
50%	Male	47%
	Female	42%
	Joint	17%
40%	Male	45%
	Female	40%
	Joint	17%

Observing the figures in Table 35.7, we can conclude that an equity allocation of 60% to 70% would be near the optimum asset mix for the retiree.

Conclusion:

VA–GMIBs are one of the most useful income classes in our toolbox. They convert the longevity and market risks to inflation risk like GMWBLs. However, their annuitization feature makes them a different income class.

Deal only with insurance companies with the highest ratings and the best balance sheets. All you are buying is a promise; do your best to search for a company that can deliver that promise. Make sure to understand all the benefits and options before you buy a VA–GMIB. Read the prospectus carefully.

Endnote: After the 2008 market crash, during the spring of 2009, many insurers suspended their GMIB plans. The information in this chapter might be useful if you already hold such plans, but not too useful for plans that will be offered in the future.

Chapter 37

Buy Term Annuity, Invest the Rest

With this strategy, the retiree buys a term certain annuity to cover his income needs for a number of years. The remaining assets are invested. The expectation is, by the time the annuity expires, the growth of the investment portfolio will be sufficient to finance further withdrawals for the remainder of the retiree's life.

Let's look at an example.

Example 37.1

Steve, 65, is just retiring. He has $1,000,000 savings for retirement; he needs annually $40,000 in current dollars. He wants his plan to last until age 95.

Case A: Steve keeps an investment portfolio to finance his retirement. In his investment portfolio, equities grows at the same rate as the S&P500 index, plus 2% for dividends, less 2% management fees for a net alpha of 0%. His fixed income yields same as the historical 6-month CD rate plus 0.5%. The asset mix for the investment portfolio is 50% equity and 50% fixed income.

The following chart depicts the aftcast since 1900. The aftcast indicates that the probability of running out of money by 95 is 31%, which is not good.

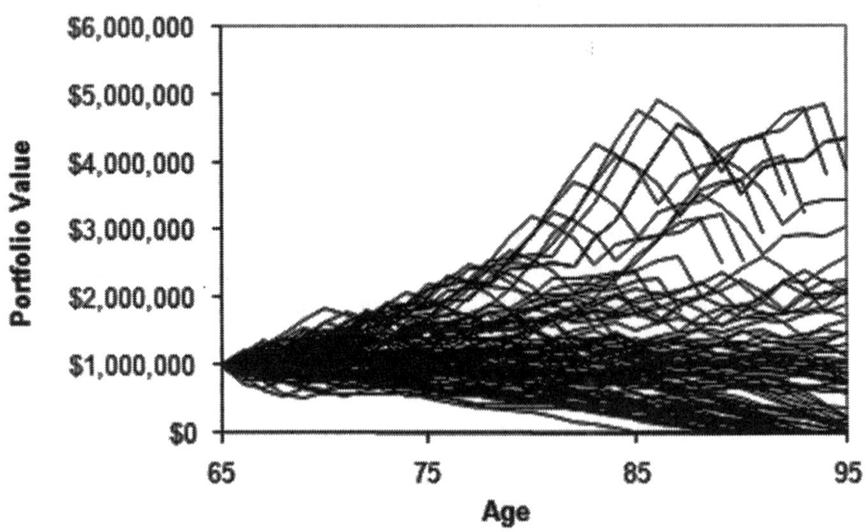

Case B: Steve tries a different strategy. He buys a 10-year term annuity that pays $40,000 each year, indexed by 3% annually. This annuity costs him $380,800.

He has $619,200 remaining in his investment portfolio.

Question: Does this strategy secure a lifelong income?

During the first 10 years, there are essentially no withdrawals from the investment portfolio. However, a small amount of cash may be taken out of or added to the investments when the inflation rate is different than the 3% assumed during that time.

The following chart depicts the aftcast. For the first 10 years (the area marked as "A"), while the term annuity pays the required income, the investment portfolio grows. After that (area marked as "B"), the income is withdrawn from the investment bucket. The problem is, if Steve is unlucky, the growth of his investment during that 10-year time period is insufficient to fund his retirement.

The probability of running out of money by 95 is 34% which is slightly higher than mot buying the term certain annuity. In this case, the "buy term annuity and invest the rest" strategy did not work either.

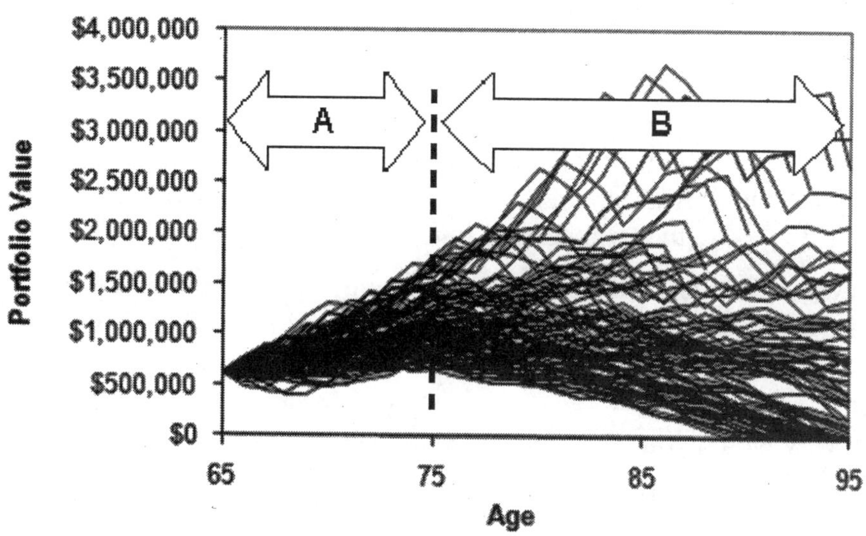

What is the effect of varying the asset mix and the term of the annuity? Table 37.1 shows the probability of depletion for various combinations of asset mix and annuity term for Example 37.1.

Table 37.1: The impact of asset allocation and term length, IWR 4%:

Asset Mix: (Equity/ Fixed Income)	No Term Annuity	With Term–Annuity		
		Term: 10 years	Term: 15 years	Term: 20 years
	Probability of Depletion by Age 95:			
0 / 100	21%	21%	20%	29%
30 / 70	21%	18%	18%	26%
50 / 50	31%	34%	34%	31%
70 / 30	45%	45%	41%	36%
100 / 0	53%	50%	46%	45%

Table 37.1 demonstrates that at a 4% initial withdrawal rate, the optimum asset mix is near 30% equity and 70% fixed income with 10 or 15 years of annuity term. However, for withdrawal rates higher than 4%, both the effect of asset allocation and the length of the term of the annuity are insignificant. There was practically no difference if you use 40/60 or 100/0 asset mix or a 5–year or 15–year term for the annuity.

> The first rule of thumb:
> In a normal interest environment, the "Buy Term-Annuity, Invest the Rest" strategy will work only if your withdrawals are below the sustainable withdrawal rate *without* the term certain annuity.
>
> If your withdrawal rate is larger than the SWR, buying a term annuity with your precious capital will not create a successful plan in a normal interest environment.

That being the case, why would you buy a term certain annuity?

The purpose of the term annuity is to buy time. This moves the income adequacy problem into the future. It gives you temporary peace of mind. In the meantime, you are hoping that interest rates go up and you can buy a life annuity cheaper at a later date. Or, if you die during the term of the annuity, your estate might end up with a larger amount of money and the problem of lifelong income would then be solved!

The second rule of thumb:
If the implied interest rate of the 10–year term annuity exceeds the effective growth rate of the *unlucky* distribution portfolio by 1% or more, then including a term certain annuity in your plan will usually increase portfolio longevity.

If the implied interest rate of the annuity (term or life) exceeds the effective growth rate of the *median* distribution portfolio, then including an annuity (term or life) in your retirement plan will likely be more advantageous.

See Table 20.1 for the effective growth rate of various distribution portfolios.

The implied interest rates for the term annuities that I used in Example 37.1 were 3.36%, 4.20% and 4.50% for the 10–year, 15–year and 20–year term annuities, respectively. These are the current rates as of May, 2009. In historical terms, these interest rates are relatively low.

I recalculated the effect of interest rates as shown in Table 37.2. You can see how a term certain annuity in a higher interest environment can reduce the probability of depletion of the investment portfolio. Keep in mind that these figures apply only to Example 37.1. You need to analyze each case using the actual, current annuity quotes.

Table 37.2: The impact of interest rate, asset mix 50/50, IWR 4%:

Implied Interest Rate of the Term–certain Annuity	No Term Annuity	With Term–Annuity		
		Term: 10 years	Term: 15 years	Term: 20 years
	Probability of Depletion by Age 95:			
Current	31%	34%	34%	31%
Current +1%	31%	30%	16%	11%
Current +2%	31%	24%	8%	3%
Current +3%	31%	20%	0%	0%

The third rule of thumb:
In a higher interest rate environment, buy the longer term annuity with payments indexed.

In a low interest environment, either ignore the "Buy Term Annuity, Invest the Rest" strategy altogether, or buy a shorter term annuity (perhaps 5 years) with flat payments (no indexation).

Keep in mind one important point: the notion that this strategy can work better in high interest rate environments, can be misleading. You need to look at the entire picture. If interest rates are high, that is probably because the risk of inflation is high. Equities do not thrive in such environments, so whatever you save in the cost of buying the term annuity, you may already have lost in your investment portfolio.

On the other hand, if interest rates are low, that is probably because the risk of inflation is low. Equities generally do well in such environments, so whatever additional amount you pay to buy the term annuity; you might have even better gains in your investment portfolio. In retirement planning, you cannot treat a single event in isolation because each event affects all other events.

Let us continue with Example 37.1. We want to look at what happens after Steve's term annuity expires.

Example 37.2

Continuing from Example 37.1: Ten years later...

Steve is now 75. His term annuity has just expired. He needs $56,000 annual income, in current dollars. He wants to review his plan. His remaining retirement time horizon is now 20 years.

There are three general categories of outcome:

- Steve was lucky (top decile)
- Steve was unlucky (bottom decile)
- Steve had average luck (median)

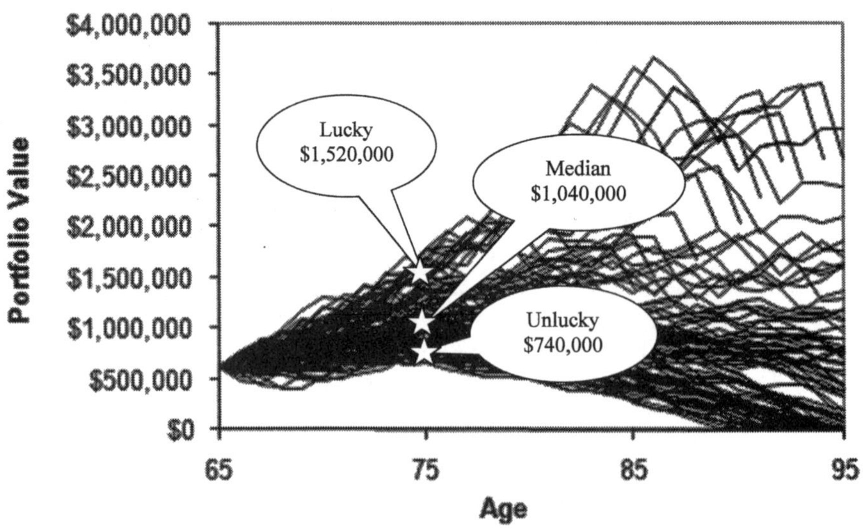

Case A: Steve was lucky:

During the last 10 years Steve was lucky. His portfolio grew well and it is now worth $1,520,000. The chart below shows the aftcast. It indicates that Steve's investment portfolio can finance his retirement. At age 75, SWR is 5.2% (from Table 17.9), so he can increase his pay to $79,040 starting at age 76 (5.2% of $1.52 million).

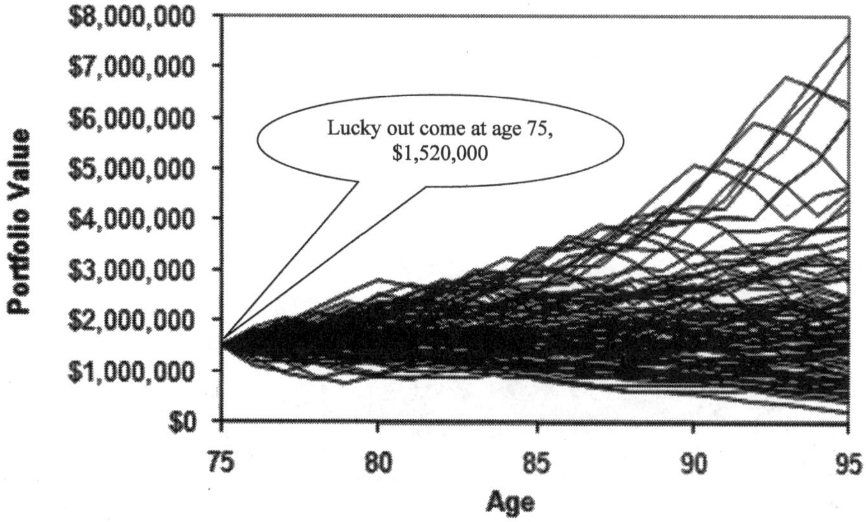

Case B: Steve was unlucky:

During the last 10 years Steve was unlucky. His portfolio did not do well and it is now worth $740,000. This amount is unlikely to finance his retirement until age 95. The probability of portfolio depletion by age 95 is 70%. How do you solve this problem? You have to wait until Chapter 41, The Zone Strategy for the answer.

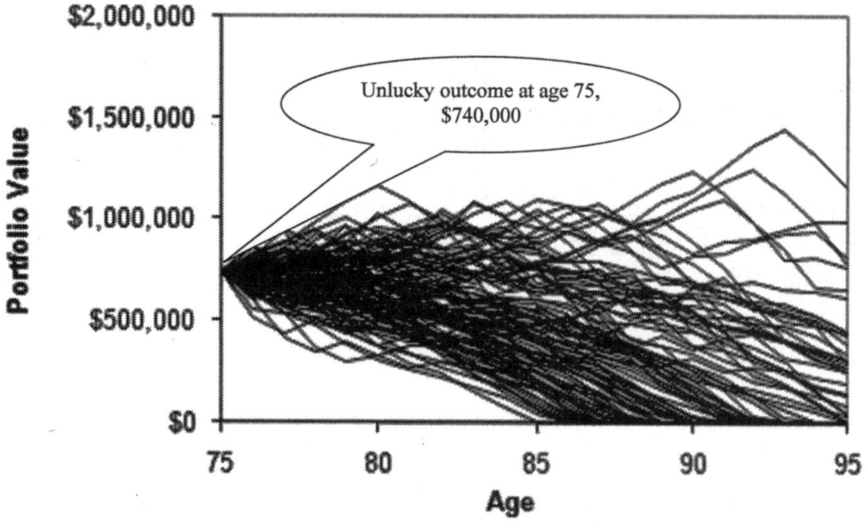

Case C: Steve had average luck:

During the last 10 years Steve had average luck. His portfolio grew to $1,040,000. This amount is insufficient to finance his retirement until age 95. The probability of portfolio depletion by age 95 is 37%. Again, you have to wait until Chapter 41, The Zone Strategy for the solution.

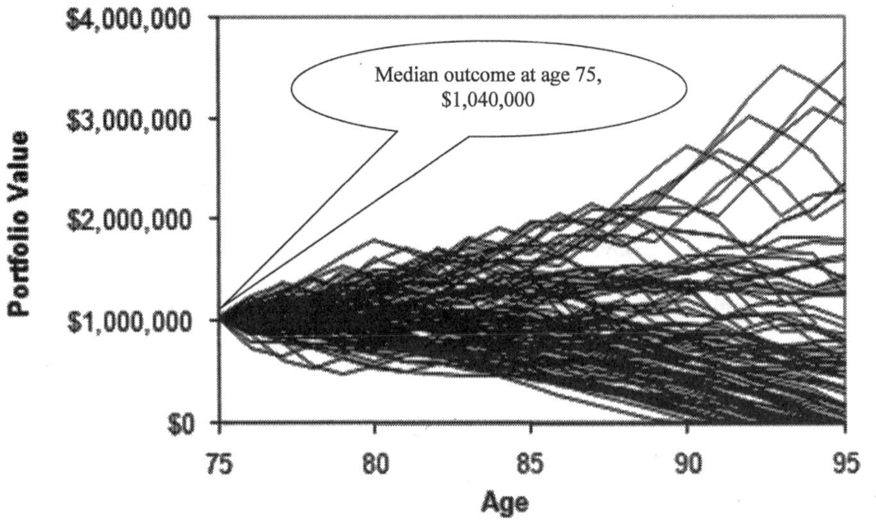

Conclusion:

The "Buy Term Annuity, Invest the Rest" strategy can work in high interest rate environments. Keep in mind that it does not solve the underlying problem, but only postpones it for a while.

Of the three financial risks of retirement, it covers the market risk temporarily, it may or may not cover the inflation risk and it definitely does not cover the longevity risk. As a result, if savings are insufficient to begin with, this strategy is unlikely to work successfully most of the time.

Chapter 38

Asset Dedication

Here is what the asset dedication strategy attempts to accomplish: set aside sufficient funds to meet the income needs for a certain number of years. Call this the "money bucket". Keep investments in a separate "investment bucket". Withdraw income only from the money bucket while the investment bucket grows.

The expectation is that by the time the money bucket dries up, the growth in the investment bucket will be sufficient to finance further withdrawals for the remainder of the retiree's life.

In theory this sounds wonderful. In reality, if the buckets are too small or if they are leaking, this strategy fails. The question is: how large are the buckets you need? What is the optimum size for each bucket? As with any financial strategy, the devil is always in the details.

Typically, the separation of buckets is only notional and imaginary. Assets are invested in a suitable asset mix, say 60% equity and 40% fixed income. In addition, there is one constraint: the fixed income portion of the portfolio can never hold less than a specific number of years of income. That is what constitutes the money bucket. Unlike the "Buy Term Annuity, Invest the Rest" strategy, with asset dedication, both the money bucket and investment bucket are usually within the same portfolio.

Example 38.1

Richard, 65, is just retiring. He has $1,000,000 savings for retirement; he needs annually $40,000 in current dollars. He wants his plan last until age 95.

His equities grow the same as the S&P500 index, plus 2% for dividends, less 2% management fees for a net alpha of 0%. His fixed income yields same as the historical 6-month CD rate plus 0.5%. His asset mix is 50% equity and 50% fixed income.

The following chart depicts the aftcast since 1900. It indicates that the probability of running out of money by 95 is 31%, which is not good.

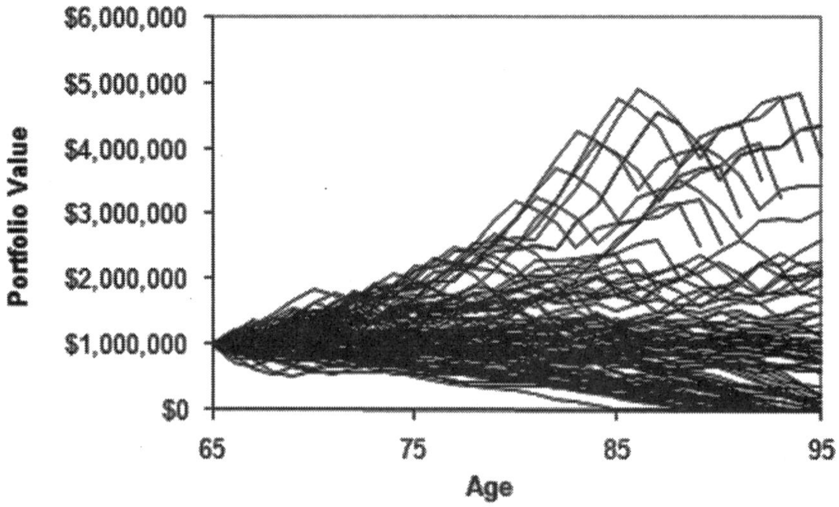

So, unhappy with this aftcast, Richard tries the asset dedication strategy. In his fixed income portion, he decides to keep at least 7 years' worth of withdrawals. That is about $280,000, calculated as $40,000 x 7, not counting inflation adjustments.

Does this asset dedication strategy secure a lifelong income? Here is the aftcast:

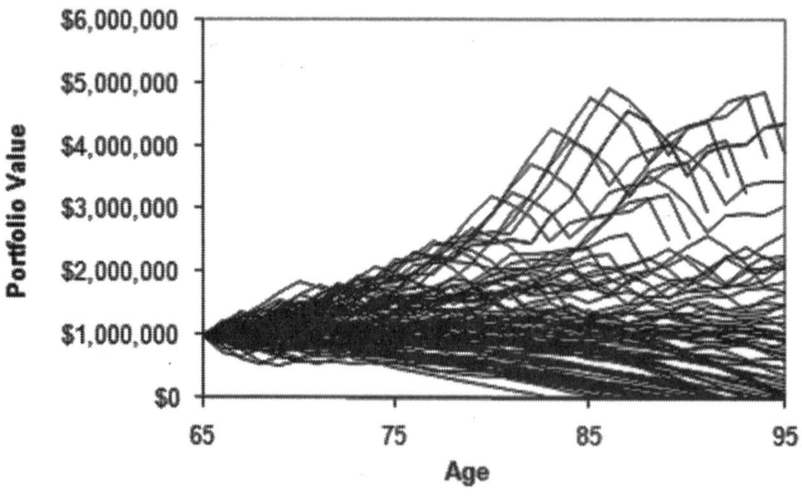

The aftcast indicates that the probability of running out of money by 95 increased from 31% to 43%. This asset dedication strategy does not work for Richard.

Here is the average asset mix over his retirement time horizon:

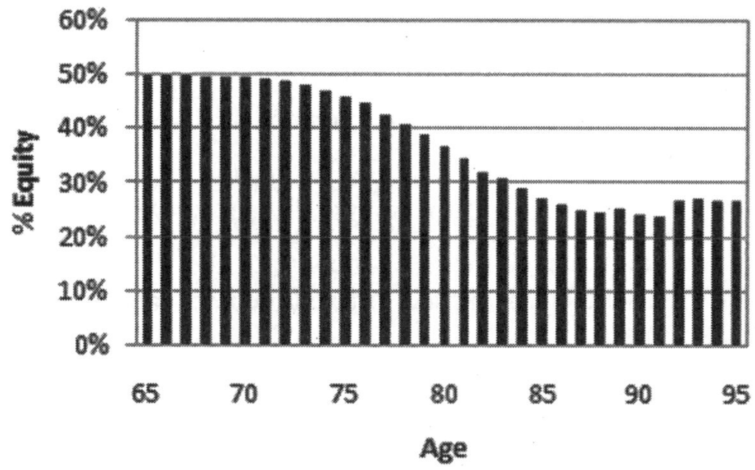

What happens is this: the asset dedication strategy dictates that at least $280,000, or 28% of Richard's initial portfolio is kept in the fixed income portfolio. That is no problem, because 50% of his portfolio is already in fixed income.

As time goes on, if Richard is lucky, his portfolio increases in value and he still maintains 50% fixed income. The "minimum 7-year fixed income" rule never kicks in.

But if he is unlucky, then his portfolio value goes down. As the portfolio value decreases, coupled with increasing withdrawals (inflation), more of the portfolio is allocated (dedicated) to fixed income. On average -as seen on the column chart above- more and more money is allocated to fixed income as time goes on. This reduced the chances of portfolio recovery after an unlucky streak.

This strategy made things worse for Richard. The following chart depicts the probability of receiving full income during his retirement. The standard strategic asset allocation outperforms the asset dedication strategy.

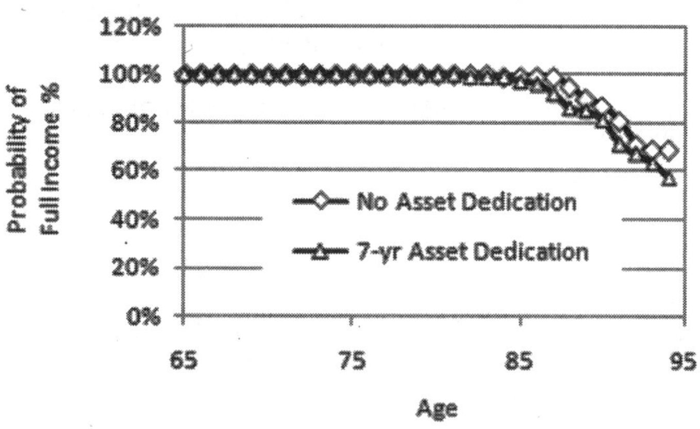

Let me give you a different perspective: a retiree walks in. He has $1 million in his investment portfolio. He needs $60,000 annual income from his portfolio, indexed to inflation.

- Case A: You believe in strategic asset allocation.

  His risks profile points to an asset mix of 40% equity and 60% fixed income (including cash). Thus, $600,000 is allocated in fixed income and $400,000 is allocated in equities.

- Case B: You believe in asset dedication and use a 10–year money bucket.

  You decide to dedicate 10 years of income to the fixed income portion of the portfolio. Thus, $600,000 is placed to fixed income, calculated as ten years times $60,000. The remainder, $400,000 is invested in equities.

What is the difference between Case A and Case B? Initially, there is no difference. Both portfolios have essentially the same dollar amounts invested in equities and in fixed income.

After some years, in Case B, if the retiree is unlucky, then more of his money is allocated to fixed income. This is a similar pattern to age–based asset allocation, even though that was not your original intent. So, why would you expect a better outcome using the asset dedication strategy? If your pie is the same size, it just does not matter how you slice it. Unless you export the risk elsewhere, there is no reason to expect an improvement.

If the retiree is lucky, in Case B, the equity assets grow. But for that, you don't need an asset dedication. A standard, run–of the–mill strategic asset allocation method will work just as well. When you are lucky, just about anything works.

Table 38.1 shows the sustainable asset multiplier for the asset dedication strategy.

Table 38.1: Sustainable asset multiplier, portfolio size required for $10,000 annual income fully indexed to CPI. Portfolio: 50% equity (S&P500 index, alpha–0%), 50% fixed income (yield: 6–month CD plus 0.5%)

Time Horizon	Minimum Portfolio Size Required for $10,000 annual income indexed fully to CPI, maximum 10% probability of depletion			
	No dedication	5–year dedication	10–year dedication	15–year dedication
20 years	$212,000	$216,000	$214,000	$214,000
30 years	$281,000	$285,000	$300,000	$327,000
40 years	$346,000	$347,000	$364,000	$388,000

Conclusion:

The most critical factor in retirement planning is having sufficient savings to finance both the retirement and the time value of fluctuations. Did I say this before? If savings are not sufficient, short of exporting the risk, no amount of wise strategy –that is legal– can save the day.

Asset dedication is a catchy phrase. Some advisors use it, hoping and wishing that it will work. Some of their arguments and strategies may be very compelling. But like many other "logical" ideas, in real life, this strategy performs worse than traditional strategic asset allocation.

A 65–year old retiree with a time horizon of 30 years holding a 7–year asset dedication portfolio gets about the same portfolio life as your plain vanilla age–based asset allocation strategy. Asset dedication strategy is not the magic elixir that it is made out to be. I consider it another marketing tool, nothing more, nothing less. It helps us to hang on to your assets a little longer[81].

Pay no heed to it.

[81] Our financial industry estimates that it makes collectively about $200 billion per year on your retirement savings in U.S.A. and Canada. That may be on the low side.

Chapter 39

Withdrawal Strategies Based on Performance

During a planning meeting with a client, if it turns out that the client's assets appear insufficient for lifelong income, then my first suggestion is delaying his retirement. In some cases, working two extra years can turn an unsuccessful plan into a successful one.

Some clients feel uncomfortable with delaying their retirement age. Some are simply unable to do so. My next best suggestion is to reduce withdrawals to below the sustainable withdrawal rate. Invariably, the client responds with one of the following questions:

1. "If I reduce my withdrawals by 20% during bad years in the market, can I then have a lifelong income?" This strategy is called "reduction in bad markets".
2. "If I reduce my withdrawals by 30% as soon as my withdrawals exceed 8% of the portfolio value, can I then have a lifelong income?" This strategy is called "reduction after withdrawals become excessive".
3. "If I take out no more than the growth of the portfolio, can I then have lifelong income?" This strategy is called "limiting withdrawals to the portfolio's growth".
4. "If I take out no more than 10% of the current portfolio value, can I then have a lifelong income?" This strategy is called "limiting withdrawals to a percentage of the portfolio value".

The questions are not always worded exactly like this, but they generally fit into one of these four categories. In this chapter, I will analyze these withdrawal strategies.

Reduction in Bad Markets:

> "If I reduce my withdrawals by 20% during bad years in the market, can I then have a lifelong income?"

My answer is, "If your withdrawals are higher than the sustainable rates, then income reduction in bad years will not help. If you want the portfolio to last longer, you must reduce periodic withdrawals to below the sustainable withdrawal rate throughout the entire retirement, not just during adverse times."

If the withdrawal rate is above sustainable rates, it is likely that your portfolio will run out of money during retirement. If you follow this strategy, it might stretch the portfolio life in some cases a little longer. However, this is usually not as significant as Monte Carlo simulators forecast.

Let's look at how each asset class behaves when withdrawals are reduced after "bad" performance.

Equity:

Let's assume that you are holding 100% equities. Your strategy is to reduce your withdrawals in the year following a negative annual return. We use the historical DJIA index return with 2% average dividend, 0.5% management fees, for a net alpha of 1.5%. We also use the historical inflation rate. The initial withdrawal rate is 6%, starting at age 65. Table 39.1 demonstrates the probability of portfolio depletion by age 95, a 30–year time horizon.

Table 39.1: Reducing withdrawals in the year following a negative year, initial withdrawal rate is 6%, 100% DJIA

Amount of Reduction	Probability of Depletion by age 95
No Reduction	70%
10% Reduction	68%
20% Reduction	63%
30% Reduction	60%
50% Reduction	55%

As the reduction percentage is increased, the probability of depletion decreases. Nevertheless, this strategy did not convert an unacceptable retirement plan into an acceptable one.

When we talk about reduced withdrawals, another point we need to consider is the frequency and the length of these "pay cuts". You might be able to handle an income reduction of 20% for one year, but probably not if it lasts for three years. Or, you may be happy if this reduction happens once every five years, but not every other year.

The market history shows that there would be a pay cut 36% of the time until the portfolio finally expires. As for the duration, here are the numbers:

- The probability of a pay cut lasting one year is about 16%
- The probability of a pay cut lasting two years is 5%
- The probability of a pay cut lasting three years is 2%
- The probability of a pay cut lasting four years is 1%

Figures in Table 39.1 are based on a 6% initial withdrawal rate. Table 39.2 shows the impact of reducing withdrawals for different initial withdrawal rates.

Table 39.2: Probability of depletion by the 30th year of retirement, withdrawals reduced in the year following a negative growth year.

Initial Withdrawal Rate	No Reduction	10% Reduction	20% Reduction	30% Reduction
	Probability of depletion by year 30			
4%	44%	38%	31%	26%
6%	70%	68%	63%	60%
8%	93%	90%	84%	80%
10%	100%	100%	98%	96%

What happens if you tighten the definition of "bad" market? For example, let's use 8.8% as our threshold, the historical average growth rate. So, instead of giving yourself a pay cut after a losing year, you give yourself a pay cut when the portfolio growth is less than 8.8%. Table 39.3 shows the results. In reality, raising the threshold did not change the outcome in any meaningful way.

Table 39.3: Reducing withdrawals when portfolio growth rate is less than 8.8%, initial withdrawal rate of 6%

Amount of Reduction	Probability of Depletion by age 95
No Reduction	70%
10% Reduction	68%
20% Reduction	60%
30% Reduction	59%
50% Reduction	51%

It is important to recognize that as long as regular withdrawals are above the sustainable withdrawal rate, reducing them in response to "bad" performance makes little difference in an equity portfolio. Once you are stuck in an adverse secular trend and your retirement portfolio starts losing money, it is generally irreversible. In such cases, the portfolio runs out of money, no matter what.

After the 2008 market crash, the Canadian government promptly reduced the minimum mandatory withdrawals from retirement accounts by 25%. So, if you were required to withdraw $10,000 during 2008, you were now allowed to withdraw only $7,500 without a tax penalty. What is the effect of this gesture for the retiree? Practically nothing.

Fixed Income:

Does it help to reduce withdrawals in a bond portfolio? For the aftcast of a bond portfolio return, we use the historical 6–month CD interest rate plus 0.5% for each year since 1900.

Let's assume you can reduce your withdrawals in any year following a bond portfolio return of 5.1% (historical average) or lower in the previous year. Table 39.4 demonstrates the probability of portfolio depletion by age 95. Table 39.5 shows the impact of reducing withdrawals for different initial withdrawal rates.

Table 39.4: Reducing withdrawals when portfolio growth rate is less than 5.1%, all fixed–income, initial withdrawal rate of 6%

Amount of Reduction	Probability of Depletion by age 95
No Reduction	96%
10% Reduction	94%
20% Reduction	88%
30% Reduction	84%
50% Reduction	41%

Table 39.5: Probability of depletion by 30th year of retirement, 100% fixed income portfolio, withdrawals reduced during years if previous year 's growth rate is less than 5.1%

Initial Withdrawal Rate	No Reduction	10% Reduction	20% Reduction	30% Reduction
	Probability of depletion by year 30			
4%	21%	19%	19%	13%
6%	96%	94%	88%	84%
8%	100%	100%	100%	98%
10%	100%	100%	100%	100%

Inflation Indexed Bonds:

Does reducing withdrawals help in a portfolio of inflation–indexed bonds? For the aftcast of an inflation–indexed bond portfolio return, we use the historical inflation rate plus 1% for each year since 1900.

Let's assume that you can reduce your withdrawals in any year if in the previous year the CPI was higher than the historical average of 3.2%. Table 39.6 demonstrates the probability of portfolio depletion by age 95. Table 39.7 shows the impact of reducing withdrawals for different initial withdrawal rates.

Table 39.6: Reducing withdrawals in any year if in the previous year the CPI exceeds 3.2%, 100% inflation indexed bond portfolio with real interest rate of 1.5%, initial withdrawal rate of 6%

Amount of Reduction	Probability of Depletion by age 95
No Reduction	100%
10% Reduction	100%
20% Reduction	100%
30% Reduction	100%
50% Reduction	100%

Table 39.7: Probability of depletion by the 30th year of retirement, reducing withdrawals in any year if in the previous year the CPI exceeds 3.2%, 100% inflation indexed bond portfolio with real interest rate of 1.0%

Initial Withdrawal Rate	No Reduction	10% Reduction	20% Reduction	30% Reduction
	Probability of depletion by year 30			
3%	0%	0%	0%	0%
4%	63%	0%	0%	0%
6%	100%	100%	100%	100%
8%	100%	100%	100%	100%
10%	100%	100%	100%	100%

We observe that there is no benefit in following a reduced withdrawal strategy for inflation–indexed bond portfolios, just as we observed with equities and conventional bonds, unless withdrawals are already very close to the sustainable rate.

Example 39.1

Don, 65, is just retiring. He has $1,000,000 savings for his retirement. He needs in current dollars $50,000 annually. He wants his plan to last until age 95.

His asset mix is 50% equity and 50% fixed income. His equities grow the same as the S&P500 index, plus 2% for dividends, less 2% management fees for a net alpha of 0%. His fixed income yields the same as historical 6-month CD rate plus 0.5%.

The aftcast since 1900 indicates that the probability of running out of money by 95 is 68%, which is too high. Here is the aftcast of portfolio assets:

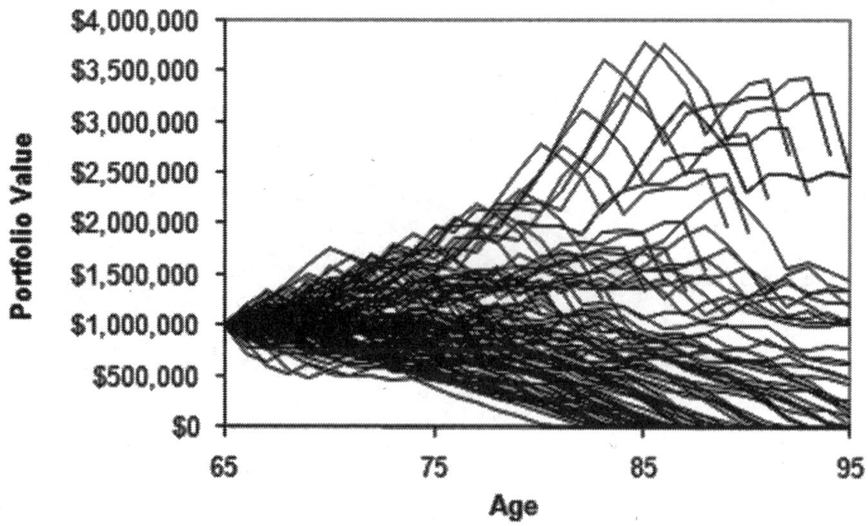

Here is the aftcast depicting the probability of receiving the required income:

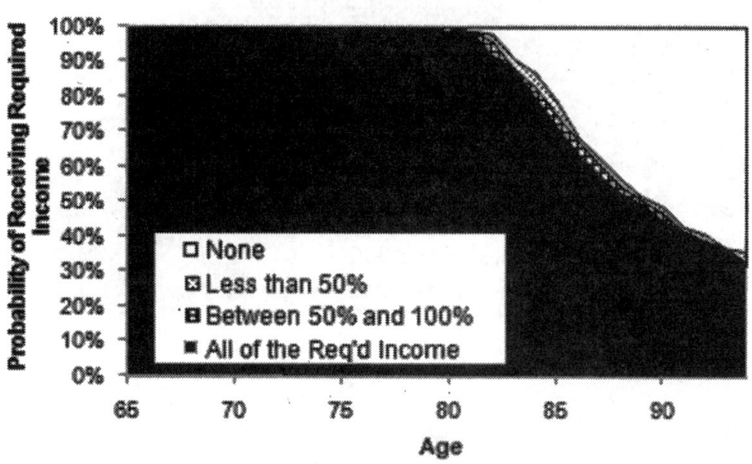

Don decides to reduce his withdrawals by 30% in any year following a "bad year". He defines a "bad year" when his portfolio grows by less than 3%.

How does this affect his retirement income? How does it affect his portfolio assets?

By following this strategy, his probability of depletion by age 95 decreased from 68% to 58%, not a significant improvement. For that little improvement, Don had a pay cut about 35% of the time.

The chart below depicts the aftcast of the portfolio value:

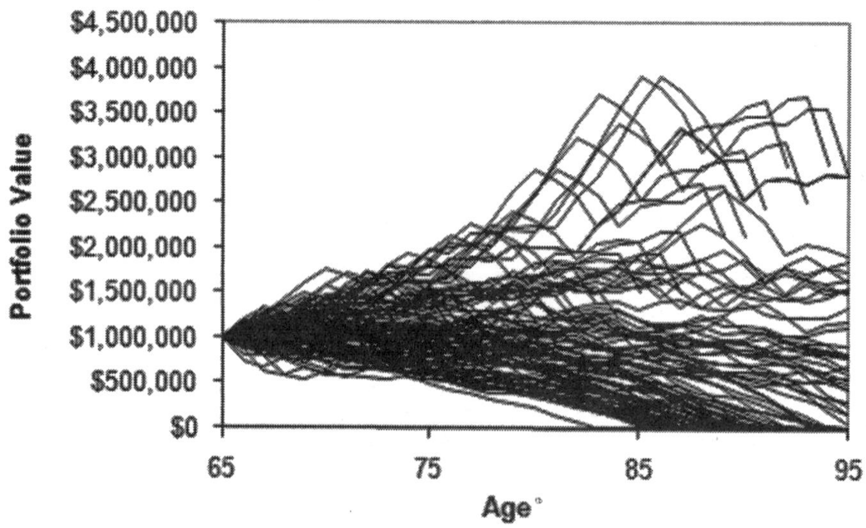

Here is the aftcast depicting the probability of receiving the required income:

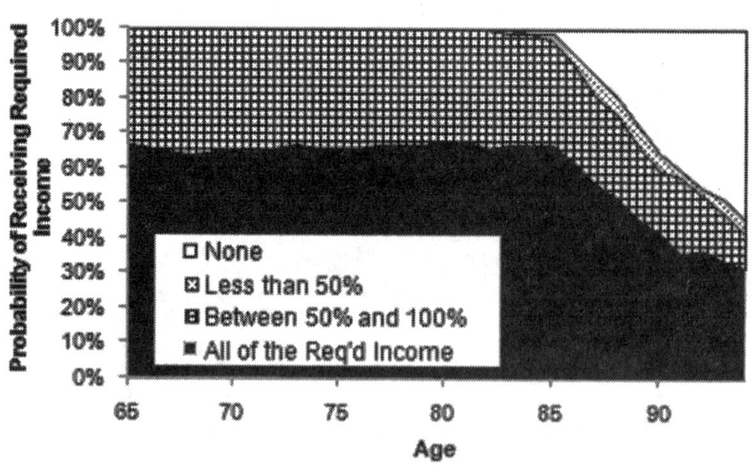

Reduction after Withdrawals Become Excessive:

> "If I reduce my withdrawals by 30% as soon as my withdrawals exceed 8% of the portfolio value, can I then have a lifelong income?"

My answer is "If your withdrawals are higher than sustainable to start with, then waiting until they are even more excessive before reducing them will not help at all. If you want the portfolio to last during your retirement, your periodic withdrawals must be below sustainable, starting from the first day of your retirement."

We discussed earlier the irreversible effects of an excessive withdrawals rate. I don't want to waste your time, showing you tables and charts. I will just give you an example.

Example 39.2

Continuing with Example 39.1, Don decides to follow a different withdrawal reduction strategy.

He decides to reduce his withdrawals by 25% for the rest of his life once his withdrawals reach 8% of the current portfolio value.

How does this affect his retirement income? How does it affect his portfolio assets?

By following this strategy, his probability of depletion by age 95 decreased from 68% to 43%, not enough to declare victory. The chart below depicts the aftcast of Don's portfolio assets.

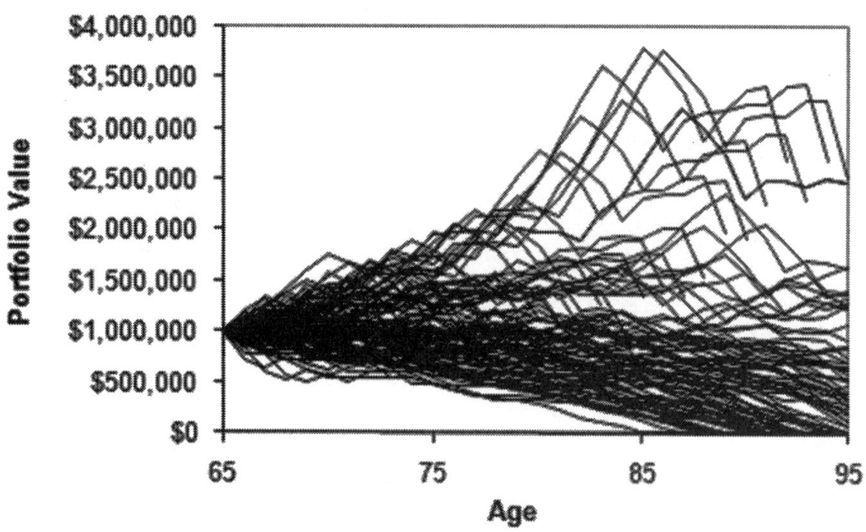

Here is the aftcast depicting the probability of receiving the required income:

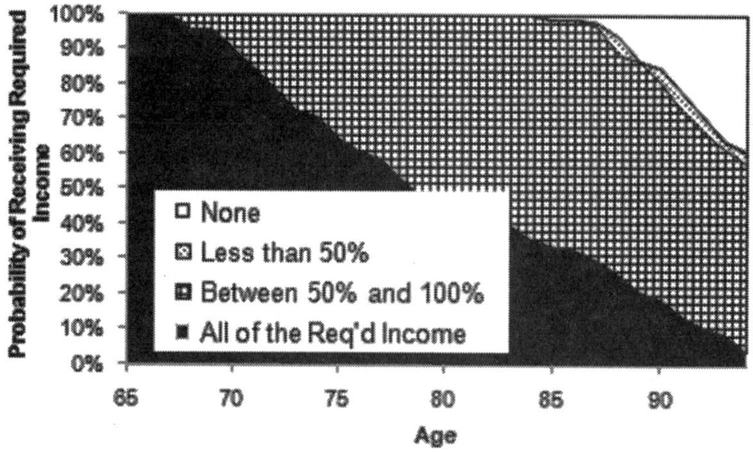

The aftcast of both assets and income indicates that this income reduction strategy fails miserably. That is because there is no significant gain in the outcome.

Limiting Withdrawals to Portfolio's Growth:

> "If I take out no more than the growth of the portfolio, can I then have lifelong income?"

My answer is, "You will definitely have a lifelong income. The only problem is, your income may be much less than you think most of the time!"

The income level varies greatly from year to year. Some researchers take this strategy, run some simulations and then conclude that it is a viable strategy. However, because they are not the ones sitting at the kitchen table across from the client, they cannot comprehend the serious consequences of a loss of real income. Clients want consistent income.

Let's continue with Don's example.

Example 39.3

Continuing with Example 39.1, Don decides to follow a different withdrawal reduction strategy.

He decides to withdraw $50,000 annually, but not exceeding the growth of his portfolio. If his portfolio has a negative year, he will take no withdrawals in the following year. If his portfolio grows by $32,000, he will take $32,000 in the following year. If his portfolio grows by $132,000, he will take up to $50,000 in the following year, indexed to inflation.

How does this affect his retirement income? How does it affect his portfolio assets?

By following this strategy, his portfolio never depletes. The chart below depicts the aftcast of Don's portfolio assets.

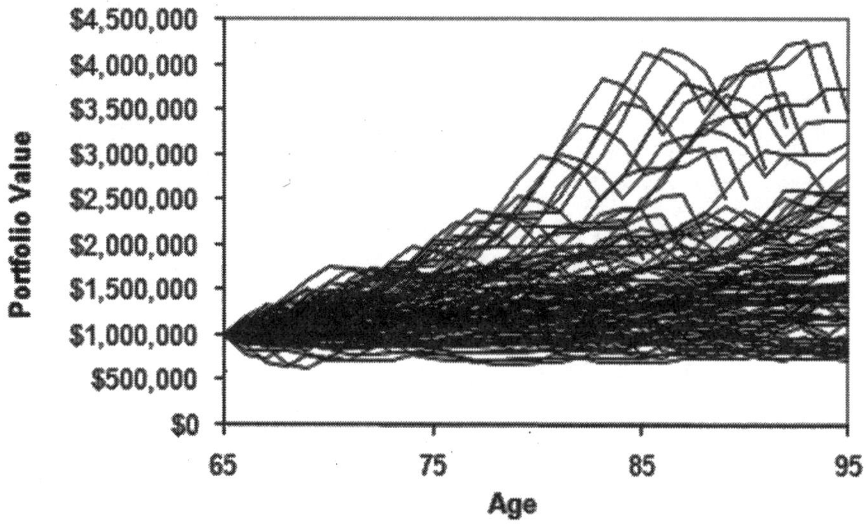

Here is the aftcast depicting the probability of receiving the required income:

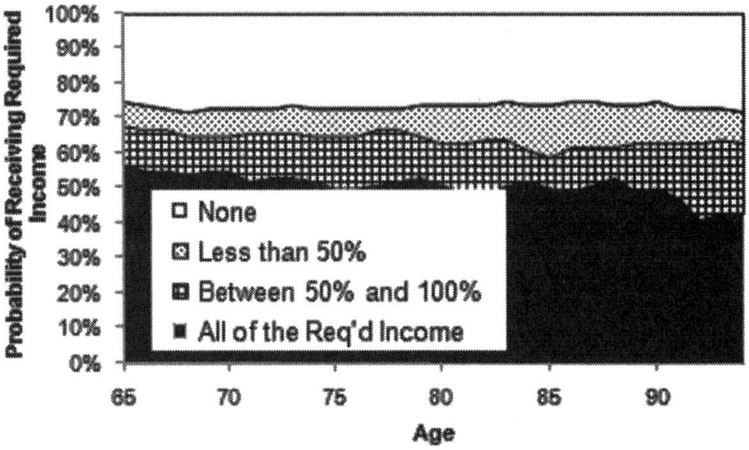

Don had full income about 50% of the time. About 30% of the time, he had no income. Just for the sake of preserving assets, his cash flow was seriously impeded.

The aftcast indicates that this income reduction strategy also fails miserably.

In the previous chapter, we discussed asset dedication. Here we see it again: if the required withdrawal rate exceeds the sustainable rate, the growth of assets will not be sufficient to top off the money bucket in the asset dedication strategy.

Limiting Withdrawals to a Percentage of the Portfolio Value:

> "If I take out no more than 10% of the current portfolio value, can I then have a lifelong income?"

My answer is, "You will have a lifelong income for sure. As a matter of fact, you can take 90% of your portfolio each year and you will still have a lifelong income. The only problem is, your income will diminish significantly as time goes on!"

While the portfolio never depletes, the income level will generally drop each year. Let's continue with Don's example.

Example 39.4

Continuing with Example 39.1, Don decides to follow a different withdrawal reduction strategy.

He decides to withdraw $50,000 annually in current dollars, but not exceeding 8% of his portfolio value in the preceding year.

How does this affect his retirement income? How does it affect his portfolio assets?

By following this strategy, his portfolio never depletes. The chart below depicts the aftcast of Don's portfolio assets.

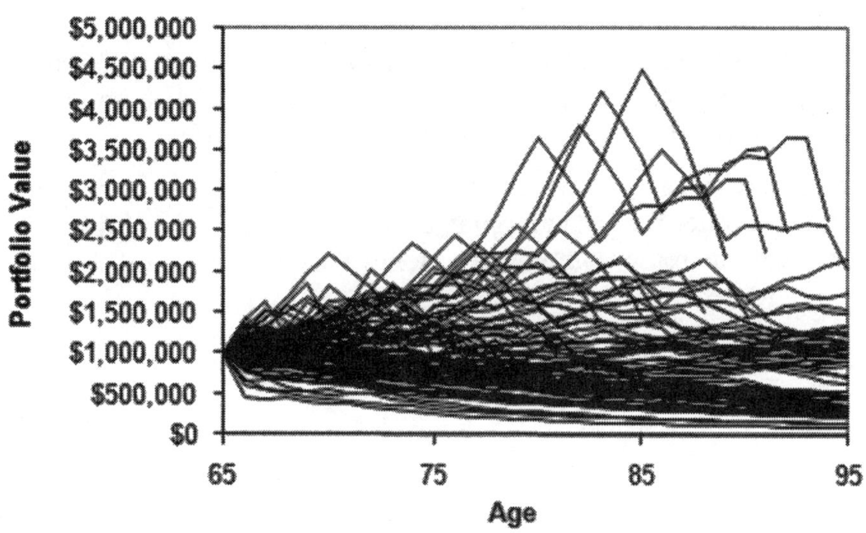

Here is the aftcast depicting the probability of receiving the required income:

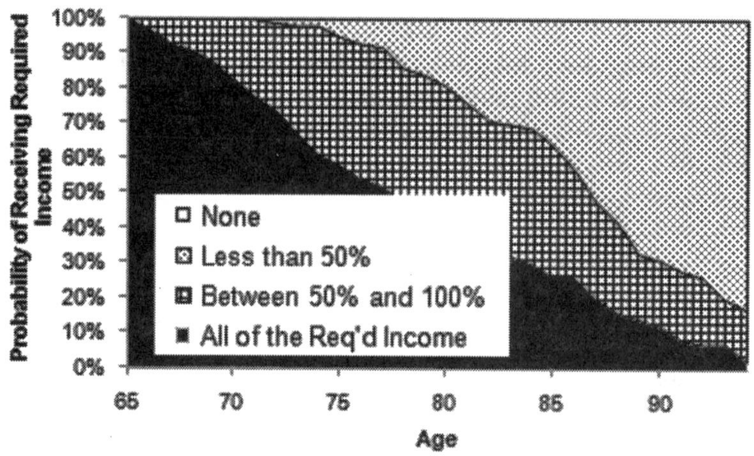

After the first year, the probability of receiving the full income decreased steadily from 100% at age 65 to 2% at age 95.

The aftcast indicates that this income reduction strategy does not work.

Conclusion:

History shows that strategies that are based on the reduction of withdrawals driven by events, do not work. If you want your portfolio to last for life, then you need to maintain your withdrawals below the sustainable rate throughout your life.

If you count on luck and it later turns out that you are not lucky, it is usually too late. I suggest doing it the other way around; plan on being unlucky and if it turns out that you are lucky, only then increase withdrawals. Believe me; it works much more safely that way.

Chapter 40

Budgeting for Retirement

In my early years in retirement planning, budgeting for retirement was one of the most time–consuming events. I would sit down with both spouses, go over their expenses and try to figure out how much income they would need in their retirement years.

What happened time after time is that somewhere between "donations" and "recreational expenses", one spouse disagreed with the other about how much he or she spends. Suddenly, those golf trips or the container full of expensive shoes in the basement became the only reason for their retirement blues. I was turning into a perfect catalyst for starting some of the meanest fights between two seemingly loving partners.

I do not like fights, especially between spouses. Therefore, I stopped doing any budgeting for clients. If someone calls me for retirement advice, I mail my "Retirement Cash Flow Worksheet and Budget"(see Appendix B). I ask them to fill out their budget in their own privacy and bring it to our first meeting. I make sure to tell them that it is very important that they fill it out.

Now, my job is a lot easier. Occasionally, if a client comes in without filling out the form, then I cancel the meeting. There is no point in trying to make a retirement plan if the client is unwilling, unable or too lazy to figure out his/her basic expenses.

The first step is to add up your expenses at the start of your retirement. Go to Appendix B and fill out your expenses for each line item. If a line item is an essential expense, such as property tax, then place a check mark in the box to the right of the line item. Add up all *required expenses* and then add up all *essential expenses*. Calculate out your average tax rate and add this figure to the total.

Now you have the current value of your expenses. If you are not already retired, you need to calculate the future value of your current expenses. Use the inflation multiplier table, Table 40.1. You will need to assume an inflation rate for the years until your retirement starts. Calculate the future value of your expenses by multiplying the current value of expenses with the inflation multiplier from Table 40.1.

Table 40.1: Inflation multiplier

Number of Years until Retirement	Assumed Inflation 2%	Assumed Inflation 3%	Assumed Inflation 4%	Assumed Inflation 5%
		Inflation Multiplier:		
0	1.00	1.00	1.00	1.00
2	1.04	1.06	1.08	1.10
4	1.08	1.13	1.17	1.22
6	1.13	1.19	1.27	1.34
8	1.17	1.27	1.37	1.48
10	1.22	1.34	1.48	1.63
15	1.35	1.56	1.80	2.08
20	1.49	1.81	2.19	2.65

Example 40.1

Jim, 55, is planning to retire at age 65. He calculates the current value of his total required expenses as $58,000. He calculates the current value of his essential expenses as $50,000. Assuming a 3% inflation rate going forward, what is the future value of his expenses at retirement?

Jim has ten years until retirement. Under the 3% inflation column, the inflation factor is 1.34.

Therefore, the future value of his total required expenses is $78,000 calculated as $58,000 multiplied by 1.34 (nearest thousand dollars). The future value of his essential expenses is $67,000 calculated as $50,000 multiplied by 1.34. By the time Jim retires at age 65, he will need $67,000 in then current dollars to meet his essential retirement lifestyle needs.

Once you have calculated the future value of all expenses, the next step is to make a list of all income after retirement from all sources in future dollars. Include all government and company pensions, rental income, royalty income, existing annuities and income from other sources. Do not include any income from your savings.

Now, calculate your shortfall, the difference between the total projected income at retirement and your total expenses in future dollars.

If your projected income is higher than your projected expenses, then you have a surplus. That is good news. You do not really need retirement planning (other than planning for contingencies), but you likely need tax planning and estate planning.

If your projected income is lower than your projected required expenses, then you have a shortfall. Your retirement savings must cover this shortfall.

> Example 40.2
>
> Continuing with example 40.1, Jim calculates that at age 65, his income from all sources other than his retirement savings will be $35,000.
>
> What is his shortfall?
>
> - Based on total required expenses of $78,000, his shortfall is $43,000 calculated as $78,000 minus $35,000.
> - Based on total essential expenses of $67,000, his shortfall is $32,000 calculated as $67,000 minus $35,000.

The last step is to check how much savings you need to finance the shortfall during your retirement. We use Table 17.10, which depicts the minimum portfolio size required at the optimum asset mix for a $10,000 income requirement.

> Example 40.3
>
> Continuing with example 40.2, Jim wants to know the portfolio amount that he needs at age 65 to finance his retirement for 30 years, from age 65 until age 95.
>
> How much savings does he need?
>
> From Table 17.10, we read that he needs savings of $263,200 for each $10,000 annual income.
>
> - Based on total required expenses, his shortfall is $43,000. He needs to have $1,132,000 (nearest thousand dollars) by the time he reaches age 65 calculated as $263,200 times $43,000 divided by $10,000.
> - Based on total essential expenses, his shortfall is $32,000. He needs to have $842,000 (nearest thousand dollars) by the time he reaches age 65 calculated as $263,200 times $32,000 divided by $10,000.

You might want to calculate how much savings you need to purchase a life annuity to provide you with lifelong income, instead of financing it through an investment portfolio. For that, we use Table 33.1, which depicts the cost of a single premium life annuity for a $10,000 income requirement.

> Example 40.4
>
> Continuing with example 40.3, Jim wants to know how much money he would need to buy a single premium immediate life annuity at age 65. The annuity payments are indexed to CPI.
>
> How much savings does he need?
>
> From Table 33.1, we read that he needs savings of $187,812 for a single life annuity with minimum 15-year guarantee period, for each $10,000 annual income.
>
> - Based on total required expenses, his shortfall is $43,000. He needs to have $808,000 (nearest thousand dollars) by the time he reaches age 65 calculated as $187,812 times $43,000 divided by $10,000.
> - Based on total essential expenses, his shortfall is $32,000. He needs to have $601,000 (nearest thousand dollars) by the time he reaches age 65 calculated as $187,812 times $32,000 divided by $10,000.

Conclusion:

There are four steps for calculating the savings required at the time of retirement:

1. Estimate all your expenses (required and essential) in future dollars
2. Estimate your annual income from all sources during retirement, excepting the income from your retirement savings, in future dollars
3. Calculate the shortfall, if any, that needs to be provided by the retirement savings
4. Calculate how much savings you need in your portfolio to finance this shortfall. If do not have sufficient savings in a portfolio, then consider a life annuity to finance your retirement.

Keep in mind that Table 17.10 is based on a 10% probability of portfolio depletion by age 95. Therefore, the portfolio values (required and essential) that we calculated using figures from Table 17.10 are the absolute minimum portfolio savings required at the time of retirement. If you choose the life annuity route, make sure to use actual quotes, as the figures in Table 33.1 are for general guidance only.

Chapter 41

The Zone Strategy

Everything you have read in this book so far guides you in one direction: ignore the popular wisdom and hype. Design your own "personal" pension for your retirement. Unless you create your own pension, you are exposed to the risk of running out of money during your retirement.

After calculating how much income you need from your retirement savings, you need to think about how to create that income for life. It is often a difficult decision and it must be made *before* you commence your retirement. Some people leave that decision until after retirement and then only when significant market events shock them. *You* have to be in control of your decisions, not the markets. Once you prepare your retirement plan, and how to allocate to the various income classes, do not allow market events to alter them.

You need to ask yourself if you have the capacity for financing your retirement. Your capacity to retire has two components:

1. The emotional capacity
2. The financial capacity

In the context of retirement finances, emotional capacity refers to how you react to market events. Choices about asset and income allocation, investment types, annuities and many other decisions depend on this emotional capacity. It is a very important aspect of planning.

Financial capacity refers to your ability to finance your retirement for life. If you do not have sufficient financial capacity, no amount of emotional capacity will improve the outcome. You can be as aggressive as you want with your investments, you might be able to take any market downturn in stride, and you might have been very successful in your own business decisions. But when we talk about retirement planning, emotional capacity always plays second fiddle to financial capacity.

Much of the advice from the financial industry places retirees at great risk. That is because they try to convince you that if you are brave enough to weather market volatility, you will be OK in the long term. Throughout this book, I have demonstrated that it is not so. Your courage to weather volatility has nothing to do with the ill effects of the time value of fluctuations.

Before dreaming about creating a scholarship in your name or donating a new cancer wing to your local hospital, before talking about the wisdom of asset allocation, before you can talk about investing large cap or small cap, before you can talk about investing in Canada or in China, you must first quantify your financial capacity. It is the critical path in retirement planning.

Your financial capacity dictates
how much emotional capacity you need during retirement.

Without adequate financial capacity,
your emotional capacity has no meaning.

Therefore, your first and foremost task is to evaluate your financial capacity. The zone strategy is a simple system that will help you determine it precisely. It is about finding *realistic and reliable* strategies for lifelong income. It is not about plugging some average numbers into a retirement calculator and saying, "On average, Mr. Client, you should be OK". It is not about running a Monte Carlo simulator a million times during your lunch break and then saying, "According to our sophisticated mathematical models, Mr. Client, you should be OK". The averages and simulators just don't cut it.

You have several choices as to where to generate your retirement income: You can withdraw income from an investment portfolio. You can buy one or more of the different types of annuities with a lifelong guaranteed pay. What works for one person might be disastrous for the other. The zone strategy helps you define and create your own personal pension through appropriate income allocation decisions.

How do you decide how much to allocate and to which income class? How do you create your own personal pension? Here is what the zone strategy can do for you:

For retirees and advisors:

- It gives a precise guideline about when risk must be exported to create a lifelong income.
- It tells you exactly how much risk to export.
- It indicates whether you have an accumulation or decumulation portfolio during retirement. This can help you accomplish your estate plan with less hype and more truth.

For advisors:

- In your initial meetings, the zone strategy guides you exactly to which emotion to focus on: hope or fear.
- It helps filter out potential problem situations with pinpoint accuracy.
- It helps you save a tremendous amount of time.

Information Required for the Zone Strategy:

For the zone strategy, you need three pieces of information:

1. The first question is directed to yourself: "How much income do I want to withdraw from my retirement savings?"

   We call this the *withdrawal rate,* WR for short. This is the shortfall we calculated in Chapter 40.

2. The second question is directed to your portfolio: "Mr. Portfolio, how much income can you pay me for the rest of my life?"

   This is the *sustainable withdrawal rate*, SWR for short.

3. The third question is directed to the insurance company: "Mr. Insurance Company, if I were to give you all my retirement assets, how much would you pay me for the rest of my life?"

   This is the *annuity rate*, AR for short. For the sake of simplicity, we will use figures from Table 33.1 for a full–CPI–indexed annuity. Keep in mind that annuity rates change daily. You need to ask for a quote from an insurance company.

Once you have the WR, SWR and the AR, you can define the zones.

Defining the Zones:

Let's assume that you have $1 million in your retirement savings and you are planning for 30 years of withdrawals. The SWR is $38,000 in the first year (Table 17.9), indexed to inflation annually. The annuity quote indicates that the insurance company would pay $53,000 in the first year, indexed to inflation annually[82].

The annuity rate is always higher than the sustainable withdrawal rate. That is because with an annuity, the market and longevity risks are pooled. When the risk is pooled, the same amount of capital can supply a larger payout.

There are three zones: The red, green and gray zone. Your financial capacity is indicated in one of these zones. Figure 41.1 depicts these zones graphically.

[82] Here, we use numbers from Table 33.1 for simplicity and traceability. The annuity pays $10,000 in the first year for a premium of $187,812 (single male, age 65, full annual CPI indexation, 15–year minimum guarantee period). Therefore, a $1 million premium pays in the first year $53,000, calculated as $10,000 / $187,812 X $1,000,000 (nearest one thousand dollars)

Figure 41.1: The red, green and gray zones

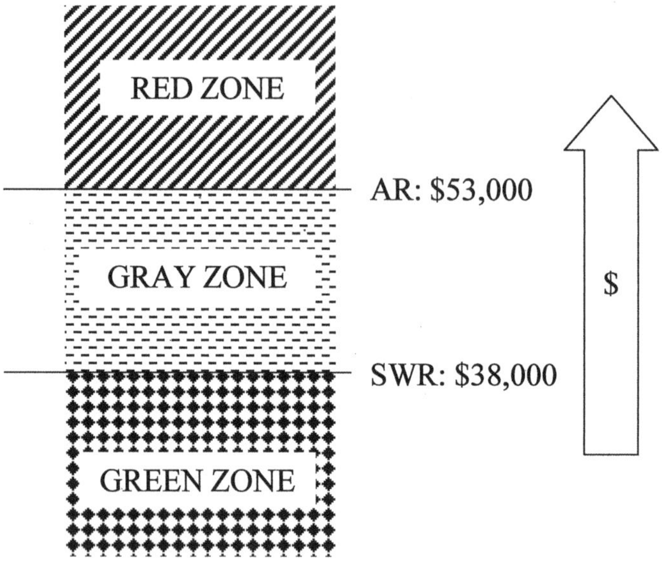

Your entire retirement income allocation strategy depends on which zone you are in. Here is how you can establish your zone:

1. If your withdrawal rate (WR) is lower than the sustainable withdrawal rate (SWR), then you are in the *green* zone. You have *abundant* savings.
2. If your withdrawal rate is greater than the annuity rate (AR), then you are in the *red* zone. You have *insufficient* savings.
3. If your withdrawal rate is between SWR and AR, then you are in the *gray* zone. You have *sufficient* savings.

Accumulation or Decumulation:

Some people use the term "decumulation stage" to describe the "distribution stage". This is incorrect. Decumulation refers to asset value, distribution refers to cash outflow. Just because you take money out of a portfolio does not necessarily mean its value will decline. You could be taking out money while the portfolio value increases.

The zone strategy tells you exactly whether your portfolio will be accumulating or decumulating during the distribution stage.

- If you are in the green zone, your portfolio will be accumulating. If you are lucky, it will accumulate at a steeper rate, otherwise it will accumulate at a slower rate.
- If you are in the red zone, your portfolio will be decumulating. If you are lucky, it will last a little longer, otherwise it will deplete sooner.
- If you are in the gray zone, your portfolio may be accumulating or decumulating, depending on your luck.

Figure 41.2: Zones of accumulation and decumulation in distribution portfolios

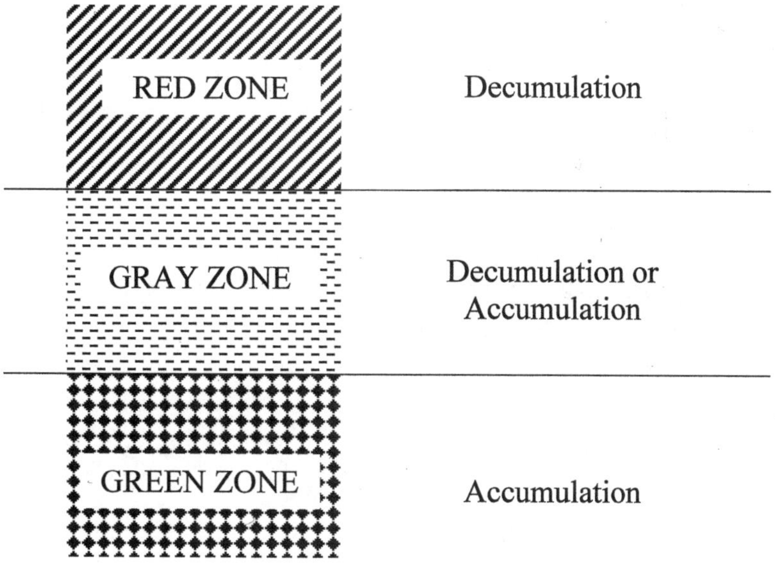

Hope or Fear:

When we market our strategies, we rely on two basic human emotions: hope and fear. Generally, advisors from the investment background downplay market calamities. They want you to look at long-term charts and sell you hope.

On the other hand, those from an insurance background generally market their products by creating a fear of running out of money during your retirement years.

If you are an advisor, then you know how important it is to focus on the correct emotion. If you try to sell fear to someone who needs $100,000/year from his $20 million portfolio, he will not even listen to you – rightfully so. You can (and should) sell only hope to this person, not fear.

On the other hand, if you try to sell hope to someone who needs $100,000/year from his $1 million portfolio, then you might be setting up the biggest disappointment for this client and the largest liability for your practice. You should sell only fear to this person, and not hope.

The zone strategy tells you exactly which emotion to sell: If your client is in the green zone, then sell hope. Otherwise, sell fear.

Figure 41.3: Zones of hope and fear in distribution portfolios

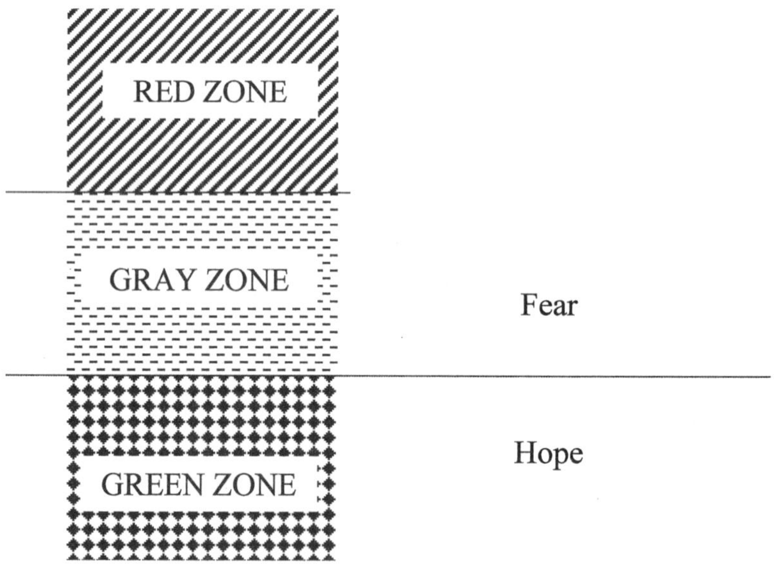

Export or Retain the Risk:

There are three financial risks of retirement: longevity risk, market risk, and inflation risk. When you buy a life annuity with payments indexed to CPI, you are in effect exporting these risks to the insurance company. Keep in mind that the insurance company is a for–profit organization; transferring risk to them costs you money. For example, if you are buying a life annuity, you have to part with your capital permanently.

By definition, if you are in the green zone, then your portfolio has sufficient reserves to cover the longevity, market and inflation risks. For you, the **volatility of returns** is the deciding factor, which can be handled with proper asset allocation and diversification. You do not need to export these risks to an insurance company. Only if you want to feel extra safe, you can export risks partially or fully, and you will still have money left to invest.

However, in the gray and red zones you have no choice. Your investment portfolio does not have sufficient reserves to cover longevity, market and inflation risks. For you, the **sequence of returns** is the deciding factor and that cannot be fixed within the investment portfolio. In the gray zone, you need to allot *part* of your assets to annuities. In the red zone, your *entire* assets are used to purchase annuities.

Figure 41.4: Zones of exporting or retaining financial risks of retirement

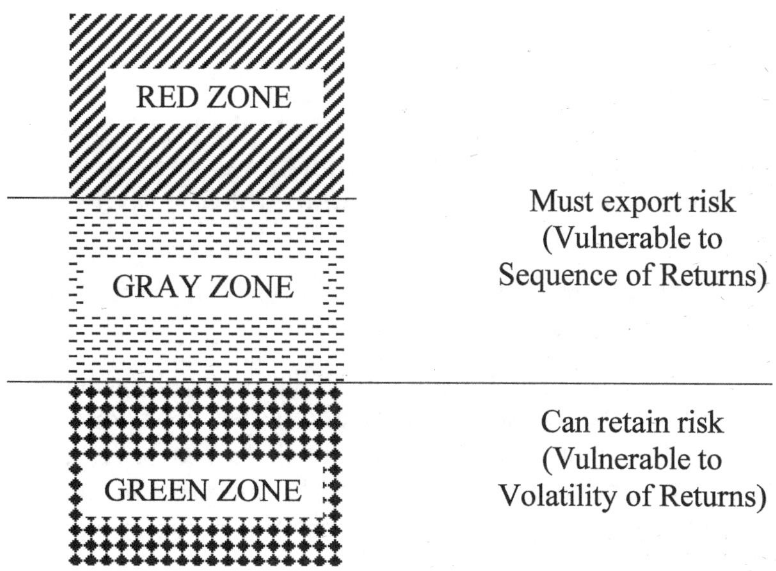

Calculating Your Zone:

Now that you know the basics of the zone strategy, Figure 41.5 gives you a more detailed set of numbers for the zone borders.

Figure 41.5: Adequacy of retirement savings for each dollar of income at the beginning of retirement

❷ Annuity Rates (AR):

	Age: 55	Age: 65	Age: 75
Male	4.0%	5.3%	7.3%
Female	3.7%	4.8%	6.8%
Joint	3.4%	4.3%	6.0%

❶ Sustainable Withdrawal Rates (SWR):

	Age: 55	Age: 65	Age: 75
U.S.A.	3.0%	3.7%	4.8%
Canada	3.0%	3.7%	5.2%
Japan	3.0%	3.7%	5.0%
UK	2.6%	3.2%	4.4%
Australia	2.8%	3.5%	5.1%

❶ SWR: The numbers on the small table pointing to the border between the green zone and the gray zone indicate the sustainable withdrawal rate –in percentage– from an investment portfolio[83]. It is based on a time horizon that spans from the age indicated until age 95.

Multiply the SWR percentage from the table by your total retirement assets. This gives you the SWR in dollar amount.

If your withdrawal rate is greater than the dollar amount of SWR: It makes little difference what asset allocation you use, how diversified your portfolio is, what income strategy you prefer, how many years of cash buckets you have, whether you have a $10,000 retirement account or are running a $10 billion pension fund, there is only one thing to do: **You must export the risk**. Your portfolio does not cover the time value of fluctuations.

[83] The SWR is based on 10% probability of depletion by the age of death, i.e. 90% survival rate. Asset mix: 40% equity, 60% fixed income. Equity: index return, S&P500 for USA, SP/TSX for Canada, Nikkei225 for Japan, FTSE AllShr for UK and ASX AllOrd for Australia. Fixed Income: historical 6–month CD yields plus 0.5%. These figures are slightly different than those in Chapter 17, Sustainable Withdrawal Rate; because I am using simpler portfolios here (no inflation indexed bonds in the mix, annual rebalancing).

If your withdrawal rate is lower than the SWR: You are in the green zone and you have abundant savings. Your portfolio covers the time value of fluctuations.

❷ AR: The numbers on the small table pointing to the border between the red zone and the gray zone indicate the annuity rate for a CPI– indexed life annuity[84].

Multiply the AR percentage from the table by your total retirement savings. This gives you the AR in dollars.

If your withdrawal rate is greater than the dollar amount of the AR: Payments from a life annuity will not be sufficient to sustain your financial needs during your retirement. You will have to change your retirement plans. You cannot have the income you want for life without either delaying your retirement, or cutting back your expenses, or supplementing your income from other sources (part–time work or your own business) during your retirement. You are in the red zone and you have insufficient savings.

If your withdrawal rate is between AR and SWR: You are in the gray zone. You have sufficient savings provided that you export risk.

Keep in mind that these numbers are based on current annuity rates at the time of writing. The annuity rates vary every day. If you want more accuracy, then you need to use fresh annuity quotes for your analysis.

Example 41.1

Two single men (Keith, 60, and Phil, 65), a single woman (Jane, 70), and a couple (Rick and Susan, each 65), all recently retired, were sitting around a table discussing their retirement at the local coffee shop.

Keith says he needs $34,000 of income annually from his retirement savings. His portfolio contains mostly US investments. He has $926,000 in his portfolio.

Phil says he needs only $16,000 of income annually from his retirement savings. His portfolio contains mostly Canadian investments. He has $484,000 in his portfolio.

Jane says she needs $24,000 of income annually from her retirement savings. Her portfolio contains mostly US investments. She has $385,000 in her portfolio.

Rick and Susan say they need $70,000 of income annually from their retirement savings. Their portfolio contains mostly US investments. They have $4 million of investable assets that they can use for retirement.

Calculate whether each party has adequate savings, if they can reasonably expect to leave any money to their children, if they should export or retain risk and if they should worry about lifelong income.

[84] Rates based on Standard Life annuity quotes, June 12, 2009, full CPI indexation at the anniversary of purchase. Minimum guarantee period is 10 years. For the joint annuity, both spouses are at the same age and there is no reduction of payments when the first spouse dies.

Keith: age 60, WR: $34,000, Assets: $926,000

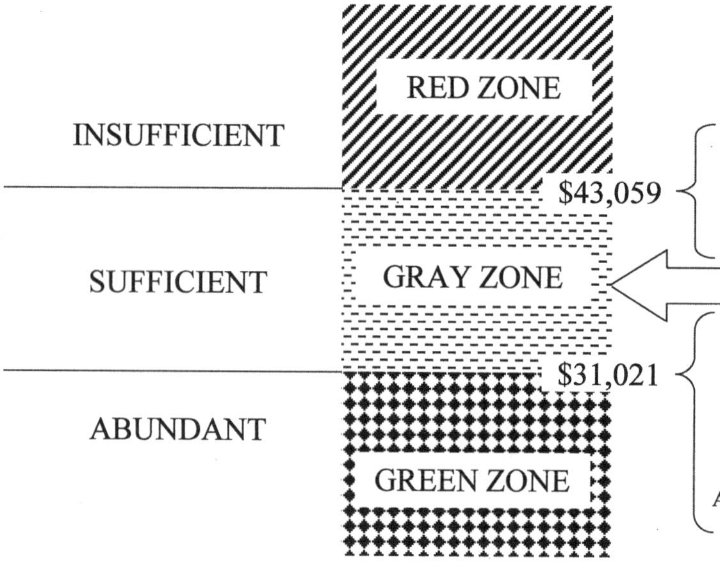

Annuity Rates (AR):

	Age: 55	Age: 65	Age: 75
Male	4.0%	5.3%	7.3%
Female	3.7%	4.8%	6.8%
Joint	3.4%	4.3%	6.0%

Sustainable Withdrawal Rates (SWR):

	Age: 55	Age: 65	Age: 75
U.S.A.	3.0%	3.7%	4.8%
Canada	3.0%	3.7%	5.2%
Japan	3.0%	3.7%	5.0%
UK	2.6%	3.2%	4.4%
Australia	2.8%	3.5%	5.1%

Keith is 60 years of age. On the table we have only ages 55 and 65. So, we interpolate the SWR and AR for age 60.

AR is calculated as 4.65%, halfway between 4.0% and 5.3%. In dollars, AR is $43,059, calculated as 4.65% of $926,000.

SWR is calculated as 3.35%, halfway between 3.0% and 3.7%. In dollars, SWR is $31,021, calculated as 3.35% of $926,000.

Keith's WR ($34,000) is between his AR ($43,059) and SWR ($31,021); therefore he is in the gray zone.

He must export his risk by buying some life annuity. If he is lucky, there will be money left to children, but this is far from certain. He should worry about lifelong income and he must review his plan each year or more often, if there is a significant change in his financial situation.

Phil: age 65, WR: $16,000, Assets: $484,000

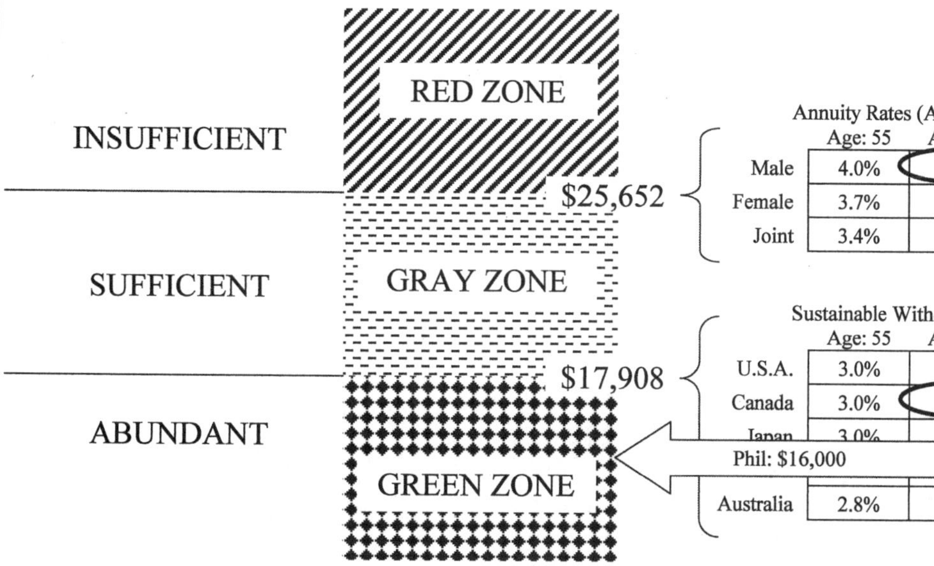

Annuity Rates (AR):

	Age: 55	Age: 65	Age: 75
Male	4.0%	5.3%	7.3%
Female	3.7%	4.8%	6.8%
Joint	3.4%	4.3%	6.0%

Sustainable Withdrawal Rates (SWR):

	Age: 55	Age: 65	Age: 75
U.S.A.	3.0%	3.7%	4.8%
Canada	3.0%	3.7%	5.2%
Japan	3.0%	3.7%	5.0%
[illegible]	[illegible]	3.2%	4.4%
Australia	2.8%	3.5%	5.1%

AR is 5.3%. In dollars, AR is $25,652, calculated as 5.3% of $484,000.

SWR is 3.7%. In dollars, SWR is $17,908, calculated as 3.7% of $484,000.

Phil's WR ($16,000) is lower than his SWR ($17,908); therefore he is in the green zone.

His investment portfolio is large enough to cover longevity, market and inflations risks. He does not need to buy a life annuity unless if he wishes to do so. Most likely, there will be money left to children. He should not worry about lifelong income He should review his plan at least annually, or whenever there are significant changes to his financial situation.

Jane: age 70, WR: $24,000, Assets: $385,000

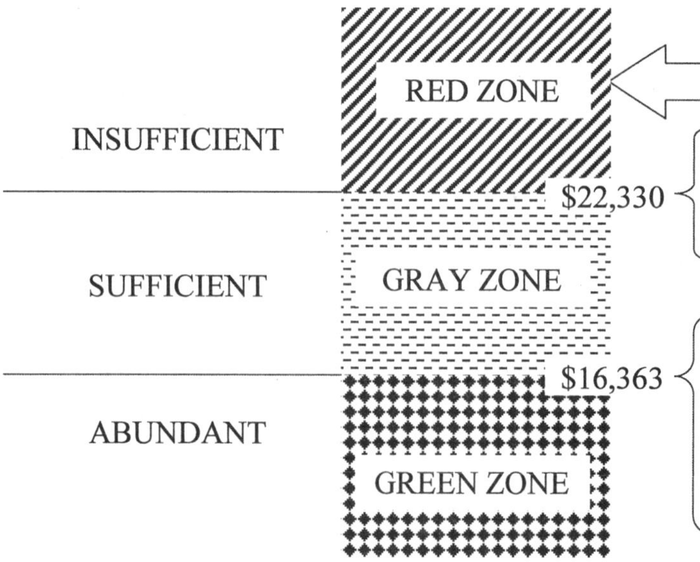

Annuity Rates (AR):

	Age: 55	Age: 65	Age: 75
Male	4.0%	5.3%	7.3%
Female	3.7%	4.8%	6.8%
Joint	3.4%	4.3%	6.0%

Sustainable Withdrawal Rates (SWR):

	Age: 55	Age: 65	Age: 75
U.S.A.	3.0%	3.7%	4.8%
Canada	3.0%	3.7%	5.2%
Japan	3.0%	3.7%	5.0%
UK	2.6%	3.2%	4.4%
Australia	2.8%	3.5%	5.1%

Jane is 70 years of age. On the table we have only ages 65 and 75. Therefore, we interpolate the SWR and AR for age 70.

AR is calculated as 5.8%, halfway between 4.8% and 6.8%. In dollars, AR is $22,330, calculated as 5.8% of $385,000.

SWR is calculated as 4.25%, halfway between 3.7% and 4.8%. In dollars, SWR is $16,363, calculated as 4.25% of $385,000.

Jane's WR ($24,000) is larger than her AR ($22,330); therefore she is in the red zone.

Her investment portfolio is too small to cover longevity, market and inflation risks. She must buy a life annuity. Even then, payments from the life annuity will not be sufficient to cover her income needs. She must cut back her expenses by 7%, calculated as ($24,000 - $22,330) / $24,000 x 100%.

There will be no money left for children. Once the life annuity is purchased, there is no need to review the plan each year; she just has to live within her means with the income from the annuity.

Rick and Susan: age 65, WR: $70,000, Assets: $4,000,000

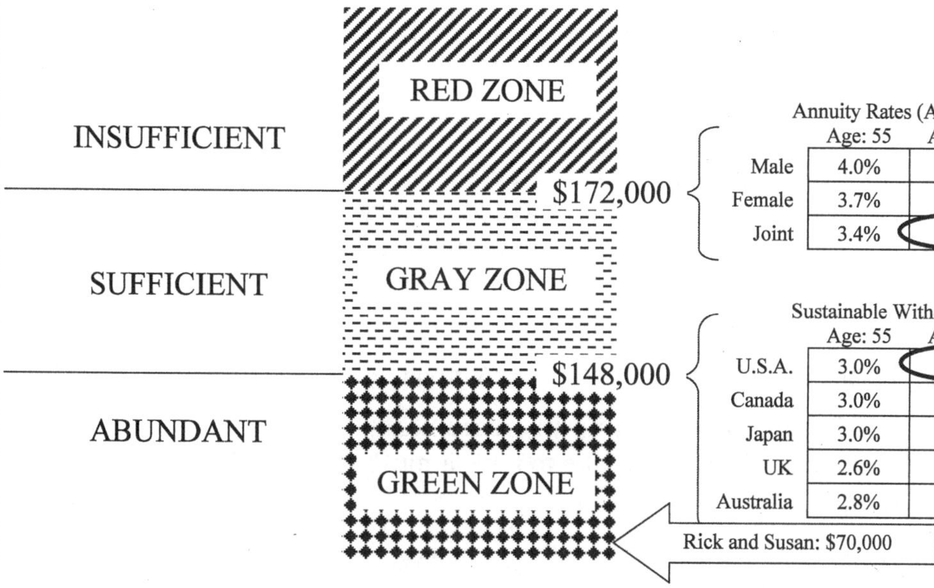

Annuity Rates (AR):

	Age: 55	Age: 65	Age: 75
Male	4.0%	5.3%	7.3%
Female	3.7%	4.8%	6.8%
Joint	3.4%	4.3%	6.0%

Sustainable Withdrawal Rates (SWR):

	Age: 55	Age: 65	Age: 75
U.S.A.	3.0%	3.7%	4.8%
Canada	3.0%	3.7%	5.2%
Japan	3.0%	3.7%	5.0%
UK	2.6%	3.2%	4.4%
Australia	2.8%	3.5%	5.1%

AR is 4.3%. In dollars, AR is $172,000, calculated as 4.3% of $4,000,000.

SWR is 3.7%. In dollars, SWR is $148,000, calculated as 3.7% of $4,000,000.

Rick and Susan's WR ($70,000) is much lower than their SWR ($148,000); therefore they are deep in the green zone.

Their investment portfolio is large enough to cover longevity, market and inflation risks. They do not need to buy life annuity. They should plan on leaving behind a large estate. They do not need to worry about lifelong income. An annual review of the plan is still recommended for investment, estate and tax planning purposes, or if there are very significant changes to their financial situation.

Calculating Your Zone – A Simpler Method:

The method of calculating your zone, the one I described above, involves calculating annuity rate and sustainable withdrawal rate percentages and then multiplying those by your assets. So, you have to do two calculations. For me, that is too much work. Here is a method that has only one calculation.

Picture this: A client comes in for a retirement plan. I am meeting him for the first time. After the introductions, we may have a small talk that goes something like this:

Client: "I'd like you to prepare my retirement plan".
JO: "Great, thank you for coming. I would be very happy to."
Client: "I am 65 years old. I would like to retire now."
JO: "I am all ears. Can I get a cup of coffee for you?"
Client: "Sure. Cream and sugar please."

I go and get the coffee. We continue with our conversation:

Client: "I have $1 million savings for my retirement"
JO: "That is great. Would you like to have a muffin with your coffee?"
Client: "O.K."

I go and get the muffin. We continue with our conversation:

JO: "How much do you want to take out from your savings each year?"
Client: "$100,000"
JO: "Thank you for coming to see me. I don't think I can help you. Have a wonderful day. Good bye!"

Excluding the time I spent for my two trips to the kitchen, the entire "discovery process" took about 15 seconds. Within that short period of time I was able to determine whether or not I could help him. I did only one calculation in my head to determine if this person was in the red zone, green zone or the gray zone. I could have wasted several hours going over his retirement dreams and inspirations. I did not. My entire loss was confined to one cup of coffee, one muffin and a few minutes of my time.

How do I determine the zone so easily? Divide the client's assets by his first year's withdrawal. We call this the client's asset multiplier (CAM). In the conversation above, the CAM is 10, calculated as $1 million (his retirement assets) divided by $100,000 (his required income).

Here are the rules for a 65–year old male: If his CAM is below 20, then he is in the red zone. It his CAM is above 27, he is in the green zone. If his CAM is between 20 and 27, then he is in the gray zone. It can't get simpler than that.

Figures 41.6 through 41.8 give you the zones for a male, for a female and for a couple.

Figure 41.6: Adequacy of retirement savings using the asset multiplier for a male

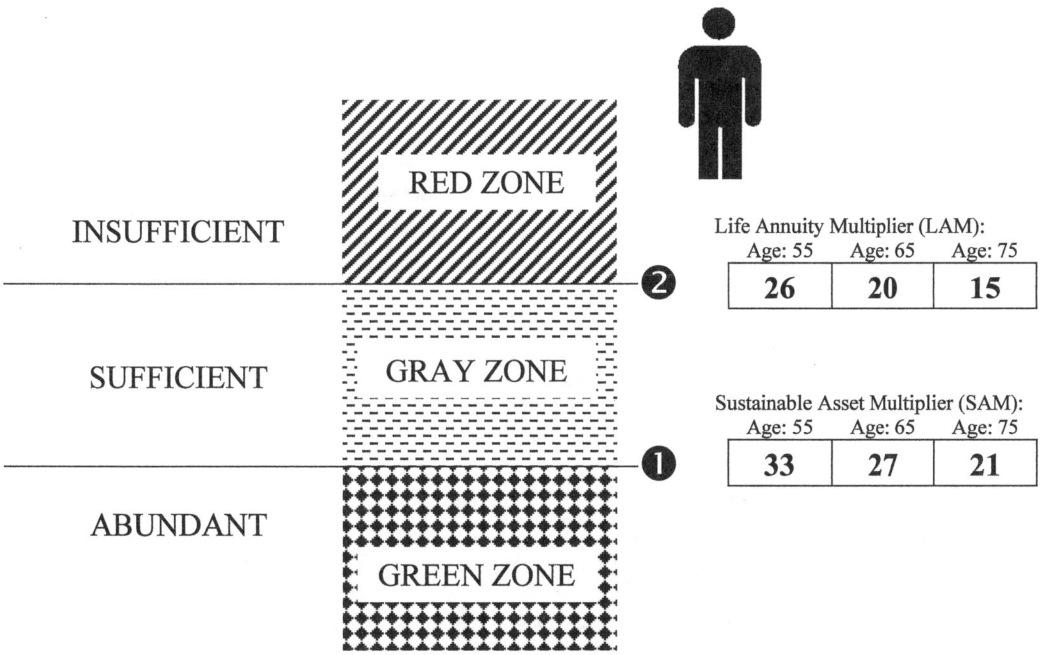

❶ SAM: The numbers on the small table are the sustainable asset multiplier (SAM). This is the minimum portfolio value required to generate one dollar of income, indexed to CPI each year, starting at the age indicated and ending at age 95.

<u>If your asset multiplier, CAM, is less than SAM</u>: It makes little difference what asset allocation you use, how diversified your portfolio is, what income strategy you like, how many years of cash buckets you have, whether you have a $10,000 retirement account or are running a $10 billion pension fund, there is only one thing to do: **You must export the risk.**

<u>If your CAM is larger than your SAM</u>: You are in the green zone and you have abundant savings.

❷ LAM: The numbers on the small table pointing to the border between the red zone and the gray zone indicate Life Annuity Multiplier (LAM). This is the premium you need to pay to purchase a life annuity that pays one dollar of income per year, indexed to CPI, starting at the indicated age.

<u>If your CAM is less than your LAM</u>: Payments from a life annuity will not be sufficient to sustain your financial needs during your retirement. You will have to modify your retirement plans. You cannot have the income you want for life without either delaying your retirement, cutting back your expenses, or supplementing your income from other sources (part–time work or business) during your retirement. You are in the red zone and you have insufficient savings.

<u>If your CAM is between your LAM and SAM:</u> You are in the gray zone. You have sufficient savings provided that you export risk.

Figure 41.7: Adequacy of retirement savings using the asset multiplier for a female

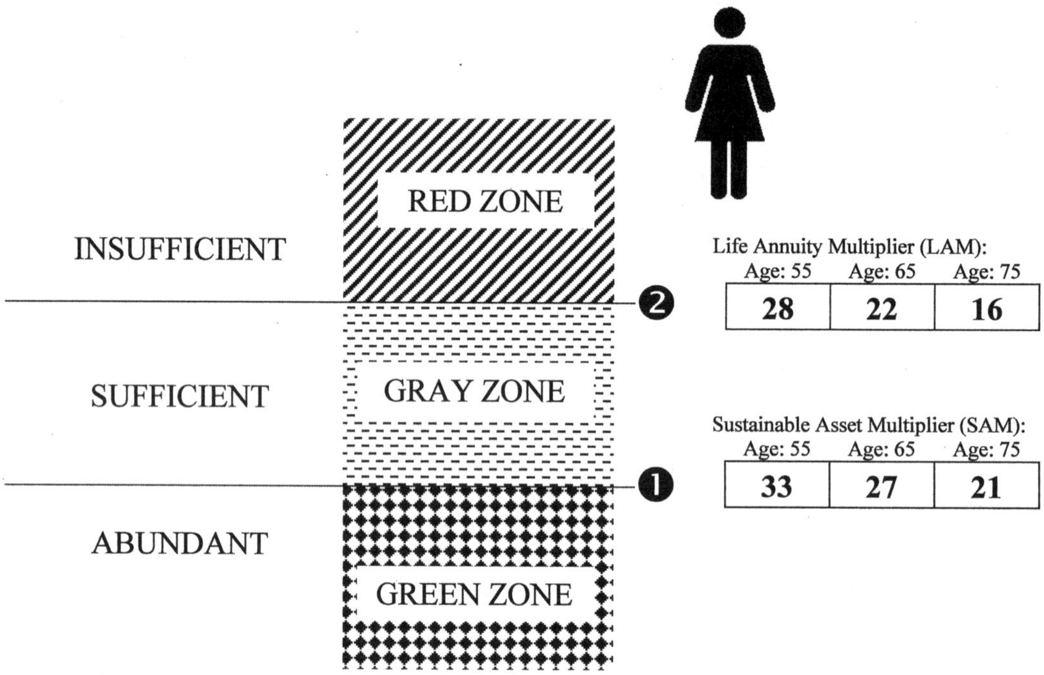

Figure 41.8: Adequacy of retirement savings using the asset multiplier for a couple (each spouse is at the same age)

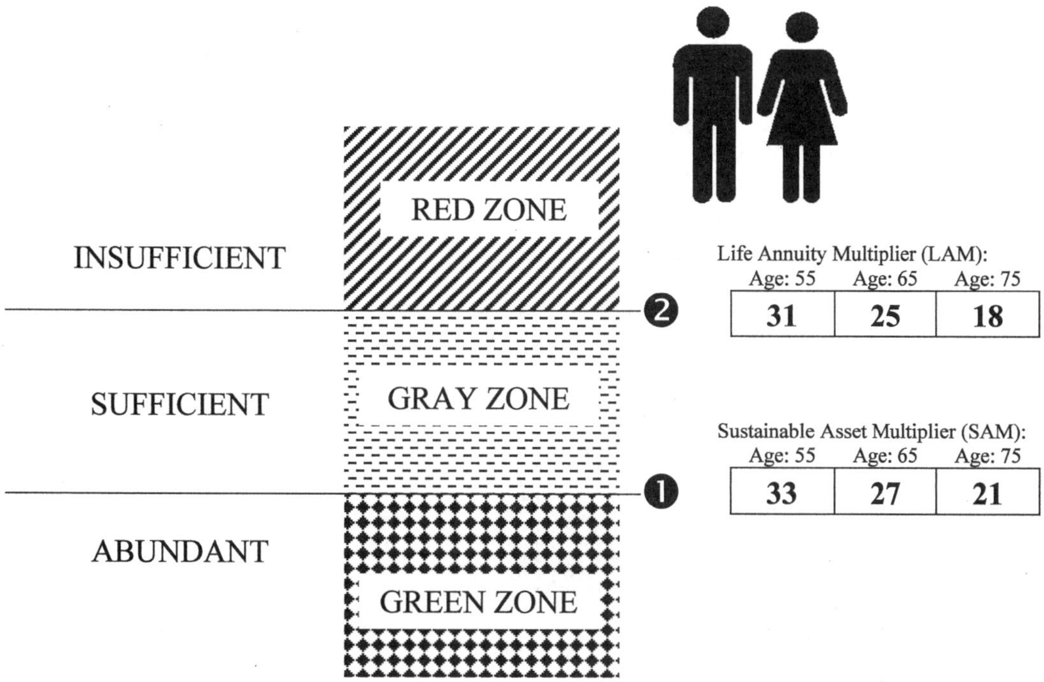

Example 41.2

Two single men (Keith, 60, and Phil, 65), a single woman (Jane, 70), and a couple (Rick and Susan, each 65) were sitting around a table discussing their recent retirement at the local coffee shop.

Keith says he needs $34,000 of income annually from his retirement savings. His portfolio contains mostly US investments. He has $926,000 in his portfolio.

Phil says he needs only $16,000 of income annually from his retirement savings. His portfolio contains mostly Canadian investments. He has $484,000 in his portfolio.

Jane says she needs $24,000 of income annually from her retirement savings. Her portfolio contains mostly US investments. She has $385,000 in her portfolio.

Rick and Susan say they need $70,000 of income annually from their retirement savings. Their portfolio contains mostly US investments. They have $4 million of investable assets that they can use for retirement.

Calculate each party's zone.

Keith: age 60, CAM: $926,000 / $34,000 = 27.2

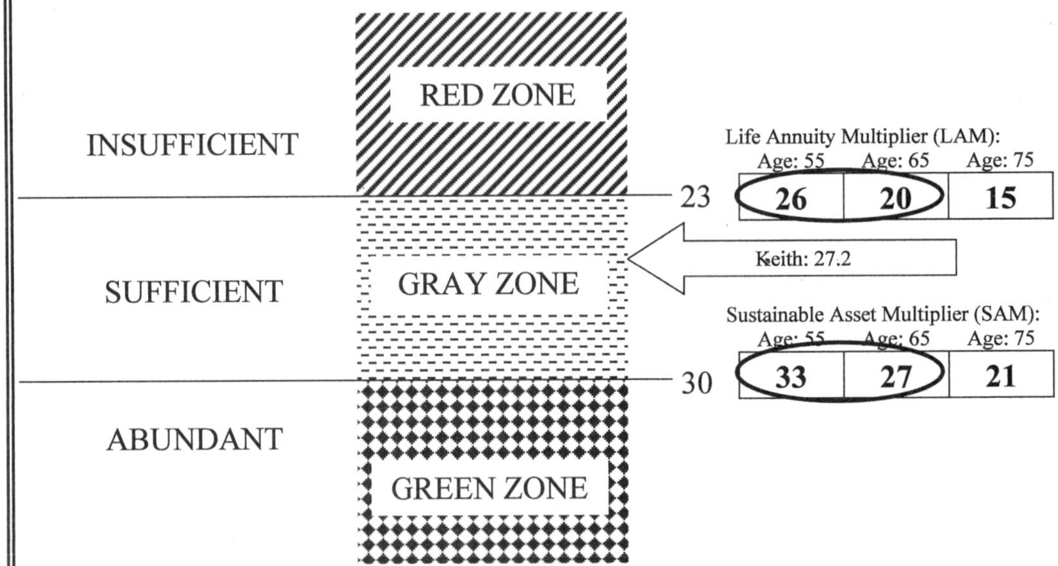

Keith is in the gray zone.

Phil: age 65, CAM = $484,000 / $16,000 = 30.3

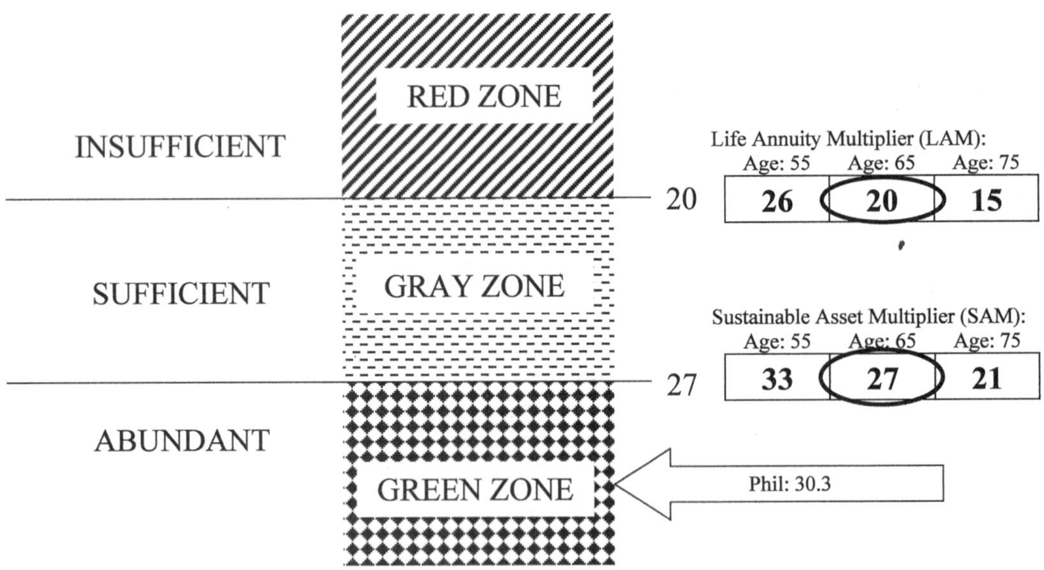

Phil is in the green zone.

Jane: age 70, CAM = $385,000 / $24,000 = 16.0

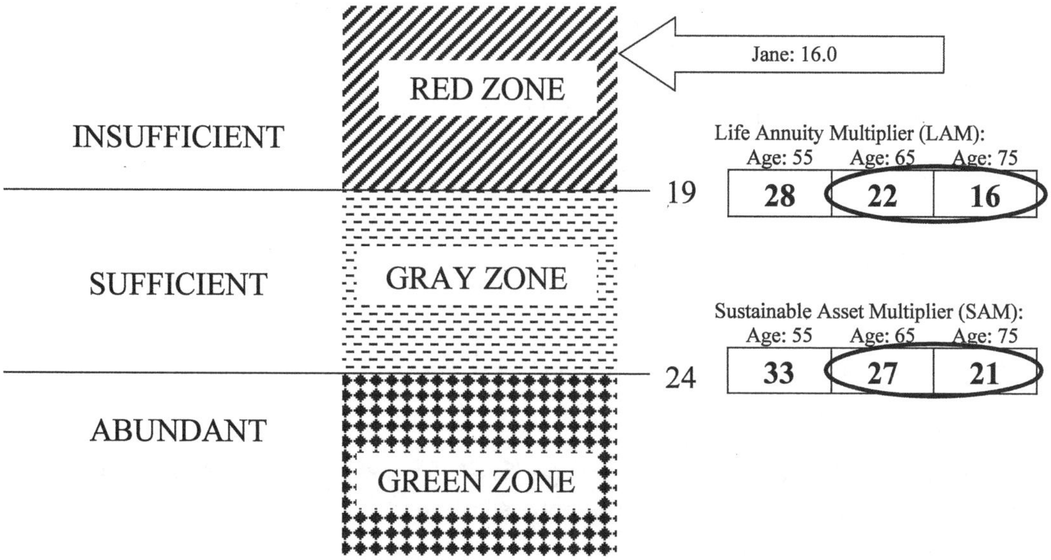

Jane is in the red zone.

Rick and Susan: age 65, CAM = $4,000,000 / $70,000 = 57.1

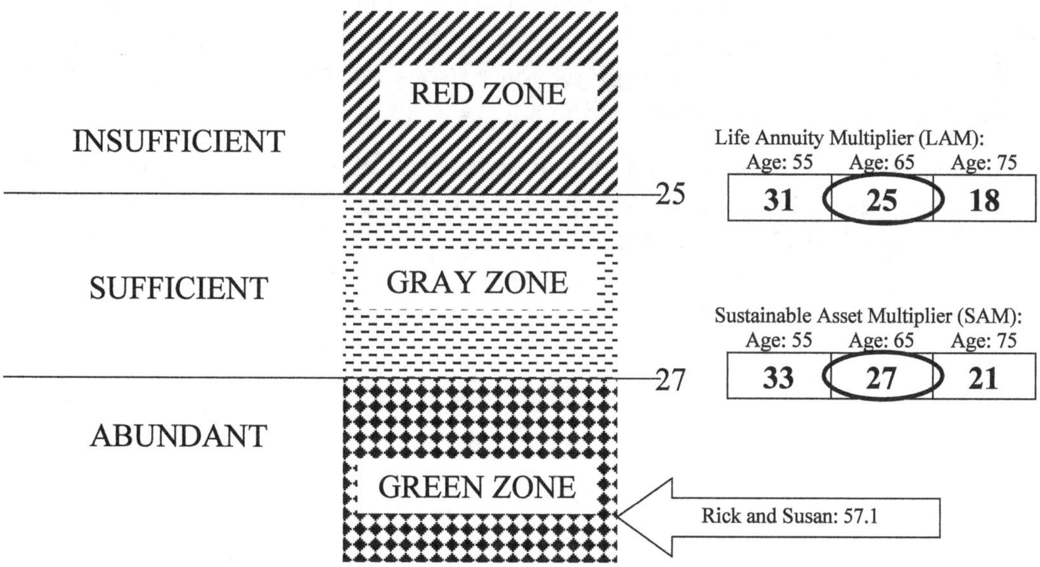

Rick and Susan are deep in the green zone.

Example 41.3

Continuing from Example 37.2:

> Steve is now 75 years old. He needs $56,000 annual income. His LAM is 15, his SAM is 21.

Case B: Steve was unlucky. He now has $740,000 in his portfolio.

> CAM = $740,000 / $56,000 = 13.2
>
> Steve's CAM is less than his LAM. Therefore, he is in the red zone. See in Chapter 44 the red zone solutions.

Case C: Steve had average returns. He has now $1,040,000 in his portfolio.

> CAM = $1,040,000 / $56,000 = 18.6
>
> Steve's CAM is between his LAM and his SAM. Therefore, he is in the gray zone. See in Chapter 43 for the gray zone solutions.

Conclusion:

Your zone tells you just about everything you need to know about the adequacy of your retirement savings. It gives you guidance as to whether you should export or retain the three financial risks of retirement. It gives you reasons whether you should be fearful of running out of money or hopeful of leaving a legacy.

Now that you know your zone, let us look at different lifelong income strategies. Chapter 42 covers the green zone strategies, Chapter 43 covers the gray zone strategies and Chapter 44 covers the red zone strategies.

Green Zone Strategies

If your withdrawal rate (WR) is lower than the sustainable withdrawal rate (SWR), then you are in the green zone. Alternatively, if your asset ratio (CAM) is greater than the sustainable asset multiplier (SAM), you are in the green zone.

Here are highlights of the green zone:

- Among the three zones, the green zone is the best zone to be in.
- Expect a lifelong income.
- Your portfolio can finance your retirement and the time value of fluctuations.
- You have abundant reserves to cover longevity, market and inflation risks.
- You have a number of choices among different strategies.
- You can switch your income allocation strategy during your retirement and still remain in the green zone.
- Your distribution portfolio will likely still be accumulating.
- You have reasonable leeway to make use of the classic ideas, such as asset allocation, diversification, benefits of dividends or even some technical analysis in your investment decisions.
- Of the two primal emotions (hope and fear), hope is on your side. You don't need to fear running out of money as long as your withdrawals continue as planned.
- Expect that your portfolio will grow and assets will be passed on to your children or to other beneficiaries after your death.
- If you are close to the border of the gray zone, consider long–term care insurance to contain expenses during the final years of life.
- Annually review your budget, portfolio performance and income allocation strategy.
- Your most important financial planning issues are tax and estate planning. Many people focus on portfolio costs that are only a couple of percent of the portfolio, instead of focusing on the tax bite. If not planned properly, taxes can do a lot more damage to your wealth than portfolio costs. Plan accordingly.

Practice Management Tips for Advisors:

Here are a few tips for managing your green zone clients:

- One of the perpetual fads in the advisory business is to pursue high net worth clients. Keep in mind that what matters most is not the size of assets, but how fast those assets are drained. Being in the green zone is a good indication that the client will likely be a good source of revenue for you, as long as you can create the "normal" index returns and as long as you can maintain his/her trust.
- Do not try to motivate a green zone client with "fear", but with "hope".

- Green zone clients generally possess good money management skills. Your time is better spent with them than with red zone clients. One client in the green zone can create more revenue than five clients in the red zone.
- In the green zone, almost any income allocation or withdrawal strategy works.
- Pay a lot of attention to tax and estate planning.
- Clients in the green zone generally carry the lowest risk for your practice.

Worked Examples:

In the following pages, I walk you through examples in the green zone. The first task is to determine if the retiree is in the green zone, red zone or gray zone. After that, we proceed to aftcasting different strategies of creating lifelong income.

Example 42.1 - Zone Analysis

Dan is 65 years old, just retiring. He has $1.1 million in his portfolio, earmarked for retirement. He needs $30,000 each year, indexed to inflation. He needs income for 30 years until age 95. What zone is Dan in?

Dan's numbers are:

- CAM = $1,100,000 / $30,000 = 36.7
- SAM = 27 (from table in Figure 41.6)
- LAM = 20 (from table in Figure 41.6)

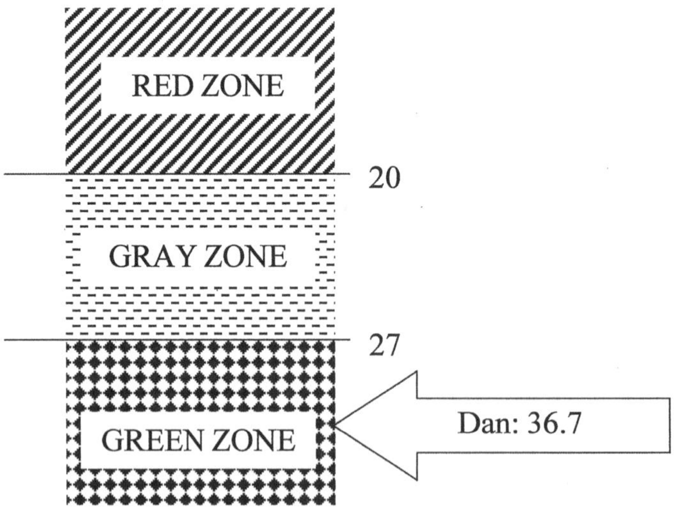

Dan is in the green zone. With proper asset allocation, he has abundant savings available in his investment portfolio to cover all three financial risks of retirement.

Example 42.2 - Investment Portfolio

Continuing with Example 42.1, Dan wants to generate his income from his portfolio.

His asset allocation is 40% DJIA and 60% fixed income, rebalanced annually. On the equity side, he expects the index return. On the fixed income side, he expects a return of 0.5% over and above the historical 6-month CD rates after all management fees.

What does the aftcast indicate?

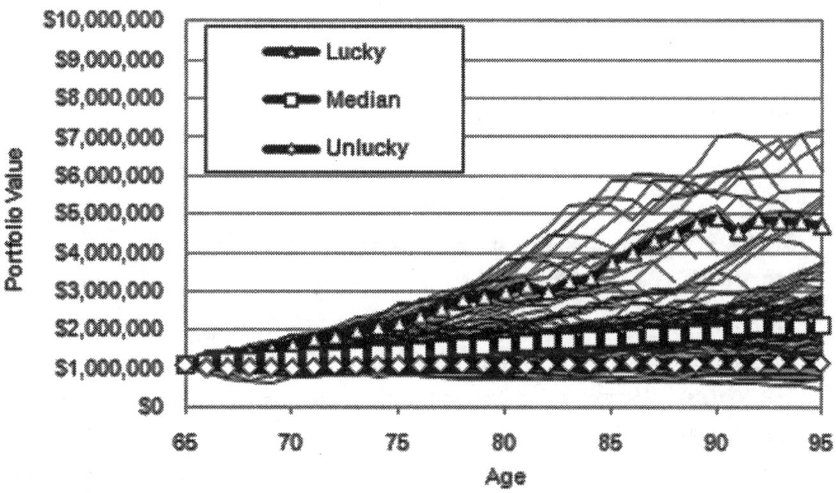

The aftcast indicates that at age 95, Dan's portfolio might be worth $4.7 million if he is lucky and $1.1 million if he is unlucky. The median portfolio was worth $2.1 million at age 95.

This income allocation generates lifelong, CPI-indexed income 100% of the time.

Example 42.3 - Straight Life Annuity and Investment Portfolio

Continuing with Example 42.1, Dan does not want to take chances with his retirement income. He wants to buy a straight life annuity that costs $384,000 and pays $30,000 annually for the rest of his life. He cashes out some of his investments to pay the premium for this life annuity. Payments are constant for life. He will lose his purchasing power over time. Therefore, he intends to withdraw any inflation deficiency from his remaining investment portfolio.

After buying this annuity, his remaining assets are invested 40% in DJIA and 60% in fixed income, rebalanced annually. On the equity side, he expects the index return. On the fixed income side, he expects a return of 0.5% over and above the historical 6-month CD rates after all management fees.

What does the aftcast indicate?

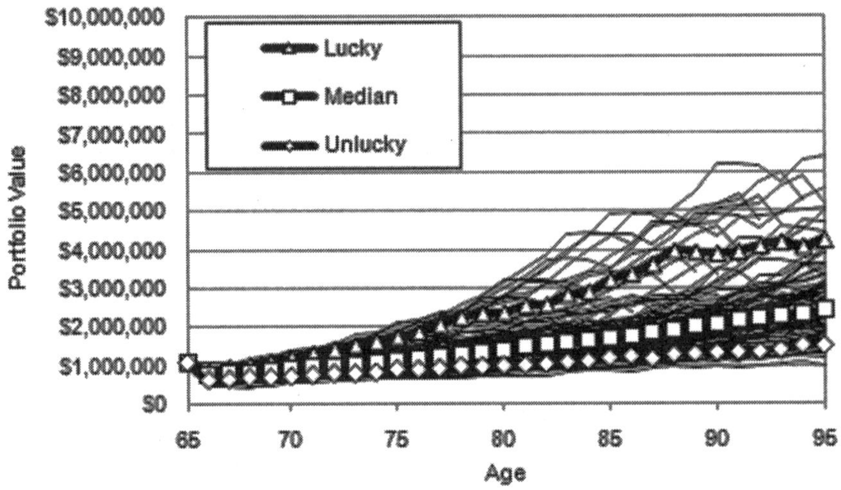

The aftcast indicates that at age 95, Dan's portfolio might be worth $4.6 million if he is lucky and $1.6 million if he is unlucky. The median portfolio was worth $2.5 million at age 95. If he lives until 95, i.e. beyond his average life expectancy, the median portfolio would be about $400,000 richer, just because he exported longevity and market risks and retained the inflation risk.

This income allocation generates lifelong, CPI-indexed income 100% of the time.

Example 42.4 - 3% Indexed Life Annuity and Investment Portfolio

Continuing with Example 42.1, Dan wants to buy a life annuity that pays $30,000 annually, indexed by 3% each year. This annuity costs $546,000. If and when the inflation is higher than 3%, he plans to withdraw any deficiency from his remaining investment portfolio.

After buying this annuity, his remaining assets are invested 50% in DJIA and 50% in fixed income, rebalanced annually. On the equity side, he expects the index return. On the fixed income side, he expects a return of 0.5% over and above the historical 6-month CD rates after all management fees.

What does the aftcast indicate?

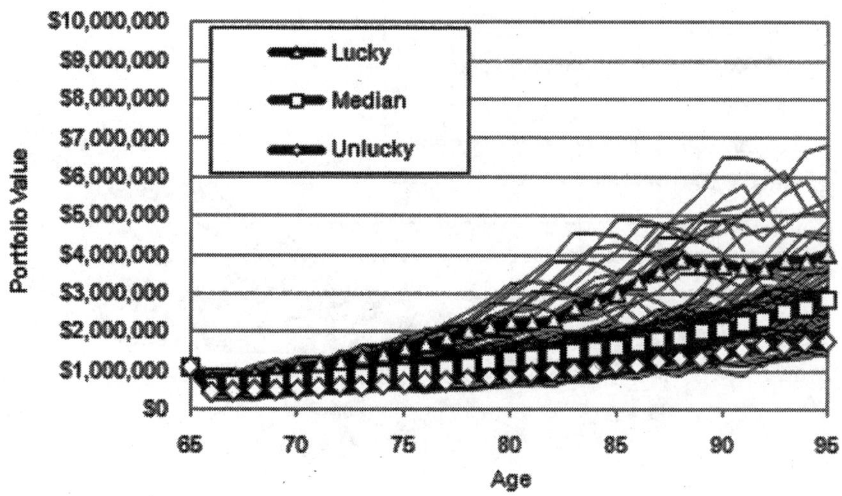

The aftcast indicates that at age 95, Dan's portfolio might be worth $4.0 million if he is lucky and $1.8 million if he is unlucky. The median portfolio was worth $2.8 million at age 95.

This income allocation generates lifelong, CPI-indexed income 100% of the time.

Example 42.5 - CPI-Indexed Life Annuity and Investment Portfolio

Continuing with Example 42.1, Dan does not want to take chances. He wants to buy a life annuity that pays $30,000 annually, fully indexed to CPI. This annuity costs $565,000.

Since annuity payments are indexed to inflation, he does not need to make any withdrawals from his investment portfolio. His asset allocation is 50% DJIA and 50% fixed income, rebalanced annually. On the equity side, he expects the index return. On the fixed income side, he expects a return of 0.5% over and above the historical 6-month CD rates after all management fees.

What does the aftcast indicate?

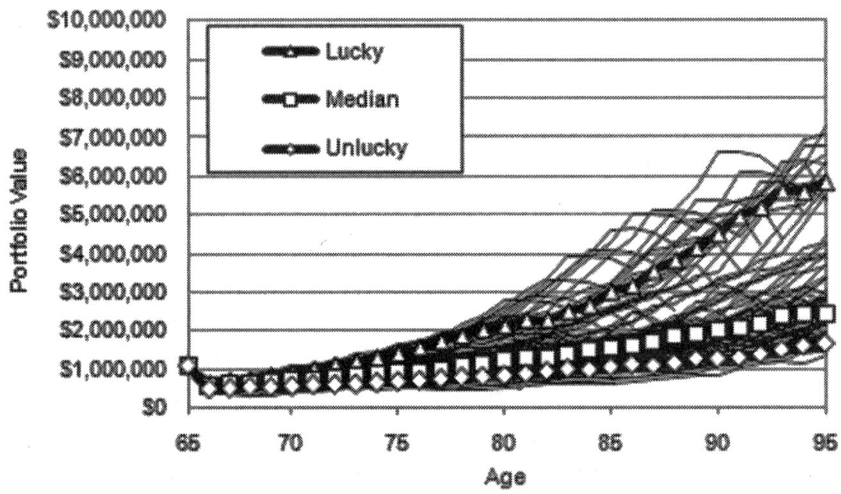

The aftcast indicates that at age 95, Dan's portfolio might be worth $5.8 million if he is lucky and $1.7 million if he is unlucky. The median portfolio was worth $2.5 million at age 95.

This income allocation generates lifelong, CPI-indexed income 100% of the time.

Example 42.6 - Ten-Year Term Annuity and Investment Portfolio

Continuing with Example 42.1, Dan decides to buy a term annuity that pays $30,000 annually for 10 years. It costs $285,000 to buy this annuity. Since this term annuity payments are not increasing, he will lose his purchasing power over time. Therefore, he intends to withdraw any inflation deficiency from his remaining investment portfolio. After the expiry of his term annuity, Dan plans to withdraw income from his portfolio only. He hopes that his portfolio will increase during those ten years.

His remaining portfolio assets -after buying the term annuity- are invested 40% in DJIA and 60% in fixed income, rebalanced annually. On the equity side, he expects the index return. On the fixed income side, he expects a return of 0.5% over and above the historical 6-month CD rates after all management fees.

What does the aftcast indicate?

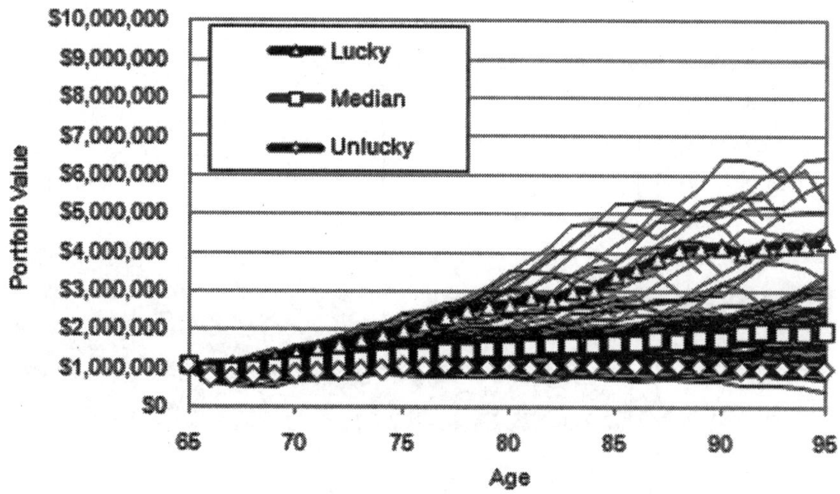

The aftcast indicates that at age 95, Dan's portfolio might be worth $4.3 million if he is lucky and $1 million if he is unlucky. The median portfolio was worth $1.9 million at age 95.

This income allocation generates lifelong, CPI-indexed income 100% of the time.

Example 42.7 - Variable Annuity with GMWBL and Investment Portfolio

Continuing with Example 42.1, Dan decides to buy a variable annuity with GMWB. This VA-GMWB guarantees a minimum of 5% of the guaranteed withdrawal base (GWB) annually. He places $600,000 to the GMWBL (80% equity and 20% fixed income) that initially pays $30,000/year. The annuity payments might increase if there are any step-up resets.

Since the VA-GMWBL payments are not indexed to CPI, Dan will have to withdraw any inflation deficiency from his remaining investment portfolio.

His remaining portfolio assets are $400,000 and they are invested 40% in DJIA and 60% in fixed income, rebalanced annually. On the equity side, he expects the index return. On the fixed income side, he expects a return of 0.5% over and above the historical 6-month CD rates after all management fees.

What does the aftcast indicate?

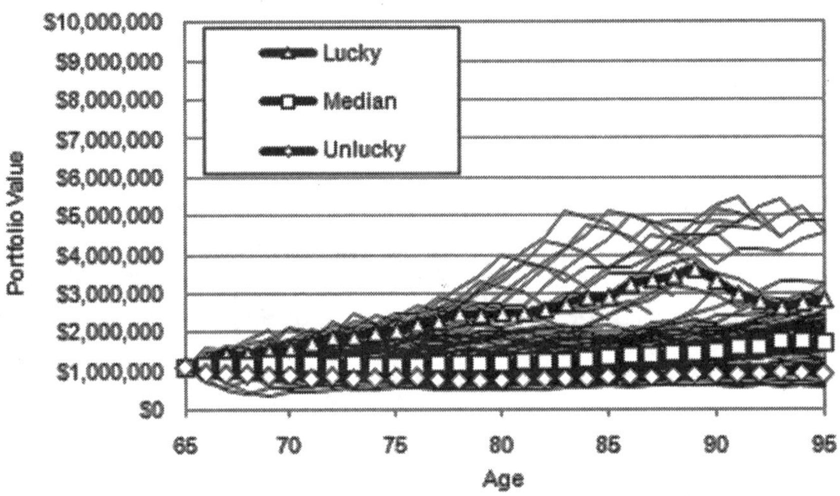

The aftcast indicates that at age 95, Dan's portfolio might be worth $2.8 million if he is lucky and $900,000 if he is unlucky. The median portfolio was worth $1.7 million at age 95.

This income allocation generates lifelong, CPI-indexed income 100% of the time.

Example 42.8 - Variable Annuity with GMIB and Investment Portfolio

Continuing with Example 42.1, Dan decides to buy a variable annuity with GMIB. This guarantees a minimum of 6% of the guaranteed income base (GIB) annually. Dan places $500,000 to the GMIB (80% equity and 20% fixed income) that initially pays $30,000/year. The annuity payments might increase if there are any step-up resets until age 75. The annuitization occurs when the portfolio runs out of money, or at age 85, whichever comes first.

Since the VA-GMIB payments are not indexed to the CPI, Dan will have to withdraw any inflation deficiency from his remaining investment portfolio.

His remaining portfolio assets are invested 40% in DJIA and 60% in fixed income, rebalanced annually. On the equity side, he expects the index return. On the fixed income side, he expects a return of 0.5% over and above the historical 6-month CD rates after all management fees.

What does the aftcast indicate?

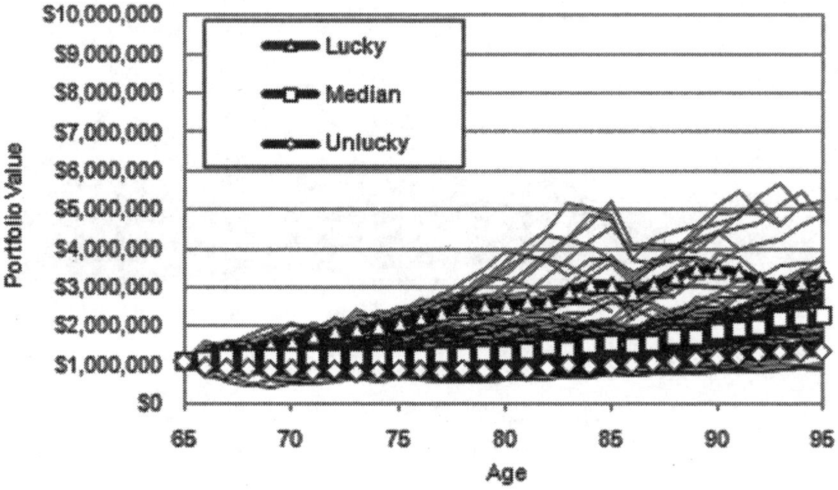

The aftcast indicates that at age 95, Dan's portfolio might be worth $3.4 million if he is lucky and $1.4 million if he is unlucky. The median portfolio was worth $2.3 million at age 95.

This income allocation generates lifelong, CPI-indexed income 100% of the time.

Example 42.9 - Ten-Year Asset Dedication

Continuing with Example 42.1, Dan decides to follow an asset dedication strategy. He holds 10 years of income in the fixed income portion of his portfolio. He invests the remainder of his portfolio in equities (DJIA index only). He rebalances his asset mix every 4 years, at the end of the Presidential election year.

His fixed income asset mix is 30% cash, 30% conventional bonds and 40% inflation indexed bonds. On the conventional bonds, he expects a return of 0.5% over and above the historical 6-month CD rates after all management fees. On the inflation-indexed bonds, he expects a real yield of 1% over and above the historical inflation rate after all management fees.

What does the aftcast indicate?

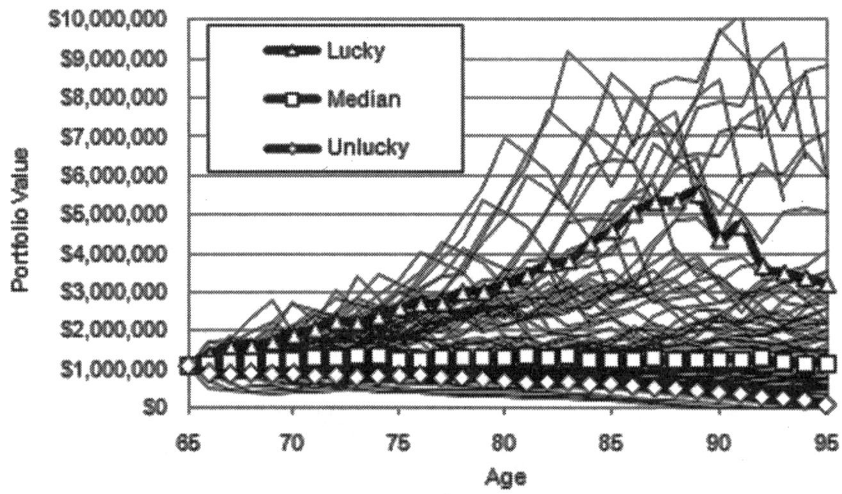

The aftcast indicates that at age 95, Dan's portfolio might be worth $3.2 million if he is lucky and $95,000 if he is unlucky. The median portfolio was worth $1.1 million at age 95.

This income allocation generated lifelong, CPI-indexed income 92% of the time.

Example 42.10 - Straight Life Annuity Ladder and Investment Portfolio

Same as Example 42.3, but Dan spreads his annuity purchase over 10 years. He buys at ages 65, 70, and 75 a straight life annuity, costing $134,000, $121,000, and $108,000, respectively. Each rung of the annuity pays $10,000 per year for life, totaling to $30,000 per year. He cashes out some of his investments to pay the premiums for these life annuities. Payments from each annuity are constant for life. He will lose his purchasing power over time. Therefore, he intends to withdraw any inflation deficiency from his remaining investment portfolio.

His remaining assets are invested 40% in DJIA and 60% in fixed income, rebalanced annually. On the equity side, he expects the index return. On the fixed income side, he expects a return of 0.5% over and above the historical 6-month CD rates after all management fees.

What does the aftcast indicate?

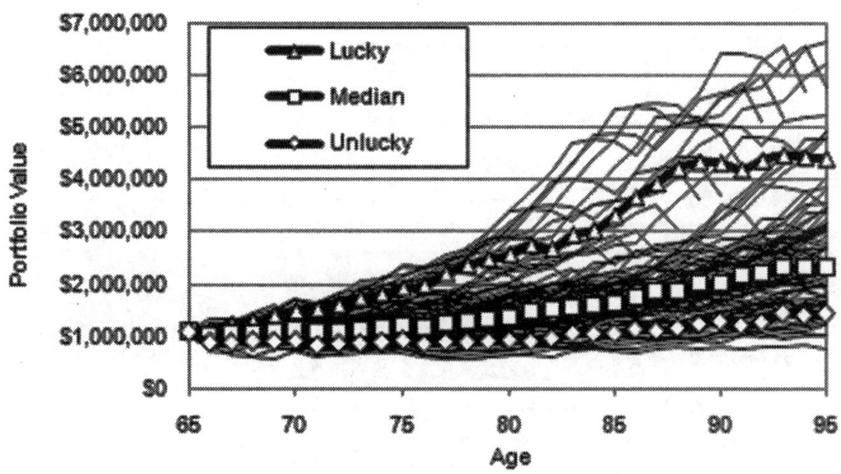

The aftcast indicates that at age 95, Dan's portfolio might be worth $4.4 million if he is lucky and $1.4 million if he is unlucky. The median portfolio was worth $2.3 million at age 95.

This income allocation generates lifelong, CPI-indexed income 100% of the time.

Example 42.11 - CPI-Indexed Life Annuity Ladder and Investment Portfolio

Same as Example 42.5, but Dan spreads his annuity purchase over 10 years. He buys at ages 65, 70, and 75 a CPI-indexed life annuity, costing $186,000, $159,000, and $136,000, respectively. Each rung of the annuity pays $10,000 per year for life, totaling to $30,000 per year, indexed fully to CPI annually. He cashes out some of his investments to pay the premiums for these life annuities.

Because he is spreading the annuity purchase over time, there may be some deficiency of income for inflation over time. Therefore, he intends to withdraw any inflation deficiency from his remaining investment portfolio.

His asset allocation is 40% DJIA and 60% fixed income, rebalanced annually. On the equity side, he expects the index return. On the fixed income side, he expects a return of 0.5% over and above the historical 6-month CD rates after all management fees.

What does the aftcast indicate?

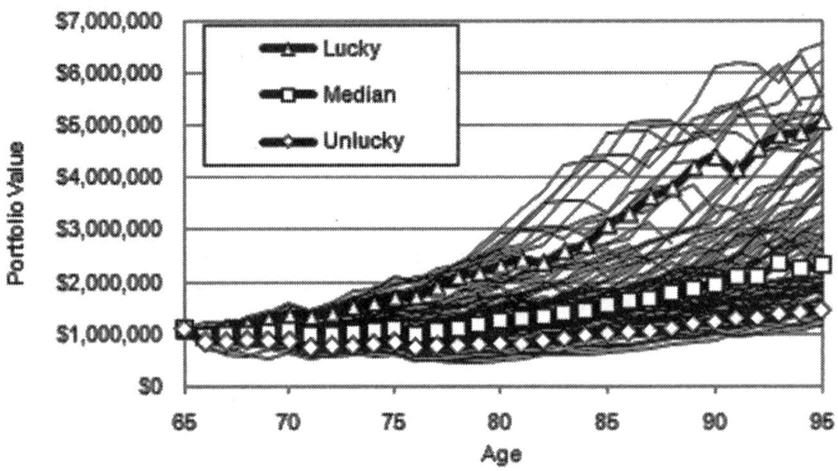

The aftcast indicates that at age 95, Dan's portfolio might be worth $5.1 million if he is lucky and $1.5 million if he is unlucky. The median portfolio was worth $2.3 million at age 95.

This income allocation generates lifelong, CPI-indexed income 100% of the time.

Example 42.12 - Bond Portfolio

Continuing with Example 42.1, Dan holds only bonds in his portfolio, no stocks. His asset allocation is 50% conventional bonds and 50% inflation indexed bonds.

For his conventional bonds, he expects a return of 0.5% over and above the historical 6-month CD rates after all management fees. For his inflation-indexed bonds, he expects a return of 1% over and above the historical inflation rate after all management fees. He holds bonds until maturity; ignore any capital gains and losses during the holding time period.

What does the aftcast indicate?

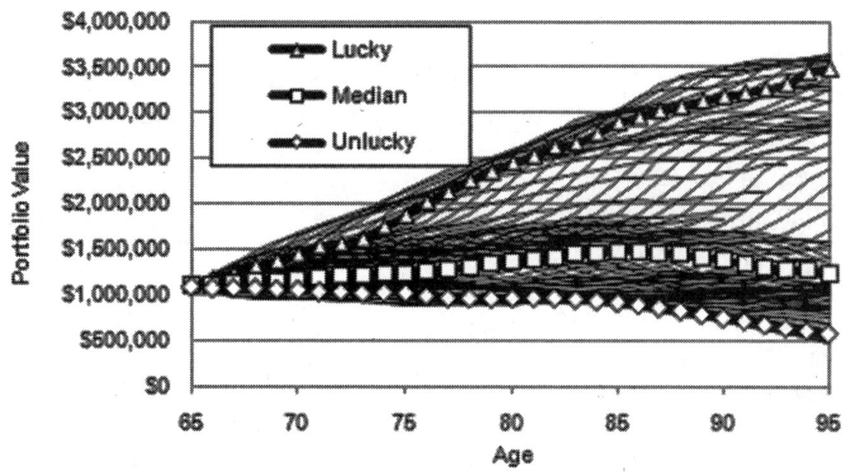

The aftcast indicates that at age 95, Dan's portfolio might be worth $3.5 million if he is lucky and $600,000 if he is unlucky. The median portfolio was worth $1.2 million at age 95.

This income allocation generates lifelong, CPI-indexed income 100% of the time.

Compare the income allocation examples in the green zone:

	Portfolio Value at Age 95			Probability of full income at age 94
	Unlucky	Median	Lucky	
Example 42.2 Investment Portfolio	$1.1 million	$2.1 million	$4.7 million	100%
Example 42.3 Straight Life Annuity and Investment Portfolio	$1.6 million	$2.5 million	$4.6 million	100%
Example 42.4 3% Indexed Life Annuity and Investment Portfolio	$1.8 million	$2.8 million	$4.0 million	100%
Example 42.5 CPI-Indexed Life Annuity and Investment Portfolio	$1.7 million	$2.5 million	$5.8 million	100%
Example 42.6 10-Year Term Annuity and Investment Portfolio	$1.0 million	$1.9 million	$4.3 million	100%
Example 42.7 VA-GMWBL and Investment Portfolio	$0.9 million	$1.7 million	$2.8 million	100%
Example 42.8 VA-GMIB and Investment Portfolio	$1.4 million	$2.3 million	$3.4 million	100%
Example 42.9 Ten-Year Asset Dedication	$0.1 million	$1.1 million	$3.2 million	93%
Example 42.10 Straight Life Annuity Ladder and Investment Portfolio	$1.4 million	$2.3 million	$4.4 million	100%
Example 42.11 CPI-Indexed Life Annuity Ladder and Investment Portfolio	$1.5 million	$2.3 million	$5.1 million	100%
Example 42.12 Bond Portfolio	$0.6 million	$1.2 million	$3.5 million	100%

Conclusion:

If you are in the green zone, then any reasonable income allocation strategy works. If you want additional income security, you can build ladders for annuities, VA–GMWB's and VA–GMIB's. The rungs of the ladders can be one year apart or several years apart. You have the freedom to choose any strategy that makes sense.

You do not need any miracles and you do not need to take unusual risks. Ordinary market index within a balanced portfolio provides a lifelong income, and then some. If you do not like the risks of the equity markets at all and you don't like annuities, in many cases a bond portfolio will give you all you need, provided that your are in the green zone and don't live beyond age 94.

If you expect to live long, then combining the investment portfolio with a life annuity with indexed payments will provide the highest estate value at age 95.

As I noted in Chapter 38, asset dedication performed poorest because by being less conservative in early years, it created a larger exposure to the sequence of returns. By being more conservative in later years, it hindered protection against inflation.

The green zone is the ideal zone for any retiree. If you are an advisor, they are your ideal clients. Unfortunately, there are not too many of them around. The average baby boomer either is or will soon be in the red zone.

The same is true for most private and public pension funds. Many are also in the red zone or soon will be because of the prevailing faulty financial models and the defective financial culture.

Chapter 43

Gray Zone Strategies

If your withdrawal rate (WR) is between the sustainable withdrawal rate (SWR) and the annuity rate (AR), then you are in the gray zone. Alternatively, if your asset ratio (CAM) is between the sustainable asset multiplier (SAM) and the life annuity multiplier (LAM), you are in the gray zone.

I would like to mention an important point about the life annuity multiplier (LAM), which draws the border between the red zone and the gray zone. To cover the inflation risk in the gray zone, you need to use the annuity rate that will buy you a CPI–indexed life annuity for calculating the LAM. Otherwise, the gray zone strategies will cover the longevity and market risks, but not the inflation risk.

Only if the inflation risk is not important to you, can you calculate the LAM using an annuity rate for an annuity where payments are not indexed to the CPI.

Here they are highlights of the gray zone:

- Expect a lifelong income, but you must export the risk.
- Your portfolio can finance your retirement, but it is unlikely that it can finance the time value of fluctuations.
- You have insufficient reserves to cover longevity, market and inflation risks. You must export these risks to an insurance company.
- You have little choice among different strategies.
- Your distribution portfolio may be accumulating or decumulating. You will not know which one it is until several years after the start of retirement.
- You must stay away from any fancy or complicated investments. It is important to keep everything simple, with portfolio costs as small as possible.
- Of the two primal emotions (hope and fear), design for fear. Use strategies that alleviate or remove the fear of running out of money during retirement.
- There may or may not be any estate left for children or other beneficiaries after your death.
- The only sure way of leaving an estate is buying a life insurance. If you already have life insurance, keep it.
- Buy long–term care insurance to cover the costs of the final years of life in a nursing home.
- Review your budget, portfolio performance and income allocation strategy after major economic and family events, and at least annually.

Practice Management Tips for Advisors:

Here are a few tips for managing your gray zone clients:

- If a prospect is in the gray zone and he is not willing to follow your advice on exporting part of the risk to create a lifelong income, don't waste your time. Try to educate him about the consequences. If he still ignores your counsel, don't accept him as a client; politely show him the door.
- If a client is in the gray zone and he does not follow your advice on income allocation, he will likely run out of money during retirement. Ask him to find another advisor.
- Clients in the gray zone carry a higher risk than your clients in the green zone. Make sure to have regular reviews and updates.
- Design for "fear" and plan for unlucky outcomes. If, after one or two market cycles, it turns out that the client is lucky, you may then want to cultivate hope, modify income allocation, and even allow an increase of withdrawals.
- Make sure to discuss life annuity and long–term care insurance with your client.

Worked Examples:

In the following pages, I walk you through gray zone examples.

Example 43.1 - Zone Analysis

Mike is 65 years old, just retiring. He has $960,000 in his portfolio, all earmarked for his retirement. He needs $40,000 each year, indexed to inflation. He needs income for 30 years until age 95.

What zone is Mike in?

Mike's numbers are:

- CAM = $960,000 / $40,000 = 24
- SAM = 27 (from table in Figure 41.6)
- LAM = 20 (from table in Figure 41.6)

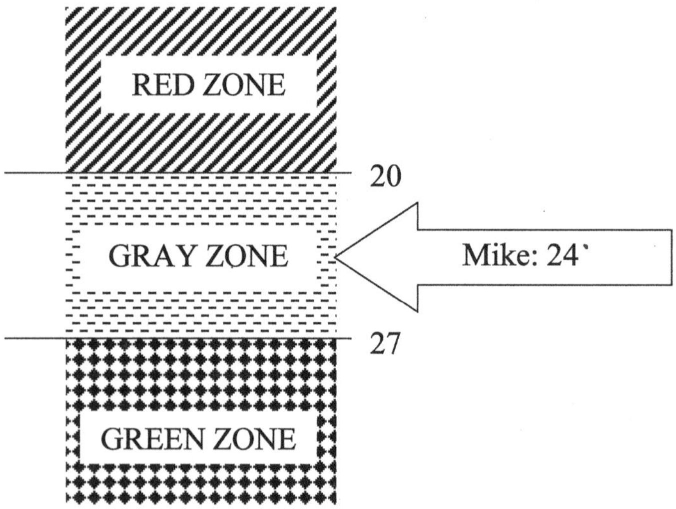

Mike is in the gray zone. He can have lifelong income only if he exports risk.

What does not work?

What works in the green zone does not necessarily work in the gray zone. Any income allocation strategy that does not export the adequate amount of longevity, market and inflation risks might fail. If you delay passing these risks to insurance companies at the beginning of your retirement, you would then be at the mercy of your luck factor.

Remembering that for a proper retirement plan, we want the probability of depletion of the portfolio to remain at or below 10% at the age of death. We also want the probability of receiving the full required income to remain above 90% throughout retirement in a properly designed plan.

Let's first take the numbers from Example 43.1 and apply them to each strategy that we ran in the green zone in the previous chapter. As such, Example 43.2 uses the same strategy as Example 42.2, except that we use Mike's numbers instead of Dan's numbers.

	Probability of Depletion by age 85	Probability of Depletion by age 95	Probability of full income at age 94
Example 43.2 Investment Portfolio	0%	29%	70%
Example 43.3 Straight Life Annuity and Investment Portfolio	0%	11%	89%
Example 43.4 3% Indexed Life Annuity and Investment Portfolio	4%	15%	85%
Example 43.5 CPI-Indexed Life Annuity and Investment Portfolio	0%	0%	100%
Example 43.6 10-Year Term Annuity and Investment Portfolio	1%	50%	50%
Example 43.7 VA-GMWBL and Investment Portfolio	26%	53%	38%
Example 43.8 VA-GMIB and Investment Portfolio	11%	33%	68%
Example 43.9 Ten-Year Asset Dedication	8%	61%	38%
Example 43.10 Straight Life Annuity Ladder and Investment Portfolio	1%	18%	82%
Example 43.11 CPI-Indexed Life Annuity Ladder and Investment Portfolio	0%	5%	95%
Example 43.12 Bond Portfolio	0%	30%	70%

Notice that, in the green zone examples in the previous chapter, I listed the portfolio values for lucky, median and unlucky outcomes. There, I showed the probability of depletion and the probability of full income. That is because, once you are in the gray zone, you are in the survival mode and portfolio values are not important. In this mode, only the probability of depletion and the probability of full income are important.

What do you notice in the examples above? Only two income allocation strategies met our criteria of an acceptable retirement plan in the gray zone.

Example 43.5 worked perfectly. It is the combination of the life annuity with payments indexed to CPI and the investment portfolio. Example 43.11 is also workable. The difference between the two is the laddering of the annuity purchases. No other strategy worked well enough for a robust and acceptable retirement plan, not even the life annuity with payments indexed by 3% annually (Example 43.4).

I have said this a few times in this book; because it is important, I'll say it again: ignore any cookie cutter solutions, such as "allocate 1/3 to a life annuity, 1/3 to investments and 1/3 to variable annuities." Or something like, "allocate 2/3 of your assets to inflation indexed bonds and 1/3 to conventional bonds." Or "buy a 10–year term annuity, invest the rest." None of these will work in the gray zone unless you get lucky. Each case is different; you need to run a number of different scenarios for each retiree to find the optimum income allocation strategy.

Any income allocation strategy that does not export the adequate amount of risk is exposed to failure. Any delay in passing these risks to insurance companies at the beginning of retirement may have dire consequences in the gray zone.

So, let's calculate how much risk we need to export.

Terminology – Asset Allotment:

Let me clarify one thing about the terminology that I use: It is tempting to call the process of dividing up assets into different income classes as "asset allocation". After all, we already use this term in the accumulation stage.

However, I do not like to use "asset allocation" in this context for two reasons. The first reason is this: in the current investment jargon, the term "asset allocation" refers to how much money one places in equities, bonds, cash, etc., in an investment portfolio. This is not what we are doing here.

The second reason is this: the term "asset allocation" might imply that you have assets. However, when you are doing an income allocation, you might not have any assets left afterwards. For example, when you buy a life annuity, you exchange your assets for a lifelong cash flow. You no longer own these assets. Therefore, using the term "asset allocation" might not be the perfect way of describing this process of allocating dollars to various income classes.

Instead, I use the term "asset allotment" to describe how much of the assets are placed in any one of these income classes. It reduces the element of confusion.

The Perfect Mix:

In the February, 2003 issue of the *Financial Planning* magazine, an article of mine was published. That article described exactly how much risk you need to export in the gray zone. The editor of the magazine named the article "The Perfect Mix". I liked that name, so I called this formula my "Perfect Mix" formula.

Here is the perfect mix formula to calculate how much of the assets should be allocated to buy a life annuity in the gray zone. It is the percentage of total retirement assets:

$$\text{Minimum Annuity Allocation\%} = \frac{(SAM-CAM)}{(SAM-LAM)} \times 100\% \qquad \text{(Equation 43.1)}$$

Example 43.13

Calculate the percentage of his retirement assets that Mike needs to allocate to buy a life annuity with payments indexed to CPI.

Using Equation 43.1, we calculate:

$$\text{Minimum Annuity Allocation\%} = \frac{(27-24)}{(27-20)} \times 100\% = 43\%$$

Mike has $960,000, so he needs to purchase a life annuity with $412,800 of his money, calculated as 43% of $960,000. This is the minimum amount of life annuity that he needs to buy. The payments from this annuity at age 65 will be $20,640 (calculated as $412,800 / 20), indexed to CPI in all subsequent years.

This would leave him a portfolio of $547,200, calculated as $960,000 less $412,800. The withdrawals from this portfolio would be $19,360 at age 65. His initial withdrawal rate from his portfolio is 3.5%.

Here is Mike's aftcast:

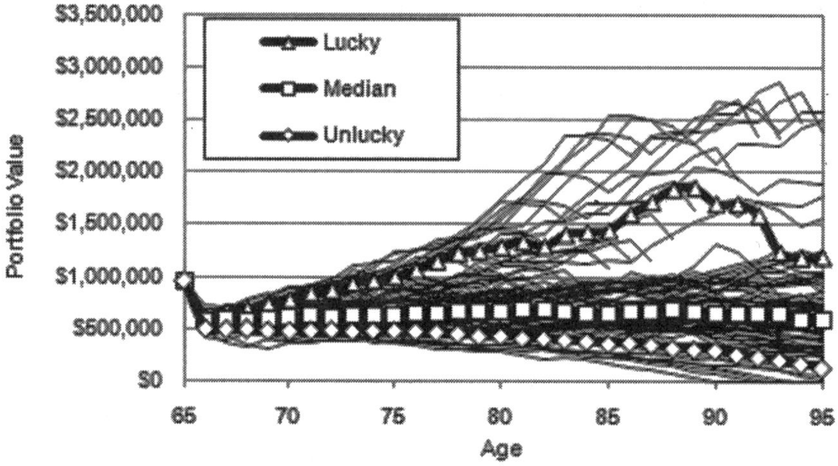

The aftcast indicates that at age 95, Mike's portfolio might be worth $1.2 million if he is lucky and $134,000 if he is unlucky. The median portfolio was worth $590,000 at age 95.

This income allocation generates lifelong, CPI-indexed income 95% of the time. If he realizes he is unlucky in future years, he will have plenty of opportunity to buy an additional life annuity for further risk reduction.

Example 43.14

Being in the gray zone, Mike can certainly buy a larger amount of life annuity.

Say, he wants his life annuity to cover his entire income need, which is $40,000 / year. This annuity would cost him $800,000, calculated as $40,000 X 20. (SAM=20).

His remaining portfolio would then be $160,000. With no withdrawals from it, it is in effect an accumulation portfolio. The median portfolio is gradually increasing over the years, instead of staying flat, as was the case with Example 43.13.

Here is Mike's aftcast:

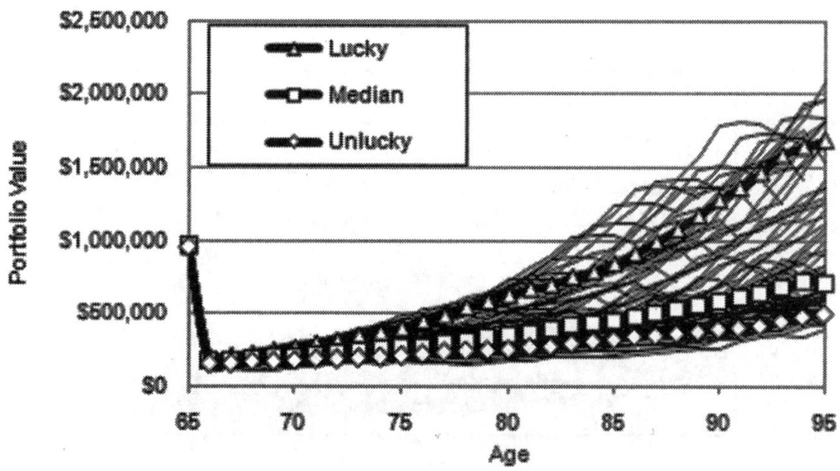

The aftcast indicates that at age 95, Mike's portfolio might be worth $1.7 million if he is lucky and $500,000 if he is unlucky. The median portfolio was worth $700,000 at age 95.

This income allocation generates lifelong, CPI-indexed income 100% of the time.

Laddering the Perfect Mix:

Be careful when laddering annuities in the gray zone. It is gender sensitive; what works for a male, may not work for a female or for a joint–and–last survivor annuity. That is because the annuity rates can be significantly different for different genders. Analyze each aftcast based on its own numbers and don't assume anything.

Example 43.15

Mike may also try laddering his annuity purchases. At age 65, he buys a life annuity for $300,000. At age 70, he buys another annuity for $150,000. Let's look at his aftcast:

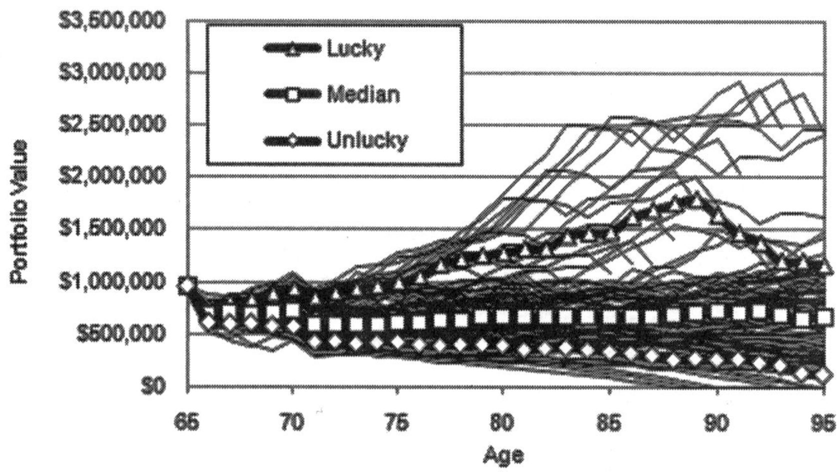

The aftcast indicates that at age 95, Mike's portfolio might be worth $1.2 million if he is lucky and $120,000 if he is unlucky. The median portfolio was worth $670,000 at age 95.

This income allocation generates lifelong, CPI-indexed income 93% of the time. In the gray zone, it is generally not a good idea to ladder annuities too far apart.

Variability of Income:

Now, let us go one step beyond the perfect mix formula: when you are calculating your retirement expenses, you may want to distinguish between essential and non–essential expenses. The worksheet in Appendix B can help you make such a distinction. For example, you might find that you require $55,000 for your essential expenses and $5,000 as your non–essential expenses.

If you are flexible with your non–essential expenses, then you may want to purchase income classes with varying income. Being flexible, even on a small portion of your income, can be beneficial in many ways:

- a lower annuity premium
- a potentially larger estate value
- a more attractive tax benefit (prescribed life annuities)
- a potentially higher future payout

In previous chapters, we covered income classes where the real income varies over time. They are:

- life annuities that are not fully indexed to CPI – Chapter 33
- variable pay annuities (VPA) – Chapter 34
- guaranteed minimum withdrawal benefits (GMWBL) – Chapter 35
- guaranteed minimum income benefits (GMIB) – Chapter 36

Let us look at each of these income classes. Keep in mind, everything in this chapter is for the gray zone. If you are in the green zone or red zone, the formulas and the strategies below do not apply to you.

<u>Life Annuities that are not fully indexed to CPI:</u>

The income from life annuities that are not fully indexed to CPI loses its purchasing power over time. That is because the payments either remain the same or increase at a lower rate than the prevailing inflation. Over time, this real income gap grows. While your income is not exposed to longevity or market risks, the inflation risk is present.

This may be a desirable feature in situations where non–essential income is neither required nor desired. You may want to allocate $5,000/year to travelling. It may be important to travel (and spend that $5,000) in the early years of retirement, but as you get older you may not want to travel as much. You may not care about preserving your purchasing power over time. You can just buy a straight life annuity at a significantly lower cost than a fully indexed life annuity. This would fulfill your objective of gradually decreasing purchasing power over time.

Figure 34.1 depicts the downside variability of payments in real dollars as a percentage of the starting amount from a straight life annuity (no increase in payments). In the worst–case scenario, the real income was about 21% of the initial amount.

Figure 34.1 Downside variability of income for straight life annuity, no increase of payments

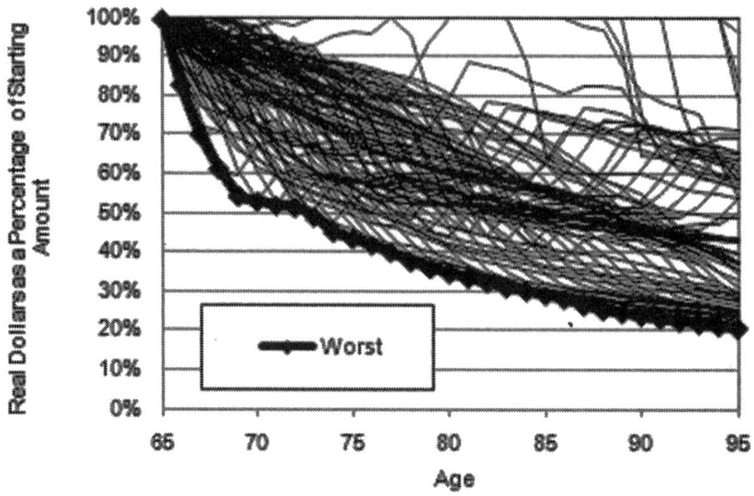

Table 34.1 indicates the worst real income percentages (WCRI) for various indexation rates of the life annuity payments.

Table 34.1: Downside variability of income for straight life annuity

Indexation of Life Annuity Payments	Worst–case Real Income (WCRI) as percentage of starting amount at age 85	at age 95
0%	29%	21%
1%	36%	28%
2%	43%	38%
3%	53%	50%

Later on, we will use these worst–case real income (WCRI) numbers in income allocation calculations.

Variable Pay Annuity:

The income from the VPA depends on market performance. If markets perform well, your income can increase greatly. On the other hand, in bad markets, you income can decrease significantly. These large swings can start immediately after buying the VPA. While your income is not subject to longevity risk, it has a large element of both market risk and inflation risk.

If you are willing to endure large swings of income for your non–essential expenses starting right after retirement, then VPA may be a good choice for you. If you choose an anticipated investment return (AIR) that is 3% or higher, the cost of the VPA can be about the same or lower than the straight life annuity, yet it has potential for a higher income.

Figure 34.2 depicts the downside variability of VPA payments in real dollars as a percentage of the starting amount. In the worst–case scenario, the real income was about 33% of the initial amount. This number is slightly different for different values of AIR, genders, and different notional asset mixes. However, we will use 33% as our WCRI for all VPAs.

Figure 34.2: Downside variability of income for VPA, 3% AIR

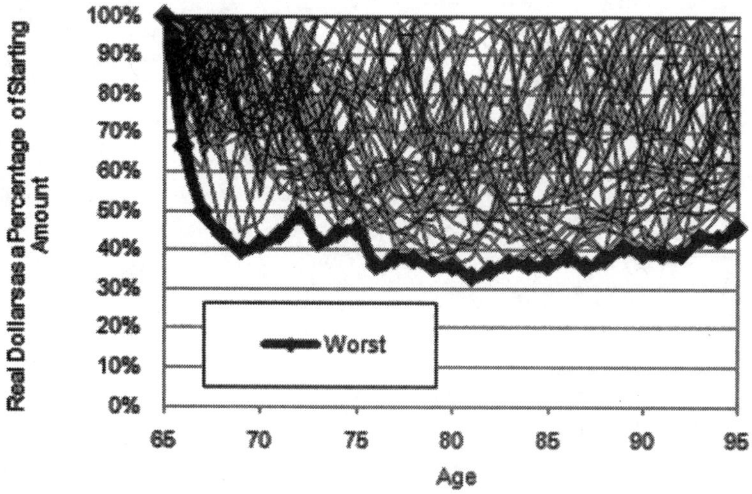

Variable Annuity with GMWBL:
The income from the VA–GMWBL will gradually erode over time. The benefit of the GMWBL is that your assets belong to you. You can cash them out at any time, subject to some fees and penalties. If your estate is important to you, and you can endure a loss of purchasing power gradually over time, then you may want to allocate some of your assets to this income class.

Figure 34.3 depicts the downside variability of GMWBL payments in real dollars as a percentage of the starting amount. In the worst–case scenario, the real income was about 21% of the initial amount. This WCRI is same as the straight life annuity, i.e. in the worst case, income from a GMWBL stayed flat.

Figure 34.3: Downside variability of income for GMWBL, 5% guaranteed rate

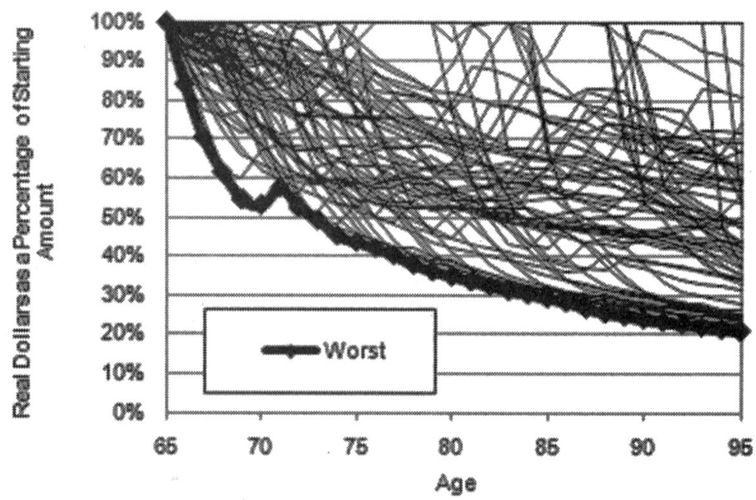

Variable Annuity with GMIB:
Similar to GMWBL, the income from the GMIB will gradually erode over time. When you annuitize, you will see a "pop" in income, but after that, the income remains constant. The benefit of the GMIB is that your assets belong to you until annuitization. Compared to GMWBL, the payments are generally higher. You can cash it out at any time until the annuitization, subject to some fees and charges. If your estate is important to you, and loss of purchasing power is tolerable, then you may want to allocate some of your assets to this income class.

Figure 34.4 depicts the downside variability of GMIB payments in real dollars as a percentage of the starting amount. The WCRI was about 25% of the initial amount, slightly better than the GMWBL.

Figure 34.4: Downside variability of income for GMIB, 6% guaranteed rate, no step–up after age 75, annuitized at age 85 or upon depletion of assets

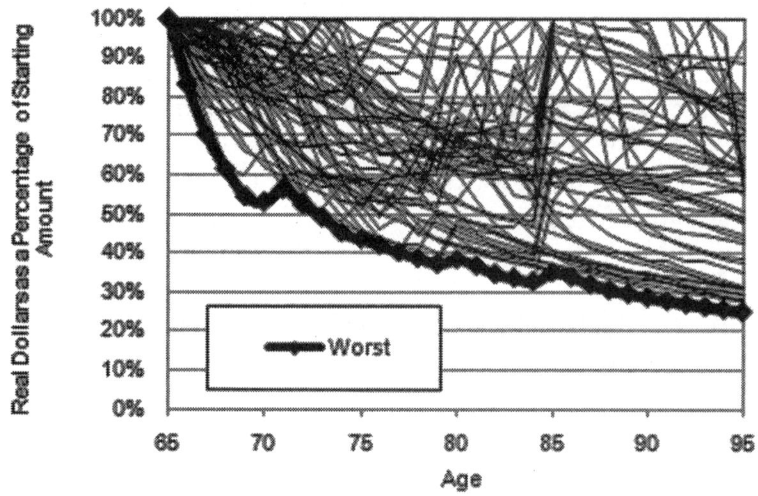

A "More Perfect Mix":

I first wrote about combining an investment portfolio, a CPI–indexed life annuity and a VPA in an article published in the *Financial Planning* magazine in June, 2003. This was a follow up to my "The Perfect Mix" article. The same editor aptly named this second article, "A More Perfect Mix". I will use the same name. Remember, it works only in the gray zone and only if you are willing to tolerate some fluctuation in your income.

How do we calculate how much to allot to each income class?

There are three steps for the "more perfect mix". In the first step, we calculate how much to allot to the income class with the variable income stream. This income stream may come from any one of the four income classes mentioned above (a life annuity not indexed to CPI, a VPA, a GMWBL or a GMIB). I call this equation "Otar's First Equation".

Otar's First Equation:

$$\$VI = \frac{\$NEI}{(100-WCRI) \times PR} \text{ X } 100 \qquad \text{(Equation 43.2)}$$

where:

$VI	is the dollar amount that needs to be allotted to the income class with variable payouts (one of the four income classes: life annuity, VPA, GMWBL or GMIB)
$NEI	is the dollar amount of the non–essential income required
WCRI	is the worst–case real income for each income class
PR	is the annuity rate or payment rate from this income class as a fraction of the premium, for example 0.05 for GMWBL or 0.07 from a straight life annuity

The second step is to calculate the dollar amount to allot to a CPI–indexed life annuity. This, I call "Otar's Second Equation".

Otar's Second Equation:

$$\$LA = \frac{\$NEI + \$EI - (SWR \times \$TS) + [\$VI \times (SWR - PR)]}{LR - SWR} \qquad \text{(Equation 43.3)}$$

where:

$LA	is the dollar amount to allot to the CPI–indexed life annuity
$EI	is the dollar amount of the essential income required
SWR	is the sustainable withdrawal rate (from Table 17.9)
$TS	is the total retirement assets available
LR	is the annuity rate in the first year for the CPI–indexed life annuity as a fraction of the premium

In the last step, we calculate the remaining assets to allot to the investment portfolio:

$$\$IP = \$TS - \$VI - \$LA \qquad \text{(Equation 43.4)}$$

where:

$IP	is the dollar amount to allot to the investment portfolio

Note that if the non–essential income ($NEI) is zero, then Equation 43.2 reverts to zero and Equation 43.3 reverts to the "perfect mix" equation.

Let's work through examples.

Example 43.16 - Gray Zone Solutions - Straight Life Annuity

Gavin is 65 years old, just retiring. He has $960,000 in his portfolio, all earmarked for his retirement. He needs $36,000 each year, indexed to inflation. This is for his essential expenses. He also needs $4,000 each year for travelling, a non-essential expense.

He needs income for 30 years until age 95.

1. In what zone is Gavin?

   Gavin's numbers are:

   - WR = $36,000 + $4,000 = $40,000
   - AR = 5.3% (from table in Figure 41.5) x $960,000 = $50,880
   - SWR = 3.7% (from table in Figure 41.5) x $960,000 = $35,520

   The WR is between AR and SWR, so Gavin is in the gray zone.

2. Calculate Gavin's income allocation, assuming he buys a straight life annuity for the non-essential income.

   This straight life annuity pays $7,100 annual income for life, no increases, for a premium of $100,000. The worst-case real income, WCRI for a straight life annuity is 21% (Table 34.1). The payment rate PR is 0.071, calculated as $7,100 / $100,000

   Otar's First Equation:

$$\$VI = \frac{\$NEI}{(100 - WCRI) \times PR} \text{ X } 100$$

$$\$VI = \frac{\$4{,}000}{(100 - 21) \times 0.071} \text{ X } 100 = \$71{,}314$$

   Gavin allots $71,314 to the straight life annuity.

   Otar's Second Equation:

$$\$LA = \frac{\$NEI + \$EI - (SWR \times \$TS) + [\$VI \times (SWR - PR)]}{LR - SWR}$$

$$\$LA = \frac{\$4{,}000 + \$36{,}000 - (0.037 \times \$960{,}000) + [\$71{,}314 \times (0.037 - 0.071)]}{0.053 - 0.037}$$

   $LA = $128,438

   Gavin allots $128,438 to the CPI-indexed life annuity.

The remaining assets are allotted to the investment portfolio:

$IP = $TS - $VI - $LA

$IP = $960,000 - $71,314 - $128,438 = $760,248

Gavin allots $760,248 to his investment portfolio.

Asset Allotment:

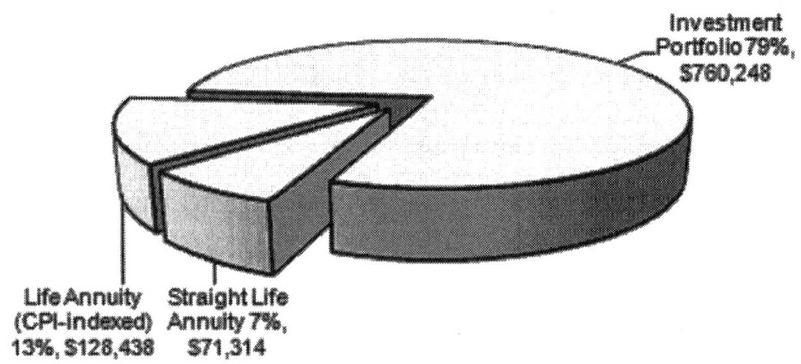

Check if Gavin meets his income needs:

The straight life annuity pays $5,063 (7.1% of $71,314), the CPI-indexed life annuity pays $6,808 (5.3% of $128,438), and investment portfolio provides $28,129 (3.7% of $760,248) in the first year.

They add up to $40,000, which is what Gavin wants.

Income Allocation:

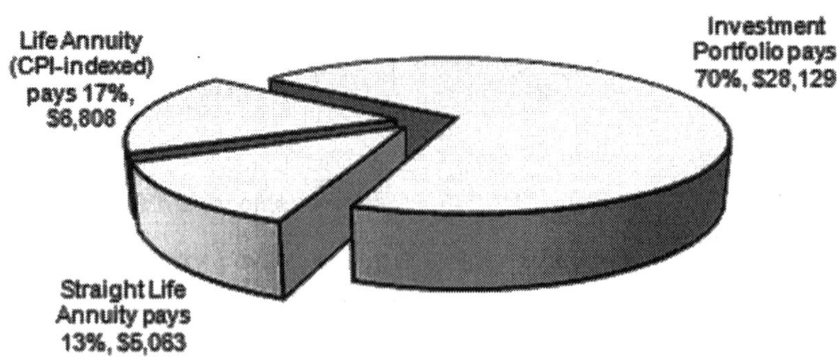

What happens in the worst-case situation? The straight life annuity pays (in current dollars) $1,063 (21% of $5,063) and the other income sources remain the same. The total for the worst case is exactly $36,000 ($1,063 + $6,808 + $28,129).

This is exactly how much Gavin wants for his essential income requirement. Here is his aftcast:

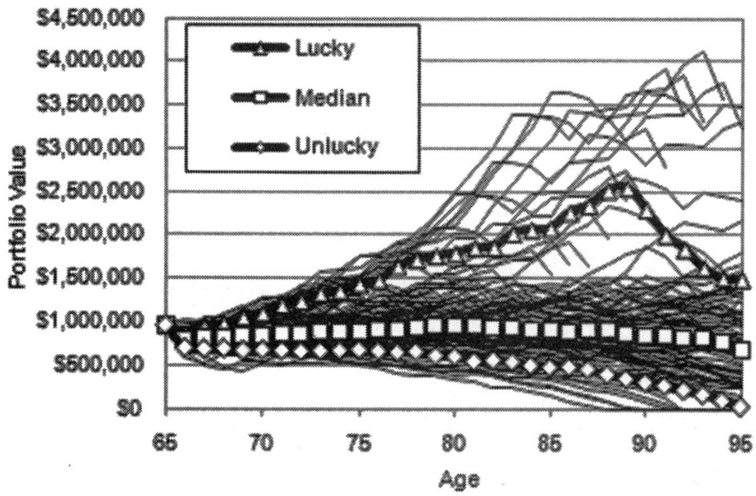

Example 43.17 - Gray Zone Solutions - Straight Life Annuity

Same as Example 43.16, except that Gavin does not care much about his non-essential expenses after **age 85**. The worst-case real income, WCRI, for a straight life annuity is 29% (Table 34.1) for age 85. The payment rate PR is 0.071, calculated as \$7,100 / \$100,000

Otar's First Equation:

$$\$VI = \frac{\$4{,}000}{(100-29)\times 0.071} \text{ X } 100 = \$79{,}349$$

Gavin allots \$79,349 to the straight life annuity.

Otar's Second Equation:

$$\$LA = \frac{\$4{,}000 + \$36{,}000 - (0.037 \times \$960{,}000) + [\$79{,}349 \times (0.037 - 0.071)]}{0.053 - 0.037}$$

$$\$LA = \$111{,}383$$

Gavin allots \$111,383 to the CPI-indexed life annuity.

The remaining assets are allotted to the investment portfolio:

$\$IP = \$960{,}000 - \$79{,}349 - \$111{,}383 = \$769{,}268$

Gavin allots \$769,268 to his investment portfolio.

Asset Allotment:

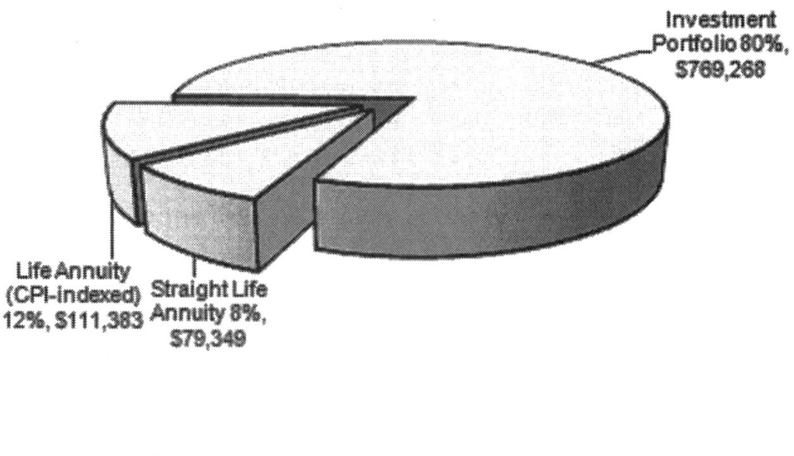

Check if Gavin meets his income needs:

The straight life annuity pays $5,634 (7.1% of $79,349), the CPI-indexed life annuity pays $5,903 (5.3% of $111,383), and the investment portfolio provides $28,463 (3.7% of $769,268) in the first year.

They add up to $40,000, which is what Gavin wants.

Income Allocation:

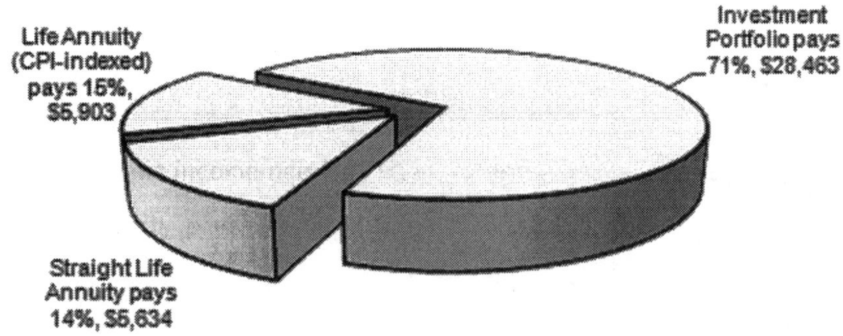

What happens at age 85 in the worst case? The straight life annuity pays (in current dollars) $1,634 (29% of $5,634) and the other income sources stay the same. The total for the worst case is exactly $36,000 ($1,634 + $5,903 + $28,463).

This is exactly how much Gavin wants for his essential income requirement at age 85.

What happens at age 95 in the worst case? The straight life annuity pays (in current dollars) $1,183 (21% of $5,634) and the other income sources stay the same. The total for the worst case is $35,549 ($1,183 + $5,903 + $28,463), a shortfall of $451 /year ($36,000 minus $35,549) of his essential income needs in current dollars.

However, compared to Example 43.16, he has $9,020 more in his investment portfolio (calculated as $769,268 minus $760,248). This can easily finance this shortfall that might potentially occur in the worst-case situation.

Example 43.18 - Gray Zone Solutions - VPA

Same as Example 43.16, except that Gavin buys a variable pay annuity with 3% AIR. The annuity quote indicates that the VPA initially pays \$5,400 / year for a premium of \$100,000. The worst-case real income, WCRI, for a VPA is 33%. The payment rate, PR, is 0.054, calculated as \$5,400 / \$100,000

Calculate Gavin's income allocation,

Otar's First Equation:

$$\$VI = \frac{\$4{,}000}{(100-33)\times 0.054} \text{ X } 100 = \$110{,}558$$

Gavin allots \$110,558 to the VPA.

Otar's Second Equation:

$$\$LA = \frac{\$4{,}000 + \$36{,}000 - (0.037\times\$960{,}000) + [\$110{,}558\times(0.037-0.054)]}{0.053-0.037}$$

$\$LA = \$162{,}563$

Gavin allots \$162,563 to the CPI-indexed life annuity. The remaining assets are allotted to the investment portfolio:

$\$IP = \$960{,}000 - \$110{,}558 - \$162{,}563 = \$686{,}879$

Gavin allots \$686,879 to his investment portfolio.

Asset Allotment:

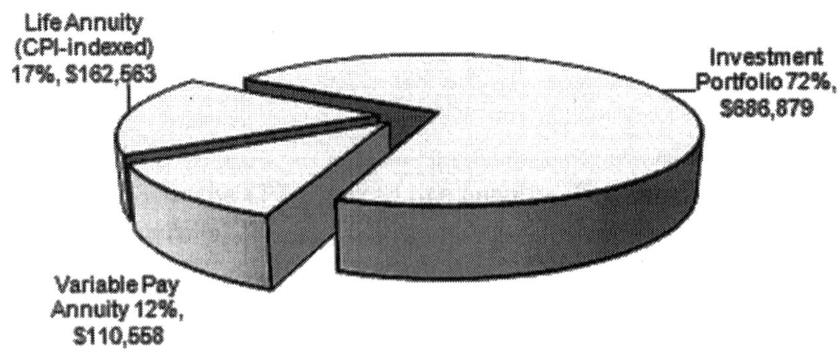

Check if Gavin meets his income needs:

The VPA pays $5,970 (5.4% of $110,558), the CPI-indexed life annuity pays $8,616 (5.3% of $162,563), and the investment portfolio provides $25,414 (3.7% of $686,879) in the first year.

They add up to $40,000, which is what Gavin wants.

Income Allocation:

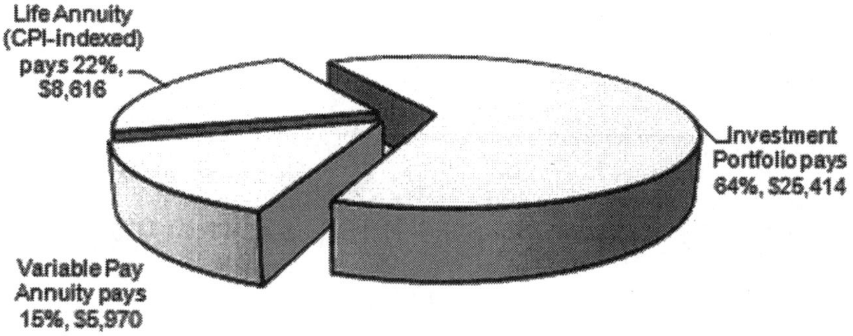

What happens in the worst-case situation? The VPA pays (in current dollars) $1,970 (33% of $5,970) and the other income sources remain the same. The total for the worst case is exactly $36,000 ($1,970 + $8,616 + $25,414).

This is exactly how much Gavin wants for his essential income requirement. Here is his aftcast:

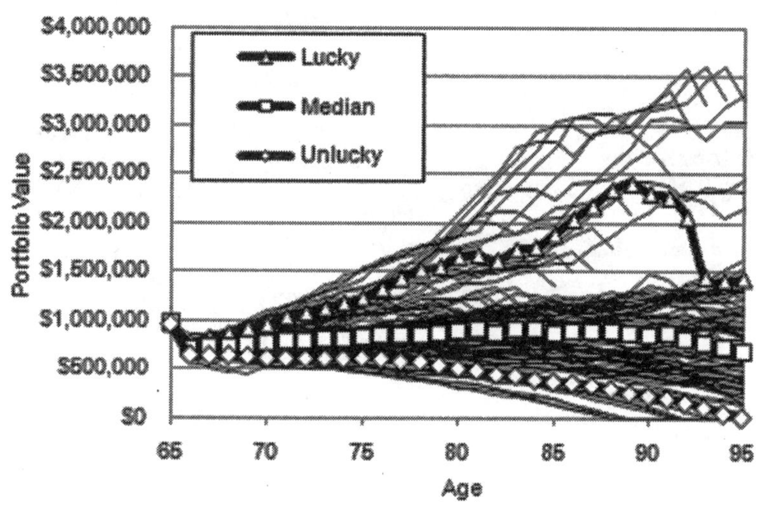

Example 43.19 - Gray Zone Solutions - GMWBL

Same as Example 43.16, except that Gavin buys a VA-GMWBL which has 5% guaranteed payments for life. It has potential for step-up increases. The WCRI for a GMWBL is 21%. The payment rate, PR, is 0.05.

Calculate Gavin's income allocation, assuming he buys a GMWBL for the non-essential income.

Otar's First Equation:

$$\$VI = \frac{\$4{,}000}{(100-21)\times 0.05} \text{ X } 100 = \$101{,}266$$

Gavin allots $101,266 to GMWBL.

Otar's Second Equation:

$$\$LA = \frac{\$4{,}000 + \$36{,}000 - (0.037 \times \$960{,}000) + [\$101{,}266 \times (0.037 - 0.05)]}{0.053 - 0.037}$$

$$\$LA = \$197{,}721$$

Gavin allots $197,721 to the CPI-indexed life annuity. The remaining assets are allotted to the investment portfolio:

$$\$IP = \$960{,}000 - \$101{,}266 - \$197{,}721 = \$661{,}013$$

Gavin allots $661,013 to his investment portfolio.

Asset Allotment:

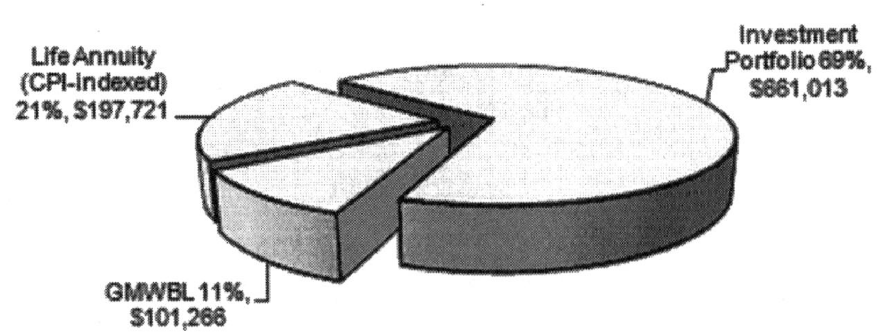

Check if Gavin meets his income needs:

The GMWBL pays $5,063 (5.0% of $101,266), the CPI-indexed life annuity pays $10,479 (5.3% of $197,721), and the investment portfolio provides $24,458 (3.7% of $661,013) in the first year.

They add up to $40,000, which is what Gavin wants.

Income Allocation:

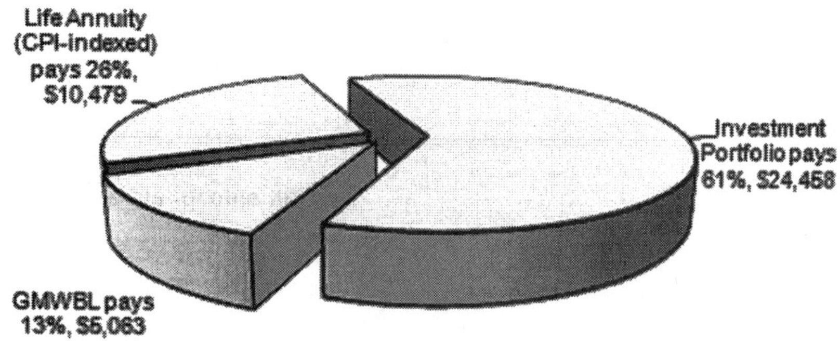

What happens in the worst-case situation? The GMWBL pays (in current dollars) $1,063 (21% of $5,063) and the other income sources stay the same. The total for the worst case is exactly $36,000 ($1,063 + $10,479 + $24,458).

This is exactly how much Gavin wants for his essential income requirement. Here is his aftcast:

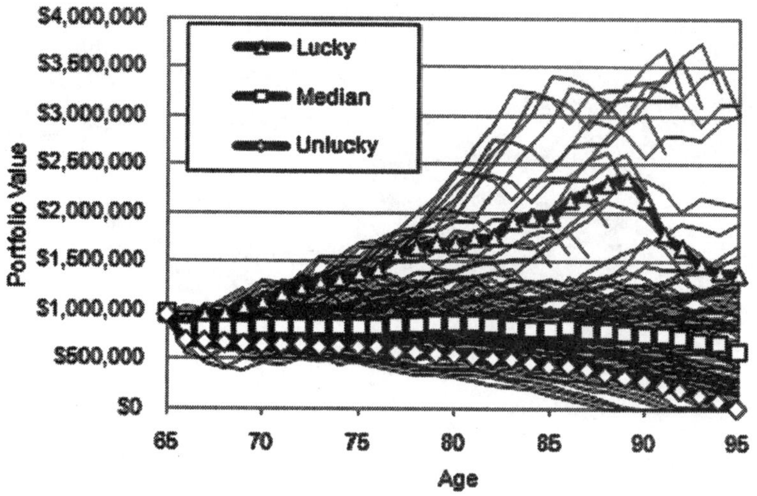

Example 43.20 - *Gray Zone Solutions - GMIB*

Same as Example 43.16, except that Gavin buys a VA-GMIB which has 6% guaranteed payments for life and must be annuitized at age 85. It pays potentially higher amounts in the future. The WCRI for a GMIB is 25%. The PR is 0.06.

Calculate Gavin's income allocation, assuming he buys the GMIB for the non-essential income.

Otar's First Equation:

$$\$VI = \frac{\$4{,}000}{(100-25)\times 0.06} \text{ X } 100 = \$88{,}889$$

Gavin allots $88,889 to the GMIB.

Otar's Second Equation:

$$\$LA = \frac{\$4{,}000 + \$36{,}000 - (0.037 \times \$960{,}000) + [\$88{,}889 \times (0.037 - 0.06)]}{0.053 - 0.037}$$

$$\$LA = \$152{,}222$$

Gavin allots $152,222 to the CPI-indexed life annuity. The remaining assets are allotted to the investment portfolio:

$$\$IP = \$960{,}000 - \$88{,}889 - \$152{,}222 = \$718{,}889$$

Gavin allots $718,889 to his investment portfolio.

Asset Allotment:

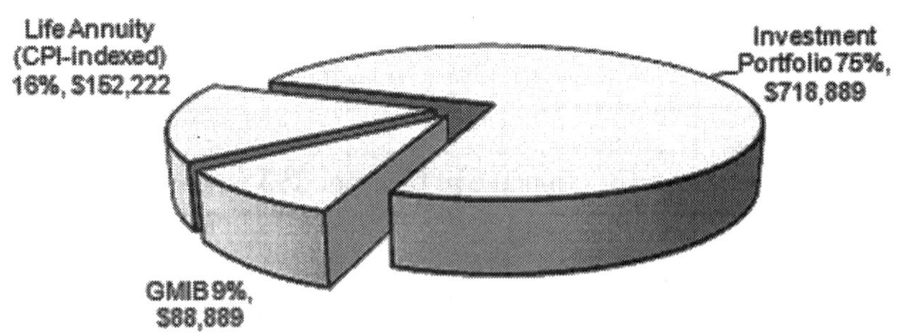

Check if Gavin meets his income needs:

The GMIB pays $5,333 (6% of $88,889), the CPI-indexed life annuity pays $8,068 (5.3% of $152,222), and the investment portfolio provides $26,599 (3.7% of $718,889) in the first year.

They add up to $40,000, which is what Gavin wants.

Income Allocation:

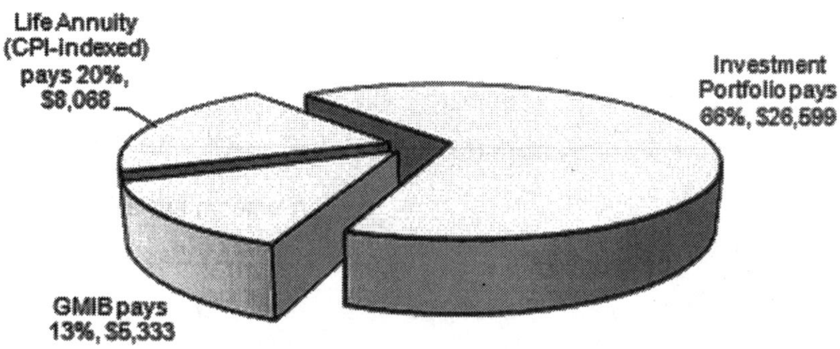

What happens in the worst-case situation? The GMIB pays (in current dollars) $1,333 (25% of $5,333) and the other income sources stay the same. The total for the worst case is exactly $36,000 ($1,333 + $8,068 + $26,599).

This is exactly how much Gavin wants for his essential income requirement. Here is his aftcast:

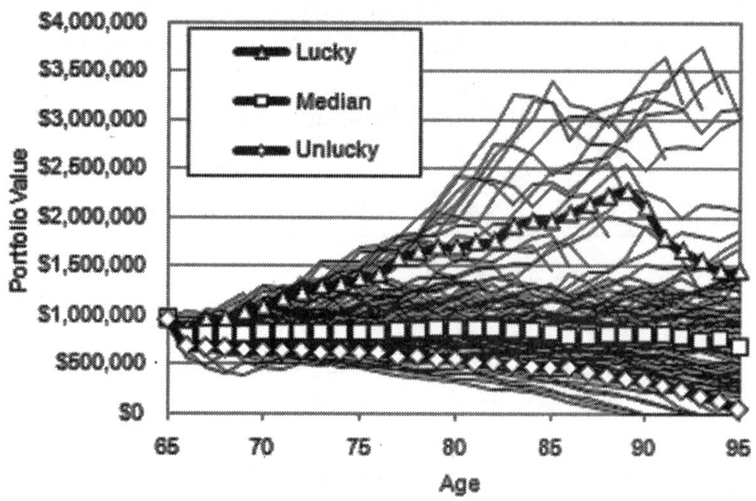

Summary of Gray Zone Solutions - Asset allotment in gray zone solutions.

Annual Income - Required $40,000, income is NOT variable

Asset Allotment to each Income Class:

	Investment Portfolio	CPI-Indexed Life Annuity	Other Income Class
Example 43.13	$547,200	$412,800	N/A

Annual Income - Essential: $36,000, Non-Essential $4,000

Asset Allotment to each Income Class:

	Investment Portfolio	CPI-Indexed Life Annuity	Other Income Class
Example 43.16	$760,248	$128,438	$71,314 Straight Life Annuity
Example 43.17	$769,268	$111,383	$79,349 Straight Life Annuity
Example 43.18	$686,879	$162,563	$110,558 VPA
Example 43.19	$661,013	$197,721	$101,266 GMWBL
Example 43.20	$718,889	$152,222	$88,889 GMIB

In the examples above (43.16 through 43.20), we calculated how much to allot to only one income class that pays the non–essential part of the income. However, you don't have to limit yourself to a single income class; you can divide it up into as many as you wish. Here are the steps:

1. Decide how you want to divide risk to each income class.
2. Use Otar's first equation to calculate how many dollars you need to allot to each income class.
3. Figure out how much to allot to a CPI–indexed life annuity using Equation 43.5.

$$\$LA = \frac{\$NEI + \$EI - (SWR \times \$TS) + \sum[\$VI \times (SWR\text{–}PR)]}{LR\text{–}SWR} \qquad \text{(Equation 43.5)}$$

4. Finally, use Equation 43.4 to calculate how much to allot to the investment portfolio.

The next example shows how you can have five different income classes: a straight life annuity, a VA–GMWBL, a VA–GMIB, a CPI–indexed life annuity and an investment portfolio.

Example 43.21 - Gray Zone Solutions - Multiple Income Classes

Same as Example 43.16, except Gavin wants his non-essential income of $4,000/year to come from three different income classes, risk divided equally.

VA-GMIB has 6% guaranteed payments for life and must be annuitized at age 85. The WCRI for a GMIB is 25%. The PR is 0.06.

GMWBL has 5% guaranteed payments for life. It pays potentially higher amounts in the future. The WCRI for a GMWBL is 21%. The PR is 0.05.

The straight life annuity pays $7,100 annual income for life, no increases, for a premium of $100,000. The worst-case real income, WCRI, for a straight life annuity is 21% (Table 34.1). The PR is 0.071.

1. Calculate Gavin's asset allotment to the VA-GMIB using Otar's First Equation:

$$\$VI = \frac{(\frac{\$4{,}000}{3})}{(100-25) \times 0.06} \text{ X } 100 = \$29{,}630$$

Gavin allots $29,630 to VA-GMIB.

2. Calculate Gavin's asset allotment to the VA-GMWBL using Otar's First Equation:

$$\$VI = \frac{(\frac{\$4{,}000}{3})}{(100-21) \times 0.05} \text{ X } 100 = \$33{,}755$$

Gavin allots $33,755 to VA-GMWBL.

3. Calculate Gavin's asset allotment to the straight life annuity using Otar's First Equation:

$$\$VI = \frac{(\frac{\$4{,}000}{3})}{(100-21) \times 0.071} \text{ X } 100 = \$23{,}771$$

Gavin allots $23,771 to straight life annuity.

Now, calculate the total contribution of these three income classes for Equation 43.5:

$$\$LA = \frac{\$NEI + \$EI - (SWR \times \$TS) + \sum [\$VI \times (SWR - PR)]}{LR - SWR}$$

Calculate the sum from each income class with variable payments

$$\underbrace{\$29{,}630 \times (0.037 - 0.06)}_{\text{VA-GMIB}} + \underbrace{\$33{,}755 \times (0.037 - 0.05)}_{\text{VA-GMWBL}} + \underbrace{\$23{,}771 \times (0.037 - 0.071)}_{\text{Straight Life Annuity}}$$

= -\$681 - \$439 - \$808

= - \$1,928

Otar's Second Equation becomes:

$$\$LA = \frac{\$4{,}000 + \$36{,}000 - (0.037 \times \$960{,}000) + [-\$1{,}928]}{0.053 - 0.037}$$

$LA = \$159,500

Gavin allots \$159,500 to the CPI-indexed life annuity. The remaining assets are allotted to the investment portfolio:

$IP = \$960,000 - \$29,630 - \$33,755 - \$23,771 - \$159,500 = \$713,344

Gavin allots \$713,344 to his investment portfolio.

Asset Allotment:

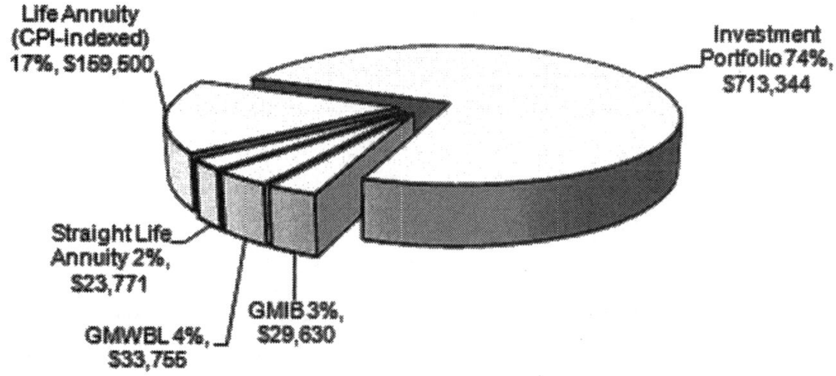

Check if Gavin meets his income needs:

The GMIB pays $1,778 (6% of $29,630), the GMWBL pays $1,688 (5% of $33,755), the straight life annuity pays $1,688 (7.1% of $23,771), the CPI-indexed life annuity pays $8,454 (5.3% of $159,500), and the investment portfolio provides $26,394 (3.7% of $713,344) in the first year.

They add up to $40,000 (excluding the rounding error), which is what Gavin wants.

Income Allocation:

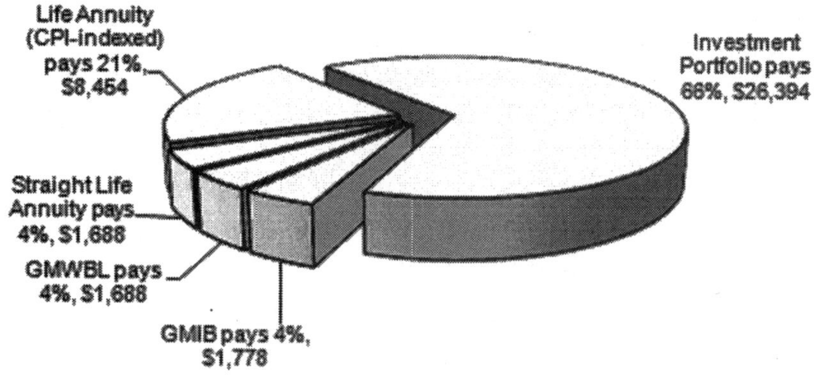

What happens in the worst-case situation?

The GMIB pays (in current dollars) $445 (25% of $1,778), the GMWBL pays $354 (21% of $1,688), the straight life annuity pays $354 (21% of $1,688). The other income sources stay the same. The total for the worst case is exactly $36,001 ($445 + $354 + $354 + $8,454 + $26,394).

This is exactly (excluding the rounding error) how much Gavin wants for his essential income requirement.

Why would you want to diversify income classes? Because, doing so might reduce the inflation risk for the non–essential part of the income.

Keep in mind that figures in these examples are specific to this particular case. You need to use actual, up–to–date annuity quotations to calculate your own numbers. Once you have all your numbers, you can create many solutions from which to choose, as we have seen in the examples. There is never any cookie–cutter type of income allocation in retirement planning. If anyone tells you otherwise, walk away.

At this point it is important to know this: the higher the non–essential portion of your income in the total required income, the less money you need to spend on life annuities.

I admit that it is more work to separate the non–essential and the essential income needs. However, a couple of hours of work can reward you handsomely. In the preceding examples, designating 10% of his total income as non–essential allowed Gavin to retain as much as 41% more of his money inside his investment[85] portfolio, instead of handing it over to the insurance company for annuitization.

[85] In Example 43.13, a total of $547,200 is placed in the investment portfolio. In Example 43.17, a total of $769,268 was placed in the investment portfolio. The difference is 40.6%.

Conclusion:

If you are in the gray zone, then you have to be very careful with your income allocation strategy. You do not have much leeway with your retirement savings. However, with careful planning, you can have lifelong income.

In the gray zone, no strategy will work safely unless the risk is exported to an insurance company. You must purchase a sufficient amount of life annuity to bring down the level of withdrawals from the portfolio to below the sustainable rate. The perfect mix formulas help you calculate the exact amounts.

You can achieve significant improvements by separating essential and non–essential expenses. This can save you a bundle of money, allow you to keep a larger amount of your money in your investment portfolio, and reduce the dollar amount paid for life annuities. It might enable you to leave a larger estate.

If you are in the gray zone, be very leery about any strategy that does not involve some form of annuities. Many research articles I have seen involve selective historical data, unrealistic simulation models, or plainly misguided assumptions. The market history indicates that wrong strategies in the gray zone will punish the retiree severely.

Chapter 44

Red Zone Strategies

If your withdrawal rate (WR) is greater than the annuity rate (AR), then you are in the red zone. Alternatively, if your asset ratio (CAM) is less than the life annuity multiplier (LAM), you are in the red zone.

Here they are highlights of the red zone:

- The red zone is the worst zone to be in.
- Your portfolio can finance neither your retirement nor the time value of fluctuations.
- You have no reserve to cover longevity, market and inflation risks.
- If you decide to finance your retirement through your investment portfolio, your portfolio will be decumulating. You will most likely run out of money well before you die.
- Your only strategy is to buy a life annuity with your entire retirement savings.
- The lifetime income you will receive will likely be lower than you require.
- Of the two emotions (hope and fear), you have to design for fear.
- Don't count on having anything left over from your retirement savings for your children or other beneficiaries.
- If you want to leave an estate, then buy life insurance. If you already have life insurance make sure to keep it.
- Buy long–term care insurance to cover the costs of the final years of life in a nursing home.

Practice Management for Advisors:

Here are a few tips to minimize potential future problems and litigation risk, as well as to manage client expectations in the red zone:

- Pay attention to how much of your precious time you allocate to red zone clients. One client in the red zone can take more of your time than five clients in the green zone. Paradoxically, one client in the green zone will likely create more revenue than five clients in the red zone.
- If a prospect is in the red zone and he is not willing to follow your advice on buying a life annuity for a lifelong income, don't waste your time. Just don't accept him as a client and politely show him the door.
- If a current client is in the red zone and does not follow your advice on income allocation, ask him to find another advisor.
- When reviewing your client list for potential risks, clients in the red zone carry the highest risk for your practice.

- Red zone clients expect you to perform miracles because "normal" portfolio growth will not meet their financial needs. Decide what business you are in: creating miracles or giving sound advice. If you try to create miracles, it will likely backfire sooner or later, because a red zone portfolio cannot carry this risk.

Worked Examples:

In the following pages, I walk you through red zone examples.

Example 44.1 - Zone Analysis

Jim is 65 years old, just retiring. He has $720,000 in his portfolio, all earmarked for his retirement. He needs $40,000 each year, indexed to inflation. He needs income for 30 years until age 95.

What zone is Jim in?

Jim's numbers are:

- CAM = $720,000 / $40,000 = 18
- SAM = 27 (from table in Figure 41.6)
- LAM = 20 (from table in Figure 41.6)

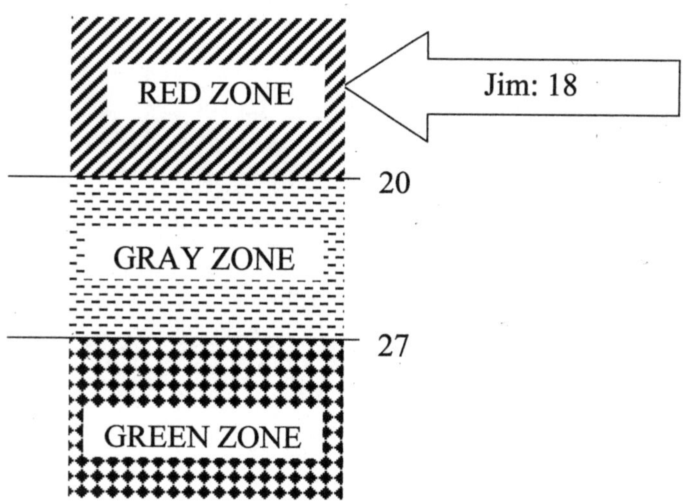

Jim is in the red zone. He can have lifelong income only if he buys a life annuity.

What does not work?

Any income allocation strategy that does not export *all* of the longevity, market and inflation risks will likely fail. If you delay passing these risks to insurance companies at the beginning of your retirement, even the luck factor cannot help you much.

Let's first take the numbers from Example 44.1 and apply them to all the strategies that we ran in the green zone in Chapter 42. Example 44.2 is the same as Example 42.2, except that we use Jim's numbers instead of Dan's numbers.

Remember that for a proper retirement plan, we want the probability of depletion of the portfolio to remain at or below 10% at the age of death. We also want the probability of receiving the full required income to remain above 90% throughout retirement in a properly designed plan.

What do you notice in this? No income allocation strategy meets our criteria of an acceptable retirement plan in the red zone.

	Probability of Depletion		Probability of full income at age 94
	by age 85	by age 95	
Example 44.2 Investment Portfolio	32%	85%	14%
Example 44.3 Straight Life Annuity and Investment Portfolio	29%	68%	33%
Example 44.4 3% Indexed Life Annuity and Investment Portfolio	N/A	N/A	0%
Example 44.5 CPI-Indexed Life Annuity and Investment Portfolio	N/A	N/A	0%
Example 44.6 10-Year Term Annuity and Investment Portfolio	43%	94%	6%
Example 44.7 VA-GMWBL and Investment Portfolio	44%	75%	14%
Example 44.8 VA-GMIB and Investment Portfolio	37%	64%	36%
Example 44.9 Ten-Year Asset Dedication	38%	90%	10%
Example 44.10 Straight Life Annuity Ladder and Investment Portfolio	41%	73%	27%
Example 44.11 CPI-Indexed Life Annuity Ladder and Investment Portfolio	N/A	N/A	0%
Example 44.12 Bond Portfolio	18%	100%	0%

None of the income allocation strategies worked for Jim. He is in the red zone, wants $40,000 income annually, indexed to inflation, from his portfolio of $720,000 starting at age 65.

Remedies:

Sometimes, with a few adjustments you can move from the red zone into the gray zone, even to the green zone.

If Already Retired:

If you are already retired, then you need to slow down withdrawals from your portfolio. Withdrawals can be reduced by cutting back expenditures and/or by finding part time work to supplement retirement income.

Going back to Example 44.4, this life annuity cost Jim $728,000. It generates $40,000 with 3% annual indexation of payments. However, Jim has only $720,000 in his account. So, he needs to cut back his withdrawals by about 1.1%, to $39,560 at age 65, calculated as $40,000 X $720,000 / $728,000. This is a small sacrifice, but it does solve the longevity and market risks. However, it does not fully cover the inflation risk.

If Jim wants to cover his inflation risk fully, then he needs to buy a life annuity with payments indexed fully to CPI, which is Example 44.5. This life annuity cost Jim about $753,000. However, he has only $720,000 in his account. So, he needs to cut back his withdrawals by about 4.4%, to $38,247 at age 65, calculated as $40,000 X $720,000 / $753,000. Again, this is a small sacrifice for covering all of the longevity, market and inflation risks for life.

Do not ladder annuities in the red zone. That increases the risk significantly. Just buy what you need in one installment and move on. Do not wait for the interest rates to go up. Time is your enemy, you cannot play market timing with interest rates. If you were to ladder your annuity purchase in Example 44.11, you would then have to cut back your income to about $31,000, a 23% reduction for lifelong income, just for the luxury of laddering the annuity.

If Still Working:

If you are still working then the most effective way of moving out of the red zone is to delay retirement. I have seen cases where one or two additional years of working, moves the outcome from the red zone to the green zone.

For example, in Example 44.2, you need to work until age 74 if you want to generate lifelong income from your investment portfolio. However, with a life annuity with CPI–indexed payments, you may be able to retire at age 66. If you really want to leave an estate, it would probably be a lot cheaper to buy life insurance and retire 8 years sooner.

Conclusion:

If you are in the red zone, then you must export all of the risk to an insurance company. For secure lifelong income, all your savings must be allocated to life annuities. You will need to cut back your expenses, because even if you use all your savings to buy a life annuity, the payments will be lower than the withdrawal rate that you were hoping for.

The most effective remedy is to delay retirement. A few extra years in the accumulation stage can create a significant difference in your retirement finances.

If you are in the red zone, you are not alone. The average baby boomer is in the red zone. Most pension funds –private or public– are in the red zone. It is a crowded place.

Chapter 45

The Final Word

Thank you for reading this book. I am glad I was able to share my research on retirement planning with you. I hope it helped you understand the math based on market history. Now, perhaps it will be easier to recognize some of the nonsense in our business.

I realize that I repeated some of my opinions and conclusions more often than I should have. Forgive me for that. When I first discovered the importance of the luck factor, sequence of returns, the time value of fluctuations, the unimportance of asset allocation or diversification, the detrimental results of Monte Carlo simulators or the Gaussian mindset, I just could not believe it. I played with my spreadsheets based on the actual market history endlessly during the last nine years. Each time I discovered another angle, it took me a long time to fully realize its implications for the millions of retirees. Many times, in conferences and so–called "educational" seminars, I felt like shouting "What nonsense are you talking about?"

So here are a few of my basic closing thoughts.

- Debt and Leveraging: stay out of debt. In life, there are only two occasions you might want to consider borrowing: to finance your first home and your education. Other than that, stay away from borrowing and leveraging.
- Work: do what you love and love what you do. And if you love what you do, don't just retire because you hit a certain age. Keep on doing it; you'll be happier, healthier and richer.
- Trust others only as much as you need to and only after they fully earn it.
- Keep your life simple. Stick to stocks, bonds, inflation–indexed bonds, cash. That is all you need. Complicated investments can blow up in your face.
- Learn to differentiate between what is important and what is essential. You can ignore everything else.
- Emergency funds: put aside a minimum of one year's living expenses in the bank. Do not touch it for travel, hobbies or other "important" expenses. This is for emergencies *only*. Yes, it will sit there for years doing nothing. That is OK.
- Investment education: make this an ongoing process.
- If you have the time, discipline and inclination, you may want to follow a few simple technical analysis signals. If you can avoid large losses, markets take care of growth. I use moving averages, MACD, RSI. You don't need anything more complicated than that
- If you don't have the time or inclination to do it yourself, then find a good advisor.

- Don't believe everything you read in any research, article, book or media. Avoid any investment research article which includes words like "Monte Carlo, simulation, mathematical model, proprietary model, hot fund managers, hot sectors, assumed average, forecast, market history of 30 years (30 years is too short to be called a history)", and so on.
- Fads: our financial industry always comes up with new marketing ploys, new products, and new names. Learn to recognize them. Don't fall for fads of any kind.
- If you are a do–it–yourselfer: 1. Do not put more than 5% of the account value in one company stock; 2. when in doubt, get out; 3. the best time to recover from a mistake is the first time you realize you might have made a mistake; 4. do not let a profit turn into a loss; 5. avoid big losses.
- The average person has little or no hope of achieving anywhere close to index returns. Most mutual fund managers are either no different than the average investor, or worse. There are plenty of ETF's available. You can put together a well–diversified portfolio with four or five different ETFs. I prefer broad based fundamental index funds.
- Don't pay too much attention to books and articles about the behavioral psychology of investing. They are for losers trying to figure out why they keep losing money. If you can't make money after ten trades in a row, give up. Build a *conservative* ETF portfolio and hang on to it.
- Ignore any retirement plan that includes a forecast. No assumed growth rate, no assumed inflation, no Monte Carlo models, no "black box" models. Use aftcast only.
- Review your financial situation regularly.
- If following a buy and hold strategy, never allocate more than 50% of your assets to equities in any portfolio, ever.
- Relax. My father slept for about thirty minutes every day after lunch. He lived in generally good health until age 95. I started doing the same after his death three years ago. I regret that I did not start it sooner. I recommend it to everyone.

Your Advisor:

When I first started fifteen years ago, I had to fill out a "Know Your Client" form, a.k.a. KYC, one for each client. At that time, it was only one page long. Now, I have to fill out a KYC for each account of each client. Now, I have three or four different KYCs for the same client. And the KYC form has grown from one page to four pages.

I used to spend 10% of my time filling out forms. Now I spend about 40% of my client time for that. I became a foot soldier in an army of confidential data collectors. At each client meeting it seems I am handing over more forms to sign. I often wonder what a client thinks when I push another form in front of him, asking him to sign that he was not a president, a cabinet minister, a judge, a member of parliament, etc. in a foreign country on the PEFP (politically exposed foreign persons) form, each and every year.

I am expected to spend a lot of time gathering data for my compliance department, and ultimately for the army of lawyers in the government. How can you expect me to do what you hired me for in the first place? Honestly, I have no good answer for you. I am too busy filling out forms.

In my opinion, the available educational curriculum for the advisor is mediocre at best. Looking back to my fifteen years as a financial advisor, I participated in too many seminars, conferences and workshops offered by the "biggest and the best" of investment companies, mutual funds, national associations, academia and others. I have yet to experience one event that did not include some of the myths produced by common academic wisdom. Every event I went to, there was always one or more presenter reciting the wisdom of asset allocation, efficient frontier, or yet another simulator model; all of which are based on the Gaussian mindset. After that much junk indoctrination, even the smartest advisor starts believing this propaganda. The frontline advisors need unbiased, usable, and pertinent knowledge. When I sit down with a client, he does not care if the inventor of a strategy won a prize in some distant Scandinavian[86] country. All he cares about is the sustainability of his own retirement. Fortunately, having an engineering background helped me to shut out a lot of this nonsense. I did my own research for one reason: to enable me to analyze my own personal retirement. I was lucky to have the patience, opportunity and craving to share my findings with you and others.

You need advisors to help you prepare a financial plan, a retirement plan, an estate plan and a risk management plan. They will give you guidance in your financial decisions. I have met many good advisors at conferences. Most of them are honorable people. They try their best to educate themselves and then to give you the advice you need. Treat them with respect.

The reality is, markets fluctuate. After a serious downturn, many investors are disappointed and angry with their advisors. That is understandable. The financial professionals end up looking like the barbers performing surgery in medieval ages[87]. That is the way it goes. Still, treat your advisor with respect.

Proper retirement planning requires that we let the market history provide us with two outcomes: lucky and unlucky. As demonstrated throughout this book, when we consider two extreme outcomes based on market history, we can expect the reality to lie somewhere in between. If your plan does not include extreme outcomes, find another planner.

---

[86] no offense intended to any foreign country or their institutions

[87] no offense intended for the hair care profession.

Pension Funds:

This book is not about pensions, but this may be a good place to express my thoughts on pensions anyway.

There are two types of pension funds: Defined Benefit and Defined Contribution. With most defined benefit plans, the employer alone is responsible for the market risk. When it blows up, then the risk is sometimes transferred to all taxpayers for the benefit of the few. Many private and public defined benefit pension funds are in the red zone. Many more will soon be in the red zone because of the prevailing faulty financial models and the defective financial culture.

On the other hand, the defined contribution pensions download and spread the risk to many individuals and therefore have a better chance of survival over the long term.

What puzzles me most is this: Why should an employer, be it a company or the government, fully assume the stock market risk that it has no control over? As absurd as it is to pass a law banning hurricanes, you cannot legislate an average market growth into any pension. Yet in a roundabout way, this is exactly what is happening. That is why most defined benefit pensions –given enough time– will eventually fail.

Defined benefit pension funds ought to be either closed down or converted to the defined contribution type. Just admit that they were a financial catastrophe for employers, taxpayers and shareowners, add it to the long list of our failed social experiments – like feudalism, dictatorship or communism–, apologize to affected parties, and move on. Companies already have enough on their plate to deal with. They should not and they cannot continue underwriting the stock market risk. Why should an average taxpayer holding two jobs, working day and night trying to make ends meet, pay the financial industry billions and billions of dollars for an illusion of unattainable dreams? Yes, it is a puzzle for me.

What is not a puzzle is the math: say you are the pension sponsor, i.e. the company with a defined contribution pension plan. Ignore all long–term growth rates that your actuaries and investment managers are proposing to you. Ask your actuary to use an "average" 3.7% annual growth rate, which is halfway between the historical unlucky and median effective growth rates (Table 20.3). Calculate your annual pension obligation based on this 3.7% annual growth rate for the next 10 years. Do the same calculation again, this time using a 1.8% annual growth rate for the next 4 years. If you are comfortable with such payments for both of these periods, then your plan might work. Otherwise, shut it down.

Conclusion:

To be honest, I hate the time value of fluctuations. It ruins everything. I wish I had never discovered it. For that, I blame the premature frost that killed my cabbage crop 47 years ago.

Good Luck!

Source Data

Column A: End of year
Column B: Interest Rate %, 1900–1987, courtesy of "Market Volatility", by Robert J. Schiller, MIT Press, [1997], page 440–441, data series 4
Column C: Annual inflation %, (U.S. Bureau of Labor Statistics, wholesale price index for the years between 1900–1913, the consumer price index after 1913)
Column D: Annual percent change of DJIA
Column E: Annual percent change of S&P500
Column F: Annual percent change of SP/TSX
Column G: Annual percent change of FTSE–AllShares
Column H: Annual percent change of Nikkei225
Column I: Annual percent change of ASX–All Ordinaires

A	B	C	D	E	F	G	H	I
1900	4.64	8.10	7.01%	16.28%		–0.90%		5.66%
1901	4.30	–2.62	–8.70%	14.85%		–4.95%		–0.11%
1902	4.72	6.15	–0.42%	4.19%		–1.29%		0.33%
1903	5.50	2.54	–23.61%	–21.04%		–5.56%		9.28%
1904	4.34	2.47	41.74%	26.20%		2.48%		11.99%
1905	4.17	–2.41	38.20%	17.08%		6.22%		7.49%
1906	5.47	3.53	–1.92%	–3.14%		–0.44%		7.22%
1907	6.23	5.46	–37.73%	–28.35%		–14.74%		3.48%
1908	5.32	–4.21	46.64%	32.26%		8.13%		11.14%
1909	3.65	7.77	14.97%	11.26%		4.77%		9.62%
1910	5.26	4.08	–17.86%	–8.04%		–2.51%		4.73%
1911	4.00	–7.83	0.39%	–1.62%		0.33%		5.63%
1912	4.35	6.54	7.58%	1.97%		–0.88%		1.33%
1913	5.65	0.92	–10.34%	–10.00%		–6.69%		4.44%
1914	4.64	1.00	–30.72%	–10.63%		–6.89%		9.91%
1915	3.65	2.00	81.66%	24.73%		–5.10%	51.99%	–1.67%
1916	3.64	12.60	–4.19%	2.57%		0.54%	29.63%	–10.33%
1917	4.25	18.10	–21.71%	–24.66%		–10.55%	–0.50%	1.46%
1918	5.98	20.40	10.51%	8.88%		10.95%	1.96%	5.87%
1919	5.36	14.50	30.45%	12.48%	30.45%	2.46%	27.06%	7.46%
1920	7.30	2.60	–32.90%	–19.48%	–10.60%	–13.27%	–48.83%	12.10%
1921	7.44	–10.80	12.72%	2.67%	–5.43%	–5.41%	5.25%	1.92%
1922	4.58	–2.30	21.74%	21.92%	15.15%	17.59%	–17.00%	13.95%
1923	4.96	2.40	–3.25%	–0.79%	3.19%	2.01%	–4.76%	16.17%
1924	4.34	0.00	26.16%	19.82%	6.01%	9.50%	7.10%	5.02%
1925	3.87	3.50	30.00%	19.57%	22.68%	4.42%	14.36%	7.26%
1926	4.28	–1.10	0.34%	5.93%	16.80%	2.41%	–2.54%	11.17%
1927	4.26	–2.30	28.75%	30.82%	38.99%	8.24%	–5.25%	7.65%
1928	4.64	–1.20	48.22%	41.81%	27.50%	8.09%	–0.66%	8.69%
1929	6.01	0.60	–17.17%	–12.67%	–14.76%	–7.35%	–16.88%	5.78%
1930	4.15	–6.40	–33.77%	–26.39%	–34.12%	–19.44%	–21.11%	–29.28%
1931	2.43	–9.30	–52.67%	–48.06%	–37.15%	–23.46%	–3.21%	–16.06%
1932	3.36	–10.30	–23.07%	–14.58%	–20.83%	5.59%	86.30%	19.64%
1933	1.46	0.80	66.69%	48.66%	46.79%	27.20%	12.50%	22.81%
1934	1.01	1.50	4.14%	–12.14%	–0.74%	8.29%	–5.33%	16.74%
1935	0.75	3.00	38.53%	48.60%	22.55%	7.81%	4.52%	12.71%

A	B	C	D	E	F	G	H	I
1936	0.75	1.40	24.82%	27.83%	26.46%	13.85%	6.46%	11.92%
1937	0.88	2.90	–32.82%	–35.70%	–26.38%	–19.30%	3.87%	11.37%
1938	0.88	–2.80	28.06%	10.52%	4.58%	–14.24%	–9.83%	–7.66%
1939	0.56	0.00	–2.92%	–1.60%	1.97%	0.78%	33.57%	–4.48%
1940	0.56	0.70	–12.72%	–14.23%	–20.90%	–12.99%	–16.77%	–1.25%
1941	0.53	9.90	–15.38%	–15.36%	–8.25%	22.62%	13.42%	–0.92%
1942	0.63	9.00	7.61%	12.99%	6.45%	18.59%	0.64%	–9.49%
1943	0.69	3.00	13.81%	17.44%	18.55%	8.05%	–1.40%	18.46%
1944	0.72	2.30	12.09%	13.84%	12.42%	10.68%	–0.69%	3.20%
1945	0.75	2.20	26.65%	33.58%	35.81%	–0.58%	–3.08%	5.43%
1946	0.76	18.10	–8.14%	–15.59%	0.40%	18.12%	–29.14%	12.33%
1947	1.01	8.80	2.23%	–2.50%	–4.61%	–2.73%	36.87%	10.69%
1948	1.35	3.00	–2.13%	3.57%	5.90%	–4.00%	85.30%	5.20%
1949	1.58	–2.10	12.88%	9.90%	14.59%	–13.88%	50.89%	–3.99%
1950	1.32	5.90	17.63%	25.65%	39.91%	6.36%	–7.28%	20.19%
1951	2.12	6.00	14.37%	14.05%	17.79%	2.42%	62.95%	18.03%
1952	2.39	0.80	8.42%	8.23%	–5.63%	–5.06%	118.38%	–24.61%
1953	2.58	0.70	–3.77%	–2.75%	–3.12%	15.98%	4.22%	0.34%
1954	1.80	–0.70	43.96%	39.83%	32.24%	34.49%	–5.78%	11.87%
1955	1.81	0.40	20.77%	24.02%	22.63%	1.58%	19.55%	9.50%
1956	3.21	3.00	2.27%	2.90%	5.31%	–9.00%	29.00%	–1.13%
1957	3.86	2.90	–12.77%	–9.49%	–23.52%	–3.33%	–13.58%	12.47%
1958	2.54	1.80	33.96%	35.26%	26.75%	33.18%	40.46%	8.56%
1959	3.74	1.70	16.40%	4.33%	1.35%	43.40%	31.26%	24.63%
1960	4.28	1.40	–9.34%	0.14%	–1.86%	–4.71%	55.07%	21.81%
1961	2.91	0.70	18.71%	23.13%	28.66%	–2.52%	5.59%	–7.89%
1962	3.39	1.30	–10.81%	–11.81%	–10.25%	–1.81%	–0.85%	0.67%
1963	3.50	1.60	17.00%	18.89%	11.72%	10.60%	–13.75%	9.50%
1964	4.09	1.00	14.57%	12.97%	21.46%	–10.00%	–0.70%	12.44%
1965	4.46	1.90	10.88%	9.06%	3.23%	6.73%	16.55%	–12.20%
1966	5.44	3.50	–18.94%	–13.09%	–10.40%	–9.31%	2.42%	–0.62%
1967	5.55	3.00	15.20%	20.09%	13.89%	28.98%	–11.61%	17.24%
1968	6.17	4.70	4.27%	7.66%	18.20%	43.36%	33.61%	43.61%
1969	8.05	6.20	–15.19%	–11.36%	–4.06%	–15.19%	37.56%	9.98%
1970	9.11	5.60	4.82%	0.10%	–7.08%	–7.52%	–15.76%	–4.18%
1971	5.66	3.30	6.11%	10.79%	4.54%	41.93%	36.57%	–16.48%
1972	4.62	3.40	14.58%	15.63%	23.83%	12.82%	91.91%	20.20%
1973	7.93	8.70	–16.58%	–17.37%	–2.69%	–31.36%	–17.30%	–6.50%
1974	11.03	12.30	–27.57%	–29.72%	–29.25%	–55.34%	–11.37%	–25.81%
1975	7.24	6.90	38.32%	31.55%	12.91%	136.33%	14.18%	–5.94%
1976	5.70	4.90	17.86%	19.15%	6.08%	–3.87%	14.51%	23.77%
1977	5.28	6.70	–17.27%	–11.50%	4.75%	41.18%	–2.51%	–4.09%
1978	7.78	9.00	–3.15%	1.06%	23.63%	2.65%	23.35%	13.32%
1979	10.88	13.30	4.19%	12.31%	38.41%	4.35%	9.46%	23.13%
1980	11.37	12.50	14.93%	25.77%	25.12%	27.07%	8.33%	49.36%
1981	17.63	8.90	–9.23%	–9.73%	–13.86%	7.24%	7.95%	4.16%
1982	14.6	3.80	19.60%	14.76%	0.20%	22.07%	4.36%	–23.64%
1983	9.37	3.80	20.27%	17.27%	30.35%	23.10%	23.42%	26.28%
1984	11.11	3.90	–3.74%	1.40%	–5.96%	26.02%	16.66%	23.39%
1985	8.35	3.80	27.66%	26.33%	20.84%	15.18%	13.61%	39.01%
1986	7.31	1.10	22.58%	14.62%	5.71%	22.34%	42.61%	39.18%
1987	6.55	4.40	2.26%	2.03%	3.06%	4.16%	15.31%	–15.99%
1988	7.91	4.40	11.85%	12.40%	7.28%	6.48%	39.86%	23.42%
1989	9.08	4.60	26.96%	27.25%	17.10%	30.01%	29.04%	8.09%
1990	8.17	6.10	–4.34%	–6.56%	–17.96%	–14.31%	–38.72%	–21.20%

A	B	C	D	E	F	G	H	I
1991	5.91	3.10	20.32%	26.31%	7.85%	15.06%	–3.63%	22.55%
1992	3.76	2.90	4.17%	4.46%	–4.61%	14.83%	–26.36%	–5.64%
1993	3.28	2.70	13.72%	7.06%	28.98%	23.35%	2.91%	51.21%
1994	4.96	2.70	2.14%	–1.54%	–2.50%	–9.55%	13.24%	–20.78%
1995	5.98	2.50	33.45%	34.11%	11.86%	18.48%	0.74%	25.01%
1996	5.47	3.30	26.01%	20.26%	25.74%	11.71%	–2.55%	5.91%
1997	5.73	1.70	22.64%	31.01%	13.03%	19.73%	–21.19%	9.61%
1998	5.44	1.60	16.10%	26.67%	–3.19%	10.91%	–9.28%	8.92%
1999	5.46	2.70	25.22%	19.53%	29.72%	21.25%	36.79%	6.99%
2000	6.20	3.40	–6.18%	–10.14%	6.18%	–7.97%	–27.19%	6.31%
2001	3.50	1.60	–7.09%	–13.04%	–13.94%	–15.41%	–23.53%	3.42%
2002	1.80	2.40	–16.76%	–23.37%	–13.97%	–24.97%	–18.63%	–13.77%
2003	1.17	1.90	25.31%	26.38%	24.29%	16.57%	24.45%	11.86%
2004	1.95	3.30	3.2%	9.0%	12.5%	9.2%	7.6%	25.1%
2005	3.73	3.40	–0.61%	3.00%	21.91%	18.10%	40.23%	18.84%
2006	4.70	2.50	16.28%	13.60%	14.51%	13.14%	6.91%	15.65%
2007	4.74	4.10	6.43%	3.55%	7.17%	2.04%	–11.13%	13.77%
2008	3.19	0.10	–33.84%	–38.49%	–35.03%	–32.78%	–42.12%	–43.01%

Retirement Expenses Worksheet

Date: ____________________

	Monthly $	Annual $	Essential?
Housing			
Mortgage	______	______	☐
(Final payment date of the mortgage ______________)			
Rent paid	______	______	☐
Condominium Fees	______	______	☐
Property Insurance	______	______	☐
Property Tax	______	______	☐
Heat	______	______	☐
Water	______	______	☐
Electricity	______	______	☐
Security & Alarm	______	______	☐
Maintenance & Repairs	______	______	☐
Other	______	______	☐
Other	______	______	☐
TOTAL Housing Expenses		______	❶
TOTAL **Essential** Housing Expenses		______	❶ $
Household and Living Expenses:			
Food, Groceries	______	______	☐
Dry Cleaning & Laundry	______	______	☐
Decorating & Painting	______	______	☐
Carpet Cleaning	______	______	☐
Gardening	______	______	☐
Pool Care	______	______	☐
Pet Care	______	______	☐
Kennel	______	______	☐
Maid Service	______	______	☐
Computer Equipment & Maintenance	______	______	☐
Pocket Money	______	______	☐
Clothing	______	______	☐
Footwear	______	______	☐
Dependent Support 1	______	______	☐

	Monthly $	Annual $	Essential?
Dependent Support 2	___________	_____________	☐
Anniversary Gifts	___________	_____________	☐
Seasonal Gifts	___________	_____________	☐
Other Gifts	___________	_____________	☐
Donations	___________	_____________	☐
Other	___________	_____________	☐
Other	___________	_____________	☐

TOTAL Household and Living Expenses .... _____________ ❷

TOTAL **Essential** Household and Living Expenses .... _____________ ❷

Transportation Expenses:

	Monthly $	Annual $	Essential?
Car Loan Payments	___________	_____________	☐
(Final payment date of the car loan: ______________________________)			
Lease Payments	___________	_____________	☐
Maintenance & Repairs	___________	_____________	☐
License Fees	___________	_____________	☐
Gasoline	___________	_____________	☐
Oil Change	___________	_____________	☐
Parking	___________	_____________	☐
Car Insurance	___________	_____________	☐
Car Rental	___________	_____________	☐
Public Transportation	___________	_____________	☐
Other	___________	_____________	☐
Other	___________	_____________	☐

TOTAL Transportation Expenses................................. _____________ ❸

TOTAL **Essential** Transportation Expenses................. _____________ ❸

Investment Expenses:

	Monthly $	Annual $	Essential?
Investment Loan Payments	___________	_____________	☐
(Final payment date of the investment loan: ______________________)			
Professional Fees: Accounting	___________	_____________	☐
Professional Fees: Legal	___________	_____________	☐
Professional Fees: Other	___________	_____________	☐
Investment related Subscriptions	___________	_____________	☐
Other	___________	_____________	☐
Other	___________	_____________	☐

	Monthly $	Annual $	Essential?	
TOTAL Investment Expenses		____		❹
TOTAL **Essential** Investment Expenses		____		❹
Personal and Health Care Expenses:				
Hair Care	____	____	☐	
Beauty Supplies	____	____	☐	
Personal Care	____	____	☐	
Manicure, Pedicure	____	____	☐	
Doctors	____	____	☐	
Dentists	____	____	☐	
Prescription Drugs	____	____	☐	
Nutritional Supplements, Vitamins	____	____	☐	
Visiting Home Care	____	____	☐	
Live–in Home Care	____	____	☐	
Medical & Support Equipment	____	____	☐	
Other	____	____	☐	
Other	____	____	☐	
TOTAL Personal & Health Care Expenses		____		❺
TOTAL **Essential** Personal & Health Care Expenses		____		❺
Communication Expenses:				
Telephone	____	____	☐	
Mobile Phone	____	____	☐	
Cable TV	____	____	☐	
Satellite TV	____	____	☐	
Pay TV	____	____	☐	
Internet	____	____	☐	
Other	____	____	☐	
Other	____	____	☐	
TOTAL Communication Expenses		____		❻
TOTAL **Essential** Communication Expenses		____		❻

	Monthly $	Annual $	Essential?
Personal Insurance Expenses:			
Life Insurance 1	___________	_____________	☐
(Final premium payment date, if any : ____________________)			
Life Insurance 2	___________	_____________	☐
(Final premium payment date, if any : ____________________)			
Life Insurance 3	___________	_____________	☐
(Final premium payment date, if any : ____________________)			
Life Insurance 4	___________	_____________	☐
(Final premium payment date, if any : ____________________)			
Long Term Care Insurance 1	___________	_____________	☐
(Final premium payment date, if any : ____________________)			
Long Term Care Insurance 2	___________	_____________	☐
(Final premium payment date, if any : ____________________)			
Critical Illness Insurance 1.................	___________	_____________	☐
(Final premium payment date, if any : ____________________)			
Critical Illness Insurance 2.................	___________	_____________	☐
(Final premium payment date, if any : ____________________)			
Health / Dental Care 1........................	___________	_____________	☐
Health / Dental Care 2........................	___________	_____________	☐
Other	___________	_____________	☐
Other	___________	_____________	☐
TOTAL Personal Insurance Expenses		_____________	❼
TOTAL **Essential** Personal Insurance Expenses..........		_____________	❼
Recreational & Entertainment Expenses:			
Clubs	___________	_____________	☐
Travel	___________	_____________	☐
Camping	___________	_____________	☐
Sports Equipment	___________	_____________	☐
Books	___________	_____________	☐
Newspapers	___________	_____________	☐
Adult Education	___________	_____________	☐
Hobbies	___________	_____________	☐
Hobbies	___________	_____________	☐
Hobbies	___________	_____________	☐
Dining Out	___________	_____________	☐
Entertaining at Home	___________	_____________	☐
Theatre, Ballet, Concerts	___________	_____________	☐
Sports Events	___________	_____________	☐
Tobacco	___________	_____________	☐
Alcohol	___________	_____________	☐

	Monthly $	Annual $	Essential?
Other	________	________	☐
Other	________	________	☐

TOTAL Recreational and Entertainment Expenses....... ________ ❽

TOTAL **Essential** Rec. and Entertainment Expenses.... ________ ❽ 💰

Add up all your Expenses:	Required:	Essential:
Housing .... ❶	________	❶ 💰 ________
Household and Living Expenses .... ❷	________	❷ 💰 ________
Transportation Expenses .... ❸	________	❸ 💰 ________
Investment Expenses .... ❹	________	❹ 💰 ________
Health Care Expenses .... ❺	________	❺ 💰 ________
Communication Expenses .... ❻	________	❻ 💰 ________
Personal Insurance Expenses .... ❼	________	❼ 💰 ________
Recreational & Entertainment Expenses ...... ❽	________	❽ 💰 ________
TOTAL EXPENSES .... ❾	________	❾ 💰 ________

Plus Estimated Income Taxes ________

(add estimated income taxes to total expenses box below)

	Required:	Essential:
TOTAL EXPENSES including income taxes:	________	________

Other Potential Expense Considerations:

- Buy a car every ____ years starting at age _____ until age ____.
- Increase Health Care Expenses by $ _____ after age ____.
- Increase Health Care Expenses again by $ _____ after age ______.
- Decrease Travel expenses by $ ______ after age _______.
- Sell house at age ______
- Move to nursing home at age ____

Index

E

F

G

H

I

J

K

L

M

N

O

P

R

S

T

U

V

W